Why Do You Need This New Edition?

If you're wondering why you should buy this new edition of *Communication Counts*, here are seven good reasons!

1. New **Learning Outcomes** begin each chapter to help you efficiently preview, study, and review key chapter concepts and skills.

2. Newly **integrated ethics coverage** emphasizes that communication is not only strategic but also ethical and underscores pitfalls of communication (and how to avoid them).

3. New **Chapter 10: Informative Speaking** and **Chapter 11: Persuasive Speaking** help you focus on and master these two important types of public speaking.

4. Fully revised and updated **Chapter 14: Mass Communication and Computer Mediated Communication** addresses the increasing importance of technology and networking to society and, more often than not, to college students who are considered "digital natives."

5. Newly designed **graphics program** shows concepts visually and engages non-traditional learners.

6. Three engaging types of boxes in each chapter (**Communication Counts in Your Career, Communication Counts in Your College Experience,** and **Communication Counts in Your Life**) highlight relevant connections between communication and your life—both in the classroom and as you prepare for your career.

7. New **Culture Counts icon** draws attention to the connection between culture and communication, integrating issues of diversity throughout the textbook.

PEARSON

Communication Counts in College, Career, and Life

Communication Counts in College, Career, and Life

Second Edition

David Worley

Indiana State University

Debra Worley

Indiana State University

Laura Soldner

Northern Michigan University

PEARSON

Boston   Columbus   Indianapolis   New York   San Francisco   Upper Saddle River
Amsterdam   Cape Town   Dubai   London   Madrid   Milan   Munich   Paris   Montréal   Toronto
Delhi   Mexico City   São Paulo   Sydney   Hong Kong   Seoul   Singapore   Taipei   Tokyo

Editor-in-Chief, Communication: Karon Bowers
Senior Acquisitions Editor: Melissa Mashburn
Editorial Assistant: Megan Sweeney
Director of Development: Eileen Calabro
Developmental Editor: Kristen Desmond LeFevre
Marketing Manager: Blair Zoe Tuckman
Senior Digital Editor: Paul DeLuca
Digital Editor: Lisa Dotson
Associate Developmental Editor: Angela Mallowes
Production Manager: Raegan Keida Heerema
Associate Managing Editor: Bayani Mendoza de Leon
Managing Editor: Linda Mihatov Behrens
Project Coordination, Text Design, and Electronic Page Makeup: Integra
Senior Cover Design Manager/Cover Designer: Nancy Danahy
Cover Image: © Dwight Cendrowski / Alamy Image
Permission Coordinator: Lee Scher/Annette Linder
Photo Researcher: Bill Smith Group
Senior Manufacturing Buyer: Mary Ann Gloriande
Printer and Binder: R. R. Donnelley/Willard
Cover Printer: Lehigh-Phoenix Color/Hagerstown

Credits and acknowledgments borrowed from other sources and reproduced, with permission, in this textbook appear on page 329.

Library of Congress Cataloging-in-Publication Data

Worley, David (David W.)
 Communication counts in college, career, and life/David Worley, Debra Worley, Laura Soldne.—2nd ed.
  p. cm.
 Rev. ed. of: Communication counts : getting it right in college and life. 2007.
 ISBN-13: 978-0-205-83013-8
 ISBN-10: 0-205-83013-7
 1. Communication in education. 2. Interpersonal communication. 3. Universities and colleges.
 I. Worley, Debra. II. Soldner, Laura. III. Worley, David (David W.) Communication counts. IV. Title.
 LB1033.5.W665 2012
 370.1'4—dc22
                                                                                              2011007450

1 2 3 4 5 6 7 8 9 10—RRD—14 13 12 11

ISBN-13: 978-0-205-83013-8
ISBN-10:   0-205-83013-7

CONTENTS

CHAPTER 13
Communication in Organizations   275

CHAPTER 14
Mass Communication and Computer
Mediated Communication   299

PREFACE

OUR VISION

As the title of this book suggests, *communication counts*, communication counts in professions and personal relationships. But communication also counts in the college experience—which provides the focus for this book. Conceptually, we integrate essential content for the hybrid basic communication course with college students' lived experiences. Specifically, we focus on how communication principles and practices can assist students in their college years and later in their personal and professional lives.

We are pleased to offer a second edition of this book that blends thought, practice, and interest in helping students develop communication knowledge and skills. We, the authors, are teachers at heart, and we see this book as an extension of our passion for teaching; we wrote this book for students. We have worked to make this material relevant to students through fresh examples, content reorganization, and applications to daily experience. However, we also believe this book will appeal to both beginning and veteran teachers who seek to make the basic communication course relevant to students' lives.

WHAT'S NEW IN THIS EDITION?

This second edition offers new, fresh examples to which students can relate while also reorganizing information in response to your feedback. We have made significant changes as a result of reviewer suggestions, and we hope you will find the changes helpful to your teaching and your students' learning.

New Features

- Chapter-opening **learning outcomes** list each concept and skill that students will encounter as they read the chapter, allowing them to more efficiently preview, study, and review key chapter concepts and skills.
- Redesigned **concept maps** at the start of each chapter give students a visual guide to follow through the chapter.

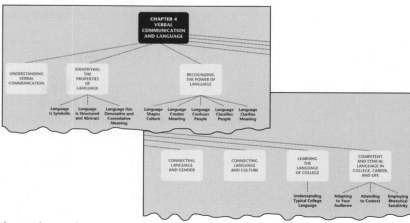

- **Coverage of ethics** has been integrated throughout the text to emphasize its critical importance and to open students' eyes to the pitfalls of unethical communication (complete with suggestions on how to avoid those pitfalls).

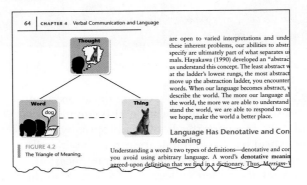

■ An updated and redesigned **graphics program** enhances text discussions in each chapter—showing concepts visually and engaging both traditional and nontraditional learners.

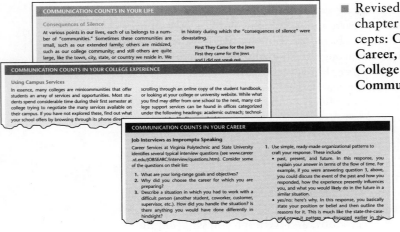

■ Revised feature boxes appear in each chapter and are organized around concepts: **Communication Counts in Your Career, Communication Counts in Your College Experience,** and **Communication Counts in Your Life.** These boxes provide students with interesting and relevant connections between communication and their lives, college experiences, and careers.

■ **Culture Counts** To draw attention to the critically important connections between culture and communication, the new **Culture Counts icon** is placed in the margins throughout chapters to note areas where the discussion at hand integrates issues of diversity and culture.

New in Each Chapter

■ **Chapter 1: Appreciating and Understanding Communication** provides a fresh description of human communication—as a uniquely creative human enterprise—and streamlined coverage of communication models. Expanded coverage of *feedback* points out that it is both verbal and nonverbal and it can be positive, negative, intentional, unintentional, understood, misunderstood, or a combination of these. Revised coverage of *noise* now goes beyond external noise to include two types of internal noise: physiological (body) and psychological (mind).

■ **Chapter 2: Perception: Self, Others, and Communication** presents a new skills-based discussion of dealing with perceptual challenges, and expanded coverage of *impression management* discusses its potential negative consequences (along with its positive outcomes). New coverage of *Standpoint Theory* helps students understand how time and space impact the way in which we view the world.

■ **Chapter 3: Effective Listening** offers revised coverage that relates the Listening Model to the Perceptual Model introduced in Chapter 2. Expanded coverage of *critical listening* explains how students can use this strategy for success in the classroom, on the job, or in their everyday lives.

- **Chapter 4: Verbal Communication and Language** includes new coverage of *ethnocentrism, hate speech,* and *gendered language.*
- **Chapter 5: Nonverbal Communication** opens with a new section on the power of nonverbal communication, emphasizing that how we act in a given situation may reveal far more than our words do. There is new coverage of *paralanguage, proxemics,* and *silence.*
- **Chapter 6: Understanding Interpersonal Communication** provides streamlined coverage of *Knapp's Relational Model.* New sections include *Gendered Relationship Language* and *Intimacy and Impression Management.*
- **Chapter 7: Practicing Effective Interpersonal Communication** applies the concept of intimacy to integrate essential interpersonal communication principles—such as conflict—providing a focus for various concepts. Newly streamlined coverage of *Interpersonal Communication Dialectics* opens the chapter, including a skills-based section called *Strategies for Managing Dialectics in Your Relationships.*
- **Chapter 8: Public Speaking: Process, Purposes, Topics, and Audiences** offers new coverage and abundant examples of both draft and revised *thesis statements* for informative, persuasive, and special occasion speeches. There is expanded coverage of gathering information, including conducting interviews and recording personal observations. Also included is updated coverage of how to evaluate resources, including Internet and media resources.
- **Chapter 9: Organization, Supporting Material, Delivery, and Visual Aids** provides fully revised and enriched instruction on outlining and the principles of effective organization, replete with extended examples from sample student speeches.
- **Chapter 10: Informative Speaking** presents all-new coverage detailing the types of informative speeches and how to go about researching, constructing, and delivering them—including extensive examples throughout.
- **Chapter 11: Persuasive Speaking** is the all-new counterpart to Chapter 10, providing parallel coverage and examples of persuasive speaking.
- **Chapter 12: Groups in Discussion** provides a specific context for understanding group concepts and practices, especially as they apply to college and university life. This chapter offers expanded coverage of *problem-solving groups, social groups, learning groups,* and *therapy groups* and makes a clear distinction between *teams* and *groups.*
- **Chapter 13: Communication in Organizations** offers a unique discussion of organizational communication, helping students recognize the importance of navigating organizations, including colleges and universities, to succeed. Also included are updated information on interviewing—from an organizational communication framework—and streamlined coverage of the *Systems Model.*
- **Chapter 14: Mass Communication and Computer Mediated Communication** is fully revised and updated to address the critical importance of technology and networking to society and students' lives.

TO OUR COLLEAGUES

Together, we have invested decades of our professional lives learning, teaching, reading, writing, and researching to produce this book. Foremost, however, this book is the fruit of our classroom teaching in basic communication courses, our long-term association with first-year initiatives, and our ongoing interactions with the growing population of mature learners returning to college. With the help of our publisher, editors, and reviewers, we have produced what we hope you will find to be a well-written, useful text that will help *you* help students find their voices and engage their various learning environments while also thinking ahead to their future lives when they complete their studies.

In this text, we assert that students' college experience is an authentic context—not a "waiting room" for real life after college. Therefore, the illustrations and applications we offer draw on the actual world of college students; we demonstrate how communication principles are relevant here and now for college students. However, we also identify how the communication concepts and skills learned in college transfer to social and professional spheres after graduation.

We also wish to emphasize that this book is not about competing with college success texts and teachers but about cooperating with them by confirming the significance of their work and applying what we have learned from them through illustration and integration. We have worked diligently to relate communication knowledge and skills with college success principles to stress the relevance between the two. Given the numerous learning community initiatives springing up on campuses across the United States, we believe this text offers a strategic pedagogical tool to link college success courses and basic communication courses, as we have been doing in our pedagogical practice for a number of years, without compromising the unique content of either.

Making *Communication Count* in Life Means Tapping into Students' Lived Experiences

We emphasize issues of concern for both traditional and nontraditional students as they navigate their lives by:

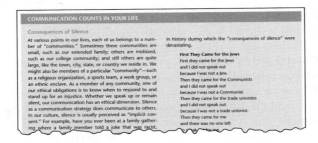

■ Providing relevant connections that students can make between communication and their lives in the *Communication Counts in Your Life* boxes in each chapter.

■ Drawing attention to the connection between culture and communication with the *Culture Counts* icon—integrating issues of diversity throughout the textbook.

■ Integrating principles of ethical communication in each chapter.

Making *Communication Count* in College Means Applying Communication Theories and Skills in the Here and Now

We emphasize issues of concern for both traditional and nontraditional students as they navigate their college experience by:

■ Relating students' college experiences to communication principles and practices in the *Communication Counts in Your College Experience* boxes in each chapter.

■ Providing relevant, engaging, up-to-date examples as well as visual materials such as photos, tables, and figures to help emphasize and illustrate key concepts.

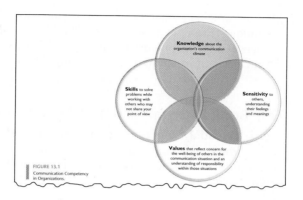

FIGURE 13.1
Communication Competency in Organizations.

■ Opening each chapter with a clear learning outcome grid and a graphic depiction of the content.

■ Concluding each chapter with valuable resources, including a summary to help students identify key points, a list of key terms, discussion questions, and exercises to assist students and teachers in applying the information.

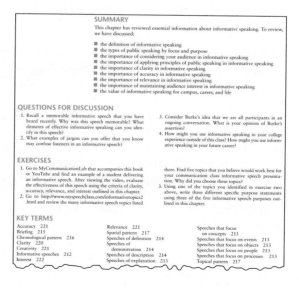

■ Focusing students' attention on the importance of groups in discussion in Chapter 12—providing a specific context for understanding group concepts and practices, especially as they apply to the college experience.

Making *Communication Count* in Career Means Thinking Ahead to Success in Future Contexts

We emphasize issues of concern for both traditional and nontraditional students as they plan for their careers by:

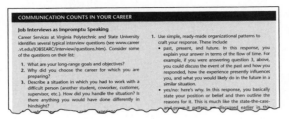

- Linking practical and conceptual issues between communication and the world of work in our *Communication Counts in Your Career* boxes in each chapter.

- Emphasizing the importance of organizational communication in Chapter 13—a unique feature in a hybrid text. This chapter helps students recognize the importance of navigating organizations, including work environments, to succeed and includes information on interviewing.

This Book Is Organized into Four Major Sections

Unit I: Essential Communication Elements   This unit offers an overview of basic communication theory, including descriptions of communication, self and perception in communication, listening, and verbal and nonverbal communication.

Unit II: Interpersonal Communication   This unit considers essential interpersonal communication concepts to help students understand interpersonal communication conceptually and practically.

Unit III: Public Communication   This unit provides an overview of the essential aspects of public speaking by focusing on the process of developing, supporting, organizing, and delivering informative and persuasive speeches. We have reorganized the content in this section to provide more concrete information about public speaking. You will find many new examples that help illustrate public speaking concepts and practices, along with unique chapters focused on informative and persuasive speaking.

Unit IV: Groups, Organizations, and Mass Communication   This unit incorporates fundamental information about the theory and practice of effective communication in groups, organizations, and mass communication.

This book takes a contextual approach, beginning with basic communication concepts and, for the most part, moving concentrically to increasingly larger contexts. Therefore, after reviewing important communication concepts, we move from a discussion of interpersonal communication to public speaking and then to small group, organizational, and mass communication. However, the book is written so that teachers do not need to move through the book as it is organized but can easily assign the sections in the order that best fits their pedagogical purposes.

TO STUDENTS

How many times have you sat in a college class and wondered, "How does this relate to my major or, for that matter, to my life?" You may be asking the same question about *this* course and this textbook. You need to know that we—the authors of this book—have worked hard to provide you with a textbook that answers this question. Within these pages we offer you the essential knowledge critical to developing a fundamental grasp of communication principles and practice. Whether you are a recent graduate of high school or an adult returning to school while juggling multiple responsibilities, we wrote this text with *you* in mind because we want you to see the significant role communication plays in your everyday life as a college student.

This text focuses on how you can use communication in your college life as you move from learning experiences in the classroom into your home or residence hall conversations, campus organizational meetings, community placements for service learning and internships, and eventually professional life in the working world. Of course, this text will only help you if you read it and use it! So, we encourage you to make the most of this resource and this course to enhance your success in college, work, and everyday life.

In this second edition, we have provided fresh, up-to-date examples; integrated communication ethics throughout each chapter; and added individual chapters on informative and persuasive public speaking. We believe these changes will enhance the value of the text and its usefulness to you in this course and in your future academic, personal, and professional life.

David Worley
Debra Worley
Laura Soldner

RESOURCES IN PRINT AND ONLINE

NAME OF SUPPLEMENT	AVAILABLE	INSTRUCTOR OR STUDENT SUPPLEMENT	DESCRIPTION
Instructor's Manual and Test Bank (ISBN: 0-205-13324-X)	Online	Instructor Supplement	Prepared by Jennifer Walton, Ohio Northern University, the Instructor's Manual includes a wealth of resources for each chapter. There is an annotated Instructional Outline that matches the PowerPoint™ presentation package and can be used for planning, developing, and delivering lectures. Discussion questions, designed to increase student engagement, can be used for assignments, essay questions, or as review questions for an exam (sample answers are provided). There are also activities and suggestions for additional resources. The Test Bank contains more than 500 multiple-choice, true/ false, completion, and matching questions organized by chapter. Each question is referenced by topic, skill, and page. Available at www.pearsonhighered.com/irc (access code required).
MyTest (ISBN: 0-205-22050-9)	Online	Instructor Supplement	This flexible, online test-generating software includes all questions found in the test bank portion of the Instructor's Manual and Test Bank, allowing instructors to create their own personalized exams. Instructors can also edit any of the existing test questions and add their own questions. Other special features of this program include random generation of test questions, creation of alternate versions of the same test, scrambling of question sequence, and test preview before printing. Available at www.pearsonmytest.com (access code required).
PowerPoint™ Presentation Package (ISBN: 0-205-22051-7)	Online	Instructor Supplement	Prepared by Jennifer Walton, Ohio Northern University, this text-specific package provides a basis for your lecture with PowerPoint™ slides for each chapter of the book. Available at www.pearsonhighered.com/irc (access code required).
Pearson Introduction to Communication Video Library	VHS/DVD	Instructor Supplement	Pearson's Introduction to Communication Video Library contains a range of videos from which adopters can choose. The videos feature a variety of topics and scenarios for communication foundations, interpersonal communication, small group communication, and public speaking. Please contact your Pearson representative for details and a complete list of videos and their contents to choose which would be most useful to your course. Some restrictions apply.
Lecture Questions for Clickers for Introduction to Communication (ISBN: 0-205-54723-0)	Online	Instructor Supplement	Prepared by Keri Moe, El Paso Community College, this is an assortment of questions and activities covering culture, listening, interviewing, public speaking, interpersonal conflict and more are presented in PowerPoint™. These slides will help liven up your lectures and can be used along with the Personal Response System to get students more involved in the material. Available at www.pearsonhighered.com/irc (access code required).
Preparing Visual Aids for Presentations, Fifth Edition (ISBN: 0-205-61115-X)	In Print	Student Supplement	Prepared by Dan Cavanaugh, this 32-page visual booklet provides a host of ideas for using today's multimedia tools to improve presentations, including suggestions for planning a presentation, guidelines for designing visual aids and storyboarding, and a walkthrough that shows how to prepare a visual display using PowerPoint™ (available for purchase).

NAME OF SUPPLEMENT	AVAILABLE	INSTRUCTOR OR STUDENT SUPPLEMENT	DESCRIPTION
Pearson Introduction to Communication Study Site (Open access)	Online	Student Supplement	This open-access, student resource features practice tests, learning objectives, and weblinks organized around the major topics typically covered in the Introduction to Communication course. Available at www.pearsonintrocommunication.com.
Study Card for Introduction to Speech Communication (ISBN: 0-205-47438-1)	In Print	Student Supplement	Colorful, affordable, and packed with useful information, the Pearson study cards make studying easier, more efficient, and more enjoyable. Course information is distilled down to the basics, helping students quickly master the fundamentals, review a subject for understanding, or prepare for an exam. Because they're laminated for durability, they can be kept for years to come and pulled out whenever students need a quick review (available for purchase).
MySearchLab with eText	Online	Instructor & Student Supplement	**MySearchLab** with eText features access to the EBSCO ContentSelect database and Associated Press news feeds, and step-by-step tutorials which offer complete overviews of the entire writing and research process. **MySearchLab** with eText also includes numerous course- and book-specific media tools, including our video upload tool, MediaShare, MyOutline, video clips, chapter assessments, and flashcards. For more information, please see details on the following page.

MySearchLab

MySearchLab is an interactive website that features an eText, access to the EBSCO ContentSelect database and Associated Press news feeds, and step-by-step tutorials which offer complete overviews of the entire writing and research process. **MySearchLab** is designed to amplify a traditional course in numerous ways or to administer a course online. Additionally, **MySearchLab** offers course specific tools to enrich learning and help students succeed.

eText: Identical in content and design to the printed text, the Pearson eText provides access to the book wherever and whenever it is needed. Students can take notes and highlight within their eText, just like a traditional book.

MediaShare: A cutting-edge video upload tool that allows students to upload speeches, interpersonal role plays, and group assignments, for instructors and classmates to watch (whether face-to-face or online) and provide online feedback and comments. Customizable rubrics can be attached for further evaluation and grading purposes. Grades can be imported into most learning management systems. Structured much like a social networking site, MediaShare can help promote a sense of community among students.

MyOutline: This valuable tool provides step-by-step guidance and structure for writing an effective outline, along with a detailed help section to assist students in understanding the elements of an outline and how all the pieces fit together. Students can download and email completed outlines to instructors, save for future editing or print – even print as notecards. Instructors can choose from our templates or create their own structure for students to use.

Video Clips: These portray various communication scenarios as well as sample student and professional speeches which offer students models of the types of speeches they are learning to design and deliver. Interactive videos contain essay questions to encourage students to think critically, evaluate and apply knowledge learned.

Online Quizzes: Chapter quizzes test student comprehension, are automatically graded, and grades flow directly to an online gradebook.

Chapter-specific Content: Each chapter contains Learning Objectives, Chapter Summaries, Quizzes, and Flashcards. These can be used to enhance comprehension, help students review key terms, prepare for tests, and retain what they've learned.

To order this book with MySearchLab access at no extra charge use ISBN 0-205-24516-1 Learn more at www.mysearchlab.com

ACKNOWLEDGMENTS

This book is the result of the labor and investment of many individuals. We are grateful to all who have contributed to its development. First, we wish to thank the students who have shared classroom life with us and have taught us as we have worked to teach them. We are equally grateful to the many teachers and professors who invested their knowledge and pedagogical expertise in us during our years of education; their contributions live on in us and through us in our students. More specifically, we thank our families, friends, and colleagues who have supported us in this endeavor. Dr. Jennifer Walton, a former graduate student and teaching assistant at Indiana State University, is due a special word of thanks for her excellent work on many of the instructor's supplements. Thank you, Jenny! We are especially grateful to the excellent staff at Pearson, including Karon Bowers, Editor-in-Chief; Kristen Desmond LeFevre, Development Editor; Megan Sweeney, Editorial Assistant; and Raegan Heerema, Project Manager.

REVIEWERS

We also want to thank all of the reviewers who read through and offered excellent suggestions for improving various drafts of our manuscript. Our sincere thanks to the following:

Linda Jean Anthon, Valencia Community College
Jacki Brucher Moore, Kirkwood Community College
Mark Buckholz, New Mexico State University at Carlsbad
Melissa Crawford, University of Central Arkansas
Isabel Del Pino-Allen, Miami Dade College
Robert Dixon, St. Louis Community College at Meramec
Christopher Goble, Monmouth College
Teresa M. Hayes, DeVry University
Jeffrey S. Hillard, College of Mount St. Joseph
Emily Holler, Kennesaw State University
Susan A. Holton, Bridgewater State College
Mary E. Hurley, St. Louis Community College at Forest Park
Charles J. Korn, George Mason University
Shirley Maase, Chesapeake College
JJ McIntyre, University of Central Arkansas
Jim Parker, Vanderbilt University
Ané Pearman, ECPI College of Technology
Lisa Peterson, Boise State University
Jeff Pierson, Bridgewater State College
Rebecca S. Robideaux, Boise State University
Darci Slaten, University of Arizona
Eric W. Trumbull, PhD, Northern Virginia Community College–Woodbridge
John T. Warren, Bowling Green State University

Dr. David W. Worley is a former Professor and Chairperson in the Department of Communication at Indiana State University in Terre Haute, Indiana. He also served as Director of Communication 101, a hybrid basic oral communication course required of all graduates at Indiana State University for 15 years. He received his PhD from Southern Illinois University at Carbondale, with a concentration in communication education. Dr. Worley is the recipient of the Central States Communication Association Outstanding New Teacher Award, the Caleb Mills Distinguished Teaching Award at Indiana State University, the Excellence in Education Teaching Award from the College of Arts and Sciences at Indiana State University, and the Federation Prize from the Central States Communication Association. He teaches courses in communication education, research methods, and cross-cultural communication. His research interests include disability and communication, communication education, and instructional communication. He has published in *Communication Education, Communication Studies, Communication Quarterly, Review of Communication, Journal of the Association for Communication Administration, Basic Communication Course Annual,* and *Iowa Journal of Communication.* He is the outgoing editor of *Basic Communication Course Annual* and a regular contributor at the National Communication Association and the Central States Communication Association Annual Conventions.

Dr. Debra Worley is a former Professor of Communication at Indiana State University, where she began teaching in 1999. She received her doctorate from Wayne State University. Dr. Worley is the recipient of the Caleb Mills Distinguished Teaching Award, the Excellence in Education award, and the Distinguished Service Award from Indiana State University, as well as the Federation Prize from Central States Communication Association. She teaches courses in organizational communication, public relations, and communication ethics. Dr. Worley has presented lectures on communication in the workplace and has published articles in *Communication Studies, Public Relations Review, Journal of Business Ethics,* and *Basic Communication Course Annual.* She has also served on the editorial boards of *Communication Teacher* and *Journal of Applied Communication Research.*

Professor Laura Soldner is a Full Professor in the Department of English at Northern Michigan University, where she serves as Director of Composition as well as Learning and Study Skills Specialist. Professor Soldner graduated from the University of Wisconsin–Madison and has spent three decades teaching incoming freshmen through graduate students. In 2010, she was honored by the International Reading Association's College Literacy and Learning Special Interest Group with its Outstanding Commitment to College Reading and Study Skills Award. Additionally, Professor Soldner received NMU's Excellence in Teaching Award in 2006; served as the Director of NMU's First-Year Experience Program, a nationally recognized freshman transition program; received Alpha Lambda Delta's (national freshman honor society) Advisor of the Year Award; and was a semifinalist for the National Outstanding First-Year Advocate Award. Professor Soldner also publishes and presents regularly at national and international venues.

CHAPTER 1

Appreciating and Understanding Human Communication

LEARNING OUTCOMES After reading this chapter, you will have:

the **Knowledge** to...   and the **Skills** to...

THINK ABOUT COMMUNICATION, page 3

Appreciate the importance of communication in your college experience, career, and life after college.

- Realize that your competence as a communicator impacts every relationship you will have in your lifetime.

LEARNING ABOUT COMMUNICATION, page 5

Understand the foundational concepts and characteristics of human communication.

- Appreciate how words, utterances, and body movements make human communication unique.
- Identify common communication misunderstandings and strive to avoid them.

- Understand the communication components of sender, message, receiver, feedback, context, noise, and motivation.
- Know that we are continuously acting as senders and receivers of communication (as in the transactional model).

LINKING ETHICS AND COMMUNICATION, page 12

Value the relationship between ethics and communication.

- Practice honesty, truthfulness, and fairness as key principles of ethical communication.

BECOMING A COMPETENT AND ETHICAL COMMUNICATOR IN COLLEGE, CAREER, AND LIFE, page 15

Develop into a capable and moral communicator.

- Exhibit tolerance in interactions with others.
- Engage in dialogue to communicate with—not at—others.

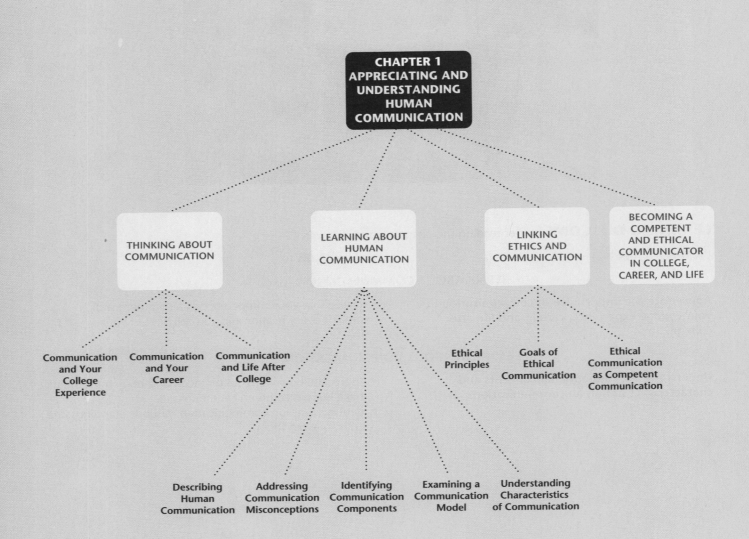

THINKING ABOUT COMMUNICATION

As you begin your experience as a college student, you are learning "how to do college." Perhaps you have already faced some challenges this term as you have learned to manage your academic, financial, family, and personal responsibilities as a college student. Although not all of the problems you face are communication related, many of them are, as Johnson, Staton, and Jorgensen-Earp (1995) report in their study of first-year students.

Human communication is complex and multidimensional. Miscommunications and misunderstandings are inevitable, but learning more about the components of communication and about different communication models will equip you with the skills to ease some of these problems. Moreover, understanding the characteristics of communication and clarifying some misconceptions will also help you to become a better communicator in your college and personal life and in your professional career. Before we begin our investigation of some fundamental communication concepts, let's discuss the relationships between communication, your college experiences, and your life outside the classroom.

Communication and Your College Experience

Whether you are a first-year student, a mature learner, or a returning student who "knows how to do school," college will present you with opportunities for intellectual, social, and personal growth.

Many of the challenges and opportunities you will face as a student-learner are linked with communication, for example:

- Listening to professors explain concepts you need to know
- Engaging in class discussions
- Establishing friendships with other students with whom you can socialize, study, or complete group projects
- Developing a comfortable working relationship with your academic advisor
- Posing questions to and talking with professors, staff, and administrators
- Expressing your opinions and insights clearly in class discussions
- Negotiating your relationships with significant others and family members
- Addressing relevant campus and community issues that concern you

Research confirms the importance of communication in college—given that college students spend 69 percent of their time engaged in speaking and listening (Barker, Edwards, Gaines, Gladney, & Holley 1980). Therefore, appreciating the role communication plays in the college experience and developing your oral communication skills will help you make the most of the experience. We sincerely hope this text will help you understand and apply important principles of communication here and now.

College also brings with it numerous challenges. You must develop the essential academic skills necessary to learn, and you must identify, set, and achieve personal and career goals. You will want to develop meaningful relationships with your peers, professors, and other important people on campus, including staff and administrators. There will be many opportunities to become involved in campus life—which means you must choose if, how, and where to become involved. In addition, you must decide how to finance your education and make choices about your behaviors and their consequences. Whether you are a recent high school graduate or an adult learner, you will face these and other issues.

Although it is too simplistic to assert that communication is the key to dealing with *all* of the situations you are likely to encounter, communication does play a key role in adapting to and navigating through the college experience. We'll emphasize the value of becoming a creative, competent communicator as you engage the college experience throughout this text.

For example, as a student-learner, you are required to employ a wide range of communication skills. We use the term *student-learner* because being enrolled as a student doesn't necessarily mean you are a learner. At least two issues impact whether you become a student-learner or just a student.

First, remaining in college is a challenge. According to the National Center for Education Statistics, in 2000–2001, 58 percent of students who began college as first-year students graduated within six years. Noel, Levitz, and Saluri (1985) suggest that students decide during the first six weeks of college whether they will stay or leave. Factors that influence this decision include homesickness, separation from long-time friends, a new living environment, and changes in diet. In addition to this, you must decide how to spend free time, how to manage money, whether to go to class, and how to meet academic expectations unlike any you have ever faced. Such pressures put some first-year students in danger of never assuming their role as a student-learner because they are tempted to drop out of college before having to make the difficult transition. When you grow discouraged, remember that college can affect your earning potential. According to the National Center for Education Statistics *Outcomes of Education* report, in 2002 men with a bachelor's degree earned more than $22,000 more per year than men with only a high school diploma; women with a bachelor's degree earned more than $15,000 more per year than those with only a high school diploma.

Second, those who stay in college must engage learning—meaning you must attend class regularly; complete required homework; learn to use the library; use a variety of technologies; and develop your listening, writing, and speaking skills. Moreover, you need to become involved in campus life (Astin 1985) and the local community, navigate the financial aid system, and develop supportive relationships with other student-learners and faculty (Terenzini et al. 1996). As you move ahead in becoming a student-learner, you must learn and use several new skills. Communicating effectively with others is essential to learning these skills.

Although mature learners do not necessarily face the same specific challenges as recent high school graduates, you face equally difficult obstacles. These often include managing time to meet work and family responsibilities while setting aside sufficient time to study. Managing money also presents challenges, especially if you have taken a leave of absence or quit your job in order to complete your degree. You may also feel a considerable amount of fear about whether or not you can succeed in the college environment (Brown 1996). Many of you are likely experiencing other significant personal changes as you begin college, which may include dealing with a divorce, becoming a single parent, changing your career, or facing an "empty nest" when your children have moved out (Aslanian 1996). Even though you may truly want to learn, distractions abound.

Communication and Your Career

Although college ends, learning does not. We continue to learn throughout our entire lives. Likewise, we also continue to rely on communication in our personal, professional, and public lives.

Relationships with other people are often our greatest sources of both joy and pain. Later in this book, we will talk more about personal relationships and the important role communication plays in them. At this point, however, it is sufficient to note that both during and after college, healthy relationships with romantic partners, friends, family, and coworkers require effective, appropriate, and creative communication. Communication plays an equally important role in our professional lives. Surveys confirm that competent communication skills, including speaking, listening, and writing, are among the top skills required by employers. Listening can improve opportunities for advancing at work (Sypher, Bostrom, & Seibert 1989) and is identified as an important skill by Fortune 500 companies (Wolvin & Coakley 1991). Although you may think that your chosen career does not entail using communication skills on a regular basis, we encourage you to talk with a seasoned professional in your field of interest. In all probability, you will find that every career path calls for effective, creative communication skills (see the box "Communication Counts in Your Career: Effective Communication Is the Key to Getting and Keeping a Job") in order to interview well for a job; make presentations to clients, customers, or colleagues; and work with a team to complete a project. For example, the *Scientist* (Richman 2002) reports that communication skills are crucial to obtaining a job in science-related fields. Gardner and Jewler (2003) note that "regardless of which career you choose, people are likely to judge your effectiveness—at least in part—by your speaking skills" (p. 137).

Competent communication skills, including speaking, listening, and writing, are among the top skills required by employees.

COMMUNICATION COUNTS IN YOUR CAREER

Effective Communication Is the Key to Getting and Keeping a Job

You may be saying, "Okay, I get it. I need to communicate well to get and keep a job. I've heard this over and over." Perhaps you've heard it so often because it is fundamentally true. In a report from North Carolina State University titled "Communication in the Workplace: What Can NCSU Students Expect?" employers from a variety of businesses all confirm that oral communication plays an important role in recruitment, job success, and promotion. This survey indicates that 95 percent of employer respondents perceived oral communication as *very important* and *important* for promotion and for job success, and 87 percent of respondents perceived it to be important for promotion. In other words, if you want to get, keep, and progress in a job, according to these employers, you need to have strong oral communication skills.

Source: "The Importance of Oral Communication in the Workplace" from *English for Specific Purposes,* Vol. 21, 2002, pp. 41–57 (48). Reprinted by permission of Elsevier.

Communication and Life After College

Although your personal and professional lives are important, you also share in the public life of your communities, states, and nations. In order to participate in the privileges and responsibilities of a democracy, you must communicate. For example, listening carefully to candidates' positions on issues of critical importance allows you to obtain vital information that helps you choose how to vote. Or, you may be motivated to speak to a local school board about an issue that impacts public education in your community. Situations of public concern will likely prompt you to engage the communication process as a result of your role as citizen.

Now that we have considered the importance of communication to our lives in college and in future careers, let's get a better understanding of some of the basic yet vital kinds of information about human communication. We will start with thinking about the nature of human communication.

LEARNING ABOUT COMMUNICATION

In this chapter, we will learn about human communication by describing the phrase *human communication*, by clarifying popular misconceptions about communication, by identifying important components of communication, by reviewing models of communication, and by explaining characteristics of communication. We hope this variety of approaches will help you develop an understanding of the complexity, creativity, and challenge of human communication.

Describing Human Communication

Definitions of *communication* abound. Dance and Larson (1976) identify over 100 definitions of communication. The sheer number of definitions suggests the difficulty of defining the term. Furthermore, when we define any term, by the very nature of the act, we specify and thereby limit the concept. This is useful and necessary in many instances, but human communication is flexible and situational by nature and, therefore, difficult to define. Consequently, it may be better to say that we can *describe* human communication in a variety of ways in order to assist our understanding.

Human communication may be described as "negotiating symbolic meaning." This statement identifies important ideas for us to consider. First, this book focuses on *human* communication. Researchers in the sciences, particularly those who study animal behavior, have theorized that animals communicate in many ways. Those of you who have pets can probably attest to the fact that you "understand" your pets' "communication." Animals may have their own languages, but here we focus on the nature of human communication.

Second, communication is **symbolic**. This means that humans use words (verbal communication), vocal utterances (oral communication), or body movements (nonverbal communication) to represent a host of referents (that to which one refers). For example, verbal communication uses words like *chair*. The spelling, sound, and definition of this symbol is arbitrary because there is no firm reason why the word *chair* should not be spelled

Human communication ■ Negotiating symbolic meaning.

Symbolic ■ Using words, vocal utterances, or body movement to represent a host of referents.

Paralanguage (or vocalics) ■ The vocal sounds we make such as pitch, volume, emphasis, or other similar sounds.

Fidelity ■ Greater clarity.

chare or the first two letters pronounced as "sh" rather than "ch," or even used to refer to a completely different object than a piece of furniture upon which one sits. Because we have agreed upon the conventions of language or the rules that guide language, we use verbal symbols to communicate. Oral communication or vocal utterances may also act as symbols. Consider, for example, the sound we make when we gasp. A gasp is actually a sharp intake of air that creates a whispery sound using our mouth, lips, and vocal cords. A gasp is not a word, so it is not verbal communication; however, a noise or an utterance can be classified as oral communication. When you hear a gasp or respond with a gasp, what does this communicate? Usually it implies or denotes surprise or shock. Therefore, when a novelist writes, "She gasped at the sight before her," we understand the behavior, and this cues us to expect the writer to describe the shocking scene the character observes.

Vocal utterances—like a gasp—typically fall within the area of symbolic nonverbal communication called *paralanguage* or *vocalics*. **Paralanguage, or vocalics,** refers to the qualities of the vocal sounds we make, such as pitch, volume, and emphasis. However, we usually think of nonverbal communication as facial or bodily movement. Facial movements like frowns, smiles, or grimaces communicate feelings. Gestures represent words, give directions, or express feelings. Although we will further discuss nonverbal communication in Chapter 5, it is important at this point to understand that nonverbal communication is symbolic—that is, nonverbal communication represents or accompanies a word, a feeling, an object, or some other referent. For example, the simple act of pointing is symbolic as we give others directions or focus their attention. We can also express our pleasure or displeasure when we give a thumbs-up or a thumbs-down.

We use symbols like these to construct *meaning* and to create a shared understanding with one another. However, this meaning is not always clear! Imagine that your professor says to your class, "We will have a quiz next week." After taking the quiz, a classmate exclaims, "I thought this was supposed to be a quiz. This was an exam!" What makes the difference between a quiz and an exam? The difference is not arbitrary; it is a matter of the meaning we attach to the symbols. In your classmate's mind, a quiz is a short, relatively easy, focused assessment. In your professor's mind, it is also a shorter, focused assessment, but not as short, focused, or easy as your classmate expected! Different meanings for the same symbol, therefore, created miscommunication. The point is this: Symbols carry meaning, but *we* create the meaning as a result of our prior experience and expectations. We will add more information about verbal communication later in Chapter 4, but for now, consider this important idea: *People, not symbols, create meaning.*

Because human communication rests on symbols that carry a variety of personal meanings, communication must be negotiated. In other words, when we communicate with one another, we seek to create shared understanding. This does not mean that we have exactly the same definitions for every verbal, oral, and nonverbal symbol but that we find common ground that allows us to share greater clarity or **fidelity**. As you likely know, this is not always easily done. Myers and Myers' (1992) humorous summary makes the point well: "I know you believe you understand what you think I said, but I am not sure you realize that what you heard is not what I meant!" How many times have you felt this way? We must consciously work at creating shared meaning. There are numerous strategies we can employ to enhance shared meaning, which we will discuss throughout this text, but it is important to realize early that *when we communicate with one another, we are negotiating meaning.*

Addressing Communication Misconceptions

Because each of us "learns" communication more by practice than by "formal" learning, at least until we are in the later stages of school, we tend to develop a number of misconceptions about communication. Some of these are passed to us from family or friends, and some we simply assume because we model the behavior of others. Skillful and effective communicators are people who accurately understand each other and who share meaning. So letting go of misconceptions can assist us in better understanding ourselves and others. Let's consider some of the most common misconceptions about communication.

MISCONCEPTION #1: COMMUNICATION IS EXACT Exactness in communication is impossible. As we have stressed throughout this chapter, communication requires creative negotiation, not transmission or translation. Because of our unique backgrounds and experiences, the limitations of symbols, and the nature of meaning, we can never avoid miscommunication or the hard work required to negotiate meaning. It is unrealistic to think that we can attain perfect precision with our communication skills. Although we can certainly improve our skills and learn how to reduce miscommunication and enhance fidelity, or greater clarity, we can never achieve exactness. Have you ever witnessed a verbal argument between two friends and then tried to talk to them about what happened? Is your memory of the incident the same as theirs? It is our personal and unique interpretation of a communication exchange that prevents us from remembering the exact same incident. But while exactness may not be possible, the more we try to share our experiences the better we can understand others and improve our own accuracy.

MISCONCEPTION #2: MORE COMMUNICATION IS BETTER COMMUNICATION Even though communication is fundamentally important to every part of our lives, we should not assume that increasing the *amount* of communication results in greater benefit. More is not always better, because communication is governed by the law of diminishing returns—that is, increasing the quantity of the communication may actually compromise its quality. For instance, some of you may have debated about enrolling in college this semester. You may have talked about it repeatedly and still not made a decision until almost the beginning of the term. As a result, when you decided to enroll in college, you found that you had *talked* about the decision rather than made the decision and therefore had a more difficult time registering for the classes you wanted because they were already full. In this case, less talk and more action would have helped. Therefore, *more* communication does not always equal *better* communication.

Sometimes increasing the quantity of communication diminishes its quality.

MISCONCEPTION #3: COMMUNICATION SOLVES ALL CONFLICTS Communication does not solve all conflicts. Often people speak of communication as a cure for all ills. You have likely heard the following assertions: *People would have better health if they just communicated their feelings more. Relationships would be stronger and more satisfying if parents, partners, and friends opened up to one another. International tensions would be reduced if representatives from the affected nations engaged in peaceful negotiation.* Even though all of these assertions have some degree of validity, they are not absolutely true. Communication does not necessarily cure health or relational and national conflicts. Communication can increase understanding and get us closer to sharing meaning. Communication may help people and nations to identify difficulties and discover ways to address conflicts, but it is not a magic elixir that will cure all problems. To believe otherwise is to misunderstand communication. Communication can also potentially increase conflict if the goal of the communicators is *not* to share meaning but to win at all costs in the conflict. Perhaps it is better to say that effective and competent communication can increase our chances of understanding and of developing positive relationships, but communication is not a guarantee of success.

Identifying Communication Components

In order to better understand how communication is symbolic and how it is used to negotiate meaning, consider the components of communication. These include communicators (a sender and a receiver), a message, feedback, a channel, a context, noise, and motivation.

COMMUNICATORS   A **sender** is the originator of a message, whereas a **receiver** is the target or recipient of the message. The sender creates a message using a system of symbols the receiver will understand, such as a shared language. The receiver interprets the message. To put it another way, the sender and receiver constitute the *who* in the communication process; they are both communicators.

MESSAGE   The **message** is twofold (Watzlawick, Beavin, & Jackson 1967). First, the message is the *what* of the communication process. It constitutes the content one person wants to share with someone; it is the topic or substance of communication. Second, the message reflects the relationship that exists between the people communicating. For instance, although both your romantic partner and your mother may tell you, "I love you," there is an obvious difference in the meanings because of the nature of the relationships.

Sender ■ The originator of a message.

Receiver ■ The target or recipient of the message.

Message ■ The content one person seeks to share with another; the topic or substance of communication.

Feedback ■ A verbal or nonverbal response to communication.

Channel ■ The means by which a message is delivered from the sender to the receiver; the medium by which the message travels.

Context ■ A specific environment that includes a number of situational factors including physical, cultural, linguistic, social, temporal, and personal aspects.

Culture ■ "The learned patterns of perception, values, and behaviors, shared by a group of people that is also dynamic and homogenous" (Martin & Nakayama 2001, 23).

Noise ■ Any interference that occurs as people communicate.

Motivation ■ The reason or *why* of communication.

Instrumental (or functional) communication ■ Communication that achieves practical ends.

Relational communication ■ Communication that expresses emotions, strengthens bonds with others, or secures a sense of belonging.

Human communication is the process of negotiating symbolic meaning.

FEEDBACK   As Schramm (1955) emphasized, when people communicate, they respond to one another. Something as little as a smile or a frown can be a clear and powerful response—feedback—to another's message. This response—whether verbal or nonverbal—constitutes **feedback**. Feedback, therefore, is also a message, although it is typically a responsive message the receiver provides to the sender and may be positive or negative in tone, unintentional or intentional, understood or misunderstood, or a combination of these elements. Feedback—like *message*—may also be thought of as a part of the *what* in the communication process.

CHANNEL   The **channel** is the *how* of communication. It is the medium by which the message travels from the sender to the receiver. When people communicate face-to-face, the air carries the messages they send and receive. However, other channels include written letters, telephone calls, video conferencing, e-mail, instant messaging (IM), text messaging (SMS), and other emerging computer-mediated communication tools.

All communication occurs in a **context** or a specific environment that involves several situational factors, including physical, cultural, linguistic, social, temporal, and personal aspects. For example, **culture**—"the learned patterns of perception, values, and behaviors, shared by a group of people that is also dynamic and heterogeneous" (Martin & Nakayama 2001, 23)—affects our communication context through the native language we speak and customs, such as shaking hands. However, there are less obvious cultural influences that affect the context our communication. For example, our culture determines whether certain topics or terms are appropriate for casual or intimate conversation or even whether we should speak or remain silent. In other words, our culture "programs" us to communicate according to particular patterns that are imbued with unconscious ideas and ideals.

Consider, for example, how students communicate differently in the library than in the commons. What are some of the differences? Why do these differences exist? How does the physical arrangement, the cultural expectations, the social significance, or the time of day impact communication in these two very different spaces? Are you likely to hear different types of language used in these locations? Why? By reflecting on these questions, you can see that *where* and *when* communication takes place directly impact the nature of the communication.

NOISE   **Noise** refers to any interference that occurs as we communicate. This interference may be external (physical) or internal (psychological). For example, consider an early morning summer class where the groundskeeper is mowing the grass outside. Suddenly, a riding mower becomes the object of interest for a number of students. The external noise of the mower interferes with the communication in the classroom. Internal distractions such as being preoccupied with a problem or excited about an upcoming event also interfere with communication. How many times have you sat in class feeling worried, bored, sleepy, or hungry and suddenly realized that you had missed an important lecture point? In these instances you were experiencing internal interference or noise. (See the box "Communication Counts in Your Life: Concentration.")

MOTIVATION   **Motivation** is the final component of communication that we will examine. Motivation is our incentive for communication—the reason we listen, speak, or concentrate on our own thoughts or another's talk. Human communication, as we have already suggested, is a creative endeavor that arises from a variety of motives. When we communicate to achieve practical ends, we are engaging in **instrumental** or **functional communication**. For example, when you ask a classmate, "Can I copy your notes from the last class I missed?" you are engaged in instrumental communication. Other times, we communicate to express our emotions, strengthen bonds with others, or secure a sense of belonging; in these cases we are engaging in **relational communication**. For example, hanging

COMMUNICATION COUNTS IN YOUR LIFE

Concentration

Can't concentrate?
Lose your train of thought?
Find your mind wandering all the time?
Can't remember what you've been reading or studying?

These are all examples of mental noise that interferes with learning. How do you deal with this noise in order to more effectively engage your learning in college? To start, you can learn to improve your concentration; this can reduce frustration and earn you better grades. But improving your concentration requires developing methods of monitoring your attention span and redirecting your focus. Eliminating or minimizing distractions is a good place to start.

Reducing External and Internal Noise

You can often control external distractions by changing locations or arranging set study times. Internal distractions, however, are much more difficult to control because they interfere with your concentration and focus. To combat both types of distractions, try employing one or more of the following suggestions.

Combating External Noise

ESTABLISH A "DISTRACTION-FREE" STUDY AREA Find a study location away from your dormitory room, apartment, or home. Find a location on campus, in the community, or in your building that you find conducive for studying. Think of your study time as your "part-time" job. Go there and put in your hours.

TAKE CARE OF YOUR PHYSICAL NEEDS Overlooking your needs for rest, nutrition, exercise, and relaxation can cause concentration problems. Make sure that you are taking care of your body's needs so that your mind can do its work.

INSTITUTE REGULAR STUDY TIMES Start paying attention to your level of concentration throughout the day and in various settings. Are you able to concentrate better at certain times of days and in particular locations? Determining when and where you are at your peak levels of concentration will help you to set regular study times throughout the week.

BE HONEST WITH THOSE WHO ARE IMPORTANT TO YOU Let roommates, spouses, children, parents, and others involved in your life know that you need privacy and quiet to get your studies done.

Fighting Internal Noise

Here are some things you can try.

DEVELOP A "PURGE" LIST In order to get worries off your mind, begin your study session by jotting down on a piece of paper everything that's on your mind (i.e., needing milk and bread from the store, paying your telephone bill, worrying about your aunt's surgery). Keep this paper nearby while you study; when you find yourself getting distracted, you can "unload" these distractions and concentrate on your studies.

PAY ATTENTION TO CONCENTRATION When you begin to study or read, jot down the time you begin in the margin of your text or notes (i.e., 4:12 P.M.). Begin studying. Note when your attention begins to wander and write down that time (4:19 P.M.). Repeat the process when you begin again.

In sum, improving your concentration can help you accomplish more work in less time, reduce your levels of frustration and anxiety, and prepare you to function more effectively in your chosen field. Unfortunately, noise is more likely to increase as you take on additional responsibilities, so finding ways to enhance your attention span now will help you in college and will assist you in your profession.

out with your friends may include small talk, jokes, or serious conversations that help to express how you feel about one another while also reinforcing your ties to one another. Whatever the reason we communicate, there *is* a motive. This constitutes the *why* of communication—yet another important component of the communication process. These components of communication help us analyze most human communication and are summarized in Table 1.1. The following question helps summarize the components while providing us with a way to carefully observe almost any communication situation: *Who* (sender/receiver) is talking, listening, or responding to *whom* (receiver/sender), about *what* (content), *where* (context), *when* (context), *how* (channel), and *why* (motivation)?

Examining a Communication Model

In order to see the relationships between these various components of communication, let's take a look at a model of the communication process known as the **transactional model** (Wood 2001). If you observe people talking with one another, it soon becomes apparent that while we do take turns, sometimes we talk simultaneously or we may even interrupt or talk over one another. Even if we are not speaking at the same time, we still send nonverbal messages while we communicate. We send and receive messages simultaneously and therefore act as senders *and* receivers at the same time, as depicted in Figure 1.1

Transactional model ■ Depicts communication in which people act simultaneously as senders and receivers.

TABLE 1.1

COMPONENTS OF COMMUNICATION

WHO	Sender	Creates messages using symbols
	Receiver	Interprets symbols and assigns meanings
WHAT	Message	The content or the topic
		Indicates the relationship between sender and receiver
HOW	Feedback	Responsive message
	Channel	Means by which the message is delivered
		Examples: e-mail, letters, IM, videotape
WHERE	Context	The situation where communication occurs
WHEN	Context	The time of the communication
WHEN/WHERE	Noise	Interferences with communication
WHY	Motivation	Instrumental or functional—practical reasons
		Relational—connecting to others

Culture Counts

As the transactional model shows, the communication context surrounds the entire process of communication and therefore influences every aspect of the process. That's because context impacts the kinds of meanings people create, especially if the communicators share similar or have very different personal experiences (Wood 2001). For example, think of the challenges international students encounter in studying at universities in the United States. They face many strange contexts because their prior experiences include different native languages, climates, foods, holidays, values, and beliefs. Because of so many contextual changes, international students face **culture shock,** which Martin and Nakayama (2002) define as "a relatively short-term feeling of disorientation, or discomfort due to the unfamiliarity of surroundings and the lack of familiar cues in the environment" (89). An international student recently described her experience of studying in the United States by saying, "I feel invisible," while another said, "Learning in English is like trying to see through a gauzy cloth; everything was there but nothing was clear. Over time, it was like the cloth was being removed so that I could see what was going on around me." These students express the overwhelming challenges in understanding the context for communication in English, which is a significant factor in communication, as depicted by the transactional model.

The transactional model helps us relate the components of communication to one another, while also identifying some important characteristics of communication. However,

Culture shock ■ A relatively short-term feeling of disorientation or discomfort due to the unfamiliarity of surroundings and the lack of familiar cues in the environment.

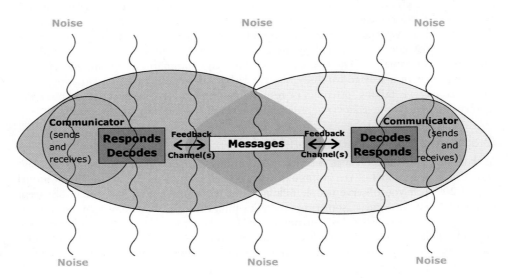

Transactional Communication Model

there are additional characteristics that will further clarify our understanding of communication, which we consider next.

Understanding Characteristics of Communication

As the linked loop in the transactional model suggests, communication is a **process**. In order to think carefully about communication, we divide and diagram the process into components. However, in reality communication is not a series of separate acts but is ongoing; it is not like a series of single frames examined one at a time but more like a movie in which the frames flow together. To illustrate, before coming to college, you probably spent a great deal of time thinking about which college to attend, what college life would be like, and how your life might change. Your thinking was probably influenced quite heavily by your life experiences and by the people with whom you spent a lot of your time. In other words, the communication you experienced before coming to college has impacted your current expectations and behaviors now that you are attending college; it also has influenced how you communicate with others about your college experience and will continue to influence this in the future.

International students encounter numerous challenges in understanding English given the influence of the context of communication, as the transactional model illustrates.

To take another example, if you have a best friend, you probably share a special communication code you have created as a result of prior communication with each other. Therefore, the two of you enjoy verbal or nonverbal shorthand: a word, phrase, or name holds special significance for both of you and creates a predictable reaction, even if you have not seen each other for a long period of time. This demonstrates that communication is indeed a process, because what you have shared before continues to influence your communication in the present and in the future.

COMMUNICATION IS SYMBOLIC   As communicators, we "interpret" words, gestures, and other symbols into messages.

COMMUNICATION IS TRANSACTIONAL   Whenever we communicate, we build on prior thoughts, experiences, and relationships so that we are changing through our communication with others.

COMMUNICATION IS CONTEXTUAL   We communicate differently depending on where we are and with whom we are communicating.

COMMUNICATION IS COMPLEX   Given what we have already discovered about the nature of human communication, this may already be apparent. As one student commented, "I never realized communication was so complicated!" Communication is **complex** because it requires people with possibly very different backgrounds and experiences to use ambiguous symbols to cocreate meaning in an environment that may be very noisy. It is noisy because we are considering what we think of the other person, what he or she might think of us, and what he or she might think we think of them. If this sentence makes you a little confused, it's because communication often requires us to wade through a very complex set of thoughts and feelings as we interpret meaning.

COMMUNICATION IS INTENTIONAL AND UNINTENTIONAL   **Intentionality** refers to what we plan or propose to do. The word suggests that we make choices and then act on them. Consider this question: Do we communicate even when we don't intend to do so? Watzlawick, Beavin, and Jackson (1967) contend that "one cannot *not* communicate." They believe that we communicate regardless of whether we choose to do so. Other communication theorists distinguish communication from communicative behavior. These scholars contend that communication is, by definition, always intentional or purposeful behavior. Have you ever been totally misunderstood and not known why? Think about what happened. In all likelihood, something you said or did was misinterpreted. To put it in terms we introduced earlier, the receiver of your message attached an intended meaning to your words or behavior that was, in fact, not your intention at all.

Communication may also be unintentional. Consider the example of an elementary school student in music class, listening to a group of his classmates practicing for an

Process ■ An ongoing activity.

Complex ■ Incorporating intention, relation, context, and ethics.

Intentional ■ Purposeful.

upcoming spring concert. As the group sang, the student rubbed his nose with his right hand. The teacher stopped the class and verbally rebuked him for the behavior. The young boy was astonished; he scratched his nose because it itched, but the teacher interpreted the behavior to mean that the student thought the group's singing "stunk." This example not only illustrates communication that is unintentional but also that communication is a process, because this event continued to influence the student's communication with his teacher during and after elementary school.

COMMUNICATION IS RELATIONAL AND CONTEXTUAL   As we explained earlier, communication includes both **content** and **relational dimensions.** We communicate information or a request, and we indicate how we feel about others in the manner in which we share the information or present the request. Although we may not be aware of it, we tell others how we view our relationships with them when we communicate. If a faculty member asks students to complete an assignment and invites questions and offers help, he or she is demonstrating that he or she recognizes the interpersonal quality of a teacher–student relationship. However, if a faculty member gives an assignment and does not allow an opportunity for questions, tells students to work problems out for themselves, or threatens to lower the students' grades if they pose questions or ask for help, the instructor communicates a very different view of his or her relationship with students by emphasizing the superior–subordinate roles of teacher and student.

To be successful in college, you must learn how to read these cues and respond accordingly from term to term as you meet new teachers. Even though this may at first seem relatively simple, learning to read relational messages is actually quite complicated. It becomes even more complicated when people have days when they do not feel well or are frustrated or overwhelmed and, as a result, act out of character. For example, a teacher who has been helpful and approachable all term may one day, in a stressful moment, become irritable and speak more firmly with students. No doubt his or her students ask, "What happened? I thought the teacher liked us! What did we do wrong?" Suddenly, the relational message shifts and communication becomes more complex.

COMMUNICATION IS ETHICAL   When we are faced with asking what is the *right* way or the *best* way to communicate in a given situation, we are dealing with the ethics of communication. If we seek to escape or ignore these questions, we have made a clear ethical choice. Consider these important questions about communication ethics: Is it ever appropriate to lie to someone? Should you confront a speaker in a public setting if you know his or her argument relies on false or misused information? Is it wise to tell your best friend that his partner is cheating on him? Should your campus allow all groups, even hate groups, to speak freely on campus? What is the best way to respond to a university employee who becomes verbally abusive when you ask to speak to her manager? Making these and other decisions about what is the right or appropriate communication in a given situation requires considerable wisdom and skill and makes communication even more complex! We discuss ethical communication further in the following section.

LINKING ETHICS AND COMMUNICATION

According to ethics professor Thomas Nilsen (1966), "As a subject of study, **ethics** deals with questions about the meaning of 'good' and 'bad,' 'right' and 'wrong,' and 'moral obligation'" (1). What does ethics have to do with communication? At the very least—as this definition asserts—communicators who are not coerced into a communication situation must understand and accept responsibility for the outcome of their communication interaction. Beyond that, ethics is fundamental to communication because any time our communication affects another, we are responsible for the outcome. In our daily interactions, we directly and sometimes dramatically affect others through our explanations, instructions, endearments, approval, rebuke, courtesy, and so on.

Instead of taking for granted that we "know" how others will react to our communication and that we "know" they won't be "harmed," we should think critically about our communication before we act. For example, is it wrong to tell a lie in order to spare someone's feelings? Should we tell the "whole" truth in all situations? If not, then under what circumstances is it acceptable to lie? What is a "lie" anyway? Are we lying when we let someone draw erroneous conclusions from something we said without attempting to clarify their misunderstanding? These questions are basic to any understanding of the role ethics plays in our communication.

How do we analyze a situation in order to make ethical communication decisions? First we examine our basic beliefs and values. These become the principles that provide a foundation for what is important to us and are derived from a wide variety of sources in our lives: family, church, school, friendships, media, organizations, and so on.

Ethical Principles

Perhaps the two primary principles that each of us will use when making decisions concern **honesty** and **truthfulness**. (The ethical principles discussed in this section are summarized in Table 1.2). Ethicist Sissela Bok (1978) explains, "There is great risk [in discussing truth and truthfulness] of not seeing the crucial differences between two domains: the *moral* domain of intended truthfulness and deception, and the much vaster domain of truth and falsity in general. The moral question of whether you are lying or not is not *settled* by establishing the truth or falsity of what you say. In order to settle this question, we must know whether you *intend your statement to mislead*" (6). In other words, to lie is to intentionally mislead another—by telling someone something that you know to be untrue or by withholding information that would change another's interpretation of the information. Whenever we intentionally manipulate information, we lie. Bok suggests, "A false person is not one merely wrong or mistaken or incorrect; it is one who is intentionally deceitful or treacherous or disloyal" (8).

Most of us cannot imagine a society in which *lying* is the norm. In order to function in our society, we must trust to some degree that what others say is true. For example, on the first day of your communication class, did you presume that your instructor would tell you the truth regarding the course's requirements? When you filled out your application for college, did you presume that the individuals reading that application would believe you were telling the truth? In the beginning stages of relationship development, we need to balance our expectations of "truthfulness" with our knowledge that some individuals, in some circumstances, do lie. Without some degree of trust, however, we would never be able to develop relationships of any significance. Thus, in order to survive, individuals in society must generally regard truthfulness as a central virtue.

Following the principles of honesty and truthfulness are the related principles of **confidentiality** (keeping secrets and confidences when requested). We learn early in our lives that keeping a promise or a secret is fundamental to successful relationships. Think about the individuals in your life to whom you act faithfully and whose promises you keep. The common denominator in each of these relationships is the degree of established trust between you and them. In turn, trust ensures fidelity and confidentiality.

Fairness is related to the principles of honesty and truthfulness, and it takes many forms. We may say something is *fair* if every person receives similar treatment. We may believe a situation is *fair* if the reward is commensurate with the effort or if the "punishment fits the crime." Or we may believe that fairness means those having more resources providing for

Honesty and truthfulness ■ Telling the truth and not withholding the truth.

Confidentiality ■ Keeping secrets and confidences when requested.

Fairness ■ The ethical quality of being equitable; free of favoritism or bias; acting impartially and justly, according to accepted standards.

TABLE 1.2

ETHICAL PRINCIPLES IN COMMUNICATION

Principle	Definition	Example
Honesty & Truthfulness	Telling the truth and not withholding the truth	Not lying to or misleading friends
Fidelity	Keeping promises and acting faithfully	Completing your share of group work which you agreed to do
Confidentiality	Keeping secrets and confidences when requested	Guarding friends' private information
Fairness	Appropriate treatment for everyone	A professor offering *all* students extra credit opportunities
Significant Choice	Sufficient information to make good choices	Knowing enough about college policies so that you can make an effective decision

Significant choice ■ Having sufficient information about a situation to make a "good" decision.

those with less. Regardless of your personal concept of fairness, we use this principle in making effective and ethical decisions. Think about what you believe is a "fair" grade for a course. Should fairness be decided only by doing assignments "correctly," or should other considerations such as completing work on time, neatness, and amount of research weigh in the grade? Should special consideration be given to those with certain circumstances such as illness, personal problems, or other coursework? These are ethical questions both you and your instructors will consider at some point during your college experience.

Finally, **significant choice** is a principle central to our democratic process. *Significant choice* means having sufficient information about a situation to make a "good" decision. It also speaks to our ability to make choices for ourselves. America's democracy requires that individuals become involved in the political and social processes that ground our society. Most of us consider significant choice a right. We may become angry, frustrated, and hostile when we perceive that others are keeping secrets from us or are withholding information critical to our ability to make good decisions. Significant choice is based on respect for individuals. Providing information in order to make rational, effective decisions means we value people as decision makers. If information is withheld, our autonomy (self-determination) is in jeopardy. When our autonomy is jeopardized, we resent the lack of respect this represents.

While significant choice is fundamental to our democracy, it is also fundamental to our intimate, interpersonal relationships. In good faith, we ground our closest relationships on exchanging truthful, complete information. When we discover that we can no longer trust someone we confided in, our whole world seems out of alignment. In order to develop healthy personalities and self-concepts, we need to believe that those important to us are providing us with complete and truthful information. Thus, it is in these close interpersonal relationships that a special sensitivity to ethical communication must be exercised.

Goals of Ethical Communication

Ethicists James Jaksa and Michael Pritchard provide four overriding goals for studying the ethics of communication:

■ First, a study of ethics *stimulates our moral imagination*. Each of us needs to be prepared for meeting the moral challenges that will inevitably confront us in our families, our jobs, and our lives. If we see that in any situation where we make a decision about rightness or wrongness, we are using our moral imagination, we can become better at making judgments and decisions.

■ Second, studying ethics helps us understand and *recognize ethical issues* in a given situation. Unless we recognize an issue in terms of its consequences for ourselves and others, we are bound to underestimate the impact of a decision. What are the consequences to our own sense of self when we lie to our employer? Do we begin to lose respect for our own trustworthiness?

■ Third, the more time we spend examining fundamental ethical concepts and principles, the more we *develop the analytical skills* necessary to make more effective and ethical decisions. When we analyze a situation thoroughly, we can see how our decisions impact others and we take greater responsibility for our choices. Complex ethical decisions require more than a simplistic assessment of a situation and a "quick fix." We can develop the ability to look at a much wider range of individuals affected by a decision when we enhance our ability to analyze a situation thoroughly.

Competent and ethical communication call for interpersonal respect, sensitivity, listening, tolerance for disagreement and dialogue.

■ Finally, developing effective and competent communication skills such as good listening, thinking reflectively about our and others' communication, and maintaining interpersonal sensitivity allows us to more effectively *tolerate disagreement* and differences of choice in others. This tolerance prevents us from labeling our choices as "moral" and opposite choices as "immoral." When we can truly look at another's decision from his or her experience—religious, political, economic, or any other—we may begin to understand why others communicate in the ways they do. This does not mean we automatically agree with their position but that we understand and tolerate it.

Ethical Communication as Competent Communication

Ethical communicators are more competent communicators. We hope that you are taking a class in human communication, in part, to become a more effective and competent communicator because *the success of every relationship in your lifetime will depend on your communication competence.* Whether it is your partner, coworker, best friend, boss, children, parents, or mechanic, you will need to communicate ethically and competently. Communication competence occurs when individuals communicate in ways that are responsible, effective, and appropriate that result in shared meaning between communicators. (Table 1.3 summarizes important information about competent communication.) Can you see that competence includes an ethical component? "Appropriateness" and "responsibility" ask us to make choices about our communication behavior for ourselves and others. Today, we extend communication competence expectations to relationships that are negotiated exclusively in a computer-mediated environment, where there is no face-to-face interaction. We believe that the basic definition of *competence* does not change simply because the channel of communication is computer-mediated.

TABLE 1.3

GUIDELINES FOR COMPETENT COMMUNICATION

- Knowledge of rules, norms, expectations, similarities, and differences among communicators and communication situations
- Sensitivity to and respect for others as humans, not as objects to be manipulated in a communication interaction
- Awareness and understanding of the ethical standards needed to judge the moral correctness and appropriateness of our communication

BECOMING A COMPETENT AND ETHICAL COMMUNICATOR IN COLLEGE, CAREER, AND LIFE

As a college student, you are immersed in a community in which a broad array of moral issues confront you daily. For example, what is your school's policy on each of the following issues?

Academic dishonesty or plagiarism
Tolerance and hate speech
Privacy and security
Drinking and drug use

On a more personal level, what do you believe characterizes true friendship during college? Have you modified your value system in terms of appropriateness of sexual intimacy in college relationships? What roles do prior sources of your ethical guidelines play now that you are in college? Finally, how tolerant are you of the ideas, feelings, and behaviors of others?

Tolerance at a basic level implies respect for one another. Respect doesn't mean we must agree with everything someone else says or does but simply that we believe every human being has value. And because they have value, they are entitled to equal treatment, rights, and justice. Because we respect others, we also tolerate differences in viewpoint and choices—again, not because we agree with the choice or point of view but because we believe humans are moral agents who are responsible for their own decisions. Respect doesn't mean that we permit people to violate the rights of others; tolerance doesn't mean we tolerate intolerance. The *Credo for Ethical Communication* developed by the National Communication Association (NCA) illustrates this clearly: "We condemn communication that degrades individuals and humanity through distortion, intimidation, coercion, and violence and through the expression of intolerance and hatred."

The NCA credo is the ethical code endorsed by the largest communication association in the United States (see the box, "Communication Counts in Your College Experience: The National Communication Association Credo for Ethical Communication"). Ultimately, the credo provides a set of principles that allows each of us to support the notion of **dialogue** as a foundation of effective, competent, and ethical communication. In dialogue, we communicate with each other, not to each other. Strike and Moss (1997, 194) provide four reasons to support dialogue as fundamental to effective communication:

1. Dialogue makes moral judgments more reasonable by bringing evidence and argument to bear on our opinions.
2. Dialogue is a way of affirming the equal right of people to participate in decisions that affect them.

Tolerance ■ Respect for one another.

Dialogue ■ Communicating with each other, not to each other.

The National Communication Association Credo for Ethical Communication

The statement that follows is from the National Communication Association and outlines ethical communication (see www.natcom.org/policies/External/EthicalComm.htm). How well do you think this statement captures the ethics of communication? How might this statement inform or influence your communication practices?

Questions of right and wrong arise whenever people communicate. Ethical communication is fundamental to responsible thinking, decision making, and the development of relationships and communities within and across contexts, cultures, channels, and media. Moreover, ethical communication enhances human worth and dignity by fostering truthfulness, fairness, responsibility, personal integrity, and respect for self and others. We believe that unethical communication threatens the quality of all communication and consequently the well-being of individuals and the society in which we live. Therefore we, the members of the National Communication Association, endorse and are committed to practicing the following principles of ethical communication:

- We advocate truthfulness, accuracy, honesty, and reason as essential to the integrity of communication.
- We endorse freedom of expression, diversity of perspective, and tolerance of dissent to achieve the informed

and responsible decision making fundamental to a civil society.

- We strive to understand and respect other communicators before evaluating and responding to their messages.
- We promote access to communication resources and opportunities as necessary to fulfill human potential and contribute to the well-being of families, communities, and society.
- We promote communication climates of caring and mutual understanding that respect the unique needs and characteristics of individual communicators.
- We condemn communication that degrades individuals and humanity through distortion, intimidation, coercion, and violence, and through the expression of intolerance and hatred.
- We are committed to the courageous expression of personal convictions in pursuit of fairness and justice.
- We advocate sharing information, opinions, and feelings when facing significant choices while also respecting privacy and confidentiality.
- We accept responsibility for the short- and long-term consequences for our own communication and expect the same of others.

Source: Reprinted by permission of the National Communication Association.

Dialogue is one of the primary characteristics of communication in professional settings.

3. Dialogue recognizes that sometimes what counts as the right thing to do is the product of an open and uncoerced agreement—a contract.
4. Dialogue accepts people's right to their own understanding of the meaning of respect and helps us to understand one another.

Strike and Moss summarize their support of dialogue by saying, "Why dialogue? Your character depends upon it" (195). As a college student, a professional, a family member, and a citizen, your character represents your moral decision making. For example, someone who tells a lie once is not usually perceived as "a liar," but someone who habitually tells lies is perceived as having a weak or untrustworthy character. Ethicist Karen Lebacqz suggests, "[E]ach choice about what to do is also a choice about whom to be—or, more accurately, whom to become" (1985, 83). Our character, then, is the accumulation of our choices about what it means to be a moral and ethical person.

Dialogue, however, is not just about speaking with others. Communicating with yourself is also important. While we understand that you have multiple goals for your college experience, we believe that your college education is primarily about learning. While this learning takes many forms, your academic performance remains vitally important. Research confirms that a reciprocal relationship exists between how you perceive yourself and your academic success (Bassett & Smythe 1979). In their research, Gage and Berliner (1992) assert that a positive sense of self alone is not enough to ensure academic success; self-esteem is not a panacea. However, a positive attitude is crucial. Seligman (1996) suggests that optimism is an important variable that ultimately impacts self-concept and academic achievement. Moreover, Bandura (1997) notes that self-efficacy is an important measure of academic success. Specifically, research suggests that when you increase your sense of self-expectancy, based on your prior academic experience, you can impact your success in specific subject areas like math, science, or reading.

So, what does all this mean for you? Believing in yourself is important; equal measures of positive attitude, personal expectation, and hard work are vital to academic success. Because you can't rely on positive thinking alone to graduate, you must be realistic about your strengths and weaknesses and respond accordingly. You can do this by monitoring and adjusting your self-perceptions based on external and internal feedback and using what you learn to strengthen your performance in college. Part of this process includes communicating with yourself by setting realistic goals and engaging in positive self-talk, which we will talk about more later. For now, remember that the messages you give yourself impact your level of success. As we noted at the beginning of this chapter, developing effective communication skills is vital to your college experience and to your future after you complete your education. Consider the story of Mike, an engineer who designs computer chips used in wildlife tracking equipment. Mike spends much of his day sitting at a computer and manipulating technical programs. It may seem as if he does not need to rely on communication with others; however, he also interacts with customers and makes presentations at scientific conferences and trade shows. He also regularly teaches classes at his church and voices his opinions about political issues that concern him. At one point Mike observed, "I would never have developed the confidence and ability to organize and express my thoughts if I had not taken a basic speech course in college. What I learned there has helped me think, write, and speak as nothing else ever has. I used these skills while I was in college, and I continue to use them in my life and work every day." While you may not share Mike's exact experience and while the course you are enrolled in is but one introductory course to human communication, remember that this course and future courses in communication can help you navigate college with greater ease and assist you in developing skills that will aid you for a lifetime—especially if you begin applying them now. As a first step in your learning the skills of effective communication, consider this: Take a few seconds before you provide feedback to another's communication so that you can consider whether you are interpreting the other's experience appropriately or whether you are judging without considering all of the issues important to an ethical response. We encourage you, then, to begin working on your communication skills today to enhance your success in college and later.

SUMMARY

In this chapter we introduced the important role communication plays in our college environment and in our personal, professional, and public lives. Rather than define human communication, we have offered various ways to describe it. As a result, we have established that human communication is a creative negotiated process. The following list highlights the major ideas in this chapter:

- Human communication includes senders, receivers, messages, feedback, channels, contexts, noise, and motivation.
- The transactional model best represents the human communication process, and it emphasizes the importance of context.
- Communication is a symbolic, transactional, contextual, complex, intentional or unintentional, relational, and ethical process that includes both relational and content messages.
- There are numerous misconceptions about communication.

QUESTIONS FOR DISCUSSION

1. In what ways have you used oral communication to enhance your learning as a college student?
2. Provide personal examples that illustrate this phrase: "When we communicate with one another, we are negotiating meaning."
3. How might a different channel influence how a message is understood? Give examples of messages that might have different interpretations depending on the channel used to send and receive the message.
4. Some people argue that animals are better communicators than people. Do you agree? Why or why not? How might animals and people communicate differently if, indeed, you believe animals communicate?

EXERCISES

1. Think of a time when you have been misunderstood. Using at least two of the concepts from this chapter, write a brief paragraph that explains why this misunderstanding took place.

2. You have had considerable experience with a variety of teachers during your 12-plus years of education. Without naming any teacher, identify one of your teachers who you believe was an effective communicator and one who was not as effective. Analyze the communication characteristics of these two teachers. Write a one-page essay explaining your analysis.

3. Assume that you want to break up with a romantic partner whom you have been dating for several months. Analyze this communication situation drawing on the information you have read in this chapter. How will you do this? What kinds of messages will you develop? What channels will you use? Where will you explain your decision? What ethical issues will you need to consider?

KEY TERMS

Channel 8
Complex 11
Confidentiality 13
Content dimension 12
Context 8
Culture 8
Culture shock 10
Dialogue 15
Ethics 12
Fairness 13

Feedback 8
Fidelity 6
Honesty and truthfulness 13
Human communication 5
Instrumental (or functional) communication 8
Intentional 11
Message 7
Motivation 8
Noise 8

Paralanguage (or vocalics) 6
Process 11
Receiver 7
Relational communication 8
Relational dimension 12
Sender 7
Significant choice 14
Symbolic 5
Tolerance 15
Transactional model 9

REFERENCES

Aslanian, C. B. 1996. *Adult learning in America: Why and how adults go back to school.* Washington, DC: Office of Adult Learning Services, the College Board.

Astin, A. W. 1985. *Achieving educational excellence.* San Francisco: Jossey-Bass.

Barker, L., Edwards, B. R., Gaines, C., Gladney, K., and Holley, F. 1980. An investigation of the proportional time spent in various communication activities by college students. *Journal of Applied Communication Research* 8:101–110.

Bandura, A., 1997. *Self-efficacy: The exercise of control.* New York: Freeman.

Bassett, R., and Smythe, M. J. 1979. *Communication and instruction.* New York: Harper & Row.

Bok, S. 1978. *Lying: Moral choice in public and private life.* New York: Vintage Books.

Brown, A. C. 1996. Older & better: Back to the classroom (Minneapolis-St. Paul) *Star Tribune.* Online (www.startribune.com/mcu/projects/learning/content/story2.html).

Dance, F. X. E., and Larson, C. E. 1976. *The functions of human communication: A theoretical approach.* New York: Holt, Rinehart and Winston.

Gage, N., and Berliner, D. 1992. *Educational psychology.* 5th ed. Boston: Houghton Mifflin.

Gardner, J. N., and Jewler, A. J. 2003. *Your college experience: Strategies for success.* 5th ed. Belmont, CA: Wadsworth.

Johnson, G. M., Staton, A. Q., and Jorgensen-Earp, C. R. 1995. An ecological perspective on the transition of new university freshmen. *Communication Education* 44:336–352.

Lebacqz, K. 1985. *Professional ethics: Power and paradox.* Nashville: Abingdon Press.

Myers, G. E., and Myers, M. T. 1992. *The dynamics of human communication: A laboratory approach.* 6th ed. Boston: McGraw-Hill.

Martin, J. N., and Nakayama, T. K. 2001. *Experiencing intercultural communication: An introduction.* Mountain View, CA: Mayfield.

National Center for Education Statistics. (n.d.). *Digest of education statistics for 2002: All levels of education.* Retrieved June 2, 2010, from http://nces.ed.gov/fastfacts/display.asp?id=40

Nilsen, T. R. 1966. *Ethics of speech communication.* New York: Bobbs-Merril.

Noel, L., Levitz, R., and Saluri, D., eds. 1985. A study of first-generation college students and their families. *American Journal of Education* X:144–170.

Richman, J. 2002. The news journal of the life scientist. *Scientist* 16(18):42.

Schramm, W. 1955. *The process and effects of mass communication.* Urbana: University of Illinois Press.

Seligman, M. 1996. *The optimistic child: How learned optimism protects children from depression.* New York: Houghton Mifflin.

Strike, K. A., and Moss, P. A. 1997. *Ethics and college student life.* Boston: Allyn and Bacon.

Sypher, B. D., Bostrom, R. N., and Seibert, J. H. 1989. Listening communication abilities and success at work. *Journal of Business Communication* 25:293–303.

Terenzini, P. T., Rendon, L. I., Millar, S. B., Upcraft, M. L., Gregg, P. L., Jamolo, R. Jr., and Allison, K. W. 1996. Making transition to college. In *Teaching on solid ground: Using scholarship to improve practice,* eds. R. J. Menges, M. Weimer, and associates, 43–73. San Francisco: Jossey-Bass.

Watzlawick, P., Beavin, J., and Jackson, D. D. 1967. *Pragmatics of human communication.* New York: Norton.

Wolvin, A. D., and Coakley, C. G. 1991. A survey of the status of listening and training in some Fortune 500 companies. *Communication Education* 40:52–164.

Wood, J. T. 2001. *Communication mosaics: An introduction to the field of communication.* Belmont, CA: Wadsworth.

CHAPTER 2 Perception: Self, Others, and Communication

LEARNING OUTCOMES After reading this chapter, you will have:

the **Knowledge** to...   and the **Skills** to...

UNDERSTANDING THE PROCESS OF PERCEPTION, page 21

Comprehend the five stages of the perception process.

- Note what attracts your attention and how you select what to focus on.
- Become aware of your scripts or mental organizational patterns that arrange and inform your behavior.
- Understand how you assign meaning and value through interpreting and evaluating your perceptions.

FACING PERCEPTUAL CHALLENGES, page 23

Recognize potential challenges with perception.

- Realize how prior experiences shape your thinking.
- Avoid using stereotypes when drawing conclusions.
- Remain open-minded and guard against selectivity.
- Consider how your cognitive orientation influences your preferences.

CONNECTING PERCEPTION AND COMMUNICATION: A RECIPROCAL RELATIONSHIP, page 25

Understand reciprocal relationship between perception and communication.

Use your perceptual skills to improve your communication with others.

- Be aware of how your self-concept, self-esteem, and self-fulfilling prophecies impact how you perceive yourself and others.
- Use positive self-talk to enhance your self-image and mental health.
- Realize how others shape your ideas and perceptions.

- Avoid comparing yourself negatively to others.
- Develop a positive self-image.
- Avoid internalizing others' self-appraisal; be your own person.

IMPROVING YOUR PERCEPTUAL SKILLS, page 32

Employ specific strategies to enhance your perceptual abilities.

- Guard against perceptual errors by checking the facts.
- Gather additional information before forming conclusions.
- Use perception checking by asking questions first without making judgments.
- Adjust your perceptions, understanding that time and circumstances influence perception.
- Practice empathy by respecting other points of view.

ENACTING COMPETENT AND ETHICAL PERCEPTION IN COLLEGE, CAREER, AND LIFE, page 34

Understand how to form competent and ethical perceptions.

- Be mindful of how family, religion, and culture shape your perceptions and ethical decision making.

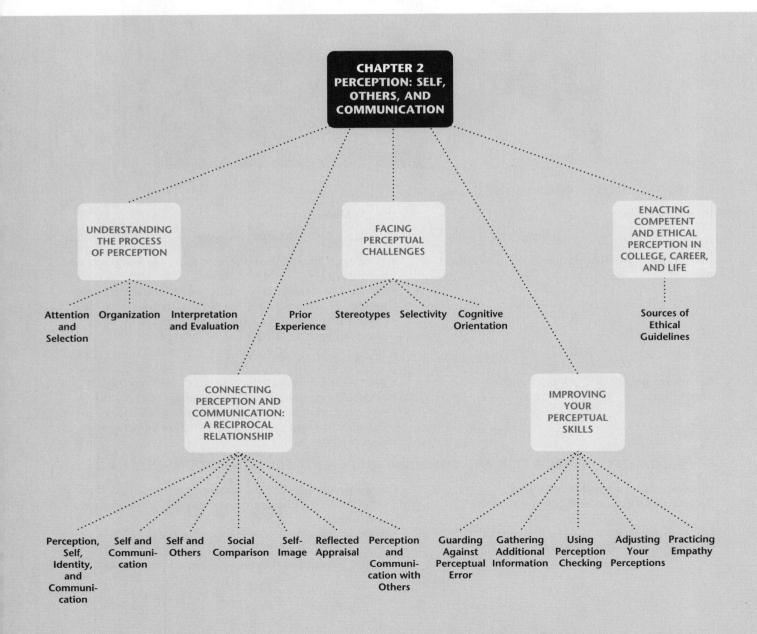

UNDERSTANDING THE PROCESS OF PERCEPTION

CLARENCE: "Wow, that tastes great!"

BRAD: "Are you kidding? I don't know how you stomach that stuff!"

LATISHA: "Why would anybody ever wear an outfit like that?"

ROBIN: "Come on! It's a cool dress."

JOEY: "Let's get in line again. I love riding this roller coaster."

ANN: "No way! I can't stand those gigantic drops and upside-down turns!"

In each of these examples, both people tasted the same food, saw the same dress, and rode the same amusement park ride, and yet they had completely different responses. You have probably heard or been engaged in conversations like these before. You may experience the same tastes, sights, or movements but perceive them very differently than someone else. For example, you and your roommate may disagree about the "best" time of the day. Maybe you're a morning person, while your roommate is a night owl. So, you want to study at 11:00 A.M., before class, and he wants to study at 11:00 P.M. While 11:00 is the same number on your clocks, it means completely different things to each of you: You perceive time differently. In this chapter, we discuss the process of perception and its problems, consider the reciprocal relationship between communication and perception, examine self-perception and the perception of others, and suggest ways to apply the chapter's insights to college, career, and life contexts.

Perception is the process of becoming aware of people, events, or objects and then attaching meaning to your awareness. For instance, when you step into a crowded room and all conversations stop, you may have the sense that you've interrupted something. In another example, if the person to whom you are speaking takes a step backward, you may recognize that you are standing too close in that specific situation. Each of these examples illustrates perception, and the process of perception involves attention, selection, organization, interpretation, and evaluation. Let's consider each of these steps in the process in Figure 2.1.

Attention and Selection

Attention—the first stage in the perception process—refers to something that causes you to be aware of a stimulus around you. For example, you may pass someone on your way to class who is wearing an appealing fragrance that stimulates your sense of smell. You are bombarded by a host of stimuli every day that involve your senses of sight, smell, hearing, taste, and touch. A colorful bouquet of carnations, a freshly baked pizza, a blaring car alarm, a warm chocolate chip cookie, or the rough stubble on a beloved grandfather's face—these stimuli surround you all the time.

Perception ■ The process of becoming aware of people, events, or objects and attaching meaning to that awareness.

Attention ■ The first stage of perception; awareness of certain stimuli.

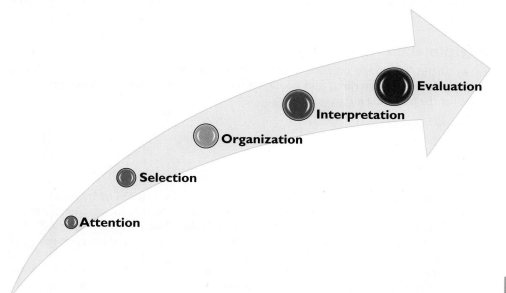

FIGURE 2.1
The Perception Process.

Attention and selection make your friends "stand out" in a crowded hallway.

Culture Counts

Selection ■ The second stage of perception; focusing on specific stimuli.

Scripts ■ Mental organization patterns that help arrange information and inform behavior.

Interpret ■ Assign meaning to information.

Evaluate ■ Decide on the worth or value of information.

While you may be aware of all these stimuli, you do not consciously attend to them all; you select some over others. **Selection,** the second stage of perception, refers to those stimuli that you focus on (Devito 2008). Depending on your exposure, you will retain only certain things. Because your attention is limited, your perception will focus on specific stimuli. For example, you probably attend to stimuli that impress you in some way—you notice the smell of fresh bread coming from a cafeteria because you are hungry. In this case, you select stimuli related to your needs. You may also pay attention to sensory information because of your interests. For example, while you are heading across campus, you see a good friend walking with a group of students. Despite the crowd around her, you focus on your friend to see if she is wearing the new baseball cap you bought her. You also tend to select stimuli that are intense or novel. For instance, if you hear a bloodcurdling scream in the middle of the night, you'll wake up with an adrenaline rush. The intensity and uniqueness of the experience grab your attention.

Organization

Organization—the third step in the process of perception—helps us understand the world around us. Because we are surrounded by so many stimuli, we seek to organize them in order to help make sense of our world and reduce uncertainty (Berger 1979).

We organize our perceptions according to prior experience, particularly to the principle or similarity and difference, and we rely on patterns. For example, in a parking lot full of cars, you typically perceive just a mass of cars rather than different makes and models. However, if you are looking for your own car, you will scan the mass of cars looking only for the red one or the one with a tennis ball on the antenna.

You also rely on **scripts** or mental organizational patterns to help arrange information and inform behavior. For instance, different cultures have unique greeting and leave-taking behaviors that convey certain meanings. When Korean students come to the United States to study and greet their professors for the first time, they often bow and then shake hands. In the Korean culture and in other Asian cultures, bowing is the appropriate way to greet someone of higher status. U.S. professors, unaware of this cultural script, may return the bow, working off their own script, which reads, "Mirror the greeting you receive." In this case, the cultural scripts collide, because if the professor bows, the students will be required to bow once more, only more deeply than the first time. As you can see, we respond to observed behaviors by drawing on our own experiences and the mental scripts we have created from our cultural backgrounds. Often, these differing perceptions cause confusion or uncertainty.

Interpretation and Evaluation

As we attend, select, and organize information, we also interpret and evaluate it—that is, we assign meaning (**interpret**) and decide on the information's worth or value (**evaluate**). Consider the following information:

1,500,000
€1,500,000
£1,500,000
$1,500,000

Which piece of information holds the most meaning and value for you? If you live in the European Union, the second number has greater meaning and value. If you live in the United Kingdom, the third symbol is more meaningful. And if you live in the United States, the fourth number holds more value. Of course, the process of interpretation and evaluation is more complex than this simple illustration.

Interpretation—the fourth step in the perception process—requires you to determine meaning. This assignment of meaning can be done quickly, as in the previous example, or it may take more deliberation. In another example, if you came upon a picnic table in a

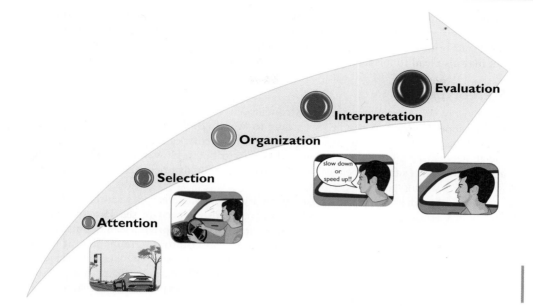

FIGURE 2.2
The Perception Process
in Action.

park with a brightly colored tablecloth, helium balloons, and a layer cake, it would be safe to assume that you were witnessing preparations for a birthday party or some other celebration. These external signs helped you to figure out the most likely cause for this park scenario.

The final step in the process of perception is evaluation, the determination of meaning or value. Once we have attended to new stimuli, selected the most critical information, organized the message, and interpreted its meaning, we need to assign importance to the information. For example as Figure 2.2 shows, if we are zooming down the road and see a yellow light ahead (attention), we take note (selection) of our speed and the distance to the stoplight, and decide whether to slow down or speed up (interpretation). If we braked rather than accelerating and narrowly missed the vehicle starting into the intersection, we can congratulate ourselves (evaluation) on avoiding an accident.

As we will discuss in Chapter 4, language encompasses layers of meaning, which are interpreted and evaluated. To make the point simply, consider the word *snaps*. What does this word make you think of—a sound, a type of candy, a fastener on clothing, or a photograph? Depending on where you live and how you were raised, the word *snaps* will have different meanings for you. This example illustrates an important point that we will consider next: Perception has limitations and problems.

FACING PERCEPTUAL CHALLENGES

In reality, everyone's perception is limited. While people with physical, cognitive, or learning disabilities are often thought of as challenged, in reality, we are all limited. For example, some people have a stronger sense of taste, hearing, or smell, while others have greater visual acuity. In fact, as we age, our senses become more limited. Furthermore, if we compare ourselves to other species, we discover that our hearing, for example, pales in comparison to that of an owl, a whale, or a dog. Beyond physical challenges, sometimes we face perceptual challenges because our past experiences differ significantly from those around us. We may also have differing expectations on what we think is the best course of action or the best outcome for something, or our self-concept may be marred by bad experiences in the past, so we may be unable to fully perceive what is truly happening.

Still, most perceptual challenges are not linked to these limits but to prior experience, stereotypes, selectivity, and cognitive orientation.

Prior Experience

As we noted in our discussion of scripts, our prior experiences frame our perceptions. For example, you may avoid going to the dentist because you once had a very painful tooth extraction and, as a result, you are frightened and anxious about future dentist visits.

Stereotypes ■ Conclusions drawn from generalizations; predictive generalizations about people or situations.

Prejudice ■ A definitive negative attitude toward a group.

Discrimination ■ Unfair treatment of a given group of people based on prejudice.

In another example, if your experiences with older people have been friendly, encouraging, and enjoyable, you may be more likely to get to know your elderly neighbors. In short, our prior experiences with specific events, people, or places frame our perceptions but may also lead to misperceptions, stereotypes, prejudice, and discrimination.

Stereotypes

When people use **stereotypes,** they draw conclusions about individuals based on a generalization about a group of people. According to Wood (2009) stereotypes are "predictive generalizations about people or situations" (43). Stereotypes may be based on ethnic, racial, gender, sexual, religious, or even physical attributes. However, not all stereotypes are negative. For example, the idea that "Hispanics are family oriented and warmhearted" is a positive stereotype.

While they may help us organize information neatly, stereotypes can be both good and bad. Certainly they can engender positive ideals, as seen in the Hispanic family example, but they can also create false categories that lead to **prejudice,** a definitive negative attitude toward a given group, which in turn can lead to **discrimination,** or unfair treatment of a given group of people. As a result, a host of "isms" may ensue, including ageism, sexism, racism, ableism, and ethnocentrism. All of these "isms" rest on the assumption that one group is superior to another, which supports harmful stereotypes that lead to prejudice and discrimination.

Keep in mind that prejudice—whether positive or negative—can blind individuals or groups to alternate beliefs. For example, if you were raised in India under the traditional caste system, you would likely hold specific beliefs about people in each of the five castes, or classes of Indian society. You might espouse the belief that people are born into, associate within, and die in a certain caste, and you would likely understand why a member of the merchant class (Vaishya) would never socialize with an "untouchable" (Harijan). In short, if you believe that a certain group of people is better than another, you harbor prejudicial attitudes.

Selectivity

As we noted in our discussion of the process of perception, you select certain stimuli more than others. This leads to a perceptual challenge: You tend to see what you choose to see. In other words, your experiences, cultures, beliefs, values, and other factors cause you to focus on the information that you find the most comfortable, credible, or compelling. Therefore, if you expect a certain person or group of people to behave in a particular manner, you will see exactly what you expect. This creates a potentially vicious cycle: Your perceptions create your expectations, and your expectations confirm your perceptions. Psychologist Abraham Maslow once noted, "It is tempting, if the only tool you have is a hammer, to treat everything as if it were a nail" (1966, 15). Selectivity, then,

TABLE 2.1

ARE YOU LEFT-BRAINED OR RIGHT-BRAINED?

Do you prefer information that is ...		
logical, orderly, well planned, evidence based, and written?	or	visual, feeling based, and shared conversationally?
If you answered "yes," you are likely **left-brained.** In this class, you will probably find outlining, organizing, and supporting your ideas relatively easy.		If you answered "yes," you are likely **right-brained.** In this class, you will probably find ideas about interpersonal communication particularly interesting and share your feelings easily in class discussions.

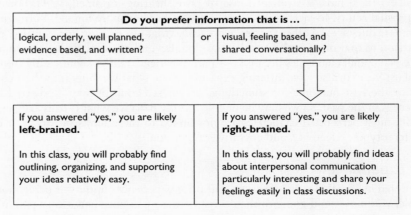

TABLE 2.2

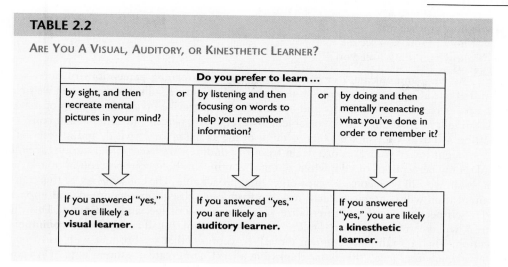

ARE YOU A VISUAL, AUDITORY, OR KINESTHETIC LEARNER?

Do you prefer to learn ...				
by sight, and then recreate mental pictures in your mind?	or	by listening and then focusing on words to help you remember information?	or	by doing and then mentally reenacting what you've done in order to remember it?
If you answered "yes," you are likely a **visual learner.**		If you answered "yes," you are likely an **auditory learner.**		If you answered "yes," you are likely a **kinesthetic learner.**

makes it very difficult to gain new information or insight; this hinders open-mindedness and perception checks, both of which we will discuss later in this chapter.

Cognitive Orientation

Cognitive orientation refers to how you process information and is directly tied to perception. We usually think of cognitive orientation as *learning style* or brain dominance. **Brain dominance** refers to the side of the brain you tend to use. Table 2.1 shows a list of qualities that may help you determine your learning style or perceptual preference.

Brain dominance is also reflected in our learning styles. There are various learning styles, which we cover in depth in other chapters. However, to simplify, think of yourself as a visual, auditory, or kinesthetic learner. Table 2.2 summarizes information about these learning styles.

What does cognitive orientation have to do with perception? Because you "see" information in a particular fashion, you are likely to positively perceive information that is organized according to your preferences and negatively perceive information that is, in your view, disorganized. For example, if you are a left-brain, auditory learner, you probably have a negative impression of a professor whose lectures are not well organized and whose assignments ask you to create a visual product such as a collage or a diagram. On the other hand, if you are a right-brained, visual learner, you are likely to find this same professor an excellent teacher.

These orientations can create tensions between people. However, you can develop your skills to compensate for your orientations and avoid the problems that may result. One way to do this is by taking courses or engaging in activities that don't necessarily match your cognitive orientations. Even though they would be challenging, these classes or activities will help you become a well-rounded learner. To summarize, differing cognitive orientations determine your preferred ways of attending, selecting, organizing, interpreting, and evaluating the multiple stimuli in the world around you, and they frame your perceptions about your world. These perceptions, in turn, guide your responses and create learning and relational challenges.

CONNECTING PERCEPTION AND COMMUNICATION: A RECIPROCAL RELATIONSHIP

Now that you have a basic understanding of the process and challenges of perception, you can think more about the impact that perception and communication have on each other. Campbell and Hepler (1970) assert that every communication encounter includes six people:

- how I see myself
- how you see yourself
- how I see you

Cognitive orientation ■ How a person processes information—visual, auditory, or kinesthetic; also termed *learning style.*

Brain dominance ■ Refers to the side of the brain a person is more likely to use, left (logic and writing based) or right (visual and feeling based).

Intrapersonal communication ■
Internalizing messages and communicating with yourself about yourself; also termed *self-talk*.

Self ■ The sum of your personality, character, and identity.

■ how you see me
■ how I think you see me
■ how you think I see you

As we communicate, our prior, immediate, and ongoing perceptions of ourselves and of one another inform our communication. As Figure 2.3 illustrates, if when we first meet I perceive you as friendly and open, then I might strike up a conversation or make small talk in an attempt to be sociable. However, if you perceive my attempts at conversation as intrusive, you are likely to think of me as pushy or forward, and in response you might lower your eyes or refrain from responding. After our initial meeting, I will adapt my perceptions of you, while you may continue to hold your perception of me. As a result, we will both consider each other unapproachable. The consequence of this communication will continue because it will inform our subsequent encounters and impact our self-perceptions: I will internalize your impression of me, and vice versa. This, in turn, will create a round of self-talk, or what some scholars call **intrapersonal communication**. This self-talk may confirm the self-perceptions that we brought with us to our initial encounter (e.g., "Everyone thinks I'm a jerk!") or create questions (e.g., "Do people respond to me like this because there's something wrong with me?"). Perception and communication, then, are reciprocal: One influences the other.

Because perception's influence on communication is a dynamic process, in order to understand it more completely, let's consider how we perceive ourselves and others.

Perception, Self, Identity, and Communication

How you perceive yourself influences how you communicate with yourself and with others. We use the term **self** to mean the combination of personality, character, and

FIGURE 2.3

Perceptions Inform Our Communication.

identity—all of what makes you you. In order to understand self-perception, we must think about three important related concepts: self-concept, self-esteem, and self-fulfilling prophecy.

Self-concept refers to the relatively stable mental image you hold of yourself; this self-image includes how you view your personality as well as your strengths and weaknesses. Your self-concept is like a compass that always points to your perceived "true personality." For example, if you believe that you are a shy person, that belief is part of your perceived self-concept. **Self-esteem,** on the other hand, refers to how you *feel* about yourself, or the value or worth you place on yourself. Some refer to self-esteem as *self-respect.* To expand on the previous example, if you believe you are *too* shy, then you are evaluating a part of your perceived self-concept, which affects your self-esteem accordingly.

Self-concept and self-esteem influence each other because who you believe you are influences how worthy you feel, and how worthy you feel influences who you believe you are. These powerful psychological influences can lead to **self-fulfilling prophecies,** events that are more likely to transpire because you expect them to. For example, if you expect to do poorly on your first speech in this class, you increase the likelihood that you will, indeed, not do as well as you could had you not expected a substandard performance. If you possess low self-esteem, you are likely to fall prey to the power of negative self-fulfilling prophecies: Your expectation becomes your reality.

While these are important and powerful concepts, it is important to clarify that you cannot suddenly become proficient in a given area simply by thinking more positively about yourself. Rather, first you must become aware of your strengths and weaknesses. Know what you do well and what requires more work on your part. Then set realistic goals, accomplish those goals, and congratulate yourself for reaching them. This will provide a strong sense of self and self-worth based on sound expectations, thereby creating a motivating self-fulfilling prophecy. The box "Communication Counts in Your Career: Using the Self-Fulfilling Prophecy" reviews another way to think about self-fulfilling prophecy as you move into the world of work and provides insights for your college career.

Self and Communication

As you interact with others and examine yourself, you internalize messages and communicate with yourself about yourself. As we have noted, some people refer to this as *self-talk,* or

Self-talk has a powerful impact on your self-concept and mental health.

Self-concept ■ The relatively stable mental image a person holds of himself or herself.

Self-esteem ■ The value or worth a person places on himself or herself.

Self-fulfilling prophecies ■ Events that are more likely to transpire because someone expects them to.

COMMUNICATION COUNTS IN YOUR CAREER

Using the Self-Fulfilling Prophecy

Read the following article by Max Garfinkle of Capability Snapshots, Inc., a Canadian organizational consulting firm (see www.capsnap.com/max/maxarticle1.asp?ID=7). After you read the article, reflect on the questions at the end of this box.

Expectations Shape Reality

In 1932 the American public lost faith in the ability of the banks to guarantee their deposits. People ran to the banks trying to get their money out before the banks became insolvent. This mass behavior did indeed force banks, even those with sufficient funds, to close their doors on frantic depositors.

The sociologist Robert K. Merton coined the term "the self-fulfilling prophecy" to explain this turn of events. Once the public perceived the situation as a threat, their subsequent behavior turned those fears into a reality. He defined a self-fulfilling prophecy as "a false definition of a situation evoking a new behavior which makes the originally false perception come true."

However, self-fulfilling prophecies can be based on true as well as false definitions of a situation. They can be used for positive as well as for negative outcomes. Another sociologist, W. I. Thomas, stated this fundamental truth about human nature: "If men define situations as real, they are real in their consequences." In essence, expectations shape reality.

The nature of the expectation of success by an individual, a group, or an organization as a whole leads to the kind of striving that is likely to result in outcomes supporting the initial prophecy. This principle can be demonstrated by viewing the sales achievements of four types of salespersons:

• The *average achiever* sets limited goals and puts forth moderate effort to achieve these goals. The prophecy is fulfilled with the achievement of these limited goals.

(continued)

- The *outstanding achiever* sets stretch goals and puts forth strenuous effort to achieve these goals. Again, the prophecy is fulfilled with the achievement of the stretch goals.
- The *anxious achiever* sets limited goals and puts forth strenuous effort. The salesperson is afraid to aspire higher for fear of failure. The self-fulfilling prophecy is based on the expectation that hard work is needed to assure even limited success.
- The *self-deflating achiever* sets stretch goals to gain approval, but puts forth only moderate effort, never coming near to the goals set. This sales rep starts with an expectation of personal inadequacy that gets reinforced by continuously disappointing performance. Even the moderate effort is more a show of work, more a display of rote behavior than of looking after the essentials.

Types of Managers

This concept of a "self-fulfilling prophecy" can be applied to the leadership behavior of any manager by keeping in mind one distinction. The sales rep sets *personal* goals and is *personally* responsible for his/her own effort. The manager sets the direction toward *unit* goals [department, division] and endeavors to mobilize *unit-wide* effort on behalf of these goals. Leadership effectiveness is determined by the extent that the unit achieves its unit goals. There are four types of managers analogous to the four types of sales reps:

- The *average* manager sets limited goals for the unit and mobilizes moderate unit-wide efforts to achieve these limited goals.
- The *outstanding* manager sets stretch goals for the unit and mobilizes strenuous unit-wide efforts to achieve these strenuous goals.
- The *anxious* manager sets limited goals for the unit and mobilizes strenuous unit-wide efforts to achieve these limited goals. What a waste of potential!
- The *self-defeating* manager sets stretch goals for the unit but mobilizes only moderate unit-wide effort. The unit learns not to take the stretch goals too seriously.

In both situations we can portray a 2 3 2 table based on the interaction between "Level of Aspiration" and "Degree of Effort," leading to four prototypical cases. The following table illustrates these cases.

Four Types of Achievers			
		Level of Aspiration	
		Limited Goals	Stretch Goals
Degree of Effort	Moderate	AVERAGE	SELF-DEFEATING
	Strenuous	ANXIOUS	OUTSTANDING

Coaching Managers

The leader who understands the dynamics of the self-fulfilling prophecy can use it to coach managers to become outstanding achievers. The process is a gradual, step-by-step change.

- The self-defeating manager can be helped to become an average manager. The leader has to put this manager on a "guaranteed success" program, lowering the goals to make them fit the actual moderate effort. The expectations of failure, disappointment, and a sense of personal inadequacy have to be broken. Once success comes to be expected, the moderate efforts become more functional, replacing the earlier superficial style.
- The average manager has to pass through the stage of being an anxious manager en route toward eventually becoming an outstanding achiever. The leader has to help the manager get his/her unit to put forth more strenuous effort while still retaining limited goals. The unit comes to expect success as a result of the hard work.
- The anxious manager, whose unit is accustomed to strenuous effort, can now be converted into an outstanding manager. The leader has to help the manager gradually raise the bar and let go of the security blanket of readily achievable targets. Not only the manager but also the whole unit becomes higher performing, constantly trying to surpass its best achievements.

- Outstanding managers and units should have their successes recognized and be properly compensated.

For the sales rep the difference between moderate and strenuous effort lies in the effort to cultivate the personal competencies required for sales success. For the manager of a unit, the difference between modest and strenuous effort lies in the effort to build unit capabilities required for unit success.

The CEO directs toward organization goals and endeavors to mobilize organization-wide effort on behalf of these goals. For the CEO, the difference between modest and strenuous effort lies in the effort to build organization capabilities essential for strategic success.

Expectations lead to efforts to shape reality in the direction of the expectations.

Questions

1. What is Garfinkle's main point?
2. How is this point relevant to your future career, even if you do not intend to enter business?
3. How can Garfinkle's insights assist you as you complete your college education? To help in answering this question, review the table in the article.

Source: "Using the Self-Fulfilling Prophesy: Expectations Shape Reality," by Max Garfinkle, www.capsnap.com. Reprinted by permission of CSI Diagnostics, Inc.

intrapersonal communication. Some argue that intrapersonal communication is not authentic communication, but we can all agree that self-talk certainly occurs; indeed, emerging research reveals that intrapersonal communication is a viable field of inquiry in the discipline of communication (see Aitken & Shedletsky 1995). Perhaps more importantly, however, research indicates that self-talk has a powerful impact on the state of your self-concept and mental health, even after suffering traumatic life events (see Kubany et al. 2004). For example, after the death of a loved one, you will be extremely sad. Instead of berating yourself for being weak or emotional, you could tell yourself, "Feeling this sadness is normal and is to be expected. I just need to work through these feelings as part of my grief." Intrapersonal communication, therefore, helps frame and form our self-perception.

Self and Others

Your self-perception does not exist in a vacuum: Your self-perception develops as you interact with others, and your self-concept and self-esteem develop as you communicate. When other people praise your abilities or point out the areas where you need to develop your skills, you take this information to heart and, especially after repeated similar responses, adjust your self-concept. Therefore, your self-concept is relatively stable; however, it changes as you learn more about yourself from others. Likewise, your self-esteem increases when others affirm your value and worth as a person. Of course, if people put you down, make fun of you, or disconfirm your worth, your self-esteem suffers.

In addition to understanding how one's self concept is relatively stable but shaped by experiences and relationships, it is important to understand the role played by the **generalized other,** the common expectations within a social group that dictate acceptable beliefs and actions. For instance, in countries where the media is highly restricted, like Iran, what the general public hears about European and North American elections is tightly controlled by the ruling government. As a result of this control, announcers and journalists must operate within accepted political, religious, social, and cultural norms decrying the West as corrupt. In this example, the generalized other—the attitude of the larger community—acts to control the information media specialists are allowed to broadcast or publish. As you can see in the box "Communication Counts in Your Life: The Influence of Culture on Perception," the power of culture to influence perceptions is critical to understanding and appreciating cultural differences.

Culture Counts

Generalized other ■ The common expectations within a social group that dictate acceptable beliefs and actions.

Social Comparison

Social comparison, or how we see ourselves in comparison to others, also impacts our self-esteem (Festinger 1954). Typically, you compare yourself to people who are

Social comparison ■ How a person sees himself or herself in comparison with others.

COMMUNICATION COUNTS IN YOUR LIFE

The Influence of Culture on Perception

Culture is like a lens through which we view the world. It includes our background, values, beliefs, and attitudes gleaned from our upbringing and shared with us by others with whom we live. These influences, like the tools a lens crafter uses to make eyeglasses, affect the way our cultural lens is ground. Consequently, our perceptions are formed by our cultures.

Samovar and Porter (2001) explain this difference in generalized terms that may not necessarily equally apply to all cultural groups or individuals within cultures. In the United States, for example, most people hold to individualism and believe in independence. This individuality in turn gives rise to a strong sense of self-concept and self-esteem. However, in many Asian countries, people emphasize collectivism; the group and especially the family are more important than individuals. Therefore, many Asians value

self-effacement, cooperation, and responsiveness to others' needs.

Think about how these different cultural perspectives might, for example, influence whom you choose to marry. In the United States, while you may be concerned to some degree with what family members think, for the most part, marriage is a decision between two individual people. In other words, you perceive marriage as an individualized decision. However, in many cultures around the world, marriage is a family decision. In fact, in many cultures, marriages are arranged by parents and family members. In these cultures, marriage is perceived as a collective decision that includes family members' insights, opinions, and involvement.

To summarize, culture powerfully influences our perceptions, which, in turn, directly impacts our communication, choices, and behavior.

Though your self-concept is relatively stable, it is shaped by your relationships with others.

like you, but if you engage in *upward social comparison*—meaning you compare yourself to people you perceive to be superior—then your self-esteem will plummet. For example, if you compare your speaking abilities with those of Martin Luther King Jr., you are likely to come away severely disappointed. On the other hand, if you engage in *downward social comparison*—meaning you compare yourself to someone whom you find less impressive—then your self-esteem grows. For example, if you compare your speaking abilities with those of an average ninth grader, you are likely to come away with an inflated sense of self-esteem. The goal is to set your sights on realistic comparisons and those you can grow into appropriately. Setting your sights too low will keep you from growing; but setting your sights too high will keep you from achieving your goals, and you will spend considerable time disappointed in yourself.

The media plays a significant role in how we view ourselves in comparison to others. Comments on online discussion boards, video clips on YouTube, photos on magazine covers, and famous superstars on screen all impact not only how we see ourselves but also how we view ourselves in comparison to others. A study conducted by Bessenoff (2006) found that female undergraduates who were exposed to thin-ideal media experienced decreased body satisfaction, negative mood, increased depression, and lowered self-esteem.

To illustrate further, several studies (see Abell & Richards 1996; Faith, Leon, & Allison 1997) note that people, especially adolescents, evaluate their body images by comparing themselves with others (Rosenblum & Lewis 1999). Additionally, media, including magazines (Jones, Vigfusdottir, & Lee 2004) and television (Botta 1999) influence how male and female children and adolescents view their bodies. Research indicates that eating disorders and other body-image difficulties are also linked to the results of social comparison (Cash & Deagle 1997) and influence self-esteem (Abell & Richards 1996). In short, social comparison is a powerful method for determining our self-concept and self-worth and can dramatically influence our behavior.

Self-Image

Self-image can be defined as the mental picture you have of yourself or your sense of identity, talents, and value. Feeling a greater sense of self-worth has been associated with higher rates of academic achievement and retention for all students but particularly for African Americans (Allen 1988). Because of the many challenges facing college students on a daily basis, building and maintaining a positive self-image is essential. Your self-image is built upon the sum of your experiences and interactions. How you see yourself, how others react to you, and how you interact with the world all impacts the mental picture you carry of yourself.

Your self-image is impacted by your family, friends, coworkers, classmates, teachers, neighbors, and others. As a result of your relationships with these significant people in your life, you establish a set of beliefs and attitudes about who you are, based on what you "see" reflected in these relationships. We develop a picture of what we think others see in us, and from that picture we then develop a set of expectations for ourselves. We then "live" these expectations. For example, if our parents believed we were smart, we internalized this reflection and enacted that understanding. Our self-image is the result of our beliefs relating to our appearance, what type of status we think we have relative to others, and how much we like ourselves or how much we believe others like us. These all come from our assessment of others' "reflections" of us.

Self-image ■ Mental picture a person has of himself or herself, relatively stable over time.

Reflected appraisal ■ Accepting how others define or describe you.

Reflected Appraisal

Reflected appraisal refers to accepting how others define or describe you, and this impacts self-perception. So, for example, you may compare how much you weigh with how much others your age weigh and conclude that you are either "too thin" or "too fat"; this is social comparison. If you then comment to your best friend, "You know, I think I'm too skinny," and your friend says, "Yeah, I think you are too," then you may reflect this appraisal; you internalize what others say. Of course, this is not automatic, because you may also respond with greater **self-efficacy**—meaning you are less likely to reflect others' appraisals and, as a result, can cope with setbacks, accomplish your goals, enhance your sense of well-being, and possess a greater sense of self-control over situations (Bandura 1994). Therefore, while social comparison and reflected appraisal exert powerful influences, you can balance their potency by having a sense of greater self-efficacy. To summarize, your perceptions are dynamic and formed by your experiences and by your interactions with others and how you respond to these influences.

Perception and Communication with Others

Given the reciprocal link between perception and communication, it is not surprising that we communicate with others based on our perceptions and that we adjust our perceptions of others based on communication encounters. For example, you perceive Kendra, who is in your math class, as someone who truly understands college algebra. Consequently, you are more likely to ask her questions about course content. However, if you approach Susan and discover that she is dismissive and unfriendly, you will probably change your perceptions and actively avoid any future communication with her. In other words, your original perception motivates you to communicate, but your subsequent communication alters your perceptions and affects future communication. This simple illustration demonstrates the reciprocal power of perception and communication.

We communicate based on our self-perceptions, and we interact with others based on our perceptions of them. Specifically, as you observe others, you rely on your perceptual biases and attributions in order to make conclusions about them. Let's consider these ideas in greater detail.

Observation   When you walk into a new class at the beginning of a new academic term, you probably look for people you already know and try to find out some things about the professor. In other words, you begin to observe the people around you and start drawing conclusions about them; you engage in the process of perception. For example, if a male professor came to the first class of the semester wearing a white shirt, a black tie, a black jacket and pants, and highly polished black shoes, what would be your first impression? No doubt you would draw some conclusions about his personality just from his attire, because how teachers dress impacts students' perceptions (Morris, Gorham, Cohen, & Huffman 1996).

According to **implicit personality theory,** we rely on deductions based on a combination of physical characteristics, personality traits, and behavior to draw conclusions about others (Bruner & Taguiri 1954). Specifically, we tend to believe that certain traits, behaviors, or personality characteristics go together, and we draw several conclusions about an individual based on observing a single factor; this is termed the **halo effect.** The halo effect occurs when you take one outstanding trait and create an overly favorable perception of the whole personality. Therefore, you may conclude that the professor wearing a blue cardigan and open-necked shirt is relaxed, open, and friendly, based only on his attire. Whatever your perceptions, you draw conclusions based on limited observation.

Perceptual Influences   Why do we organize and interpret our perceptions of others in patterns such as those seen in the previous example? Knowing more about scripts, closure, and attributions can help you understand this process more clearly. Scripts, as we noted earlier, are mental organizational patterns we use to help us move more easily through the world. For example, you have expectations about what to do when you get into an elevator: You step to the back, face forward,

Self-efficacy ■ Sense of self.

Implicit personality theory ■ The idea that people rely on deductions based on a combination of physical characteristics, personality traits, and behaviors to draw conclusions about others.

Halo effect ■ Drawing conclusions about an individual after observing a single factor based on the belief that certain traits, behaviors, and personality characteristics belong together.

Dressing up for an interview and adopting a positive outlook favorably influence others' perceptions of you.

TABLE 2.3

ATTRIBUTION BIASES

Bias	Explanation	Example
Fundamental Attribution Error	Overestimating internal factors to the exclusion of external factors	"I know Jared is late to dinner because he didn't plan time well, not because he's stuck in traffic."
Self-Serving Bias	Overestimating external factors to explain personal failure and overestimating internal factors to explain reasons for personal praise	"I did well on the test because I studied really hard" versus "I did poorly on the test because the professor wrote an unfair test."
Attractiveness Bias	Thinking better of people who we find physically attractive as compared to people we find unattractive	"Sharon is really beautiful *and* she's also nice; it's just not her fault that she can't seem to pass math."
Similarity Bias	Thinking others we like are similar to us; attributing our own motivations to someone else	"Jeff and I are a lot alike; I bet he really likes J. R. R. Tolkien books as much as I do."

and stand apart from others. Such scripts inform our perceptions of others. If someone enters an elevator and faces you, you are likely to question the appropriateness of this person's behavior because he or she violated a nonverbal communication norm.

We also rely on **closure,** or filling in the blanks. For example, what if you saw the following on a license plate?

HNRS STDNT

Even though there are no vowels on the license plate, you would probably conclude that the plate reads "HONORS STUDENT." In other words, you provide the missing information. So when we first meet others, we draw conclusions, or **first impressions,** and then fill in the blanks. To illustrate, when you go for an interview and meet your prospective boss, you may say to yourself, "She seems very nice; I think I'd like working with her." Based on your first impression, you fill in the blanks about the kind of boss you think she will be.

Additionally, we rely on **attributions,** or assigning meanings to actions. Attribution theory is based on Heider's (1944) work on social perception that suggests we assign meanings to others' behavior based on either external or internal explanations. So, for example, if you like the woman who is nominated as the representative for nontraditional students on your campus, you are likely to attribute her success to her skills or personality. If, on the other hand, she loses the election, you are likely to attribute her lack of success to external factors, such as poor advertising. However, if you dislike the nominee and she wins the election, you are likely to say it was because the other candidates were weak; whereas, if she loses the election, you are likely to blame her. Interestingly, this tendency results in a series of perceptual biases, which are summarized in Table 2.3. The point is that our perceptions are highly influenced by limited observations, scripts, closure, and attribution.

IMPROVING YOUR PERCEPTUAL SKILLS

You have probably had the unfortunate experience of discovering that your first impressions about someone were totally wrong. To use a previous example, upon meeting your prospective new boss for the first time, you may conclude that she will be pleasant to work with, only to later discover that she is more focused on her own career and sacrifices the well-being of others to ensure that she succeeds. According to the Standpoint Theory, where you are in time and space impacts the way in which you view the world. For example, at the turn of the century, hat etiquette dictated that a man remove his hat when encountering a lady. To refuse to do so would have been not only impolite but also a sign of a poor upbringing. Over the last 100 years, this practice has fallen out of favor. Can you imagine the strange looks a man would draw in a college classroom today if he were to remove his cap when his female classmates arrived? Because our reality is constructed by

Closure ■ Filling in the blanks.

First impressions ■ Conclusions based on an initial meeting.

Attributions ■ Meanings assigned to actions.

the time, place, and culture in which we live, we need to recognize that our worldviews and standpoints are partial and biased. In this example, our views on actions considered chivalrous in the early 1900s but peculiar today allows us to see that one's standpoint influences perception.

Certainly perceptions can change depending on what stand you take—especially when it comes to first impressions. How can you improve your initial and subsequent perceptions and, thereby, enhance your communication abilities? Consider these suggestions.

Guarding Against Perceptual Error

It is easy for us to absolve ourselves of responsibility. For example, if you insist, "I know what I saw" and contend that your conclusions are valid, you give little room for error. However, because you know that perceptions can be erroneous, it is helpful to recognize that you might have a different perspective than someone else. What you might accept as fact may simply be an inference on your part. Be sure to fact-check to support your ideas on solid information rather than on opinion or conjecture. Also, acknowledge that perceptions matter because we treat them as reality. In fact, some argue that perception *is* reality. To guard against perceptual errors, it is important to consider others' perceptions and to be open to ideas other than your own.

Gathering Additional Information

As we have explained in this section, knowing more can often adjust your perceptions. So, rather than taking first impressions at face value or drawing conclusions based on limited information, seek multiple sources of information that can help you adjust your perspectives. Of course, talking with others is one of the best ways to do this. While you may be uncertain about or uncomfortable talking with others who are different from you, doing so can help you glean important information and help you avoid stereotypes that lead to discrimination and prejudice.

Using Perception Checking

One of the best ways to avoid perceptual error is to use **perception checking.** Perception checking is based on a simple but powerful communication principle: Ask questions first and make statements later. Here's how it works:

1. Describe the behavior you observe that you wish to clarify (Example: "It seems like you're really down today.")
2. Offer at least two possible explanations for the observed behavior (Example: "Maybe you're just extra tired today, or perhaps something is wrong.")
3. Ask a clarifying question (Example: "Is there something you'd like to talk about?")

Notice how this approach acknowledges your perceptions but also recognizes that there may be multiple explanations for them, without assuming that your perceptions are necessarily accurate. Moreover, this approach encourages communication as a way to clarify your perceptions while also potentially advancing the development of a relationship with another person.

Adjusting Your Perceptions

As you glean additional information and clarify your perceptions, you can adjust your perceptions. By practicing some simple principles, you can learn to adjust your perceptions and avoid the potential pitfalls we have identified. In the book, *People in Quandaries*, Johnson (1946) offers two such principles: dating and indexing. **Dating** refers to assigning specific time periods to perceptions to emphasize that perceptions can shift over time. Consider these contrasting examples:

UNDATED STATEMENT: Professor Lambert is concerned about student success.

DATED STATEMENT: Professor Lambert was concerned with student success when I took interpersonal communication with her *last year*.

Notice that this statement adjusts perception based on personal experience in a specific time frame.

Perception checking ■ A process that acknowledges initial perceptions but also recognizes that there may be multiple explanations for them.

Dating ■ Assigning specific time periods to perceptions in order to emphasize that perceptions can shift over time.

We communicate concern, warmth, acceptance, support, and trust because human beings have value.

Indexing qualifies generalizations when they are applied to specific circumstances. Consider these contrasting examples:

GENERALIZED STATEMENT: You'll have a hard time in Professor Lambert's interpersonal communication class. I sure did!

INDEXED STATEMENT: While I had a hard time in Professor Lambert's interpersonal communication class, *you may do better than I did.*

Notice the difference in the two statements: The first generalizes the speaker's experience to everyone else's, while the second recognizes that not everyone may share the same experience. Qualifying your thinking and speaking in this manner allows you to avoid some of the problems associated with perception by recognizing that perceptions change over time and circumstances.

Practicing Empathy

Empathy, or seeing experiences from someone else's perspective, helps you avoid drawing firm conclusions without considering how others may see a given situation. Even though you may disagree with someone else's perceptions, by practicing empathy, you demonstrate respect for another person, enlarge your perspective, glean additional information, and check your perceptual biases. As a result, you are more likely to communicate ethically. Reflecting on the box "Communication Counts in Your College Experience: Understanding Differing Values" can assist you in developing an understanding of different points of view, which can increase your ability to empathize with others.

ENACTING COMPETENT AND ETHICAL PERCEPTION IN COLLEGE, CAREER, AND LIFE

As you pursue your college degree, career path, and life's goals, the power of perception will play a significant role. While we have mentioned these connections throughout this chapter, we want to highlight some important areas.

Sources of Ethical Guidelines

For most of us, our earliest perception of ethical behavior comes from our families. Our family is the first source that helped us develop our beliefs and values. We learn our basic sense of right and wrong from our family environment, where our behaviors are either

Indexing ■ Qualifying generalizations when they are applied to specific circumstances.

Empathy ■ A purposeful attempt to understand another person's perspective.

COMMUNICATION COUNTS IN YOUR COLLEGE EXPERIENCE

Understanding Differing Values

Should people live their lives focused on spiritual matters, career aspirations, or family expectations? Should people use the natural world as they see fit, actively protect the natural world, or seek to strike a balance? The answers to these and similar queries are valuable because they reveal what you believe the world should be like. Answers also differ depending on the background from which you originate. Consider these five important questions created from research by Kluckhohn and Strodtbeck (1961):

1. What is human nature?
2. What is the relationship between humans and nature?
3. What is the relationship between humans?
4. What is the preferred form of activity?
5. What is the orientation toward time?

The following chart shows the range of cultural answers to these questions, according to these authors' research. As you read this chart, where do you place yourself? Can you think of people from different cultures whose answers are likely to be different from yours? Why might the answers differ?

	Question	Alternatives		
#1	**Evil:** People are basically evil; evil must be controlled	**Mixed:** People are both good and bad when born	**Good:** People are basically good
#2	**Controlled by nature:** People have little control over nature; nature decides your life	**Harmony with nature:** People are one with nature; nature is one's partner in life	**Humans control nature:** Humans dominate nature and should use it for their own purposes
#3	**Authoritarian:** Clear lines of authority are followed and dominate relationships (e.g., patriarchy)	**Group-oriented:** Individual goals and wishes are less important than group goals and wishes	**Individualism:** Individual goals and wishes are more important than group goals and wishes
#4	**Being:** Emphasizes who you are and encourages free expression of emotion and desires	**Growing:** Emphasizes becoming who you are through growth; encourages self-expression along with self-control	**Doing:** Emphasizes action; emphasizes self-expression measured by external criteria, not by self
#5	**Past:** Traditions and customs matter most; they should be carefully followed	**Present:** What matters is here and now; yesterday is gone; tomorrow is not here yet	**Future:** Think about tomorrow and plan for it; be prepared for what is ahead

Source: Kluckhohn, F. K. & Strodtbeck, F. L. from *Variations in Value Orientations.* Evanston, IL: Row, Peterson, 1961.

encouraged or discouraged. Many of us probably received more instructions on what *not* to do rather than on what to do. Our parents emphasized behavior that affected our health or safety (i.e., look both ways before crossing the street), discouraged behavior that disturbed others (i.e., don't interrupt when someone else is speaking), and attempted to deter behavior that differed from "accepted" conduct (i.e., don't use profanity). Our parents' standpoints on right and wrong influenced what we perceive as appropriate or inappropriate, and so we generally conform to those perceptions.

Our religious background or church affiliation may also provide us with a definitive source of ethics. If your family did not attend a church or identify with a specific religion, perhaps other types of authority (police, politicians, etc.) became a significant source of the "do nots" in your life. Teachers are some of the most significant authority figures who impact our sense of right and wrong. Can you identify a teacher who had a significant impact on you? How did he or she treat you? Was this person concerned about you as an individual? In addition to your teachers, the school you attended was most likely full of "rules of conduct" that provided stability and consistency throughout your childhood (even if you didn't think all the rules were necessary). Whatever the source, some kind of authority helped you develop a belief and value system and a sense of right and wrong.

Another source of ethical guidelines or values is our culture. For most of us, culture comes through mediated channels: radio, television, the Internet, and so on. We learn what individuals and groups outside of our geographic areas, religious training, cultural background, or educational upbringing believe should guide ethical perception and reflection. Think about your favorite television program. How does this show portray values regarding relationships? Would you define these values as "good"? The view of our larger culture often provides us with a dramatically different understanding of right and wrong or provides us with differences of opinion on what is right and wrong. We may learn that some of our early sources of information about morality (i.e., family) were not always "right." We may also learn that what is considered right at one time may be wrong at another; right and wrong are not fixed categories. Laws and rules vary from place to place and from person to person, and they are often adapted to new circumstances. Think about issues such as slavery, segregation, or women's right to vote. In each of these cases, the "right" or "ethical" position within our culture has changed substantially over time. To illustrate, religious institutions may modify their moral prescriptions from generation to generation to respond to changing social conditions. For example, many religions that were male dominated now accept women as ministers.

Because the sources of our beliefs and values change as our standpoints mature, we may face internal conflict as we use a wider variety of sources to make critical, ethical decisions—that is, given the influences in our lives, we may question what we once perceived to be right or wrong, or may change our opinions. (The box "Communication Counts in Your College Experience: Understanding Differing Values" on page 35 provides more information about how we grow morally and ethically.) One of the most difficult issues for many college students is how to respond to the broader range of values and beliefs they are exposed to in college classes, civic organizations, campus media, and so on. Is it "ethical" to maintain your previously established beliefs and values under all circumstances? Or is it more "ethical" to adjust your perceptions and values to new situations, such as when meeting new people and learning new concepts and skills? These are not simple questions. Evaluating one's ethics is difficult and often confusing. It may also be seen as threatening to others who may not approve of changes in our thought processes or actions. Despite these obstacles, one of the steps in becoming an adult is establishing one's own value system; whether you are aware of it or not, you are likely in the midst of this process now.

SUMMARY

In this chapter, we focused on the important role of perception and communication. Specifically we have noted that

- perception is a process that includes attention, selection, organization, evaluation, and interpretation;
- perception is challenging due to prior experience, stereotypes, selectivity, and cognitive orientation;
- a reciprocal relationship exists between perception and communication;
- there are important concepts related to self-perception, including self-concept, self-esteem, self-fulfilling prophesies, social comparison, reflected appraisal, self-image, and self-efficacy, as well as their impact on communication with self and others;
- as we observe others, we rely on our perceptual biases and attributions in order to make conclusions about them;
- perceptual flaws can be strategically offset by using tactics such as guarding against perceptual errors, gathering more information, using perception checking, adjusting our perceptions, and practicing empathy;
- college, career, and life are all significantly impacted by the power of perception.

QUESTIONS FOR DISCUSSION

1. Identify a stereotype that you have relied upon, and explain how this stereotype proved to be helpful or harmful.
2. Provide your own example of the intersection of self-concept, self-esteem, and self-fulfilling prophecy. If appropriate, draw on your own experience to illustrate the connection.
3. Using the principles of appropriate self-disclosure, analyze a time when someone inappropriately self-disclosed

information to you. What principles did they violate? How? What advice would you offer them now, given what you have learned in this chapter?

4. Evaluate our discussion of the role of self-perception and academic success. Do you agree or disagree with our analysis? Why?

EXERCISES

1. Interview someone who is in a career similar to the one you would like to have after you graduate. What are his or her perceptions of work? How does this influence his or her sense of self and success?

2. Identify a time in your life when you misperceived someone else. How were you wrong? Why were you wrong? How might you use the principles in this chapter to help you avoid this same misperception in the future?

KEY TERMS

Attention   21
Attributions   32
Brain dominance   25
Closure   32
Cognitive orientation   25
Dating   33
Discrimination   24
Empathy   34
Evaluate   22
First impressions   32

Generalized other   29
Halo effect   31
Implicit personality theory   31
Indexing   34
Interpret   22
Intrapersonal communication   26
Perception   21
Perception checking   33
Prejudice   24
Reflected appraisal   30

Scripts   22
Selection   22
Self   26
Self-concept   27
Self-efficacy   31
Self-esteem   27
Self-fulfilling prophecies   27
Self-image   30
Social comparison   29
Stereotypes   24

REFERENCES

Abell, S. C., and Richards, M. H. 1996. The relationship between body shape satisfaction and self-esteem: An investigation of gender and class difference. *Journal of Youth and Adolescence* 25:691–703.

Aitken, J., and Shedletsky, L., eds. 1995. *Intrapersonal communication processes.* Plymouth, MI: The Speech Communication Association and Midnight Oil Multimedia.

Allen, W. R. (1988). Black students in higher education: Toward improved access, adjustment, and achievement. *Urban Review, 20,* 16–188.

Bandura, A. 1994. Self-efficacy. In *Encyclopedia of human behavior,* ed. V. S. Ramachaudran, Vol. 4, 71–81. New York: Academic Press.

Berger, C. R. 1979. Beyond initial interaction: Uncertainty, understanding and the development of interpersonal relationships. In *Language and social psychology,* eds. H. Giles and R. St. Clair. Oxford: Basil Blackwell.

Bessenoff, G. R. 2006. Can the media affect us? Social comparison, self-discrepancy, and the thin ideal? *Psychology of Women Quarterly* 30(3):239–251.

Botta, R. A. 1999. Television images and adolescent girls' body image disturbance. *Journal of Communication* 49:22–41.

Bruner, J. S., and Taguiri, R. 1954. The perception of people. In *Handbook of social psychology,* ed. G. Lindzey, Vol. 2. Reading, MA: Addison-Wesley.

Campbell, J., and Hepler, H. 1970. *Dimensions in communication: Readings.* Belmont, CA: Wadsworth.

Cash, T. F., and Deagle, E. A. 1997. The nature and extent of body-image disturbances in anorexia nervosa and bulimia nervosa: A meta-analysis. *International Journal of Eating Disorders* 22:107–125.

Devito, J. 2008. *The interpersonal communication book.* 12th ed. Boston: Pearson Allyn & Bacon Longman.

Faith, M. S., Leon, M. A., and Allison, D. B. 1997. The effects of self-generated comparison targets, BMI, and social comparison tendencies on body image appraisal. *Eating Disorders* 5:128–140.

Festinger, L. 1954. A theory of social comparison processes. *Human Relations* 7:117–140.

Garfinkle, M. 2004. Using the self-fulfilling prophecy: Expectations shape reality. Retrieved October 10, 2004, from www.capsnap.com/max/maxarticle1.asp?ID=7.

Goffman, E. 1959. *The presentation of self in everyday life.* New York: Doubleday.

Grammatis, Y. 1998. *Learning styles.* Chatsworth, CA: Chaminade College Preparatory. Retrieved July 29, 2006, from www.chaminade.org/inspire/learnstl.htm.

Heider, F. 1944. Social perception and phenomenal causality. *Psychological Review* 51:358–374.

Johnson, W. 1946. *People in quandaries: The semantics of personal adjustment.* San Francisco, CA: International Society for General Semantics.

Jones, D. C., Vigfusdottir, T. H., and Lee, Y. 2004. Body image and the appearance culture among adolescent girls and boys: An examination of friend conversations, peer criticism, appearance magazines and internalization of appearance ideals. *Journal of Adolescent Research* 19:323–329.

Kubany, E. D., Hill, E. E., Owens, J. A., Iannce-Spencer, C., McCaig, M. A., Tremayne, K. J., and Williams, P. L. 2004. Cognitive trauma therapy for battered women with PTSD (CTT-BW). *Journal of Consulting and Clinical Psychology* 72(1):3–18.

Lim, B. 1996. Student expectations of professors. *The Teaching Professor* 10(4):3–4. In *Communication for the classroom teacher,* P. Cooper and C. Simonds, 58: 2003. Boston: Allyn and Bacon.

Luft, J. 1970. *Group processes: An introduction to group dynamics.* Palo Alto, CA: Mayfield.

Maslow, A. 1966. *Psychology of Science: A Rennaissance.* New York: Harper & Row.

Morris, T. L., Gorham, J., Cohen, S. H., and Huffman, D. 1996. Fashion in the classroom: Effects of attire on student perceptions of instructors in college classes. *Communication Education* 45:135–148.

Rosenblum, G. D., and Lewis, M. 1999. The relations among body image, physical attractiveness, and body mass in adolescence. *Child Development* 70(1): 50–64.

Samovar, L. A., and Porter, R. E. 2001. *Communication between cultures.* Belmont, CA: Wadsworth.

Schaubroeck, J., Jones, J. R., and Xie, J. L. 2001. Individual differences in utilizing control to cope with job demands: Effects on susceptibility to infectious disease. *Journal of Applied Psychology* 86(2):265–278.

Sheldon, W. H. 1942. *The varieties of temperament: A psychology of constitutional differences.* New York: Harper & Brothers.

Seligman, M. 1996. *The optimistic child: How learned optimism protects children from depression.* New York: Houghton Mifflin.

Wood, J. T. 2009. *Communication in our lives.* Chapel Hill, NC: University of North Carolina.

CHAPTER 3

Effective Listening

LEARNING OUTCOMES After reading this chapter, you will have:

the **Knowledge** to . . .

and the **Skills** to . . .

UNDERSTANDING LISTENING, page 42

Understand the difference between listening and hearing.

- Be mindful that hearing is an auditory process and listening is a mental process.

OVERCOMING OUR RELUCTANCE TO LISTEN, page 43

Recognize listening challenges.

- Weigh the appropriateness and trustworthiness of a sender's message.
- Make sure that your channels (number and nature) reinforce your message.
- Avoid overloading; simplify your messages.
- Consider your receiver when formulating your message.
- Take into account contextual or cultural differences when communicating.
- Use gender-neutral language.

Identify barriers to listening.

- Be attentive; don't pseudolisten.
- Listen to the full message; don't select only parts to attend to.
- Keep your emotions in check; don't respond defensively.
- Listen authentically; don't plan to ambush or attack what others say.
- Share equally; don't dominate the conversation.

LEARNING TO LISTEN EFFECTIVELY, page 48

Learn to listen well in various listening situations.

- Engage in pleasurable listening to enjoy an experience.
- Use informational listening to discern others' messages.
- Practice relational listening and rhetorical sensitivity in order to understand, support, and empathize with others.
- Use evaluative listening to judge a message's accuracy, trustworthiness, or usefulness.

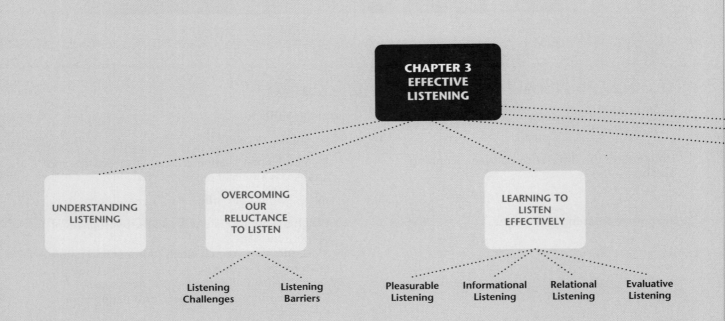

REAPING THE REWARDS OF LISTENING, page 52

Realize the benefits of listening.

- Find value and enjoyment in listening well.
- Notice an improvement in your understanding during listening.
- Experience enhanced empathy when communicating with others.
- Receive heightened respect and civility from others.

USING LISTENING TO ENHANCE LEARNING, page 54

Enhance your college experience with better listening and self-management.

- Listen carefully to faculty and staff instructions.
- Reduce forgetting during instruction by coming prepared and taking clear notes.
- Keep all class handouts and information.
- Get and stay organized by using a three-ring binder and daily/weekly/monthly calendars.

BECOMING A COMPETENT AND ETHICAL LISTENER IN COLLEGE, CAREER, AND LIFE, page 55

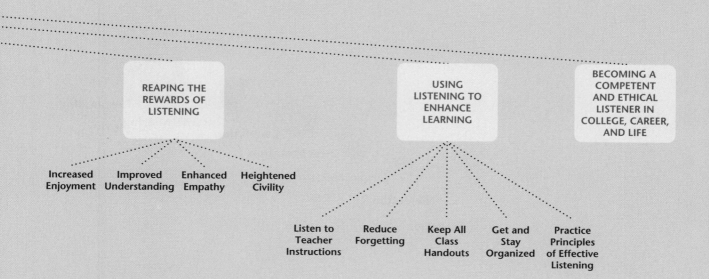

UNDERSTANDING LISTENING

A few years ago, one of your authors invited the dean of the college to attend an orientation for new graduate teaching assistants in order to welcome them to the campus. In his remarks, the dean noted that he had recently returned from a symposium on preparing college students for the workplace, where academics and business professionals alike agreed that *listening* is the primary communication skill college graduates need but seem to lack the most.

Certainly, listening is the communication skill we use the most and learn the least about. In this chapter, we highlight the importance of listening in the communication process. As we explained in Chapter 1, *human communication* is a transactional process in which we create and share meaning. As with other aspects of communication, listening is reciprocal; it is important to listen and be listened to. Therefore, we need our parents, partners, professors, and peers to listen to us, and they need us to pay attention to them. In this chapter we will focus specifically on receiving messages, even though both sending and receiving messages happen simultaneously. Listening is hard work. Although it might seem that listening is a physical process of hearing sounds, listening is much more. **Hearing** is a physical process that allows us to perceive sounds in our environment. **Listening,** however, is a mental process that requires us to be **mindful** in order to create meaning (Wood 1997). When we are mindful, we are paying attention. Notice that this phrase assumes that we are *paying* attention. In other words, it costs us to listen.

In order to truly listen, we must follow the steps of perception that we discussed in Chapter 2. We must *pay attention*, *select stimuli* to focus on, *organize* our thinking based on what we know, *interpret* what we encounter, and *evaluate* the experience. For example, you might be listening to a conversation that is going on down the hall or in another room. You may have caught a man's particularly deep voice (attention) and you might have paid closer attention (selection) to his words "free food." From past experience (organization), you determine that it is best to stop what you are doing and find out what is going on (interpretation) in order to save yourself some time and some money (evaluation) getting your own lunch later.

Listening, however, is not merely an auditory process related to your hearing; it is a mental process as well. When you engage in a furious texting session, you have "listened" and responded to your friend's messages. When you watch a YouTube video and then relate the story to a friend, you "listened" to what was presented, engaged in mental processing, remembered what you saw, and conveyed what you "heard" to another person.

As Figure 3.1 shows, the listening process is a continuation of the perception process in Chapter 2, made up of seven overlapping stages, and each stage is integrally related to the

Hearing ■ The physical process that allows people to perceive sounds.

Listening ■ The mental process that requires mindfulness in order to create meaning.

Mindful ■ Paying attention.

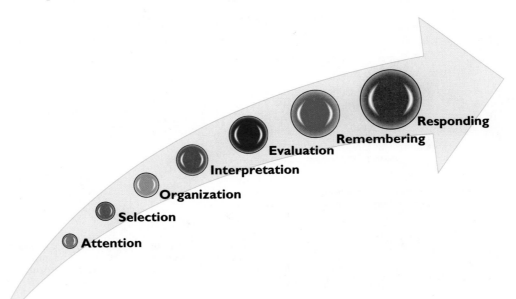

FIGURE 3.1
The Listening Model.

others. At any point in this process, we may encounter various types of noise that interfere with, or even block, our ability to listen effectively. Consider each of these stages briefly:

- *Attending* is paying close attention to the sounds that we choose.
- *Selecting* is choosing to focus on certain sounds.
- *Organizing* is how we arrange the sounds to make the words or symbols.
- *Interpreting* is assigning meaning to the sounds we choose and pay attention to.
- *Evaluating* is analyzing and making decisions or judgments about the sounds we choose, attend to, and understand.
- *Remembering* is retaining the sounds we have chosen, attended to, understood, and evaluated for later recall.
- *Responding* is offering feedback to the sounds that we have chosen, attended to, understood, evaluated, and remembered.

OVERCOMING OUR RELUCTANCE TO LISTEN

Think about how you pay attention to a lecture in one of your general education classes as opposed to a conversation with a person you find attractive. You probably pay closer attention to your attractive acquaintance than to your professor's lecture because you find this person much more interesting, unique, or appealing. While this does not necessarily mean the lecture is boring, it does mean that when compared to an enjoyable conversation, you are more reluctant to listen to the lecture. By understanding our reluctance to listen and the challenges associated with this reluctance, we can develop strategies to improve our listening skills.

Listening Challenges

Listening is difficult because it is a complex process. At times, that complexity has the potential to challenge our ability to listen effectively.

To identify listening challenges, let's look at the communication model we examined in Chapter 1—made up of sender, message, channel, receiver, feedback, noise, and context (see page 10). To better understand listening challenges, let's reconsider these elements and identify how particular aspects of each of these elements contribute to these challenges.

SENDER-BASED CHALLENGES Sometimes we face listening challenges because of the sender's credibility or clarity. The credibility, or **ethos**, of a communicator is determined by the listener's perception of his or her goodwill, trustworthiness, competence, and appropriateness. If we believe a sender has our best interest at heart, we consider him or her to have goodwill. For example, you are more likely to trust the advice of your best friend than that of someone you do not know very well because you probably believe that your best friend is truly interested in your welfare. Moreover, if you believe someone is honest, you're likely to consider him or her trustworthy. For example, you are probably more likely to loan money to someone you believe will pay you back than to someone who has not returned the money you loaned out two weeks ago. In other words, these two borrowers' different levels of honesty make a difference in their respective trustworthiness and how reliable you perceive their promises to be.

Listening is impacted by our perceptions of the sender's competence and appropriateness. While **competent** people know what they are talking about, speakers who are sensitive to the audience and the occasion demonstrate **appropriateness**. For example, graduation speakers are usually chosen because of their reputations, intelligence, or success. However, some speakers seem to forget that students attend graduations to receive their diplomas, not to listen to speakers, and end up speaking too long! In this instance, the speaker may be competent but is insensitive to the occasion and the audience.

Ethos ■ A speaker's credibility, based on the perception of his or her goodwill, trustworthiness, competence, and appropriateness.

Competent ■ Possessing the necessary and expected combination of qualifications, knowledge, skills, and abilities.

Appropriateness ■ Possessing sensitivity suitably expressed toward a particular person, audience, or context.

Was your graduation speaker's message memorable? How so?

Sound bite ■ A brief statement taken from an audiotape or videotape and broadcast especially during a news report.*

When a speaker embodies competence, appropriateness, goodwill, and trustworthiness, we are more likely to pay attention to the message because we consider the speaker credible. Likewise, if a speaker uses clear language that we understand and seeks feedback from us to ensure that we *do* understand, we are also more likely to listen. The standards of goodwill, trustworthiness, competence, and appropriateness apply to others, and they also apply to *us* when we send messages. If we are credible, clear communicators, we help others listen to us.

CHANNEL-BASED CHALLENGES   As we discussed in Chapter 1, we use channels to share messages with one another, including verbal and nonverbal communication shared via mass media. When we think of the relationship between listening and channels, focusing on the *nature* and the *number* of channels helps us understand this relationship and the listening challenges that may occur.

The Number of Channels.   The *number* of channels we use can either enhance or complicate listening. When we use multiple channels, we enhance the likelihood that others will listen. For example, think about how difficult it is to create shared meaning when you play a game like *Pictionary* or charades, in which players rely only on the nonverbal channel to send or interpret messages. It is difficult not to speak as we attempt to cue others in this game because we know that if we were to add the verbal channel (spoken words) to the nonverbal channel (gestures) our partners would be more apt to guess correctly.

Additionally, think about the conclusions you make about professors or peers based on their speech or appearance. For instance, we may find a teacher who speaks very slowly or with a strong nasal quality quite annoying. On the other hand, peers who dress stylishly or who are physically attractive are more likely to catch our attention; studies indicate that even from childhood, we are more likely to listen to them because we find them appealing (Ramsey & Langlois 2002). To overcome this challenge, try to avoid drawing conclusions based solely on nonverbal channels like vocal quality and attire. Instead, work to gather additional information, including *how* a person speaks and *what* the person says. If you pay attention to multiple communication channels, you can enhance your effectiveness as a listener.

The Nature of Channels.   Consider the *nature* of the channels that influence our listening. What we mean is that each channel influences how we interpret meaning. If all you know about a particular class comes from reading only the syllabus, you may draw incorrect inferences about the course. However, by asking questions of the teacher or talking with other students who have taken the class, you can gain additional information that will help you draw better conclusions.

By using both the written and oral verbal channels, you can adjust your perceptions and overcome channel-based challenges. The lessons in this section, then, are simple but important:

- Use more than one channel to enhance your listening and to ensure that you send clear messages that help others listen to you.
- Use more than one type of channel to enhance your listening and to ensure that you send clear messages that help others listen to you.

To further illustrate these two important listening skills, think about how media influences your listening. Much of television advertising and news programs rely on the **sound bite,** which *Merriam-Webster's Collegiate Dictionary* defines as "a brief statement, as by a politician, taken from an audiotape or videotape and broadcast especially during a news report." This approach may initially help you gain information; however, reducing complex ideas, events, or feelings to brief messages tends to compromise rather than help us listen. To overcome the listening challenges sound bites present, try gathering additional information through reading, talking with others, or listening to other

*Definition of "sound bites" used by permission. From *Merriam-Webster's Collegiate® Dictionary*, 11th Edition © 2011 by Merriam-Webster, Incorporated (www.Merriam-Webster.com).

media sources that offer in-depth information about a given issue. As you do this, you add listening channels and you improve your listening effectiveness. Likewise, while we may use sound bites to catch others' attention, by using additional channels, we can ensure that others receive our messages clearly and completely.

MESSAGE-BASED CHALLENGES Messages also impact your listening.

Message Overload. Receiving too many messages at the same time creates **message overload** and makes it more difficult to listen. Perhaps you experience message overload in the classroom. Given that college students spend up to 53 percent of their time in listening (Barker, Edwards, Gaines, Gladney, & Holley 1980), you probably often feel like a fully saturated sponge, even though

Message overload can impact our personal relationships. How is it impacting yours?

your brain is very capable of processing more information. Consequently, listening to additional information becomes practically impossible as you work to process a lot of information in a short period of time. You can overcome this problem simply by focusing on the messages that are critical in any moment; your brain is capable of managing overload with focus.

Message Complexity. **Message complexity** also creates a listening challenge. For example, think about the most difficult course you are taking this semester. It probably contains complex ideas, numerous details, or new skills. In short, the course contains many complex messages that require you to listen carefully and consistently. We all find this difficult to do. One of your authors remembers taking Greek as a first-year student in college. Here is his experience:

> Trying to master a new alphabet and learn vocabulary and grammar was difficult enough. But when the teacher used English grammar as a way to help students understand the equivalent parts of speech in Greek, I was utterly lost! In other words, language got in the way of learning language!

This anecdote indicates another problem with listening to some messages. At times, words themselves present a listening barrier. Complex vocabulary, technical jargon, or loaded words make it more difficult to listen. To overcome these types of message-based challenges, strive to use simple, direct language, and avoid using **trigger words**—words that stimulate a negative emotional reaction in listeners—to help others listen to you.

RECEIVER-BASED CHALLENGES As listeners, we face numerous challenges receiving messages. For example, after a conversation with a friend, have you ever found that you had little recall of what your friend said? What happened? Perhaps your mind raced ahead, given that you can think much faster than your friend can speak. During this time gap, your mind easily wandered and you ceased to listen. Maybe you were preoccupied with other matters, such as an upcoming event or concern about how well you did on a recent exam. You may have been cold, hot, or hungry, or maybe you had a headache. External and internal physical noise may have distracted you from listening. You may have also found your friend difficult to hear or understand and decided that what she was saying was not important anyway. Or you may have assumed that you already knew what she was going to say and thought, "I've heard this all before!" In any case, you made a prejudgment and ceased to listen.

You may also have experienced **receiver apprehension** or "the fear of misinterpreting, inadequately processing, and/or not being able to adjust psychologically to messages sent by others" (Wheeless 1975, 263). However, whatever the explanation, all of the listening challenges discussed in this section are receiver-based difficulties—that is, the primary source of your listening problem was *you*, not the sender's ethos, too few channels, or complex messages with troublesome language. You did not listen because you did not effectively manage physical or mental noise. This is not a matter of blame but of responsibility. In other words, sometimes we do not listen because we are physically or mentally

Message overload ■ Receiving too many messages at the same time, making it difficult to listen.

Message complexity ■ Containing complicated ideas, numerous details, or new skills.

Trigger words ■ Words that stimulate a negative emotional reaction in listeners.

Receiver apprehension ■ The fear of misinterpreting, inadequately processing, and/or not being able to adjust psychologically to messages sent by others.

Co-cultures ■ Cultures that exist within a more dominant culture.

Culture Counts

distracted or we choose not to listen. You can overcome these challenges by asking questions of the speaker to make sure that what he or she said is what you understood.

CONTEXT-BASED CHALLENGES   Remember from Chapter 1 that *context* refers to the various environments that surround a given communication event, including the physical, linguistic, cultural, and social environments. Each of these environments potentially creates listening challenges. Obviously, if we are unable to hear a message because of physical noise, we cannot listen. Simply changing the physical environment by moving to another space, turning down the CD player, or turning off the television can help to overcome this type of context-based listening challenge.

If we do not share the same language with someone, it may be impossible to truly listen. As a result, the linguistic environment creates a listening barrier. We may be able to hear what is said but be unable to understand. As our communities increasingly become multicultural, linguistic barriers are more likely to appear. And even when people of other ethnic backgrounds speak English, their accents may make it challenging for us to listen. For example, some students find it difficult to understand international students or teachers who speak accented English. Moreover, **co-cultures,** or cultures that exist within a more dominant culture (Martin & Nakayama 2001), may use words in unique ways or speak with dialects that sound foreign to our ears. If we focus on these differences, we are likely to be distracted from listening.

Cultural environments also impact listening. An international colleague explains that he chose to stay in the United States to teach because he enjoys student-teacher interaction. He was not inclined to return to the lecture-based teaching typically found in his native country. In his culture, listening includes limited feedback from students. Note how the role of listening shifts in this example. Students in Japan and in many other nations are expected to absorb information from the professor by listening to lectures. While lecture is very common in college classrooms in the United States, discussion, small group projects, and other interactive instructional methods are used more often. In this case, listening becomes a matter of attending to and absorbing information and of dealing with numerous voices, offering more personal feedback and evaluating ideas, considering opinions, and learning information.

The cultural context that influences classroom communication in Japan and the United States creates different types of listening challenges. In Japanese higher education, passive listening is the norm; it requires students to attend carefully to the presentation of information. However, in U.S. college classrooms, students are expected to actively engage in listening by providing immediate feedback through exchanging and examining ideas (Martin & Nakayama 2001). To overcome the challenges of context and culture, spend time initially in these new environments by watching how others interact; then ask questions to clarify your understanding of the cultural or contextual rules operating in that environment.

In addition to issues related to culture and context, gendered communication creates challenges to our understanding and interpretation of others. Deborah Tannen (1990) notes how gender influences or impacts listening. In her book *You Just Don't Understand: Women and Men in Conversation*, Tannen suggests that men, in general, interrupt their conversational partners more often than women and prefer to focus more on information; women, in general, emphasize relational issues and focus more on people. As listeners, then, women are prone to provide support for their conversational partners by giving encouraging feedback (smiles, nods, or vocal support), while men are less likely to provide supportive feedback and even interrupt their conversational partners more often. Why do these listening differences exist? Are men, by nature, rude? Are women, by nature, more nurturing? Making such assumptions indicates a failure to understand the influence of the social context and overgeneralizes. Most likely, men and women speak and listen differently because of the ways in which they are socialized. In short, the social context dramatically impacts how people listen. We speak more of this in Chapters 7 and 8, but for now you should understand that to overcome these challenges you should begin with the belief that while we differ in the ways we communicate, there is not a "right" way to communicate. We are all different, and we can find shared meaning through these differences. See "Communication Counts in Your Life: Are You Listening?" for tips on understanding contextual challenges in communication.

Listening Barriers

Understanding barriers to effective listening is the first step in gaining the skills we need to improve our listening effectiveness. In this section, we identify several barriers to effective listening.

PSEUDOLISTENING   As professors, we often see students in our classes who appear to be listening but are not. They may keep eye contact with us, nod, or even smile, while they are actually mentally far removed from the classroom conversation. As another example, perhaps your boss or coworker tries to give you the impression he is listening, when in fact he cannot repeat what you have said. This is termed **pseudolistening,** or pretending to listen. When we encounter individuals who we believe are pseudolistening to us, we feel devalued—diminished in their eyes. After all, if they really thought what we said was important, they'd truly listen, right? We are all probably guilty of pseudolistening at some time, but to become effective and ethical communicators we must understand that pseudolistening can damage relationships and hamper shared meaning. If you are distracted when another person is speaking, ask the person if you can speak later when you are able to concentrate on his or her needs and conversation.

SELECTIVE LISTENING   **Selective listening** occurs when we focus on parts of a message that appeal to us because we either like or dislike the topic. Think of how often you fail to listen to a friend, romantic partner, or family member until he or she mentions something that you find particularly interesting. Or, conversely, you may tune out something that you find distasteful or difficult to handle. In such instances, you are listening selectively.

You can also be engaged in selective listening—as well as viewing—of particular forms of mass media. You are selectively listening when you log on to msnbc.com for the latest news, listen to "All Things Considered" on NPR (National Public Radio), or watch the latest reality TV show. To ensure that you are not prejudging or discounting another person's thoughts and ideas without appropriate consideration, spend a little time with his or her point of view before you decide not to listen.

DEFENSIVE LISTENING   "I can't believe you would say something like that to me!" Have you ever received this kind of a response and wondered what you said to provoke it? Perhaps you know people who often respond this way. These people are likely engaged in **defensive listening,** which is the practice of attributing criticism, hostility, or attacks to the comments of others even when these comments were not meant to be offensive. Low self-esteem, feelings of inadequacy, or an assumption that another person distrusts us may prompt defensive listening.

Pseudolistening ■ Pretending to listen.

Selective listening ■ Occurs when listeners focus on parts of a message that appeals to them because they like or dislike the topic at hand.

Defensive listening ■ The practice of attributing criticism, hostility, or attacks to the comments of others even when they are not intended.

As listeners, we need to remain open and consider other points of view.

Ambushing ■ Occurs when a person listens carefully in order to attack what the speaker says.

Authentic listening ■ Seeking to truly understand the intent, feelings, and perspective of a speaker's message.

Dominating ■ Occurs when others consistently refocus attention on themselves, even if they must interrupt others to do so; also termed *monopolizing* or *stage hogging*.

Pleasurable listening ■ Listening for appreciation.

Informational listening ■ Listening to discern.

When you encounter a defensive listener, stop and calmly clarify your meaning. You cannot guarantee that he or she will modify an interpretation, but you can at least clarify your intentions.

AMBUSHING   **Ambushing** is essentially the opposite of defensive listening and occurs when we listen carefully to others so we can attack what they say. While listening includes evaluating what others say, evaluation is not equivalent to attack. When we engage in **authentic listening,** we attempt to truly understand a person's intended message—not actively look for ways that we can attack his or her position. While we may disagree with someone's position, our purpose in constructive listening is not to find ammunition for our conversational war but to give a "fair hearing" and respond accordingly. The key to avoiding an ambush on someone's ideas or thoughts is to believe, fundamentally, that we all have the right to a point of view. Competent communicators do *not* think their point of view or assessment of a situation is the *only* right one. We do have a right to our points of view, but we do not have the right to attack those of others. When we attack or ambush others, we are really attacking them as persons because our goal is to undermine and devalue their ideas.

DOMINATING   **Dominating,** also termed *monopolizing* or *stage hogging,* happens when others consistently refocus attention on themselves, even if they must interrupt others to do so. Dominators may use interruptions like, "Well, if you think that's something, let me tell you what happened to *me.*" Unlike supportive listeners who interrupt to clarify or encourage another to continue to speak, dominators interrupt to recapture the conversation. One of your authors worked with a colleague who dominated conversations so often that at one point he confronted the colleague kindly and said, "I don't know if you realize it or not, but you simply don't listen to me. Every time I try to speak with you, you interrupt or talk over me." Interestingly, this colleague received the information very well, but even during the conversation, when his dominating behavior was explicitly mentioned, he continued to control the conversation. This person did not even listen closely enough to accept constructive criticism about his listening behaviors! If you spend at least the same amount of time listening as you do speaking, you will be less likely to dominate a conversation. As with avoiding ambushing, if you believe in the inherent value of all communicators, not just in yourself, you will be more likely to listen effectively and share the conversational stage fairly and appropriately.

LEARNING TO LISTEN EFFECTIVELY

We will now turn our focus to some specific, practical strategies that you can employ to improve your listening skills. To understand these strategies, we need to understand the basic types of listening: *pleasurable listening, informational listening, relational listening,* and *evaluative listening.*

Pleasurable Listening

When we listen to music, television, or a joke, we are engaged in **pleasurable listening,** or listening for appreciation. This type of listening calls for less focused concentration but still requires us to tune in to the source. In short, you can't fully enjoy much of your world without truly listening. What makes music pleasurable? We seem to focus easily on something we love. It is because we truly tune in when we care. The next time you are listening for pure pleasure, stop and ask yourself why this is so easy. Focus on what makes you tune in and use that sense of care and pleasure to increase your listening skills in other listening contexts.

Informational Listening

When people are seeking to understand others' messages, they are engaged in **informational listening,** or listening to discern. As a college student, it is especially important that you develop a keen ability to listen for information. When you attend class, talk with your RA about housing regulations, obtain financial aid information, or visit the student health center, you are listening to information. Consider these suggestions to improve your informational listening skills.

FOCUS ON THE SPEAKER   Position yourself so that you can easily make eye contact with the speaker. When your mind begins to wander, catch yourself and refocus your attention on the speaker. Make it your aim to understand what the speaker has to say rather than on how she says it or her appearance. Later in the interpersonal chapters we discuss how to truly focus on another person in a way that confirms him or her. But for now, simply think about sitting so you are in direct line of sight to the speaker or nodding to show that you are following his or her train of thought.

SEEK TO UNDERSTAND THE MESSAGE   Look for main ideas rather than details. In a lecture, take notes and seek to organize the information in a way that helps you understand and remember it. Use memory devices such as acronyms and acrostics. You can do this by listing a series of key words and then using the first letter of each word to make a memory aid. Ask questions as you listen but without interrupting the speaker inappropriately. Simple questions for clarification are easy and don't interrupt the flow of the speaker. Finally, don't judge the value of the message by your impression of the speaker. The box "Communication Counts in Your College Experience: Use a Recall/Cue System of Note-Taking" offers some helpful suggestions for improving note-taking.

AVOID ALLOWING THE CHANNEL TO DECIDE HOW YOU LISTEN   You may find a lecture with visual aids, demonstrations, or dynamic delivery more interesting. However, do not allow your preferences to decide whether you listen. Choose to listen regardless of the channels being used, even though you may find it challenging.

MONITOR YOUR RECEPTION   Avoid trying to read speakers' minds or concluding that you already know or dislike what they are going to say. Because you can listen much faster than someone can speak, use this lag time to pose clarifying questions or summarize main points in your notes. Getting enough rest and attending to those hunger pangs will also help you monitor your listening.

COMMUNICATION COUNTS IN YOUR COLLEGE EXPERIENCE

Use a Recall/Cue System of Note-Taking

Using a recall/cue system with your notes is one way to make your outline notes work harder for you—it makes them easier to review and helps you retain information. John Gardner and his colleagues A. Jerome Jewler and Betsy Barefoot (2007) describe the recall/cue system of note-taking in the seventh edition of their book *Your College Experience: Strategies for Success.* The steps are as follows:

1. *Set up your notebook paper.* Draw a line from the top of your page to the bottom about two inches in from the left-hand margin. This will divide your paper into two parts: the recall/cue space (on the left side of the paper) and the note-taking area.
2. *Take outline lecture notes.* Jot down your notes as you normally would, using the right-hand two-thirds of your sheet. Be sure to use good outline format by employing indentation and spacing to help you see relationships among main points and details.
3. *Set aside a brief, daily study session to review notes and develop recall cues.*
4. *Write the main ideas in the recall column.* Gardner et al. (2007) suggest that you review the notes you took in lecture for five or ten minutes first. Then, they suggest you go back through your notes and identify or highlight key terms or phrases and then write them in the recall column next to the material they represent.
5. *Use the recall column to review your ideas.* Cover up the notes on the right-hand side of your page with a blank piece of paper and use the prompts from the recall column to review your material. Reciting *out loud* or writing out the ideas on the sheet you are using to cover the right-hand side of the notes are excellent ways to actively learn the material rather than passively review it.
6. *Review the previous day's notes just before the next class session.* Arrive at class early, and take a few moments to review your two-column notes. Again, begin by covering up the right-hand side and only using the recall cues on the left-hand side to trigger or prompt your review. This will help you not only to review the material you've previously covered but also to prepare for what will be covered next in class.

If you have back-to-back classes and can't review immediately before class, try doing your periodic review during breakfast, in the hallway before class, riding the bus to school, or while doing a load of laundry. Using little bits of time to review prior to and after class will increase your understanding and will help you retain the information in your notes.

Conversing with others going through the same things you are helps you to feel welcome and supported.

REDUCE CONTEXTUAL DISTRACTIONS   Dress appropriately for the physical environment. Think ahead to where you'll be and how you can be comfortable. Seat yourself away from as many physical distractions as possible. Mentally block out background noise. Don't become so focused on the words the speaker uses or the ways in which the speaker forms words that you miss the message.

AVOID POOR LISTENING BEHAVIORS   Don't pretend to listen or listen only to those parts of the message you like or that you find interesting. Give speakers the benefit of the doubt rather than assuming they are opposed to you or that you need to find fault with the message.

Relational Listening

In **relational listening,** we listen to understand, support, and empathize with others. As noted in Chapter 2, **empathy** refers to an attempt to understand other people's perspectives and to place yourself in their situation. When we listen relationally, we focus on the feelings, needs, and desires of others as they attempt to make decisions, solve problems, or get to know each other better. Later in this chapter, we will focus more on listening and learning, and we will provide additional insights about empathetic listening. Meanwhile, here are some skills you can use to enhance listening in your relationships.

TRY TO UNDERSTAND   When you listen to what others say, you may respond in any number of ways. Sometimes you may make quick *judgments* that are either positive ("Hey, that's a good plan!") or negative ("That's a really stupid way to feel!"). Or you may offer *advice* ("Well, if I were you, I would...."). At other times, you may provide an *analysis* of the situation ("As I think about it, it seems to me that the real problem here is...") or pose *questions* that help the other person think about the issue at hand ("Why do you think this happened at this particular point in time?").

While any of these responses may be helpful in certain situations, initially it is best to attend to what the other person has to say. To let others know you are listening, you can offer various forms of feedback. **Paraphrase** or restate the speaker's ideas or feelings in your own words. This can help you check your understanding while also assuring the speaker you are listening. Try, "If I understand what you're saying, you think...." and state your own interpretation; then ask if that is what the speaker meant.

ENCOURAGE OTHERS TO SHARE   Responses like "Tell me more about...," "Uh-huh," and "I see" prompt speakers to reveal what they are thinking or feeling and add important clarifications that will help you understand them better. Even a brief silence offers the speaker a chance to share more information.

OFFER SUPPORT   As someone once noted, "People don't care how much we know until they know how much we care." In other words, the people who are important in our lives need to know that we are committed to them regardless of their problems or decisions. Providing verbal and nonverbal feedback—such as posing questions, paraphrasing, encouraging responses, maintaining eye contact, smiling, nodding, and touching (when appropriate)—communicates interpersonal support.

SELECT A SAFE ENVIRONMENT   Some information is much too personal to share in a public setting. Recently, two of your authors were in a restaurant where a man and woman were arguing about their relationship. They were talking so loudly about personal issues that we became uncomfortable both for them and for ourselves. We encourage you to deal with personal issues in private so that you can listen and respond appropriately.

TAKE YOUR LEAD FROM THE OTHER PERSON   Often conversational partners will ask for your evaluation or opinion if they want it. Therefore, it's best to wait until you are invited to share your viewpoint. Even then, however, it is important to weigh your

Relational listening ■ Listening to understand, support, and empathize with others.

Empathy ■ A purposeful attempt to understand another person's perspective.

Paraphrase ■ Restating someone's ideas or feelings in your own words.

COMMUNICATION COUNTS IN YOUR CAREER

Rhetorical Sensitivity

The idea of rhetorical sensitivity rests on the belief that all people hold attitudes toward communication—that is, they like to talk with others, they dislike talking with others, or they think everyone who tries to start a conversation is after something, and so on. Rhetorical sensitivity embraces a particular approach composed of the following assumptions:

- When talking, people should *balance* their needs and the needs of others.
- People should sharply distinguish between all thoughts and thoughts-for-communication.
- People should assume that there are many different ways to say the same thing.

- There is no "real self," as each of us is composed of multiple selves and we speak with multiple voices.
- Flexibility, strategy-making, and adaptation to others are the keys to successful communication.

Rhetorical sensitivity is ultimately expressed through our ability to adapt to the widest range of social activity and to employ the communication methods required in that communication moment. We understand the widest range of communication skills and apply what is needed to the context, the person, the relationship, and the values of the parties involved.

We encourage you to complete the RHETSEN in order to learn more about yourself and to get a sense of your attitudes toward communication.

words carefully. Listen carefully to the response they want; don't assume they want a full blown critique when they've asked for a simple yes or no or basic agreement. Essentially, think first of the other person and then respond.

PRACTICE RHETORICAL SENSITIVITY **Rhetorical sensitivity,** a concept developed by Hart, Carlson, and Eadie (1980), refers to "concern for self, concern for others, and a situational attitude" as cited in Littlejohn (1996, 107). In other words, as we listen empathetically, we are focused on ourselves, the other person, and the situation; in this way, we can provide appropriate, supportive verbal and nonverbal feedback to the speaker. As we discuss in the box "Communication Counts in Your Career: Rhetorical Sensitivity," rhetorical sensitivity increases accuracy in perceptions and enhances listening. It comes with experience and practice, and ultimately enhances the success of relationships through more effective communication. We will elaborate on this concept further in Chapter 4.

Evaluative Listening

Evaluative listening refers to analyzing a message in order to judge its validity, reliability, or usefulness. Evaluative listening critiques information, viewpoints, opinions, and evidence. Rather than accepting a message at face value, evaluative listeners carefully think about a message and weigh its merit. To perform successfully in the classroom, on the job, or in your everyday life, you need to engage in **critical listening,** a form of evaluative listening that involves analysis, synthesis, and judgment. Because you are responsible for what is covered in a lecture, required in the workplace, or expected at home, you need to listen critically to decide how to respond. Though critical listening involves judgment, it is essential that you strive to understand the other person before forming an opinion, arriving at a conclusion, or making a decision.

As a college student, you are bombarded with many media messages that attempt to persuade you to purchase certain products or services because they are "cool." For example, think about how the media influences the clothes we choose to wear or what kinds of music we listen to. While you make personal choices dependent on your unique preferences, your choices are framed in part by your peers' choices. These choices are directly influenced by various advertisements and marketing initiatives sponsored by businesses that seek to persuade you to purchase their products or services. When you listen critically, however, you can be aware of these messages and can evaluate them for yourself, given your own preferences or the state of your checking account.

While the products or services we buy may not be critically important decisions (unless we are creating an unmanageable debt), other issues are much more important and can potentially affect our safety and the well-being of our society. For instance, certain hate groups or gangs have become more prevalent on college campuses and seek to

Rhetorical sensitivity ■ Concern for self, concern for others, and a situational attitude.

Evaluative listening ■ Analyzing a message in order to judge its validity, reliability, or usefulness; also termed *critical listening.*

Critical listening ■ A form of listening that involves analysis, synthesis, and judgment.

recruit students as new members. Are you acquainted with the messages of such groups? Do you accept their claims? If so, why? If not, why not? As an evaluative listener, you must be aware of these messages and analyze them carefully. Here are some skills to help you listen evaluatively (you will find others in Chapter 9).

LISTEN BEFORE YOU EVALUATE   Before we can judge a message's quality, we must first understand that message. Just because a message comes from the media, a particular group, or a certain person does not mean that the message is necessarily suspect or reliable. By seeking to first understand the message, we are better able to assess its merit.

CONSIDER THE SOURCE   Even though the source may not cause us to doubt or accept a message's validity, we must consider the credibility of the message's originator. Is the source biased? Does the source have a known agenda that impacts the message? Is the source competent? Is the source trustworthy? Does the source have a reputation for good-will toward the audience? Does the source use appropriate messages for the occasion? Asking such questions will help you think about the validity, reliability, or usefulness of the message.

CONSIDER THE EVIDENCE   Is the evidence accurate or recent? Is there a sufficient amount of evidence? Is the evidence drawn from an unbiased source? Is the evidence open to multiple interpretations? Does the evidence include an appeal to emotions or does it include reason and logic? Asking questions like these can help you evaluate the claims that others make.

CONSIDER THE REASONING   It is important that an evaluative listener think about how a source develops an argument. Does the speaker focus on attacking another person or addressing the issue? Does the speaker draw hasty conclusions without sufficient evidence? Does the speaker appeal to popular opinion or use the argument, "Everybody is doing it"? Does the speaker appeal to an authority as being "right"? Does the speaker draw a cause-effect relationship that is not necessarily valid? Does the speaker present a case as being an either/or situation without considering other possible alternatives? Asking these kinds of questions can help you begin to understand whether the speaker's reasoning is sound. We will discuss faulty reason in more depth in Chapter 9.

REAPING THE REWARDS OF LISTENING

Why should we listen? While there are many possible answers, we will address four primary benefits of listening. Learning to listen well can increase our enjoyment, improve our understanding, enhance our empathy, and heighten civility.

Increased Enjoyment

As we have discussed, enjoyment and listening are linked. However, the more carefully we attend to stimuli like the tones, pitches, or words a speaker uses, the more enjoyment we are likely to obtain. For example, as you learn more about music as a part of your general education, you will likely have a new appreciation for a greater range of music because you can listen to it with an attuned ear. This does not, of course, mean that you will suddenly prefer Beethoven over your favorite popular music artist, but you can gain more enjoyment from a variety of music by listening more carefully to what makes each genre unique. Learning to stretch your listening preferences can truly increase your enjoyment.

Improved Understanding

Consider this scenario: A student questions a grade he received in a communication class because it was affected by his unexplained, excessive absenteeism. The attendance policy was clearly explained in the syllabus for the course, orally reinforced by his instructor, and even separately detailed in a document specially written for the student to clarify the policy. However, the student still did not abide by the policy, explain his absenteeism, or even speak with his instructor about the situation as the syllabus directed him to do. Moreover, when the policy was explained to the student in greater detail and he was given a fresh start in the course, he continued to miss class. As a result, his grade was considerably reduced. In short, if the student had listened, he would have understood the policy and been able to keep a higher grade. Listening, then, is vital to improving our understanding of many types of information.

In the workplace, practicing civility, empathy, and understanding not only make us better listeners but better colleagues as well.

Whether we are learning information in the classroom, on the job, or in conversation with others, improved listening will help us better understand ourselves and others and the situations we encounter every day. With improved understanding, we can make decisions, answer questions, and solve or even prevent problems. This can mean improved grades, job promotions, or higher salaries. It can also mean better work situations or personal relationships with others. Such rewards are certainly worth the effort of listening with greater care to the information we encounter.

Enhanced Empathy

Nothing brings more pleasure—or pain—than personal relationships. Empathy is one of the most important skills we can develop to gain the most from relationships. Earlier we noted that *empathy* refers to the ability to feel as another person feels or to see as another person sees. This complex behavior includes our choices, intelligence, and emotion—that is, we must seek to understand and appreciate another person's perceptions. Listening is a vital first step in this process. When we listen carefully to what others say and cue into the words and the manner in which they are spoken, we start to develop empathy. As we do so, we increase the pleasure in our relationships because we can build relationships founded on shared understandings.

Furthermore, when we are hurt by relationships, we also learn from our own experience how others feel in similar situations. We can, as a result of our experiences with pain, enter into others' disappointments and provide genuinely meaningful support by listening and empathizing.

Additionally, by developing empathy, we are more likely to gain the acceptance and appreciation of others. Although we do not empathize to increase our own influence or to have others affirm us, when we learn to listen to others carefully and compassionately, we nevertheless are likely to enhance our skills in empathy and gain the acceptance and affirmation of others. In other words, empathy has reciprocal benefits.

Heightened Civility

How easy it is to become angry, rude, and self-centered! All of us understand this tendency. We also know that as the world becomes more diverse and people of different cultures, backgrounds, and lifestyles interact more frequently, the potential for personal and large-scale conflict escalates. Road rage and ethnic or cultural wars are examples of this kind of conflict. Sadly, **civility**—an attitude of respect for other people as unique individuals—is often uncommon both in the world at large and in our own communities. For example, recently in the Midwest, a college student killed several international students in a series of drive-by shootings before committing suicide. Investigators revealed that this young man had connections with a right-wing group that stressed white supremacy as a central tenant of its belief system. These ideas had so influenced this young man's thinking that he exploded in a violent manner.

In response to this disturbing trend of violence, Arnett and Arneson (1999) propose dialogic civility as a communicative antidote to the despair, cynicism, and cycle of hatred

Civility ■ An attitude of respect for other people as unique individuals.

Dialogic civility ■ A set of communication behaviors that include understanding the importance of public dialogue, the need for respect for one another, the extension of a sense of grace to one another, and the commitment to keep the conversation going.

that too often mars contemporary life. **Dialogic civility** refers to a set of communication behaviors that include understanding the importance of public dialogue, respecting one another, extending grace to one another, and committing to keeping the conversation going (Worley & Worley 2000). As Arnett and Arneson phrase it, we need to "reach out to one another using behaviors that are civil and that keep the conversation going in the midst of difference" (76).

But this is easier said than done. How can we begin such a seemingly complex process? The first step is to begin to genuinely listen to one another. Genuine listening communicates respect and provides us with important opportunities to gain understanding and develop empathy. Civil communication begins with practicing the principles of effective listening and results in social and personal benefits. After all, isn't it fair to listen to what someone else has to say before we decide how to respond? To do less is unethical and uncivil for all concerned.

USING LISTENING TO ENHANCE LEARNING

To this point we have thought about the reluctance to listen, the requirements for listening, and the rewards of listening. But how is this information relevant to your experience as a college student? As a college student, you spend the majority of your time listening to lectures, PowerPoint presentations, guest speakers, and the like, according to Anderson and Armbruster (1986). But how well do you really understand and remember what you hear? We have already addressed the importance of listening; now let's think about your role in the listening process and how you can enhance your abilities to learn by listening.

As we noted earlier, you invest a tremendous amount of your time listening in college. Particularly, you are called upon to listen both inside and outside the classroom as you negotiate your college experience. Here are some suggestions to help you sharpen your abilities to learn through listening.

Listen to Teacher Instructions

Listening to and interacting with professors and peers helps us understand and remember what we are learning.

College professors usually have syllabi or course outlines that explain major assignments and their due dates. They also often explain the assignments and reinforce the due dates orally. Be sure to cue in to this information. It is your responsibility to understand what you are to do and when you are to have assignments completed. Explaining that you didn't know an assignment was due or that you missed class the day a test or quiz was given will not generally persuade professors to give you an opportunity to make up the work. Improve your abilities to follow direction by getting to class before your professor arrives, listening carefully, jotting down important reminders, checking your syllabi regularly, and making notes on handouts as your professor goes over them.

Reduce Forgetting

Studies indicate that we generally lose 50 percent of what we learn or hear within the first hour after encountering the new material and that we normally lose 70 percent of what we heard 72 hours after hearing it (McWhorter 2006). Therefore, to combat forgetting, you must find ways to capture and retain as much information as possible during lectures and other learning situations. One way to retain more during a lecture is to print out any notes or handouts the professor has available before going to lecture so that you can listen more to the concepts and ideas he or she is presenting rather than trying to write down everything that is being said. Also, be sure to review your notes periodically throughout the week—not just right before tests and quizzes—to reduce forgetting and increase understanding. For more information about a specific style of note-taking that may enhance your understanding and retention, see the Campus Link: Use a Recall/Cue System of Note-Taking.

Keep All Class Handouts

If your instructor gives you copies of notes or provides you with written instructions for assignments, keep a copy of this information. It will help you listen to any oral explanations and remind you of important ideas as you prepare to complete assignments. Be sure to date both your notes and your handouts so that you can pair them for more comprehensive studying. Your professor may also distribute class handouts, assignments, or notes via the Web, so be sure to print off or save them for future study sessions.

Get and Stay Organized

Staying organized in college takes time; however, the end results—better grades— make the extra effort worthwhile. Being able to get right to work or to find the right handout will save priceless study time and unnecessary frustration. Be sure to purchase a good three-ring binder, two inches wide or larger; section dividers; and a three-hole punch. Use the tabs to delineate the different courses you are taking or units you are studying in a certain subject. Keep all your subjects and materials (lecture notes, handouts, returned work, textbook notes) in this binder. This way you'll always have all your materials with you, and you can review them when you have extra time.

Additionally, many students find that noting important dates on a calendar or assignment notebook helps them keep track of their workload. You can also use a calendar or the programs on your computer to remind you of other appointments, meetings, or social events. Practicing these organizational skills will help you prepare to enter the world of work where organizational skills are even more important.

Practice the Principles of Effective Informational Listening

Earlier in this chapter, we offered guidelines and skills that will help you listen for information. Using these will truly help you in the classroom. Consider writing short reminders about these principles on a 3 × 5 card and putting them in your notebook for easy review. Effective listening, like most habits, requires persistent practice. Do you consider yourself a good listener? Could you use some additional listening practice?

BECOMING A COMPETENT AND ETHICAL LISTENER IN COLLEGE, CAREER, AND LIFE

You need to listen to various people in a variety of places—on campus, on the job, or in your daily life. When you need assistance with a particular question or problem, you will often receive information about where to go or with whom to speak. By paying careful attention, you can save time, energy, and frustration for yourself and others. For example, financial aid is often confusing given the number of forms and the amount of information you need to gather. While some of the complexity that accompanies financial aid is inevitable, with careful and cordial listening, you can avoid unnecessary complications and frustrations. Specifically, consider the following suggestions:

- *Ask the person's name with whom you are speaking.* Being able to address someone by name personalizes your encounter and allows you to get to know someone in that office.
- *Ask clarifying questions.* If you don't understand the information, ask questions until you do understand. Try to rephrase what you've heard to make sure that you have heard correctly. You might try saying, "If I heard you correctly, you want me to do three things..." or "So, what I need to do is.... Is that correct?"
- *Practice civility.* When you are confused or frustrated, it is easy to become angry or rude. Take a deep breath and remember that if you want the information you need, it is best to avoid anger or outbursts, especially if the person with whom you are speaking is in the best position to help you.

■ *Jot down notes.* As we noted earlier, psychological studies indicate that we all have problems with forgetfulness. Jotting down names, numbers, addresses, or directions will give you a better chance of recalling important information, and you will tend to listen better as you initially receive the information.

Practicing these suggestions for civil and ethical communication will enhance your interactions in any setting, be it school, work, home, and community.

SUMMARY

In this chapter, we have emphasized that listening is vital in human communication. In doing so, we have stressed these main ideas:

■ There are many challenges that listeners face that are based on several factors—sender, channel, message, receiver, context, and social.

■ Some barriers to listening include pseudolistening, selective listening, defensive listening, ambushing, and dominating.

■ The rewards for listening—enjoyment, understanding, empathy, and civility—are significant enough to encourage us to become effective listeners.

■ Improved listening abilities will pay dividends in your college experience, your professional life, and your personal relationships.

QUESTIONS FOR DISCUSSION

1. Consider this scenario: John and Gloria are sharing a deep-dish pizza in the Student Center. As they decide who should have the last slice, John says, "Professor Raja is so frustrating. I had to miss two labs for my aunt's funeral, and she won't let me make up the time. Now, my grade is really suffering."

   "Have you talked to her about it?" Gloria inquires.

   "I tried! I showed her the obituary and tried to get her to understand how important my aunt was to me, but she just wouldn't listen. And to top it off, I'm not sure she even understands what I'm saying because she doesn't speak English all that well to begin with. Then, because she speaks English with that funny accent, when she does try to explain why she won't excuse my absences, I have the same problem understanding her as I do when she lectures in class. I don't know what to do. If I don't get at least a B in that class, it could affect my financial aid, and then my parents will freak for sure!"

   What listening problems do you identify in this scenario? What suggestions do you have for Jack, Gloria, and Dr. Raja in order to improve their listening?

2. Consider the remainder of this scenario: After his lunch conversation with Gloria, John went to his communication course where his teacher explained the idea of using multiple channels to help ensure shared meaning between communicators. John realized that he had only tried talking to Professor Raja and had never attempted to use another channel. Immediately after class, he went to the computer lab and sent an e-mail message to Professor Raja, trying to be as respectful as possible and to explain his concerns. What is your opinion of John's new course of action? Given the principles in this chapter, what additional advice would you offer him? What other communication strategies may help him resolve this situation in a manner that is mutually acceptable to both him and his professor?

3. Why is listening transactional?

4. Where do you find the greatest listening challenges on your campus? Why? What strategies are offered in this chapter that might help you improve your listening in this context?

5. Recall a recent incident when you and your friend, roommate, or parent strongly disagreed with each other. What listening challenges did you face in this situation? How would listening relationally help you deal with this situation more effectively when it occurs again?

6. What do you think about the current state of civility in our society? Does this impact your personal experience? Do the ideas that we offer here sound helpful? What role does communication play in helping to enhance civility in our interactions with others? What additional suggestions would you offer?

EXERCISES

1. Listen to the song "American Pie." Write down the lyrics as you listen. Did you encounter difficulties writing these lyrics? Analyze any specific problems with listening that you encountered.

2. Using this chapter's model for listening, analyze a recent lecture in one of your classes. How does each stage apply to the listening process in this situation? What specific listening challenges do you face in listening to lectures? How might you improve your listening in this situation?

3. In pairs, tell a story about a recent time when you believe that someone with whom you were speaking was not listening. How do you know he or she was not listening?

How did this make you feel? What lessons for your own listening can you draw from this experience?

4. To understand pleasurable listening and its relationship to family communication, tell one of your favorite family stories to a small group of your classmates. Make sure the story is appropriate to repeat to others. After telling the story, discuss as a group some of the following questions:

   a. When does your family engage in storytelling?
   b. Who surfaces as the "orator" in your family?
   c. In addition to pleasurable listening, what listening skills are enhanced by storytelling? Explain.
   d. What are some of the stories you have heard that have stayed with you all your life? Who was the storyteller? How did these stories make you feel about the storyteller? What have you learned about the person? What did they teach you through their stories?
   e. Do you see yourself as a storyteller for your family? Why or why not? (Bowles & Gee 2000).

5. In order to practice listening nonjudgmentally, Collins (2000) suggests that we get interested in something so that we can attend to ideas or feelings of others as they talk. She refers to this as "playing the inner game of listening." To do this, try the following exercise: Engage in a conversation in pairs. One partner should be the "talker" and the other the "listener." The talker should talk for three to five minutes about anything he or she wishes. The listener should close his or her eyes and listen for the talker's interest level while focusing on a way to become truly interested in what the talker is saying. After three to five minutes, the listener should reflect on the following questions: On a scale of zero to ten, how interested is the talker? How do you know? What other observations can you make about the person talking? Do not share your observations yet, but make some notes about your insights. Now reverse roles and repeat the exercise. Once again, the listener should jot down notes about his or her observations. Next, together discuss your observations: What did you hear? How did you get interested in what the talker was saying? How did you change your personal listening experience to make it more fulfilling? What kind of inner games did you find yourself engaging in to improve your interest level and your listening?

6. Interview five to ten peers who are not in your class about their listening behaviors. Write down their responses to the following questions. When you have completed all the interviews, summarize the responses for each question by noting what is similar or unique among them.

   a. What is the main reason you listen to classroom lectures?
   b. During which class period of the day do you listen best?
   c. What physical classroom characteristics influence your listening the most?
   d. Where do you sit in the classroom if you really want to listen to what is being said?
   e. What single characteristic of the instructor most influences your listening?
   f. What single characteristic of your own most influences your listening?
   g. What single behavior on your part helps you listen?
   h. What single characteristic about the lecture or message most influences your listening?

KEY TERMS

Ambushing 48
Appropriateness 43
Authentic listening 48
Civility 53
Co-cultures 46
Competent 43
Critical listening 51
Defensive listening 47
Dialogic civility 54
Dominating 48

Empathy 50
Ethos 43
Evaluative listening 51
Hearing 42
Informational listening 48
Listening 42
Message complexity 45
Message overload 45
Mindful 42

Paraphrase 50
Pleasurable listening 48
Pseudolistening 47
Receiver apprehension 45
Relational listening 50
Rhetorical sensitivity 51
Selective listening 47
Sound bite 44
Trigger words 45

REFERENCES

Anderson, T. H., and Armbruster, B. B. 1986. *The value of taking notes.* (Reading Education Report No. 374). Champaign: University of Illinois at Urbana-Champaign, Center for the Study of Reading.

Arnett, R. C., and Arneson, P. 1999. *Dialogic civility in a cynical age.* Albany, NY: State University of New York Press.

Barker, L., Edwards, R., Gaines, C., Gladney, K., and Holley, F. 1980. An investigation of the proportional time spent in various communication activities by college students. *Journal of Applied Communication Research* 8:101–110.

Bowles, K., and Gee, F. H. 2000. *The benefits of storytelling to listening.* Retrieved May 18, 2004, from www.listen.org/pages/exercises.html.

Collins, J. 2000. *Listening nonjudgmentally.* Retrieved May 18, 2004, from www.listen.org/pages/exercises.html.

Gardner, J., Jewler, A. J., and Barefoot, B. 2007. *Your college experience: Strategies for success.* 7th ed. Belmont, CA: Thomson Wadsworth.

Hart, R. P., Carlson, R. E., and Eadie, W. F. 1980. Attitudes toward communication and the assessment of rhetorical sensitivity. *Communication Monographs* 47(1):1–22.

Littlejohn, S. 1996. *Theories of human communication*. 5th ed. New York: Wadsworth.

Martin, J. N., and Nakayama, T. K. 2001. *Experiencing intercultural communication: An introduction*. Mountain View, CA: Mayfield.

McWhorter, K. 2006. *College reading and study skills*. 5th ed. Upper Saddle River, NJ: Pearson Education.

Ramsey, J. L., and Langlois, J. H. 2002. Effects of the "beauty is good" stereotype on children's information processing. *Journal of Experimental Child Psychology* 81:320–340.

Tannen, D. 1990. *You just don't understand: Women and men in conversation*. New York: William Morrow.

Wheeless, L. R. 1975. An investigation of receiver apprehension and social context dimensions of communication apprehension. *The Speech Teacher* 24:261–268.

Wood, J. 1997. Diversity in dialogue: Communication between friends. In *Ethics of communication in an age of diversity*, eds. J. Makau, and R. Arnett, 5–26. Urbana: University of Illinois Press.

Worley, D. W., and Worley, D. A. 2000. *On religious wars: Wieman's concept of creative interchange and Arnett and Arneson's dialogic civility*. Paper presented at the Sixth Annual Communication Ethics Conference. Gull Lake, MI.

CHAPTER 4

Verbal Communication and Language

LEARNING OUTCOMES After reading this chapter, you will have:

the **Knowledge** to...

and the **Skills** to...

UNDERSTANDING VERBAL COMMUNICATION, page 62

Be able to explain the meaning of verbal and nonverbal communication.

- Make sure your verbal messages are reinforced by your nonverbal behaviors.
- Know that each person is unique and that we cannot truly know the full meaning of another's message.

IDENTIFYING THE PROPERTIES OF LANGUAGE, page 62

Understand the properties of language and their impacts on verbal communication.

- Use symbolic language that clearly and concretely conveys your message.
- Employ a sentence structure that is easy to understand.
- Guard against using language with negative or ambiguous connotations.

RECOGNIZING THE POWER OF LANGUAGE, page 64

Be mindful of the power of language.

- Realize that language is shaped by culture.
- Remember that shared experiences with others create unique meanings for those involved.
- Avoid confusion by refraining from using equivocal (uncertain) or ambiguous (unclear) language.
- Refuse to use doublespeak or euphemisms to "soften" or mask your message.
- Resist classifying people based on stereotypes.
- Clarify your meaning in clear, direct language.

CONNECTING LANGUAGE AND GENDER, page 70

Heighten awareness of gender in verbal communication.

- Use gender-neutral language.

CONNECTING LANGUAGE AND CULTURE, page 71

Understand the challenges of language in cultural contexts.

- Interpret language with care, understanding that messages are interpreted differently in different contexts as well as in individualist or collectivists cultures.

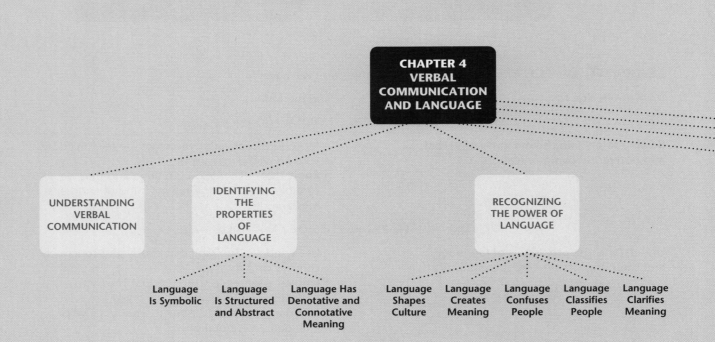

LEARNING THE LANGUAGE OF COLLEGE, page 72

Become familiar with verbal language used in college.

- Ask your classmates, roommates, or your instructors to explain unfamiliar terms and concepts.

USING LANGUAGE COMPETENTLY AND ETHICALLY IN COLLEGE, CAREER, AND LIFE, page 73

Develop skills in the competent and ethical use of language.

- Consider your communication context and avoid unfamiliar jargon.
- Use confirming language ("I find your point easy to understand" or "I like how you have wrapped up your argument").
- Practice rhetorical sensitivity by adapting your message to the specific contexts.

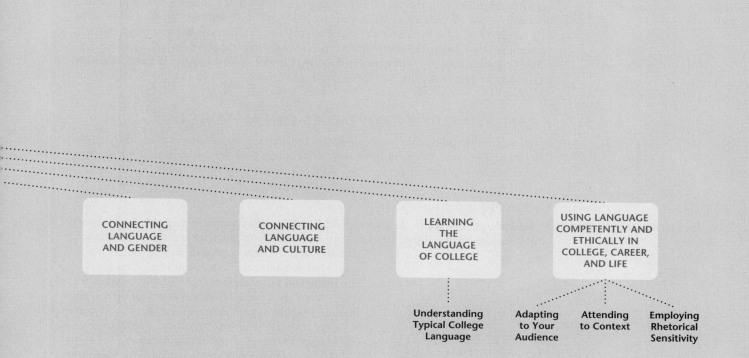

CONNECTING LANGUAGE AND GENDER

CONNECTING LANGUAGE AND CULTURE

LEARNING THE LANGUAGE OF COLLEGE

USING LANGUAGE COMPETENTLY AND ETHICALLY IN COLLEGE, CAREER, AND LIFE

Understanding Typical College Language

Adapting to Your Audience

Attending to Context

Employing Rhetorical Sensitivity

UNDERSTANDING VERBAL COMMUNICATION

We live in a world of words. Actually, it is more accurate to say that we live in many worlds of words. This is because language is embedded in a particular culture. To put it another way, there are some words that can be translated into a different language and others for which there is no direct translation.

In this chapter, we explore the nature of language and its impact on our lives. Although we sometimes take for granted that people who "speak our language" will understand the words we use, we must also understand that each of us creates personal meaning for our language; therefore, our meaning can never exactly match the meaning of another person. It is also important to emphasize that it is impossible to study either verbal or nonverbal communication in isolation. When we communicate, we experience all of the verbal and nonverbal elements together. When you engage in conversation, your tone of voice communicates to the listener important information about how to interpret your words: as a joke, as a serious remark, or as sarcasm.

Verbal communication involves the sending and receiving of messages with words. **Nonverbal communication,** on the other hand, involves the sending and receiving of wordless messages. Nonverbal messages can be communicated through body language, posture, gestures, facial expressions, or eye contact. Figure 4.1 shows communication scholar John Stewart's (1995) notion of a continuum of verbal and nonverbal elements of communication. At the "primary verbal" end of the continuum are written words; at the opposite end are "primary nonverbal" elements such as gestures, facial expression, touch, and appearance. At the continuum's midpoint are what Stewart refers to as "mixed" elements, including vocal pacing, pause, loudness, and silence. Stewart emphasizes the relationship between the two when he suggests, "the verbal and nonverbal elements of communication are completely interdependent, which means that the verbal affects the nonverbal and the nonverbal affects the verbal, but that neither *determines* the meaning of the other" (52). We discuss the nature of verbal communication in this chapter and the nature of nonverbal communication in Chapter 5.

We use words to describe ourselves, and the ways we describe ourselves both reflect and are a reflection of our self-concept. In turn, our self-concept influences how we dress, behave, and interact. In this sense, language is an activity that influences who you are and how you behave. Words affect what we perceive; they reduce uncertainty; they allow us to express abstract, complex ideas; and they both promote human contact and create barriers between persons. Language allows us to express feelings and emotions as well as assert individual and social identity. Our personal meaning can be explained by the fact that language has certain properties we need to understand.

Verbal communication ■ Involves the sending and receiving of messages with words.

Nonverbal communication ■ Involves the sending and receiving of wordless messages that can be communicated by body language, postures, gestures, facial expressions, and eye contact.

Symbolic ■ Representative of a particular thing, idea, concept, or event.

Arbitrary ■ Created in individual persons or through cultural associations.

IDENTIFYING THE PROPERTIES OF LANGUAGE

In this section we discuss the basic properties of language, continuing our discussion from Chapter 1. The symbolic, arbitrary nature of language is important to a more substantive understanding of how humans, not the words themselves, create meaning.

Language is Symbolic

As we discussed in Chapter 1, language is **symbolic.** In other words, a particular set of letters represents a particular thing, idea, concept, or event. Thus, language is a system of symbols that allows us to relate sounds or writing to meaning in ways that facilitate our understanding of each other and ourselves. But there is no relationship between the symbols and the "thing." Symbols stand for things, but they are not "the thing." A map, for example, is a symbolic representation of the "territory" you are traveling; it is not the actual route or destination.

These language symbols are **arbitrary.** Meaning is created in individual persons or through cultural associations. Meaning does not exist in a word. Did you ever stop to think about who decides which symbols stand for which things? For example, why

FIGURE 4.1

Stewart's Verbal-Nonverbal Continuum.

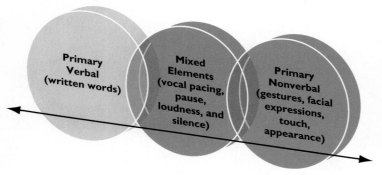

Primary Verbal (written words)

Mixed Elements (vocal pacing, pause, loudness, and silence)

Primary Nonverbal (gestures, facial expressions, touch, appearance)

do the letters *D-O-G* stand for the four-legged, drooling pet we love? At some point in history, someone used these letters to describe this animal. Over time, and by mutual consent, more people used this set of symbols to refer to the animal. And we now know this is the "correct" set of symbols for our pet because the dictionary uses these letters to represent the word for this animal. This combination of letters for this animal is also what we learned in school. In preschool or kindergarten we might have had flash cards with a picture of the animal on one side and the letters *D-O-G* on the other. We had books that explained that the picture should be referred to by the word *dog*. However, in French-speaking countries, the symbols for this animal are *CHIEN*; in Spanish, *PERRO* or *PERRA*, depending upon whether the dog is male or female; and in Chinese, *QUAN*.

EMERGENCY EXIT
NOTAUSGANG
SORTIE DE SECOURS
SALIDA DE EMERGENCIA
非常口

Though our words may differ, their meanings are the same.

When we forget that the word is not the thing, we engage in *reification*—the act of regarding something that is intangible or abstract as tangible or concrete. We may also think of it as characterized by consistent parts of a static entity. Take the example of the word "woman." What is a woman? If you attempt to describe this "thing" as having certain parts or certain characteristics, you have engaged in reification. A woman is not a thing to be described. A woman is a person with distinctive and often unique feelings, thoughts, and behaviors. Reification of words causes potentially damaging misunderstanding. When we reify a word, we often engage in what is called *bypassing*—using different words with the same meaning or the same words with different meanings. Instead of making sure we understand what a speaker intends by a word or what a listener interprets in a word, we "pass each other by." Stewart and Logan (1993) describe what may be the most catastrophic example of bypassing, which occurred at the end of WWII:

> Before the United States dropped atomic bombs on Hiroshima and Nagasaki, the Japanese government knew that they had lost the war. Government leaders were meeting almost constantly, and they had agreed to surrender; the only question was exactly when and how. Surrender negotiations were also under way with Russia, which meant the Japanese government had received detailed ultimatums from both Russia and the Allied Forces. So as not to upset the negotiations with Russia, the Japanese cabinet decided that their first response to the Allied ultimatum would be noncommittal. The key word in its reply was *mokusatsu*, a term which can be translated as "no comment." Unfortunately, the Japanese word is made up of two characters, one meaning "silence" or "ignore." Allied translators understood the Japanese to have "ignored" the ultimatum and were furious. The punishment came quickly, tens of thousands of people died, and the world was propelled into an age of weapons we still haven't completely figured out how to manage. (115)

Language is Structured and Abstract

It is impossible to speak of language and the meaning we develop without understanding that language is **structured.** The way we put words together into sentences (syntax), sentences into paragraphs, and paragraphs into essays is governed by a set of rules that is culture bound. Individuals who are bilingual or trilingual understand how different the structure of languages can be. A change in a sentence's structure affects how the meaning will be interpreted.

Communication theorists Ogden and Richards (1993) developed a "triangle of meaning" to help us understand how language works. As Figure 4.2 shows, the triangle explains the relationship between the *thought*, the *word*, and the *thing*. The symbol/word is designated to refer to some thought or feeling. The symbol stands for or references the actual object or what the symbol stands for. Thoughts and feelings are shaped by past experience. The solid line between the word and the thought implies a direct connection between the letters we see (word) and our interpretation (thought) of the word. The solid line between the thought and the thing implies a direct relationship as well. However, the dotted line between the word and the thing tells us that there is no direct connection.

Language is also **abstract.** Some words are clear, simple, and commonly understood across a particular cultural group. Other words or concepts are much more complex and

Structured ■ Governed by a set of rules.

Abstract ■ Complex and open to varied interpretations and understanding.

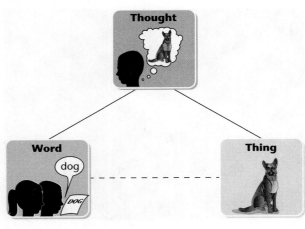

FIGURE 4.2
The Triangle of Meaning.

are open to varied interpretations and understandings. Despite these inherent problems, our abilities to abstract, categorize, and specify are ultimately part of what separates us from "lower" animals. Hayakawa (1990) developed an "abstraction ladder" to help us understand this concept. The least abstract words are positioned at the ladder's lowest rungs, the most abstract at the top. As you move up the abstraction ladder, you encounter more meanings for words. When our language becomes abstract, we are better able to describe the world. The more our language allows us to describe the world, the more we are able to understand it. When we understand the world, we are able to respond to our environment and, we hope, make the world a better place.

Language Has Denotative and Connotative Meaning

Understanding a word's two types of definitions—denotative and connotative—can help you avoid using arbitrary language. A word's **denotative meaning** is the objective, agreed-upon definition that we find in a dictionary. Thus, *Merriam-Webster's Collegiate Dictionary* defines *dog* as "a highly variable domestic mammal (*Canis familiaris*) closely related to the gray wolf" or "a male" or "a worthless or contemptible person."* So how do we decide which is the correct or fitting definition?

We have to understand that each of us has some personal history or cultural experience that will influence the meaning we create for the word. This is our **connotative meaning**. Our connotative meaning is subjective and individual and built on our experiences with that word. For example, have you ever owned a dog? Was it your best friend, a beast that shared space in your house, or a being to fear? Was it large, small, friendly, mean, loving, standoffish, young, old, thin, fat? When you think of a dog, does a specific mental picture come to mind? The connotative meaning we give to words, symbols, and "things" originated within this personal relationship. For each word, we create a set of personal "signifiers" that become a set of characteristics for the word. For many of us, "dog" is something we "signify" as loving, loyal, funny, or protective. It may be our best buddy, a comforting friend, or even a member of the family. For others, a dog is something we signify as ferocious, mean, dangerous, hurtful, or wild. Depending on your experience with dogs, your signifiers for *dog* could be very different from either of these lists. Thus, some words have many connotative definitions, especially concepts such as freedom, love, and justice; other words may have fewer connotations—for example, *chair, book,* or *apartment.*

Because language allows us to **associate** or signify language in very personal ways, we must understand how some words have enormous power in our relationships, cultures, and lives. Words become meaningful to us through a very complex process of association over time. When we are children, the associations we make between words and things are simple; later in life, we expand our range of associations with a word to create more complex combinations of meanings. For example, to a child, water may be associated with a bath or a drink from a faucet. The child may be conscious of the water's temperature and may have experiences with it, such as playing in a pool or running under a sprinkler. Later in life, we can associate water with experiences both in our lives and beyond the immediate world in which we live. For example, we may associate it with massive flooding, beachside vacations, community picnics, or with the place where we fell in love, were rejuvenated at a retreat, or spread a loved one's ashes. In sum, competent communicators need to be aware of the associations of the words they use.

Denotative meaning ■ The objective, agreed-upon definition of a word.

Connotative meaning ■ The meaning of a word as influenced by an individual's personal history or cultural experience.

Associate ■ Signify language.

RECOGNIZING THE POWER OF LANGUAGE

Many of you have heard the childhood saying, "Sticks and stones may break my bones, but names will never hurt me." Do you believe this is true? Do words sometimes hurt? Of course they do. Language allows us to do more than just convey facts

*Definition of "dog" used by permission. From *Merriam-Webster's Collegiate® Dictionary,* 11th Edition © 2011 by Merriam-Webster, Incorporated (www.Merriam-Webster.com).

TABLE 4.1

EIGHT FUNCTIONS OF LANGUAGE

1 • Language allows us to "conquer silence," thus allowing us to reduce fear. Through language, we reduce our uncertainty about ourselves, others, and relationships.

2 • Language allows us to express and control emotion. By talking about emotions, we can regulate them.

3 • Language can either reveal or hide out thoughts and motives. We can "tell it like it is," or we can "tell it like we want another to know."

4 • Language permits us to either connect with or avoid others. Language bridges differences or divides.

5 • Language enables us to be unique individuals, to create our own "style." We can grow closer to others by "sharing" a language or vocabulary.

6 • Language allows us to share information. Sharing with others allows us to feel we belong.

7 • Language allows us to control and be controlled by the world. Once we name or describe something, we know what to expect from it.

8 • Language can be used to monitor or analyze our communication. As human beings, we have the power of "metacommunication" —we can "talk about our talk."

or find information. Trenholm and Jensen (1992) suggest that there are eight basic functions of language in Table 4.1.

To illustrate, you may have been in situations where a family member needs immediate medical attention. Imagine that you are sitting in a hospital sitting room waiting for word from the doctor on your family member's condition. Following Trenholm and Jensen's functions of language model, it is likely that:

- By talking about how we are feeling, some of us would try to "conquer" the silence (Function #1).
- By sharing our hopeful reassurances and mutual concerns, we can connect with one another (Function #2).
- In identifying our hopes and fears, we can gain some control over what is happening to us in this tense and uncertain situation (Function #3).
- We can connect on a more emotionally fulfilling basis during this time of stress (Function #4).
- During emotional stress we are also, perhaps inevitably, our most unique selves, which we communicate through the way we deal with a crisis (Function #5).
- Sharing our innermost feelings in a time of crisis brings a sense of belonging (Function #6).
- And, perhaps most importantly, through language in this time, we may feel a better sense of control over what may be a tense and frightening time (Function #7).
- For some of us, how we "talk about our talk" in a stressful time can also help us to "control" the situation (Function #8).

Authoritative nature of language
■ The rules of communication with particular others in certain communication contexts as dictated by language.

Language Shapes Culture

Language has the power to *shape culture* and has the potential to create who we are and how we define ourselves and are defined by others. We need to understand the **authoritative nature of language.** Language is authoritative because it tells us the rules of communication with particular others in certain communication contexts. It tells us who

Culture Counts

In the workplace, we often use specialized language and information.

people are, their position in society, and how we should interact with them. Sometimes these rules are appropriate and understood by individuals across the entire culture; at other times, they create barriers between individuals and groups.

Edward Sapir and Benjamin Lee Whorf (1956) developed the **Sapir-Whorf hypothesis;** they theorize that language is the most significant factor in determining what we see in the world and how we think and evaluate what we see. At a very basic level, this means that if we do not have a word to describe something, we do not see it as important. Once we have developed words to describe a phenomenon, we can discuss, analyze, label, and evaluate it. Language is bound by culture, a system of symbols governed by the rules and patterns of the culture.

Think about the word *work*. What does this signify to you? In your experience, is work something you must do to survive? Is it something you take for granted or depend on to make ends meet? Is your work your life? Or is your life your work? What is the difference between these two questions? Do you believe in the "Protestant work ethic"—the moral value of hard work? Is work what we do so we'll have the money to really enjoy life? Is work the ticket to respect and self-esteem? How you signify *work* will influence almost every other aspect of your life. It will determine what you study in college and what career you aspire to. It will influence the friendships you create and the romantic partners you have. It will influence how you analyze and evaluate public policies such as welfare and affirmative action. It will, perhaps, even impact your civic engagement and determine which political party you support.

Language Creates Meaning

As an element of culture, language helps us *create meaning*. And we, in turn, use that meaning to modify, adapt, and change our culture. We use it to create, maintain, and evaluate relationships. Each generation in the United States creates its own language to establish its place and to create a unique impact on our culture. In the '60s, we were "anti-establishment," we wanted to "ban the bomb," and we wanted to "make love not war." In the '70s we thought our favorite celebrities were "far out!" We wanted to "find ourselves" through counseling and encounter groups. In the '80s and '90s a new and unique vocabulary developed as well. What would you describe as the unique elements of language today? Media images, TV sitcoms and reality shows, and trends also create and change culture through language.

Any *Seinfeld* fan will remember the phrase, "yada yada yada," which was the essence of an entire episode and which became one of the show's "signature" phrases. *Merriam-Webster's Collegiate Dictionary* defines "yada yada yada" as "boring or empty talk" and "often used interjectionally especially in recounting words regarded as too dull or predictable to be worth repeating."* Why *yada yada yada*? When the writers of *Seinfeld* were developing the script, they thought the phrase sounded right for the characters. Although the *Seinfeld* writers were not the first to use this phrase, their incorporation of this funny utterance on an episode of a TV sitcom has come to have its own place in our language. We now have a term describing a behavior that we did not have before. We have named it, we can understand it, and we can create meaning from it. It has become part of our shared popular cultural experience.

Language Confuses People

Language also has the *power to confuse* us, especially if it is **equivocal.** Equivocation includes language that is **ambiguous.** Sometimes there are so many different meanings for a

Sapir-Whorf hypothesis ■
Language is the most significant factor in determining what we see in the world and how we think about and evaluate what we see.

Equivocal (or ambiguous) ■
Having multiple meanings.

*Definition of "yada yada yada" used by permission. From *Merriam-Webster's Collegiate® Dictionary,* 11th Edition © 2011 by Merriam-Webster, Incorporated (www.Merriam-Webster.com).

word that we do not know which one to choose. Using language ambiguously can be seen as a form of language power, because occasionally we might be intentionally ambiguous in order to deceive someone strategically. Sometimes we are ambiguous with language because we are careless or because we don't want to hurt someone's feelings. What does it mean when your instructor says you are a "good" speaker? Our students often tell us they want to be communication professionals because they are "good" with people. What does that mean? Our dog is "good with people." Does this mean he would make a great communication professional? When people say, "Hi, how are you?" are they asking for a summary of your health and well-being, or do they mean "hello"? When a politician says, "Vote for me because I care about this country," what does he or she mean by "care" or "country"?

What do the words *almost never, frequently, seldom, now and then,* or *occasionally* mean? How many are *a few, several, not many,* or *a lot*? Each of these words or phrases is open to interpretation based on the context, the individuals in conversation, and the relationship between those individuals. Language, thus, is often very subjective. The following are headlines taken from newspapers and news reports in the last 20 years:

"Man Found Dead in Graveyard"
"Local Man Has Largest Horns in Texas"
"20-Year Friendship Ends at Altar"
"Massive Organ Draws a Crowd"

Sometimes a word is ambiguous because its meaning or interpretation has changed over time. For example, what does the word *gay* mean? *Merriam-Webster's Collegiate Dictionary* provides the following definitions: (1) happily excited; (2) bright, lively; (3) given to social pleasures; (4) homosexual.* The most common meaning of the word *gay* today is "homosexual," but the other three meanings are correct, although they are associated with a different time in history and are thus "dated."

Competent and effective communicators know that there is a difference between "what words mean" and "what people mean by words." And competent communicators also know that you should never assume that you understand what people actually mean in their ambiguous language. When words do not have a clear meaning, it is a good idea to ask for clarification.

Other forms of ambiguous communication used to confuse or soften meaning are doublespeak and euphemisms. **Doublespeak** obscures the speaker's true meaning or intention—as in the term "downsizing" for "firing of many employees" or the deliberately ambiguous phrase "wet work" for "assassination." A **euphemism** is a strategic word choice, often used to "soften" reality or be "sensitive" to another person. For example, we might say that someone has "passed away" instead of "died," or we say that someone has gotten "pink-slipped" rather than "laid off." Euphemisms are considered to be more socially acceptable alternatives to direct speech. If your friend asks, "How do you like my new hairstyle?" and you don't like it but want to spare her feelings, you might reply, "It's really unique!" rather than saying something more direct like, "It really makes your ears stand out."

As we mentioned earlier in this chapter, according to Hayakawa's (1990) abstraction ladder, when individuals can avoid ambiguity and increase specificity, they can enhance their communication with others. For example, rather than simply saying, "people" (an abstract noun) need to be aware of their surroundings, you might refer to "women" (a broad class of nouns). To target your message even further, you might wish to specify "teenage women" (a specific category of nouns) and even further to "teenage women in their first year of college" (specific identifiable nouns). By using the most specific terms possible, you can avoid confusion and ambiguity.

Language Classifies People

Language also has the power to *classify people*. We must not underestimate the power of **labels**—which tell us about a group to which someone belongs. For example, which of the following labels most correctly identifies your political philosophy: *liberal, democratic, socialist, republican, libertarian, conservative, communist, fascist, internationalist,*

Doublespeak ■ Language deliberately constructed to disguise or distort its actual meaning.

Euphemism ■ Language used to soften or be sensitive to another person.

Labels ■ Words used to classify.

*Definition of "gay" used by permission. From *Merriam-Webster's Collegiate® Dictionary,* 11th Edition © 2011 by Merriam-Webster, Incorporated (www.Merriam-Webster.com).

COMMUNICATION COUNTS IN YOUR LIFE

Gender Labels

Have you ever noticed how many terms or labels are used to describe men and women? Think of the categories listed below. For each category, make a list for men and women. How many can you think of for each?

    Food (e.g., cupcake, sweetcakes, sucker, etc.)
    Animals (e.g., ham, pig, cow, chicken, pussycat, etc.)
    Plants (e.g., clinging vine, rose, etc.)

Playthings or toys (e.g., dollface, Barbie, etc.)

Does one list look longer than another? Are more of the terms associated with men or women positive? Negative? Are some dominant and others passive? What are the implications of any "imbalance" in your lists? What is the objective of using these labels to describe men and women?

Stereotypes ■ Oversimplified categories that people associate individuals with in order to reduce uncertainty about them.

Racism ■ Prejudicial feelings or beliefs we use to create labels that define and demean a group.

Ethnocentrism ■ The view that one's own culture or group is the center of the universe.

Hate speech ■ Speech aimed at attacking or denigrating the status of entire groups—whites, blacks, Jews, homosexuals, and so forth.

utilitarian, environmentalist, or *nationalist*? What does it mean to say that someone is a *liberal* or a *conservative*? It depends upon your position, doesn't it? Does the word *liberal* refer to someone who is tolerant and open minded, or does it mean someone radical and pushy? Does the word *conservative* refer to someone who is closed minded or fiscally responsible? Labels are most powerful when you are the one who controls the definition associated with them. If you are the one stuck with the label, especially an incorrect one, you may become angry and resentful at someone who attempts to define you as something you are not. The box "Communication Counts in Your Life: Gender Labels" provides opportunities for further exploration of the power of labels.

    Stereotypes are a more extreme form of classifying people. Some stereotypes are just oversimplified categories in which we classify individuals to reduce uncertainty about them. When we meet someone for the first time, we often rely on stereotypes to determine how we should approach or interact with them. We attempt to find a "rule" that will help us act appropriately with that person. For example, what are the "rules" for approaching your professor for the first time? Should you approach male and female professors differently? Does it make a difference if you are much younger than your professor or if you are a nontraditional student who is about the same age? If your roommate is from Southeast Asia, how should you establish the physical territories you each will inhabit in the dorm room? If you are on a predominantly commuter campus and want to create a carpool to school, which individuals would you be most comfortable approaching about sharing rides? In each of these examples, we use a "group" as a baseline to provide information about how we should communicate with one another.

    Some stereotypes, however, are not mild. As we saw in Chapter 2, *prejudice* is a definitive negative attitude toward a given group. According to the Conflict Research Consortium at the University of Colorado, "prejudice can lead parties to view their opponents as threatening adversaries who are inherently inferior or are actively pursuing immoral objectives. Such prejudices lead the parties to view others as enemies who must be actively opposed. This results in a persistent level of destructive tension that can easily escalate into a highly destructive, all-out confrontation" (www.colorado.edu/conflict/peace/treatment/prejred.htm).

    Some prejudice arises from ignorance regarding a particular group and is often the result of fear or hatred. **Racism** stems from the beliefs that people from particular racial groups have qualities and abilities that are superior or inferior to others. Once we have created stereotypes that result in prejudicial feelings or beliefs, we create labels that define and demean that group. **Ethnocentrism** is the view that one's own culture or group is the center of the universe—the most valuable, the most advanced, and the most moral. Ethnocentrists view their culture as having the "best" of everything and label individuals from other groups with such terms as *alien, intruder, foreigner, outsider, newcomer,* or *immigrant.* When ethnocentrism becomes extreme, language can deteriorate into **hate speech.** Hate speech is commonly used by individuals or groups to express their belief that their point of view and their place in society is superior and to express their need to develop a "pure" society (one that includes only members of their cultural group). Hate speech attacks or denigrates the status of entire groups—whites, blacks, Jews, homosexuals, and so on.

Culture Counts

COMMUNICATION COUNTS IN YOUR COLLEGE EXPERIENCE

Combating Hate Speech on Campus

Find your college's student handbook and locate any information regarding hate speech on campus. Is there a definition of hate speech in the handbook? Are there policies that sanction hate speech?

Locate the student handbooks from a range of colleges in your state or region. How do they compare to your campus handbook with regard to definitions of and rules or policies regarding hate speech? Are there similarities or differences in the definitions, standards, or degree of punishment (or lack thereof) for violations?

Should such speech be stifled? Read more about it in the box "Communication Counts in Your College Experience: Combating Hate Speech on Campus."

Regardless of the targeted group, the goal of hate speech is to humiliate and harm with words. Hate speech hurts those who send hateful messages as well as those who receive them. It hurts cultures in which it occurs, creating community divisions; it may also cause some groups to become more isolated, fearful, or dangerous.

Sexism is a form of prejudice regarding issues of gender, expectations of what is appropriate feminine and masculine behavior, and assertions on gender superiority. **Heterosexism** is a form of prejudice regarding issues of sexual orientation and the question of whether attraction to the same sex is a choice. Both sexism and heterosexism create tensions in relationships when individuals "impose" on others certain characteristics or moral values. Sexism and heterosexism are particularly harmful forms of prejudice that prevent people from truly knowing one another as individual, valuable human beings. In the box "Communication Counts in Your Career: Creating Nonsexist Environments," we explore ways to eliminate sexist language at work and in our daily lives.

The enormous power of labels and stereotypes lies in their ability to influence our attitudes and, ultimately, our actions. If our attitudes about an individual's sexual orientation, ethnicity, or religion are based on stereotypes, we may refrain from establishing relationships with them. How many times in your life have you tried *not* to get to know someone because of your stereotypes? If we are honest with ourselves, we will admit that the answer may be many times. Thus, our *attitudes* influence our *behaviors*, which in turn are *communicated* to the individuals we stereotype—through our words and actions and by what we *do not* say and what we *do not* do.

Sexism ■ A form of prejudice regarding issues of gender, expectations of what is appropriate female and male behavior, and assertions on gender superiority.

Heterosexism ■ A form of prejudice regarding issues of sexual orientation and the issue of whether a person's attraction to the same or opposite sex is one of choice or not.

Language Clarifies Meaning

Much of this discussion has been focused on the negative power of language. Yet it is important to remember that competent communicators use language to *clarify meaning*, create relationships, and break down the barriers that separate us. When we expand our language, we enhance our relationships and our lives. The more words we have to describe and analyze a situation, an object, or a concept, the more opportunities we have to know the world and ourselves, to understand the past and present, and to predict the future.

Language is the fundamental building block to all relationships. Education is fundamentally about developing more sophisticated language that we can use to generate new ways of thinking, products to market, and services to provide. More precise language may also help us to make the world better by reducing the misunderstandings between people who speak "different languages."

Whether you are learning on campus or online, there is a plethora of new language to get used to.

COMMUNICATION COUNTS IN YOUR CAREER

Creating Nonsexist Environments

A greater equality exists in terms of job access today than in the past, but there is not always agreement about what that means for the communication behavior of women and men in the workplace. Is there such a thing as "women's work" or "men's work"? Should men try to adopt a more "feminine" style of leadership? Should women be more masculine or feminine in the workplace? What are the rules?

Should men "walk on eggshells" in the workplace to avoid inadvertent sexual harassment? What is a sexist remark? Here are some suggestions for both women and men in nonsexist treatment of all persons in a workplace:

- Avoid typecasting in careers and activities and in hiring policies. (Are all of your secretaries female but the administrative assistants male?)
- Represent members of both sexes as whole human beings: masculine characteristics as well as feminine characteristics.
- Pay closer attention to your words; take responsibility for your words and for the meanings you and others may ascribe to them. Clarify, ask questions.

- Accord women and men the same respect and avoid either trivializing women or describing them by physical attributes when men are described by mental attributes:
- Avoid sexual innuendos.
- Avoid references to the general "ineptness" of men in the home.
- Treat women as part of the rule, not the exception; for example, avoid terms like "woman doctor."
- Avoid describing women as needing male permission to act.
- Address individuals using gender-neutral language.
- Use inclusive language (i.e., "humankind").
- When confronted by what you perceive to be sexist language, regardless of your gender, address the situation by
  - focusing on the event, not the person;
  - offering positive criticism;
  - owning your thoughts and feelings;
  - stating your concern for the other;
  - being specific and using examples; and
  - avoiding mind reading.

CONNECTING LANGUAGE AND GENDER

Some theorists believe that the first "language barrier" each of us must negotiate is the "different world of words" inhabited by men and women. Sociolinguist Deborah Tannen (1990) suggests that the ways in which boys and girls grow up and the language used to socialize them are primary factors in our tendency to misunderstand one another.

It is important to recognize the distinctions between the words *sex* and *gender*. A person's *sex* is a biological factor based on the chromosomes in our DNA. A person's *gender* is a social construct that creates a set of expectations for appropriate behavior. Language, according to Tannen, is "gendered." Women and men, she suggests, approach the world differently. Men often approach the world as individuals in a hierarchical social order in which they are either one-up or one-down. They commonly use negotiation to maintain the upper hand, take charge of situations, or solve problems and offer solutions. Conversely, women often view the world as a network of connections. Their conversations are negotiations for closeness, confirmation, and support. They protect themselves from others' attempts to push them away, struggle to preserve intimacy, and work to avoid isolation.

The language used by men tends to conform to a "hierarchy of power," and the language used by women tends to conform to a "hierarchy of friendship." These are different but equally valid language styles. It's important to remember that trying to treat women's and men's language "the same" hurts both sides. Both of these approaches to conversation and relationships are means to the same end. Both status (masculinity) and connection (femininity) can be used to get things done through talking.

At the same time, it is important to understand that women and men often have very different reasons for carrying on a conversation. Men tend to converse to impart information (report talk); women converse to indicate relationship (rapport talk). Women are also more likely to exchange personal and relational talk than men. For example, in your experience, is a man or a woman more likely to talk about a troubling experience? Who is more likely to share a secret? Who is more likely to give advice? Who is more likely to challenge an expert in a public forum? If you answered "woman" to the first two questions and "man" to the second two, you already understand the differences between rapport talk and report talk. Understanding how women and men engage in conversations and use language is the first step. Realizing how our language creates inequality in perceptions is also

Spending time with friends is a way women support and encourage one another.

important. As a competent communicator, you should strive to use gender-neutral language to create a more inclusive culture, using such terms as *mail carrier* (instead of *mailman*), *firefighter* (instead of *fireman*), *police officer* (instead of *policeman*), *worker* (instead of *workman*), and *chairperson* (instead of *chairman*). When we modify our language, we modify our cultural expectations and build bridges that bring us closer together in our relationships and in our understanding of one another.

CONNECTING LANGUAGE AND CULTURE

Each culture in the world has developed a language that assists its members in creating meaning. **Linguistic determinism** is a term used to describe the power of language to influence interpretations of the world in a specific culture. For example, the Inuit tribes in northern Canada have more than 50 words for *snow*. In the world of the Inuit, the ability to make fine distinctions between the type of snowfall and snow pack is a life-and-death issue. Here are just a few examples:

Culture Counts

Inuit snow lexemes

1. apun—*snow*
2. apingaut—*first snowfall*
3. aput—*spread-out snow*
4. kanik—*frost*
5. anigruak—*frost on a living surface*
6. ayak—*snow on clothes*
7. kannik—*snowflake*
8. nutagak—*powder snow*
9. aniu—*packed snow*
10. aniuvak—*snowbank*

(Retrieved July 12, 2006, from www.ucalgary.ca/~kmuldrew/cryo_course/snow_words.html)

Language is the element of culture that allows people to develop values and beliefs and to name them. Language allows us to share our customs, which binds individuals together into a collective identity.

At its most powerful, culture provides us the road map for what we should pay attention to and what we should ignore. Once our values, beliefs, and customs are developed and named, culture affects our role identity, telling us how to categorize individuals inside our culture. Culture affects how we use language to identify our goals and how we achieve

Linguistic determinism ■ The power of language to influence interpretations of the world in a specific culture.

Individualist cultures ■ Cultures that emphasize the importance of individual success.

Collectivist cultures ■ Cultures that emphasize the group, not the individual.

those goals. Finally, culture explains how we should evaluate the aspects of communication competence. When we communicate with individuals who have been acculturated by a different set of values, beliefs, and customs, we must make a greater effort to understand and clarify meaning. Intercultural conversations require new rules for negotiating meaning.

One of the most interesting and important intersections of language and culture is the degree to which a culture has an individualist or collectivist orientation. Reynolds and Valentine (2004) suggest that **individualist cultures** like the United States and Great Britain emphasize the importance of individual success. Values such as freedom, independence, and autonomy are at the heart of these cultures. Language in individualist cultures is direct. U.S. citizens are known for "speaking their minds" when in conversation with others, and U.S. history books are filled with the stories of adventurous individuals who have fought against incredible odds to prevail and succeed.

In contrast, according to Reynolds and Valentine, **collectivist cultures** emphasize the group, not the individual. Harmony within the group is highly valued. In conversation, politeness is often a goal. Language is indirect and implicit, and communicators depend more often on what is not spoken. Words are less important to the overall meaning within an interaction than are the nonverbal elements. Silence has more value in collectivist cultures. The Japanese proverb "You have two ears and one mouth" implies that listening is twice as important as speaking. Important values in collectivist cultures include stability, tradition, and authority. For example, in Japan, exchanging business cards is one of the first and most important interactions in a business transaction. This is because one's title determines the nature of the interaction with that person. The businessperson with the lower rank must perform the lower bow. In contrast to English, the Sino-Tibetan family of languages, spoken by most Asian cultures, "is multi-valued, complex, and subtle, allowing for many shades of gray. There is no firm belief in objective reality; language seeks to capture impression, an overall emotional quality, and subjective, experiential thinking. Communication is fluid, indirect, inexplicit, nonlinear, and self-effacing" (61).

LEARNING THE LANGUAGE OF COLLEGE

As a student on a college campus, you are experiencing a unique communication "culture" every day. The language of college will provide you with some of the most potentially satisfying and perhaps frustrating experiences of your life thus far. In some ways, learning this new language is as alien as any other foreign language.

Understanding Typical College Language

What is "typical" college or academic language? College language incorporates a wide range of topics and a jargon that can create a sense of community but can also cause misunderstanding. Let's explore the titles people have on your campus. In your classroom, you might have an instructor, an adjunct, a teaching assistant, an assistant professor, an associate professor, a full professor, or even a dean. What is the difference between these titles? One of the primary differences is the type of degree the person holds. Instructors, typically, do not have what is called a "terminal degree" or the highest degree that can be obtained in a particular field—doctor of philosophy, doctor of education, doctor of arts, jurist doctorate, or doctor of psychology; these are the individuals who should be addressed by "Doctor." Another factor that distinguishes the title is the number of years that person has been teaching at the institution and whether he or she has received tenure (meaning the person has a permanent appointment or "job security"). Most assistant professors do not have tenure; normally, associate and full professors do. In either case, rhetorically sensitive communicators are encouraged to address all their teachers as "Professor" unless advised otherwise. This title of respect is always correct.

If you do not know exactly what you want to study, there are offices on your campus where people can help you. You may have a Career Center where you can explore a range of options with regard to your field. When you identify the degree you want to obtain, you must declare your major and in many cases your minor, or secondary area of study. Your program of study might be housed in a school or a college. Your degree may be in the arts, humanities, social sciences, natural sciences, education, technology, business, health, sports, medicine, or law. Once you have a major, you will be assigned an advisor who will assist you in choosing classes and identifying career goals.

Outside of the classroom, you may have already dealt with people in Admissions (who helped you with your entrance into your school) and Student Affairs. Student Affairs professionals may be those you encounter in Housing and Residence Life, Student Activities, Diversity Services, and the like.

If you are on a residential campus (where some students live in dorms or student housing on campus), you will likely have met the coordinators or supervisors called *resident advisors* (RAs) or *resident directors* (RDs). If you attend a primarily commuter campus (where most students drive to and from classes), you will probably find Commuter Student offices where staff members can assist you with issues like transportation and child care. The Financial Aid office is where you fill out paperwork to request grants (assistance you do not pay back), loans (financial assistance you must pay back), or work-study (payment you receive for work you do on campus). Other offices provide information about scholarships (gifts of tuition, books, or other assistance to candidates who qualify under certain conditions).

Navigating your way around campus and understanding the language takes time and patience.

The key to successfully negotiating the college campus "world of words" is to think of the experience as similar to the cross-cultural communication experience. Learn where the important offices, services, and professionals are, and be sure to ask faculty and staff to explain this new world's jargon to you—much of which is likely conveyed in your college's student handbook.

USING LANGUAGE COMPETENTLY AND ETHICALLY IN COLLEGE, CAREER, AND LIFE

If we are to begin to distinguish between "what words mean" and "what people mean by words," then we must understand the numerous influences on how we create meaning and some of the pitfalls to competent and effective communication. One of the first characteristics of competent and ethical use of language is understanding and adapting to one's audience.

Adapting to Your Audience

What does it mean to "adapt to your audience" when using language? At a very basic level, it means understanding the cultural influences that play a role in how someone interprets meaning. To understand how a different culture influences the interpretations of its members, you need to understand the influences of your own culture on your interpretation. You must recognize the cultural or ethnocentric stereotypes you have regarding the value of a particular worldview. For example, consider some of your personal biases. Do you think that elderly people are burdensome, that the working poor deserve low pay, or that only the best and brightest students should get college scholarships? One of the results of failing to recognize the cultural and other biases we have is called **mindlessness**. Someone who is communicating in a "mindless" way uses habitual or scripted ways of communicating regardless of the others in the communication experience. Mindless communication uses stereotyped categories to make inferences about others instead of attempting to clarify in a specific communication situation what others mean or understand.

In contrast, competent communicators operate from a perspective of **mindfulness**. Mindful communicators are willing to create new categories of meaning and understanding for communicating in new situations. They choose words carefully and, when communicating cross-culturally, select simple, concrete words with commonly recognized meanings. Mindful communicators also try to avoid jargon and "buzzwords" that create confusion and misunderstanding.

Mindful communicators are open to new information, are aware of more than one perspective, and are able to make finer distinctions about individual differences of interpretation. They take greater care to accommodate the other in the conversation, to "meet them halfway." Active listening is a sign of competent and mindful communication and is characteristic of rhetorically sensitive communicators.

Culture Counts

Mindlessness ■ The use of fairly habitual or scripted ways of communicating regardless of the others in the communication experience.

Mindfulness ■ Willingness to create new categories of meaning and understanding in communicating in new situations.

When you are mindful, you are fully present in your interactions with others.

In developing the ability to be mindful of your communication, you must make an effort to examine your thoughts and actions critically, looking for new solutions, new explanations, and new perspectives on language and its impact on your communication success. Finally, mindful communicators make an effort to be aware of the impact of the communication context on meaning and interpretation.

Attending to Context

As we discussed in Chapter 1, the communication context is a critical element in the communication model. Context is critical to how we understand and create meaning. To become a competent communicator, we must understand the cultural "rules" that impose themselves on a particular communication context. When is it appropriate, for example, to use jargon? **Jargon** is a vocabulary that is shared by members of a group to create a sense of community among its members. It becomes a sort of "shorthand" for individuals, allowing for more efficient communication. For example, consider the jargon terms of these individuals:

> **Politicians:** wonk, GOP, spin
> **Police officers:** 10-4, perpetrator, JD
> **Attorneys:** briefs, subpoena, motion
> **Newspaper editors:** pica, layout, production, paste-up, storyboards

Jargon can be the source of much misunderstanding by individuals who are not members of the group. To identify whether using jargon is appropriate or inappropriate, ask yourself whether the intention is to include or to exclude.

Employing Rhetorical Sensitivity

As we discussed in Chapter 3, communicators who use **rhetorical sensitivity** adapt to the widest range of communication experiences with skill and consider the most appropriate response based on a comprehensive understanding of the entire communication experience. Imagine you are hired at your "ideal job." You have been in this position for two months. As a part of your orientation to the job, you have been reviewing a variety of print materials produced by your company. In chatting with your boss one day, she asks for your opinion of the materials in general. You do not think they are very interesting, visually appealing, or representative of the organization overall. What do you tell her? In constructing a rhetorically sensitive response, what are the critical questions you must ask yourself about this communication situation?

In addition to knowing how to adapt your language to the specific context, rhetorical sensitivity also includes taking risks in exploring and communicating in a broad range of communication contexts. Rhetorically sensitive communicators are curious about others and attempt to explore their beliefs, values, and worldviews. Curiosity about others

Jargon ■ A language strategy used by a specific group to create a sense of community among group members.

Rhetorical sensitivity ■ The ability to adapt to the widest range of communication experiences with skill, considering the most appropriate response based on a comprehensive understanding of the entire communication experience.

does not imply that we are abandoning our beliefs and values; it merely allows us to broaden our vocabulary and to expand our ways of analyzing, explaining, and interpreting the world.

Rhetorically sensitive communicators characterize their conversation with **confirming language.** Confirming language acknowledges the other person. Individuals who use confirming language clearly and directly support the contributions of another person (i.e., "That was a great idea, Michelle." or "Angelo, we haven't heard your position on this issue; would you like to share it with us?"). Communicators who use confirmation ask questions and respond directly. In contrast, **disconfirming language** evaluates or judges the contributions of others (i.e., "That's a stupid idea" or "Doesn't somebody have a *good* idea for a change?").

A final characteristic of rhetorically sensitive communicators is that they take responsibility for their own feelings, thoughts, beliefs, and actions. Instead of blaming others for a thought or feeling (i.e., "You make me mad."), rhetorically sensitive and competent communicators take ownership of the ways they create meaning (i.e., "I feel angry when you ignore me."). Ownership of individual thoughts, feelings, and actions translates blame (a "you" message) into responsibility (an "I" message). Stewart and Logan (1993) suggest that true understanding of the close connection between what you say and who you are is critical to respectful language. Thus, they suggest to "watch your tongue...be careful about your speech; revere talk for what it is—a direct reflection and a clear indication of who you are and what's important to you. Talk is how you make yourself present to others" (70).

Confirming language ■ Language that acknowledges and directly supports the contributions of another person.

Disconfirming language ■ Language that evaluates or judges the contributions of others.

SUMMARY

Effective communication involves negotiating a "world of words." In this chapter, we have identified the following concepts important to your understanding of effective and rhetorically sensitive verbal communication:

- Each of us creates personal meaning for our language, and, therefore, our meaning can never exactly match the meaning of another person.
- When we communicate, we experience all of the verbal and nonverbal elements together.
- Language is symbolic. A particular set of letters together comes to represent a particular thing, idea, concept, or event. Symbols are arbitrary. Meaning is created in individual persons or through cultural associations.
- Language is structured. The way we put words together into sentences and sentences into paragraphs and paragraphs into essays is governed by a set of rules that is culture bound.
- Language is abstract. Some words are clear and simple, and the meaning for the word is shared across a particular cultural group.
- The *denotative definition* is the one we find in our language dictionary.
- The *connotative definition* is the personal, experiential meaning we have for a word.
- Language allows us to be associative.
- The Sapir-Whorf hypothesis theorizes that language is the most significant factor in determining what we see in the world and how we think and evaluate what we see.
- Language is equivocal and often ambiguous. Doublespeak is language deliberately constructed to disguise or distort its actual meaning.
- A euphemism is also a strategic choice, but it is most often used to "soften" or be sensitive to another speaker.
- Language is gendered. Women and men, who usually grow up in different worlds of words, have different purposes for verbal communication and often very different styles.
- *Linguistic determinism* is a term used to describe the power of language to influence interpretations of the world in a specific culture, whether the culture is individualistic or collectivistic.
- Ethnocentrism is the view that "my" culture or group is the center of the universe and is the most valuable, the most advanced, and the most moral. When cultural ethnocentrism becomes extreme, language can deteriorate into hate speech.
- Competent communicators operate from a perspective of mindfulness.
- *Rhetorical sensitivity* is the term used to describe the ability to skillfully adapt to the widest range of communication experiences.

QUESTIONS FOR DISCUSSION

1. In your experience, how are men's friendships (with men) and women's friendships (with women) similar and different? To what degree do you believe the stereotypes (i.e., of female "nurturance/passivity" and male "logic/aggressiveness") have affected patterns of communication in your friendships?
2. Why is it important to understand the ways in which our language influences our words and actions? Can you think of times when you were communicating with a person from another culture and one or the other of you confused meanings?
3. What are some of the best reasons for using ambiguous language? Consider corporations' slogans or logos. For example, what does Ford's company slogan, "Quality is Job 1," mean?
4. What is reification? Can you think of an example from your experience?
5. How are language and perception interrelated?
6. Have you heard anyone on your campus use hate speech? What was your response?

EXERCISES

1. Develop a Top Ten list of U.S. cultural rules for conversation between women and men who are interested in a potential romantic relationship.
2. Do you belong to a group or organization on or off campus? Identify the jargon used by members of the group. Describe an experience where use of jargon by a group member caused misunderstanding by someone who was an "outsider."
3. Translate the following statements from "you" language to "I" language:
■ You hurt my feelings.
■ You make me sick.
■ You are embarrassing me.
■ You make me happy.
4. Make a list of ten terms that describe you. Identify the origin of the descriptor. In other words, is this a label that has been imposed by another (parent, friend, media) or one you have created independently?
5. Identify the jargon on your campus that creates the most confusion among students. Who might help you to "learn" the jargon?

KEY TERMS

Abstract 63
Arbitrary 62
Associate 64
Authoritative nature of language 65
Collectivist cultures 72
Confirming language 75
Connotative meaning 64
Denotative meaning 64
Disconfirming language 75
Doublespeak 67

Equivocal (or ambiguous) 66
Ethnocentrism 68
Euphemism 67
Hate speech 68
Heterosexism 69
Individualist cultures 72
Jargon 74
Labels 67
Linguistic determinism 71
Mindfulness 73

Mindlessness 73
Nonverbal communication 62
Racism 68
Rhetorical sensitivity 74
Sapir-Whorf hypothesis 66
Sexism 69
Stereotypes 68
Structured 63
Symbolic 62
Verbal communication 62

REFERENCES

Dobkin, B. A., and Pace, R. C. 2003. *Communication in a changing world: An introduction to theory and practice.* New York: McGraw-Hill.
Hayakawa, S. I. 1990. *Language in thought and action.* 5th ed. New York: Harcourt Brace.
Ogden, C. K., and Richards, I. A. 1993. *The meaning of meaning.* New York: Morrow.
Reynolds, S., and Valentine, D. 2004. *Guide to cross-cultural communication.* Upper Saddle River, NJ: Pearson/Prentice Hall.
Stewart, J. 1995. Verbal communicating. In *Bridges not walls,* ed. J. Stewart, 50–53. New York: McGraw-Hill.
Stewart, J., and Logan, C. 1993. *Together: Communicating interpersonally.* New York: McGraw-Hill.
Tannen, D. 1990. *You just don't understand: Women and men in conversation.* New York: Ballantine Books.
The Real Mother Goose, 2004. Available at www.gutenberg.org/files/ 10607/10607-h/10607-h.htm.
Trenholm, S., and Jensen, A. 1992. *Interpersonal communication.* 2nd ed. Belmont, CA: Wadsworth.
Whorf, B. 1956. *Language, thought, and reality,* ed. J. Carroll. Cambridge, MA: MIT Press.

CHAPTER 5

Nonverbal Communication

LEARNING OUTCOMES After reading this chapter, you will have:

the **Knowledge** to. . .   and the **Skills** to. . .

UNDERSTANDING NONVERBAL COMMUNICATION, page 80

Understand the power of nonverbal communication.

Distinguish between nonverbal and verbal communication.

- Remember that what you do is more powerful than what you say.
- Craft communication where the nonverbal and verbal messages are congruent or reinforce one another.

IDENTIFYING THE PROPERTIES OF NONVERBAL COMMUNICATION, page 81

Explain the properties of nonverbal communication.

- Ensure that your nonverbal communication modifies your message by complementing or clarifying its meaning.
- Be mindful of how your eyes and facial expressions show feelings.
- Be sensitive to turn-taking cues in your interactions with others.

CLASSIFYING THE TYPES OF NONVERBAL COMMUNICATION, page 83

Know the nine types of nonverbal communication and understand how they impact communication.

- Ensure your body movements (kinesics), gestures, affect displays, and physical mannerisms match the message you are sending.
- Understand that physical characteristics such as attractiveness and physique impact communication.
- Be sensitive to the "rules" about touch (haptics) in various contexts and cultures.
- Understand how proxemics (space, environment, and territory issues) color nonverbal communication.
- Moderate the volume, pitch, and rate (elements of paralanguage) according to your communication context.
- Avoid fillers or disfluencies (*umm, ah*).
- Use silence consciously (to signal your displeasure, offer your consent, prompt another to speak, and the like).
- Be aware of how clothing, body adornment, and passions (artifacts) reveal information about yourself and others.
- Know how you and others are impacted by olfactics (smell).
- Be conscious as to how (chronemics) time is seen in various communication contexts.

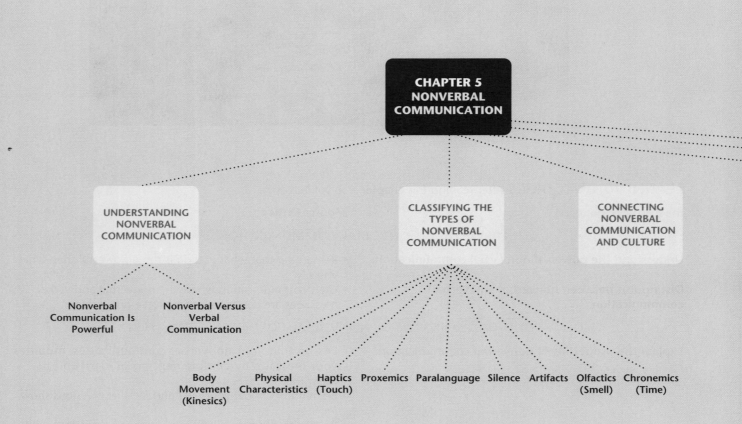

CONNECTING NONVERBAL COMMUNICATION AND GENDER, page 91

Realize how nonverbal communication is impacted by gender.

- Be conscious of masculine and feminine uses of space and territory, fashion, touch, and eye contact.

CONNECTING NONVERBAL COMMUNICATION AND CULTURE, page 93

Appreciate how nonverbal communication is shaped by culture.

- Exercise cultural sensitivity to differences in distance and space (high-contact vs. low-contact), time (monochromic vs. polychromic), eye contact, and touch.

BECOMING A COMPETENT AND ETHICAL NONVERBAL COMMUNICATOR IN COLLEGE, CAREER, AND LIFE, page 94

Identify ethical issues surrounding the communication of nonverbal messages.

Attend to the consequences of your nonverbal communication.

Understand the value of nonverbal messages that result in mutual understanding and shared meaning.

- Improve your self-presentation by adopting an "available attitude."
- Be mindful and respectful of others.
- Use immediacy (responding with a smile, an encouraging nod, and direct language) to put others at ease.
- Ensure your verbal and nonverbal messages are congruent and match.

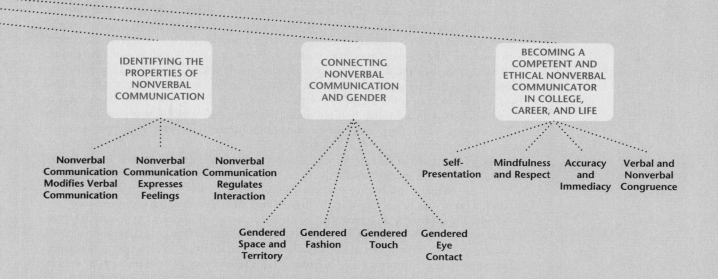

UNDERSTANDING NONVERBAL COMMUNICATION

As we saw in Chapter 4, *nonverbal communication* involves sending and receiving of wordless messages. Nonverbal messages can be communicated through body language, posture, gestures, facial expressions, and eye contact.

Nonverbal Communication Is Powerful

You may have heard the saying, "What you do is more important than what you *say*." How we act in a given situation reveals far more than our words. Callero (2005) said, "Nonverbal communication is not a mystical or magical thing. It is a rational—even logical—process by which people convey information by means other than words" (279).

Just as spoken words have the power to harm or heal, so too do nonverbal expressions. Wordless expressions also convey great meaning. When your significant other turns away from you when you are speaking, fiddles with a cell phone, or starts straightening a stack of newspapers on the table, the nonverbal message he or she might be sending to you may be, "You aren't important to me," or "I'm bored with this conversation." Though these specific words are not spoken aloud, their message is conveyed clearly through actions.

The loudness or softness of our voices, the closeness or distance from which we stand near others, the way we gesture with our hands, the facial expressions we use—all reveal far more than our spoken words.

Nonverbal Communication Versus Verbal Communication

Verbal and nonverbal communication are intricately woven together, and when we create meaning about our own or another's communication behavior, we cannot separate the two. Many times our verbal and nonverbal communication "match"—what communication scholars call **congruent messages.** Congruence in nonverbal communication means that your nonverbal cues match your verbal message. Whether you are giving a presentation to a group or visiting with a friend, it is important that your nonverbal communication mirrors your spoken message. For example, if you tell your boyfriend, "I hate you!" in a loud voice, accompanied by direct eye contact and hands folded over your chest, he's likely to believe you because your verbal and nonverbal messages are congruent.

At other times, however, messages don't match, and our communication is made up of **incongruent messages.** For example, if you tell your boyfriend, "I hate you!" in a joking voice with a smile on your face, he's more apt to understand that that you are kidding because your messages are incongruent. One of the most significant differences between verbal and nonverbal communication concerns structure. Verbal communication is highly structured. We learn verbal communication by understanding and applying the formal rules of grammar to generate "correct" speaking and writing. Nonverbal communication, in contrast, has no formal structure. Thus, a variety of different meanings can be assigned to any nonverbal message. For example, in English, if you want to discuss how you love your pet, you begin the sentence with the subject and verb, and then the adjectives and adverbs usually follow. "I love my cat a lot!" In most European languages, the order or structure of the sentence is rearranged. However, if you want to nonverbally show that you love your pet, there are many ways to do so, such as with a big hug, a huge smile, wrestling on the floor; just about any form of nonverbal "affection" will work to communicate how you feel. No structure needed.

Culture Counts

As we discussed in Chapter 4, verbal communication is culture bound. In the United States, most people speak English; the French speak French; the Russians speak Russian; and so on. While some nonverbal symbols or gestures have meaning that is culture bound, a large number of nonverbal symbols and messages have universal meaning. For example, some of what we consider "innate" communication (facial expressions denoting happiness, fear, disgust, or surprise) is interpreted similarly across many cultures. We consider this type of nonverbal communication innate because infants use these expressions prior to any "learning" and because infants from every culture use similar expressions. Nonverbal communication is a continuous communication phenomenon. We don't "stop" communicating nonverbally, even when we stop talking; thus, we are always communicating. Therefore, we cannot not communicate. Verbal communication, however, occurs in discrete, often disconnected, units. Related to this characteristic is the fact that verbal communication is always "intentional." We speak because we choose to. Nonverbal communication, however, can be both intentional and unintentional. Much of our nonverbal communication is spontaneous and occurs outside of our awareness.

A final distinction between verbal and nonverbal communication concerns the "what" that is communicated through verbal and nonverbal means. Verbal communication, for example, expresses primarily factual information. The nonverbal dimension adds feeling or relational information that creates meaning in our communication interactions.

IDENTIFYING THE PROPERTIES OF NONVERBAL COMMUNICATION

Another way to clarify the relationship between verbal and nonverbal communication is to consider the three primary functions of nonverbal messages: to modify verbal communication, to express feeling, and to regulate interaction.

Nonverbal Communication Modifies Verbal Communication

As Table 5.1 shows, nonverbal communication serves to *modify* verbal communication in four basic ways:

1. to *complement* or *clarify* (congruence),
2. to *contradict* (incongruence),
3. to *repeat* or *reinforce*, and
4. to *substitute* for verbal messages.

When verbal and nonverbal message are congruent, they "match" in meaning; but when they are incongruent, they do not match, and the listener may be confused in how to interpret them. For example, when you give someone directions to a destination, your nonverbal hand gestures and body movements complement your oral instructions. When you shout, "I am NOT angry!" your nonverbal message contradicts your verbal message. When you are immersed in a conversation and want to make your point clear, your hand gestures again reinforce the verbal message. And, finally, sometimes our nonverbal message replaces a verbal message, such as nodding your head instead of saying, "Yes." These nonverbal messages are very important, especially when trying to determine if a person is telling the truth.

TABLE 5.1

NONVERBAL COMMUNICATION MODIFIES VERBAL COMMUNICATION IN FOUR WAYS

1 To complement or clarify verbal messages (congruence)
• Example: When you give someone directions to a destination, your nonverbal hand gestures and body movements (pointing, etc.)complement your oral instructions.

2 To contradict verbal messages (incongruence)
• Example: When you cross your arms and shout, "I am NOT angry!" your nonverbal message (crossing your arms and shouting) contradicts your verbal message.

3 To repeat or reinforce verbal messages
• Example: When you nod your head while saying "yes," your nonverbal message (nodding your head) reinforces your verbal message.

4 To subsitute for verbal messages
• Example: When you nod your head instead of saying "yes," your nonverbal message (nodding your head) serves as a substitute for a verbal message.

TABLE 5.2

THREE RELATIONAL DIMENSIONS OF NONVERBAL COMMUNICATION

1
The degree of like or dislike we have for another
• Example: When we like someone, we tend to sit closer to him or her, look him or her in the eye, smile, or nod our heads in response.

2
Our perceptions of the status or power within the relationship
• Example: When communicating with a superior at work, we express our status in a variety of nonverbal means such as not keeping a superviser waiting or allowing the boss more "speaking time" in a conversation.

3
Our degree of awareness or responsiveness—sometimes called "attending to"—to the other
• Example: When we disagree with what someone has to say, we may cross our arms and turn our bodies away from him or her to show that we are disinterested.

Emoticons ■ Expressions of emotion in Internet communication.

Often, our eyes and face tell more about how we are feeling than our words do.

Nonverbal Communication Expresses Feelings

Nonverbal communication gives us tools to *express our feelings*. Three relational dimensions, as shown in Table 5.2, may be communicated through our nonverbal messages: (1) the degree of like or dislike we have for another, (2) our perceptions of the status or power within the relationship, and (3) our degree of awareness or responsiveness—sometimes called "attending to"—to the other.

Our eyes and facial expressions are the primary channels of nonverbal communication regarding attending to (or not attending to) another. When communicating using technology, **emoticons**—or expressions of emotion in electronic communication—are able to convey nonverbal messages as well.

Nonverbal Communication Regulates Interaction

We use nonverbal communication to *regulate interaction*. As children, most of us learn the "rules of interaction"; however, for some individuals, this is a lifelong struggle. These rules of interaction, unfortunately, are not written down somewhere but are learned intuitively through experience. Communicators learn to regulate interactions in two crucial ways: by using **turn-taking cues** and **start/stop cues**. To illustrate, when we run into friends on our way to class, we know that the appropriate way to begin an interaction is to attempt to make eye contact. Sometimes we recognize them before they see us, and we will perhaps tap them on the shoulder to get their attention. Later in the interaction, we use our eyes and voices to signal that we are finished with our turn in a conversation, or we signal that we want to add to the conversation through facial expression, eye movements, hand gestures, and body movement.

Each of these functions of nonverbal communication highlights the importance of understanding communication as a complex "package." It also highlights that while there are no formal rules regarding the appropriateness of nonverbal communication, there are implicit or intuitively understood informal norms that guide our interactions. These norms affect all types of nonverbal behavior, from

COMMUNICATION COUNTS IN YOUR COLLEGE EXPERIENCE

Nonverbal Communication in "Casual" and "Involved" Dating

In a study conducted by Knox, McGinty, and Zusman (2003), 233 never-married undergraduates at a large southeastern university completed a 45-item questionnaire designed to assess nonverbal and verbal communication differences in "involved" and "casual" dating relationships. Two-thirds (67.3 percent) of the respondents were female; 32.7 percent were male. In regard to relationship status, most (56.6 percent) were casual daters with 43.4 percent dating someone exclusively, engaged, or married (referred to as involved). Whites made up 78 percent of the sample, blacks 20 percent, and individuals of mixed race/heritage 2 percent.

Findings revealed that "involved" daters, females, and whites are significantly more likely to be concerned about nonverbal communication than "casual" daters, males, and blacks. Analysis of the data revealed several significant findings:

1. Involved daters value nonverbal communication more than casual daters.
2. Involved daters work on nonverbal behavior more than casual daters and are more likely than casual daters to "work hard" to ensure that their nonverbal behavior reinforced their verbal behavior.
3. Partners of involved daters also worked on nonverbal communication more.
4. Involved daters are "less confused than casual daters" when their partner says one thing and does another.

5. Involved daters are happier than casual daters. Respondents were told that the lower the number they assigned, the higher their satisfaction. The mean value for the "involved" and "casual" daters was 3.08 and 5.08, respectively.
6. Females value nonverbal behavior more than males. When females were compared with males, the females were significantly more likely than males to report that nonverbal behavior "should" be regarded as important.
7. Females engage in more nonverbal behavior. When females are compared to males, females were more likely to look their partners straight in the eye and to nod their heads when their partners spoke.
8. Whites value nonverbal behavior more. Whites are significantly more likely than blacks to believe that nonverbal behavior is and should be important to a relationship. The hypothesis regarding this finding is that blacks face enormous pressure to adapt to the mainstream white culture, even with little to no attention given to nonverbal communication. Hence, blacks may feel more predisposed to believe in the verbal—the literal. Meanwhile, whites may feel no such pressure and feel more "free" to focus on nonverbal aspects of communication.

Source: From "Nonverbal and verbal communication in 'involved' and 'casual' relationships among college students." *College Student Journal,* March 2003, by Kristen McGinty, David Knox, and Marty E. Zusman. Reprinted with permission of Project Innovation, Inc.

eye contact to styles of dress to arrangement of our living spaces. Most of us know immediately when someone has violated a nonverbal communication norm such as standing too close to someone in a checkout line or staring directly at a stranger. Let's explore some of these types of nonverbal communication and their roles in our interactions. Before doing so, we urge you to check out the box on "Communication Counts in Your College Experience: Nonverbal Communication in 'Casual' and 'Involved' Dating" to examine some of your own relationships in light of your nonverbal communication practices.

Let's examine the types of nonverbal communication to get a better sense of what nonverbal communication is and how it impacts our interactions with others.

Turn-taking cues ■ Cues such as eye contact, touch, and voice that communicate that the other may now take his or her turn in the conversation.

Start/stop cues ■ Cues that regulate interaction in a conversation.

CLASSIFYING THE TYPES OF NONVERBAL COMMUNICATION

Knapp (1978) created a list of nonverbal communication types to assist us in understanding the role of nonverbal messages in the communication process: kinesics (body movement), physical characteristics, haptics (touch), paralanguage, and proxemics (use of space). We add the concept of time as nonverbal communication to Knapp's list. At the same time, we are mindful of Knapp's suggestion that we should not study nonverbal communication in "discrete" units; rather we should understand the important role that nonverbal communication plays in the "total communication system, the tremendous quantity of information cues it gives in any particular situation, and . . . its use in fundamental areas of our daily life" (38).

Kinesics ■ Body behaviors including the eyes, face, gestures, and posture.

Emblems ■ Communication behaviors that substitute for words.

Illustrators ■ Communication behaviors that accompany words to add vividness or power to them.

Affect displays ■ The facial movements or expressions that convey emotional meaning as well as the posture or gesture cues that convey our emotions at any given moment.

Adaptors ■ A wide range of movements intended to hide or "manage" emotions that we do not want to communicate directly.

Self-adaptors ■ Ways in which we manipulate our bodies that show emotions.

Object-adaptors ■ Ways we manipulate objects that show emotions.

Regulators ■ Cues on turn-taking in conversations.

Body Movement (Kinesics)

The term **kinesics** refers to a broad range of messages communicated through the human body, including the eyes, face, gestures, and posture. Kinesics, or body behaviors, assist communicators in several ways, including the use of emblems, illustrators, affect displays, and adaptors.

EMBLEMS   **Emblems** are communication behaviors that substitute for words and have a specific verbal translation. Some examples are nodding your head to communicate "yes," using the A-OK gesture, giving the slash across your throat to communicate "cut," raising your hand to signal you wish to speak, or holding your hand to your ear to say, "Speak up. I can't hear you."

ILLUSTRATORS   **Illustrators** accompany our words to add vividness or power to what we're saying. Illustrators include our use of gestures when speaking. Many people use their hands continuously while they speak, and others use few gestures. These gestures do not have a specific meaning in and of themselves; they simply add meaning to the total message. When you provide someone directions to a building on your campus, you might both speak the route you want him to take and use your hands and arms to point in the direction you want him to go. When we say "yes" to someone, we usually also shake our head up and down.

AFFECT DISPLAYS   **Affect displays** are the facial movements or expressions—as well as posture or gesture cues—that convey our emotions. Consider the ways we communicate anger, happiness, sadness, fear, and disgust. Anger shows in our eyes (the glare), our face (the intense frown), our clenched fists, and our rigid body posture. Happiness shows in our raised eyebrows, our wide smile, our open arms, and our loud laughter.

ADAPTORS   **Adaptors** include a wide range of movements that are intended to hide or "manage" emotions that we do not want to communicate directly. Adaptors come in two forms: self-adaptors and object-adaptors.

Self-adaptors are the ways in which we manipulate our body, such as chewing nails, twisting hair, cracking knuckles, or biting the inside of our cheeks. When we experience anxiety, stress, uncertainty, or other negative feelings, we use adaptors to help us reduce these feelings.

Object-adaptors serve a similar purpose, except we manipulate an object such as a pencil or pen, our glasses, or a cigarette. What each of these kinesic movements or adaptors have in common is that they operate primarily at the subconscious level (of the sender). The adaptors can either help or hinder our communication effectiveness, depending on the communication context or relationship. Because we usually communicate these messages unconsciously, and because receivers are usually more aware of these messages than the sender, we may be sending messages we do not really want to send. For example, have you ever watched someone who you believed was lying nervously manipulate pencils, pens, or other objects?

REGULATORS   **Regulators** serve to cue in the participants in a communication interaction about turn-taking in the conversation. For example, we usually raise our voices slightly at the end of a sentence when we ask a question. Sometimes this means we are looking for an answer. If not, we use our bodies to cue the listener to the fact that we are speaking rhetorically and will continue our conversation. When we're done speaking, we look to the listener for his or her response.

Facial expressions and eye contact are particularly important in nonverbal communication. Ekman (1972) proposed that individuals can identify seven human emotions simply from facial expressions. These include sadness, happiness, anger, fear, surprise, disgust, and anger. While Ekman's ideas are still being debated and tested, over the decades since he first proposed his model of human emotions, Ekman and his colleagues continued to study emotion. If, as we and many researchers suggest, verbal communication is the "content" of the message, while nonverbal communication is the "relationship" dimension of the message, then facial expressions and eye contact are where we seek first to "discover" what a speaker feels about us personally and where we communicate most clearly how we feel about another.

Think about a time when someone was speaking to you but refused to make eye contact. Her words might have sounded nice, but something about her refusing to look you in the eye made you hesitate to believe her words. We look for kindness particularly in the eyes and the face. Fundamentally, emotions communicate feelings, and feelings are at the heart of relationships.

Physical Characteristics

This category of nonverbal behavior includes characteristics like physical attractiveness and body shape, size, and color.

PHYSICAL ATTRACTIVENESS   Perhaps more than any other factor in nonverbal communication, we are bombarded daily with information about what constitutes "attractiveness" in our culture. In fact, every culture has standards about what is seen as attractive or unattractive. Consider how much time you spend each day "preparing" yourself to be seen by others. How often do you see someone who looks like you represented in the mass media?

For many years, scholars have researched the role of attractiveness in human communication. Studies have shown that attractiveness matters in many communication interactions like job interviews, dating, and marriage and that it impacts persuasion, attitude change, and perceived credibility (Watkins & Johnston 2002). This does not mean that you have to look like a cover model to get a job. It just means our perceptions of others are influenced by their physical characteristics.

BODY SHAPE, SIZE, AND COLOR   Body shape and height, for example, influence our perceptions of someone's personality. Research suggests that individuals with "soft, round, fatter" body shapes are more often seen as easygoing, happy, and good-natured. Individuals with a "tall, thin, fragile" build are seen as more tense and nervous, more conscientious, and more meticulous than others. And, finally, those with a "strong, muscular, athletic" build are more often seen as adventurous, mature, and self-reliant. In other words, we seem to have a "physique-temperament stereotype" (Knapp 1978, 165).

We also seem to be overly conscious of body color. The tremendous growth in tanning salons attests to the fact that many individuals are unhappy with their skin color. We are also aware of the racial and ethnic stereotypes associated with people of color.

Even when studying, our unconscious nonverbal communications convey messages about how we are feeling.

Haptics (Touch)

Touch, or *haptics*, is perhaps one of the most powerful methods of communicating nonverbally; it is the most basic form of communication and the one we learn first. Positive touch is at the very heart of our most intimate and accepting relationships, and when touch turns violent and negative, it has the greatest power to hurt, both physically and mentally. Forms of touch (haptics) can include embraces, handshakes, high fives, shoulder pats, and hand holding, among others.

Touch is perhaps the most "regulated" of our nonverbal behaviors, although this regulation occurs more through cultural and family norms than through official "rules" of touch behavior. Touch is also one of the most contextualized nonverbal behaviors. As Figure 5.1 shows, in Western cultures touch is directly related to the situation in which it occurs. For example, we endure *functional/professional touch* when we go to our hairstylist, chiropractor, or physician. We engage in *social/polite touch* when we shake hands with a stranger or an acquaintance. We hug or kiss a dear friend whom we have not seen in a long time during *friendship/warmth touch*. Finally, we engage in *love/intimacy touch* within our most personal and meaningful relationships.

FIGURE 5.1

Types of Touching in Western Cultures.

Proxemics ■ The study of the use of space to communicate.

Yet touch communicates much more. For example, we communicate status and power differences with our touch (high-status individuals touch lower-status individuals more than the reverse). The ways we interpret the meaning of touch are impacted by when (in what context), where (on our bodies), how long, and in what manner we are touched.

It is important to note that the amount of touching differs from country to country and culture to culture. For example, Italians are known for their frequent use of touch, from openly greeting one another with two kisses, one on each cheek, to walking arm and arm on the piazza or city square. In contrast, the British are known for their reserve in not showing emotion; as a result, their gestures are more restrained. They would be more likely to greet one another with a handshake than an embrace.

Proxemics

Maintaining direct eye contact and turning toward the person you are speaking with conveys your openness to other viewpoints.

Proxemics, or the study of spatial environments in which people communicate, includes a number of dimensions. At one level, *proxemics* refers to communication messages within environmental settings such as lighting, noise, color, textures, and temperature. At another level, proxemics includes aspects of our "territoriality" or "ownership" of certain physical spaces. Finally, proxemics includes what anthropologist Edward T. Hall (1959, 1966) referred to as "personal space." What areas of your world can you truly call your own—your dorm room, apartment, office, or garage? When you walk into a classroom, do you sit in the same seat each day of class? When you go to the library, do you spread your books, papers, book bag, or other personal items out on the table so that no one will "invade" your space? Have you ever found yourself crowded in a room or elevator and felt uncomfortable because people were too close? Each of these questions reflects the importance of understanding how proxemics is part of our nonverbal communication behavior.

ENVIRONMENTAL FACTORS Environmental factors have a great deal to do with how we perceive the spaces around us. The openness of a building's architecture, the amount of order or disorder (clutter) therein, and the placement of objects in space all reveal information about its inhabitants. Have you ever noticed, for example, that restaurants or bars are the most comfortable places in an airport? Why? If you are more comfortable in those areas of the airport, you are more likely to spend money. Look around your campus. Can you locate the president's office? How many administrative assistants must you speak to before you can see him or her? What do the offices of your faculty look like? Some are probably large, include windows, or are nicely decorated. Others perhaps are in a basement and are dark and maybe even damp. Which ones are the most inviting to you as a student? Think of your classrooms. What color are the walls? How old is the furniture? Is there a particular smell? There is a relationship between the classroom environment and your level of motivation to learn. Recognizing that some environments are not conducive to learning may assist students, faculty, and staff in helping to create more effective surroundings to enhance learning.

TERRITORIALITY   **Territoriality** is a term coined by ethologists, scientists who study animal behavior. Many animals stake out a particular territory, mark it, and declare ownership. Humans also "mark" their territories. The closer we are to home, the more territorial we are. Territory is something we don't often think about until someone "invades" it. When we feel invaded, we respond. Sometimes we react by defending our territory; sometimes we try to insulate ourselves from further invasion and withdraw. Have you ever seen someone in your library spread his or her materials out on a table, go to retrieve a book, and return to find someone else "sharing" his or her space? How does the person returning react?

HALL'S ZONES OF PERSONAL SPACE   The final element of proxemics refers to our personal or "informal" space. As shown in Figure 5.2, Hall (1966) identifies four types, or zones, of personal space—intimate, personal, social, and public—that are particularly relevant in Western cultures. **Intimate space,** which Hall suggests is from 0 to about 18 inches around ourselves, is the zone into which we allow only those with whom we are most intimate, such as a parent, lover, child, or close friend. Do you feel odd in crowded elevators where you have no room to move? What do you do? Our discomfort in this type of situation reflects the fact that when strangers are in our intimate zone, we respond negatively. **Personal space,** Hall's second zone, ranges from 18 inches to about 4 feet around ourselves. In this space, we are comfortable with good friends and family. **Social space** ranges from about 4 to 12 feet around ourselves, and we reserve this zone for impersonal business, classroom, and general interactions. Finally, **public space** ranges from 12 feet around ourselves to the limits of our visibility or hearing. Public performances or presentations fall into this spatial zone. It is important to understand that Hall developed his zones based on his observations of adult, middle-class Americans and that the actual limits of each zone vary by geographic region, culture, gender, age, and other factors.

Paralanguage

Paralanguage, or **vocalics,** is how the voice communicates without the use of words. *How* we use our voice matters. The qualities of the voice (loudness, pitch, rate, and pacing) are an extremely important part of how we create meaning in communication.

Volume, or loudness, also affects how we perceive another. We view someone who is too loud as boisterous and pushy; we view someone whose voice is too soft as meek or ineffectual. **Pitch** refers to how high or low a voice is. We associate higher voices with femininity and lower voices with masculinity. When we meet someone who does not "match" this expectation, we alter our perceptions about him or her. **Rate** is the speed at which one speaks, and this affects our perception of the speaker's attitude or intelligence. For example, someone from the Midwest might meet a New Yorker and conclude that this person is pushy and loud ("I couldn't get a word in!"). The New Yorker, on the other hand, might think the Midwesterner is slow and dull because that person doesn't seem capable of contributing to the conversation. Our perceptions of "appropriateness" related to the pacing or the manner and speed of speech are also very much dependent on the situation. The delivery of speech can vary dramatically, as evidenced in the pacing of classroom instruction, funeral eulogies, and auction bidding.

Territoriality ■ The characteristic of marking one's environment.

Intimate space ■ The zone of comfort only for those with whom a person is most intimate, such as a parent, lover, child, or close friend; about 0 to 18 inches.

Personal space ■ The zone of comfort for family and good friends; about 18 inches to 4 feet.

Social space ■ The zone of comfort for impersonal business, classroom, and general interactions; about 4 to 12 feet.

Public space ■ The widest zone of comfort, for public performances and presentations; 12 feet to the limits of our visibility or hearing.

Vocalics ■ How the voice communicates without the use of words.

Pitch ■ How high or low a voice is.

Rate (of speech) ■ The speed with which we speak.

FIGURE 5.2

Hall's Zones of Personal Space.

Source: From "Personal Spaces for Social Interaction," in *Right Attitudes: Ideas for Impact* by Nagesh Belludi, http://www.rightsattitudes.com. Reprinted by permission of the author.

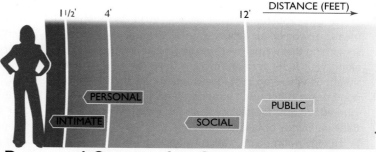

Personal Spaces for Social Interaction

Disfluencies ■ The fillers that some individuals add within their conversations (e.g., *um, uh, you know*).

Silence ■ Stillness or the absence of sound.

DISFLUENCIES Vocalizations such as crying, whispering, moaning, screaming, laughing, and whining are also important in paralanguage. Fillers or "disfluencies" are included in this category. **Disfluencies** are the "fillers" that some individuals add within their conversations, such as *um, uh, you know, hmm, ahh,* and others. Having too many of these in our conversation may signal to others that we are nervous, anxious, or unprepared. Many senders fail to "hear" their disfluencies, but receivers hear every one of them; in fact, sometimes we are so distracted by these disfluencies that we no longer hear the message itself. Ultimately, it is important to understand what your vocal qualities communicate about you because your voice has a powerful influence on others' perceptions of you.

Silence

Silence is stillness or the absence of sound. As Callero (2005) notes in his book, *The Power of Nonverbal Communication: How You Act Is More Important Than What You Say*, "Sometimes what you *don't* say is more important than what you *do* say" (61). To illustrate, if you want to convey your displeasure about the restaurant your friend has suggested, your response could be silence, signaling your lack of interest. In another example, if you remain silent when witnessing the harassment of someone in the hall of your building, your nonverbal message could be interpreted as one of acceptance or support of the action. In each of these instances, silence was a communication choice—a willful nonverbal action that conveyed a wordless message. Exactly what that nonverbal message means and how it could be evaluated is open to debate, however. See the box "Communication Counts in Your Life: Consequences of Silence" to learn how silence functions in communities.

COMMUNICATION COUNTS IN YOUR LIFE

Consequences of Silence

At various points in our lives, each of us belongs to a number of "communities." Sometimes these communities are small, such as our extended family; others are midsized, such as our college community; and still others are quite large, like the town, city, state, or country we reside in. We might also be members of a particular "community"—such as a religious organization, a sports team, a work group, or an ethnic enclave. As a member of any community, one of our ethical obligations is to know when to respond to and stand up for an injustice. Whether we speak up or remain silent, our communication has an ethical dimension. Silence as a communication strategy does communicate to others. In our culture, silence is usually perceived as "implicit consent." For example, have you ever been at a family gathering where a family member told a joke that was racist, sexist, or sexually inappropriate? Did you speak up and confront the joke-teller about the inappropriateness of the joke? Most of us do not. But what we often fail to realize is that our silence tells the joke-teller we think these types of jokes are OK.

We can probably think of several situations in which a friend, coworker, or fellow church member said or did something that we believed was inappropriate, but we went along with it for fear of "rocking the boat." What about situations where an individual requests assistance and we don't respond because "someone else will do it"? Have you ignored requests for help because you didn't want others to think differently or badly of you?

The following poem, which has several forms and about which there remains some controversy, refers to one situation

in history during which the "consequences of silence" were devastating.

First They Came for the Jews
First they came for the Jews
and I did not speak out
because I was not a Jew.
Then they came for the Communists
and I did not speak out
because I was not a Communist.
Then they came for the trade unionists
and I did not speak out
because I was not a trade unionist.
Then they came for me
and there was no one left
to speak out for me.

–Pastor Martin Niemöller

An important consideration in terms of ethical responsibilities as part of a community is the concept of *social justice*. According to the Center for Economic and Social Justice (www.cesj.org/thirdway/economicjustice-defined.htm), "Social justice encompasses economic justice. Social justice is the virtue which guides us in creating those organized human interactions we call institutions. In turn, social institutions, when justly organized, provide us with access to what is good for the person, both individually and in our associations with others. Social justice also imposes on each of us a personal responsibility to work with others to design and continually perfect our institutions as tools for personal and social development."

College classrooms and campuses provide many opportunities to observe silence in action. If you ask a favorite professor a question and she responds with silence, she may actually be encouraging you to try to answer you own question. If you go to the student service center and are told that your check is late and the clerk looks at you in silence when you ask when you can expect it to come in, the nonverbal message here may be that she has no idea and that there is nothing more to discuss.

Silence is also a powerful nonverbal tool in negotiations. Most of us are not used to using silence as a nonverbal cue to reinforce the strength of our message, our reluctance to change our minds, or our signal to end a conversation. Many of us are not used to silence and often fill the gaps of quiet with words—often unplanned words. In negotiation, silence often cues that you are being thoughtful about your upcoming response or that you wish the other person to speak. Once you get accustomed to using silence as a nonverbal tool, it can help reinforce your verbal communication.

Artifacts

The way we dress and the adornments we choose affect the perceptions of those with whom we interact, and research suggests that our dress also affects our self-image. Therefore, our clothing and **artifacts** are both a reflection of our self-image and a means of communicating messages about ourselves.

Our clothes may encourage or discourage certain patterns and types of communication. What is your perception of someone who wears an "inappropriate" outfit? Have you ever been in a situation where you were either overdressed or underdressed? How did you feel? Aiken (1963) conducted research to determine whether there is any relationship between clothing selection and personality traits. The results of his study suggest that clothing is related to personality. For example, Aiken found that males and females who scored high in clothing consciousness were more guarded, inhibited, and compliant when confronted by authority figures. Both males and females who scored low in clothing practicality were considered independent, serious, mature, and aloof. In other words, those scoring high in clothing consciousness would be more likely to dress like those around them and take cues in what to wear from their superiors. Individuals with low clothing consciousness would be less likely to conform to the attire of those around them and would be more likely to experiment with what they wear.

In addition to the relationship between clothing, self-concept, and personality, research also suggests that we intentionally communicate through personal artifacts such as badges, tattoos, jewelry, and cosmetics. These types of artifacts reveal the values, beliefs, hobbies, status, or life style of the wearer. Consider your groups of friends at home, at work, or at school. What types of artifacts do they display and what do these say about the wearer? Does your manager at work wear a small Star of David around her neck? Does the person who drives your bus wear his ball cap to the side? Does your science professor wear worn out Birkenstocks to class every day? What do these nonverbal artifacts tell you about the individuals you encounter on a daily basis?

Although we do not know exactly *how* we communicate through these artifacts, we do know that our appearance impacts the ways we communicate and how we interpret the messages communicated by others. We know that our looks impact our ability to influence others and that we have developed a set of stereotypes related to physical appearance.

Olfactics (Smell)

Olfactics—the influence of the smell in human communication—also plays an important role in nonverbal communication. Americans react negatively to body odor, bad breath, or soiled clothing and go to extraordinary lengths to be "clean." Many other cultures, however, consider Americans' obsession with masking body odor to be unnatural. One interesting finding in the research on cross-cultural communication suggests that people from cultures that include little meat (Chinese and other Asian cultures) feel that people who consume meat on a regular basis (Europeans and Americans) emit a very offensive odor (Samovar and Porter 2001). Some research also suggests that our sense of smell is the most acute at producing past memories. In the 1996

Artifacts ■ A person's dress and adornments, which are a reflection of self-image and a means of communicating messages about the wearer.

Olfactics ■ The influence of smell in human communication.

Culture Counts

Artifacts, like sorority shirts and jackets, reflect who we are and what we think about ourselves.

film *Michael*, John Travolta plays an archangel who is sent to Earth to help the main characters mend their broken hearts. In one scene, in a bar, Michael attracts a number of women to the dance floor and each one is attracted to him because he evokes in each the most cherished smell from their childhoods (freshly baked cookies, pie, etc.). Can you think of a recent time when a smell evoked a familiar and cherished memory?

Chronemics (Time)

Chronemics refers to the study of how people use time as a nonverbal communication channel. There are two ways we can discuss how we think about and interpret communication behavior chronemically. First is our psychological time orientation. There are three main categories of time orientation: past, present, and future. Do you spend more time contemplating past experiences, activities in your present life, or events that may transpire in the future? Are you always on time or chronically late? Do you wear a watch or refuse to own one? Are you "preoccupied" by time, or do you give it little consideration? Do you complete tasks ahead of time or wait until the last minute? What does your orientation toward time and your use of time say about you? What messages are you sending others about how you value their time?

We also communicate status and power differences through time. Higher-status individuals keep lower-status individuals waiting. For example, does your campus have a "rule" about how long you should wait in a classroom for an instructor to arrive? Often it depends on the instructor's rank. On some campuses, students are advised to wait five minutes for a nontenured faculty member and ten minutes for a tenured faculty member!

We can also distinguish between "formal" and "informal" time. Our **formal time** is most likely scheduled. During formal time, we schedule for certain exchanges of services and goods. For example, we call for appointments with doctors, lawyers, psychologists, counselors, hairstylists, and so on. In contrast, our **informal time** is often spontaneous. During our informal time, we are more likely to drop in on a friend, call a friend at the spur of the moment just to chat, or decide to go for a walk with a colleague.

While this has been but a brief look at a number of nonverbal communication behaviors, by now you should understand that nonverbal messages are equal to, if not more powerful than, verbal messages. Nonverbal communication comes in many forms.

Chronemics ■ The study of how people use time as a nonverbal communication channel.

Formal time ■ Scheduled time; used for appointments with paid professionals such as doctors, lawyers, and psychologists.

Informal time ■ Unscheduled time, often spontaneous; used for activities like dropping in on a friend or calling someone just to chat.

The most competent communicators exhibit sensitivity and interpret the complexities of nonverbal messages. There are, however, two additional concepts to understanding and interpreting nonverbal cues: gender and culture.

CONNECTING NONVERBAL COMMUNICATION AND GENDER

Women and men often communicate verbally in dissimilar ways and interpret communication behavior differently. Nonverbal communication is no exception.

Julia T. Wood's studies (1998) explain that communication produces and reproduces cultural definitions of masculinity and femininity and reveal gender. One's views of what is considered masculine or what is considered feminine begin at childhood and are reinforced throughout one's life. Masculine and feminine cultures differ dramatically in when, how, and why individuals of either gender use communication. Thus, in order to communicate effectively across cultures and genders, we must bridge these gaps by striving to understand more about these communication styles.

One of the most remarkable distinctions in feminine nonverbal communication behavior is that its users are usually more sensitive to the nuances of nonverbal communication. Stewart, Cooper, and Friedley (2002) suggest that one of the reasons for this may be that mothers display and encourage a wider range of emotions with girls than with boys. Because girls are exposed to a wider range of emotional communication as infants, it is thought that they are more likely to "read" that emotional communication as adults. Hall (1976) asserts that greater nonverbal sensitivity is required of individuals who are oppressed in society. Thus, women and minorities are more likely to be better at interpreting nonverbal behavior to survive the inequities still operating in our society. While there is not absolute agreement on whether either of these theories is correct, they both acknowledge that feminine and masculine nonverbal messages differ. How these differences manifest themselves on the job are shown in the box "Communication Counts in Your Career: Gender and Nonverbal Communication in the Workplace."

Culture Counts

COMMUNICATION COUNTS IN YOUR CAREER

Gender and Nonverbal Communication in the Workplace

Consider the following table, which shows differences between women and men regarding nonverbal communication. What are the implications for these "gendered" differences in nonverbal communication in the workplace? According to Deborah Tannen (1995), in her book *Talking 9 to 5*, those who speak in ways that claim attention tend to be heard more often, and their suggestions are more likely to influence decision making. In the following table, which set of styles is more likely to be heard? Who is perceived as more credible and assertive?

Females	Males
Stand closer to each other in conversation	Maintain greater distance from each other
Use more eye contact	Use less eye contact
Use more facial expression and are generally more expressive	Reveal less emotion through facial expressions
More likely to return a smile when smiled at—generally smile more	Smile less often
Take up less space—hold legs more closely together and keep arms close to their bodies	Tend to have legs apart and hold arms farther from their bodies
Use fewer gestures overall—use more gestures with men than with other women	Use more gestures in general social situations—use about the same amount of gestures with women or men
Are approached by both sexes more closely	Have more negative reactions to crowding
More likely to lower eyes, avert eyes, look away, and watch another speaker while listening	More likely to look or stare aggressively at others and look elsewhere while speaking
More likely to wear more constraining, formfitting clothing	More likely to wear loose, comfortable clothing

How many gender differences can you detect in these two women's communication?

Gendered Space and Territory

Let's examine some instances in which gender conveys nonverbal messages. For example, in terms of personal space and territory, individuals with masculine nonverbal traits tend to control more area and invade another's personal space more freely. When a man and woman sit next to each other in a movie theater or airplane, men usually use the armrest. Women are also more likely to cede to an intrusion of personal space whereas a male will likely confront or counter such an intrusion.

Gendered Fashion

Regarding fashion, are expectations the same for men and women? Today, women wear jeans, pants, and suits; yet it is not socially acceptable, in most Western cultures, for men to wear skirts and dresses. Why is this? Men and women also have different ranges of colors that are acceptable. For example, how do people react when they see a little boy wearing pink? Do reactions differ based on where people live? How acceptable is it for a man to wear a flowered shirt, a lavender tie, or colorful socks? Men and women also wear different clothing styles. Men wear looser, more comfortable clothes in more contexts. Women, on the other hand, tend to wear more constraining clothes in more form-fitting styles. Consider how these customs, colors, and contexts impact masculine and feminine communication. How many examples can you cite that illustrate gender's influence on communication?

Gendered Touch

Gender also influences other nonverbal behaviors such as touching, eye contact, and movement. In childrearing, parents touch female children more than male children and use more gentle touch with girls than they do with boys. From these early experiences, girls see touch as a signal support whereas boys learn that touch conveys control. Can you think of instances from your life where this may have caused confusion in your relationships?

In a study of gendered touch in social settings, Henley (1973) found that males were more likely to touch females than females to touch males. Henley found that in public settings, males also initiated touching more often than females. A study done by Hall and Veccia (1990) revealed that women touch women more often than men touched men; however, male to female touching exceeded both other groups. Males were more likely to touch with their hands, while females were more likely to engage in touching of other sorts (embraces, kisses, shoulder touches). Based on the information from these two studies, how does your group compare?

Gendered Eye Contact

Considering eye contact, who looks at whom more often? Surprisingly, women use more eye contact than men. Regarding movement, what is the role of nodding the head in conversations between women and men? Women tend to nod to signal, "I hear you," whereas men tend to nod to signal, "I agree with you." Think about the potential misunderstanding that could occur in this situation. Women also tend to smile more than men and use a smile in the same way they use a head nod—to communicate listening.

These examples show that gender differences and expectations exist in nonverbal communication. In general, women read more nonverbal cues into communication situations than men. Expectations for appropriate nonverbal communication are gendered. Recognizing the differences, however, may lead to a broader range of behaviors and interpretations of nonverbal cues, which may decrease the potential for misunderstanding and miscommunication.

CONNECTING NONVERBAL COMMUNICATION AND CULTURE

While different cultures may share some of the same nonverbal communication cues, the interpretation of those nonverbal cues is culture bound. As a result, understanding the ways culture influences nonverbal communication and interpretation is important to developing effective communication skills. Becoming more sensitive to differences in nonverbal cues across cultures is one of the most important competencies you can develop.

In the same way that cultures exist on a continuum in regard to verbal behavior, as we discussed in the previous chapter, they also exist on a nonverbal continuum from high contact to low contact. **High-contact cultures** are those that engage in communication that encourages interaction, physical proximity, large gestures, and warm greetings such as hugs and kisses. **Low-contact cultures** maintain more distance, use smaller gestures, and give more formal greetings. Hugs and kisses are reserved for intimate relationships and nonpublic spaces. The personal space for individuals in high-contact cultures (Arabic, Latin American, Mediterranean) is less than for low-contact cultures (American, German, Scandinavian). As we discussed earlier, issues related to time are culture bound. Cultures exist on a time (chronemic) continuum, ranging from monochronic to polychronic. Individuals from **monochronic cultures** (American, English, Swiss) prefer to do one thing at a time, concentrating on a linear approach to a task. People from these cultures value being on time and tend to develop a larger number of short-term relationships. People from **polychronic cultures** (Bolivian, African, Samoan) prefer to do many things at once. Time is a much more flexible concept, and being on time is based on the relationship or commitment between people. The appropriateness of another nonverbal behavior, direct eye contact, also varies a great deal from culture to culture. Very direct eye contact is highly valued in the Middle East, Latin America, and most of North America. A more moderate level of eye contact is expected in Northern Europe and Britain. Minimal eye contact is considered appropriate in Southeast Asia, India, and Native American cultures (Chaney and Martin 2004).

Cultures also differ in the ways individuals greet and touch each other (haptics). For example, in Hindu cultures, individuals greet each other with hands together and head bowed to indicate respect. In Thailand and Laos, a similar gesture is used to show respect for higher-status individuals. Of course, in the United States we greet with a handshake (if in business or formal settings), as do people in the Netherlands, France, and some Asian countries. In many Mediterranean and Eastern European cultures, individuals greet each other (even strangers) with kisses on both cheeks, hugs, and shoulder pats (Reynolds and Valentine 2004).

High-contact cultures ■ Cultures that engage in communication that encourages interaction, physical proximity, large gestures, and warm greetings (e.g., Arab, Latin American, and Mediterranean).

Low-contact cultures ■ Cultures that maintain more distance, use smaller gestures, and more formal greetings (e.g., American, German, Scandinavian).

Monochronic cultures ■ Cultures that generally prefer a linear approach to activities (e.g., American, English, Swiss).

Polychronic cultures ■ Cultures that generally prefer to do multiple things at once and view time as a flexible concept (e.g., Bolivian, African, Samoan).

Culture Counts

Self-presentation ■ The ways in which a person presents some of the more personal aspects of himself or herself.

Immediacy ■ Behaviors such as direct eye contact, smiling, and facing the other person directly, and using vocal variety.

These are but a few examples of the distinctive cultural expectations for a variety of nonverbal behaviors. There are countless ways in which nonverbal communication differs across cultures, and understanding these cross-cultural differences enhances your communication skills in personal, business, and social relationships.

BECOMING A COMPETENT AND ETHICAL NONVERBAL COMMUNICATOR IN COLLEGE, CAREER, AND LIFE

There are ethical issues surrounding the communication of nonverbal messages. Competent and ethical communicators attend to the consequences of their nonverbal communication. Next, we discuss three ways an ethical communicator can ensure that nonverbal messages result in mutual understanding and shared meaning in the communication interaction.

Self-Presentation

Stewart and Logan (1993) suggest that you can enhance the quality and ethicality of your interpersonal communication by attending to the ways in which you present personal aspects of yourself. These authors identify three "distinct attitudes" that can improve your **self-presentation**. First, you must adopt an "availability attitude" toward your interactions. Being available to another means that you present your concerns and questions and attend to the concerns and topics of another. There are critically important nonverbal availability skills that may enhance your interpersonal relationships: Direct eye contact, for example, is an important indicator of availability in Western cultures. Facial expressions that show interest in the other also enhance the quality of interaction. Body orientation that meets the other openly and directly also communicates attention and availability. Being on time for appointments communicates a subtle but critical message that the other's time and needs are important.

The second attitude is flexibility. When we are flexible, we create meanings for the verbal and nonverbal messages that are tentative, open to new information, and dependent on perception-checking before understanding is assured. When confronted by unclear or uncertain nonverbal messages, re-maining open to the possibility of new interpretations, to different cultural foundations, or to gendered interpretations will improve relationships.

The final attitude is commitment to the conversation. Commitment does not mean you must agree with every message the other person communicates. Instead, commitment means being involved in the interaction and communicating that you value the other, whether or not you agree with him or her.

Mindfulness and Respect

Good friends are mindful and respectful of each other's opinions and ideas.

When we are consciously aware of our nonverbal messages and pay attention to how others interpret them, we are being "mindful" of our communication. The opposite of mindfulness is thoughtlessness—not paying attention to what we communicate verbally and nonverbally. Thoughtlessness is often reflected in our habitual communication behaviors. Stereotyping others' communication is one form of thoughtlessness. When we are willing to create fresh categories instead of relying on stereotypes, when we are open to new information, and when we are available to others' perspectives, we are engaging in mindful and respectful communication.

Accuracy and Immediacy

For each of us, interacting with someone new is likely to produce a certain level of anxiety. We may worry about what this newcomer may think about us or about our ability to communicate effectively. Engaging in nonverbal behaviors that communicate **immediacy** will help to lower your anxiety and enhance the ethicality of your communication. Some examples of nonverbal immediacy behaviors include using direct eye contact, showing a smile, facing the other directly, and using vocal variety. The results of using these nonverbal immediacy behaviors are increased accuracy and understanding of the messages you send as well as increased accuracy of your interpretations of others' messages.

Verbal and Nonverbal Congruence

Effective communicators look for congruence (a match) between verbal and nonverbal communication cues. Note the person's eye contact, body posture, tone of voice, gestures, and the like when he or she is speaking with you. Do these nonverbal behaviors match what he or she is saying, or is there a mismatch between them? If someone tells you he doesn't care if you go to the movies this evening but says it in a half-hearted way and avoids eye contact, you are getting incongruent or mismatched messages that tell you something is on his mind or that he really does care where you go. It is important also to pay attention to the feedback you receive when communicating with others and make adaptations when necessary. In this instance, it would be important to say, "Your voice tells me that you aren't interested in the movies. Would you like to do something else?" Monitoring your communication and responses, as well as those of others, will help you become more aware of the nonverbal cues you send when speaking with others. Self-monitoring is an important skill that will help you respond appropriately in given situations.

PAY ATTENTION TO INCONSISTENCIES   Nonverbal communication should reinforce what is being said. If you get the feeling that someone isn't being honest or that something is "off," you may be picking up on a mismatch between verbal and nonverbal cues. Is the person saying one thing and his or her body language saying something else? For example, is the person telling you "yes" while shaking his or her head no?

As a new or returning student, the success of your communication in college and beyond frequently depends on your ability to negotiate the complex communication relationships that surround you. Understanding and using the recommendations discussed in this chapter can help you negotiate the relationships you create and wish to maintain in college and in life. Chaney and Martin (2004) suggest that

> effective negotiators are observant, patient, adaptable, and good listeners. They appreciate the humor in a situation but are careful to use humor only when appropriate. Good negotiators are mentally sharp. They think before they speak, and they are careful to speak in an agreeable, civil manner. ... Good negotiators praise what is praiseworthy and refrain from criticizing anything about the [other] negotiators. (197)

What are the important relationships you must negotiate during your college experience? You will encounter teachers; roommates; family members; financial aid personnel; records and registration personnel; and individuals in student life, the health center, the counseling center, and many more areas. Each of us comes to these negotiations with a "cultural mind-set" that influences what and how we perceive another. How you attend to the nonverbal messages within each of these negotiations will dramatically impact your success in college and in the world beyond your college experience.

As Chaney and Martin suggest above, being an observant, patient, and careful listener is important. What are other important nonverbal cues you must be aware of about yourself and observe in others in college? In the following true story about your author's encounter with students in a group project, what cues were being sent?

> Scenario: A group of students in a communication class is assigned to work on a project; its task is to develop a communication plan to increase student-voter turnout for the upcoming election. Prior to beginning the project, the team develops a contract that delineates responsibilities for each member of the team. The contract spells out what each member must do for the project and what principles guide interactions between group members. During the first weeks of the project, one group member is habitually late turning in work and routinely turns in work that other team members perceive as substandard (i.e., not edited carefully, lacking major portions of a section, etc.). This group member also misses several meetings without contacting fellow group members and

shows up bleary-eyed and half-asleep. When confronted by other group members about violating the contract, this group member responds with angry facial expressions, stony silence, and crossed arms.

If you were the teacher, what would you think about this communication exchange? What responsibilities do group members have to negotiate in this situation? What role should the teacher play to monitor the negotiation? What role does nonverbal communication play in the success or failure of the negotiation?

This situation actually occurred in the college context, but it could just as easily have occurred in the workplace. Does the changed context of the situation alter the responsibilities of the participants? If so, how? Clearly this situation escalated into a significant conflict for all participants, including the wayward group member. In Chapter 8, we cover conflict management and ways to manage conflict successfully. The self-presentation skills of this errant student played a critical role in the escalation of this conflict. Mindfulness and immediacy are lacking in this communication situation as well.

To ensure greater success and accuracy in the creation and interpretation of nonverbal communication, we must pay careful attention to the detailed nonverbal messages within the environment of the communication. These messages include such things as setting, space, and decor, as well as eye contact, facial expressions, body posture, personal artifacts, touch, and vocal variety. Developing the habit of perception-checking will enhance your ability to negotiate the complex relationships in college and in the world beyond.

SUMMARY

In this chapter, we have identified concepts important to your understanding of effective and ethical nonverbal communication, including these important points:

- We define *nonverbal communication* as sending and receiving wordless messages.
- Verbal and nonverbal messages can be congruent or incongruent.
- Nonverbal communication serves to modify verbal communication, to express our feelings about a number of relational dimensions, and to regulate interaction.
- Kinesic messages are those communicated through the human body, including the eyes, face, gestures, and posture.
- Touch, or haptics, is perhaps one of the most powerful methods of communicating nonverbally.
- Paralanguage, or vocalics, is the use of the voice to communicate.
- Proxemics, or the study of the use of space to communicate, includes how environmental settings such as lighting, noise, color, textures, temperature, and so on affect our communication, as well as how aspects of our "territoriality" or "ownership" of certain physical spaces and our own personal space are shown.
- *Chronemics* refers to the study of how people use time as a nonverbal communication channel.
- *Olfactics* refers to communication based on smell.
- Women are usually more sensitive to the nuances of nonverbal communication than men.
- High-contact cultures are those that engage in communication that encourages interaction, physical proximity, large gestures, and warm greetings with hugs and kisses.
- Low-contact cultures maintain more distance and use smaller gestures and more formal greetings.
- Self-presentation includes three important "attitudes"—availability, flexibility, and commitment.
- When we are consciously aware of our nonverbal messages and pay attention to how others interpret them, we are being "mindful" of our communication.
- Engaging in nonverbal behaviors that communicate immediacy will help to lower your anxiety and enhance the ethicality of your communication.

QUESTIONS FOR DISCUSSION

1. Do you remember when and how you "learned" nonverbal behavior and what certain nonverbal cues meant? Explain some of the lessons you learned in childhood.
2. We argue that women are more sensitive to nonverbal cues than men. Do you agree? Why or why not?
3. Have you ever been accused of sending a sexual signal when you did not? How is this possible?
4. Think about the places in your home that are yours (others are not allowed or must seek permission to enter). What are they? If you have a life partner, what are his or her spaces? How are they similar or different to yours?
5. Think about the people who keep you waiting in your life. What can you say about them in terms of education, status, importance, and so on. Who do you keep waiting? Why?
6. What is the most appropriate clothing to wear for a job interview? What are the reasons for wearing particular attire in that communication setting? What are you trying to communicate to the prospective employer through your mode of dress?
7. What is the difference between a "gaze" and a "stare"? Who stares more—women or men? Why do women tend to smile more than men?

EXERCISES

1. A young man is fairly successful at getting first dates, but second and third dates are extremely rare. The general consensus is that he is cold, unemotional, and, especially, unromantic. What advice for nonverbal communication would you give him to make him a more successful dating partner? What nonverbal dating faults would you point out? Organize your advice around the following areas of nonverbal communication: body communication, facial and eye communication, spatial communication, and tactile communication.
2. In a group, identify how the following attitudes are communicated nonverbally. Be as specific as possible: machismo, sexism, love, hatred, loneliness, happiness, dogmatism, authority, high status, sensuousness.
3. In a group, identify as precisely as possible what individuals from Canada, China, England, Saudi Arabia, Japan, Brazil, and Germany would say is the time frame for the following list of terms:

- Immediately
- Soon
- Right away
- As soon as possible
- Later today
- In the near future

4. Draw a diagram of your ideal office. Where is it located in the building in which you work? What is the decor like? Who will be allowed to enter without your permission?
5. Identify three rules of body communication and gesture operating in U.S. culture that are uniquely masculine. [Note: Rules may be conceived of as prescriptive (indicating what should be done) or as proscriptive (indicating what should not be done)]. Identify three rules of body communication and gesture in U.S. culture that are uniquely feminine.

KEY TERMS

Adaptors 84	Immediacy 94	Proxemics 86
Affect displays 84	Incongruent messages 80	Public space 87
Artifacts 89	Informal time 90	Rate (of speech) 87
Chronemics 90	Intimate space 87	Regulators 84
Congruent messages 80	Kinesics 84	Self-adaptors 84
Disfluencies 88	Low-contact cultures 93	Self-presentation 94
Emblems 84	Monochronic cultures 93	Silence 88
Emoticons 82	Object-adaptors 84	Social space 87
Formal time 90	Olfactics 89	Start/stop cues 82
High-contact	Personal space 87	Territoriality 87
cultures 93	Pitch 87	Turn-taking cues 82
Illustrators 84	Polychronic cultures 93	Vocalics 87

REFERENCES

Aiken, L. 1963. The relationship of dress to selected measures of personality in undergraduate women. *Journal of Social Psychology* 59:119–128.

Callero, H. H. 2005. *The power of nonverbal communication: How you act is more important than what you say.* Aberdeen, WA: Silver Lake Publishing.

Chaney, L. H., and Martin, J. S. 2004. *Intercultural business communication*. 3rd ed. Upper Saddle River, New Jersey: Pearson Prentice Hall.

Ekman, P. 1972. Universal and cultural differences in facial expressions of emotions. In J. K. Cole, ed. *Nebraska Symposium on Motivation 1971*, 207–283. Lincoln, NE: University of Nebraska Press.

Hall, E. T. 1959. *The silent language*. Garden City, NY: Doubleday.

Hall, E. T. 1966. *The hidden dimension*. Garden City, NY: Doubleday.

Hall, E. T. 1976. *Beyond culture*. Garden City, NY: Anchor Press.

Hall, J. A. & Veccia, E. M. 1990. More "touching" observations: New insights on men, women, and interpersonal touch. *Journal of Personality and Social Psychology* 59: 1155–1162.

Henley, N. M. 1973. Status and sex: Some touching observations. *Bulletin of the Psychonomic Society* 2:91–93.

Knapp, M. L. 1978. *Nonverbal communication in human interaction*. 2nd ed. New York: Holt, Rinehart and Winston.

Knox, D., McGinty, K., and Zusman, M. E. March 2003. Nonverbal and verbal communication in "involved" and "casual" relationships among college students. *College Student Journal* 68–71.

Reynolds, S., and Valentine, D. 2004. *Guide to cross-cultural communication*. Upper Saddle River, New Jersey: Pearson Prentice Hall.

Samovar, L. A., and Porter, R. E. 2001. *Communication between cultures*. 4th ed. Belmont, CA: Wadsworth.

Stewart, J., and Logan, C. 1993. *Together: Communicating interpersonally*. 4th ed. New York: McGraw-Hill.

Stewart, P. J., Cooper, L. P., and Friedley, A. D. 2002. *Communication and gender*. Boston: Allyn and Bacon.

Tannen, D. 1995. *Talking 9 to 5*. New York: Harper.

Watkins, L. and Johston, L. 2002. Screening job applicants: The impact of physical attractiveness and application quality. *International Journal of Selection and Assessment*, 8, 76–84.

Wood, J. T. 1998. Gender communication and culture. In Samovar, L. S., & Porter, R. E. *Intercultural communication: A reader*. Stanford, CT: Wadsworth. What nonverbal messages are conveyed in this business meeting?

CHAPTER

6 Understanding Interpersonal Communication

LEARNING OUTCOMES After reading this chapter, you will have:

the **Knowledge** to. . .   and the **Skills** to. . .

RECOGNIZING THE DIFFERENCE BETWEEN IMPERSONAL AND INTERPERSONAL COMMUNICATION, page 102

Understand the disparities between impersonal and interpersonal communication.

- Know that interpersonal communication exists in a continuum from impersonal to interpersonal.
- Realize that interpersonal communication is rule-bound by culture, society, and relationship-specific rules.

UNDERSTANDING INTIMACY AS A KEY CONCEPT OF INTERPERSONAL COMMUNICATION, page 103

Understand intimacy and its role in interpersonal communication.

- Be aware of how attraction influences your interpersonal communication.
- Consider how your various needs are fulfilled in your different interpersonal relationships.
- Take note of how much self-disclosure you are comfortable with as you manage others' impressions of you.

99

IDENTIFYING THE STAGES OF RELATIONSHIP DEVELOPMENT AND DISSOLUTION, page 110

Identify the stages of relationship building.

Identify the stages of relationship termination.
Understand Duck's Relational Dissolution Model.

- Examine the various stages you may be at in your relationship building.
- Evaluate relationships that have ended or are in the process of ending.
- Apply Duck's Relational Dissolution Model to relationships you, your friends, or family have experienced.

DEVELOPING RELATIONSHIPS BETWEEN PROFESSORS AND STUDENTS, page 115

Recognize the relationship cycle between professors and students.

- Consider your relationship with your instructors this term in light of the stages of initiating, experimenting, and intensifying.

CONNECTING GENDER AND INTERPERSONAL COMMUNICATION, page 116

Appreciate differences in masculine and feminine communication and language.

- Use gender-neutral language.
- Examine your use of masculine and feminine language.

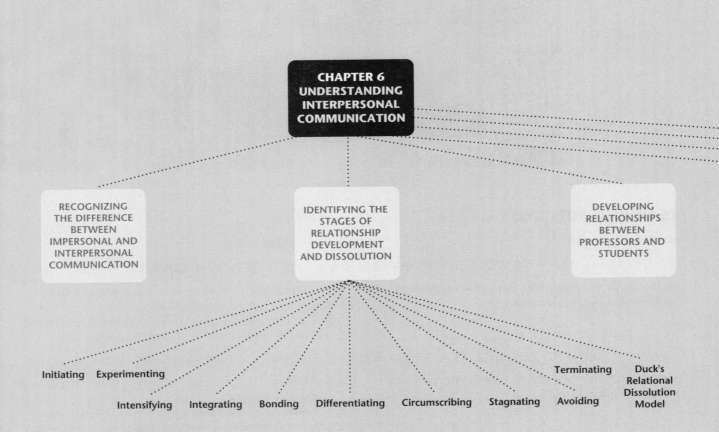

CONNECTING CULTURE AND INTERPERSONAL COMMUNICATION, page 117

Be aware of cultural differences in interpersonal communication.

- Evaluate your family and home community to determine if it is low-context or high-context and consider why this is so.

BECOMING A COMPETENT AND ETHICAL INTERPERSONAL COMMUNICATOR IN COLLEGE, CAREER, AND LIFE, page 118

Become a capable and moral communicator.

- Practice authentic and respectful interpersonal communication at school, on the job, and in everyday life.

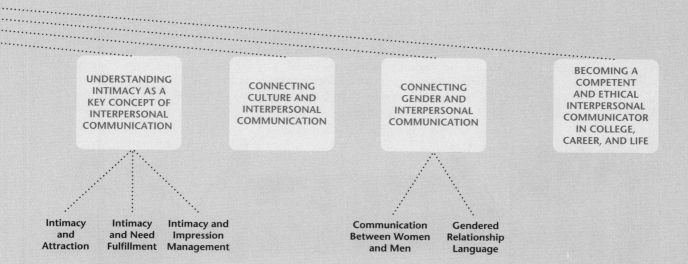

Interpersonal (dyadic) communication ■ A relationship context involving two persons (a *dyad*).

Impersonal communication ■ Information exchange that lacks depth, is superficial.

Developmental approach ■ Includes three levels of rules—cultural, sociological, and psychological—that tell us how to communicate with others.

Cultural rules ■ General rules that apply to all members of a culture.

Sociological rules ■ Rules that apply to individuals in a particular group.

RECOGNIZING THE DIFFERENCE BETWEEN IMPERSONAL AND INTERPERSONAL COMMUNICATION

Our lives are shaped by the varied and often complex relationships we have with others. From the very first relationships we develop within our families, we branch out to create relationships with friends, schoolmates, coworkers, lovers, and others. Some develop into long-term, intimate relationships while others are short-lived. What factors influence the longevity of some relationships and not others? This chapter discusses several issues that impact our competence as communicators in our interpersonal relationships. At one level, **interpersonal (dyadic) communication** can be defined as a relationship context involving two persons, or a *dyad*. *Inter-* is a prefix that means "between." Interpersonal communication, then, refers to communication between two persons, usually face-to-face. With the advent of new social media, however, interpersonal communication can also be mediated. Interpersonal communication can occur just between two people or within a group, and these can occur with the assistance of technology even when the people are not in the same "space." But not all interpersonal communication, or communication in dyads, is equally interpersonal. A more useful way to understand interpersonal communication is to distinguish it from impersonal communication.

Think of interpersonal and impersonal communication as two ends of a relationship continuum, as shown in Figure 6.1. Both require interaction with at least one other person. At the interpersonal communication end of the continuum, we exchange information that is intended to build relationships, add depth and understanding in the relationship. But at the **impersonal communication** end of the continuum, the information we exchange with the other person is superficial, lacks depth, and does not provide us or the other person with any authentic information.

The degree to which we develop relationships beyond impersonal interaction depends on many factors described throughout this text—such as self-disclosure (this chapter), self-concept (Chapter 2), and listening (Chapter 3).

Miller and Steinberg (1975) outline the **developmental approach** to interpersonal communication. They identify three levels of "rules" that tell us how to communicate with others (see Figure 6.2).

Cultural rules are general rules we apply to all members of a culture. When most Americans meet a stranger for the first time, they are usually polite, shake hands, exchange names, and choose topics that are very general, like the weather. Cultural rules include a society's beliefs, values, and language. For example, although some Americans feel a person who doesn't make eye contact is untrustworthy, in some cultures, not making eye contact is a sign of respect for someone's age, position, or experience. A student from South Africa found it difficult to make eye contact with others because in his background, eye contact invited confrontation, not interest or engagement. Another student, who had worked in Russia for several months, found that if he made eye contact, especially with women, his intentions were misread as a sexual overture.

We use **sociological rules** with individuals who belong to certain groups. For example, you communicate one way with other college students and another way with faculty members. We associate the set of rules with the group, and each group's rules are different.

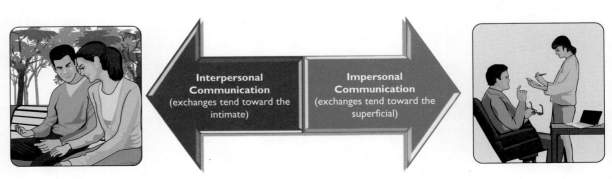

FIGURE 6.1
The Interpersonal-Impersonal Communication Continuum.

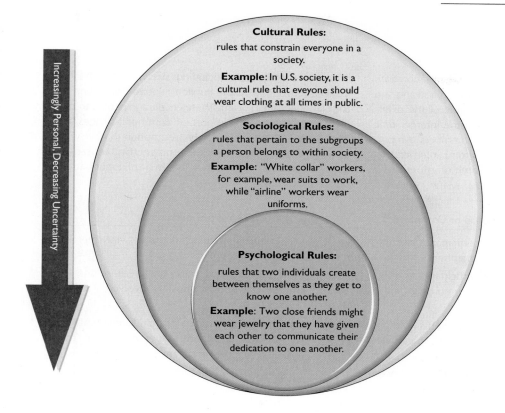

Increasingly Personal, Decreasing Uncertainty

Cultural Rules:
rules that constrain everyone in a society.

Example: In U.S. society, it is a cultural rule that eveyone should wear clothing at all times in public.

Sociological Rules:
rules that pertain to the subgroups a person belongs to within society.

Example: "White collar" workers, for example, wear suits to work, while "airline" workers wear uniforms.

Psychological Rules:
rules that two individuals create between themselves as they get to know one another.

Example: Two close friends might wear jewelry that they have given each other to communicate their dedication to one another.

FIGURE 6.2
Miller and Steinberg's Rules of Interpersonal Communication.

We use **psychological rules** when we begin to learn something about a person as an individual. These rules are developed by the individuals and are unique to that relationship. We joke around with friends or "insult" them. We sit closer to them or maybe even develop our own language that others outside the relationship cannot understand. As Miller and Steinberg suggest, the more we develop a relationship beyond exchanging basic factual information and begin to tell others about our feelings, values, dreams, and goals, the more we move toward a truly interpersonal relationship. The more we move away from a general, culturally proscribed set of rules for interaction to more personal ones, the more we are willing to invest ourselves in the relationship; likewise, the more confident we are in disclosing personal, intimate information, the more interpersonal the relationship. The more we listen to others, the more we can respond to them with appropriate, timely, relationship-based information, thereby expanding and developing the relationship interpersonally.

Psychological rules ■ Rules that apply to the specific relationship we have with another.

Intimacy ■ The process of coming to know the other and yourself as a relationship develops.

Rules govern our interactions with one another.

UNDERSTANDING INTIMACY AS A KEY CONCEPT OF INTERPERSONAL COMMUNICATION

So what motivates you to continue a relationship beyond the impersonal level? Fundamentally, we are motivated to continue those relationships that help us develop a more comfortable, confident sense of self. The more comfortable we are in establishing *intimacy* with another person, the more likely the relationship will grow beyond impersonal communication. In this sense, we do not primarily mean physical intimacy but the process of coming to know the other and yourself as the relationship develops. We refer to **intimacy** as the willingness to risk sharing information to create a unique and personal relationship.

As you can see in the box "Communication Counts in Your Life: Interpersonal Relationships and Community," the "intimacy" that may develop within a community of people has a profound impact on the ways people perceive themselves as "belonging" to a place.

COMMUNICATION COUNTS IN YOUR LIFE

Interpersonal Relationships and Community

This chart (taken from www.communitycollaboration. net/id53.htm) identifies the differences between a strong and a weak sense of community. Note how many of the differences are directly related to the nature of the interpersonal relationships that exist among community members. We cannot have strong communities without strong interpersonal relationships that are based on shared common ground and the ability to dialogue with one another. Many structured

initiatives already exist, including study circles, the Public Conversations Project, the Public Dialogue Consortium, and the National Issues Forum. These encourage people to gather for conversation about important community issues. However, these endeavors rest on the assumption that we will not just talk to one another but with one another, consequently developing relationships that will form a solid foundation for our communities.

Indicator	Strong Sense of Community	Weak Sense of Community
Sense of membership	The active participants proudly display symbols of membership in the community.	The active participants do not view themselves as a community.
Mutual importance	The active participants recognize, cherish, and support the contributions of each other.	Participants are active only because one or a few powerful persons are involved.
Shared world views	The active participants hold common beliefs and promote shared values important to them.	The active participants hold fundamentally different beliefs and values and cannot reconcile their differences.
Bonding/networking	The active participants enjoy one another and look forward to time spent together.	The active participants have no affinity for each other, and relationships are formal or superficial.
Mutual responsibility for the community	The survival and health of the community is a primary concern of all its active participants.	One or only a few persons struggle to keep the group together.

Source: From *Effective Community Mobilization, Lessons from Experience.* Published by the Department of Health and Human Services Substance Abuse and Mental Health Services Administration.

Attraction ■ One of the factors that motivates individuals toward intimacy in an interpersonal relationship.

Intimacy and Attraction

Several factors influence and motivate us toward intimacy in developing interpersonal relationships. One is **attraction**. Attraction, as most of us know, is the draw or appeal of another, sometimes without explanation. It becomes our desire for another; we are enticed to be near him or her. At a very basic level, each of us is *attracted* to some individuals and not others. Every individual, for example, develops a basic criterion for what makes others physically attractive. Our society places a great emphasis on physical beauty as a measure of attractiveness. Each individual, in turn, identifies certain physical characteristics with what he or she finds attractive. But other issues impact how we identify another as "attractive." For example, we are attracted to those who share our values, hobbies, or personality characteristics and to those in close physical proximity to us. The sheer "opportunity factor" of proximity means we will have greater opportunities to get to know others if we often run into them in classes, in apartments or residence halls, or in groups we belong to. We are also attracted to those who share our past or present experiences. We are motivated to develop relationships more interpersonally when we have something in common. And, finally, we are attracted to those who assist us in achieving goals. Is there a group or organization you want to be involved with because you admire its work? Do you want to position yourself to advance in your career? Or do you simply want to be associated with certain people? For example, if you want to be a member of the Greek society on your campus, on what basis do you choose the sorority or fraternity you will join? On the other hand, if you have no interest in being a member of a Greek organization, why not? Or if you are a mature learner, have you sought out organizations on your campus where you can meet other students like yourself? What is the basis of your decision to seek or not seek such engagement?

We are much more likely to be attracted to individuals who help us achieve these kinds of goals. So, the more knowledge we have of others and the more attraction we feel toward them, the more likely we are to develop those relationships interpersonally.

While each of these elements of attraction moves *us* toward developing interpersonal relationships, our expectations for how *others* will act also influences our motivation to maintain or continue those relationships. Our expectations of a friend may differ vastly from those we expect of a life partner. Thus, the more we invest of ourselves in an interpersonal relationship, the more expectations we have for the other in that relationship. However, this, too, may shift depending on one's culture. For example, many people throughout the world use the word *friend* to describe what many U.S. residents would call a *close friend* (Martin & Nakayama 2001). Additionally, research verifies that different concepts of friendship exist within specific ethnic or cultural groups (Elbedour, Shulman, & Peri 1997; You & Malley-Morrison 2000), within age groups (Adams, Blieszner, & DeVries 2000), and among people with and without physical disabilities (Meyer et al. 1998; Novak 1993). Moreover, such differences impact how well people perceive one another's communication ability (Collier 1996) and even the topics they will engage in during friendly conversation (Goodwin & Lee 1994).

Intimacy and Need Fulfillment

Clearly we are more attracted to some individuals than others, and an important consideration in deciding how, where, and with whom we develop relationships involves what those relationships do for us. The function of an interpersonal relationship in our lives is to fulfill our various needs. Abraham Maslow and William Schutz are two theorists who have studied our needs and how we fulfill them.

MASLOW'S HIERARCHY OF NEEDS   Abraham Maslow (1970) developed a hierarchy that classifies our needs into seven categories: physiological, security and safety, love and belonging, self-esteem, knowing and understanding, aesthetics, and self-actualization. Maslow believed that each of the levels provides us with certain motivations that characterize our behavior. These motivations constrain our behavior until we have fulfilled those needs. The categories are hierarchical in the sense that we must be at least partially fulfilled at each level in order to move toward a higher level (see Figure 6.3). In other words, we must fulfill our physiological needs before we are motivated to fulfill our safety needs.

When we are willing to engage in dialogue with another, we increase the potential for a meaningful relationship.

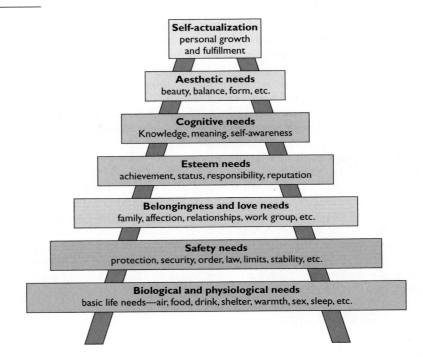

FIGURE 6.3

Maslow's Hierarchy of Needs.

Source: Maslow, Abraham. *Motivation and Personality.* New York: HarperCollins, © 1954.

Physiological needs ■ Biological needs necessary to sustain life, including air, water, food, sleep, and sex.

Safety and security needs ■ Feeling free from violence and feeling a sense of stability in life.

Love and belonging needs ■ The need for affection, support, approval, and love from friends and family.

Self-esteem needs ■ The needs for confidence or self-worth; they motivate individuals toward success.

Physiological Needs. **Physiological needs** are biological needs necessary to sustain life and include air, food, water, sleep, and sex. Once we satisfy these basic needs, we can address our needs for safety and security. How we meet these needs impacts our well-being. In turn, our well-being impacts our ability to develop and maintain healthy relationships.

Safety and Security Needs. **Safety and security needs** include feeling free from violence and having a sense of stability in our lives. Safety needs are physical; security needs are psychological. For many of us, physiological and safety concerns are not issues because we live in fairly safe neighborhoods and have food and shelter. However, many people in the world are not so lucky. Abject poverty and lack of affordable housing cause individuals and families to spend a considerable amount of time simply trying to find enough to eat or a place to sleep. Just a few hundred miles off U.S. shores you can encounter indescribable poverty in countries like Haiti, Guatemala, and Honduras.

And we are not exempt from this problem within our own country. Consider the number of people today in the United States who live in homeless shelters. According to the Urban Institute (2000), 2.3 million people, or 1 percent of the population, face homelessness at least one time during any given year. In addition, the rate of people living in poverty is 6.3 percent. We may take for granted our livable houses or apartments, while thousands of families in this country go without decent, affordable housing and may even lack indoor plumbing.

Love and Belonging Needs. So for most of us, our behavior is not motivated by physiological or safety and security needs. Maslow believed that after we meet these first two levels of needs, we then seek to fulfill **love and belonging needs.** *Love and belonging* refer to our needs for affection, support, approval, and love from friends and family. This level of motivation is perhaps the most significant in our search for meaningful interpersonal relationships. Many of us have felt strong support and love from our families all our lives, while others have had these needs withheld or provided only conditionally. After some of our needs for love and belonging have been satisfied, we move toward the need for self-esteem and respect.

Self-Esteem Needs. **Self-esteem needs** are our needs for confidence or self-worth; they motivate us toward our careers and toward accumulating the things in life that show we are successful, such as homes, cars, and other worldly goods. Have you identified a career goal? What type of job do you think you are suited for and that would give you satisfaction? Think about what you have accumulated in your life to date and what you still yearn for, and consider all the advertisements you see on a daily basis that portray "successful" people in our culture. Consider the importance of what people *think* of you. Are you liked and respected? By whom? Whose respect matters to you? Your parents? Your teachers? Your friends? Your boss? Much of your behavior is motivated by these important, and perhaps as-yet unsatisfied, self-esteem needs. Consider the shoes you are wearing today. People prefer certain styles over others. For example, students often wear brand-name athletic shoes. Why? What motivates college students to choose certain kinds of shoes over others? While it may seem that shoes and self-esteem are hardly related, on closer examination, perhaps they *are* related, because how others perceive us, including whether we wear the right shoes, influences how we think of ourselves.

Knowledge and Understanding Needs. When we have partially satisfied the need for self-esteem and respect, Maslow's hierarchy suggests that we move toward the need for knowing and understanding and the need for aesthetics and beauty. **Knowledge and understanding needs** make us curious about the world and about others. We seek out others, develop relationships, and expand our knowledge just because it is possible to do so and because we feel more confident about ourselves with that knowledge. Some of the greatest learning occurs by interacting with our peers. For example, your authors go to conferences, attend professional development meetings, and chat at lunch with colleagues because we have learned how much we can gain from our colleagues and peers. Moreover, we have found that we learn from our students every semester! Curiosity and conversation are the ways to connect with others and to enhance our learning. Look at the students sitting near you in class; imagine all the knowledge they have that you do not. There's only one way to tap into their knowledge and experience—communicate with them! Ask questions. Engage a conversation. You may be pleasantly surprised at what you'll learn, and besides, you may make some friends.

Aesthetic Needs. According to Maslow, **aesthetic needs** encompass the need to see beauty for its own sake. Have you ever been on a vacation and just stopped to enjoy a view? Do you remember the feeling you had standing there and surveying what was before you? To truly appreciate what we see before us, we need to understand and value what is inside us. To illustrate, while you may consider some of your general education courses to be less important than those directly related to your major, these courses provide you the opportunity to meet aesthetic needs as described by Maslow because you will have the opportunity to examine various forms of art, including poems, paintings, theatrical productions, and musical scores.

Self-Actualization Needs. The level of self-actualization is the highest level of motivation, according to Maslow. Maslow described **self-actualization needs** as encompassing our drive to be the best we can be and to live our lives in the best ways we know how. At this level, we are comfortable and satisfied with who we are, where we are, and what we have achieved. This level is actually quite difficult to achieve, and many of us spend our entire lives searching for true fulfillment.

SCHUTZ'S THEORY OF INTERPERSONAL NEEDS   William Schutz (1958) identified three interpersonal needs that motivate us: *affection, inclusion,* and *control.*

The Need for Affection. Like Maslow, Schutz identified our need for affection as basic to our development of relationships. We need to feel liked, loved, and respected. We join groups for this purpose, and we seek out friends and life partners because of these needs. While some people develop those affectionate relationships on their own, others may contract with a dating service or ask friends to "set them up." Essentially, we seek out emotional commitments because we cannot feel truly satisfied without them, even though they may often be unsatisfying in the long run. And although we make mistakes in some of our relationships, we still try to find "the one" for us.

The Need for Inclusion. Schutz also identified our need for inclusion as a primary motivator of our behavior. We need to feel that we are making a difference, that we have some significance in the world or in someone else's life. Think of the types of groups you would most like to join or be involved with. Do you seek out this group because of what might be changed or improved in your community (i.e., Habitat for Humanity, Boys and

---

Knowledge and understanding needs ■ Needs that make individuals curious about the world and about others.

Aesthetic needs ■ The highest level of needs; the need to see beauty for its own sake.

Self-actualization needs ■ Encompass an individual's drive to be the best that he or she can be.

Girls Clubs of America, etc.)? You may also have an opportunity to join a variety of campus groups, including service, academic, student government, religious, or Greek groups. You should find groups that are in harmony with your personal goals or interests because these groups can add a great deal to your academic experience and can meet your need for inclusion. A student recently told us, "When I first came to campus, I made a lot of friends, and then most of them joined a sorority during their first year at school. I didn't really want to join a sorority, but after a year, I did, because I lost contact with so many of the friends I made my first year." You will be faced with these decisions, and you will need to think clearly about what *you* want to do.

If you are returning to school later in life, you too will face similar decisions. Although you may not be faced with joining a sorority, you will likely have to juggle time between study and your family, friends, or social groups within and outside of college. Clearly, some of us are more motivated to be "joiners" than others. Schutz suggests that we each have a different level of needing to belong, which makes us more or less social.

The Need for Control.   Finally, Schutz identifies our need for control as a primary motivator. At a basic level, this means we must be able to predict what will happen to us in our jobs, in our relationships, and in our lives. But taken to a higher level, our need for control encompasses our need to be leaders and to be responsible for jobs and tasks. Some of us are more motivated toward leadership than others, which may result in new challenges or opportunities in our college experience.

Each of these needs—affection, inclusion, control—motivates our communication and development of relationships with others. These needs also motivate us to gain knowledge of the world and our role in it. Knowing these needs exist and understanding how much of each need we must fulfill can help us understand why we seek out certain relationships and not others. In the next section, we explore how intimacy affects our self-perceptions and how we manage our own and others' perceptions of us.

Intimacy and Impression Management

Our needs affect our motivation toward intimacy, and our self-perception influences how we communicate with others in developing that intimacy. We share our self-perceptions (how we see ourselves) through **self-disclosure,** which is the process of purposefully sharing personal information with others. If you feel good about yourself, you are more likely to disclose information. However, if you doubt yourself or feel unworthy, you are more likely to be protective, uncertain, or guarded.

Self-disclosure ■ When we tell someone something about our self that they would not know unless we told them.

A variety of needs motivate our communication and development of relationships with others.

THE JOHARI WINDOW   The **Johari Window,** named for its creators Jo Luft and Harry Ingham, provides a way for you to analyze your level of self-disclosure (Luft 1970). Figure 6.4 depicts their model, which contains four quadrants or panes. The *open* pane refers to all the information that both you and someone else knows about you—information you have self-disclosed; the *hidden* pane contains information you have not disclosed to anyone; the *blind* pane contains information that others may know about you that you do not know about yourself; and the *unknown* pane refers to information that neither you nor anyone else knows. As you self-disclose and receive feedback from others, the various panes enlarge so that others learn more about you and you learn more about yourself. However, how you view yourself will impact what and how much information you disclose and to whom you disclose it. In other words, your sense of self will, in part, determine the size of the panes in your personal Johari Window.

	Known to Self	Not known to Self
Known to Others	1 OPEN	2 BLIND
Not known to Others	3 HIDDEN	4 UNKNOWN

FIGURE 6.4
The Johari Window.

Source: "The Johari Window" from *Group Processes: An Iintroduction to Group Dynamics* by J. Luft. Reprinted by permission of the McGraw-Hill Companies.

THE SOCIAL PENETRATION MODEL   The **social penetration model** (Altman & Taylor 1973) provides yet another way to think about self-disclosure. As Figure 6.5 shows, this model (also termed the *onion model*) depicts self-disclosure as a process that gradually reveals both breadth and depth of information. We are like onions in that we have layers, which we reveal as we get to know one another. In this process, we disclose more information about ourselves and include a broader range of topics and more detailed information about these topics. However, the depth and breadth of these revelations relates directly to our self-concept.

IMPRESSION MANAGEMENT   We adjust our self-disclosure as a result of our self-concept, and we monitor our interactions with others. **Impression management** (Goffman 1959) refers to strategies we use to positively influence others toward us. Some refer to this as *self-enhancement* or "putting your best foot forward." This is not dishonest; it is a conscious attempt to make a positive impact on others. For example, if you interview for a job, you should be well-groomed, speak articulately, and be ready to sell yourself to a prospective employer. However, your self-concept will influence how you manage your impressions. If you judge yourself unworthy, you may appear and act in a manner that more likely ensures you will not get the job.

While most of us use impression management to enhance and positively influence others honestly, some individuals choose to "enhance" themselves in ways that are precariously close to lying. Many of us have chosen to withhold information from someone to create a positive impression. What is the line between withholding information and

Johari Window ■ A model for understanding levels and types of self-disclosure.

Social penetration model ■ A model depicting self-disclosure as a process that gradually reveals both breadth and depth of information.

Impression management ■ Strategies we use to positively influence others.

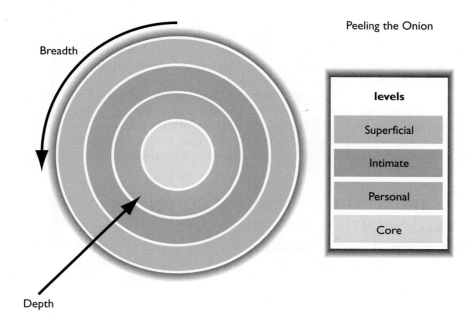

Peeling the Onion

Breadth

Depth

levels

Superficial

Intimate

Personal

Core

FIGURE 6.5
The Social Penetration Model.

Source: From *Business Communication* by Scott McLean, http://static.flatworldknowledge.com. Copyright 2010 Flat World Knowledge, Inc. Reprinted by permission.

COMMUNICATION COUNTS IN YOUR COLLEGE EXPERIENCE

Truthfulness and Romance

Many of you, especially those of you who do not have a life partner, are likely excited about the prospects of dating and romance during your college years. However, have you thought about what you expect from a college romance? Research regarding romantic relationships suggests that being able to trust your partner is vitally important and that intentional deception brings a number of results, including "(1) a strong effect on beliefs about the honesty of the other in the relationship, (2) negative emotional responses, (3) communication patterns of either avoidance or engagement, and (4) consequences for relationships, such as terminating or continuing them" (Jang, Smith, & Levine 2002, 236).

Although college romances may not endure, working toward honest, open relationships is important. All of your authors have talked with students who have been devastated by broken relationships. However, in our experience, when a partner has been deceived in some manner, the hurt is multiplied. We have seen students lose focus, become depressed, and even quit school because they have been so deeply hurt by a relationship that ended due to deception. Moreover, these students often find it difficult to trust others again and, understandably, become very self-protective. So, how can you enjoy dating and interacting with potential partners and maintain honesty? Here are some suggested communication strategies for you to consider:

1. **Be honest with yourself.** Before you can be truthful with others, you must be honest with yourself about the kind of relationship you want. This will depend on your personality, your other life commitments, your age, and other factors. However, it is important that you have a clear sense of where you are in your own life and how much energy you wish to place in a relationship at this point. In other words, you need to have clear communication with yourself.

2. **Share your intentions.** If you're interested in having a good time and getting to know someone but not interested in a romantic commitment, make this clear from the outset. Don't let a dating partner assume your intentions; make them known in an appropriate way.

3. **Communicate courageously and kindly.** At some point, you may have to break up with someone. Whatever the reason, if you are no longer interested in dating someone or continuing a relationship, have the courage to say so as kindly as you can.

4. **Ask for forgiveness.** People make mistakes, and sometimes we may lie or break a trust. If this happens, you can continue trying to deceive or you can admit your wrongdoing, ask for forgiveness, work toward repairing the relationship, or end the relationship. All in all, people are human, and many of life's most important lessons are learned painfully as we grow.

lying by omission? When we intentionally withhold information to create a false impression, we have crossed the boundary into lying. When we overtly fabricate a persona or personality to avoid disclosing who we really are, we have chosen to create a distorted impression—a lie.

Quite another approach to impression management is to only "hint" at who we are but to never truly self-disclose. Perhaps you have encountered someone who never really told you much about who they are, what they think, and how they feel? We must be willing to share of ourselves to others as they share themselves with us. This is the key to developing appropriate intimacy in our relationships. Therefore, it is important to manage your impressions toward others and your self-image so that you can present your best self without feeling fake or phony. As you can see in the box "Communication Counts in Your College Experience: Truthfulness and Romance," self-disclosure and sharing your intentions honestly can mean the difference between true intimacy in romantic relationships and an encounter that becomes a "one-night stand." In the next section we explore the phases or stages of relationship development.

IDENTIFYING THE STAGES OF RELATIONSHIP DEVELOPMENT AND DISSOLUTION

Knapp and Vangelisti (1992) have developed a ten-step model to describe the stages of relationship development and dissolution (see Figure 6.6). These stages can assist us in seeing how increasing and decreasing levels of intimacy impact the way relationships succeed or fail.

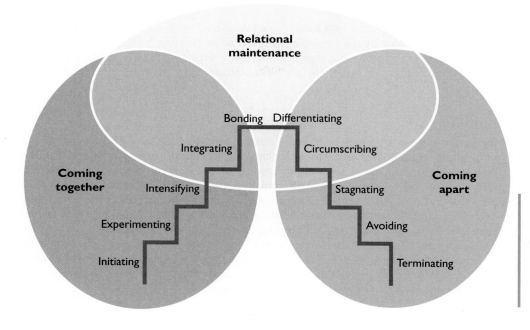

FIGURE 6.6

Knapp's Relational Development and Dissolution Model.

Source: Knapp & Vangelisti, *Interpersonal Communication and Human Relationships,* Figure 2.1 "Staircase Model of Interaction Stages" p. 53, © 1992. Reproduced by permission of Pearson Education, Inc.

Initiating

In the **initiating stage** of relationship development, the parties involved attempt to create an impression. Each pays careful attention to the other in an attempt to pick up any cues that would provide information about who the other is and how the other will respond.

For some, this is one of the most difficult stages of the relationship. Like the apprehension many of us feel when giving a public presentation, we may feel significant apprehension in any social setting where we meet another for the first time. This **social anxiety** can be quite difficult for people to overcome. Anxiety, in general, is caused by uncertainty. Uncertainty is "what we don't know about a situation" and "what we don't know about how the other will react" in the encounter. Our inability to predict what the other might do in a social situation threatens our self-concept and self-esteem because we fear being seen as foolish, incompetent, or stupid. Social anxiety often stems from how we compare ourselves to others and from the fact that these **social comparisons** may find us lacking in a certain area. Social anxiety also stems from what we see or think we see about ourselves reflected in the eyes of others, and the more importance we invest in others' perceptions of us, the more anxiety we are likely to feel.

Experimenting

If some initial positive responses help to reduce our anxiety, we will be more likely to continue to the **experimenting stage**. Each individual in the dyad cautiously begins to look for commonalities, primarily through small talk, or what some communication scholars term **phatic communication** (introduced by Malinowski 1923). The primary goal at this stage is to reduce some of the uncertainty that comes from not knowing the other. This is a critical stage in relationship development because our "first impressions" often determine very quickly whether or not there is reason to develop the relationship.

Intensifying

If we decide to continue, we move to the **intensifying stage,** and we finally risk disclosing in a more personal manner. The relationship is often more relaxed, and we feel free to joke and tease. We begin to speak in terms of "we" instead of "I." We develop a level of comfort with the other because we can now predict how that person will respond to our self-disclosure. This is often the most exciting and satisfying period because both parties are having fun investing time and energy in the relationship.

Initiating stage ■ The stage of a relationship in which the parties attempt to create an impression.

Social anxiety ■ A feeling of apprehension in any social setting in which an individual meets another for the first time.

Experimenting stage ■ The stage of a relationship in which individuals begin to look for commonalities.

Phatic communication ■ Small talk.

Intensifying stage ■ The stage of a relationship in which individuals begin to disclose in a more personal manner.

Integrating stage ■ The stage of a relationship in which two individuals become a couple.

Bonding stage ■ The stage of a relationship that signifies to the outside world a commitment to maintain intimacy.

Differentiating stage ■ A relationship stage that occurs when one or more of the parties withholds or retreats from intimacy.

Circumscribing stage ■ A relationship stage in which the parties' communication with each other is significantly lessened.

Stagnating stage ■ A relationship stage in which communication disappears.

Integrating

In the **integrating stage,** the two individuals become a "couple." Outsiders to the relationship begin to identify the two as a "couple" or as "friends." The two have become so familiar with each other that they begin to speak their own language. They are often so synchronous that nonverbal signals communicate more between them than verbal signals.

Bonding

At this point, the parties in the dyad may want to publicly ritualize their movement into the **bonding stage.** Lovers unite through a marriage ceremony. Friends may create a different type of ritual to show their ultimate commitment to each other. For example, the notion of "blood brothers" emerged from the practice of two friends intermingling their blood as a physical sign of interpersonal commitment. Similarly, those who join sororities or fraternities speak of one another as "brother" and "sister" as a way to linguistically formalize a bonded relationship. Some religious groups also use family labels, such as "brother," "sister," or "father," to express their interpersonal bonds. In any case, the bonding stage signifies to the outside world a commitment to maintaining intimacy. At this point, the parties have worked out several critical issues in terms of the expected communication patterns of the relationship.

Differentiating

Rituals signify bonding and mark a commitment to maintain an intimate relationship.

If one or more parties begin to *withhold* or *retreat* from intimacy in a relationship, the relationship may enter the **differentiating stage.** It is often at this point that some of a partner's behavioral traits go from tolerable to annoying or when activities that used to be enjoyable are now something you simply endure. Instead of using "we" or "us," you may start saying "you" or "I." One of the major causes of relationship differentiation is lack of negotiation. Sometimes in our rush to develop relationships, we ignore some of our partner's behaviors because we don't want to appear too critical. If, however, you or your partner is unwilling to negotiate critical dialectic issues, that we discuss in Chapter 7, the relationship will inevitably move to the differentiating stage.

Circumscribing

If differentiation continues and the parties are still unwilling to renegotiate, then the relationship may move to the **circumscribing stage.** The most significant characteristic of this stage is that the parties' communication with each other is significantly lessened. Instead of communicating about critical issues, the issues are ignored or identified as "off limits." Ultimately, this lack of communication means significantly fewer expressions of commitment between the parties.

Stagnating

If this lack of communication continues, the parties quickly move to the **stagnating stage.** For the most part, communication disappears or becomes awkward or overly formal. Also, individuals will engage in virtually no activities together. They may continue to inhabit the same living space, but each acts as if communication with the other is a waste of time. Perhaps at some time in your life you have either received or given the "cold shoulder treatment" or the "silent treatment" as an indication of relational dissatisfaction; this is an early form of stagnating that can eventually spiral downward to the avoiding stage if not addressed.

Avoiding

When the relationship gets to the **avoiding stage,** each individual goes his or her own way or makes independent decisions without consulting or communicating with the other. What has been subtle avoidance now becomes more direct. One of the parties will move out, or if that is impossible, psychological avoidance becomes more direct. In the case of friends, one of the individuals may stop answering the phone or be too busy to get together.

Terminating

Ultimately, this spiral continues to the **terminating stage** if no significant intervention is attempted. Sometimes the termination is a relief; sometimes, however, it is the most painful experience imaginable. Ultimately, the communication in this stage focuses on all the partners' faults and problems and on what may happen in the future to either or both parties.

Knapp and Vangelisti's model describes the potential process that relationships may evolve through, but the process is not inevitable. Moreover, each dyad, and each individual in that dyad, has the opportunity to change the course of the relationship if he or she chooses. Each dyad is unique in the speed with which the stages are negotiated and the degree of success within that negotiation. It is also true that individuals in a dyad are often not in the same stage as their partner during the course of the relationship. The degree of relationship success or failure and the speed of the process are determined by the ability of the individuals in the dyad to negotiate the dialectics previously described.

While the stages of relational development are seen as exciting, stimulating, and satisfying, the stages of relational dissolution, or the "coming apart" phases of relationships, are more often characterized by anger, insecurity, and pain. The communication skills used by the partners during the dissolution phases significantly impact the effectiveness of the process and the ability to successfully engage in future intimate relationships. To achieve competent and effective communication, partners must be honest, empathetic, and adaptable to the constraints of the situation. Each partner must be willing to talk openly without accusation. As hard as this might sound, the more each partner represses his or her feelings or engages in hurtful, aggressive accusations, the more painful and long-lasting the consequences of the breakup.

The development, maintenance, and dissolution of relationships impact your everyday life, especially in terms of your friendships or romantic relationships. Many of you can testify to the excitement and subsequent pain of becoming good friends with someone in your class, dorm, neighborhood, or workplace, only to have the relationship end in disappointment. And you may also know the pain of a romantic relationship that did not last. Relationships are complex, and many factors play a role in why they dissolve. One factor that has been gaining significant attention in the last few years is the increase in dating violence. As we discuss in the box "Communication Counts in Your College Experience: Violence in Interpersonal Relationships," the causes of violence in relationships stem from a variety of issues related to self-esteem and family dynamics. But there are ways that romantic partners can create the building-blocks for long-term, successful romance.

Duck's Relational Dissolution Model

Duck's (1982) **relational dissolution model** provides another perspective with which to view the stages of relationship dissolution. Duck describes four types of behavior that individuals engage in when a relationship is ending.

INTRAPSYCHIC PHASE   Individuals must first come to terms with their sense of "grievance and distress" at the possibility of relational dissolution and at a partner's faults and weaknesses. Duck calls this the **intrapsychic phase** (*intra* meaning "within"). In this stage, partners will explore the costs and benefits of staying and leaving. They will review the relationship over and over in their minds and will engage in a sort of cost-benefit analysis, comparing the "costs" of the other partner's faults and weaknesses with the

Avoiding stage ■ A relationship stage in which parties go their separate ways.

Terminating stage ■ Occurs when no significant intervention is attempted at the avoiding stage.

Relational dissolution model ■ Identifies the intrapsychic, dyadic, social, and grave-dressing phases of relationship dissolution.

Intrapsychic phase ■ The stage in which an individual explores the costs and benefits of leaving a relationship.

COMMUNICATION COUNTS IN YOUR COLLEGE EXPERIENCE

Violence in Interpersonal Relationships

More than four in ten college students have been the victim of relationship violence by a partner, friend, or acquaintance, according to a study in 2008 titled "Relationship Violence Common in College," according to WebMD (www.webmd.com).

"All forms of relationship violence are prevalent among male and female college students; almost half of the students [studied] had experienced relationship violence at some point in their lives, more than one-third had experienced violence before college and one-quarter had experienced violence during college," writes researcher Christine M. Forke, MSN, CRNP, of the Children's Hospital of Philadelphia and colleagues in the July issue of *Archives of Pediatrics & Adolescent Medicine.*

In another article, "Rejection Sensitivity and Male Violence in Romantic Relationships," Downey, Feldman, and Ayduk (2005) discuss a propensity toward violence in romantic relationships called "rejection sensitivity." The authors suggest rejection sensitivity is the disposition to anxiously expect, readily perceive, and intensely react to rejection by significant others.

They suggest that rejection sensitivity may create vulnerability and enhance the chances of violence within intimate relationships. "Rejection-sensitive men may attempt to prevent anticipated rejection by reducing their investment in intimate relationships" or "they may become highly invested in intimate relationships in search of an unconditionally supportive partner. Their low threshold for perceiving and overreacting to rejection, however, heightens their risk of responding aggressively to their partners' negative or ambiguous behavior." The authors found that "among college men who reported relatively high investment in romantic relationships, anxious expectations of rejection predicted dating violence. Among men who reported relatively low investment in romantic relationships, anxious expectations of rejection predicted reduced involvement in discretionary close relationships with friends and romantic partners and, more generally, increased distress in and avoidance of social situations" (45).

So why does it seem that romantic relationships seem to be at higher risk for violence today?

Many researchers feel that early exposure to a violent environment is likely to lead to domestic violence situations later in life. In addition, feelings of insecurity, abandonment anxiety, and intimacy issues are also likely to plague these romantic connections.

So, what can be done to help relationships start on the right track? Consider these suggestions:

- Practice respect and appreciation for one another. Your partner probably does something every day that you can be thankful for, so just pay a bit of attention. When these positive things happen, express your thanks for what your partner does or says.
- Find the things you enjoy and engage in these together. Investigate new activities that you may enjoy sharing so that you can increase your options.
- Don't be afraid to apologize. In any relationship, we may, at times, hurt our partner's feelings or disappoint them. Expressing our regret when this occurs helps to create a trusting relationship.

Source: www.utexas.edu.

"benefits" of staying in the relationship. This is a sort of "what's in it for me" approach to analyzing the relationship.

DYADIC PHASE While the intrapsychic phase is an introspective, individualistic phase, the next step, the **dyadic phase,** involves the other partner. Partners confront each other, talk about the relationship's strengths and problems, and try to find ways to fix what is wrong. Sometimes this phase involves the parties sitting down together to calmly explore what is bothering them. At other times, the confrontation may be loaded with emotion, accusation, and insult.

SOCIAL PHASE The third phase, the **social phase,** involves talking with friends and family about the possibility or actuality of the dissolution. This social phase is a sort of test to see how others will react to the potential breakup. The partners will also explore what others feel should be the nature of the relationship with the "former" partner after they break up.

GRAVE-DRESSING PHASE Finally, Duck describes the last stage in the dissolution process as the **grave-dressing phase.** In this phase, partners must come to terms with their perceptions of the relationship, the problems that occurred, who was at fault, and how they should "remember" the relationship. This involves a sort of perception-checking of self and others in order to make sense of how and why the breakup occurred. Duck believes we must compare our feelings to others who are important to us to help confirm our decisions or our rationalizations about the relationship.

Dyadic phase ■ The stage in which partners confront one another, talk about the relationship's strengths and problems, and try to identify solutions to the problems.

Social phase ■ The stage in which partners discuss the possibility or actuality of dissolving the relationship with friends and family.

Grave-dressing phase ■ The stage in which each partner must come to terms with his or her perceptions of the relationship, its problems, and how to remember the relationship.

DEVELOPING RELATIONSHIPS BETWEEN PROFESSORS AND STUDENTS

Although friendships and romantic relationships are important in your college experience, your relationships with your professors are equally important. Cooper and Simonds (2003) adapt and apply Knapp's relational development model to teacher–student relationships. Teachers and students *initiate* relationships on the first day of class, when first impressions play an important role. So if you are a student who is in the habit of missing the first class, you may want to think again. You leave a first impression by your absence—especially if you have not contacted your professor ahead of time to explain your nonattendance.

Teachers and students also engage in *experimenting* as they develop relationships. This phase is earmarked by testing: Students test teachers to discern their expectations, while teachers test students to assess who they are, what they want from a class, and what might be the best teaching methods for reaching the students. After initiating and testing have been charted, teachers and students may *intensify* their relationships. No doubt you have had a teacher who has left a long-lasting impression on you. You probably developed a different level of intimacy with this teacher that permitted you both to get to know each other in a more personal and yet appropriate fashion. In short, you got to know this teacher as a person as well as an instructor, just as the teacher got to know you. This experience illustrates intensification well.

According to Cooper and Simonds (2003), while your friendship with a teacher may exist beyond your classroom interaction, eventually all teacher–student relationships deteriorate and dissolve. In other words, unlike other interpersonal relationships, teacher–student relationships have definitive endings because all courses or programs end. If the friendship continues beyond the course or program, the relationship has moved to a different level, but the teacher–student bond is no longer motivating the relationship. Others would argue that during the lifetime of this relationship, there is always recognition of this relational dialectic as fundamentally important to both parties. The box "Communication Counts in Your College Experience: Important Characteristics of a Positive Student–Teacher Relationship" helps identify some communication characteristics that will help you find a teacher with whom you can develop a mentoring or interpersonally warm relationship.

COMMUNICATION COUNTS IN YOUR COLLEGE EXPERIENCE

Important Characteristics of a Positive Student–Teacher Relationship

Here is a series of questions that will help you determine if your professor has the characteristics that will enable you to have a positive, helpful mentoring relationship with him or her:

1. **Does the professor truly listen?** Even if we can hear, we do not necessarily listen. Good mentors know how to actively listen, which means they are involved in the communication process and refuse to be distracted; they focus on you and can empathize with you. A true mentor is someone who listens, frequently asks questions, encourages you to say more, paraphrases your comments, and clarifies your comments by posing questions. Listeners will be nonverbally supportive; they will typically make eye contact, smile, nod their head, and lean forward.

2. **Is the professor immediate?** *Immediacy* refers to both nonverbal and verbal behaviors that indicate that one is approachable, friendly, warm, and available for communication (see Andersen 1979). Therefore, immediate professors are people who strike you as likable and approachable. They may, for example, regularly invite students to visit during office hours or stop by as needed. Take them up on the offer!

3. **Does the professor appropriately self-disclose?** *Self-disclosure* means telling people something about yourself that they would not otherwise know. Professors who disclose appropriate information about themselves are more likely to be open to being known and getting to know others.

4. **Is the professor credible?** According to Cooper and Simonds (2003), credibility consists of competence and character. In other words, a credible professor demonstrates expert knowledge in a given field and, at the same time, is someone you perceive as trustworthy, ethical, and concerned for others' well-being. A good mentor is someone who has the knowledge you need and who has your best interests at heart.

5. **Does the professor use power appropriately?** Teachers possess considerable power in their ability to influence students (Barraclough & Stewart 1992). Research demonstrates that teachers can use different types of power, which, in turn, impact student learning (see McCroskey & Richmond 1983; Richmond, McCroskey, Kearney, & Plax 1987). To have an effective mentoring relationship with a professor, you need someone who will advise you—not dominate you.

CONNECTING GENDER AND INTERPERSONAL COMMUNICATION

Communication Between Women and Men

Our discussion of the differences in communication between women and men thus far in this text might suggest that women and men inhabit different worlds of feelings, thoughts, and behaviors. Many researchers have suggested that is, in fact, the case. We have reported on the work of Deborah Tannen (1990), which suggests that boys and girls grow up in "different worlds of words" and that this difference significantly impacts communication styles in adults. Boys, for example, learn to play with other boys in groups where the goal is to see who can be at the top of the status hierarchy; they show their status by being "better than" the other boys. Girls, by contrast, are more likely to play in smaller groups or pairs where the goal is to see how they can be more "like" each other. While boys work through *status* issues in their play, girls are more focused on *connection*. Adults who have grown up in a world focused on status may attempt to manage conflict by showing their knowledge and experience as "experts" who have all the information needed to "solve" a problem. For men, intimacy develops from what partners "do" with each other. That may mean responding to their female partners by trying to "fix" a problem.

Having grown up in a world of connection, adult females may attempt to manage conflict by showing how their feelings and experiences are similar to another. Women tend to focus more on feelings to manage conflict while men tend to focus more on facts. Women rarely want to be told how to "fix" a problem; instead they want to share with their partner and to hear his feelings in order to develop closeness and intimacy. So who's right and who's wrong here? Neither. But to understand each other and to manage conflict successfully, both women and men need to understand these differences in style.

Gendered Relationship Language

Women and men, then, "speak" different language and develop relationships differently. Both of these approaches to conversation and relationships are a means to the same end. Both status (male) and connection (female) can be used to get things done by talking. Most meaning in conversation does not reside in the words spoken but is filled in by the person listening. Yet it is important to understand that women and men often have very different reasons for carrying on a conversation.

Boys play in a group as a way to improve their individual status.

For men and women, relationship development begins with different reasons for conversation. Men tend to converse to impart information (report talk); women converse to indicate relationship (rapport talk). Women are also more likely to exchange personal and relational talk than men. For example, in your experience, is a man or a woman more likely to talk about a troubling experience? Who is more likely to share a secret? Who is more likely to give advice? Who is more likely to challenge an expert in a public forum? If you answered "woman" to the first two questions and "man" to the second two, you can understand the differences between rapport talk (women) and report talk (men). Understanding how women and men engage in conversations and use language is the first step to understanding relationship development between the sexes.

Other distinguishing characteristics of male and female language include vocabulary, adjective use, and use of questions and hedges. Stewart, Cooper, and Friedley (1986) report that women, in general, have a larger number of words to describe things that interest them. For example, women use a broader array of words to describe colors and tend to use a broader array of adjectives to describe things. Women are much more likely to use words like *adorable, charming,* and *lovely* (53). Women also tend to "qualify" their language with the use of tag questions ("don't you think?" or "isn't it?") and hedges ("I wonder if" or "kind of"). These qualifiers, according to Stewart, Cooper, and Friedley, are used more by women because they have been socialized to believe that assertive language is "unladylike" or "unfeminine" (54).

In the English language, the male pronoun has historically been used to include both male and female referents, such as in *mankind, he, his*, and so on. The problem with the masculine pronoun as all-inclusive is that it isn't. When we hear, "The professor should treat all of his students fairly," we do not "see" both men and women professors; we "see" a male professor. The female professor becomes invisible. Man-linked terms are interpreted as male, not as "all." Sexist language conveys that women are less valued than men.

Gender bias in language occurs in the titles we use to address men and women. Are all men to be addressed as "Mr."? How do you address a woman? Does the fact that she is married matter in the form of address used? Should it matter? In our culture, it is still common to see a woman change her name when she gets married. This practice originated during a time when a woman was considered the legal property of a man—either her father or her husband. The use of "Mrs." to refer to a woman also dates back to a time when women were defined by their relationships to men. The use of "Ms." has been an attempt to move away from defining a woman by her relationship. For some, however, the term "Ms." is associated with "feminism," which has both positive and negative connotations, depending on your point of view.

Another way women become invisible in language is the use of masculine forms for certain titles, such as *mailman, fireman, policeman, workman, chairman,* and so on. When the female is invisible in our language, the implication is that male is "normal" and female is "other." Another common form of biased language is the use of nonparallel terms such as "man and wife" or "male students and coeds." Gender bias also shows up in language when we have different terms for males and females in the same professions, such as "actor and actress" or "tailor and seamstress" or "waiter and waitress." These are examples of how specifically female terms create a secondary category for the female profession. Men, it is implied, are the "real" thing; women are inauthentic copies.

Using these sexist terms creates artificial barriers where none exist. Engaging in direct, open discussion can reduce the frustration and misunderstanding that prevents successful relationship development. For women, this means recognizing that solutions to a problem are worth discussing. For men, this means discussing feelings in addition to solving problems. For both women and men, it means recognizing that despite the "world of words" we grow up in, we can negotiate relationships that share meaning. And it also means recognizing that neither women nor men are "right" when it comes to communicating interpersonally.

CONNECTING CULTURE AND INTERPERSONAL COMMUNICATION

Like the cultural differences in communication between women and men, there are communication style differences among individuals from diverse cultures both within and outside the United States. Assumptions, beliefs, and perceptions about communication and conflict must be recognized. For example, the United States is characterized as a **low-context culture,** where self-expression is valued and messages are primarily communicated verbally. In contrast, Asian cultures such as in China, Japan, Korea, and Malaysia are characterized as **high-context cultures,** where more value is placed on indirectness and social harmony and where nonverbal aspects of communication play a much more significant role (Gudykunst & Lee 2002; Hall 1976).

There is never only "one right way" to send a message, yet we often evaluate another's message based on "our" way of communicating. The more we know about the communication style of someone from another culture, the more opportunities we have for successfully interpreting a message's meaning and for responding appropriately to the other. It is important to understand that differences exist and to remain adaptable, especially when conflict occurs, as we discuss in Chapter 7.

Additionally, cultures share different values, perceptions, and attitudes (Martin & Nakayama 2001). These orientations inform interpersonal communication. For example, different cultures emphasize the role of the family differently. The movie *My Big Fat Greek Wedding* humorously portrays the culturally based family perspectives that can complicate romantic relationships. In this movie, the bride is enmeshed in her large, culture-bound

Culture Counts

Low-context culture ■ Culture in which individual self-expression is valued, and messages are primarily communicated verbally (e.g., the United States).

High-context culture ■ Culture in which more value is placed on indirectness and social harmony, and nonverbal aspects of communication play a significant role (e.g., China, Japan, Korea, Malaysia).

COMMUNICATION COUNTS IN YOUR COLLEGE EXPERIENCE

Intercultural Romantic Relationships

According to Martin and Nakayama (2001), there are similarities and differences in how romantic relationships are viewed in different cultures. The similarities across cultures include the importance of openness, involvement, shared nonverbal meanings, and assessment of the relationship. The differences, according to the authors, are related to distinctions between individualist and collectivist cultures. In the United States, for example, students focus on physical attraction, passion, love, and autonomy as important elements in romantic relationships. These characteristics reflect our individualist U.S. culture. In contrast, many other cultural groups focus on the importance of family acceptance of a potential partner, reflecting a more collectivist orientation. In collectivist cultures, the romantic partner's lives are likely to be much more integrated into the larger family group.

Martin and Nakayama suggest that too much individualistic orientation among Americans can be problematic when trying to balance the needs of two individuals in the relationship. An extreme individualistic perspective makes it hard for either partner to justify sacrifice or accommodation to the other. Dion and Dion (1991) suggest that the fundamental conflict of partners trying to reconcile the need for personal freedom with marital obligations is more difficult in relationships where one or both partners has an extreme individualistic orientation. These authors also suggest that individuals with an extreme individualist orientation may experience less love, care, trust, and physical attraction with their partners in their romantic relationships. In collectivist cultures, these types of relational problems are much less common.

In cross-cultural dating and romantic relationships, the degree of independence versus interdependence may be more problematic because of the difference in an individualistic versus a collectivist cultural orientation. Do you believe that cross-cultural romantic relationships can work? What recommendations would you give to an American who is beginning to date someone from Japan? What recommendations would you give to someone from Indonesia who is beginning to date an American?

family in which all activities (work and play) involve all members of the immediate and extended family. In contrast, the groom comes from a small family in which ethnicity, religion, and extended family play a minimal role in the relationships among mother, father, and son. The ways in which these families "come to know each other" involve comedic misperceptions, misunderstandings, and social blunders. Because of our enculturation, we are likely to see romantic relationships differently than people with other cultural backgrounds (Dion & Dion 1996; Quiles 2003). As the box "Communication Counts in Your College Experience: Intercultural Romantic Relationships" points out, there are similarities and differences in how romantic relationships are viewed among different cultures.

BECOMING A COMPETENT AND ETHICAL INTERPERSONAL COMMUNICATOR IN COLLEGE, CAREER, AND LIFE

Because interpersonal relationships have the greatest meaning for our personal lives and for our professional success, it is essential that we understand the ethical implications and consequences of our communication in these relationships. Because these are the most personal relationships we develop, and because we take the greatest risks in sharing ourselves with others, there also exists the greatest danger in being hurt or in hurting others. When strangers lie to us, we feel anger, but when our close friends or family members lie to us, the hurt is much deeper and lasts longer. We feel betrayed.

Ethical interpersonal communication is competent communication. When we look at another and see a unique human being who deserves consideration and care, we take the first step toward ethical interpersonal communication. When we are willing to engage in dialogue with another and to take responsibility for our communication, we increase the potential for meaningful and satisfying relationships. The foundation of ethical interpersonal communication is honest, authentic dialogue. **Authentic dialogue** (Buber 1970) is characterized by *empathy* and *confirmation*. It involves a willingness to become fully involved with the other, a belief in the equality of each participant, and a climate of supportive communication. Authentic dialogue adds a level of intimacy that helps develop our relationships in mutually satisfying ways. Finally, authentic dialogue tolerates difference and disagreement as part of

Authentic dialogue ■ Dialogue characterized by a willingness to become fully involved with the other, a belief in the equality of each participant, and a climate of supportive communication.

the process of expanding knowledge of self and others. Strong friendships, strong life partnerships, strong workplaces, and strong communities depend on interpersonal relationships that are based on shared common ground and the ability to dialogue.

Ethical and competent communication starts with you. You must explore your attraction to the other and your motivations and goals within the relationship. You must understand what motivates you within the relationship and what motivates the other. Ethical and competent communicators balance their own motives with others' motives. You must communicate effectively and appropriately with the other and remain flexible and adaptable as the relationship develops.

Whether you are a traditional student entering college right after high school or a non-traditional, mature learner, successfully negotiating the college environment necessitates understanding and applying the principles discussed in this chapter in a number of "new" interpersonal relationships. No matter what type of educational institution you are in (e.g., community college, private four-year college, public university), one of the relationships that you must negotiate is the one between you and each of your instructors. It is hard to think of these relationships as "intimate"! Yet if you are willing to share a little of yourself with your instructors, your college success, and particularly your learning, will increase (Chen 2000). This doesn't mean you should follow your instructors around every day or ask them deeply personal questions, but you should look for opportunities to develop mentoring and mutually respectful, empathetic relationships with them. Gardner and Jewler (2003) advise students to find a mentor or someone who expresses a special interest and offers meaningful support. But how do you do this? How do you develop an appropriate relationship with a professor so that you can gain the most from your academic experience?

There will be times when you need clarification and additional information on an assignment, a test, or a project. While some of your classes will take place in large lecture halls, many will be in smaller classrooms, and the climate of the class will be interactive and involve dialogue and experiential activities. You can negotiate the interpersonal communication principles we have discussed in these classes and in conversation with your instructor outside of class.

If you are a college student living away from home, you will need to negotiate new relationships with roommates. For many people, this is one of the most difficult relationships they experience in college, while others find friends for life. How you negotiate these relationships in the first weeks of your first semester will be critical to your success in many of your other relationships during college. Remember, you can control your communication and your response to others. You have some of the responsibility in the relationship's outcome. Developing effective and appropriate communication strategies in your college relationships is the best practice you could possibly have for relationships later in life.

Successfully negotiating relationships with professors and classmates directly impacts your college experience.

COMMUNICATION COUNTS IN YOUR CAREER

Randy Pausch's Advice from The Last Lecture

Randy Pausch was a professor of Computer Science, Human Computer Interaction, and Design at Carnegie Mellon University. From 1988 to 1997 he taught at the University of Virginia. He was an award-winning teacher and researcher and worked with Adobe, Google, Electronic Arts (EA), and Walt Disney Imagineering. He also pioneered the nonprofit Alice project. (Alice is an innovative 3-D environment that teaches programming to young people via storytelling and interactive game playing.) He also cofounded The Entertainment Technology Center (ETC) at Carnegie Mellon with Don Marinelli. (ETC is the premier professional graduate program for interactive entertainment as it is applies across a variety of fields.)

On September 18, 2007, Randy Pausch stepped in front of an audience of 400 people at Carnegie Mellon University to deliver a last lecture called "Really Achieving Your Childhood Dreams." With slides of his CT scans beaming out to the audience, Randy told his audience about the cancer that was devouring his pancreas and that ultimately claimed his life on July 24, 2008. On the stage that day, Randy was youthful, energetic, handsome, and often cheerfully and darkly funny. He seemed invincible. But this was a brief moment, as he himself acknowledged. Randy's lecture has become a phenomenon, as has the book he wrote based on the same principles, celebrating the dreams we all strive to make realities. To see Randy Pausch's Last Lecture, go to http://www.youtube.com/watch?v=ji5_MqicxSo.

Randy's Last Lecture focused on all of the amazing things he was grateful for in his life, including his parents, colleagues he worked with, students he remembered, opportunities that came his way, and all of the childhood dreams he dreamed and then accomplished. As the website that bears its name suggests (www.lastlecture.com) "*The Last Lecture* goes beyond the now-famous lecture to inspire us all to live each day of our lives with purpose and joy." And as Randy Pausch said, "We cannot change the cards we are dealt, just how we play the hand." How will you "play the hand you are dealt?"

Interpersonal validation ■ When someone offers to help us, expresses interest in us, or supports us.

Employers today want employees who can engage in effective and appropriate communication with coworkers, supervisors, customers, and many others. What do you want in your professional relationships? You will spend a good deal of your professional life interacting with others in the workplace. Many of you will spend more hours at work than at home. The most critical interpersonal skills needed to negotiate the numerous relationships in the workplace are the same ones that are important for ensuring college success. Does intimacy play a role in relationships at work? Yes. When you are willing to appropriately and effectively share yourself with coworkers and supervisors, ask for information and assistance, and stand up for your beliefs and values and allow others to do the same, you will develop the communication skills needed to ensure success in your career and in your long-term relationships.

In order to enjoy a successful college or workplace experience, you must develop relationships with your peers. Researchers who interviewed college students (Terenzini et al. 1993) learned that receiving interpersonal validation from friends and other students is particularly important to staying in and succeeding in college. **Interpersonal validation** occurs when someone offers to help us, expresses interest in us, or supports us. As we have already seen, listening is one way to offer such support. By listening to our peers, both at school and at work, we offer them support and develop relationships that will provide us the opportunity to be listened to when we need support. Perhaps your college has special programs, clubs, or activities that encourage you to interact with other students. If so, make use of these special opportunities and learn to develop an empathetic ear. By listening to others, you will help them and help yourself. Moreover, you will begin to develop skills that are important in your relationships with your family, life partners, and employers. Check out the box "Communication Counts in Your Career: Randy Pausch's Advice from The Last Lecture" for an example of one person who truly lived his childhood dreams; cherished his relationships with family, friends, students, and colleagues; and exemplifies the ethical and competent communicator.

SUMMARY

Interpersonal communication can be defined as another communication context involving two persons in face-to-face interaction or, more appropriately, as a developmental process involving increasing intimacy in developing a unique, personal set of rules for interaction with another. In this chapter, we have identified concepts important to your understanding of effective interpersonal communication:

- Increasing the intimacy within a relationship involves moving from cultural-level rules to sociological-level rules to psychological-level rules for appropriate behavior in the relationship.
- *Intimacy* refers to our risk-taking within the relationship as we self-disclose more feelings, beliefs, values, dreams, and expectations for the other, the relationship, and ourselves.
- We are attracted to certain others based on physical characteristics, similar attitudes and values, similar activities, and physical proximity.
- Abraham Maslow developed a hierarchy of needs that suggests we are motivated by various needs to create and maintain relationships; these needs include physiological, safety and security, love and belonging, self-esteem, knowledge and understanding, aesthetic, and self-actualization.
- William Schutz identified three basic needs that motivate individuals: affection, inclusion, and a degree of control and predictability in our lives.
- Relationships develop through five stages as intimacy is increased: initiating, experimenting, intensifying, integrating, and bonding.
- Relationship dissolution also involves five stages: differentiating, circumscribing, stagnating, avoiding, and terminating.
- Gender and cultural factors, including our use of language, impact how we develop relationships and what we expect from ourselves and from the other in the relationship.
- Ethical issues play a critical role in interpersonal relationships because of the increased risks attached to both parties when intimacy increases between the partners.
- To create and maintain effective interpersonal relationships, the partners must be more sensitive to and flexible in responding to the unique needs and expectations of the self and the other.
- Ethical and effective interpersonal relationships are characterized by open, continuous dialogue in the give-and-take between the partners.

QUESTIONS FOR DISCUSSION

1. What do you think are the most important "intimacy behaviors" between close friends? Roommates? Lovers?
2. Do you think it is possible to end a relationship without engaging in angry accusations? Can "old lovers" become "new friends"?
3. Consider the "little white lie" and its role in relationship development and dissolution. Are we more apt to tell them during the first stages of relationship development or when the relationship is more fully developed? Are little white lies ever appropriate? Why or why not?

EXERCISES

1. Think of several relationships that are important to you. Describe the nature of intimacy in each relationship. What strategies do you use to develop intimacy within these relationships? How do you maintain that intimacy? Why do you think these relationships differ in how intimacy is developed and maintained?
2. Using Miller and Steinberg's three levels of "rules" for interpersonal communication, think of a primary relationship that you are currently involved in (i.e., son or daughter, employee, parent, student, etc.) and give examples of cultural, sociological, and psychological rules that govern your communication and behavior.

KEY TERMS

Aesthetic needs   107
Attraction   104
Authentic dialogue   118
Avoiding stage   113
Bonding stage   112
Circumscribing stage   112
Cultural rules   102
Developmental approach   102
Differentiating stage   112
Dyadic phase   114
Experimenting stage   111

Grave-dressing phase   114
High-context culture   117
Impersonal communication   102
Impression management   109
Initiating stage   111
Intensifying stage   111
Integrating stage   112
Interpersonal (dyadic) communication   102
Interpersonal validation   120
Intimacy   103

Intrapsychic phase   113
Johari Window   109
Knowledge and understanding needs   107
Love and belonging needs   106
Low-context culture   117
Phatic communication   111
Physiological needs   106
Psychological rules   103
Relational dissolution model   113
Safety and security needs   106

REFERENCES

Adams, R. G., Blieszner, R., and DeVries, B. 2000. Definitions of friendship in the third age: Age, gender, and study location effects. *Journal of Aging Studies* 14(1):117–134.

Altman, I. and Taylor, D. A. (1973) *Social Penetration*, New York: Holst, Rinehart, Winston.

Andersen, J. 1979. The relationship between teacher immediacy and teaching effectiveness. In *Communication yearbook 3*, ed. D. Nimmo, 543–561. New Brunswick, NJ: Transaction Books.

Barraclough, R. A., and Stewart, R. A. 1992. Power and control: Social science perspectives. In *Power in the classroom: Communication, control, and concern*, eds. V. P. Richmond and J. C. McCroskey, 1–18. Hillsdale, NJ: Erlbaum.

Buber, M. 1970. *I and thou*. Trans. W. Kaufmann. NY: Scribner.

Chen, Z. J. 2000. The impact of teacher-student relationships on college students' learning: Exploring organizational cultures in the classroom. *Communication Quarterly* 48(2):76–84.

Collier, M. J. 1996. Communication competence problematics in ethnic friendships. *Communication Monographs* 63(4): 314–337.

Cooper, P. J., and Simonds, C. J. 2003. *Communication for the classroom teacher*. 7th ed. Boston: Allyn & Bacon.

Dion, K. K., and Dion, K. L. 1991. Psychological individualism and romantic love. *Journal of Social Behavior and Personality* 6:17–33.

Dion, K. K., and Dion, K. L. 1996. Cultural perspectives on romantic love. *Personal Relationships* 3:5–19.

Duck, S. W. 1982. A topography of relationship disengagement and dissolution. In *Personal relationships 4: Dissolving personal relationships*, ed. S. W. Duck, 1–30. London: Academic Press.

Elbedour, S., Shulman, S., and Peri, K. 1997. Adolescent intimacy: A cross-cultural study. *Journal of Cross-Cultural Psychology* 28:5.

Gardner, J. N., and Jewler, A. J. 2003. *Your college experience: Strategies for success*. 5th ed. Belmont, CA: Wadsworth.

Goffman, E. (1959). The presentation of self in everyday life. Anchor Books.

Goodwin, R., and Lee, I. 1994. Taboo topics among Chinese and English friends: A cross-cultural comparison. *Journal of Cross-Cultural Psychology* 25(3):325.

Gudykunst, W. B., and Lee, C. M. 2002. Cross-cultural communication theories. In *Handbook of international and intercultural communication*. 2nd ed., eds. W. B. Gudykunst and B. Moody, 25–50. Thousand Oaks, CA: Sage.

Hall, E. T. 1976. *Beyond culture*. Garden City, NY: Doubleday/Anchor.

Knapp, M., and Vangelisti, A. L. 1992. *Interpersonal communication and human relationships*. 2nd ed. Boston: Allyn & Bacon.

Luft, J. (1970). *Group processes; an introduction to group dynamics (2nd ed.)*. Palo Alto, California: National Press Books.

Malinowski, B. 1923. The problem of meaning in primitive languages. In *The meaning of meaning: A study of the influence of language upon thought and the science of symbolism*, eds. C. K. Ogden and I. A. Richards, 451–510. London: Routledge & Kegan Paul.

Martin, J. N., and Nakayama, T. K. 2001. *Experiencing intercultural communication: An introduction*. Mountain View, CA: Mayfield.

Maslow, A. H. 1970. *Motivation and personality*. 2nd ed. New York: Harper & Row.

McCroskey, J. C., and Richmond, V. P. 1983. Power in the classroom I: Teacher and student perceptions. *Communication Education* 32:175–184.

Meyer, L. H., Park, H., Grento-Scheyer, M., Schwartz, L. S., and Harry, B., eds. 1998. *Making friends: The Influences of culture and development*. Baltimore, MD: Paul H. Brookes.

Miller, G. R., and Steinberg, M. 1975. *Between people: A new analysis of interpersonal communication*. Chicago: Science Research Associates.

Novak A. A., ed. 1993. *Friendships and community connections between people with and without developmental disabilities*. Baltimore, MD: Paul H. Brookes.

Quiles, J. A. 2003. Romantic behaviors of university students: A cross-cultural and gender analysis in Puerto Rico and the United States. *College Student Journal* 37(3):354–367. Retrieved February 3, 2004, from www.findarticles.com/cf_dls/m0FCR/3_37/108836901/p1/article.jhtml.

Richmond, V. P., McCroskey, J. C., Kearney, P., and Plax, T. G. 1987. Power in the classroom VII: Linking behavior alteration techniques to cognitive learning. *Communication Education* 36:1–12.

Schutz, W. 1958. *Firo: A three-dimensional theory of interpersonal behavior*. New York: Holt, Rinehart & Winston.

Stewart, L. P., Cooper, P. I., & Friedley, S. A. (1986). Communication between the sexes: Sex differences and sex-role relationships. Scottdale, AZ: Gorsuch Scarisbrick.

Tannen, D. 1990. *You just don't understand: Women and men in conversation*. New York: Balantine.

Terenzini, P. T., Rendon, L. I., Upcraft, M. L., Millar, S. B., Allison, K. W., Gregg, P. L., & Jalomo, R. (1993, May). The transition to college: Diverse students, diverse stories. Paper presented at the Association for Institutional Research Forum, Chicago.

Urban Institute. February 2000. Millions still facing homelessness in a booming economy. Retrieved January 28, 2004, from www.urban.org/url.cfm? ID=900050.

You, H. S., and Malley-Morrison, K. 2000. Young adult attachment styles and intimate relationships with close friends: A cross-cultural study of Korean and Caucasian Americans. *Journal of Cross-Cultural Psychology* 31(4):528–534.

CHAPTER

7 Practicing Effective Interpersonal Communication

LEARNING OUTCOMES After reading this chapter, you will have:

the **Knowledge** to. . .

and the **Skills** to. . .

ACKNOWLEDGING THE "REALITY" OF RELATIONSHIPS, page 126

Understand the that there are no "perfect" relationships.

- Strive to develop positive and healthy relationships with others.

UNDERSTANDING INTERPERSONAL COMMUNICATION DIALECTICS, page 126

Be aware of the various dialectics that impact interpersonal communication relationships.

- Evaluate whether a relationship is complementary (based on differences) or symmetrical (based on similarity).
- Assess the level of independence, dependence, and interdependence of your communication relationships.
- Determine if you and others are exchanging confirming, disconfirming, and rejection messages.
- Work to create supportive rather than defensive communication climates.
- Gauge the levels of assertiveness, nonassertiveness, and aggressiveness in your communication relationships.

- Consider the amounts of interaction, domination, and passivity in your communication relationships.
- Be proactive in managing dialectics in your communication relationships.

APPLYING INTERPERSONAL DIALECTICS TO FAMILIES, page 129

Relate interpersonal communication dialectics to your interactions with others in varying contexts.

- Facilitate positive and supportive communication in your family.
- Be honest, open, and trustworthy in your friendships.
- Open your mind to try new experiences and form new friendships in college.
- Be a responsible and respectful member of your community.

MANAGING CONFLICT IN INTERPERSONAL RELATIONSHIPS, page 136

Learn how to manage conflict in interpersonal relationships.

- Realize that conflict is inevitable even in healthy interpersonal relationships.
- Control your emotions when expressing disagreement in intimate interpersonal relationships.

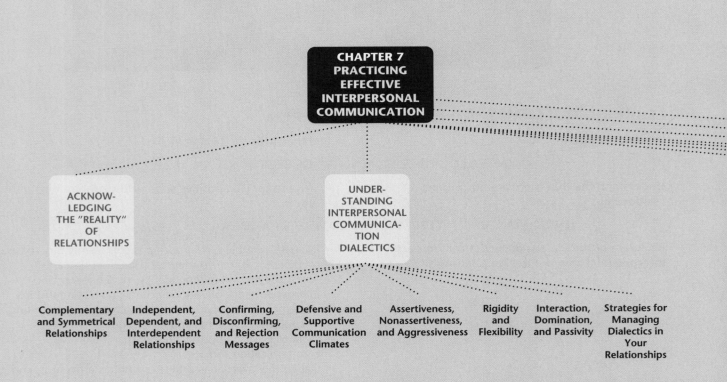

- Deal with conflict openly and honestly.
- Use conflict constructively to resolve issues.
- Avoid destructive conflict.
- Employ a conflict management style that balances concern for self with concern for others.

CREATING MORE ASSERTIVE RELATIONSHIPS, page 140

Discover how to be more self-assured in your relationships.

- Be positive, firm, confident, and involved in your interpersonal relationships.

BUILDING COMPETENT AND ETHICAL RELATIONSHIPS IN COLLEGE, CAREER, AND LIFE, page 141

Become a capable and moral relational partner.

- Use rhetorical sensitivity to adapt your message to the people, place, and time of the communication situation.
- Practice using confirming messages with those around you.

APPLYING INTERPERSONAL DIALECTICS TO FAMILIES

APPLYING INTERPERSONAL DIALECTICS TO FRIENDSHIPS

APPLYING INTERPERSONAL DIALECTICS TO COLLEGE

APPLYING INTERPERSONAL DIALECTICS TO COMMUNITIES

MANAGING CONFLICT INTERPERSONAL RELATIONSHIPS

CREATING MORE ASSERTIVE RELATIONSHIPS

BUILDING COMPETENT AND ETHICAL RELATIONSHIPS IN COLLEGE, CAREER, AND LIFE

Intimacy and Conflict

The Value of Conflict

Pseudoconflict, Destructive Conflict, and Constructive Conflict

Conflict Management Styles

ACKNOWLEDGING THE "REALITY" OF RELATIONSHIPS

Because interpersonal relationships are so important to us—whether within our families, friendships, intimate partnerships, or workplaces—many of us spend our lives searching for information that will help us create the "perfect" relationship. Go into any bookstore and you will find entire sections dedicated to books that will help us attract the perfect partner, develop lifelong friendships, or deal with a nasty boss. Television sitcoms show us "life" in an enormous variety of "normal" or "dysfunctional" relationships, depending on your point of view. One of the most recent phenomena to hit television is the so-called reality show where seemingly random strangers are stuck together in one situation or another and must "survive" the season. Have you ever noticed, though, that the purpose of the show is never to have the strangers develop positive, healthy interpersonal relationships? Such shows find every way possible to create competition, jealousy, conflict, and dissatisfaction among the participants. And if the survival of strangers together isn't bad enough, you can now potentially find and marry the man or woman of your dreams—all on television. Is the ultimate goal of these shows to find true love and long-lasting happiness in a committed partnership? Most of us don't believe so—especially when the title of the show is something like *How to Marry a Millionaire*.

Yet despite reality shows dominating in the media, healthy and long-lasting interpersonal relationships in a variety of contexts are possible. In order to develop and maintain these healthy relationships, however, we must understand how to balance a number of interpersonal dialectics, which is the focus of this chapter. Look at the box "Communication Counts in Your Life: The Spiritual Child" for a metaphor for how we develop the most positive relationships.

UNDERSTANDING INTERPERSONAL COMMUNICATION DIALECTICS

If it is to survive, each relationship must work out many **dialectics**—tension or opposition between interacting forces or elements. Every relationship must contend with several issues, or dialectics, in the negotiation of communication between the parties.

Complementary and Symmetrical Relationships

Dialectics ■ Tension or opposition between interacting forces or elements.

Complementary relationships ■ Relationships based on difference; each person brings characteristics that balance the characteristics of a relational partner.

The first issue is whether the relationship will be complementary or symmetrical in nature. **Complementary relationships** are those that are based on difference; each person brings characteristics that balance or complement those of the other. For example, you may be very logical and systematic in how you study for tests or complete assignments. You create a schedule or a checklist and mark off each task as you complete it. You begin several days before the assignment is due. Your best friend, roommate, or relational partner, however, may like to spend considerable time thinking about how to best understand the material. She may work on many assignments or tasks at the same time. At the last

---

COMMUNICATION COUNTS IN YOUR LIFE

The Spiritual Child

John Stewart, author of *Bridges, Not Walls,* uses the metaphor of the "spiritual child" to describe the process of creating and maintaining a relationship. When we meet someone for the first time, the relationship is like the birth of a child. The parents of the child are the ones who control whether the child will grow and develop into a healthy adult. All children must be fed, clothed, loved, and nurtured if they are to reach adulthood in good health. In this way, each partner in the relationship is responsible for providing what the child needs to survive. Both parties must take the time and energy required by the child. If the child is stimu-

lated, the result is a happy, growing, healthy relationship. If the child is ignored, lacks care, is confronted by aggression and disconfirmation, or is always being criticized, the relationship will stagnate and suffer and may ultimately fade away and die. In other words, communication about and to this child determines the relationship's growth, health, and longevity. Consider a relationship that is important to you. How would you describe the health of this "spiritual child"? Begin by thinking about how you communicate with the other "parent" of this child. What communication patterns can you identify?

minute, she pulls it all together and finishes the assignment. The relationship is complementary because each of you balances out the strengths and weaknesses of the other as you interact, live, or work together.

Symmetrical relationships are based on similarity; the individuals share traits, interests, and approaches to communication that are essentially alike. Perhaps you and your best friend share the same idea of what constitutes a "real" vacation: throw some clothes together, jump in the car, and drive until you get to someplace interesting. Or perhaps you both like to sit down and thoroughly plan where you'll go and what you'll see.

Independent, Dependent, and Interdependent Relationships

A second issue is the nature of independence, dependence, or interdependence the parties will have. In **independent relationships**, partners live separate and disconnected lives. In other words, they have different hobbies or interests and they may take separate vacations. Should the relationship terminate, the partners would not be dramatically impacted by the loss. In **dependent relationships**, partners rely so much on each other that their identities are enmeshed. One of the partners may not be able to make any decision without consulting the other. Should the relationship terminate, the partners would lose essential support and face an identity crisis. Parties in **interdependent relationships** rely on each other and possess mutual influence and importance, but they are not so dependent on the other that they cannot make independent decisions when warranted. Should an interdependent relationship terminate, the partners would feel the loss keenly but have sufficient personal identity to rebuild.

Confirming, Disconfirming, and Rejection Messages

A third key issue or dialectic involves the routine types of relational messages that constitute the ongoing relationships between the parties. The individuals may communicate through disconfirming, confirming, or rejection messages. **Disconfirming messages** deny a relational partner's value by refusing to acknowledge the partner's presence and the importance of the partner's communication. Messages can be disconfirming in many ways. One person might simply ignore the other or change the subject in the middle of a conversation.

Confirming messages, by contrast, value the partner's presence and contributions. We send confirming messages when we look directly at another, nod in response to a message, ask for additional information, or share a similar experience. **Rejection messages** acknowledge but do not fully accept the partner's presence and communication, such as when one person calls another's contribution "stupid" or "nonsense."

Messages possess two important characteristics: *effectiveness* and *appropriateness* (Spitzberg & Cupach 1984). Effective messages accomplish the communication's intended goal, while appropriate messages demonstrate responsiveness to the message's relational and contextual aspects. While some messages lack one or the other of these characteristics, rhetorically sensitive messages communicate both effectively and appropriately.

Defensive and Supportive Communication Climates

Related to effectiveness versus responsiveness is a fourth dialectic concerning the type of atmosphere that is maintained between the parties and that is important to the dyad. The atmosphere may be defensive or supportive. A **defensive climate** is an atmosphere in which at least one of the partners feels threatened and seeks to protect him or herself from attack. Defensiveness usually develops if a relational partner behaves in an evaluative, controlling, manipulative, uninvolved, superior, or dogmatic manner. One of the most common examples of defensiveness in a relational atmosphere occurs when one or both partners show extreme jealousy. Extremely jealous

Your success in college depends on your willingness to use confirming responses to others.

Symmetrical relationships ■ Relationships based on similarity; both individuals share traits, interests, and approaches to communication.

Independent relationships ■ Relationships in which the partners live separate and disconnected lives.

Dependent relationships ■ Relationships in which the partners rely so much on one another that their identities are enmeshed with one another.

Interdependent relationships ■ Relationships in which the partners rely on one another but are not so dependent that they cannot make independent decisions when warranted.

Disconfirming messages ■ Messages that deny the value of a relational partner by refusing to acknowledge his or her presence and communication.

Confirming messages ■ Messages that value the partner's presence and contributions.

Rejection messages ■ Messages that acknowledge the partner's presence and communication, but do not fully accept or agree with the partner.

Defensive climate ■ A climate in which partners feel threatened and seek to protect themselves from attack.

Supportive climate ■ A climate in which partners feel comfortable and secure.

Nonassertiveness ■ Feeling of powerlessness and inability to express feelings honestly and comfortably.

Assertiveness ■ Ability to communicate feelings honestly and in a straightforward manner.

Aggressiveness ■ Asserting oneself to an extreme without concern for others.

Rigidity ■ Inability to adapt and cope with changes that occur in a relationship.

Flexibility ■ Ability to adapt and alter one's behaviors to accommodate changes in a relationship.

Interaction ■ Turn-taking that allows each partner to engage in a conversation.

Dominate ■ When one partner does not allow the other to speak.

partners may question their partner's fidelity every time they interact with another person, or they may attempt to control or block their interactions with anyone outside the relationship.

A **supportive climate** is an atmosphere in which partners feel comfortable and secure. Understanding, honesty, empathy, equality, and flexibility characterize this climate. Equality and flexibility are the most critical of these qualities. Equality in the relationship means that each partner's experience, knowledge, and relational expectations will be considered when important decisions must be made. Flexibility means that both partners show a willingness to change or modify interests, plans, and expectations when circumstances change.

Author Jack Gibbs (1961) suggests that we can enhance the positive climate in relationships, particularly in group interaction, with a number of important communication strategies. We should describe a specific communication interaction instead of evaluating or judging it. We should focus on solving a problem in the communication—not attempt to control the other's interactions. We should attempt to communicate in a spontaneous fashion instead of entering the communication with a strategy of controlling the communication. We should use the values of empathy and equality when interacting with another. And, finally, Gibbs suggests that we entertain the idea that all solutions be seen as "provisional." In essence, nothing is "carved in stone" and we can reevaluate the appropriateness of a solution if new evidence or information appears. We expand on this topic more in Chapter 12.

Assertiveness, Nonassertiveness, and Aggressiveness

A fifth dialectic concerns the need for partners to negotiate the degree of **nonassertiveness, assertiveness,** or **aggressiveness** that each individual will communicate in the relationship. *Nonassertive* partners feel powerless and keep their feelings and thoughts to themselves; they are often unable to express honest feelings comfortably. *Assertive* partners know and communicate their feelings and thoughts straightforwardly and honestly with others; they do not let others speak for them or tell them how they should feel, even though they remain concerned about others' perspectives. *Aggressive* partners assert themselves to an extreme without concern for others' concerns or needs; they stand up for themselves even at another's expense. They have the tendency to force others to believe as they do and engage in verbal attack marked by strong disconfirming messages. We identify effective assertive messages and specific assertive strategies that you can incorporate into your communication later in this chapter.

Rigidity and Flexibility

Aggressive communication disregards others' needs and creates a defensive climate.

Rigid partners lack the ability to adapt and cope with changes that occur in a relationship; they possess neither the motivation nor the inclination to learn new ways of interacting. **Flexible partners,** by contrast, adapt and alter their behaviors to accommodate the changes that occur in relationships because all relationships change.

Interaction, Domination, and Passivity

Interactive conversation remains an important aspect of relational initiation and development. Turn-taking that allows each partner an opportunity to engage the conversation promotes interaction. However, when people **dominate** the conversation and do not permit their partners to speak or when one of the partners is passive, and therefore reticent or unwilling to enter the interaction, effective communication becomes virtually impossible.

Within each of these dialectics, what style is most comfortable to you? It is important to remember that the individuals in the dyad—not outsiders to the relationship—decide what will constitute the basic communication between each other. Does your style change within these dialectics in different types of relationships? Are you more passive with your romantic partner than you are with your best friend? The key to successful and competent interpersonal communication is how the individuals in the dyad negotiate the various dialectics we have discussed. The ways in which the parties negotiate and agree with each other's behavior within each dialectic will assist in maintaining and expanding the relationship over a number of years—or may contribute to the relationship's eventual dissolution.

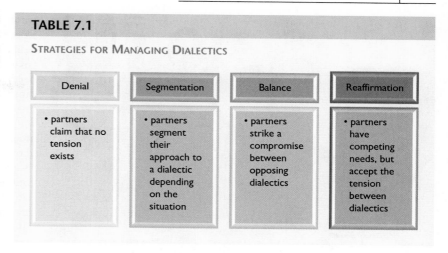

TABLE 7.1

STRATEGIES FOR MANAGING DIALECTICS

Denial	Segmentation	Balance	Reaffirmation
• partners claim that no tension exists	• partners segment their approach to a dialectic depending on the situation	• partners strike a compromise between opposing dialectics	• partners have competing needs, but accept the tension between dialectics

Strategies for Managing Dialects in Your Relationships

Negotiating and managing dialectics in your relationships reduces the tensions that block relationship development and enhance the possibilities for success. Leslie Baxter (1990) has identified four ways to deal with the dialectical tensions that we may potentially encounter in relationships: denial, segmentation, balance, and reaffirmation (see Table 7.1).

The use of denial simply means the relational partners claim that a particular tension doesn't exist. If a couple thinks they are "inseparable," their individual autonomy may be denied, for example. The use of segmentation as a strategy means that certain spheres of the relationship are treated differently. Individuals in a dyad may be autonomous at work, for example, but connected in social situations. Balance involves a compromise between two dialectics, which might mean the couple strategically identifies the nature of their autonomy and connectedness. Connectedness might mean, then, that they engage in hobbies together but do not smother one another. And, finally, reaffirmation means that the couple has competing needs for both autonomy and connection and that the tension that occurs between them is acceptable in the relationship. In this way, the couple continues to "reaffirm" both their autonomy and their connection within the relationship.

APPLYING INTERPERSONAL DIALECTICS TO FAMILIES

There are two types of families: those we are born into and those we create. The families we are born into become the fundamental building blocks of who we are at any given time. The patterns of interaction within our families are the models for the families we create. Think about the type of relationship your parents or primary caregivers modeled for you. Where did these individuals fall on the complementary/symmetrical dimension? How dependent/independent/interdependent was their relationship? What was the nature of the confirming or disconfirming communication within your family unit? Would you characterize the climate in your family as mostly supportive or mostly defensive? What degree of assertiveness did your parents or caregivers communicate to you, to each other, to others outside the immediate family? Were the rules in your family somewhat rigid or more flexible and changeable over time? Overall, was there a sense of a dominant hierarchy within your family or a feeling of more equal participation among all members?

It is important to remember that no single family dynamic is necessarily better than another. The key to successful and healthy family relationships is the agreement and cooperation among its members about these important dialectics. Healthy family communication is characterized by emotional and physical support between the members—this is a "functional" family. In a "dysfunctional" family, communication is closed, and members are not allowed to express their feelings, needs, hopes, fears, and dreams to each other.

The model your "first" family communicated to you impacts your "second," or created, family. How you approach your romantic relationships and future long-term partnerships will, to some extent, be adapted from this first model. Make a list of your basic expectations for your romantic relationships. Does your list consist primarily of what you

For some families, meals are an important time to reconnect and build family ties.

want your romantic partner to do and be for you? Does your list include what you want your partner to allow you to do and be for him or her? As we discussed in the last chapter, it is important to remember that men and women may not always have the same expectations for the relationship, particularly in terms of "the talk" that is used to negotiate healthy and long-term support of each other. Men are more likely to suppress feelings and to not talk about relationships, and this is not always healthy.

Much of our family dynamic occurs in the context of family meals. For some families, the ritual of mealtime is the most important time of the day to connect and share the happenings of the day. For some families, the most important ritual is the Sunday dinner, which may be a multigenerational activity. For other families, meals are a scattered affair where family members grab-and-go, whether they 'go' to the television, to after-school activities, or to their separate rooms. What values do children learn through what constitutes "mealtime"? When your family gathers for meals, is the value of equality operating? Are all members of the family encouraged to share equally about their day or week? Or does one member dominate the conversation and take up all of the verbal "space"? Does humility operate at family meals? How do family members show self-discipline in eating? Are members able to open up and talk about their day freely, or is conversation restricted during mealtime?

Anyone who suppresses feelings may jeopardize his or her physical health and, ultimately, a relationship. Yet disclosing feelings also has risks. Self-disclosure must be appropriate to the relationship and the immediate situation. Honestly expressing your feelings can potentially add multiple benefits to the relationship. You confirm both yourself and the other through your honesty; you set an example for the climate in the relationship with supportive and honest self-disclosure; you can become more aware of your own strengths and weaknesses in communication and of your own feelings through self-disclosure; and you can be proactive in managing conflict within the relationship.

APPLYING INTERPERSONAL DIALECTICS TO FRIENDSHIPS

We meet any number of other people on any given day. How is it that some of these people become our friends? What differentiates an "acquaintance" and a "friend"? We run into acquaintances and have a chat. We seek out friends because we like to be with them. We communicate, for the most part, only superficially with acquaintances; we self-disclose more deeply to our friends. The degree of trust that operates in a true friendship impacts how we accept each other, support each other, and even criticize each other. A strong, trusting friendship allows us to criticize each other when needed because we know the friendship can survive honest critical assessment. As the friendship moves from acquaintanceship into true friendship, we must work out important relational dialectics. Must we think alike on all things, or can we complement each other with our unique habits, quirks, and personalities? Do we have to see each other every day? Week? Year? In what ways do we need our true friends to communicate confirmation? How do we show our support to one another? Will this friendship be characterized by one person being more dominant and the other more passive? How do we negotiate each of these characteristics of the relationship?

The most effective and healthy friendships are characterized by understanding about these dialectics. Notice that we did not say "talking about" these dialectics. Some friendships seem to just naturally move into a level of comfort with the way the dialectics emerge, without the need to speak about them directly. In others, however, the friends may freely talk about expectations and comfort about some aspect of a dialectic. In both of these types of friendships, one of the most important skills for both parties in developing the health of the relationship is assertiveness. Remember that assertiveness is the ability to express rights or views without judging the rights or views of another. When you are assertive, you do not become overly sensitive to the other's point of view, and you don't take disagreements personally. You do not make *your* assertions personal or judgmental about the other. When both parties in a friendship are assertive, they can remain friends even through times of disagreement about a topic, issue, or situation.

Healthy friendships also are characterized by honest and open communication between friends. As we discuss previously, suppressing feelings and thoughts in relationships, particularly in friendships, can cause resentment that may build to the breaking point. Think about your suppression of feelings through the following metaphor, called **gunnysacking.** Each time you hold back on a thought or feeling, you put it into a gunnysack you carry on your back. Each of us carries a sack associated with each of our relationships. Think about the sacks you carry around on your back. When one is empty, it doesn't weigh anything, but every time we avoid a confrontation, swallow a criticism, or ignore a problem in that relationship, we add it to our sack. Every time we do this, the sack gets heavier. Gunnysacks can be big or small, but inevitably they fill up at some point if an individual continues to suppress his or her feelings. So what happens when the sack spills open? It may go something like this:

> Two roommates who are good friends have been living together for several months. One of the roommates likes to think of herself as neat and tidy, and she likes her living space to be free of clutter—with dishes washed and put away, laundry done in a timely manner, and a generally tidy living space. The second, however, pays very little attention to the "look" of the apartment. Clothes fall wherever they are removed, dishes pile up in the sink, and the toothpaste tube lies on the sink without the cap (you get the picture). One day, after roommate number 1 has had her fill, she explodes about the slob she lives with, focusing particularly on the toothpaste tube! Communication experts call this gunnysacking because that burlap bag has just become way too full, and the contents come spilling out in an order that defies logic. The only thing that matters to roommate number 1 is that she is fed up and unable to keep her feelings suppressed any longer.

Has this or a similar experience ever happened to you? So who is "at fault" here? What are the "rules" that have been developing between these friends over time? Is roommate number 2 completely at fault for being a slob? The answer is *no*, because the rules of the relationship have developed through the initial silence of roommate number 1 about what she expects of roommate number 2. When we suppress our thoughts and feelings, we implicitly consent to another's behavior. The box "Communication Counts in Your Career: Five Ways to Say 'I'" provides some examples of

Gunnysacking ■ Repressing feelings to the point that an individual cannot avoid "dumping" his or her feelings onto the relational partner.

COMMUNICATION COUNTS IN YOUR CAREER

Five Ways to Say "I"

Conflict is inevitable in any relationship, but how you respond verbally is within your control. Using "I" messages rather than "you" messages will help the other person hear what you have to say without feeling attacked or demeaned. Here are five ways that David Ellis, author of *Becoming a Master Student*, suggests that college students respond to conflict by using "I" messages:

1. *Observation:* describes what you can see, hear, touch, and experience and focuses on facts. Instead of saying, "You are eating like a pig," you can say, "We spent 20 dollars again this shopping trip on junk food like chips and cookies."
2. *Feelings:* describes your own feelings. Rather than saying, "You make me feel stupid," say "I feel foolish when you remember more than I do from our chemistry lecture."
3. *Wants:* describes what you want or need instead of hoping that others will guess what you want them to do or what you need from them. Avoid using the word *need*, if possible. Change your comment from, "You are so lazy around here," to "I would like you to help me with the dishes and the laundry before we go to the movies."
4. *Thoughts:* describes your thinking. Beware of "I" messages that are really judgments, such as "I think you are insensitive," or "I know that you hate my cooking." Try messages like, "I feel secure when you tell me you love me more often," or "I like it when you tell me whether or not you enjoyed the meal I cooked."
5. *Intention:* describes what you plan to do. Rather than depend on the other, state your intentions. Instead of saying, "We have a lot of chores this weekend," say, "I intend to wash the car and vacuum the carpet before studying this weekend. What would you like to do?"

ways that you can communicate more effectively in all types of relationships. You may find these skills valuable as you negotiate problems with your roommate or juggle the multiple demands of being a student, spouse, and parent because these and other issues can create conflict.

APPLYING INTERPERSONAL DIALECTICS TO COLLEGE

Whether you are entering college right after high school or returning after several years, there is a good chance that you will develop friendships and even romantic relationships during this time. These interpersonal relationships in the college context are unique in that you are exposed to a much more rich and varied group of individuals. Because many campuses are composed of persons from a wide variety of cultural, ethnic, and geographical origins, it may be more challenging to develop friendships and/or romantic relationships.

Expectations for appropriateness in interpersonal relationships are strongly influenced by culture. As we have discussed earlier in this text, culture is a pattern of perceptions, values, and behaviors shared by a group of people. In other words, culture is the unique way in which we engage in the everyday behaviors—such as eating, socializing, and creating and maintaining relationships—as American, Chinese, or French; male or female; white or Hispanic; and so on. Yet cultures are not homogeneous; they are dynamic and heterogeneous. This means that every individual in a cultural group also is unique. Race, gender, class, and sexual orientation provide additional layers of culture that impact the ways each of us negotiate the world we live in.

Cultural characteristics impact the interpersonal dialectics we have discussed. Martin and Nakayama (2001) argue that the values of a cultural group represent a worldview—a particular way of looking at the world. They distinguish between individualistic and collectivist cultural worldviews. **Individualist cultures** place more importance on the individual within certain types of relationships. These cultures value direct, open forms of communication. **Collectivist cultures** value less direct communication and tend to avoid conflict. These cultures emphasize the importance of the group (i.e., family, work, or social) and value the group's success over that of any individual in that group. Later in this text, we discuss several cultural influences on group communication.

Dutch social psychologist Geert Hofstede (1980) has identified a number of distinctions between cultural groups. One of them refers to the long- or short-term orientation to life. Some individualistic cultures are more likely to value a "short-term orientation" to life. These cultures emphasize the importance of quick results and of finding an immediate solution. Some Americans, for example, are more likely to want to establish relationships quickly by "telling all" about themselves in the first few interactions. In contrast, collectivist cultures are more likely to value a long-term orientation to life. They emphasize slowly developing relationships over time, tenaciously working toward long-term goals, and practicing the virtue of thrift. What do you think it means to be "thrifty" in developing and maintaining interpersonal relationships? Use the questions in the box "Communication Counts in Your College Experience: Expanding Your Knowledge of Cultures" to expand your opportunities to create healthy intercultural relationships. This textbox identifies websites useful for broadening your knowledge of other cultures and establishing cross-cultural friendships.

Another unique communication context operating in college concerns the relationships among faculty, staff, and students. As we will discuss later in this text, the college or campus is a unique organization with a hierarchy of power relationships. At a very basic level, instructors have the power to assign you a grade for the value of your work in their classes. Do you think it is appropriate to develop a friendship with an instructor? What should be the boundaries for appropriate interpersonal

Culture Counts

Individualistic cultures ■ Cultures that place more importance on the individual within certain types of relationships; value direct, open communication.

Collectivist cultures ■ Cultures that emphasize the importance of the group; value less direct communication and tend to avoid conflict situations.

COMMUNICATION COUNTS IN YOUR COLLEGE EXPERIENCE

Expanding Your Knowledge of Cultures

While many of you will meet individuals from across the world in your classes or jobs, there are many other ways to expand your knowledge of other cultures and establish cross-cultural friendships. Several online sites let you correspond with individuals around the world. Here are two examples:

1. Europa Pages (www.europa-pages.com/penpal_form.html): "A great way to make friends around the world and to practice your language skills is to get an international pen friend. [This] website [offers] this FREE service to everyone: students wishing to meet other language learners, teachers wanting to exchange ideas, or anyone keen to make new contacts in other countries."

2. Pen Pal Party (www.penpalparty.com/): Also offers opportunities to meet and establish friendships with others around the world.

If you were interested in establishing an online friendship that crosses cultural boundaries, how would you introduce yourself online?

relationships? Some faculty like to have students call them by their first names and are willing to tell students about their background and experience and even to disclose some information about their life history; other faculty are not. Which style are you most comfortable with? Is it appropriate for you to socialize with a faculty member outside the classroom?

Your campus may assign you to an advisor within your major's department, and this person will assist you in identifying classes that meet your major's requirements. What other expectations do you have for your advisor? Is it important for this person to know something about you personally to more effectively provide counsel on your career or life goals? Is it important for you to know something about your advisor's experience and credibility to accurately assess his or her advice? Like most communication situations on your campus, the faculty–student communication context will be varied and heterogeneous. In other words, some faculty may be more willing than others to know and understand you and to disclose information about themselves. The box "Communication Counts in Your College Experience: Working with Your Academic Advisor" offers some additional insights about advising and advisors. (You may also access information on advising at the National Academic Advising Association [NACADA] Clearinghouse of Advising Resources website at www.nacada.ksu.edu/Clearinghouse/AdvisingIssues/Core-Values.htm).

COMMUNICATION COUNTS IN YOUR COLLEGE EXPERIENCE

Working with Your Academic Advisor

Your relationship with your academic advisor is potentially one of the most important in your college career. How do you develop this relationship effectively? Consider the following when working with your academic advisor.

First, advisors hold core values, as explained by the National Academic Advising Association. One of these values is particularly important for you to consider:

Advisors are responsible to the individuals they advise

Academic advisors work to strengthen the importance, dignity, potential, and unique nature of each individual within the academic setting. Advisors' work is guided by their beliefs that students

- have diverse backgrounds that can include different ethnic, racial, domestic, and international communities; sexual orientations; ages; gender and gender identities; physical, emotional, and psychological abilities; political, religious, and educational beliefs;
- hold their own beliefs and opinions;
- are responsible for their own behaviors and the outcomes of those behaviors;
- can be successful based on their individual goals and efforts;
- have a desire to learn;
- have learning needs that vary based on individual skills, goals, responsibilities, and experiences;
- use a variety of techniques and technologies to navigate their world.

In support of these beliefs, the cooperative efforts of all who advise include, but are not limited to, providing accurate

(continued)

and timely information, communicating in useful and efficient ways, maintaining regular office hours, and offering varied contact modes.

Advising, as part of the educational process, involves helping students develop a realistic self-perception and successfully transition to the postsecondary institution. Advisors encourage, respect, and assist students in establishing their goals and objectives. Advisors seek to gain the trust of their students and strive to honor students' expectations of academic advising and its importance in their lives.

George D. Kuh, author of *Student Success in College*, states,

Academic advisors can play an integral role in promoting student success by assisting students in ways that encourage them to engage in the right kinds of activities, inside and outside the classroom. Advisors are especially important because they are among the first people new students encounter and should see regularly during their first year. (2006)

He adds that there are four important common themes regarding advising that arise from his Documenting Effective Educational Practices (DEEP) study of 20 schools, which you may wish to consider in choosing and working with your advisor:

1. **Advisors know their students well.** Subscribing to a talent development perspective on education, advisors believe their primary task is to help change students for the better by making certain they take full advantage of the institution's resources for learning. To do this, many advisors go to unusual lengths to learn as much as they can about their students—where they are from, their aspirations and talents, and when and where they need help.
2. **Advisors strive for meaningful interactions with students.** Another way advisors contribute to the quality of student learning and campus life is by helping to develop, support, and participate in mentoring programs. Mentee–mentor relationships help create close connections with one or more key persons, relationships that are especially important for students in underrepresented groups on campus. Also, because connecting *early* with advisees is essential, advisors at DEEP schools are involved in planning and delivering first-year orientation programs and experiences.
3. **Advisors help students identify pathways to academic and social success.** In addition to assisting students with choosing the right courses, advisors encourage students to take advantage of the learning and personal opportunities their school makes available. They make a point of asking students to apply what they are learning in their classes to real-life issues, thereby enhancing student learning in ways that many academic courses alone may not be able to accomplish. Among the high-quality cocurricular experiences that have powerful positive effects on students and their success are service learning, study abroad, civic engagement, internships, and experiential learning activities. Another key to navigating college effectively is for students to learn the campus culture—the traditions, rituals, and practices that communicate how and why things are done at their school.
4. **Advising and student success is considered a tag team activity.** At high-performing schools, the educational and personal development goals of advising are shared across multiple partners, not just the person "assigned" this task. Faculty, student affairs staff, and mentors along with professional academic advisors make up the multiple early alert and safety net systems for students in place at DEEP schools—particularly for students who institutional research studies indicate may be at risk of dropping out. Such team approaches go a long way toward keeping students from falling through the cracks and getting students the information they need when they need it.

Your responsibility as an advisee, then, is to make yourself available to your advisor, get to know him or her, and use your skills in assertiveness to capitalize on your advisor's values and skill. Advisors can be instrumental in helping you negotiate the political landscape that is your college campus. This individual can also be instrumental in letting you get to know his or her network of professionals, which may enhance your possibilities in landing that perfect job. And, finally, an advisor can be the most important person to write a letter of recommendation when you begin to interview for that job. The key to taking advantage of his or her expertise is your commitment to establishing a positive, assertive, and effective relationship with this important person in your college life.

Source: From "Thinking DEEPly about academic advising and student engagement," by George D. Kuh from *Academic Advising Today,* June 2006, 29, 1, 3. Reprinted by permission of the National Academic Advising Association (NACADA) and the author.

APPLYING INTERPERSONAL DIALECTICS TO COMMUNITIES

Many colleges today are attempting to incorporate a variety of service learning or problem-based learning initiatives into the life of the campus and surrounding community. Many of these initiatives have been sponsored by the American Association of Colleges and Universities (AAC&U). The AAC&U's policy is that every student deserves to receive a "liberal education," which it defines as

> one that prepares us to live responsible, productive, and creative lives in a dramatically changing world. It is an education that fosters a well-grounded intellectual resilience, a disposition toward lifelong learning, and an acceptance of responsibility for the ethical consequences of our ideas and actions. Liberal education requires that we understand the foundations of knowledge and inquiry about nature, culture, and society; that we master core skills of perception, analysis, and expression; that we cultivate a respect for truth; that we recognize the importance of historical and cultural context; and that we explore connections among formal learning, citizenship, and service to our communities. (From the Statement on Liberal Learning. Adopted by the Board of Directors of the Association of American Colleges and Universities, October 1998. Copyright © 1998 Association of American Colleges and Universities. Reprinted with permission.)

Liberal education is a student-learning and problem-centered approach to preparing students for life beyond the campus, preparing them for the issues of society and the workplace: "Quality liberal education prepares students for active participation in the private and public sectors, in a diverse democracy, and in an even more diverse community. It has the strongest impact when studies reach beyond the classroom to the larger community, asking students to apply their developing analytical skills and ethical judgment to concrete problems in the world around them, and to connect theory with the insights gained in practice" (*Greater Expectations* 2002, 26). The liberal education approach eliminates the artificial distinctions between studies deemed "liberal" (i.e., unrelated to job training) and "practical" (assumed to be related to a job). "A liberal education is practical because it develops just those capacities needed by every thinking adult: analytical skills, effective communication, practical intelligence, ethical judgment, and social responsibility" (26). To clarify, the concept of a liberal education should not be confused with a liberal arts college. Any two-year community college, four-year private college, four-year public university, research-intensive university offering advanced degrees, or any other can offer students a liberal education.

Practically speaking, this means that student work moves beyond the classroom (either using problem-based cases in classrooms or through service-learning projects in the community) to engage in the life of the community in which the campus resides. Whether your campus has this type of initiative or not, you will in your lifetime become a member of some collective community. You may be a parent negotiating with teachers and administrators in your child's school. You may purchase a house and find yourself confronted by a reassessment of property values. You may be a member of a church that has undertaken a project to assist a less-privileged group within the community. Your ability to be sensitive to the interpersonal dialectics operating within this communication context will be regularly tested. The box "Communication Counts in Your College Experience: Service Learning" provides a resource for community projects that can enhance trust and relationships among diverse groups with different interests.

COMMUNICATION COUNTS IN YOUR COLLEGE EXPERIENCE

Service Learning

You can learn a great deal about service learning from many outlets. The National Service-Learning Clearinghouse (NSLC) provides a great deal of useful information at www.servicelearning.org/. Campus Compact (www.compact.org) also offers a great deal of information. However, information is not a substitute for involvement, which is the ultimate goal of service learning. As you pursue your college education, you will likely find courses that either encourage or require you to engage in some form of service learning. While these courses may have different emphases or learning objectives, clearly understanding and actively responding to these opportunities will enhance your college experience. Following, we provide you with some basic information to help you engage service learning as you study communication and other courses.

(continued)

Definition of Service Learning

Service learning combines a service to the community, usually a nonprofit organization, with an opportunity to learn through a real-life application of concepts and content from your classes. To illustrate, when you and your peers from your health class volunteer with an after-school program to help provide physical education activities for children, this constitutes service. However, when you then draw on this service to learn about and analyze the level of physical activity of children in this specific program and the resulting health consequences, you are learning *and* serving. In some cases, service learning may emphasize *service* more than learning or emphasize *learning* more than service. In other instances, service and learning may be balanced. Whatever the configuration or course, linking service and learning is an important initiative on many campuses and one you will likely have an opportunity to engage.

Linking Service Learning and Communication

You can't truly serve or learn without developing and using appropriate and effective communication skills. As you work with others to be of service, you must learn to listen, empathize, and respond appropriately to those who may be very different from you. As you link service to learning, you must be able to think, speak, and write about your experiences. For example, in this course, you will probably deliver at least one speech. If you are engaged in service learning, you have a ready-made speech topic about which you can inform your peers (i.e., what you are learning from your service work). If you are delivering a persuasive speech, you may want to encourage your peers to volunteer their time and energy to help improve the lives of others. Regardless of whether you use your service-learning experiences for speech topics, learning the foundational principles of communication will help you serve and learn.

Conflict ■ The perception of incompatible goals.

Overt conflict ■ Confronting someone directly in a conflict.

Covert conflict ■ Where a partner hides their anger or hostility.

MANAGING CONFLICT IN INTERPERSONAL RELATIONSHIPS

The dialectics discussed earlier in this chapter can result in conflict between the relational partners. Conflict, though, is inevitable in any relationship. Partners vary in their responses to conflict, so managing conflict is essential to establishing true intimacy and in managing the various dialectics we have discussed. Understanding the value of conflict and ways to manage conflict will help you build more effective interpersonal relationships.

Intimacy and Conflict

Issues arise that lead to conflict, and partners vary in their responses to it. Some partners avoid conflict and refuse to deal with issues; they are more likely to surrender. Other partners go on the attack and seek to shift the blame or defeat the other partner; they want to win at all costs. Still other partners confront the issue to solve the problem rather than sidestep it or adopt an "I win, you lose" strategy. In order to make sure your relationships run as smoothly as possible, you must first understand the inevitability of conflict. If you try to avoid conflict, your relationships will suffer. Successful conflict management can ensure the relationship survives and grows more satisfying over time. The existence of conflict does not mean the partners in a relationship are having trouble; conflict exists because we are linked to each other, involved with each other, and connected with each other.

By definition, **conflict** is the perception of incompatible goals and the belief that for one partner to reach his or her goal, the goals of the other partner cannot be met (see Hocker & Wilmot 1997). Sometimes conflict is out in the open, but sometimes it is hidden. When we confront someone directly about a perceived conflict, the conflict is said to be **overt.** When conflict is hidden, or **covert,** we sometimes act in passive-aggressive ways that send mixed messages. For example, you may be angry at a roommate for not pulling his share of the responsibility for keeping the apartment clean or upset with your spouse or children who know you have to study yet don't take the initiative to start supper or throw in a load of laundry. You may say nothing in these situations but act coolly toward the person or people with whom you are upset. When you respond to conflict in these passive-aggressive ways, the conflict remains unresolved, and the relationship suffers.

The way an individual responds to conflict reflects past experiences, which are often a product of family history. Think about the ways your family resolves conflict. Do family members ignore the problem and hope it goes away? Is there competition to see who can "win"? Does your family encourage constructive engagement and discussion of conflict? How you manage conflict will be reflected in your words and actions. While conflict is inevitable, it is also manageable. When you approach conflict as a problem to be solved, and not a challenge for you to win at all costs, you can develop and expand your relationships with others and increase your confidence and self-esteem. A key to becoming more effective at managing conflict is the ability to be adaptable. This is easier said than done. While you may be able to control your feelings and actions during conflict, you cannot control someone else's. In the face of anger, tears, shouting, or accusation, however, we often find it difficult to remain calm. Conflict can spiral out of control if neither party in the relationship is willing to listen and adapt to the needs of the conflict situation. Perhaps even a time-out to cool down and collect your thoughts can help keep a heated conflict from becoming even more destructive. The old practice of counting to ten before you speak is still valuable.

Effectively dealing with conflict is an important aspect of any relationship.

One of the basic values that is essential in important relationships is honesty. We expect honesty in the relationship no matter what the situation. When we deceive people we care about, we lose trust in them and in the relationship. Trust is a critical building block in any interpersonal relationship. When we are trying to manage conflict, it takes courage to remain honest and to trust another. You must describe your feelings honestly and ask the other person to do the same. You must also avoid lashing out with hurtful, aggressive comments, despite how you might feel at the moment. Focus on the positive side of the relationship and its potential for better understanding of yourself and the other. When we are calm and in control of our emotions, we know this is possible. Yet, it is easy to fall back on deception when emotions run high or when we don't want to admit we've made a mistake. Obviously, there are numerous reasons why conflict can emerge in relationships. Therefore, conflict is inevitable but manageable and even potentially beneficial.

To summarize, thus far we have described several issues that reflect the complex nature of interpersonal relationships. Successful negotiation of each of the dialectics will create an atmosphere where conflict can be managed successfully and relationship development and growth can be assured. But before we leave this discussion of how to successfully negotiate these issues, there is one more issue we must explore.

The Value of Conflict

We cannot, nor should we, try to avoid all conflict. Avoiding conflict will not make problems go away. Let us look at the definition of *conflict*. First, conflict is an *expressed struggle*. This means that both parties in a conflict must recognize the conflict and communicate to the other about the conflict. Next, the conflict occurs between *interconnected* individuals. It can hardly be a conflict if the communication occurs between complete strangers who will never see each other again after their brief interaction. The parties' interconnectedness implies that these individuals mean something to each other. The relationship could be between parent and child, life partners, best friends, boss and subordinate, coworkers, teacher and student, or any configuration where the relationship matters to the parties. Finally, conflict exists because the parties see incompatibility between one person's success and another's: If I reach my goal in this situation, you cannot reach yours. You see my success as interfering with your success. We perceive that any win by one of us will be at the expense of the other. At the heart of the conflict is the critical role of *perception*, as we discussed in Chapter 2 We may be able to find a solution that meets both parties' needs, but our perceptions prevent us from seeing that as a possibility.

From the outset, we must understand that conflict has the potential to enhance the health and growth of our interpersonal relationships. If managed effectively, our

Pseudoconflict ■ Situation in which the parties are actually in agreement, but perceptions and misunderstanding prevent them from seeing the areas of agreement and compatibility.

Destructive conflict ■ Conflict in which communication escalates, and hurting one another becomes the goal.

Constructive conflict ■ Conflict in which the goal is problem solving, not hurting one another.

Collaborating style ■ Characterized by high concern for self and high concern for people.

relationships grow and prosper, becoming healthy, long-term, and satisfying. The absence of conflict is not healthy for any relationship.

Pseudoconflict, Destructive Conflict, and Constructive Conflict

Conflict is inevitable but not inevitably destructive. Some conflicts are actually only perceptual misunderstandings. **Pseudoconflict** occurs when the parties are actually in agreement, but perceptions and misunderstandings prevent them from seeing the areas of agreement and compatibility. One or more parties mistakenly believe that goal attainment is impossible for all. Pseudoconflict is easy to resolve if the parties are rhetorically sensitive to the misunderstanding. If the parties are not willing to listen to each other, however, the conflict intensifies.

Destructive conflict occurs when we allow the communication to escalate and spiral out of control. Wilmot and Hocker (2001) characterize destructive conflict as that which escalates; encourages each party to retaliate against the others; causes one or more individuals to dominate and compete with others; and increases the potential for defensiveness, inflexibility, and cross-complaints. The aim becomes to hurt another. Destructive conflict is both unethical and incompetent communication.

Obviously, there are numerous reasons why conflict can emerge in relationships. Smith and Walter (1995) identify several roadblocks that can impede the academic success of adult learners, many of which can also induce conflict:

■ Family resentment because of frequent absence from home
■ Resentment from coworkers because of absences and trying to improve one's self or one's skill
■ Resistance from a spouse who doesn't support a career change, the costs of money or time invested in attending college, or the potential for developing new friends or life directions

Acknowledging that conflict exists is one of the first steps in preventing the escalation of destructive conflict. This expression of the conflict is important. Developing skills that help prevent conflict from escalating into a "win at all costs" war of words are essential to healthy relationships. Conflict management skills are valuable as you negotiate problems with your roommate or juggle the multiple demands of being a student, spouse, and parent. Managing **constructive conflict** begins with recognizing the conflict and being willing to own one's feelings. Turning the tide of destructive conflict means you must recognize when you are being selfish and stupid and admitting this to the other. Managing constructive conflict begins with recognizing the basic importance of the relationship and valuing the relationship more than the conflict. While the parties still may disagree with each other during the conflict, the goal is one of problem solving, not hurting the other. Each participant in the conflict must be flexible and strive to find the best solution for the relationship.

Conflict Management Styles

Thomas and Kilmann (1977), drawing on the work of Blake and Mouton (1964), has identified five possible styles of managing conflict. They base these five styles on the possible combinations of two important elements: concern for self and concern for people. Figure 7.1 shows the possible combinations.

COLLABORATION   A **collaborating style** is characterized by high concern for self and high concern for people. *Collaboration* means to work together. Both parties share concern for solving a problem in a cooperative manner and consider the ultimate goal to be for both parties to win. Although both parties may initially identify different solutions to the problem, they work together to ultimately develop a solution that meets the needs of all individuals involved. The collaborating style takes work, time, and energy. Collaboration is characterized by assertiveness, perceptions of equality among the participants, belief that all parties and their opinions have value, and motivation to see the conflict through to a satisfying end. This conflict-management style is usually the most effective. However, it may not be appropriate in times of emergency, when an immediate decision must be made.

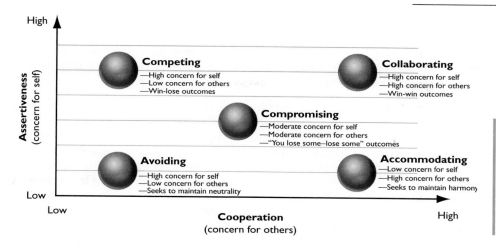

FIGURE 7.1

Five Styles of Conflict Management.

Source: From K. Thomas, "Conflict and Conflict Management," *Handbook of Industrial and Organizational Psychology,* Marvin Dunnette, editor, 1976. Adapted by permission of Leaetta Hough.

COMPETITION   A **competing style** is characterized by high concern for self and low concern for other people. Generally, individuals who use a competing style engage in a win-lose approach to the conflict. They must win, and others must lose. These individuals dominate others involved in the conflict and insist that their own opinions and solutions are more valuable than those of others. The dominating individual's communication is aggressive and depends on threats, sarcasm, overt hostility, and disconfirming statements to others. Engaging in a competing style increases the likelihood of destructive conflict.

However, under emergency situations, when an immediate decision must be made, this style might be useful. When individuals in the relationship recognize that emergencies are a part of life and have agreed that under certain circumstances one party may make a decision without communication with the other, this style may be effective. It is critical, though, to understand that this must be agreed on in advance. Here is an example. Perhaps you and your life partner have agreed that neither of you will make a major purchase, say of over $100, without discussing it with the other. But one day when you're traveling on a trip away from home, your car breaks down, and you've got to get repairs so you can meet your client and return home. The repairs, as you'd expect, are considerably more than $100. In this type of circumstance, discussing the options with your partner isn't a consideration.

ACCOMMODATION   An **accommodating style** is characterized by high concern for people and low concern for self. Individuals who accommodate other people, yield to their wishes, needs, desires, or solutions. Accommodation is associated with a nonassertive communication approach. It is effective if you really do not care about the outcome of a particular circumstance or situation as much as your partner might. For example, if you want to see a movie this weekend and there's something that your partner really wants to see but you're not interested in it, you might agree to go because you don't really care all that much. The downside of too much accommodation is the tendency to become a pushover for everyone else's ideas but never stand up for your own. The accommodating style is more likely to be used by individuals from collectivist cultures than individualistic cultures. Remember, collectivist cultures attach more value to the group than to individuals, so they are more likely to yield to the group's will.

AVOIDANCE   An **avoiding style** is characterized by low concern for self and low concern for other people. The most common behavior associated with avoidance is withdrawal—either physically or mentally. Individuals who employ this style avoid conflict by withdrawing physically or emotionally. They ignore phone calls or e-mails or simply refuse to respond to requests. Or they change the subject when an uncomfortable situation arises. Avoidance is all too common in many relationships because the parties fear that any type of confrontation will damage the relationship. Avoidance is very common in the initial stages of a relationship when one party doesn't want to be the first one to cause an argument. Unfortunately, avoidance only intensifies the possibility of a more intense conflict.

As we discussed earlier, avoidance causes us to *gunnysack* our problems and concerns. Eventually the gunnysack fills up, and the result is not pretty. In the early stages of a relationship, you may consider such behaviors to be "quirks" in your partner's

Competing style ■ Characterized by high concern for self and low concern for people.

Accommodating style ■ Characterized by low concern for self and high concern for people.

Avoiding style ■ Characterized by low concern for self and low concern for people.

Compromising style ■
Characterized by moderate concern for self and moderate concern for people.

personality—nothing major. One day, though, you're amazed to find that you've been really angry for the six months you've been picking up after him or her, and you're sick of doing it. You're tired of wiping up toothpaste from the sink, and you don't have time to fill the car up with gas (because he or she always leaves it empty). Today because you're in a hurry and late for a meeting. You explode.

COMPROMISE   The **compromising style** is characterized by moderate concern for self and moderate concern for people. When we compromise, we give up something to gain something. Compromise may be the most often used conflict management style. However, it can be very dangerous. The most critical difference between collaborating and compromising styles is the parties' degree of satisfaction with the outcome. In collaboration, we modify our decision, but we are satisfied by both the process and the outcome of the decision. In a compromise, we give something up, but we may not be particularly happy about it. We do it to expedite the situation, perhaps to avoid a drawn-out conversation or meeting. One of the most common reasons for compromise is that we are too lazy to put the energy and time into the process of collaboration. Compromise as a long-term strategy to conflict management may have the same results as accommodation. Yet compromise can be effective under some circumstances. If the parties see compromise as a short-term approach to a problem, or when the situation is not critical to either party, compromise can work. But it needs to be used only rarely and only until a more comprehensive solution can be found.

CREATING MORE ASSERTIVE RELATIONSHIPS

Assertiveness is one of the most important characteristics of healthy relationships and positive communication climates. Assertiveness is never aggressive, never powerless, never an attempt to dominate another. Assertiveness can be thought of as a "caring firmness" in our interactions with another. Assertive communicators act confidently but always see the other person as an equal partner in the communication interaction. When we are assertive we are positive, firm, confident, and involved in the conversation. But we do not talk over another or insist on our own agenda exclusively in the interaction. Table 7.2 shows suggestions for becoming an assertive communicator.

TABLE 7.2

BECOMING AN ASSERTIVE COMMUNICATOR

Tips for Becoming an Assertive Communicator:

■ Develop a value and belief system that allows you to assert yourself. Give yourself permission to be angry, to say "no," to ask for help, and to make mistakes. Avoid using tag questions ("It's really hot today, isn't it?"), disclaimers ("I may be wrong, but . . ."), and question statements ("Won't you close the door?"), which lessen the perceived assertiveness of speech.

■ Resist giving into interruptions until you have completed your thoughts. (Instead say, "Just a moment, I haven't finished.")

■ Stop self-limiting behaviors, such as smiling too much, nodding too much, tilting your head, or dropping your eyes in response to another person's gaze.

■ When saying "no," be decisive. Explain why you are refusing, but don't be overly apologetic.

■ Use "I want" or "I feel" statements. Acknowledge the other person's situation or feelings and follow with a statement in which you stand up for your rights (e.g., "I know you're X, but I feel . . .").

■ Use "I" language (this is especially useful for expressing negative feelings.) "I" language helps you focus your anger constructively and to be clear about your own feelings. For example:

   ■ Maintain direct eye contact, keep your posture open and relaxed, be sure your facial expression agrees with the message, and keep a level, well-modulated tone of voice.

■ Listen and let people know you have heard what they said. Ask questions for clarification.

■ Practice! Enlist the aid of friends and family and ask for feedback. Tackle less anxiety-evoking situations first. Build up your assertiveness muscle.

Source: From "Assertive Communication: How to Be Effectively Assertive" from the brochure *Assertive Communication* by Dr. Vivian D. Barnette created from the following works: Alberti, Robert E., and Emmons, Michael. *Your Perfect Right.* Revised edition. San Luis Obispo, CA: IMPACT, 1990. Bower, Sharon, and Bower, Gordon. *Asserting Yourself.* Reading, Massachusetts: Addison-Wesley, 1976. Bramson, Robert M. *Coping with Difficult People.* New York: Anchor/Doubleday, 1981. Butler, Pamela. *Self-Assertion for Women.* San Francisco, CA: Harper & Row, 1981 .Smith, Manual J. *When I Say No, I Feel Guilty.* New York: The Dial Press, 1975. Reprinted by permission of Dr. Vivian D. Barnette.

BUILDING COMPETENT AND ETHICAL RELATIONSHIPS IN COLLEGE, CAREER, AND LIFE

Being able to adapt your communication to the unique requirements of a particular communication context is one of the most critical skills of the competent communicator. **Rhetorical sensitivity** is the ability to adapt a message to the people, place, and timing of the communication. We are not implying that you so dramatically change your message that you compromise your ethical standards. Rhetorically sensitive communicators understand the unique elements of each communication situation and audience and adapt their messages accordingly. Morreale, Spitzberg, and Barge (2001) put it this way: "Communication is the process of making community. This means that the choices we make about how to communicate influence what we create and the kinds of personal lives, relationships, and communities we build" (22–23). Yet even when we act in the most communicatively competent manner possible, we cannot control someone else's communication behavior. As we discussed in the previous chapter, conflict is inevitable, so it is essential to have the tools to manage it effectively.

The cultural lenses through which we see the world impact the ways we manage conflict as well. In situations when directness is valued, an individual may be more likely to stake out a position in the conflict and defend it. In situations when indirectness is valued, an individual may be more likely to downplay the conflict in an attempt to "save face" (Ting-Toomey & Oetzel 2002).

Today's college classroom learning environment may be characterized by more active student involvement through small group activities and problem solving. Small groups often present unique difficulties, including interpersonal conflict as a result of personality clashes or differences of opinion. Inter-role conflicts often occur because members share some of the same responsibilities without a clear understanding of how to divide the tasks involved or because they simultaneously compete for the same functions.

Your success in college depends upon your willingness to use *confirming* responses to others both in and out of class. Your success also depends on the degree of assertiveness you can develop. *Assertiveness* means being able to ask for what you want and not giving in to others who try to make you do something you don't want to do. It means saying no when you mean no and standing up for yourself without denying other people their rights. So if you're at a party and someone shoves a beer at you and you don't want it, say so. If you've come home from a long day of work and classes and the house is a mess, tell your family that you need their help cleaning it up. If someone tries to pressure you into sexual activity and you're not ready, tell him or her how you feel. Assertiveness also means that once you explain how you feel, you are not required to repeatedly justify your feelings. Once explained, your feelings should be respected. Assertive people act responsibly and accept responsibility for what they will and will not do. It means you're not afraid to speak up, ask questions, or seek information, and you make your own decisions.

As we said early in the last chapter, interpersonal relationships are established in dyads and within groups. How group members resolve dialectical tensions will significantly impact the type of climate developed in the group. How may group members respond to conflict? In some cases, groups ignore, prevent, squelch, or, as a last resort, use a leader's status or power to suspend conflict. In most cases, collaboration, which strives for a negotiated

Rhetorical sensitivity ■ The ability to adapt a message to the people, place, and timing of the communication.

settlement between the conflicting parties, proves most beneficial to all concerned. Members focus on solving the problem rather than defending or attacking one another.

Another potential interpersonal conflict involves the nonparticipating member of a group. Groups often have members who, through disinterest, shyness, fear, selfishness, or defensiveness do not actively or verbally participate in discussion, decision making, and problem solving. Typically, such a member shows up to group meetings but says nothing and waits for others to discuss and decide issues to which they readily consent.

The flip side to this potential conflict is the overachieving member. Some group members, whether unconsciously or purposefully, seek to dominate groups with their ideas, opinions, or talk. Motivations for this behavior can range from a desire to be helpful to a desire to be the center of attention or create conflict. In any case, these people tend to bring the free exchange of ideas to a standstill and hinder the group's creativity and task functions. Some strategies for addressing both nonparticipating and over-participating members include the following:

- Assign the problem member a specific task or responsibility—especially one well suited to his or her skills or interests (e.g., "Marcie, would you please prepare a report that provides and explains the demographic of our student body so we can structure our membership drive more carefully?")
- Attend to nonverbal cues so that you sense when a member is about to speak and can respond accordingly to encourage participation or silence (e.g., "Noriko, I noticed that you frowned a bit at what Susan just said. Did you have something to add?")
- Arrange the group's seating to provide encouragement or control to members by sitting them near the leader (e.g., "Jenda, would you please sit next to me for this meeting? I may need to consult with you during the meeting, and it would be helpful to have you physically near.")
- Invite more quiet members to share their insights, thereby encouraging them to speak while helping to monitor those who may speak too much (e.g., "Jan, what do you think about using tickets to control the number of people who attend our open house?")
- Redirect the talk in the group to encourage more quiet members to share (e.g., "That's very interesting, Laughton. Thank you. Nate, what's your opinion on providing additional funds for undergraduate research projects?")
- Talk privately with the problem member (e.g., "Sally, I usually don't hear you speak up in our group on a regular basis. Is there something wrong? I would really like to hear from you." Or, "Patrick, have you noticed that it seems like some of our members are reluctant to speak up during the meeting? I was wondering if you would be willing to help me get the others members to add their thoughts by asking the quieter members questions or inviting them to speak?")
- Directly request change or voluntary self-removal of the problem member (e.g., "Mike, may I ask you to help me out? While what you share in our group is always worthwhile, would you be offended if I asked you to let others talk as well?" Or, "Joe, you really seem to have a problem relating to our group. I wonder if you would feel more comfortable working on another project or with another group. How do you feel about that?")

We elaborate on the issues of group communication in Chapter 12. Ultimately, conflict is inevitable in any relationship, but how you respond verbally is within your control. Using "I" messages rather than "you" messages will help the other person hear what you have to say without feeling attacked or demeaned.

SUMMARY

In this chapter, we have discussed the importance of applying your understanding of the dialectics of interpersonal communication in a variety of communication contexts. We have identified concepts important to your understanding of effective interpersonal communication:

- The ability of the parties to negotiate a variety of dialectics will significantly impact each partner's willingness to grow together, including complementary versus symmetrical relationships, the degree of independence of each party, what constitutes appropriate and effective messages within the relationship, and the degree of flexibility required to keep the relationship functioning.

- Individualistic cultures place more importance on the individual within certain types of relationships. Individualistic cultures value direct, open forms of communication.
- Collectivist cultures value less direct communication and tend to avoid conflict situations. Collectivist cultures emphasize the importance of the group (i.e., family, work, or social group) and value the group's success rather than any individual in that group.
- Conflict is inevitable in relationships, but it can be managed successfully.
- Pseudoconflict is when the parties actually are in agreement but perceptions and misunderstanding prevent them from seeing the areas of agreement and compatibility.
- Destructive conflict is that which escalates; encourages each party to retaliate against the other; causes one or more individuals to dominate and compete with others; and increases the potential for defensiveness, inflexibility, and cross-complaints.
- Constructive conflict begins with recognition and starts the process of managing the conflict by one individual's willingness to own his or her feelings.
- A collaborating style of conflict management is characterized by high concern for self and high concern for the other. *Collaboration* means to work together.
- A competing style of conflict management is characterized by high concern for self and low concern for the other. Generally, individuals who use a competing style engage in a win-lose approach to the conflict.
- An accommodating style of conflict management is characterized by high concern for the other and low concern for self. When we accommodate another, we yield to his or her wishes, needs, desires, or solutions.
- An avoiding style of conflict management is characterized by low concern for self and low concern for the other. The most common behavior associated with avoidance is withdrawal, either physically or mentally.
- Avoidance causes us to gunnysack our problems and concerns. Eventually our gunnysack overflows with increased destructive conflict.
- A compromising style of conflict management is characterized by moderate concern for self and moderate concern for the other. When we compromise, we give something up to gain something.
- Assertive communicators are firm, confident, and empathetic in interacting with others.
- Rhetorical sensitivity is this ability to adapt a message to the people, place, and timing of the communication.

QUESTIONS FOR DISCUSSION

1. What is the most critical issue that can cause misunderstanding within cross-cultural friendships?
2. If you are a member of the dominant cultural group in your campus, organization, or community, do you believe it is ever possible to truly understand what it feels like to live in a minority or ethnic culture?
3. Look around your campus and examine the "integration" of your institution. Are individuals of different racial,

ethnic, or religious groups interacting with each other outside of classes? Why or why not?

4. Practice with "I" messages. Imagine that you are talking with someone who has really irritated you. First, write out your messages as a "you" statement. Then convert them to "I" messages, keeping in mind Ellis's "five ways to say 'I'" ideas. Be sure to state what you observe, how you feel, and what you want in your message.

EXERCISES

1. Draw a diagram of your childhood family home and designate where and when it was acceptable to eat. What rooms were off-limits? Was mealtime a family affair conducted in a dining room, or did family members scatter to various rooms? What did you learn about the importance of family from the rituals surrounding mealtime in your home?
2. Summarize a recent conflict you had with a friend or romantic partner. Using the grid summarized in Figure 7.1, identify the strategy you used within this conflict. What other strategy might you have used to manage the conflict more successfully?

3. You have been seeing an individual who is of a different race, ethnicity, or religion. You believe that this relationship has the potential to become a deeper, long-term partnership. You have not told your parents because you believe they would be very upset. What steps might you take to continue nurturing this new relationship without causing harm to your relationship with your parents?
4. Contact your local United Way and identify a not-for-profit or social service agency in your community in need of volunteers. What communication skills are most critical to assisting you in your volunteer work for this agency?

KEY TERMS

Accommodating style   139
Aggressiveness   128
Assertiveness   128
Avoiding style   139
Collaborating style   138
Collectivist cultures   132
Competing style   139
Complementary
  relationships   126
Compromising style   140
Confirming messages   127
Conflict   136

Constructive conflict   138
Covert conflict   136
Defensive climate   127
Dependent relationships   127
Destructive conflict   138
Dialectics   126
Disconfirming messages   127
Dominate   128
Flexibility   128
Gunnysacking   131
Independent relationships   127
Individualistic cultures   132

Interaction   128
Interdependent relationships   127
Nonassertiveness   128
Overt conflict   136
Pseudoconflict   138
Rejection messages   127
Rhetorical sensitivity   141
Rigidity   128
Supportive climate   128
Symmetrical
  relationships   127

REFERENCES

Association of American Colleges and Universities. 2002. *Greater expectations: A new vision for learning as a nation goes to college.* Washington, DC: Association of American Colleges and Universities.

Baxter, L.A., (1990). Dialectical contradictions in relationship development. *Journal of Social and Personal Relationships* 7: 69–88,

Blake, R., and Mouton, J. 1964. *The managerial grid.* Houston: Gulf Publishing.

Gibbs, J. (1961). Supportive and defensive climates. *The Journal of Communication, 11(3),* 141–148.

Hocker, J. L., and Wilmot, W. W. 1997. *Interpersonal conflict.* 5th ed. New York: McGraw-Hill.

Hofstede, G. 1980. Culture's consequences: International differences in work-related values. Newbury Park, CA: Sage.

Kilmann, R. H., and K. W. Thomas "Developing a Forced-Choice Measure of Conflict-Handling Behavior: The MODE Instrument," *Educational and Psychological Measurement,* Vol. 37, No. 2 (1977), 309–325.

Kuh, G. 2006. Thinking DEEPly about academic advising and student engagement. *Academic Advising Today* 29:1, 3.

Retrieved June 15, 2006, from www.nacada.ksu.edu/AAT/NW29_2.pdf.

Martin, J. N., and Nakayama, T. K. 2001. *Experiencing intercultural communication: An introduction.* Mountain View, CA: Mayfield.

Morreale, S. P., Spitzberg, B. H., and Barge, J. K. 2001. *Human communication: Motivation, knowledge, & skills.* Belmont, CA: Wadsworth.

NACADA. 2004. NACADA statement of core values of academic advising. Retrieved June 15, 2006, from the NACADA Clearinghouse of Academic Advising Resources website, www.nacada.ksu.edu/Clearinghouse/AdvisingIssues/Core-Values.htm.

Smith, L. N., and Walter, T. L. 1995. *The adult learner's guide to college success.* Belmont, CA: Wadsworth.

Ting-Toomey, S., and Oetzel, J. G. 2002. Cross-cultural face concerns and conflict styles. In *Handbook of international and intercultural communication.* 2nd ed., eds. W. B. Gudykunst and B. Moody, 143–164. Thousand Oaks, CA: Sage.

Wilmot, W. W., and Hocker, J. L. 2001. *Interpersonal conflict.* New York: Random House.

CHAPTER 8 Public Speaking: Process, Purposes, Topics, and Audiences

LEARNING OUTCOMES After reading this chapter, you will have:

the **Knowledge** to...   and the **Skills** to...

STUDYING PUBLIC SPEAKING, page 148

Appreciate the significance of public speaking.

- Use your emerging skills as a public speaker to engage discussions to gain information, get things done, etc.

UNDERSTANDING THE PROCESS OF PUBLIC SPEAKING, page 149

Comprehend how public speaking is practiced.

- Apply the model of public speaking, from selecting a topic to presentation, making sure to cover every aspect.

IDENTIFYING PUBLIC SPEAKING PURPOSES, page 150

Become aware of the reasons for public speaking.

- Determine whether the purpose of your speech is to mark an occasion, inform, or persuade.
- Follow guidelines for preparing speeches for specific purposes.

SELECTING A SUBJECT, page 153

Know how to pick a focus.

- Use brainstorming to help you explore possible subjects.
- Consider your subjects from the various perspectives or viewpoints of your audience.

SELECTING A TOPIC, page 159

Understand how to identify a topic

- Make sure that your topic is narrowed down enough to cover appropriately.

RELATING A TOPIC TO ONE OR MORE PURPOSES, page 160

Tell how a topic connects to intentions.

- Be able to articulate the general as well as the specific purpose(s) of your speech.

WRITING A THESIS STATEMENT, page 161

Develop a thesis statement.

- Craft a thesis statement that expresses the central idea, theme, or proposition of your speech.
- Ensure that your thesis is stated clearly and directly.

GATHERING INFORMATION, page 162

Search for credible information.

- Use librarians and information specialists on your campus to find current and credible information both on- and off-line.

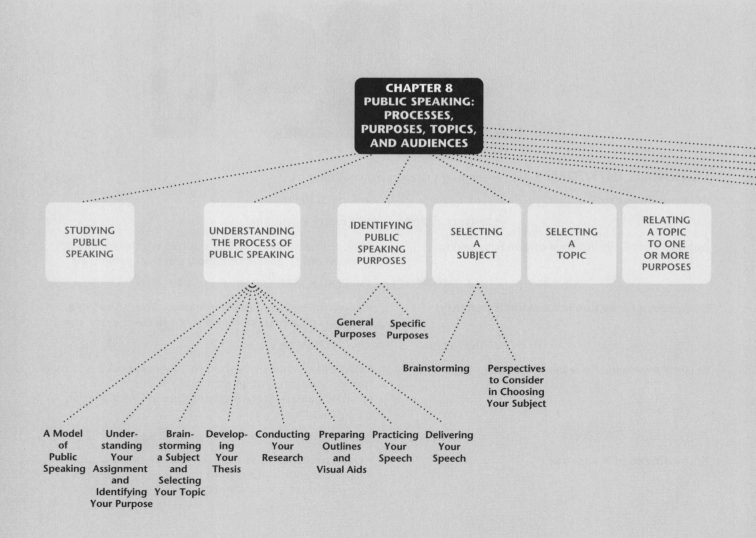

CONDUCTING INTERVIEWS AND RECORDING PERSONAL OBSERVATIONS, page 162

Know how to plan and carry out interviews and observations.

- Conduct interviews that help you answer who, why, what, where, how, and when questions.
- Decide whether or not personal observations are appropriate for your speech.

EVALUATING MATERIALS, page 164

Analyze materials critically.

- Consider the trustworthiness, accuracy, and currency of your materials.

IDENTIFYING DIFFERENT TYPES OF SPEECHES, page 165

Name and understand different types of speeches.

- Determine what kind of speech you are giving (special occasion, informative, or persuasive).

BECOMING A COMPETENT AND ETHICAL PUBLIC SPEAKER IN COLLEGE AND LIFE, page 166

Develop into a capable and principled public speaker.

- Treat all audiences, including your classroom audience as "real" audiences.
- Compose speeches that are relevant to the interests and needs of your audience.

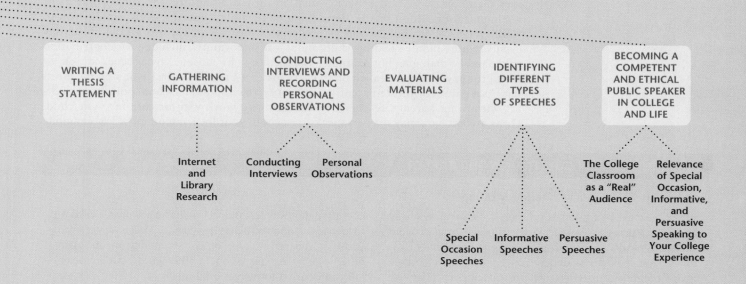

STUDYING PUBLIC SPEAKING

Preparing to give a speech helps you develop important academic skills. Although we'll discuss each of these ideas in greater detail, for now just consider the skills required to prepare an effective speech:

- Develop a simple, clear sentence that summarizes your main idea.
- Identify main ideas relevant to your thesis.
- Support your ideas adequately with current, reliable, and relevant research.
- Organize your ideas in a way that makes them accessible and reasonable.
- Articulate your ideas clearly so that others can understand your message.

While this list is incomplete, it emphasizes many of the skills you need as a college student, including engaging classroom discussion, thinking critically about what you read, supporting your ideas, and writing and speaking articulately with precision and clarity. Kanar (1998) includes the ability to make oral presentations as one of the "five essentials for classroom performance" (45). However, only 36.3 percent of 276,449 first-year students consider themselves above average in public speaking skills (Young 2004). Therefore, developing your public presentation skills is an important area of communication for you to focus on.

Studying public speaking helps you in your studies and prepares you to enter the work world. (See the box "Communication Counts in Your Career: Public Speaking as a Marketing Strategy" for additional insights.) Recent surveys confirm that effective oral communication is one of the most important job skills you can obtain (Darling & Dannels 2003; Peterson 1997). However, many students do not receive adequate communication education (Burk 2001) or resist integrating communication skills into their education (Dannels, Anson, Bullard, & Peretti 2003). Given that you will spend a great deal of your working hours listening, conversing, making presentations, working in small groups, and relating to other workers, developing your public speaking skills will provide you a keen advantage as you enter the job market.

You may be thinking, "How can public speaking help me listen, converse, work in small groups and so on? All these things? Giving a speech doesn't require me to do all these things." Public speaking is not just the actual presentation; it also requires preparation. You must gather information about your audience—often through listening and interviewing—and you must collect other forms of evidence and support. Additionally, you are most likely speaking in front of a small group and seeking to relate to your audience. Public speaking skills help you develop a wider range of abilities than you might first believe, which, in turn, are important to other contexts of communication. Additionally, developing your public speaking skills enables you to fulfill your responsibilities and privileges as a member of various groups. Everyday events require public speaking skills and, more importantly, include your contribution to the public dialogue. For example, as a member of a mosque, synagogue, church, or civic group, you may be called on to participate in a religious service or a public meeting. As a parent or future parent, you may need to respond to school policies or interact with other parents, teachers, or coaches who work with or care for your child. Or as a voter, you may need to speak to issues in your local community. For example,

COMMUNICATION COUNTS IN YOUR CAREER

Public Speaking as a Marketing Strategy

Many business professionals use public speaking as a way to contact prospective clients or customers and to build their businesses. For example, brokers often offer free investment seminars or underwrite a dinner to which they invite potential customers. At the meeting or after the meal, the broker explains some basic information about investing and then notes how he or she can assist in this important process. Doctors, dentists, attorneys, insurance agents, and other professionals are using a similar approach to identifying and recruiting new clients. They often offer to speak at service clubs or other community meetings in order to provide explanation. In other words, public speaking can be used to market a business. As a result of these endeavors, unforeseen opportunities to provide keynote speeches, conduct training sessions, or offer seminars may result.

the decisions made by lawmakers in your state directly impact the amount of tuition you pay, while state and federal laws also impact the availability of financial aid to pay your tuition. Have you been frustrated by the process of obtaining financial aid? Other than complain, what have you done about your frustration? How could you engage this issue that impacts your life and the lives of future college students? You could choose a topic like this for your informative or persuasive speech in this class so you can learn more about the issues and develop skills for addressing them. Use this communication class to engage the public dialogue. Recent information indicates (Young 2004) that many first-year students are more politically aware than in previous years, so you are likely to have an audience interested in the political and civic issues of the day in your communication class. The involvement of young voters in the most recent presidential election confirms this observation.

Public speaking skills enable you to engage not only in civic life but also in social life. At a recent wedding, the best man was expected to toast the newlyweds, even though he had not been informed of this until just after the ceremony. Sweating, literally and figuratively, he approached the minister and poured out a stream of concerns and complaints: "What am I going to do? What am I supposed to say? I've never done this before! I just can't do it. Will you please do it for me?" Although the minister tried to help him see that giving the toast was not that difficult, he utterly refused. In the end, the minister gave the toast because the best man believed he could not. While a basic communication course would not necessarily address all of this young man's concerns, he would have had some experience before an audience and would have been more prepared to toast his best friends on their wedding day.

UNDERSTANDING THE PROCESS OF PUBLIC SPEAKING

Now that we have discussed some of the advantages gained from developing your public speaking skills, let's consider a process you can use to prepare to speak.

A Model of Public Speaking

Figure 8.1 summarizes the important steps you must take to speak effectively. It emphasizes that *preparing* to speak is a *process* that requires time and energy. By referring to public speaking as a process, we are implying that you must work at developing both individual speeches and your speaking ability over time. Even people who may seem to speak with ease and assurance must employ this or a similar process. As you gain practice, you will be able to implement these steps more easily, but you will continue to use the steps in this process if you are to speak effectively.

Let's consider some key characteristics of the model as a whole in greater detail. First, the model depicts the entire public speaking process, from developing a focus for your speech to presenting it. Because we may get so involved in one aspect of the process that we forget the larger picture, this model helps us remember that in public speaking every aspect of preparation is important to the whole process.

Second, this model incorporates both single and double arrows. The single arrows indicate those aspects of preparation that logically move you forward toward the next step. The double arrow indicates that as you move forward in your preparation, you will return to a former step to refine what you previously completed. For example, consider the double arrow located between the "Developing Your Thesis" and "Conducting Your Research" steps. While you will have a rough thesis to work from, as you research you may need to refine that thesis in the process. The double arrow also emphasizes that preparation is a process requiring time, careful thought, and strategic planning. Considering each part of the model briefly permits us to examine the overall process important to public speaking.

Understanding Your Assignment and Identifying Your Purpose

You may receive an assignment to speak as a result of an invitation from a particular group, responsibilities on the job, participation in a ceremony or ritual, or as a requirement for a particular college class. The assignment also will likely identify the *purpose* of your speech. Whether or not you receive particular directions regarding your presentation

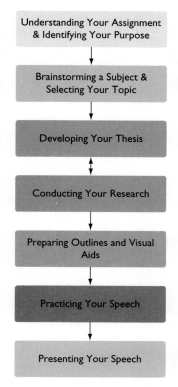

FIGURE 8.1

A Model for Speech Preparation.

you should focus on what you are seeking to accomplish in a particular speech given the occasion, audience, your expertise, and the amount of time you have to speak.

Brainstorming a Subject and Selecting Your Topic

A subject consists of a broad area of knowledge that could yield several potential topics, and a topic represents a particular and narrowed focus on that subject. Brainstorming allows you to let ideas flow without evaluating them so that you can generate many possible ideas that could yield subjects and topics as well as main ideas for your presentation.

Developing Your Thesis

A thesis statement summarizes the essence of your speech in a single, declarative sentence. The thesis is the speech's central idea, the theme to be developed, or the proposition to be proven that flows from the purpose of the speech. As you move from your topic to a thesis statement, you may find that, as the double arrow indicates, you will refine your thesis by reexamining and adapting your topic.

Conducting Your Research

If your ideas are to be clear and useful to your audience, you must develop and support them thoroughly. Research will provide you with the needed information and evidence to frame and bolster your ideas and will also help you refine your thesis, as indicated by the double arrow. In Chapter 9, we offer additional practical advice on conducting and using research.

Preparing Outlines and Visual Aids

Outlines help organize your ideas to assist in your speech's preparation and presentation, while visual aids help provide illustration and impact. In Chapter 9, we discuss organization and delivery in more detail.

Practicing Your Speech

There is no substitute for repeated, focused practice in preparing your speech. In our discussion of delivery, we suggest specific techniques that will make the most of the time you devote to practice.

Delivering Your Speech

You have planned, prepared, and practiced, and now it is time to make your presentation. We discuss the presentation element of public speaking in more detail in Chapter 9. As you can see from this brief explanation of the public speaking process, making effective presentations requires an investment of time and energy. Given the demands on your time, you will be tempted to short-circuit this process. You may even believe that you can skip some of the steps we have outlined here or disregard the entire process. Many beginning speakers think they can generate an effective presentation with minimal or even no preparation, but if you avoid or neglect this process, you will fail to gain the skills you need for academic, career, and personal success that we have outlined earlier in this chapter. As a result, you will insult your audience. How do you feel when you are listening to a speaker who rambles or who speaks in a monotone? You will make your audience just bored or frustrated if you do not adequately prepare. Therefore, we urge you to commit yourself to gleaning as much as possible from your study of public speaking. Many students will testify that they benefited greatly from making such a commitment.

IDENTIFYING PUBLIC SPEAKING PURPOSES

Why are you giving a speech? What is your purpose? Answering these questions is central to success in both your preparation and presentation. To assist you in answering these questions, consider that speeches have both general and specific purposes.

General Purposes

Some **general purposes** include

■ marking special occasions
■ informing
■ persuading

Graduation speeches, after-dinner speeches, and eulogies are examples of **special occasion speeches.** They often celebrate an event or honor people for their work or lives.

INFORMATIVE PURPOSES VERSUS PERSUASIVE PURPOSES   An **Informative speech** instructs or assists the audience in gaining understanding. Lectures and briefings are examples of informative speeches. A **persuasive speech** is meant to stimulate an audience to reaffirm or alter beliefs or encourage listeners to adopt new behaviors or continue to behave as they have in the past. While we categorize speeches according to these general purposes, it is important to note that these are, to some degree, artificial distinctions, particularly with regard to informative and persuasive speeches.

By selecting a particular topic and using specific information, even when we are not *directly* persuading, we present a particular perspective that may *indirectly* persuade. For example, a student who delivers an informative speech on creation science probably advocates a particular view about the origin of the world just by using the term *creation science* and by drawing on information from those who espouse this perspective. While the speaker may not seek to persuade us that his or her ideas are valid or that we should also believe in creation science, the topic and the evidence is, by its very nature, indirectly persuasive.

To be persuasive, persuasive speeches must use information effectively. A persuasive speech that lacks explanation and evidence, or information, will lack credibility and fail to persuade. Therefore, informative and persuasive speeches share important characteristics.

So, you may be asking, if there isn't much difference between informative and persuasive speeches, why even bother making the distinction in the first place? That's a valid question. The short answer is this: While informative and persuasive speeches share similar territory, *each kind of speech bears a different burden.* An informative speech teaches; it does not seek to convince or actuate. Any persuasion in an informative speech is clearly indirect and not purposeful. In contrast, persuasive speeches use

General purposes ■ (1) to entertain, inspire, or celebrate; (2) to inform; and (3) to persuade.

Special occasion speeches ■ Speeches that recognize a person, place, or event.

Informative speeches ■ Speeches that instruct or assist the audience in gaining understanding.

Persuasive speeches ■ Speeches that stimulate an audience to reaffirm or alter beliefs or encourage the adoption of new behaviors or the continuation of past behaviors.

TABLE 8.1

COMPARISON OF INFORMATIVE AND PERSUASIVE SPEECHES

	Informative Speech	**Persuasive Speech**
Intent of Speech	To explain, define, demonstrate *Example:* To explain the process for registering to vote	To alter belief or action, reinforce *Example:* To convince the audience to register to vote
Topic	A process, concept, or activity *Example:* Registering to vote is a simple process	A proposition or claim *Example:* Registering to vote is an important first step in participating in our democracy.
Desired Audience Response	To understand *Example:* To understand the process of how to register to vote	To believe or do *Example:* To actually register to vote
Speaker's Role	Teacher *Example:* Explaining the process for registering to vote.	Advocate *Example:* To convince the audience that registering to vote is essential to the democratic process.
Appeals	Mostly credibility and logic *Example:* I registered to vote and learned the process firsthand (credibility). I have also researched the process more thoroughly (logic).	Credibility, logic, and emotion *Example:* Registering to vote is essential for to your participation in our democracy, especially given the widespread lack of voting in our country (logic). Our forefathers gave their lives to give us this liberty and opportunity (emotion).

FIGURE 8.2

Template for Writing Specific Purpose Statements.

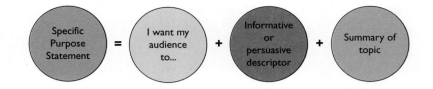

information purposefully to reinforce or change listeners' beliefs or behaviors. This is an important distinction because it helps you to envision your goal of giving either an informative or persuasive speech.

Chapters 10 and 11 will provide more information about informative and persuasive speeches. For now, Table 8.1 summarizes the key aspects of informative and persuasive speeches and notes several differences, including the intent, topic, desired audience response, role of the speaker, and types of appeals used in each type of speech.

Specific Purposes

In addition to a general purpose, your speech also needs a **specific purpose**. Obviously, if you are going to celebrate an occasion, you need to know what kind of occasion it is. If you are delivering an informative speech, it is logical to ask, "What do I want my audience to learn from this speech?" If you are delivering a persuasive speech, you may ask, "What do I want my audience to believe, or how do I want them to behave?" Answering these questions requires you to have a clear sense of your topic and have a full understanding of how your topic meshes with your purpose. We will address this link further later in this chapter. At this point, let's focus on your speech's specific purpose.

We suggest that you use a template to draft your first specific purpose statement (see Figure 8.2). Consider each aspect of this template. The clause "I want my audience to ..." allows you to focus on what you want your audience to gain from your presentation and reminds you that public speaking is an interaction between the speaker and the audience. In other words, as you consider your specific purpose statement, you must also consider how this statement relates to your intended audience. Table 8.2 provides a list of special occasion, informative, and persuasive descriptors you can use to draft your specific purpose statement.

A brief summary of your topic provides the last part of the specific purpose statement. Figure 8.3 provides an example of a specific purpose statement, showing how the parts of the statement relate.

If this were your specific purpose statement, it would reveal that your speech's general purpose is to inform and that your specific purpose is to help the audience *understand* the speech's topic.

If you used the same topic but wrote a specific purpose statement for the general purpose of persuading, consider how the statement would change: "I want my audience to agree that there are three solid reasons for not working while attending college." The opening phrase, descriptor, and topic statement in this specific purpose statement identify this as a persuasive presentation. Also, notice how the focus or burden of the speech shifts. Now

TABLE 8.2

DESCRIPTORS FOR SPECIFIC PURPOSE STATEMENTS

Special Occasion Speeches	Informative Speeches	Persuasive Speeches
Celebrate	Understand	Believe
Recognize	Learn	Agree
Remember	Know	Begin to
Enjoy	Comprehend	Cease to
Laugh at	Appreciate	Choose to
Reflect on	Absorb	Purchase
Dedicate	Explain	Select

Specific purpose ■ The purpose of a speech in relation to its specific topic.

you want the audience to agree with your position on the issue of working while attending college. Although you may use some of the same information during informative and persuasive speeches on this topic, *how* you use the information shifts. In the informative speech, you target understanding, but in the persuasive speech, you seek to lead the audience to agree with you.

How could you reframe this topic to make it a special occasion speech? Consider this specific purpose statement: "I want my audience members to celebrate their success at balancing college and employment." This statement would be suitable for a banquet or an awards ceremony where working college students are recognized for successfully balancing multiple demands. In this speech, you do not primarily explain why working and attending college simultaneously is demanding, nor do you seek to persuade your audience that both working and attending college is a problem to avoid. Rather, you celebrate the students' success at doing both even in the face of difficulties. While you may use some of the same information that you would for an informative or persuasive speech on this topic, you will employ it much differently in this speech—to enhance the celebration.

Template: Specific Purpose Statement = I want my audience to... + Informative or persuasive descriptor + Summary of topic

Example: Specific Purpose Statement = I want my audience to... + ...understand... + ...three reasons why educators believe that working while attending college negatively impacts students.

FIGURE 8.3
Example of a Specific Purpose Statement.

SELECTING A SUBJECT

Once you have a sense of your purpose and the type of speech you will deliver, you are still faced with numerous decisions in preparing your speech. Logically, the next question you need to answer is, "What will I talk about?" This requires you to consider the speech's subject and then the topic. Earlier, we noted that the **subject** is a broad area of knowledge. To begin, you must identify several such subject areas that can, in time, yield narrowed topics. Brainstorming can help you generate these subject areas.

Brainstorming

Brainstorming is a process that allows your thoughts and ideas to flow freely. Write down any possible subjects or topics that come to mind. If you have trouble getting started, use categories to jump-start the process. For example, think about people, places, events, movies, computers, books, TV, controversies, beliefs, opinions, or the latest news stories; these are all subject areas. At this point, don't eliminate any possible ideas; just write until you have no more ideas or until you have filled two or three pages with ideas. Then, begin to work through these ideas using the information in the next section. When you find a subject that has strong possibilities, circle it and move on. However, don't throw away the ideas you have worked to create; keep them in case you need to go back and consider other possibilities.

Perspectives to Consider in Choosing Your Subject

You have numerous possible subjects for your speech. Which should you choose? Consider the following perspectives as you work through the possible subjects one by one (Worley 2000). Remember to circle those that appropriately consider each of these perspectives.

THE AUDIENCE PERSPECTIVE   Begin your subject selection by considering your audience members, which is the most important perspective to consider. What issues matter to them? What questions do they have that you may be able to answer? Additionally, the **audience perspective** considers your listeners' multiple characteristics and the resulting type of audience they comprise. Audience *characteristics* include the group's demographics and psychological profiles. Audience *type* refers to the listeners' basic disposition. (Table 8.3 summarizes the information you need to

Subject ■ A broad area of knowledge.

Brainstorming ■ Allowing the thought process to flow freely.

Audience perspective ■ Considers the listeners' multiple characteristics and the resulting type of audience they comprise.

TABLE 8.3

ANALYZING YOUR AUDIENCE

The following graphic depicts the issues you need to consider in analyzing your audience to help you select an appropriate subject and narrowed topic.

AUDIENCE CHARACTERISTICS

Demographics

Age

Gender

Ethnicity

Level of education

Physical ability level

Group memberships

Psychological Profiles

Attitudes

Beliefs

Values

Learning Styles

Feelers

Watchers

Thinkers

Doers

AUDIENCE TYPES

Friendly

Neutral

Apathetic

Unsupportive

Opposed

Effective speakers always consider the audience they will address in preparing and presenting a speech.

consider about audiences.) Because analyzing your audience is essential to choosing your topic and to preparing and presenting your speech, let's consider it in more detail by briefly reviewing each of the audience characteristics; we then conclude this section by considering audience types.

The term *demographics* refers to an audience's observable or readily available characteristics—age, sex, gender, ethnicity, education level, physical ability levels, and group affiliation. Some of these characteristics are readily defined while others may be less clear. *Age* refers to how old people are, which, at least in a general sense, often influences how they look at the world because of their experiences. For example, elders who were born near the turn of the twentieth century have a very different view of the world than children born at the turn of the twenty-first century. Table 8.4 provides more information about generational differences that influence how people approach and process information.

Sex refers to whether one is biologically male or female, while *gender* refers to the learned behaviors we develop as a result of our socialization. Wood (1994) refers to *gender* as the socialized tendencies of women and men to perceive, believe, and behave

TABLE 8.4

Understanding Basic Generational Differences

1. "Baby Boomers" (born 1943 to 1960, ages 44 to 61)

Core Values	Assets	Liabilities
Optimism	Service-oriented	Not naturally "budget-minded"
Team orientation	Driven	Uncomfortable with conflict
Personal gratification	Willing to go "extra mile"	Reluctant to go against peers
Health and wellness	Good at relationships	May put process ahead of result
Personal growth	Want to please	Overly sensitive to feedback

2. Generation Xers (born 1960 to 1980, ages 24 to 44)

Core Values	Assets	Liabilities
Diversity	Adaptable	Impatient
Thinking globally	Technoliterate	Deficient in people skills
Balance	Independent	Inexperienced
Technoliteracy	Unintimidated by authority	Cynical
Fun	Creative	
Informality		
Self-reliance		
Pragmatism		

3. Generation Next, or "Y" also called "Millennials" (born since 1980, ages 24 and younger)

Core Values	Assets	Liabilities
Optimism	Collectively active	Have need of supervision/structure
Civic duty	Optimistic	Inexperienced in handling difficult people
Confidence	Tenacious	
Achievement	Heroic	
Sociability	Capable of multitasking capabilities	
Morality	Technologically savvy	
Street smarts		
Diversity		

Source: From *Generations at Work: Managing the Clash of Veterans, Boomers, Xers, and Nexters in Your Workplace,* by Ron Zemke, Claire Raines, and Bob Filipczak. AMACOM Books, 2001. Reprinted with the permission of the authors. Copyright Performance Research Associates, Minneapolis, MN. All rights reserved.

differently. Although gender roles are more flexible in contemporary society than in the past, there are still relatively stable expectations for male and female behavior (Kirtley & Weaver 1999; Sellnow & Golish 2000).

Ethnicity refers to individuals' cultural background. Although some people refer to include race as a distinguishing characteristic, race is a problematic idea because it cannot be easily defined, especially in view of the current diversity of the world (Martin & Nakayama 2005). But ethnicity, which includes a mix of characteristics such as skin color, facial features, native language, rites and rituals, and core values, helps us think more accurately about the people with whom we may speak.

Education level usually refers to the amount of formal education an audience may have received. However, education may also be thought of in terms of life experience, which should not be discounted.

Physical ability level refers to people who have disabilities, as well as the kind and degree of a disability. With the passage of the American Disabilities Act and the subsequent research that has emerged regarding the experiences of people with disabilities (see Braithwaite & Thompson 2000), we have become aware of the importance of attending to this range of audience characteristics in shaping our presentations.

Group affiliation, according to Osborn and Osborn (2000), includes membership in religious, political, social, and occupational groups. In short, knowing the kinds of groups to which your audience members belong can cue you to the types of beliefs, attitudes, and values they hold.

These demographic characteristics can help you understand your audience and, thereby, assist you in choosing a topic. For example, if you are speaking with mature, single mothers who have returned to college later in life, you have specific information about your audience that can help direct your choice of topics. On the other hand, if you are speaking with a group of teenage males who are avid listeners of rap music, you have a very different set of information about your audience. Let's assume that one of your top five topics is what you learned during a recent ten-day trip to England. You would certainly structure your speech differently for mature, single mothers than you would for the group of teenagers. For the first group, you may concentrate on government support for childcare in the UK, while for the second group you might focus on the major influence of the "British Invasion" on American music.

Stereotyping is a significant problem with this approach to audience analysis. As we've discussed before, a stereotype is a biased opinion of a group, often based on overgeneralizations. For example, thinking that all women are emotional and that all men are logical are stereotypes of both groups. Concluding that all Asian students study more than U.S. students is also a stereotype, as is believing that all college students drink heavily. Therefore, it is important to avoid making assumptions about your audience based on demographic characteristics. To return to our example, you may well find some single mothers who are interested in rap music and teenage males who are interested in childcare issues. It is important, therefore, to avoid biases in your speech preparation.

Psychological profiles include your audience's attitudes, beliefs, values, needs, and learning styles. Let's give each of these more attention.

Attitudes, *beliefs*, and *values* refer to the ethical characteristics of your audience. **Values** are deeply held convictions about the undeniable worthiness of a certain ideal. For example, after the September 11, 2001, tragedy, President Bush appealed to the value of justice in response to the terrorist acts because many U.S. citizens hold to the ideal of justice. **Beliefs** are strongly held ideas about the nature of truth. For example, some people express a belief in God, while others, of equally strong persuasion, do not believe in God. Beliefs, then, are even more specific than values. To keep to our example, some people believe in God as conceptualized by Christianity, while others believe in God as explained in Judaism, Islam, Buddhism, Hinduism, or other religions. An **attitude** refers to a favorable or negative inclination toward a person, place, event, idea, or object. For example, some people have a favorable response to NFL football and are avid fans while others find football unimportant or boring.

As you might expect, values, beliefs, and attitudes relate to one another. For example, many undergraduates are concerned about grades. In some courses, midsemester and final exam scores largely determine final grades. If you hold to the *value* of fairness, you probably *believe* that midterm and final tests should represent the content of the

Values ■ Deeply held convictions about the undeniable worthiness of a certain ideal.

Beliefs ■ Strongly held ideas about the nature of truth.

Attitude ■ A favorable or negative inclination toward a person, place, event, or object.

course as reflected in classroom lectures and assigned readings. Therefore, if you take a midterm and notice that several of the questions are not drawn from classroom lectures or the assigned readings, you may well consider this unfair and thereafter harbor a definitively unfavorable *attitude* toward the course and the instructor. In the future, if the course or the instructor is mentioned, you will probably experience a distinctively negative emotional response and communicate this to others by saying, "Don't take the course with her; she doesn't give fair tests."

As a speaker, if you deny, question, or slight your audience's values, beliefs, and attitudes, you will complicate the speaking situation. Therefore, it is important to be aware of your audience's ethical predisposition so you can build common ground with them by identifying shared values, beliefs, and attitudes. Even if, in the end, you wish to question or disagree with some of your audience's ethical positions, building common ground with them is an important step in persuasion. In other words, you need to identify common areas in order to enhance your credibility so that later you can speak with your audience about those ideas that you do not have in common. For example, your audience may not share your view that convicted prisoners should be allowed conjugal visits with their spouses. However, your audience is likely to believe in the ideal of justice. Even though your audience may disagree with your argument, you share the common value of justice, which you can use to help increase the reasonableness of your argument.

Audience *needs* refer to the basic motivations of audiences. Earlier in this book we discussed Maslow's hierarchy of needs. Recall that, according to Maslow, people have needs that range from basic physical needs to self-actualization. It is important to note that all of these needs, however, center in the self to some degree. As Osborn and Osborn (2000) explain, "People will listen, learn, and remember a message only if it relates to their needs, wants or wishes" (90).

People learn differently; they prefer to process information in different ways. There are a variety of approaches to understanding how people learn (Reiff 1992). As Sellnow (2002) explains, learning styles can be thought of as "a four-stage cycle of feeling, watching, thinking and doing" (17). As you prepare to speak, remember this important information. Even if you do not have demographic information or insight about your audience's values, beliefs, and attitudes, you can appeal to various learning styles in your audience by using anecdotes, examples, or stories that have an emotional quality. Use visuals to catch the attention of those who prefer to watch. Rely on strong evidence such as facts, statistics, or expert testimony to appeal to those who prefer to think with you as you speak. And provide an activity for your audience to appeal to those who prefer hands-on learning. This might be something as simple as completing a short survey or engaging in physical movement. If you succeed in driving home the main point of your speech in these four different ways, you will leave an impression on your audience.

TYPES OF AUDIENCES   Typically, your audience will be one of five types, depending on their characteristics and psychological profiles.

Friendly audiences are those who hold positive regard for you or your topic. If, for example, you deliver a persuasive speech, a friendly audience already agrees with your position; you already share values, attitudes, and beliefs. You will likely simply reinforce those ideas that the audience already agrees with and encourage the listeners to continue holding their position. For example, members of sororities or fraternities probably already agree in the value of the Greek system. If a speaker to a Greek audience supports this position, he or she will be speaking with a friendly audience.

In contrast, audiences toward the other end of the continuum disagree with your position or doubt your credibility; they are *opposed* to your position. In this case, you must find common ground to help the audience members appreciate an alternative perspective, even though they probably won't change their minds. To keep to our example, if your speech emphasizes the value of the Greek system for beginning college students, and your audience consists of former members of sororities and fraternities who consider the Greek system discriminatory rather than inclusive, and abusive rather than supportive, then the audience is strongly opposed to a position you are advocating.

Of course, audiences may be located at any point along the continuum and may therefore be inclined toward friendliness or opposition without being deeply committed

Personal perspective ■ Takes into account an individual's knowledge, attitudes, interests, experiences, and beliefs to help generate speech topics.

Situational perspective ■ Focuses on the context of a speech in selecting a topic.

Organizational perspective ■ Recognizes that speakers may represent an organization and, as a result, may need to be sensitive in choosing a subject.

Practical perspective ■ Considers the availability of adequate, recent research materials and time limits for the preparation and presentation of a speech.

to a definite posture. *Neutral* audiences are at the continuum's center; they remain undecided about you or your topic, although they may be interested in the topic. When addressing neutral audiences, consider offering a wide range of appeals to nudge the audience toward greater friendliness. Remember that you can always appeal to needs and learning styles as a strategy for enhancing audience responsiveness.

Unlike neutral audiences, *apathetic* audiences are disinterested in your topic and/or you as the speaker. They simply don't care. Consequently, they appear to be more opposed than they truly are. When speaking to apathetic audiences, increase their interest by relating the topic more directly to them and by delivering the speech skillfully. In other words, to overcome the "So what?" mentality of the apathetic audience, help the audience see and feel that what you have to say directly impacts their lives. Again, remembering your audience's basic needs can help you strengthen their interest.

Unsupportive audiences are not strongly opposed to a position because they possess a less definitive degree of disagreement. Unlike neutral audiences, unsupportive audiences hold a defined position on your topic, and unlike apathetic audiences, unsupportive audiences care about the topic. However, because they are less opposed to you or your position, they may be swayed by carefully crafted arguments and appeals.

By attending to the demographics, psychological profiles, and the subsequent types of your audience, you can refine your choice of subjects. After you identify those subjects that appeal to you, carefully think about your audience. What will audience members find interesting, novel, alluring, familiar, comfortable, or provocative?

THE PERSONAL PERSPECTIVE The **personal perspective** considers your knowledge, attitudes, interests, experiences, and beliefs to help generate speech topics. By choosing a subject that you are personally invested in, you can maintain your enthusiasm in both preparing and presenting your speech. However, it is essential that you select a subject that interests both your audience and you. Begin with your listeners and link your interests with theirs. A personal inventory form, which helps you identify areas of personal interest, can help you think through possible topics.

OTHER PERSPECTIVES While the audience perspective and personal perspectives are central, there are other perspectives you should consider in choosing your topic. First, the **situational perspective** focuses on the context for your speech. You must consider the time, occasion, place, and size of your audience. It's helpful to know when, where, and why you are speaking, because these will help you plan your speech carefully and select an appropriate subject and tone for delivering the speech.

Second, the **organizational perspective** recognizes that speakers may directly or indirectly represent the firm or organization for which they work; therefore, speakers may need to be sensitive to the subject they choose because there are public relations overtones related to the choice.

Third, the **practical perspective** considers the ready availability of adequate and recent research material as well as time limits for preparation and presentation of your speech. While all of us must manage our time in order to accomplish multiple tasks, college students especially must do so efficiently because they have many demands on their time. Therefore, you must be practical about your choice of subject, given the time you have to prepare for your speech; either you manage your time or your time will manage you.

Now that you have identified potential subject areas using the five perspectives we have discussed, consider the summary of these perspectives in Table 8.5 and the corresponding questions to help you analyze your chosen subjects. Then go back through your brainstorming list and write down all the circled subject areas on a piece of paper. As you read them again, rank them using the perspectives we just discussed. Which topic seems best, considering each of these perspectives? With these rankings before you, select the speech subject you find most suitable and commit to using it. You may be tempted to go back to this list and start over again, but you are likely to lose valuable preparation time if you do.

TABLE 8.5

QUESTIONS TO ASK IN CHOOSING A SUBJECT

Perspectives to Consider	Questions to Ask
Audience perspective	What does my audience consider important? What does my audience want to know? How does my audience feel about particular issues, problems, or interests? What issue is currently being debated or investigated as reported in the media?
Personal perspective	What subjects interest me? What problem concerns me? What issue would I like to learn more about? What can I learn from my personal inventory?
Situational perspective	What is the nature of the event? Where will I be speaking? At what time will I be speaking? What expectations does the audience have for this event? How many people will attend the event?
Organizational perspective	How will this subject reflect on my organization? How would the leaders in my organization want me to represent them? What subject should I avoid in order not to misrepresent my organization? What subjects may need clarification in order to offset any misperceptions of my organization?
Practical perspective	How much time do I have to speak? How soon am I to speak? How much research have I gathered? How much time will I need for additional research? What subjects do I already know a lot about? Will the subject I know a lot about interest my audience? How interested am I in the subjects I know a lot about? How motivated am I about them?

SELECTING A TOPIC

Now that you have a subject, you must narrow it to a **topic,** or the specific focus of your speech. You will not have enough time to share all the information about a given subject. Moreover, your audience does not have the patience or endurance to listen to all that information. As someone noted, "The mind can only contain what the seat can endure." So, how do you begin to narrow a subject into a topic? As our model in Figure 9.1 indicates, brainstorming can once again be very helpful. Using clean sheets of paper, again start to generate specific ideas related to your subject. Ask basic information questions like Who? When? Where? Why? How? As you did before, let your thoughts flow uninterrupted; don't exclude any possibilities. Keep your worksheet to use later in the process of developing your speech.

When you have a list of possible topics for your speech, return to the perspectives we discussed and apply them again. Which topics seem to mesh well with these perspectives? As you did with the subjects, rank the topics you have generated and commit to one. If you have carefully thought through the process, you should have confidence that the topic you have chosen will interest you and your audience and you should have sufficient enthusiasm to begin crafting your speech. As a final litmus test, ask yourself, "Do *I* truly care about this topic? Am *I* genuinely interested in this topic?" Without a personal commitment to the topic, you will lack the enthusiasm to effectively prepare and present your speech.

Topic ■ The specific focus of a speech.

COMMUNICATION COUNTS IN YOUR COLLEGE EXPERIENCE

Computer Help in Finding a Topic

Are you having problems finding a topic for your speech? Check out the following websites for assistance in finding a subject or topic. Although these sites may help you get started, remember that you must analyze your audience and adapt the topic well to them.

www.hawaii.edu/mauispeech/html/infotopichelp.html
http://wps.ablongman.com/ab_public_speaking_2/
http://www.speech-topics-help.com/

You also need to consider if your selected topic is narrow enough. A key tip here is to consider the amount of time you have to speak. Understand the time limits for the speeches you will give in this class. While these timeframes may seem long at first, the time will pass very quickly. Furthermore, as a general guideline, plan to share more information about a focused idea rather than less information about a greater number of ideas. Consider this example:

Insufficiently narrowed topic: College roommates

Sufficiently narrowed topic: How to get along with college roommates

The topic "college roommates" is much too broad because there are many possible topics related to this subject. Generate as many topics or ideas as you can about college roommates. How many emerged as you brainstormed? Now, think about strategies for getting along with college roommates. How many ideas can you generate? As you will likely see, the narrowed topic provides fewer and more specific ideas and, therefore, suggests that it is limited sufficiently. As the box "Communication Counts in Your College Experience: Computer Help in Finding a Topic" points out, there are many resources to assist you in your brainstorming and topic selection process.

RELATING A TOPIC TO ONE OR MORE PURPOSES

You now have a subject and a narrowed topic. But what is your speech's goal? Remember that the goal of your speech is related to the assignment you receive and/or the three general purposes we discussed earlier in this chapter. At this point, you must be clear on whether you are to celebrate, inform, or persuade. This defines your general purpose.

You also need a specific purpose, which you can frame by using the formula offered in Figure 8.2 on page 152. As an example, let's use the topic we identified earlier: how to get along with college roommates. Consider each of these specific purposes:

Special occasion speech: *I want my audience to laugh at ways we use to get along with college roommates.*

Informative speech: *I want my audience to understand how to get along with a college roommate.*

Persuasive speech: *I want my audience to begin to use known ways to get along with college roommates.* (This is a speech to actuate.)

OR

Persuasive speech: *I want my audience to agree with me that the known ways to get along with college roommates are useful strategies.* (This is a speech to convince.)

The general and specific purposes for a speech help to craft the topic even more clearly, although the essential topic remains the same. This reminds us that while the process of crafting a speech follows the logic identified in our model, the steps influence one another; it is an iterative process. Remember that the general and specific purposes of your speech are fundamentally important because together they are the rudder; they set the direction of your speech and help to ensure that you stay on course. You must know what you want to achieve before you can effectively reach your goal and link this purpose to your topic.

WRITING A THESIS STATEMENT

At this point in the process, you know your assignment and, therefore, your general purpose. You have also identified a subject and a topic and sufficiently narrowed the topic, and you have crafted a specific purpose statement that integrates and refines the links between your general purpose and your topic. While this statement provides you with important direction, you still need to develop its content by creating a thesis statement. A **thesis statement** summarizes the essence of your speech in a single, declarative sentence. The **thesis** is the speech's central idea, the theme to be developed, or the proposition to be proven; it is a road map for your entire presentation. A solid thesis statement should contain the single, main idea of the speech, stated in clear language and is related to the general and specific purposes of your presentation. One way to think about a thesis statement is to phrase your topic in the form of a question; the thesis should answer the question. Here's an example:

> **Question:** *How can we address the increase of childhood obesity?*
>
> **Thesis:** *We can address the increase of childhood obesity by educating parents and children about healthy eating, encouraging exercise, and enhancing physical education activities in the schools.*

Consider these thesis statements for the three main types of presentations. Note how the first statements provide a general subject area, while the second statements provide more information and the refined versions offer even more specific information and focus. Keep in mind that thesis statements develop as you move through the process of preparing your speech.

Informative Thesis Statement:

Topical thesis statement: *College roommates.*

First-draft thesis statement: *There are three important strategies that will help us get along with college roommates.*

Refined thesis statement: Getting along with college roommates can best be achieved by avoiding assumptions about what is acceptable, agreeing on mutual guidelines for behavior, and dealing with issues when they arise in an appropriate manner.

Persuasive Thesis Statement:

Topical thesis statement: *Problems with the Internet.*

First-draft thesis statement: *Parents should ensure that their children do not encounter some of the potential problems with the Internet.*

Effective thesis statement: While the Internet provides many positive opportunities, parents should monitor their children's use of the Internet to ensure that they avoid the frequent problems of the loss of personal privacy, piracy of copyright materials, and the ready availability of pornography.

Special Occasion Thesis Statement:

Topical thesis statement: *Celebrating Bob's retirement.*

First-draft thesis statement: *Bob's retirement is an appropriate time to celebrate his work at our company.*

Refined thesis statement: Bob's retirement is an appropriate time for us to celebrate his vision, energy, and dedication to our company.

At this point, you may not be sure about all of the main ideas you will incorporate into your presentation. As you can see by looking at each of the refined thesis statements, thesis statements develop as you conduct research and prepare your speech in greater detail. The first drafts are a beginning; they aren't the final draft you'll write on your preparation outline. You may well write several drafts of your thesis statement as you develop your topic. The double arrow in our model between thesis and research is a reminder that the thesis at this point is a work in progress. However, it is still important to write a first draft so you remember that your speech needs a clear, single idea from which all the other ideas flow.

Thesis statement ■ A single, declarative sentence that summarizes the essence of a speech.

Thesis ■ The central idea of a speech.

GATHERING INFORMATION

You now have a narrowed topic and a clear thesis. Now you must gather the information that will provide the substance of your speech. As you read about your specific topic, you may find information that helps you refine your thesis, identify your main ideas, and discover material that will help you develop your topic. In other words, the process of developing your speech does not necessarily move in a straight line; it may double back on itself. Effective speakers realize that they continue to refine their topic choice, specific purpose, and thesis by way of research. Be alert to how you can improve your speech as you proceed; don't get locked into a single way to approach your topic. But how do you find appropriate supporting material? To answer this question, we will now discuss where to search, how to search, and what to search for as you conduct your research. In Chapter 9 we will explore how to effectively use what you found in your research.

Internet and Library Research

There are numerous ways to find information to support your topic. These often include electronically available information. For example, you may enter key terms into an Internet search engine such as Yahoo! or Google to find some initial information. However, for the most part, the best sources are still contained in your college library. For example, databases such as ProQuest, Academic Premier, ERIC, and EBSCO will

Specialists in information technology, like your librarian, can help you search for the information you need for your speech.

often provide you with numerous and credible "hits." You can also find statistical information in such sources as *Facts on File* or leads to various periodicals and newspapers in resources such as the *Reader's Guide to Periodical Literature* or LexisNexis. Additionally, you can find materials in print resources such as books, pamphlets, or brochures.

People can also be valuable resources. Librarians can be very valuable resources to help you find material; talk with them. You may also interview a person who has strategic knowledge about your topic, or you may even draw on your own observations or experiences to help flesh out ideas. Carefully organize your materials so you can refer to them later. Even a manila folder can help keep your information together and save you time later.

CONDUCTING INTERVIEWS AND RECORDING PERSONAL OBSERVATIONS

While we address employment interviewing in Chapter 13, our focus here is to help you gather information for your presentation.

Conducting Interviews

Before gathering information from someone, you must first think about some fundamental questions: Who? Why? What? Where? How? When? Let's consider each of these questions.

WHO? You will need to identify someone who is an expert on your topic. You may, for example, want to speak with a medical doctor if you want information about the rigors of medical training. On the other hand, if you want to know about how soldiers experienced the Vietnam War, you should talk to someone who was actually deployed during the 1960s.

WHY? You need a clear focus for your interview. Why are you approaching this person with these questions? What is your purpose in the interview? What do you want to know when the interview is complete that you do not know now? Perhaps writing a simple purpose statement will help focus your thinking: "I want to know more about _____ when I am through with this interview."

WHAT?   Planning the questions you will pose in the interview is equally important. An interview schedule can help you plan your questions. As you have been thinking through your presentation, you will likely have some key ideas you want to explore in the interview. We recommend that you think about the main points of your speech and draft questions that will help you learn more about these ideas. You will also want to be ready to ask follow-up questions to ensure that you clearly understand the interviewee's answers. To illustrate, consider this example if your topic is the rigors of medical education:

> **Key question:** *What did you find to be the most challenging aspect of your medical education?*
>
> **Follow-up question:** *Why was this aspect particularly challenging?*
>
> **Follow-up question:** *What other aspects of your medical education did you find challenging?*

WHERE?   Plan to conduct the interview in a quiet, comfortable place where you will not be interrupted by people, phones, or computers. This may be the interviewee's office or a conference room. Be sure to plan ahead. You may even ask your interviewee, "Where might be the best place for us to have 30 minutes of uninterrupted time together?"

HOW?   Remember to dress appropriately, be on time, and introduce yourself to your interview if you have not previously met, and express your gratitude at the outset of the interview. Establish a friendly but professional tone, and be sure to stick to the timeframe you both agreed to for the interview. Remind the interviewee of the purpose of the interview and ask for his or her honest responses. Let the interviewee know how you will use the information. You will probably want to take notes or, better still, ask the interviewee if you may record the session for your future, private use. End the interview by thanking your interviewee. You may also want to send a follow up thank you note or email.

WHEN?   Set at mutually agreeable time and a length of time for the interview. Be sure to be sensitive to the interviewee's schedule.

Personal Observations

Personal observations refer to your own experiences interacting with others and observing life events. Often these experiences provide personal examples that offer illustrations, examples, or other information that may help you clarify an idea in your presentation. For example, you may have a job that brings you into contact with a variety of people, processes, or policies. Your participation in these situations may provide valuable insight, as long as what you share is appropriate and approved. In other words, you would not want to share sensitive, personal, or private information, but you may find a suitable illustration to help explain or illustrate an idea in your speech. Here's an example. Suppose you want to give a presentation on sexual harassment policies in the workplace and you notice that there is a large poster where you work that emphasizes this policy. You might use this as an illustration of how a company makes the policy known to employees.

While some personal observations may emerge quite naturally, you may also find it useful to intentionally observe a certain place or certain people to gain insights or examples. So, for example, if you want to talk about how college students interact within groups, you may visit the union building and simply observe how students interact with each other. Do students with certain demographics tend to sit together? What is the typical group size in the union? Do people actually tend to gather in groups, or do

Planning for and conducting effective face to face interviews can provide you with valuable information and insights.

they more often sit by themselves or with just one other person? Purposeful observation can provide you with interesting and useful information for your presentation, as long as you use it appropriately and ethically.

EVALUATING MATERIALS

After you have gathered information, you must consider its usefulness. Your research materials should be dependable and useful, so it is important to find credible sources. Not all research materials are created equal. In fact, some are outright ludicrous. If you use offensive, questionable, or suspect materials, you will compromise your credibility and lose your audience's respect and attention. In general, sources should be credible, recent, and objective. How do you evaluate a source's usefulness and credibility for your speech? Here are some guidelines:

■ Avoid "open sources" such as Wikipedia or blogs because they are not necessarily credible and may be highly prejudiced
■ Consider the source—especially ones on the Internet. These questions, suggested by David Boraks (1997), can help you evaluate them:
  • What is the site's purpose?
  • Is its information unbiased?
  • Who sponsors the site?
  • What are the organization's values or goals?
  • Can you contact the sponsors should questions arise?
  • Is the information in the site well documented?
  • Does it provide citations to sources used in obtaining the information?
  • Are individual articles signed or attributed?
  • When was the information published? Is the date of the last revision posted somewhere on the page?
  • What are the author's credentials?
  • Is the author frequently cited in other sources?
  • How does the value of the Web-based information you've found compare with other available sources, such as print?
■ Consider the author and find more about him or her. Where does the author work? Is there any personal benefit to the author for promoting a particular viewpoint? What is the personal, professional, and educational background of this author?

- What is the date of the source? In many instances information published later rather than earlier is more credible, especially when science, technology, or other rapidly changing fields are involved.
- Who published the information? Is the publisher reputable?
- Identify any bias in the information. Is there a particular tone or viewpoint that overrides the information?
- Has the information been manipulated in some fashion? For example, are the statistics clearly stated and truly representative? If nine out of ten doctors recommend a certain drug and only ten doctors were asked their opinions, the resulting statistic is misleading, although technically accurate.

Speeches of tribute ■ Speeches that celebrate a person, a group of people, or an event.

Speeches to entertain and inspire ■ Special occasion speeches that are general in nature and may occur in a variety of settings.

IDENTIFYING DIFFERENT TYPES OF SPEECHES

Now that we have considered some of the fundamental steps necessary to developing your speech, let's give more detailed consideration to special occasion, informative, and persuasive speeches.

Special Occasion Speeches

Special occasion speeches are typically given to recognize a person, place, or event. For example, **speeches of tribute** include eulogies, roasts, toasts, welcomes, and award presentations that celebrate a person or a group of people. Other special occasion speeches that focus on people include introductions, welcomes, and nominations, while dedications, ribbon-cuttings, or opening ceremonies tend to focus on a particular structure, location, or memorial. Commencement addresses and acceptance speeches celebrate a particular event. **Speeches to entertain and inspire** are general in nature and may occur in a variety of settings. For example, an organization may host an annual convention and invite a keynote speaker whose sole purpose is to inspire or entertain the organization's members. You are very likely to deliver a special occasion speech, such as a toast at a wedding, at some point in your life.

We have offered only basic information about special occasion speeches; it takes considerable time and energy to gain skill in crafting and delivering these speeches. We urge you to take additional public speaking courses to help develop your skills more thoroughly. There are also several excellent resources you can consult. We encourage you to review the references on public speaking found at the end of this chapter or to search the Internet to identify other resources.

Informative Speeches

Informative speeches include speeches of explanation, definition, and description, and briefings. Informative speeches primarily teach the audience some information that they will find valuable and interesting. You will learn more details about informative speeches in Chapter 10. At this point, keep in mind that informative speeches use credible research to provide insight, information, and illustration that help audiences understand a topic. If you choose to explain, for example, how the Internet is impacting newspapers in the United States, you are choosing to deliver an informative speech.

Offering a toast at a wedding is a common special occasion speech.

Persuasive Speeches

We will have more to say about persuasive speaking in Chapter 11. For now, keep in mind that persuasive speeches seek to change people's beliefs or behaviors or to reinforce certain beliefs or behaviors. While, like informative speeches, persuasive speeches employ credible research information, the information is purposefully used to support arguments that take a position with regard to a given topic. If you choose to talk, for example, about how the Internet is causing a lack of credible news reporting, you are posing an argument that represents a particular position that you want your audience to believe.

BECOMING A COMPETENT AND ETHICAL PUBLIC SPEAKER IN COLLEGE AND LIFE

Before we leave this chapter, it is important to emphasize that giving a speech in your communication class is an authentic and relevant speaking event.

The College Classroom as a "Real" Audience

Often students complain that giving a speech to their peers isn't "real" because the class doesn't comprise a "real" audience. This is a misunderstanding. Every aspect of a genuine speaking situation exists in your classroom. All the aspects of the communication model are present, including a speaker, listeners, a message, channels, feedback, and contexts. Furthermore, if you think of your peers as an authentic audience and plan your speech with them in mind, you can craft a speech that will engage them. What do you know about your classmates? Gathering information through surveys, class discussions, and conversations will help you get to know your classmates. Also, listen intently to your classmates' speeches; this will help you plan your speech and make genuine connections with your peers. Don't sell your peers short; they are a genuine audience.

The Relevance of Special Occasion, Informative, and Persuasive Speaking to Your College Experience

While the immediate relevance of public speaking to your coursework is evident because you are enrolled in this communication class, the various types of public speaking that we discussed earlier in this chapter extend to other aspects of your college experience. You will have numerous opportunities to use these various types of speeches in ceremonial, social, and academic settings while in college. For example, most colleges have commencement exercises that include a student speaker. While this honor is often limited to one or two students, you may be the valedictorian of your graduating class or participate in your graduation ceremony as an officer of a student organization that "passes the torch" to the next graduating class.

In other situations in college, you may be called on to present or receive an award or nominate a colleague to an office in an organization. Or you may be the person

College students are often called upon to speak in a variety of campus settings.

nominated by others to fill a position in student government or in your sorority or fraternity. If any of these situations occur, you will need to articulate your vision with other students whose votes or support you will need in order to serve your college community. In most cases, if you hold any leadership position, you will be expected to speak publicly in some manner.

Additionally, you will probably be required to deliver informative speeches in other classes—especially in institutions that emphasize speaking across the curriculum. For example, in our institutions, students give reports individually or in groups in a variety of academic areas ranging from the sciences to the humanities. In other instances, you may be called on to teach a class for a day or to develop your presentation skills in other assignments, especially if you are pursuing a career in areas such as education, business, or law that require excellent oral communication skills. In short, involvement in campus life means that you will be a public speaker. Learning public speaking skills, then, can improve your social and academic success and enhance your college experience.

As we have noted, when you graduate, you will need public speaking skills. While you may not be required to make public presentations, the variety of skills you glean from developing your public speaking skills are transferable immediately and directly to the working world. Students who work full or part time have likely already learned that the ability to speak clearly and appropriately in work settings matters to your personal satisfaction with your job as well as to the likelihood of recognition or promotion.

SUMMARY

In this introductory chapter to public speaking, we have identified some essential elements of effective public speaking. Specifically, we have

- explained why public speaking is important for the college experience and your future career;
- identified public speaking as a process and illustrated the process in a model;
- discovered how to craft an appropriate specific purpose statement;
- considered the various types of special occasion, informative, and persuasive speeches;
- explained how to select a subject and a topic using brainstorming and considering four important perspectives;
- discussed how to craft a clear, succinct thesis for your speech;
- examined the three general purposes for public speaking: to entertain, to inform, and to persuade;
- examined the relevance of the public speaking classroom audience;
- reviewed the relevance of the three types of public speaking for college and career.

QUESTIONS FOR DISCUSSION

1. Kanar (1998) asserts that making presentations is one of the five essential academic skills for students. Do you agree? Why?
2. Revisit the model for public speaking we introduced in this chapter. How might this model change if people from other cultures were constructing it? Why?

3. Evaluate Osborn and Osborn's (2000) statement: "People will listen, learn, and remember a message only if it relates to their needs, wants or wishes" (90).

EXERCISES

1. Create a list of all the ways public speaking is used as a means to inform and persuade you from day to day. What conclusions do you draw from this list about the role of public speaking in everyday life?
2. Find the text of a speech that you find interesting. You can find speech texts on the Web or in your library. For example, check a publication such as *Vital Speeches* or check these websites: www.uiowa.edu/~commstud/resources/

speech.html, links to various speakers; http://gos.sbc.edu/, speeches by women; www.americanrhetoric.com, collection of numerous American speeches; http://library.ups.edu/research/spchtxt.htm, collection of speeches. When you find a speech you like, print it out and identify its general purpose, specific purpose, subject, topic, and thesis. Highlight these and bring the speech to class for further discussion.

KEY TERMS

Attitude 156
Audience perspective 153
Beliefs 156
Brainstorming 153
General purposes 151
Informative speeches 151
Organizational perspective 158

Personal perspective 158
Persuasive speeches 151
Practical perspective 158
Situational perspective 158
Special occasion speeches 151
Specific purpose 152
Speeches of tribute 165

Speeches to entertain and
  inspire 165
Subject 153
Thesis 161
Thesis statement 161
Topic 159
Values 156

REFERENCES

Boraks, D. 1997. "How Credible Is That Site? Check It Out Before You Cite," *Charlotte [North Carolina] Observer*, 28 January.

Braithwaite, D. O., and Thompson, T. L. 2000. *Handbook of communication and people with disabilities*. Mahwah, NJ: Lawrence Erlbaum.

Burk, J. 2001. Communication apprehension among master's of business administration students: Investigating a gap in communication education. *Communication Education* 50:51–58.

Dannels, D. P., Anson, C. M., Bullard, L., and Peretti, S. 2003. Challenges in learning communication skills in chemical engineering. *Communication Education* 52:50–56.

Darling, A. L., and Dannels, D. P. 2003. Practicing engineers talk about the importance of talk: A report on the role of oral communication in the workplace. *Communication Education* 52:1–16.

Kirtley, M. D., and Weaver, J. B. 1999. Exploring the impact of gender role self-perception on communication style. *Women's Studies in Communication* 23:190.

Martin, J., and Nakayama, T. 2005. *Experiencing intercultural communication: An introduction*. 2nd ed. New York: McGraw-Hill.

Osborn, M., and Osborn, S. 2000. *Public speaking*. 5th ed. Boston, MA: Houghton Mifflin.

Peterson, M. S. 1997. Personnel interviewers' perceptions of the importance and adequacy of applicants' communication skills. *Communication Education* 46:287–291.

Reiff, J. C. 1992. *What research says to the teacher: Learning styles*. Washington, DC: National Educational Association.

Sellnow, D. D. 2002. *Public speaking: A process approach*. Fort Worth, TX: Harcourt.

Sellnow, D. D., and Golish, T. 2000. The relationship between self-disclosure speech and public speaking anxiety: Considering gender equity. *Basic Communication Course Annual* 12:28–59.

Wood, J. 1994. *Gendered lives: Communication, gender, and culture*. Belmont, CA: Wadsworth.

Worley, D. W. 2000. An acrostic for public speaking. *Basic Communication Course Annual* 12:193–209.

Young, J. R. June 30, 2004. Students' political awareness hits highest level in a decade. *Chronicle of Higher Education* A30.

CHAPTER

9 Organization, Supporting Material, Delivery, and Visual Aids

LEARNING OUTCOMES After reading this chapter, you will have:

the **Knowledge** to. . .   and the **Skills** to. . .

ORGANIZING YOUR IDEAS, page 172

Arrange your thoughts.

- Organize your ideas so that they are clear, simple, balanced, and orderly.

OUTLINING FOR EFFECTIVE SPEAKING, page 174

Order your ideas effectively.

- Use planning, working, or presentation outlines to guide your speech preparation.

IDENTIFYING PATTERNS OF ORGANIZATION, page 179

Chose an organizational pattern that suits your purpose.

- Determine which pattern or patterns (chronological, spatial, topical, problem–solution, cause–effect, motivated sequence, refutation, or state-the-case-and-prove-it) would best convey your purpose.

169

UNDERSTANDING THE PARTS OF A SPEECH, page 182

Know the various components of a speech.

- Take your time developing a strong introduction, body, and conclusion to your speech.
- Employ transitions so your ideas connect to each other and flow smoothly.

GATHERING SUPPORTING MATERIALS, page 187

Search for appropriate information and materials.

- Understand the types of supporting materials you can use and evaluate them for appropriateness.
- Build in facts, statistics, testimony, examples, and narratives to support your purpose.

CITING SOURCES, page 190

Identify sources of information correctly.

- Reveal the sources of your information openly and accurately in writing as well as in speaking.
- Guard against plagiarism.

USING VISUAL AIDS TO ENHANCE DELIVERY, page 191

Employ visual aids to augment your delivery.

- Familiarize yourself with the types of visual aids you can use to improve your delivery.
- Integrate visual aids so that they enhance your delivery.

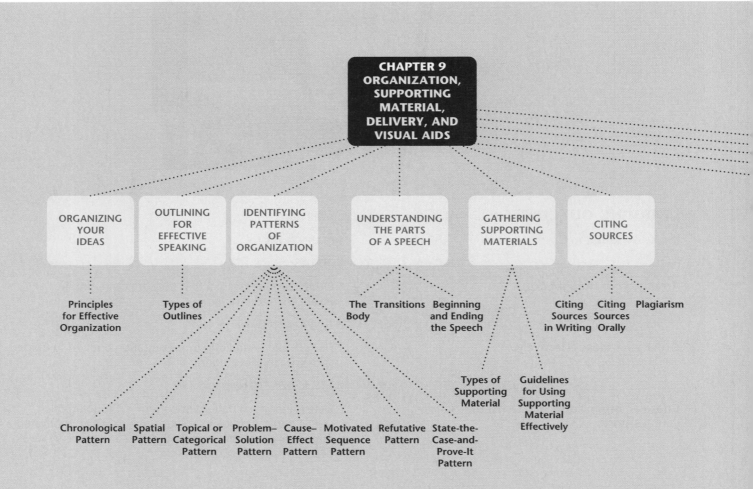

DELIVERING YOUR SPEECH EFFECTIVELY, page 196

Give an effective speech that achieves your purpose.

- Establish whether your speech will be extemporaneous, impromptu, from a manuscript, or memorized.
- Use your voice and nonverbal expressions and behaviors effectively.

DEALING WITH COMMUNICATION APPREHENSION, page 201

Cope with public speaking fears.

- Gauge your level of anxiety about public speaking and take steps to alleviate or lessen it.

PREPARING FOR EFFECTIVE DELIVERY, page 202

Practice for successful delivery.

- Rehearse your speech not only for its content but also for how you are presenting the information.
- Pause to collect your thoughts and composure before beginning your speech.

ACHIEVING COMPETENT AND ETHICAL SPEECH DELIVERY, page 205

Become a capable and ethical speaker.

- Follow the core principles for competent and ethical delivery.
- Use these principles at home, in school, at work, or in the community.

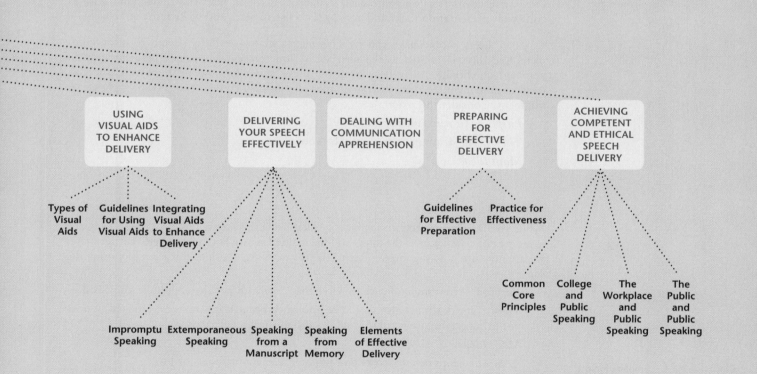

Perhaps you have heard a speaker who rambled and you could not follow what the speaker was attempting to say. Or perhaps you have heard a speaker who made strong statements without support that left you feeling like you were bludgeoned by personal opinion. Or, even more likely, you may have heard a speaker who spoke in a monotone voice and never gestured, allowing you to drift into disinterest or distraction. Or you may have seen a speaker use PowerPoint in a way that made you think, "Why didn't you just email me the slides?" If so, you have experienced the consequences of poor organization, lack of supporting material, ineffective delivery, and unappealing visual aids. In this chapter, we offer ways to help you avoid these problems and improve your effectiveness as a public speaker. Building on the ideas we shared in the previous chapter, first we consider principles of the organization of ideas.

ORGANIZING YOUR IDEAS

Put the following ideas into a logical order: (1) starting college, (2) choosing a college, and (3) applying to college. How did you arrange these ideas? Most of you probably put them in this order: (1) choosing a college, (2) applying to college, and (3) starting college. You likely put them in this order because we have been taught that events occur in chronological order. In this chapter, we consider how to organize, develop, and outline the important information in a presentation. Refer back to Figure 8.1 on page 149 where we considered the early parts of this model—namely, purpose, subject, topic, and thesis. We are now ready to discuss the continuation of this process.

Understanding and using the principles and patterns of organization will help your listeners and you. Remember that unlike reading a paragraph in a book or a magazine, your listeners have one opportunity to understand your message. If your presentation is clearly organized, they will be able to follow your speech. Additionally, clear organization can help offset any fear you may have about delivering your speech by ensuring that your speech has a clear sense of direction, thereby increasing your confidence. Moreover, understanding these principles will assist you in listening, reading, and writing more effectively (Andrews, Andrews, & Williams 1999).

Principles for Effective Organization

Organizing ideas rests on some basic principles that can help you understand how to craft your presentation ideas and assist you to listen, read, and write more effectively.

CLARITY   Ideas should have **clarity**. This means that your ideas should be clear, complete, and directly related to the purpose of your presentation. Each main thought in your speech should clearly flow from the thesis statement and relate to your speech's purpose statement. Second, each main idea should be a complete idea—not a phrase or fragment. Consider this example:

> *Purpose*: To persuade my audience
>
> *Thesis*: The death penalty should be abolished.
>
> *Main Ideas*:
>
> I. Cost
> II. Closure
> III. Deterrent

While you may be able to guess what a speaker using this sparse outline wishes to say, the ideas are not clear because the thesis and the main ideas are both incomplete. Furthermore, we are not sure how the ideas relate to the thesis. Now, consider this example, using the same topic:

> *Purpose:* I want my audience to agree that the death penalty should be abolished.
>
> *Thesis*: The death penalty should be abolished because it is not cost-efficient, it does not bring closure to victims' families, and it is not a deterrent.
>
> *Main Ideas*:
>
> I. The death penalty costs more than housing a prisoner for life.
> II. The death penalty does not bring closure to the victims' families.
> III. The death penalty is not an effective deterrent to crime.

Clarity ■ Clear, complete ideas that are directly related to the purpose of your presentation.

Notice how the ideas clearly relate to the purpose and the thesis, while they are also complete, clear thoughts.

SIMPLICITY   Read this excerpt from *Alice in Wonderland* by Lewis Carroll:

> "I quite agree with you," said the Duchess; "and the moral of that is—'Be what you would seem to be'—or, if you'd like it put more simply—'Never imagine yourself not to be otherwise than what it might appear to others that what you were or might have been was not otherwise than what you had been would have appeared to them to be otherwise.'"

In your own words, explain what the Duchess means by these words. Having difficulty? Why? As you can see, ideas are not understandable unless they are simply stated. If you use **simplicity,** you are stating your ideas in straightforward language. If you use very complex sentences, your audience will find it difficult to listen well. Attempting to sound intelligent by using as many words as possible complicates your message and typically does not impress your audience. Furthermore, if you truly know your topic well, you will be able to explain it clearly. On the other hand, if you're having difficulty explaining your ideas, you may not have a grasp of the ideas yourself. Consider these examples:

Complex	Simple
Avidly avoid ocular movement that results in plagiaristic behavior in the eyes of the proctor.	Please be sure to keep your eyes on your own paper to avoid any suspicion of cheating.
The Internet has become a quagmire of predatory possibilities resulting in nefarious consequences.	The Internet has been used to allure potential victims of crime.
Well, you know, like, the cool thing about this stuff is that you can, you know, like, listen to your tunes, like, anywhere you want.	An iPod allows you to listen to the music you like whenever and wherever you wish.

PARALLELISM   **Parallelism** refers to using similar or equivalent language to emphasize ideas. Look back to our example of clear main ideas on page 172. Note that each main idea begins with the same words: "The death penalty." This phrasing illustrates the principle of parallelism, which helps listeners identify the main ideas you wish to emphasize by phrasing them in a similar fashion. Moreover, parallelism assists clarity and simplicity.

BALANCE   As we discuss in more detail later in this chapter, your presentation should consist of a balanced combination of an introduction, body, and conclusion. **Balance** means giving each main point roughly the same importance and length. You should devote most of your speaking time to developing the ideas in the body of your speech. However, while each point may deserve the same amount of development and thereby receive *equal emphasis*, you may find that either your first or last main point requires more development. So, for example, if you are assigned a six-minute speech, you will likely spend no more than one to one and one-half minutes on the introduction and another minute on the conclusion. This leaves you about three and one-half minutes to four minutes to deliver your main ideas.

Another way to achieve balance is to order your points in terms of importance. You can use either *ascending* or *descending order*. Consider how you might use a problem–solution organizational pattern and use either ascending or descending order to address the topic of global warming. Perhaps your audience is unaware of the persistence of the problem of global warming. In this case, your *first* main point must establish the reality and persistence of this problem. Therefore, you allot more time to this first point because to support your thesis, you need to be sure that your audience is aware of the problem; this is called *descending order*. On the other hand, your audience may agree that global warming is a very real threat but needs you to identify practical solutions to the problem. In this case, your *last* main point may need more emphasis; this is called *ascending order* (Osborn & Osborn 2006).

Simplicity ■ Stating your ideas in straightforward language.

Parallelism ■ Beginning each main idea with the same words.

Balance ■ Making each main point roughly the same importance and length.

Practicality ■ Organization that helps audience understand your message.

Order ■ A clear, consistent pattern from beginning to end.

Planning outline ■ A rough collection of ideas and supporting material.

Preparation outline ■ The formal, typewritten outline that clearly identifies an introduction, body, and conclusion as well as the required portions in each section.

PRACTICALITY **Practicality** refers to choosing a particular organizational pattern to help your audience remember your message and also to help you deliver your message. For example, if your goal is to convince your audience members that they should no longer shop at big box stores because of their impact on the local economy, you will need to organize your ideas so that they help lead your audience to take this action. While you may choose from a variety of organizational options, carefully choose the one that will help you accomplish your goal. Not only will this help your audience remember and respond to your message, but it will also help you deliver your message in a convincing manner.

ORDER Your presentation should follow a logical **order**: a clear, consistent pattern—from beginning to end—that helps your audience easily comprehend your ideas. Perhaps you have listened to a professor or a visiting speaker lecture and struggled to understand what he or she was saying. Did the speaker skip from one idea to another? Were you unsure of how one thought related to another? If so, you've experienced a disorderly presentation and know how frustrating it can be, especially if you truly need to know the information. Later we will discuss organizational patterns that work well for both informative and persuasive speeches, but at this point it is important to realize that organizing your entire speech is critical to successful speaking. Developing an outline is a first step to effective organization.

OUTLINING FOR EFFECTIVE SPEAKING

To apply the principles of effective organization, we suggest you outline your ideas. An outline is an important and useful tool for organizing the ideas for your presentation. Speech outlines are like our skeletal system: They provide structure, connections, and support. Don't neglect this important aspect of speech preparation. Outlines will ensure that you develop a strong speech that your audience can follow and provide you with the necessary structure to prepare and deliver your speech effectively. You must blend all the aspects of the speech development process into a coherent whole; outlines will help you do this.

Types of Outlines

There are three types of outlines important to your speech preparation, including planning, working, and presentation outlines. We discuss each of these types of outlines in the following sections.

PLANNING OUTLINES As you develop your speech, you will probably write a rough outline as you jot down ideas and gather supporting material. Think of this as your **planning outline**. It may not look like a conventional outline and may just be a collection of notes and related ideas or a concept map, like the ones you find at the start of each chapter in this book. To help you with this process, write your topic, purpose, and thesis clearly at the top of the page and then start thinking about main ideas and how the research you have already completed might fit with each of these ideas.

WORKING OUTLINES In addition to the planning outline, you must develop a preparation and, perhaps, a presentation outline before you actually speak. A **preparation outline** is the formal, typewritten outline that clearly identifies an introduction, body, and conclusion along with the required portions in each section. This outline is the blueprint for your speech; it provides the structure and the detail for what you will say when you deliver your speech *without writing out the speech word for word*. While you will certainly work on phrasing your main points and key ideas, you should not construct a manuscript of the speech; rather, create a detailed plan of your presentation to ensure that you speak extemporaneously or conversationally.

Wise speakers and experienced speakers know that a preparation outline is essential to an effective speech. Don't shortchange yourself or your audience by taking a shortcut. Furthermore, you will, in most instances, need to hand in a copy of your preparation outline to your teacher. In many communication classes, your outline is your ticket to the front of the room because it is evidence of your preparation to address your class.

Specific Purpose: Stated in terms of audience response
Thesis:
Organizational Pattern:
Intended Audience:

Introduction

I. **Attention-Getting Device:** Full sentences giving actual attention-getter to be given in speech.
II. **Orientation Phase:** (all in complete sentences)
    A. **Point:** Statement of topic, specific purpose, and thesis
    B. **Adaptation or Link:** Reason for audience to listen
    C. **Credibility:** Explains why we should listen to you speak on this subject
    D. **Enumerated Preview:** Prestates your main points

Transition to first main point

Body

I. First main point, as stated in preview, in a complete sentence
    A. Supporting information for first main point in a complete sentence
        1. First detail of support for A in a complete sentence
        2. Second detail of support for A in a complete sentence (transition)
    B. Supporting information for first main point
        1. First detail of support for B in a complete sentence
        2. Second detail of support for B in a complete sentence (transition)
    C. Supporting information for first main point in a complete sentence

Transition statement connecting first and second main points

II. Second main point as stated in preview in a complete sentence
    A. Supporting information for second main point in a complete sentence
        1. First detail of support for A in a complete sentence
            a. Further detail of 1
            b. Further detail of 1
        2. Second detail of support for A in a complete sentence (transition)
    B. Supporting information for second main point
        1. First detail for B in a complete sentence
        2. Second detail for B in a complete sentence

Transition statement connecting second and third main points

III. Third main point as stated in preview in a complete sentence
    A. Supporting information for third main point in a complete sentence (transition)
    B. Supporting information for third main point in a complete sentence (transition)
    C. Supporting information for third main point in a complete sentence
        1. First detail of support for C in a complete sentence
            a. Further detail of 1
            b. Further detail of 1
            c. Further detail of 1
        2. Second detail of support for C in a complete sentence

Transition to conclusion

Conclusion

I. Review of main points
II. Closure

FIGURE 9.1
Outline Format Sheet.

On a technical note, the preparation outline should be typed and arranged in a proper outline format. You should also include references after the conclusion of the outline, along with citations in the outline's text. Figure 9.1 illustrates an outline format sheet that may serve as a template for writing your speech outlines. Note that the outline uses roman numerals for main ideas, capital letters for subpoints related to main ideas, arabic numbers for supporting material related to subpoints, and lowercase letters for the final level in the outline. These format rules are standard outlining procedure and can be useful in preparing for your speech and in developing an outline for research papers in other classes.

While your instructor may ask you to adapt or change the outline to some degree in order to follow the requirements of your course, the outline format sheet provides a recognized and classroom-tested pattern you can follow, and it can serve as a checklist for your outline. For additional help, consult Figure 9.2, which shows a student outline that employs the outline format sheet. The example employs full sentences, but your instructor may prefer that you use phrases or key words; this approach is illustrated in Figure 9.3. There are benefits and disadvantages to both approaches; follow the directions your instructor provides.

Specific Purpose: After my speech, my audience members will know how to get along with their roommates.

Thesis: A cooperative relationship with your roommate rests on following three important research-based tips.

Organizational Pattern: Topical

Intended Audience: Communication 101 Class

Introduction

I. **Attention-Getting Device:** They can be your best friends or your worst enemies. They can respect your space, or they can go digging through your closet. They can make your bed when you're running late, or they can pile their dirty dishes on your clean laundry. Do you know this person? It's someone who, at one time or another, we have all had to deal with—a roommate.

II. **Orientation Phase:**
   A. *Point:* Today I want to share with you three important research-based tips on how to get along with your roommate.
   B. *Adaptation:* Most of us will have to room with someone at some point. Learning how to live with someone is not only important for college life but for further relationships too.
   C. *Credibility:* A roommate can be someone you come to love and trust, or he or she can become your worst enemy. In my case, my last roommate became my worst enemy. To keep this from happening again, I have found research that identifies ways to make living with someone easier.
   D. *Enumerated Preview:* This research identifies three main ways to keep the peace while living with a roommate: don't lie, don't assume anything, and remember that each roommate should have an equal voice and equal power in the relationship.

Transition: The first way to make living with someone better is to remember not to lie.

Body

I. Lying can cause several problems while living with a roommate.
   A. According to the September 1994 issue of *Seventeen Magazine*, there are three common lies that roommates tell each other (Barry 1994, 123).
      1. The first lie roommates tell is, "I'm not uptight about neatness."
         a. If you're a slob, admit it and keep your mess to your space.
         b. If you're a neat freak, try to understand that the other person isn't like you.
      2. The second common lie is, "I don't care if guys/girls sleep over."
         a. You should set rules about what nights members of the opposite sex may spend the night.
         b. You should also set rules about how much prior notice the other person gets to find another place to sleep.
      3. "We're best friends" is the third lie roommates tend to tell.
         a. Don't feel like you have to invite your roommate to go along wherever you go.
         b. It takes a while to become friends, so take your time in developing a friendship.

FIGURE 9.2

Sample Full Sentence Preparation Outline.

B. Usually lying to your roommate creates problems for both of you.
  1. Your roommate will feel betrayed if you lie to him or her, and he or she may not trust you again.
  2. Lying creates an emotional backlash, so in the end, you will feel worse.

Transition: Lying is not the only way to miscommunicate with your roommate. Assuming anything about the person you're sharing your living space with can cause just as many problems.

II. Remembering not to assume anything about your roommate will make living together much easier ("Crowd Control," E3).
  A. You should always ask before you use anything of your roommate's.
    1. For example, one of the major problems my old roommate and I had was assuming we could always use each other's things.
      a. I thought I could borrow her Monopoly game one weekend while she was gone.
      b. She assumed she could use my computer anytime she wanted.
    2. Another example occurred when we first moved in.
      a. My roommate assumed that since my stereo took up the whole top of the bookcase, she could take the whole top of the dresser.
      b. I assumed that since she chose the bed she wanted, I had first dibs on which closet I wanted.
  B. If you're ever unsure about anything, wait until your roommate gets home and ask him or her in person!
  C. And if something happens that disturbs you, as the *Princeton Review* online recommends, speak up. If you let issues go unaddressed, they typically only get worse or continue to upset you.

Transition: Lying and assumptions create problems, but you can create a positive atmosphere in your living space by remembering that each roommate is equal.

III. The June 26, 1994, issue of the *LA Times* states that the best way to get along with your roommate is to create a place where equality rules ("Crowd Control," E4).
  A. Each roommate should always have a say in all matters.
  B. Each roommate has the right to voice his or her opinions.
  C. It is important, however, to actually talk about the issues that need to be addressed, including who will clean what parts of the room or house, how utility bills will be paid, or what guidelines you will agree to regarding having others in your room or apartment (www.college-student-life.com/dorm_life.htm).

Transition: These tips should make living with a roommate easier and more enjoyable.

Conclusion

I. Summary: Never lying, never assuming anything, and remembering that everyone is equal are three of the essentials for living with anyone.

II. Concluding Device: If you remember these suggestions, you will probably find that living with your college roommate, or even someone further down the line, can be an enjoyable and rewarding experience.

References

Barry, R. (1994, September). "Welcome to Roommate Hell." *Seventeen*, 123–4, 129.

"Crowd Control." (1994, June 27). *Los Angeles Times*, E3-4.

Living in the dorm – surviving college dorm life. *College Student Life Dot Com.* Retrieved on June 11, 2004 from http://www.college-student-life.com/dorm_life.htm.

Personal Experience, Fall 1994.

The roommate issue: eight tips for success. *The Princeton Review.* Retrieved on June 11, 2004 from http://www.princetonreview.com/college/research/articles/life/roommatetips.asp.

Specific Purpose: How to get along with roommates.
Thesis: A cooperative relationship rests on three tips.
Organizational Pattern: Topical
Intended Audience: Communication 101 Class

Introduction

I. **Attention-Getting Device:** Best friends or worst enemies? Respect your space or dig through your closet? Make your bed or pile dirty dishes on your clean laundry? Know this person? It's—a roommate.

II. **Orientation Phase:**
  A. *Point:* Tips for getting along.
  B. *Adaptation:* How to live with someone, important for college and other relationships
  C. *Credibility:* My last roommate—my worst enemy. Research on ways living with someone is easier.
  D. *Enumerated Preview:* Three main ways to keep the peace—don't lie, don't assume, and equal voice and equal power.

Transition: First don't lie.

Body

I. Lying causes problems:
  A. September 1994 issue of *Seventeen Magazine*, three common lies (Barry 1994, 123).
   1. First, "I'm not uptight about neatness."
     a. Slobs: Keep your mess.
     b. Neat-freaks: Roommate isn't you.
   2. Second, "I don't care if guys/girls sleep over."
     a. Set rules—guests.
     b. Set rules—prior notice.
   3. Third, "We're best friends".
     a. No 24/7 rule.
     b. Develop friendship.
  B. Lying creates problems.
   1. Betrayal, loss of trust.
   2. Emotional backlash; you will feel worse.

Transition: Miscommunication. Assuming causes problems.

II. Do not assume ("Crowd Control," E3).
  A. Ask before using anything.
   1. Major problem 1—assuming we could use each other's things.
     a. Her Monopoly game.
     b. My computer.
   2. Major problem 2—moving in.
     a. She assumed about stereo and bookcase.
     b. I assumed about bed and closet.
  B. Unsure? Ask!
  C. Something disturbs you, *Princeton Review* online recommends, speak up. Unaddressed issues get worse.

Transition: Create positive atmosphere: Remember equality.

III. June 26, 1994, issue of LA*Times*: The best way to get along is to create a place where equality rules ("Crowd Control," E4).
  A. Each should have a say.
  B. Each has right to his or her opinions.
  C. Talk about issues, including cleaning, bill-paying, guidelines for guests (www.college-student-life .com/dorm_life.htm).

Transition: Tips make living with roommate easier and enjoyable.

Conclusion

I. **Summary:** Never lie, never assume, and everyone is equal are three essentials.

II. **Concluding Device:** Remembering these suggestions and living with roommates, or further down the line, can be enjoyable and rewarding.

FIGURE 9.3
Sample Keyword Preparation Outline.

```
I. Lying—Seventeen, Sept. 1994

   A. neatness
        1. admit being a neat freak
        2. not everyone a neat freak
   B. opposite sex sleeping over
        1. agree on rules
        2. prior notice
   C. best friends
        1. don't always have to be together
        2. friendship takes time

Trans: From lying to assuming

II. Never assume anything—LA Times, June 27, 1994
```

FIGURE 9.4
Sample Presentation Outline Card.

PRESENTATION OUTLINES Although a preparation outline is important to planning your speech, a **presentation outline** may be useful to delivering your speech because most people get too nervous when speaking to rely solely on memory. This outline can help you stay on track. Unlike the preparation outline, the presentation outline does not contain detail; instead it contains cue words or phrases that help you recall what you have planned and practiced. Some of the important features of the presentation outline include:

1. The outline should consist of key words or phrases, *not* sentences to be read.
2. The outline should be written in letters large enough to be easily read at a glance.
3. The outline should be written on sequentially numbered note cards, not paper.

Figure 9.4 shows an example of a presentation outline card. The card illustrates how one speaker might create a presentation outline for the first main point of the speech outlined in Figure 9.2. While presentation outlines may be useful, they can also hinder delivery by inhibiting eye contact or gestures. Therefore, your instructor may require you to deliver your speech without a presentation outline to encourage you to practice and deliver your speech well. In either case, you must learn to deliver your speech without undue reliance on a presentation outline. If you are permitted to use notes, you will still need to practice sufficiently to use the cards solely as memory aids.

IDENTIFYING PATTERNS OF ORGANIZATION

As you prepare your outline and organize your ideas, you will need to follow a pattern or a way of arranging your ideas in a recognizable manner. Additionally, these patterns of thought will help you craft the flow and language of your entire speech. One of the early decisions you should make in your speech preparation is how to organize your information. There are several organizational patterns well suited to most types of speeches, although some are more suited to persuasive speeches. Consider the following patterns.

Chronological Pattern

A **chronological pattern** arranges ideas according to time. Speeches that employ this design usually move either forward or backward in time—that is, they discuss events moving from earlier to later or from later to earlier in time. For example, if you were discussing the development of country music, you might begin by talking about contemporary country music and then explain how it is similar to and different from the country music of the early days of the Grand Ole Opry.

Spatial Pattern

A **spatial pattern** relies on geographical or spatial relationships. Spatial designs include patterns such as top to bottom, east to west, front to back, or side to side. For example, if you were explaining the components in a computer, you might begin from the inside and

Presentation outline ■ The outline that contains cue words or phrases that help you recall what you have planned and practiced when you actually deliver the speech; also called the *skeletal* or *keyword outline*.

Chronological pattern ■ Speech design that arranges ideas according to time.

Spatial pattern ■ Speech design that relies on a geographical or spatial relationship.

Visual aids, such as a map, can help to plan and illustrate spatial organization.

work to the outside or vice versa. This is a spatial design. Or you might introduce students to your campus by moving from east to west; this design reflects a geographic and spatial approach. As another example, you might discuss the places of battle that occurred at Gettysburg during the Civil War.

Topical or Categorical Pattern

A **topical or categorical pattern** deals with topics or categories that relate to a main theme. For example, if you discuss the main challenges in applying for financial aid, you may choose to use a topical or categorical organizational pattern. In this case, you may choose from several challenges that would include collecting information, filling out the forms, submitting the applications at the appropriate time, communicating with your college's financial aid office, waiting for the response, and appropriately using the aid when it arrives. You probably won't have time to cover all of these related topics, so you must be sure that the ones you choose flow from your narrowed topic and thesis statement.

Problem–Solution Pattern

A **problem–solution pattern** describes or defines a problem and then offers ways that the problem may be solved. If you use this organizational pattern for an informative speech, you will avoid promoting one particular solution over another. You must explore options so that your audience understands what is available; you teach your listeners about the problem without taking a position on the advisability or applicability of any particular solution. As an example, you may examine the problem of rising tuition costs at your college and then identify possible solutions to the problem without arguing for any one solution to be adopted. However, when you describe a problem and then advocate for a particular solution, you take on a persuasive burden and change the speech's intent. Your speech then becomes persuasive. So, to keep to our example, if you identify the problem of rising tuition costs and then argue for a particular solution to this problem, you are no longer teaching; you are now advocating a position. We will have more to say about the differences between informative and persuasive speaking in the following chapters, but at this point be sure that you understand the difference in how you apply the problem–solution pattern with each type of speech.

Cause–Effect Pattern

Topical or categorical pattern ■ Speech design that deals with topics or categories that relate to a main theme.

Problem–solution pattern ■ Speech design that describes or defines a problem and then offers potential solutions.

Cause–effect pattern ■ Speech design that identifies how a certain set of conditions brings about a particular result.

A **cause–effect pattern** identifies how a certain set of conditions brings about a particular result. Or, conversely, you may use this pattern to focus on the effects and then consider the cause. The difference in the two approaches has to do with whether you discuss the cause or the effects first. The danger with this design is that you may oversimplify a serious problem and indicate only one cause, while many causes may actually create a known effect. It is also possible to infer cause and effect when no such link actually exists. When you cannot firmly establish a clear link, you should use another pattern to avoid endangering your credibility.

As with the problem–solution pattern, you must also avoid arguing a case rather than presenting insight, if the intent of your speech is to inform. For example, you may identify some of the effects of being a first-year college student (the cause). The effects may include homesickness, lack of friends, uncertainty, financial difficulties, and stress. Or you may wish to focus on other more positive effects, such as forming new friendships, intellectual growth, and future career possibilities. On the other hand, if you wish to persuade your audience, you must argue a position or a perspective. Therefore, if you wish your audience to believe that first-year college students must work through homesickness because, with time, it will pass, you must argue this case by providing evidence and possibly specific strategies to alleviate the causes of homesickness. Depending on the audience, you would adjust your ideas, evidence, and appeals. In other words, your speech about homesickness would use a different approach with parents, residential life staff, or first-year college students.

While any of the patterns we discussed to this point can be used either for an informative or persuasive speech, some additional patterns are especially applicable to persuasive speaking. These include the Monroe motivated sequence pattern, the refutative pattern, and the state-the-case-and-prove-it pattern.

Motivated Sequence Pattern

The Monroe **motivated sequence pattern** was developed by a salesman who wanted people to purchase his products and is therefore especially useful for speeches that motivate people to act. There are five sequential steps in this design. Table 9.1 summarizes each of the steps, along with the step's function and the desired audience response.

Refutative Pattern

The **refutative pattern** is particularly useful for persuasive speeches. In this approach, you present the arguments that oppose your proposition or claim and show how they are fallacious, inadequate, inconsistent, or deficient. So, for example, if you argue that gun control is necessary for increased protection of human life in the United States, you could establish your case by examining and defusing the arguments of those who oppose gun control.

To use this design, you must know your opponents' arguments well and be able to use evidence and reasoning to effectively counter them. By doing this, you are then able to establish credibility and adequacy of your position because it withstands the opposing position's ineffective arguments.

State-the-Case-and-Prove-It Pattern

The **state-the-case-and-prove-it pattern** provides a third organizational approach that is well suited to persuasive speaking. In this pattern, you set forth your proposition or claim and then systematically prove it by offering evidence and reason to support your arguments. For example, if you contend that protecting our natural environment is the first social issue we should address, you can use this design to straightforwardly state your claim and then go about providing arguments to support it with evidence and reasoning.

Although you may find a particular pattern more appealing than others, be sure to choose a pattern that helps you organize your ideas clearly and present them effectively in concert with your intended purpose. Doing so will enhance your credibility, delivery, and audience response.

Motivated sequence pattern ■ Speech design that motivates people to act.

Refutative pattern ■ Speech design that presents the arguments that oppose the speaker's proposition or claim and show how they are fallacious, inadequate, inconsistent, or deficient.

State-the-case-and-prove-it pattern ■ Speech design in which the speaker sets forth a proposition or claim and then proves it systematically by offering evidence and reason to support the arguments.

TABLE 9.1

MONROE'S MOTIVATED SEQUENCE

Step	Function	Audience Response
Attention	Getting attention	"I want to listen."
Need	Showing the need: describing the problem	"Something needs to be done (decided or felt)."
Satisfaction	Satisfying the need: presenting the solution	"This is what to do (believe, or feel) to satisfy the need."
Visualization	Picturing the results	"I can see myself enjoying the satisfaction of doing (believing or feeling) this."
Action	Requesting action or approval	"I will do (believe or feel) this."

Body ■ Consists of main points, transitions, supporting materials.

UNDERSTANDING THE PARTS OF A SPEECH

While a speech flows as a coherent whole, understanding its various parts allows you to prepare your speech in a systematic fashion. Each speech must have an introduction, a body, and a conclusion. However, in most instances you will develop the body of the speech first and then develop the introduction and conclusion. Let's consider the body of the speech first, and then we will turn our attention to beginning and ending the speech effectively.

The Body

The **body** of your speech consists of the main points, transitions, and supporting material you have gathered through your research that explains, illustrates, and bolsters your ideas. At this point you are applying the organizational pattern you have chosen as well, so the flow of your main points should reflect this choice clearly.

The main points in your speech are the primary ideas you want your audience to remember. But how do you identify, craft, and organize main points for the greatest effect? Because your main points are so important, be sure to identify strong main ideas around which to build your speech. Do this by considering your specific purpose statement that we discussed in Chapter 8; the most important ideas you want to emphasize may already be stated or implied here. For example, consider the specific purpose statement, "I want my audience to vote in the next election." With this persuasive focus, you may decide to present your speech by discussing the reasons to vote, the effects of not voting, and ways for students to vote. As you can see, you have three main points suggested by this approach, which follows a topical or categorical pattern.

In addition, as you do initial research, common themes may repeatedly occur in your reading. These repetitive ideas are probably the most important concepts to address in your speech and may, therefore, cue you as to the main ideas you should cover. If these approaches do not yield potential main ideas, brainstorming can help generate possibilities. As we noted before, in brainstorming you produce ideas without evaluating them. To identify main points, write down everything you know or would like to know about your topic and then look for themes among your ideas. These themes can yield main points.

After you identify your speech's main ideas, you are ready to write them. Main ideas should be simple, independent sentences. Rather than allowing the main ideas to become too complicated, break them into subpoints or, in some cases, divide them into additional main points. Let's return to our earlier example topic of the death penalty. Consider this summary of the topic as one speaker approached it: "The death penalty should be abolished because, contrary to popular belief, it does not cost more money to house prisoners than to execute them, it does not bring closure to the victims' families, and it is not an effective deterrent to crime." This complex sentence could be broken down into three main ideas:

Topic: The Death Penalty Should Be Abolished

Main Point I: The death penalty is not economical.

Main Point II: The death penalty does not bring closure to the victims' families.

Main Point III: The death penalty is not an effective deterrent to crime.

If the purpose of this speech extends beyond considering the abolition of the death penalty to motivating us to protest the death penalty, the organization could change and result in two main points, with supporting subpoints:

Topic: The Death Penalty Should Be Abolished

Main Point I: There are three concrete reasons to abolish the death penalty.

    Subpoint A: The death penalty is not economical.

    Subpoint B: The death penalty does not bring closure to the victims' families.

    Subpoint C: The death penalty is not an effective deterrent to crime.

Main Point II: There are three effective ways we can all protest the death penalty.

    Subpoint A: We can join a group that is anti–death penalty, such as Amnesty International.

Subpoint B: We can join an on-site protest when a state or federal execution takes place.

Subpoint C: We can write our state and federal officials.

Notice how the language of the main points is clear, simple, and parallel, which reinforces the principles we discussed in the beginning of this chapter. If you use these principles, you will help your audience listen. However, you also need to limit the number of main points. For most speeches, you usually need no more than two or three main points. Too many main points creates information overload for your audience that, in turn, creates confusion. Also, be sure to organize your main points using one of the patterns we discussed earlier. For the most part, the organizational pattern you use for your speech will help guide the organization of your main points. In the next section, we discuss various organizational techniques.

The main points of your speech are too important to leave to chance. Be sure to identify, craft, and organize them well in order to ensure the strength of your speech's body.

Transitions

Transitions ■ Provides markers between points; bridges between ideas.

Transitions within the speech provide important markers that ensure your listeners follow you as you proceed. In essence, a transition builds a listening bridge between ideas. Transitions do not provide additional information or evidence but, rather, help lead listeners from one idea to the next. Transitions are especially important in the following places within your speech:

1. between the end of the introduction and the beginning of the body,
2. between main points,
3. between subpoints within the body, and
4. at the end of the body and the beginning of the conclusion.

Moreover, there are two important elements in any transition: (1) *what* is said and (2) *how* it is said. In other words, the content and delivery of transitions are crucial to their success. The content of a transition consists of the actual words you use. Table 9.2 discusses signposts—one or two words that help direct your audience's thoughts—and Table 9.3 summarizes the purposes of longer statements that constitute various types of transitions that are discussed in Table 9.4.

Simple, direct statements such as "Now that I have talked about *X*, let me talk about *Y*" can be effective for you as you begin to develop your public speaking skills. As you gain skill, you can find more creative ways to provide transitions. Pay as much attention to your transitions as to your main ideas. In other words, solid transitions, like clear main ideas, are a part of planning and practicing your speech.

While *what* you say in a transition is important, *how* you say it is equally important. To indicate transitions, you can increase your direct eye contact, slow down your speech rate, vary your pitch, and pause either before or after stating the transition. Like every other part of your speech, practicing your delivery of transitions will help make them more effective.

Beginning and Ending the Speech

When you have your main ideas in hand, you are ready to craft your introduction and conclusion. The following sections provide more help with this planning.

TABLE 9.2

SIGNPOSTS

Signposts alert your listeners to important ideas by verbally pointing to them, much like street signs or billboards direct the attention of drivers that are typically one or two words. Here are some examples:

The first question is . . .	Don't forget . . .
Mark this idea!	This is important!
Hold on to that thought.	But what is the best solution?
The final issue is . . .	Secondly, . . .

TABLE 9.3

PURPOSES OF SPEECH TRANSITIONS

1. Transitions to summarize the main points that precede them. For example, "To this point, I have offered you a brief analysis of the problem."
2. Transitions reinforce your organizational approach, whether topical, spatial, temporal, and so on, by linking ideas together. For example, here is a transition that reemphasizes a topical approach: "Not only do persons with AIDS face economic difficulties, but they also must deal with social ostracism."
3. Transitions preview what is ahead in the upcoming main point. Consider the example above. Note that the transition summarizes one main point (the economic difficulties of persons with AIDS) while it introduces the next (the social ostracism of persons with AIDS).
4. Transitions often employ cue words like those in this list:

moreover	consequently	in the first place
furthermore	therefore	secondly
by contrast	as a result	now consider
in comparison	in view of	however
additionally	similarly	now turn to

Introduction ■ Beginning of speech—conveys first impression to audience.

THE INTRODUCTION A speech's **introduction** is vital because it conveys the first impression you give your audience. You need the introduction to

- capture your audience's attention,
- state your topic clearly by stating your thesis,
- give your audience a reason to listen,
- establish your credibility,
- offer a preview of your main points.

Capturing Your Audience's Attention.   Consider this example:

> You're lying on a beach, listening to your favorite CD. You roll over on your stomach so that you can get a little more sun on your back. The rays warm your shoulders and you drift off to sleep. You wake up a half hour later and attempt to roll over to your back.

TABLE 9.4

TYPES OF TRANSITIONS

1. **Internal Previews** offer a brief introduction of the next main point you are about to introduce. Consider this internal preview offered by a student whose speech focused on explaining the power of language to impact our attitudes toward people with disabilities.

   Example: "Not only does our use of language, such as 'wheelchair bound,' reflect our attitudes about people with disabilities, our choice of language also helps form our attitudes toward people with disabilities. Let's consider how this occurs."

2. **Internal Summaries** review the main ideas you have already presented in your speech and serve as transitions to new ideas. In particular, internal summaries are valuable between main points in a speech.

   Example: "As we have seen, persons with AIDS face many problems. Among them are, first, personal economic difficulties; second, social ostracism; and third, dealing with their own impending death. While these problems seem overwhelming, there are important steps we can take as a nation and as individuals to alleviate these problems. Let's consider some of these solutions."

You may be confused by the difference between internal previews and internal summaries. The difference is this: Internal previews review the idea that has immediately preceded the idea you want to introduce, while internal summaries review *all* the main ideas you have discussed prior to introducing a new idea. In practice, you may find internal previews useful when you're moving from a first to a second main point and internal summaries more valuable as you move from a second main point to a third main point. The important thing is to help your audience follow your thoughts with ease.

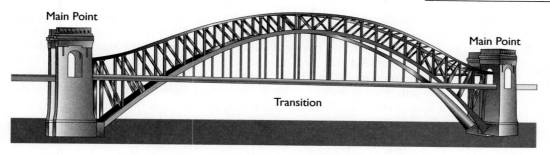

Main Point

Main Point

Transition

Transitions are like bridges that help lead your listeners from one idea to another.

Ouch! Your back is red and burned. Oops—you forgot your sunscreen! How often has this happened to you? I know it's happened to me more times than I care to count. Not only does forgetting your sunscreen result in a nasty sunburn, but it can also increase your chances of getting skin cancer. After a skin cancer scare last summer, I realized the importance of sunscreen, which helped me to learn about the long-term effects of sunburns, especially skin cancer, and the importance of sunscreen in protecting against these potentially serious effects.

Notice how the student begins by gaining attention. This is your first goal in the introduction of your presentation—attract your audience's attention. Table 9.5 provides some time-tested strategies to help you capture audience attention.

TABLE 9.5

ATTENTION-GETTING DEVICES

Strategy	Description/Example
Quote	"We have nothing to fear but fear itself."
Story	An extended narrative that is either true or hypothetical. "When I was a boy on the farm . . ."
Humor	An amusing but appropriate anecdote, saying, or one-liner. "The mind can only contain what the seat can endure. This is true for all of us to some degree but is particularly applicable to those with attention deficit disorder."
Startling statement	An arresting statement that relies on some unusual fact, statistic, or alarming choice of words. "Diabetes is an international epidemic. The disease is spreading across the world with unparalleled rapidity and is forecast to be one of the leading maladies in every part of the globe."
Greeting	A warm greeting that identifies you with the audience, establishes common ground, and expresses your appreciation. "I'm so grateful to be here since my association with this fine organization has extended over many years and has served as a continued source of personal pride."
Rhetorical questions	"Have you ever seen money fly out a window? That's what's happening every winter in your house if you don't have thermal-pane windows from Acme."
Creating curiosity	Through description, narrative, or question, the speaker does not clearly identify a referent and creates curiosity in the listeners. "The only thing he does is sit behind a highly polished mahogany desk day by day and talk on the phone. Yet he controls transactions worth millions of dollars each day that reap him enormous profits."
Illustration	A case or incident that helps the speaker point the audience toward his or her topic. "The Gulf Coast of the U.S. will never be the same since the spread of millions of gallons of oil along its beaches due the eruption of an offshore oil well in 2010."

Enumerated preview ■ Arranging the main points of a speech in numerical order (e.g., first, second, third).

Conclusion ■ Summarizes main ideas and cues listeners that the end of the speech is near.

State Your Topic Clearly by Stating Your Thesis.   After you gain attention, you should clearly state your topic by indicating the specific subject you want to address and how you intend to address it. This can be done most readily by clearly stating your thesis. However, we recommend that you avoid saying, "The thesis for my speech is ..." or "My specific purpose is ..." or "Today I want to talk with you about...." Find a creative way to state your thesis while also engaging your audience. Again, notice how the sunscreen speech example illustrates this principle. The speaker indirectly leads us to consider the importance of sunscreen by relating a personal example and linking it to something that has likely happened to us.

Give Your Audience a Reason to Listen.   Your introduction should give your audience a reason to listen. In our electronic age, most people are bombarded with hundreds of messages every hour. How can you get people to listen to *you*? Give them a good reason to. By appealing to the needs of your listeners, you can help your audience focus on what you have to say. For example, in the introduction to the sunscreen speech, the speaker addresses the audience's concern about cancer. Many people realize that wearing sunscreen is important, so they may have become immune to the message. But, if you can provide them with reasons to listen more carefully, most will likely give a fresh ear to the information.

Establish Your Credibility.   Many audience members silently ask, "Why should we listen to *you*?" To answer this question, you will need to establish your credibility. In the sunscreen speech example, the speaker refers to her personal experience with a skin cancer scare. You, too, likely possess experience or areas of expertise that can help you establish your credibility. If not, you can reference your research of the subject or your concern for the topic area and the audience. If you help your audience members trust you, they will be more likely to trust what you have to say.

Finally, your introduction should provide a clear preview of your main points before you proceed with your speech. Give the essence of your speech in simple statements to identify the path along which you intend to lead your listeners. In our example, the speaker cues us that she will focus on the long-term effects of sunburns, skin cancer, and the importance of sunscreen to protect us from these effects. There are other ways to offer your preview. Many speakers prefer what is termed an **enumerated preview**, which means arranging your main points in order (e.g., first, second, third). Here's an example of an enumerated preview for the same speech topic of skin cancer:

> The first thing to consider is the relationship between sunburns and skin cancer. Second, I'll discuss the serious risks associated with skin cancer. Third, I'll give you some practical tips on how to use the right type and amount of sunscreen in order to help you avoid this risk.

While not all speeches have such clear previews, this basic approach to speaking works well. Remember that your perspective as a speaker and your audience's perspective differ considerably. If you have adequately prepared, you know the information in your speech very well, but your listeners do not; they need clear verbal markers so they can follow your ideas and stay interested. The time-tested strategies we have shared with you for crafting an introduction will truly help you speak and will help your audience listen. Therefore, when you capture audience attention, state the thesis, give the audience a reason to listen, establish credibility, and provide a preview, the introduction to your speech tends to be very effective. As someone once said, "You only get one chance to make a first impression." As a speaker, that one chance comes with your introduction; craft it carefully.

THE CONCLUSION   While your introduction is your first impression on your listeners, your conclusion is the last. Your **conclusion** should summarize main ideas and cue your listeners that the end of the speech is near. To make the best of your last impression, your conclusion should accomplish three goals:

1. Clearly indicate that your speech is coming to a conclusion by offering a word or phrase that cues your audience that you are nearing the end. Some of our colleagues call this a "brake light." This may be something as simple as "in conclusion . . ." or "As I conclude. . . ."
2. Summarize your speech's content.
3. Bring the speech to a close so the audience knows you are finished speaking.

TABLE 9.6

STRATEGIES FOR EFFECTIVE CONCLUSIONS

Strategy	Description/Example
Quote	Uses a statement by another person that emphasizes the theme of your speech. If you are speaking on the value of silence: As one wise man advised, "Foolish people speak all that is in their minds; wise people keep a part back."
Reference to the introduction	Relates back to the words or tone found in the introduction. "An epidemic is upon us; cases of diabetes multiply daily."
Call for action	An appeal for the audience to respond in some specific way presented in the body of the speech. "As you leave today, I ask you to take this brochure about our local animal shelter and promise yourself to deliver at least one item found on the needs list in the brochure this week."
Rhetorical question	Ask the audience a "thought question." "If you were a person with AIDS, what response would you desire?"
Combination	Blends any of the above devices together for effect. "The epidemic of diabetes is a major health concern across the world. None of us is exempt. Take action and protect yourself by getting your blood sugar levels checked at the upcoming health fair this week; it's free, it's easy, and it could save your life."

Briefly review your speech's main points in one or two sentences. The conclusion should not contain any new information or a lengthy restatement of information you shared in the body. Make the summary concise and clear. Here's an example, once again using the topic of sunburns and skin cancer:

> Sunburns are, then, not just temporarily painful; they can have serious, long-term effects on your appearance and health. However, you can avoid these risks by using the appropriate type and amount of sunscreen every time you will be exposed to the sun for more than a few minutes.

Along with a summary, you must also cue your audience that you have completed your speech. This "wrap-up" gives the audience psychological closure and provides an interesting and memorable point of reference for them. See Table 9.6 for concluding devices that can help you craft a clear and compelling closure.

GATHERING SUPPORTING MATERIALS

Up to this point, we have provided essential information about the principles and practices of speech organization. We have examined the skeleton of the speech, but the ideas of your speech are not yet fleshed out. You should, by now, have already established a topic and purpose for your speech and conducted research that has informed your thesis. You are now ready to use the research you have gathered. (We discussed gathering information in the prior chapter.) First, consider the types of supporting materials you may use and then notice how we have used specific examples of these various types of supporting materials for a single speech topic: the challenges first-year college students face in their first six weeks.

Types of Supporting Material

To help you find both a sufficient number and variety of materials to support your ideas, consider the various types and effective uses of supporting materials.

FACTS   A **fact** is an objective, verifiable pieces of information, which you can typically find in sources such as encyclopedias or almanacs. For example, as you enter college for the first time, you face multiple new challenges. What you *think or feel* about these challenges is not

Fact ■ A piece of objective, verifiable information.

Finding useful, solid evidence is important to effective speaking.

a fact per se; however, that you face specific, identified challenges is a fact. Consider this example of a fact about the initial experiences of first-year college students:

> According to Woosley in 2003 writing in the College Student Journal "... researchers and practitioners have emphasized the importance of a student's initial experiences on campus and suggested that these experiences might play a critical role in a student's future success" (Woosley 2003).

Be sure to cite reliable sources when you use facts to support your ideas. We discuss how to cite sources later in this chapter, but it is important to emphasize the need for proper citation of other people's ideas.

STATISTICS   While facts are objective pieces of information, **statistics** are numeric facts that include such information as percentages, averages, or amounts of money. For example, your grade point average (GPA) is an arithmetic average that reflects how well you are performing in your classes; it is a fact. While you may not *think* your GPA accurately reflects your abilities or your performance, your opinion of your GPA is not a fact, however much you would like it to be. To take another example, the percentage of U.S. citizens who make more than $75,000 per year is also a statistic. Statistics, when used sparingly, provide strong support for certain ideas; however, it is best to place the statistic in context so your audience can appreciate the power of your information. For example, consider this statistic that illustrates the challenges first year students face in staying in school until they complete a degree:

> According to Bowler (2009) in an article in *U. S. News and World Report,* "Thirty percent of college and university students drop out after their first year. Half never graduate, and college completion rates in the United States have been stalled for more than three decades" (http://www.usnews.com/articles/education/best-colleges/2009/08/19/dropouts-loom-large-for-schools.html).

TESTIMONY   **Testimony** refers to using the words or ideas of another person to support your points. While you may paraphrase these ideas, you may choose to use **direct quotations**—repeating verbatim what someone has said. Direct quotations are most useful if the quotation is brief or especially powerful.

Of course, not all testimony is necessarily equal. **Expert testimony** refers to the insights of someone who has specialized knowledge or experience and is therefore a recognized authority on a given subject. For example, here's a quote from researchers Noel and Levitz, who have studied the first-year experience of college students for decades.

> As early as 1989, Noel and Levitz, seasoned researchers of the first-year college experience said, "The freshman's most critical transition period occurs during the first two to six weeks" (Noel & Levtiz 1989, 66).

However, at times you may not need or want expert testimony; you may want to use **lay testimony,** or the views of people who are not necessarily experts. Lay testimony

Statistics ■ Numeric facts that include such information as percentages, averages, or amounts of money.

Testimony ■ The words or ideas of another person used to support a speaker's points.

Direct quotations ■ Word-for-word repetition of what someone has said.

Expert testimony ■ The insights of someone who has specialized knowledge or experience and is therefore a recognized authority on a given subject.

Lay testimony ■ The views of a person who is not necessarily an expert.

typically focuses on peoples' feelings or opinions. Therefore, if you want to know what it feels like to be a first-year college student, you do not necessarily need an expert; you can speak with students on your campus who can share their opinions and experiences. Lay testimony is useful for helping your audience understand the human dimension of your topic, while expert testimony provides you with more objective support. It's often wise to include both in your presentation to appeal to your audience both intellectually and emotionally. Consider this example of lay testimony:

> I was so excited about leaving home and going to college. The first week was great! I enjoyed getting to know new people, learning the daily routines, and even attending class. But, by the third week, I was missing my old high school friends, my family, and my hometown; I was homesick.

EXAMPLES   **Examples** are illustrations that help make your ideas clearer and engage your audience's interest; they help your audience visualize your point. Examples can be personal, actual, or hypothetical. **Personal examples** are drawn from your own experience. Assume your speech topic is learning how to manage time as a first-year college student. You may relate an example such as this:

> I remember leaving the restaurant where I worked as a server one night after midnight, dreading the history reading assignment and the beginning speech outline I still had to complete before my class schedule, which began at 8:00 A.M. the following morning. While I tried to do both after I got back to my apartment, I couldn't stay awake. So I went to both my history and communication classes unprepared and it cost me points in both classes. After I did this a few more times, I came to grips with the reality that I would have to find ways to manage my time differently if I was going to succeed in college.

Actual examples are drawn from real-life events. For example, you may relay an illustration from current events, history, or the experiences of another person. In this case, using the time management speech topic, rather than recount your own experience, you might interview a family member or friend who is or was a first-year college student and then relay his or her experience and clearly cite your source. Here's an example, using our topic:

> I went to college on a scholarship; everything was paid for except some minimal fees. But I became discouraged after two years, gave up my scholarship, and quit. Although I made good grades, I felt like a number, not a person. I was in large classes on a huge campus and had limited social connections. I didn't join any campus organizations and commuted from home. Unknowingly, I made numerous errors in judgment that resulted in me becoming a college dropout.

In contrast, you may also use **hypothetical examples,** which are examples you create from information you have collected. Typically, hypothetical examples are created by blending events and experiences that are likely to have occurred. Again, using the previous time management example, you would relate the same information but rather than tell it in the first person, you would invite the audience to picture or imagine the scene. The phrasing therefore would change: "Imagine leaving the restaurant where you work as a server . . ." or "Imagine having a scholarship that paid for your entire college education. . . ."

NARRATIVES   **Narratives** are much like examples in that they illustrate a point or idea. However, narratives tell stories rather than relate incidents and usually have a clear introduction, body, and conclusion. Like examples, they can be stories drawn from your own life or the lives of others; in most cases these make the best stories. Folk tales, oral traditions, or children's books also offer excellent resources. In addition, you can find numerous storytelling resources online. Just remember that if you choose to tell a story, take the time to tell it well and make sure it clearly communicates the theme of your speech and engages your audience. Go to http://www.ohio.edu/univcollege/firstgeneration/upload/deardorff.pdf (Deardoff, n.d), for an example of a narrative that illustrates the challenges first-year college students face. You will

Examples ■ Illustrations that help an audience visualize your point.

Personal examples ■ Examples drawn from the speaker's own experience.

Actual examples ■ Examples drawn from real-life events.

Hypothetical examples ■ Examples created from information the speaker has collected.

Narratives ■ Stories that illustrate a point or idea; usually have a clear introduction, body, and conclusion.

Relatedness ■ Direct connectedness of your supporting materials to
your topic.

Relevance ■ Applicability and
understandability of supporting
materials to your audience.

Respect ■ Acknowledgement of
what your audience members
already know and showing them
how to draw on and adapt their
prior knowledge.

note that this is a rather long narrative. You would, therefore, choose a portion of the narrative that supports one of your main points and share only that portion, unless you had sufficient time to share the entire narrative.

Now that you have some idea of the kinds of supporting materials you can use to help flesh out your ideas, let's consider how to use them effectively. Specifically, you will need to use your supporting material well and cite your evidence clearly.

Guidelines for Using Supporting Material Effectively

You must use supporting material well to make the thesis and main points of your speech both clear and compelling. Therefore, select supporting material carefully and use it effectively to ensure that you share your message with your audience. Consider these guidelines for using your supporting material effectively.

RELATEDNESS   Imagine that you find a truly engaging story that you want to use in your presentation. Even though the story may be excellent, if it is not related and you force it to fit a point, it detracts from your presentation. **Relatedness** refers to the direct connectedness of your supporting materials to your topic. The information you choose should be directly and clearly related to your topic, your thesis, and your point. This means you should choose your supporting material with care and then craft your ideas equally carefully.

RELEVANCE   Choose material that is applicable and understandable to your audience. This is called **relevance**. Obviously, different kinds of materials appeal to groups of children, teens, and adults. Therefore, the same topic may result in a very different presentation as you adapt to your audience's interests and nature. While your thesis and main points may remain similar, the supporting material will change significantly.

RESPECT   Choose supporting materials that respect your audience's prior knowledge and their values. You can often introduce new ideas by comparing or contrasting them with established or well-known ideas. For example, assume you are speaking to your class about study strategies that will help them succeed in college. The students in your class have already developed some strategies from their prior years of schooling; however, some of these strategies may not be sufficient for the challenges of college-level work. Therefore, you can compare and contrast the strategies you wish them to consider with their default study strategies. Showing **respect** acknowledges what your audience members already know and shows them how to draw on and adapt their prior knowledge.

In addition to respecting your audience's prior knowledge, you must also be aware of their values. To avoid offending your audience, do not use supporting material that includes profanity, sexism, racism, or other offensive material, unless there is a solid reason for doing so, such as using statements that illustrate sexism or racism to clearly define the term. However, you must be very cautious in using such an approach because it may do more harm than good to your credibility. Also, use humor carefully because it can easily backfire and alienate your audience. Therefore, use appropriate, credible sources to support your main ideas. For example, consider a student who cites *Playboy* magazine as a credible source on sex education. You can easily see the difficulties such a choice might create for the audience, the speaker, and your teacher.

CITING SOURCES

As we noted earlier, clearly citing your sources is important in both researching and presenting your topic. It is therefore important to learn how to cite sources in writing and orally.

Citing Sources in Writing

You will need to cite sources in the text of your outline and in a Works Cited section at the end of your outline. (Look at Figure 9.2 again, and you will see both types of citations in this example outline.) As you gather research and prepare your outline, you should use one of several accepted forms of citation or styles. These most commonly include styles of the Modern Language Association (MLA) and the American

Psychological Association (APA), although your teacher may ask you to use another form, such as *The Chicago Manual of Style*. You can purchase style manuals, but you can also retrieve a great deal of information from online resources. For example, your college library probably has a site with this information. Or you may find it useful to take the time to complete a tutorial to learn APA or MLA found at a site such as http://library.indstate.edu/tools/tutorials/apa/index.html. The American Psychological Association also has a tutorial to learn APA basics at www.apastyle.org. Additionally, your library may have a program such at Citation 9 that you can download that will help you avoid mistakes. Also look at http://citationmachine.net for help in citing your work. For excellent examples of the various styles go to http://owl.english .purdue.edu/owl/resources/560/01.

Use the style your teacher suggests and use it consistently. While you may find it frustrating to learn, it is an important skill you need in your college career and in your future work. Also, citations enhance your credibility because they reveal that you have spent the necessary time to prepare well for your speech.

Plagiarism ■ Using someone else's ideas without giving them appropriate credit.

Citing Sources Orally

You will also need to cite sources as you speak to enhance your credibility; your audience wants to know that you have done your homework. While you do not want to include every detail of a written citation, you do need to give sufficient information to clearly identify your source and establish the credibility of your source. Consider these examples:

"According to Dr. Arnold Speckler, a practicing physician and Associate Professor at Mayo Clinic . . ."

"*Time* magazine, July 22, 1996, reports . . ."

"In the book *A Road Less Traveled*, Dr. M. Scott Peck, a respected psychiatrist and author, writes . . ."

"In a personal interview I conducted with my best friend . . ."

"A recent article in *Contemporary Education,* a journal published by Indiana State University, asserts that . . ."

Notice that each citation offers enough information to identify the source, without giving complete citation information, while also alluding to the credibility of the source where necessary. In all likelihood, your teacher will ask you to clearly cite sources as you speak and will grade you accordingly; be sure to follow your teacher's directions for oral citations

Carefully citing your sources during your speech will enhance your credibility.

Plagiarism

Failing to cite sources you use either in writing or when speaking is tantamount to stealing someone else's ideas without giving them appropriate credit: It is **plagiarism**. In many colleges, plagiarism, intentional or not, can result in severe penalties. Students have failed courses or even been academically dismissed from colleges for plagiarism. More importantly, it is unethical and illegal to use someone else's ideas, even if you change a few words, without giving him or her credit. Consult the academic dishonesty policies and talk with a librarian at your college to clarify any questions. Your teacher may also have a clear statement in the course syllabus about the consequences of plagiarism.

USING VISUAL AIDS TO ENHANCE DELIVERY

Visual aids are intended to assist the delivery of information—not replace it. Too often we have seen a visual aid *become* the speech rather than aid in its delivery. Consider the types of visual aids you may choose from, and learn some fundamental guidelines for using them and ways to effectively integrate them into your delivery.

Charts and graphs ■ Visual aids that help an audience understand *how much* and offer comparisons of parts to a whole.

Text charts ■ Posters, flip charts, writing on a chalkboard, and slides that preview or summarize key ideas.

Tables ■ Visual aids that summarize information.

Drawings ■ Visual aids that depict how things work.

Maps ■ Visual aids that help an audience understand where things occur.

Types of Visual Aids

Visual aids come in many forms, including:

- charts
- graphs
- tables
- drawings
- pictures
- maps
- photographs and slides
- objects or models
- transparencies on an overhead projector
- computer-generated presentations (e.g., PowerPoint)
- flip charts or marker/blackboards
- video clips
- segments of music
- demonstrations using people

Before you decide to use visual aids in your speech, ask yourself these two questions: First, will the visual aid help the audience understand my speech? Second, will the visual aid help my audience remember my speech? If you can answer "yes" to these questions, you should consider using the visual aid. If not, and if your visual aid simply substitutes for your content or, even worse, is an exact duplicate of what you say, then you should *not* use the visual aid. Let's look at the types of visual aids we listed above.

Charts and graphs often focus on helping an audience understand *how much* and compare parts to the whole. You may, for example, use a pie chart to demonstrate proportions (see Figure 9.5) or a bar or line graph to show your audience how trends have changed over time (see Figures 9.6 and 9.7). The Math League offers some valuable insight on the purpose and format of graphs at www.mathleague.com/help/data/data .htm. Charts also sometimes contain only text. For example, a poster, flip chart, chalkboard, and software slide that previews or summarizes key ideas or concepts are all examples of **text charts**, while **tables** help *summarize information*. In sum, text charts help listeners see a main point, while tables summarize a larger amount of information using words and sometimes graphics.

Drawings are often used to depict how things work. For example, if you are explaining the parts and functions of a personal computer, a drawing or diagram of a computer can help clarify your explanations. **Maps** focus on helping your audience understand *where* events occur or *where* landmarks are. In addition, maps may graphically explain where a given group of people lives or the geographic relationship of one

This pie chart shows the ingredients used to make a sausage and mushroom pizza. The fraction of each ingredient by weight is shown. We see that half of the pizza's weight comes from the crust. The mushrooms make up the smallest amount of the pizza by weight, since the slice corresponding to the mushrooms is smallest. Note that the sum of the decimal sizes of each slice is equal to 1 (the "whole pizza").

FIGURE 9.5

Pie Chart.

Source: From www.mathleague.com. Reprinted by permission of Mathematics Leagues, Inc.

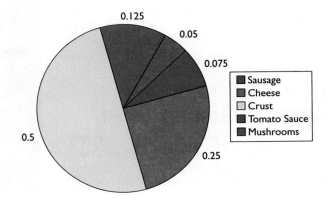

The number of police officers decreased from 1993 to 1996 but started increasing again in 1996. The graph makes it easy to compare or contrast the number of police officers for any combination of years. For example, in 2001 there were nine more police officers than in 1998.

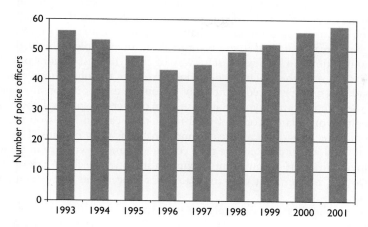

FIGURE 9.6

Number of Police Officers in Crimeville.

Source: From www.statcan.ca/english/edu/power/ch9/bargraph/bar.htm. Statistics Canada information is used with the permission of Statistics Canada. Users are forbidden to copy this material and/or redisseminate the data, in an original or modified form, for commercial purposes, without the expressed permission of Statistics Canada. Information on the availability of the wide range of data from Statistics Canada can be obtained from Statistic Canada's regional offices, its World Wide Web site at http://www.statcan.ca, and its toll-free access number 1-800-263-1136.

place to another. While we usually think of road maps that help us find directions, there are several types of maps, including physical, political, climate, economic, and topographic. However, maps typically show placement.

Photographs and slides tend to show *what* by preserving a snapshot of reality that may include, for example, a person's face, a landscape, or the action in a dramatic event. Remember, however, that a four-by-six photo you had processed at the local drugstore is not usually an effective visual aid because your audience cannot see it as you hold it, and passing it around during your speech distracts individual members of your audience.

Photographs ■ Visual aids that show what the speaker is discussing.

A line graph is used to show continuing data—how one thing is affected by another. It's clear to see how things are going by the rises and falls a line graph shows. This kind of graph is needed to show the effect of an independent variable on a dependent variable. This graph shows the number of Loggerhead turtle nests sighted on two beaches.

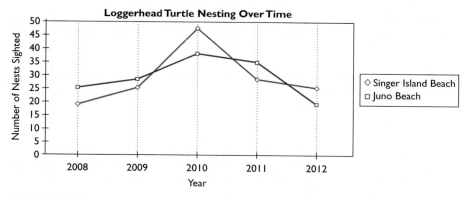

FIGURE 9.7

Line Graph.

Audio and video clips ■ Visual aids that provide examples of ideas or claims.

Demonstration ■ Visual aid that shows—sometimes with another person helping—how to do something.

PowerPoint ■ Presentation software developed by Microsoft that allows speakers to prepare a slide show to accompany a speech or presentation.

Objects or models can help your audience understand something that is multidimensional. The speaker can move the object to show its various "sides" and dimensions.

If you do not have computer capability, or if your time is limited and you have an overhead projector available, copying information onto a transparency can be useful. Other visual aids include **audio and video clips** or even a **demonstration**. Audio clips, especially music lyrics, can create a mood or enhance the power of an example or a claim. A video clip can be a great visual aid if you want to show an example or highlight some situation. A demonstration can be a very useful way of clarifying instructions or helping you explain how to *do* something. This can be fine if you are the one who is doing the demonstration and you have practiced sufficiently. If you are depending on another person to help with the demonstration, you could lose control over the speech if your "assistant" decides to alter your plans. You will need to exercise care in how you use these particular visual aids because they can create more problems than benefits if not used wisely. Using audio and visual clips can be time consuming and, if you are not familiar with the technology, can cause a significant disruption in your speech. Whatever visual aids you decide to use, be sure that they truly aid your speech and follow some basic guidelines.

Finally, what role should **PowerPoint** play in your speech? It's difficult today to find a speaker who is not using this tool. But not all who use PowerPoint use it wisely or well. Review the box called "Communication Counts in Your Life: PowerPoint as a Visual Aid" to find tips that will enhance your PowerPoint presentation and, ultimately, your entire speech.

Guidelines for Using Visual Aids

Here's a checklist you can use to help ensure that your visual aids—including PowerPoint—are well chosen, well prepared, and well used.

■ **Support not substitute.** Does your visual aid relate well to and assist in explaining your topic? Visual aids should contribute to and support a main point in your speech by making the point memorable or more powerful.

■ **Make the visual readable.** Have you prepared the visual aid so that it is readable and appeals to the eye? Choose an easily readable typeface such as Arial or Times Roman and use contrasting, dark colors so that any text is easily seen. While pastel colors may seem attractive, they "wash out" when you put them on paper or an electronic slide. Keep your visual clear, simple, and direct; avoid cluttering it with graphics or too many words. In most cases, less is better. Also, be sure it is large enough so that everyone in the audience can see. As the size of the audience increases, so must the size of the visual.

■ **Practice using the visual.** Does your visual aid need to be placed on an easel or attached with tape or a tack? If you have to hold a visual aid and refer to it, you may encounter a number of practical problems. Moreover, holding a visual inhibits your physical delivery, so tack it, tape it, or put it on an easel.

■ **Enhance the speech, do not shock the audience.** Will your visual aid draw too much attention? Visual aids should not be the focus of the speech or create unforeseen difficulties that distract the audience. This is why you should avoid using live animals, shocking pictures, or inappropriate displays or videotapes. If your aid may cause mishaps, create audience distraction, or be offensive, choose another type of aid.

■ **Use it, then lose it.** Can you keep your visual aid covered, use it, and then lay it aside? Effective visual aids will not be used for your entire speech but employed at a particular point in the speech. Therefore, keep them out of sight until you are ready to use them, and make sure you can easily retrieve them and just as easily put them aside.

■ **No handouts!** Can you avoid using handouts? Speakers who distribute handouts provide the audience with potential distractions. If you feel that handouts are useful and particularly necessary, plan to distribute them after your speech. If information from the handout is important to your speech, represent the information on a chart, overheard transparency, or blackboard.

PowerPoint as a Visual Aid

PowerPoint, presentation software developed by Microsoft to help users develop slide shows, is one of the most popular tools for presenting information. Millions of presentations in contemporary corporations today use this tool. But wait: How much of the information presented in these PowerPoint presentations really is useful?

Rule #1 for use of PowerPoint should be that you use this tool to help your *audience,* not to make *your* life easier. So if you're thinking you can just upload your whole speech in a series of slides and then read them to your audience, STOP RIGHT NOW! As with all other aspects of your speech, think first of your audience. Who are they? What do they need or want to see in the PowerPoint presentation that would help to clarify or add power to the speech? What will help them understand and remember your speech?

Consider the following tips for effective use of PowerPoint:

1. Make sure the font on each slide is big enough for the audience (all members) to read;

2. Use colors appropriately; some colors can cause "noise" for your audience, and they stop listening;
3. Don't use moving text continuously; you want your audience to stop reading and listen to you;
4. Use visuals instead of text in some of your slides; this provides variety and encourages the audience to think about what you are saying instead of reading;
5. Don't depend on slides for every section of your speech; use them selectively at appropriate sections, not continuously;
6. Keep the content of each slide to the 6 by 6 rule (six lines and six words per line per slide);
7. EDIT! EDIT! EDIT!

For more ways to enhance the look, power, and effectiveness of your PowerPoint, go to http://mason.gmu.edu/~montecin/powerpoint.html.

- **Can you do it alone?** Have you planned for any needed assistance in advance? Especially large or cumbersome visual aids may require someone else's help; be sure this is prearranged. Moreover, if you intend to conduct a demonstration that requires someone else's assistance, be sure to arrange this in advance.
- **Know your equipment.** Have you made sure that any equipment you need is readily available? At times, speakers may want to use audiovisual equipment. Be sure that these are available, economically feasible, and in good working order if you need them. In certain instances, securing equipment is prohibitively expensive; plan accordingly.
- **Practice, practice, practice.** Have you practiced with your visual aid? As with every other aspect of speech preparation, it is important to practice delivering your speech while using your visual aid. If this is not done, unforeseen problems may result.
- **Know your audience.** What does the audience expect? In some instances, your audience may expect a particular type of visual aid, such as a computerized slide show. Get a sense of the types of visual aids prior speakers have employed when addressing a given audience.

Integrating Visual Aids to Enhance Delivery

When your visual aid is ready, think about how to use it to enhance your delivery. Here are a couple of tips.

As You Begin Your Speech, Focus the Audience on You, Not Your Visual Aid   We have seen several student speakers use a visual aid to gain attention and lose the opportunity to build common ground or connect with their audience. For example, this is why we advise you to avoid using video clips. Sometimes audience members want to continue watching the movie rather than listening to you. Therefore, use the first minute of your speech to gain your audience's attention through effective use of language and delivery. Additionally, this strategy will help you gain confidence, establish eye contact, and get your speech well started, which will, in turn, help focus and energize the remainder of your speech.

USE YOUR VISUAL TO CLARIFY AN IMPORTANT IDEA IN YOUR SPEECH   While in many professional settings it is common to dim the lights and talk through a series of electronic slides, we find this approach problematic because it separates the speaker from the audience, turns a speech into a slide show with a "voice-over," and essentially omits many of the aspects of physical delivery. Avoid this approach, unless it is absolutely the expected norm. Even then, make adjustments by having the lights as bright as possible and creating significant pauses in the slide show that move the focus from the visuals to you. In general, use your visual aid to strengthen a major point in your speech and at the same time enhance audience interest.

ONLY USE THE VISUAL AIDS YOU TRULY NEED   At times, a single visual aid is sufficient for your speech, but at other times, you may need two or even more; use what you need to communicate your message effectively. Also, remember that using appropriate visual aids helps engage your audience members' attention and assists their memory. Ultimately, keep in mind that visual aids are, indeed, aids, not the substance of your speech; *you* are the speaker, and your aids are your assistants.

DELIVERING YOUR SPEECH EFFECTIVELY

A student returned from a debate angry because many students attending the event considered one side's arguments more credible than another. The student fumed, "The opposition's arguments were not as strong as the proponent's; he was just a better speaker, so a lot of the students thought he made a stronger case." This incident highlights an important point: Delivery in presentations matters. Delivery should never be a replacement for substance; however, *how* you deliver your message obviously impacts whether your audience grasps your message. We now consider the important aspects of delivery and how visual aids impact your delivery and the effectiveness of your message. To this point, if you have been following our process, you have put a lot of work into your presentation. You have found a subject, conducted research, narrowed the subject to a topic, developed a clear thesis with related main points, organized your ideas, and prepared your outlines. However, you are now ready to put all of this behind-the-scenes work onstage; you are ready to present your speech. Just as you invested time in planning and researching your speech, you must now invest time in preparing to deliver it effectively. To do so, think about the type of delivery you will employ and the various elements essential to effective delivery, as well as how you will practice this delivery. You will also need to learn how to deal with communication apprehension, which can impact your delivery.

You can deliver your speech in one of four ways: impromptu, extemporaneous, manuscript, or memorized. All of these have their uses, although in most communication classes you will likely be asked to develop your extemporaneous speaking skills. However, because you will use your speaking skills throughout your college experience and later in your career, knowing the different delivery options allows you to plan for effective presentations now and in the future.

Impromptu Speaking

Impromptu speeches are presentations that you must give in the moment, without prior planning or practice. Although you do not have time to prepare, you can quickly draw on some of the basic principles you have already learned in this textbook and from your communication course: Have a clear purpose, identify main ideas, and use your experience to provide supporting information. You may think that you will never have to give an impromptu speech. However, you may be in a meeting where you are faced with a serious issue that dramatically impacts your life, livelihood, or the well-being of your neighborhood or family. Will you sit quietly by and allow decisions to be made without your voice? If you intend to address the matter, you will be called upon to speak. Moreover, a job interview is, in reality, much like an extended impromptu speech, as explained in the box "Communication Counts in Your Career: Job Interviews as Impromptu Speaking." It is highly unlikely that you will get a job without an interview.

Impromptu speeches ■
Presentations that are given at a moment's notice, without prior planning or practice.

COMMUNICATION COUNTS IN YOUR CAREER

Job Interviews as Impromptu Speaking

Career Services at Virginia Polytechnic Institute and State University identifies several typical interview questions.* Consider some of the questions on their list:

1. What are your long-range goals and objectives?
2. Why did you choose the career for which you are preparing?
3. Describe a situation in which you had to work with a difficult person (another student, coworker, customer, supervisor, etc.). How did you handle the situation? Is there anything you would have done differently in hindsight?

4. In what ways have your college experiences prepared you for a career?
5. Describe a situation in which you worked as part of a team. What role did you take on? What went well and what didn't?
6. Do you think your grades are a good indication of your academic achievement?

*http://www.career.vt.edu/Interviewing/TypicalQuestions.html

Source: From "Typical Interview Questions," Career Services at Virginia Polytechnic Institute and State University, www.career.vt.edu/Interviewing/TypicalQuestions.html. Reprinted by permission.

Extemporaneous Speaking

Extemporaneous speeches are planned presentations that may be delivered using a keyword outline that helps you deliver your prepared comments. This mode of delivery allows you to engage your audience by employing a conversational style earmarked by effective delivery techniques. It also allows you to remain flexible and adapt to your audience, especially if they become restless.

Speaking from a Manuscript

In delivering **manuscript speeches,** you read your presentation word for word. This allows you to prepare every detail carefully, craft your use of language artfully, and time your speech exactly. If you need to be extremely careful because of language or time constraints, a manuscript speech is an appropriate choice. Beginning speakers may prefer to read presentations because they are nervous, but in most cases this compromises many of the elements of effective delivery that we will discuss later in this chapter. Therefore, your instructor will probably not allow you to read your speech to the class.

Speaking from Memory

Memorized speeches are presentations that speakers write word for word and then memorize. While memorized speeches allow for greater freedom in delivery, we do not recommend them to beginning speakers for several reasons. First, it takes considerable time to memorize even a four-minute presentation; your time is already strained as a college student. Second, if you forget a part of the speech, you are likely to be faced with disaster. Third, you are liable to recite rather than speak with your audience, which negatively impacts effective delivery. While you may find it useful to memorize certain portions of your speech, such as your introduction or the way you want to phrase your main points, memorizing the entire speech is, in most instances, not appropriate as you begin to develop your presentation skills.

Elements of Effective Delivery

Now that you have a basic understanding of the delivery types you might employ, let's consider the various elements of effective delivery before we look at some guidelines for preparation and practice. In this section, we will consider how to use your voice, face, body, and visual aids to enhance your delivery.

USING YOUR VOICE EFFECTIVELY   Have you ever sat in a lecture and drifted off to sleep? While there may be many reasons for this response, you may have been nudged into a

Extemporaneous speeches ■ Planned presentations that are delivered using a keyword outline that helps the speaker deliver his or her prepared comments.

Manuscript speeches ■ Speeches in which the speaker reads the presentation word for word.

Memorized speeches ■ Presentations that speakers write word for word and then memorize.

nap by the speaker's monotone delivery. How the speaker vocally delivers his or her message impacts how well the message is received. In like fashion, even though you may have strong content, you must engage your audience by delivering the content using appropriate breathing, volume, rate, pitch, and clarity.

Breathing. You must breathe well to deliver your speech well. Without proper breathing, you cannot use your voice effectively. Moreover, if you control your breath, you can reduce apprehension.

Volume. Appropriate **volume,** or how loudly or softly one speaks, is an important aspect of delivering a speech. If you speak too softly, the audience cannot hear you. Therefore, you must *project* your voice. Think of your voice as a ball that you must bounce off the room's back wall. While you may think you're speaking too loudly, you will often find that you need to add vocal energy to your delivery so the people in the back row can hear you. Of course, if you are in an auditorium with a microphone, you need not be as concerned with vocal projection, but in many instances you will need to project in order to be easily heard. At the same time, you must also avoid shouting, because this tends to alienate your audience. Most listeners don't want to be shouted at; they want you to speak directly and clearly with them. Of course, you can also adjust your volume at various points in your presentation for emphasis or effect. For example, if you wish to stress an idea, enhancing your volume can make this idea stand out for your listeners. In general, you should speak loudly enough to be easily heard and to add impact to certain portions of your speech.

Rate. You must consciously focus on how rapidly you are speaking, or your **rate.** If you speak too quickly, you will lose your audience through disinterest. If you speak too slowly, you will lose your audience through boredom. So what should you do? First, breathe through your diaphragm. Breathing deeply will help pace your speech rate. Second, remind yourself to slow down. You are speaking too rapidly if you stumble over words or begin to feel out of breath. If this happens, take a deep breath and slow down. We also recommend that you practice and time yourself so that you have a feel for how quickly you should speak. Let this guide your decisions as you speak.

Remember that, like volume, you can use rate for effect. For example, sports announcers respond to exciting moments in a game by increasing their rate of speech. In other words, the announcers use rate to emphasize the events. You, too, should use rate, in conjunction with volume, to emphasize important points of your speech. For example, to stress an important point, enhance your volume and slow down your rate; this will give your point vocal emphasis.

Pitch. Listen carefully to your favorite radio DJ. Notice how the DJ frequently changes the pitch of his or her voice; this is called **vocal inflection** and is the opposite of a **monotone** voice, where one rarely changes pitch. To avoid a monotone voice, we suggest that first you recognize the range of pitch you can employ. As a test, stand up, take a deep breath, and slide your voice along a musical scale. Begin at the highest tone you can produce and slide your voice down to the lowest tone you can produce. While you obviously will not want to speak with a high, falsetto voice or an abnormally low voice, this exercise can help you identify a comfortable vocal range, which still includes numerous pitches you can employ to make your speech more effective. Second, think about how you can use inflection to emphasize keywords or ideas. For example, repeat the following sentences and change your voice to emphasize the words in bold.

Volume ■ How loudly or softly one speaks.

Rate ■ How rapidly one speaks.

Vocal inflection ■ Changing the pitch of one's voice.

Monotone ■ Rarely changing the pitch of one's voice.

I just got out.

I **just** got out.

I just **got** out.

I just got **out.**

How does the meaning of the sentence change given the change in your voice? Can you add a different "tone" to each of the messages and alter the meaning yet again? For example, how might you say, "I **just** got out" with frustration or as an apology? Note how the inflection changes as you purposefully change the meaning of this simple sentence. Inflection adds emphasis, interest, and expressiveness that will help you communicate your message and engage your listeners.

Verbal Clarity. Not only do you need to speak with sufficient and varied volume, rate, and pitch, but you also need to speak clearly. We have already discussed how to use language more carefully for clarity. However, clarity is also a matter of delivery and refers, specifically, to articulation, pronunciation, and fluency. Let's consider each of these terms in greater detail.

First, **articulation** refers to saying the sounds in words clearly. For example, poor articulation occurs when "going to" becomes "gonna" and "get out of here" becomes "gitouttahere." Second, **pronunciation** refers to saying words correctly. Mispronunciation occurs frequently because of adding, subtracting, reversing, or substituting sounds, as well as accenting the wrong syllable. Yourdictionary.com (www.yourdictionary. com/library/mispron.html) provides a list of the 100 most commonly mispronounced words. Consider the examples in Table 9.7 to help you identify possible problems with clarity. **Fluency** refers to a smooth flow of speech without frequent verbal stumbles or fillers. Beginning speakers often add words such as *you know, like, okay,* or *uhs* and *ums*. While some *disfluencies* are a part of natural, conversational speech, when they are used excessively and repeatedly, they become highly distracting to listeners. We recommend that you have a solid grasp of your ideas, work carefully on the language of your speech, and omit fillers as you practice to maintain fluency. In our experience, you are most likely to insert unnecessary fillers at the beginnings and ends of sentences. To avoid this repetitive pattern, work carefully on the language of your main ideas and your transitions between these ideas. Also remember not to obsess over an occasional "uh" or "um." If you are concerned about your dialect or accent, we encourage you to talk about your concerns with your instructor.

USING YOUR FACE EFFECTIVELY   Facial delivery refers, for the most part, to **eye contact** and **facial expressions**. While eye contact, like language, differs among cultural groups, in most speaking situations, frequent, sustained, and comprehensive eye contact will help you link with your audience. This means that you should regularly share eye contact with everyone in your audience without relying on your keyword outline or note cards. Beginning speakers tend to look at their notes as a way to avoid eye contact, thus reducing their apprehension, even though they know the content of their speech well. This strategy typically backfires because they will be more apt to continue looking at their notes rather than at their audience. You may also be tempted to focus on your instructor or one friendly face in the audience, but this excludes a large portion of your audience as well. Remember, as Andrews, Andrews, and Williams (1999) point out, eye contact helps you enhance your credibility with the audience. At the same time, you can watch how your listeners respond to your presentation and adapt accordingly. Your eyes are an important gateway to audience feedback.

Additionally, think about your facial expressions. When all eyes are on you, you may become less expressive than you are in everyday conversation. Therefore, focus on

Articulation ■ Saying the sounds within words clearly.

Pronunciation ■ Saying words correctly.

Fluency ■ A smooth flow of speech without frequent stumbles or fillers.

Eye contact ■ Looking at all audience members.

Facial expressions ■ The ways in which an individual animates his or her face.

TABLE 9.7

EXAMPLES OF COMMONLY MISPRONOUNCED WORDS

Incorrect	Correct	Type of Problem
athelete	athlete	adding a sound
cannidate	candidate	dropping a sound
birfday	birthday	substituting sounds
aks	ask	reversing sounds
mis*chie*vous	*mis*chievous	misplaced accent

Gestures ■ Movements of the hands, the arms, and sometimes the shoulders, legs, or feet.

Posture ■ Overall stance.

Movement ■ Encompasses whether the speaker stands still or moves his or her entire body.

your message and allow your speech's content to help direct your facial expressions. If your speech reflects a note of humor, sorrow, or surprise and you respond accordingly, you will come across as more natural and believable; however, if you focus on practicing your nonverbal expressions, you are likely to come across as unnatural. In most instances, a smile will relax you and your audience, and your audience is likely to reciprocate, especially considering that smiling is a universal human behavior (Ekman & Friesen 1987). Of course, a smile is not always appropriate if it violates the tone or content of your speech, but it is often an effective default facial expression, especially as compared to a consistently solemn or terrified facial expression.

USING YOUR BODY EFFECTIVELY   Physical or bodily delivery typically includes gestures, posture, and movement. **Gestures** refer to movements of the hands, arms, shoulders, legs, or feet. **Posture** refers to your overall stance, whereas **movement** ranges from whether you stand still or move your entire body. With these basic definitions in hand, let's consider some principles that can enhance your physical delivery.

Just as your speech's content should direct your facial expressions, it should also give rise to natural gestures. Your gestures will help you tell a story effectively or drive home a point. Think about the size of your audience and create gestures that are in direct proportion to the size of the audience. If it is a large audience, your gestures should be enhanced and delivered in slower motion. For smaller audiences more restricted gestures are better, but their speed can be slightly quicker. But remember that forced or overly planned gestures look robotic and are distracting, if not downright laughable. We have seen beginning speakers make a point and then suddenly remember they were intending to employ a specific gesture and do so a split second after making the point. However, with practice, you can plan for some gestures that harmonize well with your speech's content. For example, if you use an ordinal approach to organization (e.g., first, second, third), you can hold up the appropriate number of fingers to help emphasize your transition between points. If you wish to emphasize a particular point, simply pointing your right index finger into the palm of your left hand helps to nonverbally underscore your point. Above all, remember to be yourself and to blend your gestures with your message.

As for your posture, stand up straight but not rigidly, flex your knees, and firmly place both feet on the floor. How you stand will tell the audience a lot about how you feel. If you are stiff, the audience will know you aren't comfortable. If you slouch over the lectern, you

Effective bodily movement enhances the appeal and power of your message.

will give the impression that you don't care much for the topic and perhaps the audience to whom you are speaking. Stand tall and be well-balanced. Lean slightly forward, toward the audience, and the audience will feel more engaged with you. You can move around the stage, but don't pace. Think about a speaker you remember as having poise and confidence. Model that mode of body language. Vary your body movement just as you vary the inflection in your voice. Some speakers visualize chewing gum on the bottom of their shoes, so the image of something tugging on their feet reminds them to move their feet purposefully. Avoid slumping or leaning on or clinging to the podium. Standing straight and keeping your knees unlocked will assist your breathing and keep you from becoming dizzy while you also strike a confident, relaxed pose.

If you wish to move as you speak, keep your movement natural and linked to your speech's content. For example, as you move from one main point to another, you may wish to step left or right to help physically reinforce your verbal transition. You can also use movement to enhance a description or to help your audience focus on a visual aid. For example, you may move from the podium to a poster, chart, or overhead transparency to point to a specific diagram or piece of information. If you do this, continue facing your audience and stand to the side of your visual aid as you draw attention to it.

The most important thing to remember is that your movement should be purposeful, not random and distracting. It should add life to the speech, enhancing your content and helping to "tell your story." Practice your speech with a friend and have him or her provide feedback about your eye contact, body movement, facial expressions, and gestures. Overall, the whole "package" should be one that flows in a consistent manner. No one part of your body movement should stand out as extreme, unusual, or distracting. Such things as playing with your hair or a pen, jingling the keys in your pocket, tapping your finger on the podium, rocking back and forth or from side to side, picking at or adjusting your clothing, or pacing all distract from your message. Focus on integrating your movement with the content of your speech and maintaining a professional, poised appearance without distracting mannerisms.

DEALING WITH COMMUNICATION APPREHENSION

An officer in the military gets ready to deliver his speech to a basic oral communication class. He begins by speaking in a clear, strong voice and appears to be doing well, until suddenly he stops speaking and runs from the room with tears streaming down his face. He explains to his teacher, "I don't know what happened; I couldn't think what to say next, and I felt everyone looking at me. I froze and couldn't keep going. Please don't make me do that again!" Many people experience "fear or anxiety associated with either real or anticipated communication with another person or persons" (McCroskey & Richmond 1979), or what we term **communication apprehension (CA)**. Researchers have studied CA and developed many insights about its origins and effects, including the fact that high CA interferes with a speaker's ability to deliver a speech. The possible combination of confused thought, sweaty palms, shaky knees, dry mouth, breathlessness, and nausea create a frightening physical and psychological reaction. If you have such reactions, we suggest speaking with your instructor, who will have strategies to assist you. However, as Dr. Michael T. Motley (1997) notes, reframing your attitude toward delivering your speech will help you begin to deal with CA. He suggests thinking of giving your speech not as a performance but as a communication event. Performances, as Motley notes, are often memorized and charged with expectations of perfection, while communication events are an ordinary part of everyday interaction and therefore do not have the same purpose or expectations as performances. The box "Communication Counts in Your Life: Dealing with Communication Apprehension" summarizes some suggested ways for dealing with CA. These strategies will give you an idea of ways to begin addressing your anxiety. You can also measure your level of anxiety about public speaking by completing the Personal Report of Public Speaking Anxiety (PRPSA) available online at www.jamescmccroskey.com/measures/prpsa.htm. Simply print the survey, complete it according to the directions, and follow the scoring directions at the bottom of the page.

Communication apprehension ■
Fear or anxiety associated with either real or anticipated communication with another person or persons.

COMMUNICATION COUNTS IN YOUR LIFE

Dealing with Communication Apprehension

Communication apprehension refers to anxiety or fear about oral communication, which people experience in a variety of communication situations, including public speaking. Some people refer to this fear as "stage fright." While most everyone feels some anxiety before speaking, there are some steps you can take to help reduce the anxiety that may hinder you from speaking as well as you would like. Using a combination of these approaches usually works best.

1. *Explanation.* In explanation, you basically seek to understand why you are afraid of public speaking. By identifying the fear, you can then face it realistically, which helps

you see that the fear is not well founded. Sometimes people say, "If I have to give a speech, I'll just die." But you realize that this won't really happen; it's an irrational fear. This understanding helps reduce fear.

2. *Rationalization.* Through rationalization, give yourself messages that replace negative thoughts with positive ones. So substitute "I'm scared to death about this" with a statement like, "I'm ready to speak; I've planned and practiced, and I can do this." When a negative thought comes to mind, immediately replace it with a positive message. Persistence in this practice reduces apprehension.

(continued)

3. *Relaxation.* Before you speak, find a quiet, comfortable place where you can sit down. Beginning with your toes, tighten, hold, and release muscles and work your way up to each area of the body, clenching and releasing your muscles. Concentrate only on your body as you tighten and release muscles; pay attention to the sensation of tension in your body. As you release the muscle tension, take deep breaths and let the tension go. This helps relieve the physical symptoms that accompany anxiety.

4. *Visualization.* How do you see yourself in your mind before you speak? Are you succeeding by speaking fluently and engaging your audience? Through visualization, you create a "mental movie" in which you picture yourself delivering a successful speech from beginning to end. In this way, you can then actually *do* what you've pictured in your mind and help reduce your fear.

5. *Education.* Often you have important things to say but lack the communication skills necessary to say them as well as you'd like. Through education such as communication classes, you can learn and develop these skills that increase your confidence. As your confidence increases, your fears decrease. By reading your text thoughtfully, attending class regularly, participating in exercises, practicing the delivery of speech, and continuing to work on your communication skills, you can reduce your communication apprehension by building your speaking skills.

Of course, you may not have high CA but still experience some measure of it. If so, please remember that this is a natural response and that you can actually use this energy to help you deliver your speech more effectively. The emotions and physical responses you experience when you are excited are very similar to those you have when you are somewhat nervous. Therefore, reframe your response from anxiety to anticipation and look forward to the opportunity to share with others what you have learned or believe. After all, how many times do you have an opportunity to present your ideas to an audience? We encourage you to seize this chance.

PREPARING FOR EFFECTIVE DELIVERY

Now that you understand the various modes of delivery and the critical elements of effective delivery, you must prepare and practice to deliver your speech effectively. This section contains some guidelines for preparation in advance and just before addressing your audience, as well as some other practical suggestions.

Guidelines for Effective Preparation

While there are several specific steps you can take to prepare for effective delivery, here are some basic guidelines to consider.

PREPARE YOUR CONTENT   While we addressed this point in detail earlier in this chapter, we again urge you to develop a clear preparation and presentation outline on a topic that you find interesting and worthwhile. Knowing what you're going to say because you have mastered the content will improve your self-confidence as a speaker. Believing that you have something important to share with your listeners is equally important to your confidence. Also, be sure to prepare any visual aids you intend to use. We will say more about visual aids later in this chapter.

PREPARE YOUR VOICE AND PRACTICE SPEAKING CLEARLY   As you practice your speech, think about how you can use the pitch and volume of your voice, the rate at which you speak, and the emphasis you place on certain words to enliven your presentation. Strive to say your words clearly and correctly. If possible, practice your speech in the room where you will deliver it and have a friend sit in the back row. Your friend can help you be sure you're speaking at an appropriate volume and rate and with sufficient vocal variety.

PREPARE YOUR BODY   As you practice your speech, think about how you can use your face, hands, posture, and bodily movement to enhance the impact of your words. While any movement needs to be natural and not forced, some planning can help you focus on your nonverbal behavior. Consider placing reminders on your keyword outline to prompt desirable gestures, facial expressions, or movement. Additionally, be sure to get a good night's rest and eat a light but nutritious breakfast, lunch, or dinner on the day you are to speak to maintain your blood sugar level and thereby provide you with needed energy.

PREPARE YOUR APPEARANCE Think about and plan how you want to be dressed and groomed for your presentation. Your appearance impacts your credibility. Wearing caps or letting long hair fall in your face can make it difficult for the audience to see your eyes and face. Your instructor may have other helpful guidelines.

PREPARE YOUR MIND It's natural to be nervous before you speak. But you can use your nervousness as energy to draw on rather than let it be "mental noise" that interferes with your presentation. Be positive. See yourself doing well. Tell yourself that your nervousness will help you think and speak better. For additional help, reread the section on communication apprehension earlier in this chapter.

PREPARE BY PRACTICING There is no substitute for regular, appropriate practice to ensure the high-quality delivery of your speech. We discuss practice in further detail in the next section.

PREPARE BEFORE YOU BEGIN Before you take the podium for your presentation, be sure nothing is in your mouth (such as gum) or hand (such as a pencil or pen); bring only what you need for the speech. After you reach the front of the room, take a moment to collect your thoughts before you begin speaking. Don't start talking before you reach the front of the room and don't continue speaking as you walk back to your seat toward the conclusion of your speech. Deliver your entire speech from the front of the room.

Practice for Effectiveness

There is simply no substitute for practice if you want to deliver your speech effectively. Consider these ideas for practice.

- Work on the parts of your speech privately and aloud. You may find it useful to practice portions of your speech in shorter time periods as you begin. For example, deliver your first main point aloud to yourself. As you do, you may find a better way to phrase your main point or to adapt your supporting material to make it more effective. You can make these changes to your outline. Then practice the major sections of your speech—specifically, the introduction, body, and conclusion.
- After you practice each major section aloud, put the entire speech together and practice it aloud. At this point, time yourself and make any changes necessary to meet the stipulated time limits or to improve the speech's flow. Make sure these are your final edits to the content of the speech.
- Continue to practice the entire speech aloud. At this point, you should have made necessary changes in the content, so focus now on delivering your content effectively. While some people recommend practicing in front of a mirror, we find this method often interferes with focusing on your message because the mirror too often prompts you to focus on yourself. However, continue to practice aloud, and be sure to use any visual aids you have prepared for the speech.
- You may wish to audio record a practice session when you are basically satisfied with the speech. Listen to yourself and identify specific aspects of your delivery you want to change. We recommend this step only if you have heard your recorded voice previously. Otherwise, you may become too distracted on hearing your recorded voice for the first time.
- As a final step, ask your roommate, a friend, or a family member to listen to your speech and provide feedback. You may also have a speech lab where you can practice and receive even more focused, helpful feedback. If you have such an opportunity, use it; research indicates that speech labs make a measurable difference in student performances and the resulting grades (Hunt & Simonds 2002).

Preparing a speech takes a considerable investment of time, but it is an investment that will pay valuable dividends in developing your skills and improving your grades. Furthermore, in many ways, the time-management skills necessary to prepare to speak effectively parallel your overall college experience, as indicated in the box "Communication Counts in Your College Experience: Time Management in Speech Preparation."

COMMUNICATION COUNTS IN YOUR COLLEGE EXPERIENCE

Time Management in Speech Preparation

To successfully complete the process of speech preparation, you must allow yourself sufficient time to brainstorm to identify your subject and topic, conduct sufficient research to construct the content of your outline and speech, and still save time for practicing aloud. In other words, you have to manage your time to be an effective speaker. The same skills required for completing your speaking assignments are also required for college and professional success. Learning how to manage your time now will yield important dividends in your college and professional careers, as well as in your communication class.

So, consider this piece of advice: *You can never FIND time; you must MAKE time.* But how do you *make* time? Consider these practical suggestions for time management for completing your speech assignments and for college and career success.

1. **Find out how you are spending your time.** Analyze where your time is going by completing a time analysis sheet. Here's a link to help you, as a college student, get started in analyzing your time: http://istudy.psu/FirstYearModules/Time/Time/TimeManagementLesson.htm. Remember that there are only 168 hours in a week. You may be surprised to find that you have more time on your hands than you thought, or, like some very busy folks, that you've exceeded the 168 hours and are overcommitted. This analysis will allow you to identify how much time to commit to preparing your speech. As a general guideline, you need two hours of preparation time for every hour you spend in class. So, if you're taking a three-semester-credit-hour communication class, you need to spend at least six hours a week studying. Effective speech preparation is likely to take even more time!

2. **Plan your time.** Once you know what activities you are currently spending your time on, you can make choices about how to spend your time in the future. Invest in a monthly and a daily planner. Begin by reading through the syllabi or course outlines for each of your classes and then record all your test, quiz, or paper due dates in your monthly planner. Use different colors for each class so you can quickly note what you must do for each of them. The major advantage of a monthly planner is that you can see what's coming up and can plan accordingly. After you've filled in your monthly planner, use your daily planner to write down all reading assignments, lecture topics, and other information. Keep your daily planner filled out at least two weeks in advance so you can keep on top of your homework load. Include your speech preparation time in your planner using the guidelines that follow.

3. **Combat procrastination.** According to McWhorter (2001), procrastination is one of the main enemies of successful time management. Here are some specific steps to help combat this enemy:

Set aside weekly plan time. Keep your monthly and daily planners up-to-date by setting aside an hour or a half-hour time block to plan each week. Use this time to update your calendars, plan what needs to be done, and set weekly and daily goals. Jot down what you wish to accomplish on a daily "sticky" note. That way you can easily add to it and will get the satisfaction of crossing off things you have accomplished. Setting realistic daily "to do" tasks provides a checklist as well as positive feedback because you will feel so much better when you can check off one of your assignments or projects.

Establish "soft" deadlines. "Soft" deadlines are due dates that you establish for yourself that allow you to complete your work ahead of time, ensuring you meet your instructor's "hard" deadline. For example, if you need to write a research paper that's due in four weeks, you could set a soft deadline to complete your research by the end of week 1, to create an outline or a rough draft by the end of week 2, and to have reworked your rough draft and completed your bibliography by the end of week 3. By setting soft deadlines, you've allowed extra time in your schedule for the real-life occurrences such as getting called into work, running out of ink cartridges for your printer, or getting clarification on your paper from your teacher.

Use these same strategies in planning your speech preparation, using specific days rather than weeks, because typically you will not have as much time to prepare your speech as to complete a research paper. So, for example, if you have a week of preparation time for your speech, identify specific goals for each day. Here's a suggested timetable, assuming you have a week's preparation time:

Day 1: Commit to a subject and topic and start your research. Consult your instructor or speech lab about your topic (two hours).

Day 2: Conduct your research and write a preliminary thesis statement (two hours).

Day 3: Complete your research, refine the preliminary thesis statement, and write your first-draft preparation outline. Start to work on your visual aids (two hours).

Day 4: Consult with your instructor or speech lab about your outline and refine your preparation outline and visual aids. Make your keyword outline and put it on note cards. Practice aloud and make changes to your note cards as you go, noting any areas that need special attention either in your use of language or your delivery goals (two hours).

Day 5: Finalize your visual aids. Practice aloud by yourself, even if it's in the shower (one hour); at a speech lab; or with your instructor and/or in front of roommates, family, or other class members using your note cards and visual aids (one hour). Make any changes to your note cards and or visual aids.

Day 6: Practice aloud and make your final draft of keyword outline cards (two hours).

Day 7: Practice aloud one more time for reinforcement as close as possible to your speech delivery time, and then deliver your speech.

Of course, you may need to adjust this schedule depending on intervening factors; that's why we offer these as soft deadlines. For example, you may need more time for research. However, if you use this schedule and adjust it as necessary, you will avoid waiting until the last minute to prepare your speech. Don't forget: An excellent speech rests on excellent preparation!

Give yourself just a few minutes to start. Often, just starting is the most difficult thing for you to do. This can be true for all sorts of activities—from starting a weight-loss program to cleaning your closet—but it is especially true when it comes to studying and preparing for your speech. If you give yourself just a few minutes to start, you may make progress on your task and find that working just a few more minutes isn't as difficult as you thought. The most important step to take when preparing your speech is to get started now!

4. **Fight disorganization.**

Use a three-ring-binder system. Rather than using separate notebooks and folders for each class, invest in a two-inch-wide D-ring binder and a three-hole punch. Buy some section dividers and loose-leaf paper as well. Create a separate section that is chronologically organized (according to the date the assignment was completed) for each of your classes in which to keep all your lecture notes, handouts, text notes, and returned work. In addition to keeping you organized, carrying your binder allows you to use brief moments to study (like between classes or when a class is canceled) and prevents you from having to run back to your residence hall or to your car to get what you need. Former students have indicated that this is the most important organizational strategy they have learned.

To assist your speech preparation, here are some additional specific organizational suggestions to consider: Keep all your work for the speech together, including your brainstorming sheets, copies of your research, your preliminary outline, and your note cards. An inexpensive folder can be a valuable organizational tool. You can save time just by having everything together in the same place. Additionally, save any research you gather under your "favorites" on your computer, save it to a disk, and e-mail articles to yourself for future use. You may also find it very useful to print hard copies of your research if you use a computer lab or the library and cannot easily access the information elsewhere. If you are using information gathered from print copies of magazines, journals, or books, photocopy the information. As you find research, carefully note the citation information so you do not have to retrieve it later; you will need this for your outline. If you are using printed information, you can always copy the page from the book, journal, or magazine that has the essential citation information. Or you can simply write down the bibliographic information on note cards and put them in your organizational folder. These simple strategies can truly save time in the long run.

ACHIEVING COMPETENT AND ETHICAL SPEECH DELIVERY

As we noted in Chapter 1, all human communication is contextualized; it occurs in unique settings. Therefore, you must adapt your delivery to a variety of settings as you continue to employ your public speaking skills. While there is a wealth of information about numerous contexts, we offer a summary and some fundamental principles for the contexts you are most likely to encounter in this section. First, we offer some reliable, time-tested principles that cut across all contexts, and then we provide some insights for the college, workplace, and public contexts.

Common Core Principles

Context is one of the essential components of any communication situation. Therefore, you should be keenly aware of public speaking contexts. We will say more about this in the next section, but at this point, consider these core principles of delivery that are applicable across contexts:

- Be clear. Your first goal in delivery is to be understandable. Speak with appropriate volume, pitch, rate, and gestures for the size of the audience and the room you are speaking in.

- Be concise. In a highly technological age, your audience is conditioned to sound bites and relatively brief oral explanations. Therefore, be conscious of the time you are allotted to speak and how you use it. Make your points as cleanly and directly as possible.
- Be correct. While some contexts are more relaxed and allow for greater flexibility in delivery, in most instances you need to use correct grammar, pronunciation, and articulation.
- Be courteous. In every speaking situation, your audience expects you to be appropriate, sensitive, and nonoffensive. Treat your audience with courtesy by avoiding any slurs that might offend.
- Be controlled. Avoid overt movement, gestures, and facial expressions that distract your audience. Smooth, flowing movements and gestures are, in most cases, appropriate and engaging. Remember that speaking is not acting or performing; it should be conversational in appearance and tone.
- Be captivating. Work at gaining and maintaining your audience's attention. Think about how you can use language and nonverbal delivery to help seize and hold attention. Sometimes this may be as simple as moving a step closer to your audience; it need not be dramatic to be effective.

College and Public Speaking

The college classroom, as we noted in Chapter 1, is a viable, real-life communication context. Rather than treat your classroom audience as a training ground for speaking to a "real audience" that you will face later in life, approach public speaking in your classes by carefully considering your audience. Given what we know about college student experiences, plan to deliver your speech energetically by employing considerable vocal variety, gestures, and strong visual aids. Moreover, Dr. Charles Schroeder (1993) suggests that present-day college students prefer concrete, well-organized information presented in a personalized manner. Consequently, think about how to make the ideas in your speech specific, clear, and practical. This will require real-life examples backed by helpful visual aids that make your ideas accessible. Additionally, carefully organize your speech so your ideas flow together, thereby allowing your audience to easily follow them. In most cases, your peers need you to lead them from one idea to another. Finally, speak with your audience in a friendly vocal tone, smile, and build common ground with them; they want a personal touch, not an overly polished orator.

The Workplace and Public Speaking

Whole courses are committed to helping you develop your skills in business and professional communication, and we highly recommend that you consider such a course in the future. It is beyond the scope of this book to offer you a complete review of speaking in the workplace, but we encourage you to read Appendix A in Andrews, Andrews, and Williams's (1999) book, which provides detailed information about workplace communication. However, here are some important delivery principles to consider that are applicable across a variety of presentations in the workplace:

- Understand the organization's culture. To craft your delivery appropriately, you must have a working knowledge of how a given business or organization is structured, how decisions are made, and how the organization's members relate to one another. There is simply no substitute for doing your homework about an organization, department, or team that you will speak with.
- Deliver your presentation extemporaneously. Prepare and practice, but be spontaneous and adapt so that you reach every audience member.
- Consider the physical context. You may be in an office, boardroom, or larger conference area; adapt your nonverbal delivery accordingly. In most instances, it is best to stand as you present, although you may sometimes be seated at a conference table.
- Use visual aids. Most organizations expect computer-generated visual support for presentations, although in some cases other forms are equally acceptable. Be sure that your aids are clean, clear, correct, and appealing to the eye; they should look truly professional. We recommend you take a workshop on how to use PowerPoint effectively.

- Respect time limits. People in organizations are faced with multiple tasks and tight deadlines; therefore, time is often strained. Remember this and reflect it in your presentation.
- Be ready to answer questions. You must have a command of the information and be ready to respond to questions in an impromptu fashion. Refer to your prepared information as much as possible to repeat and reinforce it, but be sure to maintain a cooperative, professional attitude as you respond to potentially difficult questions. Don't get rattled or—worse—angry or defensive. Monitor your nonverbal responses and adjust them to manage your impressions appropriately.

Public speaking is an important skill in the workplace.

The Public and Public Speaking

Although many of you may not see yourselves speaking publicly, life has a way of providing you with surprises. For example, your college may consider instituting a new fee to offset some of the expenses of labs or technology purchases and may plan to hold open public hearings so interested people can express their opinions. Will you speak or remain silent? While it may be easy to cynically complain, we suggest you think about a constructive response and speak up!

Much of what we have already said applies to speaking in a public forum, but we would like to emphasize some principles for delivery that are especially applicable in public forums. First, in public forums there are often differences of opinion. Therefore, it is important to present your position clearly and carefully; say what you mean as directly as you can, using clear, specific language. Pay particular attention to your articulation and pronunciation, and the vocal nonverbal elements we discussed in this chapter, because these will likely impact your credibility with the audience. Even though you may hold strong opinions about a given issue, it is important to remain controlled and rational when making your point. Ranting, raving, or accusing will allow listeners to label you a "crackpot" and disregard what you have to say.

Second, while you may have prepared comments, deliver them extemporaneously—speak with your audience; don't read to them. This will allow you to make eye contact and employ appropriate gestures to help reinforce your point.

Third, make your point clearly and concisely by using the principles of organization we discussed in this chapter. Carefully use the limited time you have.

SUMMARY

This chapter has focused on delivery and visual aids as essential elements in public speaking. In review, we have considered the following:

- Principles of effective organization, including clarity, simplicity, parallelism, balance, practicality, and orderliness;
- The introduction, body, transitions, and conclusion of a presentation and the important functions of each of these important parts of a speech;
- Various patterns of organization for both informative and persuasive speeches;
- Finding, evaluating, using, and citing various types of supporting materials to build your speech's body;
- How to avoid plagiarism;
- Planning, preparation, and presentation outlines and how to develop each;
- Alternative methods of organizing ideas, other than outlines, including concept mapping and tree outlining;
- The importance of organizational skills for college life and work;
- Types of delivery, including impromptu, extemporaneous, manuscript, and memorized;

- Elements of effective vocal delivery, specifically breathing, volume, pitch, rate, pronunciation, articulation, and fluency;
- Elements of effective physical delivery, particularly eye contact, facial expressions, gesture, posture, and movement;
- Various types of visual aids, including charts, graphs, maps, and photographs;
- Guidelines for effectively using visual aids, including PowerPoint, to assist your presentation, not overshadow it;
- Strategies for effective preparation and practice well before and just before you deliver your speech; and
- Principles and specific suggestions for speaking in college, workplace, and public contexts.

QUESTIONS FOR DISCUSSION

1. We emphasized the importance of evaluating all supporting materials, but especially online sources. Why is it necessary to carefully evaluate Internet sources?
2. What steps can you take to learn to use your library more effectively and efficiently?
3. What types of evidence appeal to you? Why? What role does your cultural background play in your preference?
4. In this chapter, we have repeatedly emphasized the value of extemporaneous speaking. To what degree do you agree with this assertion? When might extemporaneous speaking not be the best mode of delivery for you?

5. What principles of practice have you identified in playing sports, learning a video game, or playing a musical instrument that you believe are equally applicable to effective speech preparation?
6. What is your opinion of PowerPoint given your own experience as an audience member? For example, how do you react when your professor uses PowerPoint during a lecture?
7. What is your greatest challenge in effectively delivering a speech? What steps can you take to help you address this challenge and improve your skill?

EXERCISES

1. Consider this complete introduction written by a student in a basic speech course and see if you can identify the five essential components of an effective introduction:

   Have you ever not had enough money to pay the telephone bill or electricity bill? Have you ever bought a new car and wondered if you could make the payments? Have you bought something on a credit card and wished later that you hadn't? These are not uncommon occurrences, and you shouldn't feel inferior for letting things like this happen. There is one simple reason for not being prepared for these types of expenses. That is the lack or insufficiency of a personal budget. With the accounting background that I have, along with the reading that I have done, I am prepared to tell you how you can prepare a good budget. This might seem to be a tremendous undertaking at first, but it is really quite simple. To prepare a personal budget, we need to first look at some of the reasons for having a budget; then explain how you go about developing a budget; and, finally, look at some warning signs for potential poor budgeting.

   Use the following codes to identify each part of this introduction. Write one of the codes above each sentence.
   AG = attention-getter
   ST = stating the topic
   LR = listening reason
   EC = establishing credibility
   EP = enumerated preview

2. Integrate some of the principles you have learned about preparing a speech, including developing clear, main points. You've chosen the subject of social opportunities for college students in your town for an informative speech. With this subject in mind, answer the following questions:
   a. What will be the specific purpose of this speech?
   b. What topic will I develop from this subject?
   c. What is my thesis for this speech?
   d. What are the main ideas I want to share in my speech?
   e. How will I organize these main ideas? What design will be most useful?
   f. How can I craft these main ideas so they are clearly stated in parallel fashion?
   Now, write your main points and provide the appropriate outline symbols.

3. Using the death penalty topic we referred to earlier in this chapter and the following outline format, write an introduction and conclusion. Also, write transitions between the introduction and main points and the main points and the conclusion.

The Abolition of the Death Penalty
Introduction
1. Attention-getter:
2. Statement of topic:
3. Credibility:
4. Listening reason:
5. Enumerated preview:

Transition
   I. The death penalty does not cost less than housing a prisoner for life.

Transition
   II. The death penalty does not bring closure to the victims' families.

Transition

III. The death penalty is not an effective deterrent to crime.

Transition

Conclusion

1. Review of topic
2. Closure

4. Present an impromptu speech. Then engage in a mock interview with one of your peers in class, using some of the typical interview questions provided in the box "Communication Counts in Your Career: Job Interviews as Impromptu Speaking." In what ways does your experience in completing this exercise parallel delivering an

impromptu speech? How is the experience different? How does giving an impromptu speech help you with interview questions and vice versa?

5. As a relaxation technique to prepare for your speech delivery, sit comfortably in a chair. Beginning with your toes, contract the major muscle groups in your body, moving up toward your shoulders. Hold your contraction and count to ten; then slowly release the muscles. As you contract, breathe in deeply, and as you release your muscles, breathe out fully. How does this exercise affect your tension level? What differences can you tell in your body and emotional state from this exercise?

KEY TERMS

Actual examples   189
Articulation   199
Audio and video clips   194
Balance   173
Body   182
Cause–effect pattern   180
Charts and graphs   192
Chronological pattern   179
Clarity   172
Communication apprehension   201
Conclusion   186
Demonstration   194
Direct quotations   188
Drawings   192
Enumerated preview   186
Examples   189
Expert testimony   188
Extemporaneous speeches   197
Eye contact   199
Facial expressions   199
Fact   187

Fluency   199
Gestures   200
Hypothetical examples   189
Impromptu speeches   196
Introduction   184
Lay testimony   188
Manuscript speeches   197
Maps   192
Memorized speeches   197
Monotone   198
Motivated sequence pattern   181
Movement   200
Narratives   189
Order   174
Parallelism   173
Personal examples   189
Photographs   193
Plagiarism   191
Planning outline   174
Posture   200
PowerPoint   194

Practicality   174
Preparation outline   174
Presentation outline   179
Problem–solution pattern   180
Pronunciation   199
Rate   198
Refutative pattern   181
Relatedness   190
Relevance   190
Respect   190
Simplicity   173
Spatial pattern   179
State-the-case-and-prove-it pattern   181
Statistics   188
Tables   192
Testimony   188
Text charts   192
Topical or categorical pattern   180
Transitions   183
Vocal inflection   198
Volume   198

REFERENCES

Andrews, P. H., Andrews, J. R., and Williams, G. 1999. *Public speaking: Connecting you and your audience.* Boston: Houghton Mifflin.

Bowler, M. August 19, 2009. Dropouts loom large for schools. *U.S. News and World Report.* Retrieved July 19, 2010, from http://www.usnews.com/articles/education/best-colleges/2009/08/19/dropouts-loom-large-for-schools.html

Daly, J. A., and Engleberg, I. A. 2001. *Presentations in everyday life: Strategies for effective speaking.* Boston: Houghton Mifflin.

Deardoff, K. nd. First generation college student narrative. Retrieved July 19, 2010, from http://www.ohio.edu/univcollege/firstgeneration/upload/deardorff.pdf

Ekman, P., and Friesen, W. V. 1987. Universals and cultural differences in judgments of facial expressions of emotion. *Journal of Personality and Social Psychology* 53:712–717.

Hunt, S. K., and Simonds, C. J. 2002. Extending learning opportunities in the basic communication course: Exploring the

pedagogical benefits of speech laboratories. *Basic Communication Course Annual* 14:60–86.

McCroskey, J. C. & Richmond, V. P. 1979. The impact of communication apprehension on individuals in organizations. *Communication Quarterly* 27:57-61.

McWhorter, K. 2001. *College reading and study skills.* 8th ed. New York: Longman.

Motley, M.T. 1997. *Overcoming Your Fear of Public Speaking-A Proven Method.* New York: Houghton Mifflin.

Noel, L. and Levitz, R. 1989. Connecting students to institutions: Keys to retention and success. In *The Freshman Year Experience*, eds. M. L. Upcraft, J. N. Gardner, and Associates, 65–81. San Francisco: Jossey Bass Publishers.

Schroeder, C. S. 1993. New students—new learning styles. *Change* 25(5):21–26.

Woosley, S. 2003. How important are the first few weeks of college? The long term effects of initial college experiences. *College Student Journal* 37:201–208.

LEARNING OUTCOMES After reading this chapter, you will have:

the **Knowledge** to. . .   and the **Skills** to. . .

DEFINING INFORMATIVE SPEAKING, page 212

Understand informative speaking.
- Remember that the purpose of an informative speech is to explain ideas.

IDENTIFYING TYPES OF INFORMATIVE SPEECHES, page 212

Recognize the types of public speaking.
- Determine the focus and purpose of your informative speech.
- Decide whether you will use explanation, definition, demonstrations, or a combination of these methods.

ORGANIZING INFORMATIVE SPEECHES, page 216

Arrange effective informative speeches.

- Order your informative speech chronologically, spatially, or topically.

BECOMING AN EFFECTIVE AND ETHICAL INFORMATIVE SPEAKER, page 220

Achieve competence and character as a public speaker.

- Check to make sure that the information you convey to your audience is clear, accurate, relevant, interesting, and ethical.

UNDERSTANDING THE VALUE OF INFORMATIVE SPEAKING FOR COLLEGE, CAREER, AND LIFE, page 222

Value informative speaking at school, work, and beyond.

- Practice informational speaking principles to enhance your communication in college, in your career, and in your community.

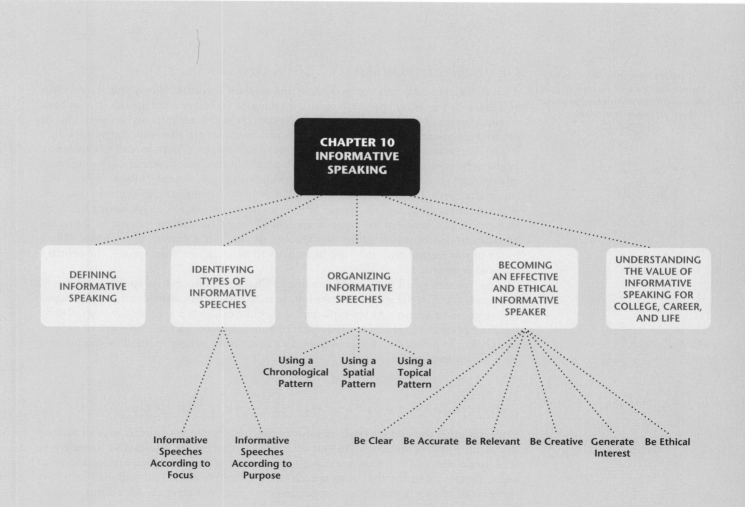

COMMUNICATION COUNTS IN YOUR COLLEGE EXPERIENCE

Approaching Lectures as Informative Speeches

Listening to lectures is a very real part of college learning. Perhaps thinking of a lecture as an informative speech may adjust your approach to lectures and help you learn more at the next class. How can this approach help? Consider these suggestions.

- Focus on the lecture's thesis. What is the topic of the lecture? Summarize in one sentence the major point of the lecture. Listen for a topic statement from your professor at the outset of the lecture.
- Listen for the lecture's main points. Pay particular attention to visual aids such as key words, objects, diagrams, or other information your professor emphasizes. Attend to what is written on the board, overhead, or included in PowerPoint slides. (Hint: If possible, ask your professor to email you his or her PowerPoint slides or visuals to ensure that you have a complete set of notes.)
- Listen for examples, stories, anecdotes, or other illustrative material. Many times a story or an example will capture

the essence of a main idea and help clarify the thesis of the lesson.

- Pay attention to the lecture's conclusion. Your professor will often repeat the topic and the main ideas of the lesson before closing class. This provides you with an important summary and gives you a thumbnail sketch of the ideas for the day.
- As soon as possible after the lecture, review your notes. Using a notation system that employs color-coding, marginal notes, or computer transcription, highlight the main ideas and important details that your professor stressed with visual aids, examples, or explanations.
- By approaching a lecture as an informative speech, you can provide important feedback to your professor. At some point, you will likely have an opportunity to provide feedback to your professor about his or her teaching. Using informative speaking principles, you can provide valuable, specific feedback that will help your professor continue to improve his or her teaching.

DEFINING INFORMATIVE SPEAKING

Informative speeches ■ Speeches in which the speaker shares information rather than attempting to sway listeners' attitudes or actions.

As a college student, you regularly hear informative speeches. When you attend class and listen to a lecture, you are typically listening to an informative speech. If you have a visiting speaker to your campus, often the speaker will share information about his or her work, organization, or life's path; such presentations are also informative speeches. If you are a member of a student organization and an officer in the organization explains how your organization will participate in homecoming, you are listening to an informative speech. Perhaps you are working while you attend college. When your supervisor gives you instructions about what or how to complete a given task, this, too, is informative speaking. The latest newscast you heard on TV or online may also be thought of as a series of informative speeches focused on various stories. In short, we are surrounded by information that reaches us through a variety of channels. While much of this information may not be structured as an informative speech, the primary purpose is informative.

As you may recall from our discussion in Chapter 8, **informative speeches** are teaching events. That is, the speaker shares information rather than attempting to sway listeners' attitudes or actions. As we explained earlier, the evidence a speaker uses may also be used in a persuasive speech, but the intent of an informative speech is to teach or explain rather than to persuade. This is an important distinction to keep in mind as you prepare your informative speech.

IDENTIFYING TYPES OF INFORMATIVE SPEECHES

Understanding the various types of informative speeches offers another way to further define informative speeches. As you understand the type of informative speech you wish to deliver, you will have greater ability to narrow your specific purpose and your topic, thereby ensuring that your speech has a definitive goal. This will also help you refine your research, craft your supporting evidence, and meet the time limit you are likely to face.

Informative Speeches According to Focus

Typically, informative speeches focus on objects, processes, concepts, people, or events. Consider each of these foci in greater detail.

Informative **speeches that focus on objects** teach listeners about something that is visible to the human eye. So, if you teach your audience about the Washington Monument, the parts of a flower, or classic automobiles, you are focusing on objects.

Informative **speeches that focus on processes** typically explain the various steps in how something is made, works, or is done. For example, if you teach your audience about how to use a particular software program, cook a gourmet dish, or scuba dive, you are focusing on a process. As you explain the process, you break the process down into steps so that your audience understands how the steps make up the process.

Informative **speeches that focus on concepts** help your audience understand ideas, especially philosophies, theories, ideologies, principles, or beliefs. If you explain the main tenets of Taoism, the primary ideas of Darwinian evolution, the notion of civil rights, or the principle of academic freedom, you are focusing on a concept.

Informative **speeches that focus on people** help the audience understand the life, work, personality, or uniqueness of another human being. The person may be a historical or contemporary figure in whom the audience is likely to be interested. For example, you may focus on someone like Susan B. Anthony as a historical figure or Hillary Rodham Clinton as contemporary figure.

Informative **speeches that focus on events** discuss particular occurrences either historically or in present time. So, for example, if you discuss the Battle of Gettysburg during the Civil War or the eruption of oil from the BP oil well in the Gulf of Mexico in 2010, you are helping your audience understand an event.

Informative Speeches According to Purpose

Informative speeches may also be understood in terms of their purposes. Review each of the examples for help with developing your informative speech.

SPEECH OF EXPLANATION   A **speech of explanation** explains and typically helps the audience understand an idea, concept, or process. For example, a speech of explanation may help listeners understand the difference between a republic and a democracy, thereby clarifying both ideas. It might also help listeners understand concepts such as spontaneous generation or the process of solving a quadratic equation. For the most part, speeches of explanation concentrate on abstract notions and are, therefore, very challenging to develop and deliver. Very often a lecture, a form of speaking with which you are well acquainted, is essentially a speech of explanation. Although some college students consider a lecture a boring presentation, it can be an engaging and interesting informative speech if it is prepared and presented effectively, as the box "Communication Counts in Your College Experience: Approaching Lectures as Informative Speeches" explains. It is important to remember that when you give speeches of explanation, you need to provide clear definitions of key terms in language that listeners can comprehend, along with numerous, relevant examples that illustrate your ideas. Consider the following example.

SAMPLE SPEECH OF EXPLANATION

Topic: The history of educating the deaf in the United States

Specific Purpose: I want my audience to understand the history of the development of deaf education in the United States

Thesis: The history of deaf education in the United States was most influenced by educational thought and legal developments.

Main Points:
I. In early U.S. history, many educators espoused oralism.
II. Later, Gallaudet, along with other educators, argued for the use of American Sign Language to educate the deaf in the United States.
III. In more recent time, legal developments have impacted deaf education in the United States.

Speeches that focus on objects
- Speeches that teach listeners about something that is visible to the human eye.

Speeches that focus on processes
- Speeches that explain the various steps in how something is made, works, or is done.

Speeches that focus on concepts
- Speeches that help your audience understand ideas, especially philosophies, theories, ideologies, principles, or beliefs.

Speeches that focus on people
- Speeches that help the audience understand the life, work, personality, or uniqueness of another human being.

Speeches that focus on events
- Speeches that discuss particular occurrences either historically or in present time.

Speeches of explanation - Speeches that explain and typically help the audience understand an idea, concept, or process.

Speeches of definition ■ Speeches that focus on helping your audience understand what a concept, process, or event means.

Speeches of demonstration ■ Speeches that concentrate on *showing* how a process is accomplished.

Speeches of description ■ Speeches that rely on mental pictures created by strategic use of pictorial language and are most likely used with speeches that focus on objects, events, and people.

SPEECH OF DEFINITION   A **speech of definition** focuses on helping your audience understand what a concept, process, or event means. To achieve this goal, you may address the connotative or denotative meanings of words, or you may analyze the history or use of key terms essential to the definition you are considering. To make your definitions clear, you may employ contrast or comparisons or identify terms that are similar to or very different from the key notion you choose to focus on. For example, although we are all acquainted with the term *justice*, on close examination, we realize that this is not an easy concept to define. A speech focused on defining *justice* would, therefore, require careful thought, specific research, and an ability to make the topic interesting for the audience. As an example, consider an informative speech on date rape that offers a legal definition of the term to help college students understand this serious and illegal behavior—without attempting to influence their opinion. Also, review this example of a different topic.

SAMPLE SPEECH OF DEFINITION

Topic: Understanding the significance of homecoming

Specific Purpose: I want my audience to understand the significance of homecoming.

Thesis: Homecoming is a time for reunion, rejoicing, and reaffirmation.

Main Points:

    I. Our university homecoming is a time of reunion, when alumni return to campus.

   II. Our university homecoming is a time of rejoicing, when we celebrate our history, the present, and the promise of the future.

  III. Our university homecoming is a time of reaffirmation of our organizational mission and values.

SPEECH OF DEMONSTRATION   A **speech of demonstration** typically concentrates on a process. Most communication teachers can point to a time when a student presented a speech titled "How to Make Scrambled Eggs" or a presentation on another mundane topic. However, speeches of demonstration can be interesting and informative. For example, do you know how to rollerblade? Obviously not everyone does—at least not with skill! Demonstrating the steps for learning how to rollerblade properly may well provide listeners with new or interesting information. However, in a demonstration speech, you do more than just *explain* how something is done; you also *show* how it is done using visual aids and movement. A student who was a scuba diver once was assigned a demonstration speech. He brought his scuba diving equipment, and by the time he finished his speech, he was attired in all of the necessary gear. Of course his speech ended with silence when he put the mouthpiece in place, peered at us through his diving mask, and opened his arms wide as if to say, "Here's what it looks like, folks!" As you can imagine, his conclusion drew a hearty laugh from his peers. Here's yet another example:

SAMPLE SPEECH OF DEMONSTRATION

Topic: How to read a textbook

Specific Purpose: I want my audience to understand how to read a textbook well.

Thesis: There are three important steps to learning how to read a textbook well.

Main Points:

    I. Review the table of contents of the book so that you understand the flow of the information in the book.

   II. Pay attention to the headings in the various chapters of the book because these identify main ideas that you will likely need to know.

  III. Note the bold terms in the text of each chapter because they are the key terms you will need to know.

SPEECH OF DESCRIPTION   **Speeches of description** rely on mental pictures created by strategic use of pictorial language and are most likely used with speeches that focus on objects, events, and people. Rather than relying heavily on visual aids to help an audience envision a scenic vista, an imposing structure, or the behavior of a certain person, the speaker uses language to help the audience "see" the color, size, shape, texture, and characteristics of the place of interest, object, event, or person. For example, consider a speech that describes the incredible poverty in Guatemala. The speech might describe how people literally fight huge, black vultures for the garbage expelled from the back of garbage trucks into the city dump and live in houses constructed of cardboard and sheets of tin. The purpose of such a speech is to paint a picture for the audience by recounting the sights, sounds, and smells of a disturbing experience. Here is this example provided in greater detail.

SAMPLE SPEECH OF DESCRIPTION

Topic: The extreme poverty in Guatemala

Specific Purpose: I want my audience to understand the extreme poverty in Guatemala.

Thesis: My trip to Guatemala exposed me to scenes of poverty I had never witnessed before.

Main Points:

I. While in Guatemala I saw poor people living in hand-made hovels with dirt floors and walls made of tree limbs, scrap wood, and old cardboard.

II. While in Guatemala I saw poor people digging through a large pile of cast-off clothes dumped in the middle of a floor in an empty store-front building to dress themselves.

III. While in Guatemala I saw poor people fighting large, black vultures that swoop down from the sky trying to get to the garbage that spews out of the back of fetid trash trucks in a Guatemalan city dump.

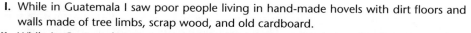

Learning a new skill, such as a medical procedure, often includes many speeches of demonstration.

BRIEFINGS Osborn and Osborn (2006) define a **briefing** as "a short presentation in an organizational setting" (343) that focuses on a process, event, or person. A briefing usually provides an update, a report on a specific project, or information necessary for others to complete a task. For example, nurses brief one another at shift changes so that patient care can continue. Marketing directors brief other members of a manufacturing company on the latest attempts to sell a particular product. Managers explain policy changes to employees. Resident assistants in college dorms provide information to other student-life personnel regarding activities or incidents on their respective floors in weekly meetings. In short, briefings occur in a variety of organizational settings to ensure that the people in the organization understand important information. Review this example.

SAMPLE BRIEFING

Topic: ABC Company's latest sales figures

Specific Purpose: I want to help my audience understand the latest information on sales figures.

Thesis: I want my coworkers to understand our latest sales figures, considering the impact of product development, sales-force productivity, and regional impact.

Main Points:

I. Our development of a range of new products has given us an edge in creating new sales.

II. Our sales force has achieved outstanding productivity with an average 10 percent increase in overall sales.

III. Our strongest regional sales occurred in the southwestern region of the United States.

Briefing ■ A short presentation in an organizational setting that focuses on a process, event, or person.

TABLE 10.1

EXAMPLES OF INFORMATIVE SPEECH FOCI AND PURPOSES

Focus	Purpose	Example
Objects	Explanation	The differences among various types of guitars
	Demonstration	How to tune a guitar
	Description	The unique style of guitarist Bryan May
Processes	Explanation	How voting impacts our day-to-day life
	Definition	Voting as a civil right
	Demonstration	How to use an electronic voting machine
	Description	The positive impact of voting on citizens' attitudes
	Briefing	How to assign proxy voting as a shareholder
Concepts	Explanation	The primary cultural results of collectivism
	Definition	Collectivism as compared to individualism
People	Description	Personality characteristics of child abductors
	Briefing	Investigative update on a particular abduction
Events	Explanation	The purpose of your college homecoming
	Description	The results of a homecoming on campus morale
	Briefing	The level of student participation in homecoming

Chronological pattern ■ The chronological pattern organizes ideas according to time.

As we have noted in our discussion, the focus and purpose of an informative speech work together. This interaction will help you have a clear sense of the specific purpose of your speech. Table 10.1 summarizes how in informative speeches, various foci and purposes intersect.

ORGANIZING INFORMATIVE SPEECHES

As we noted in Chapter 9, page 179, there are several options for organizing your informative speech. We have identified examples that illustrate some of the most common patterns used in informative speaking to help you apply these organizational patterns.

"Spending time selecting an appropriate organizational pattern for your speech is an important part of your preparation."

Using a Chronological Pattern

The **chronological pattern** organizes ideas according to time.

SAMPLE INFORMATIVE SPEECH USING A CHRONOLOGICAL PATTERN

Topic: How to get the courses you need and want in college

Specific Purpose: I want my audience members to learn how to get the courses they need and want to take to complete their college education.

Thesis: To get the courses you need and want to complete your college education, pay attention to important dates in the academic calendar.

Main Points:

I. By the fourth week of the college semester, contact your advisor for an academic advising appointment.

II. By no later than the sixth week of the semester, visit with your academic advisor and identify the courses you need to take and those you would like to take for the following semester.

III. By the eighth to tenth week of the semester, or sooner if you are permitted, register for your classes on the first day you are eligible to register.

Using a Spatial Pattern

The **spatial pattern** organizes ideas according to how they are situated in a physical space, such as geography or the layout of a building.

Spatial pattern ■ The spatial pattern organizes ideas according to how they are situated in a physical space.

Topical pattern ■ The topical pattern uses an interrelated set of subtopics directly related to the speech topic.

SAMPLE INFORMATIVE SPEECH USING A SPATIAL PATTERN

Topic: Enjoying our new recreation center

Specific Purpose: I want my audience to understand the layout of our new recreation center.

Thesis: The lay-out of our new recreation center has three levels: basement, meeting rooms/track, and workout center.

Main Points:

I. The basement level of the new recreation center has lockers, showers, a swimming pool, and two hot tubs.

II. The first level of the new recreation center has the check-in station, meeting rooms, and the walking-running track.

III. The second level of the new recreation center has weight rooms, cardio workout rooms, and a sauna.

Using a Topical Pattern

The **topical pattern** is perhaps the most common approach to informative speaking. This pattern uses an interrelated set of subtopics directly related to the speech topic.

SAMPLE INFORMATIVE SPEECH USING A TOPICAL PATTERN

Topic: The types of chocolate

Specific Purpose: I want my audience to understand the various types of chocolate.

Thesis: The various types of chocolate have various ingredients and nutritional values, and they are used for different purposes.

Main Points:

I. The various types of chocolate have a combination of ingredients that are often reflected by their names.

II. The various types of chocolate have different nutritional values.

III. The various types of chocolate are used for different purposes.

A SAMPLE ANNOTATED FULL-SENTENCE OUTLINE OF AN INFORMATIVE SPEECH

Jill Smith
COMM. 101, Sect. 19
February 19, 2008

Specific Purpose: After listening to my speech, my audience will know more about the American Cancer Society (ACS).

Organizational Pattern: Topical

Intended Audience: COMM 101 Class

This is a speech according to purpose—the purpose is to inform the audience about the ACS.

Type of organization for the speech.

The speaker begins with an example to gain attention and establish interest.

INTRODUCTION

I. **Attention Getting Device:** In the United States, cancer kills 1500 people per day and is the second leading cause of death, according to the American Cancer Society's website. The ACS also estimates that one-third of cancer deaths could be prevented by educating people about risk factors such as obesity and smoking ("Cancer Facts...").

II. **Orientation Phase:**

A. *Point:* Today I will give you information about the American Cancer Society

B. *Adaptation:* Due to the prevalence of cancer, it is very likely that everyone in this room will experience having a friend, loved one, or even yourself diagnosed with cancer at some point. Knowing more about the American Cancer Society's purpose and resources will help you to be more educated about cancer.

> The speaker establishes her credibility (ethos) here through her research support for the points she will make in the speech.

> Effective speeches are those with a clear preview of the main points of the speech.

> Strong and clear transitions help the listener to follow the speech and reinforce the main ideas in the speech.

> Facts, as evidence, are used first.

C. *Credibility:* I have researched this organization and some of the resources it offers, and I am prepared to present them to you today.

D. *Enumerated preview:* I will tell you about four major aspects of this organization. First, I will give you a brief history of the ACS and how it has grown into its modern form. Second, I will tell you about its contributions to cancer research. Third, I will discuss the educational efforts of the ACS. Last, I will tell you about some of the ways that the ACS helps cancer patients and their families.

Transition: The first important piece of information to know about this organization is how it came about and how it is structured today.

BODY

I. The ACS has a long history of working to eliminate cancer, and it has grown into a large organization.
   A. It was founded in 1913 by 10 physicians who wanted to educate the public about cancer ("ACS History").
   B. The original name for the organization was the American Society for the Control of Cancer; the name was changed to the modern one in 1945 ("ACS History").
   C. The ACS research program was established in 1946, and in 1947 it started widespread programs to educate the public about cancer ("ACS History").
   D. Today, the ACS is "one of the oldest and largest voluntary health agencies in the United States" ("ACS Fact Sheet").
   E. The ACS has a hierarchy of power and planning, including more than 3400 local offices and over 2 million volunteers ("ACS Fact Sheet").
   F. The mission statement of the modern ACS says that it is "dedicated to eliminating cancer as a major health problem by preventing cancer, saving lives, and diminishing suffering from cancer, through research, education, advocacy, and service" ("ACS Fact Sheet").

Transition: The first activity through which the ACS seeks to eradicate cancer is research.

II. The ACS funds a large amount of cancer research.
   A. In fact, it is the largest nongovernmental source of cancer research funding ("ACS Fact Sheet").
      1. It began with $1 million in 1946, and in 2005 its research budget was $131 million ("Research").
      2. Since 1946, the ACS has spent $3.1 billion on research ("Research").
   B. The ACS works to fund new scientists and help to jump-start their careers in cancer research.
      1. The ACS has funded 42 Nobel Prize winners in the early part of their careers, giving them the resources they needed to go on and make great discoveries ("ACS Fact Sheet").
   C. The ACS funds research not only on the causes and physical effects of cancer but also on the psychological ones and how best to treat the whole person and have the best quality-of-life outcomes ("Research").

Transition: Once the ACS has funded research, it is important for the public to gain any new information that is discovered, which is why the ACS mentions education in its mission statement.

III. The ACS seeks to educate the public about cancer risk factors and screenings.
   A. A major goal of the ACS is to provide "accurate, up-to-date information on cancer" ("Cancer Information Services").
      1. The ACS provides information through a 24-hour hotline, their official website, and numerous publications devoted to getting information to the people who need it ("Cancer Information Services").
      2. The ACS tries to target at-risk populations in ways that are specific to their needs and environments.
         a. For example, the ACS has started giving out educational materials on cancer screening in urban churches to target the at-risk Black urban population ("New Activities . . .").

B. The ACS also wants to make sure people know about the risk factors for cancer.
  1. The ACS recently instated the Great American Health Challenge, a program that helps people identify their cancer risk factors and take steps to correct the ones they can ("American Cancer Society . . .").
  2. Programs done in schools alert students to the importance of "developing good health habits" that can help prevent cancer in the future ("Community Programs & Services").
C. A third education goal of the ACS is to provide information about screenings to allow early detection of cancer.
  1. The ACS publishes guidelines periodically about who should get which screenings and how often (Popescu and Carmichael).
  2. There are also funds available from the ACS to help low-income people who are at risk get the screenings they need (White).

Transition: The ACS works not only to research and educate, but also to support patients and their families, mentioned as the fourth component of its mission statement.

IV. The ACS has many services to help cancer patients and their loved ones.
  A. It recently began the Patient Navigator Program, a nationwide effort to provide cancer patients with a contact person who can help them understand their disease and get the most out of their treatments ("Everett-Area Cancer Patients . . .").
  B. Another example of a patient support program run by the ACS is "Look Good . . . Feel Better," which helps female cancer patients to restore their physical appearance during and after chemotherapy ("Community Programs & Services").
  C. Another example is the summer camps that the ACS sponsors for children who have cancer ("Community Programs & Services").
  D. A final example of how the ACS supports patients is that they provide free lodging at Hope Lodges for patients who must travel far from home for treatments ("Community Programs & Services").

Transition: The American Cancer Society is a major player in the fight against cancer.

> The speaker has used a variety of sources to support her main points: facts, organizational information, news reports, and statistics.

CONCLUSION

I. *Signal:* In conclusion, the ACS works in all the ways I have mentioned to eradicate cancer in the United States and worldwide.
II. *Summary:* It has had a long history of promoting cancer awareness and is a large organization today. The ACS devotes time and resources to funding research, educating the public, and supporting cancer patients and their families.
III. *Concluding Device:* Because of this organization and others like it, the world is moving closer to a cure for cancer, and those who have been diagnosed do not have to feel confused and alone because they have an advocate in the American Cancer Society.

> The speaker concludes the summary first by restating her main points. By using an organizational system that is consistent, clear, simple, parallel, balanced, practical, and orderly, the speaker upholds elements of effective informative speaking.

REFERENCES

"ACS Fact Sheet." www.cancer.org. 8 January 2006. American Cancer Society. Retrieved February 16, 2008, from <www.cancer.org/docroot/AA/content/AA_1_2_ACS_Fact_Sheet.asp>.

"ACS History." www.cancer.org. 2 October 2006. American Cancer Society. Retrieved February 16, 2008, from <www.cancer.org/docroot/AA/content/AA_1_4_ACS_History.asp>.

"American Cancer Society Launches Campaign to Educate Americans About Cancer Risk." *Drug Week* February 23, 2007, Expanded Reporting: 190. *LexisNexis Academic.* Lexis Nexis. Indiana State University, Cunningham Memorial Library, Terre Haute, IN. Retrieved February 14, 2008, from <http://www.lexisnexis.com>.

"Cancer Facts & Figures 2008." www.cancer.org. 2008. American Cancer Society. Retrieved February 16, 2008, from <http://www.cancer.org/downloads/STT/2008CAFFfinalsecured.pdf>.

"Cancer Information Services." www.cancer.org. (n.d.). American Cancer Society. Retrieved February 16, 2008, from <www.cancer.org/docroot/AA/content/AA_2_2_Cancer_Information_Services.asp>.

"Community Programs & Services." www.cancer.org. (n.d.). American Cancer Society. Retrieved February 16, 2008, from <www.cancer.org/docroot/AA/content/AA_2_4_Community_Programs_and_Services.asp>.

"Everett-Area Cancer Patients Can More Easily Navigate Health Care System Thanks to the American Cancer Society and AstraZeneca." *Biotech Business Week* November 5, 2007, Expanded Reporting: 1909. *LexisNexis Academic*. Lexis Nexis. Indiana State University, Cunningham Memorial Library, Terre Haute, IN. Retrieved February 14, 2008 from <http://www.lexisnexis.com>.

"New Activities and Developments Reported by American Cancer Society." *Biotech Business Week* June 18, 2007, Expanded Reporting: 1755. *LexisNexis Academic*.

LexisNexis. Indiana State University, Cunningham Memorial Library, Terre Haute, IN. Retrieved February 18, 2008, from <http://www.lexisnexis.com>.

Popescu, Roxana, and Mary Carmichael. "A Guide to Predicting Your Medical Future." *Newsweek* January 21, 2008: 59. *LexisNexis Academic*. LexisNexis. Indiana State University, Cunningham Memorial Library, Terre Haute, IN. Retrieved February 18, 2008, from <http://www.lexisnexis.com>.

"Research." www.cancer.org. 2 October 2006. American Cancer Society. Retrieved February 16, 2008, from <www.cancer.org/docroot/AA/content/AA_2_1_Research.asp>.

White, Josh. "Health Tests Offered Free." *The Washington Post* 3 March 1999. Prince William Extra: V02. *LexisNexis Academic*. LexisNexis. Indiana State University, Cunningham Memorial Library, Terre Haute, IN. February 13, 2008, from <http://www.lexisnexis.com>.

BECOMING AN EFFECTIVE AND ETHICAL INFORMATIVE SPEAKER

Effective informative speaking rests on two main ideas. First, the most effective speakers are those who analyze and respond to their audiences. While this is true in all public speaking experiences, it is especially true in informative speaking. Second, effective informative speaking employs the public speaking principles that we have already discussed in earlier chapters. Consider the following guidelines that will help ensure that you consider and connect with your audience and practice solid public speaking principles.

Be Clear

Clarity in speechmaking is the process of clearly expressing your thought, and includes crafting a clear informative purpose and employing accessible language. Ask yourself this question: *In specific terms, what do I want my audience to learn from my speech?* Think carefully about your specific purpose in terms of the focus and type of your informative speech that we discussed earlier in this chapter. Write your specific informative purpose in a single, simple sentence so you have a clear informative goal in mind. Consider the following examples:

> **Unclear:** "Good informative speakers, in order to ensure that they have meticulously pondered the various cognitive approaches available to them, should eschew obfuscation."
>
> **Clearer:** "Effective informative speakers strive for clarity."

Pay close attention to the language you use as you craft your speech outline and practice your speech orally. Practically every field of human knowledge has its distinct vocabulary or jargon. Those who know this vocabulary can speak with one another using technical terms or even a type of verbal shorthand that employs acronyms. For example, think about the way medical doctors speak and write. If you have ever filled a prescription, you know there are unique symbols, like BID, that communicate to the pharmacists how often you should take the prescribed medication. However, you may not know the meaning of this or other symbols unique to the medical profession. To those who are not acquainted with a specialized vocabulary, even terms in English can sound like a foreign language or outright gibberish. Slang—the use of unique words typically known only by a given group of people who create it and use it—can also impact

Clarity ■ The process of clearly expressing your thought; includes crafting a clear informative purpose and employing accessible language.

clarity. (For a dictionary of contemporary slang, go to http://www.slangsite.com). While we may use this kind of speech with those who understand it in casual conversation, to share information effectively we need to avoid both jargon and slang unless we carefully and fully explain the meaning of such terms.

Effective informative speakers keep their overall use of language simple and direct so that everyone in the audience can understand. This does not mean that you should "speak down" to your audience; rather, you should work to state your ideas clearly. Remember that when you deliver an informative speech, you are acting as a teacher. A good teacher breaks down concepts by using clear language, careful organization, and plenty of examples, while focusing on the audience's nonverbal feedback. Consider these examples:

Technical Terminology or Jargon

Unclear: "Check the PSI of your radials by applying the TPG to the appropriate fitting, thereby measuring the resultant exertion of the internal gas against the exterior walls."

Clearer: "Check your tire pressure by pressing a tire pressure gauge on the stem of the tire."

Slang

Unclear: "Like, chill out, dude! Don't have a cow."

Clearer: "Calm down; relax!"

Be Accurate

When you deliver your informative speech, it is important that you have up-to-date, accurate information. Nothing will hurt your credibility more than to share information that the audience knows to be erroneous or purposefully slanted. **Accuracy** means that as you prepare your speech, be sure to include the most current, accurate information you can find; deliver this information accurately and as objectively as possible; and cite your sources. If you choose to directly quote a source, be sure you quote what your source said verbatim. If you choose to paraphrase, it is vital that you clearly represent the source's intended meaning.

Be Relevant

Information that is clear and accurate may still fall short of effectiveness. Listeners want to know how a topic impacts them. While you may (and should) be interested in your topic; to establish **relevancy** means that it is your job to link your topic to your audience members in such a way that they, too, are interested. For example, you may explain the latest technology for cleaning up oil spills, but many members of the audience may become obviously disinterested if you do not find a way to link this topic to them by explaining how cleaning up the oil will impact their finances, lifestyle, or enjoyment. By linking your information to the lives of your audience, you will generate attention and appeal to the listeners' needs. In turn, your audience will be more likely to remember and potentially use your information for a longer time.

Be Creative

Finding a fresh speech topic can be challenging. But creativity is important to successful speechmaking. **Creativity** means finding a novel approach to a topic that can engage your audience. Consider this example:

> We are all encouraged to volunteer. In fact, some of our classes require volunteer hours. We are told that volunteering is good for others and that as citizens privileged to get a college education we have an obligation to give our skills, time, and energy to worthwhile projects. But, I want to help you think about volunteerism differently; I would like you to think about volunteering selfishly. What can *you* gain from volunteering?

Accuracy ■ Using the most current, correct, and up-to-date information in a speech.

Relevancy ■ Linking your topic to your audience members in such a way that they, too, are interested.

Creativity ■ Finding a novel approach to a topic that can engage your audience.

Effective speakers seek to engage their audiences with relevant information and effective delivery.

Generate Interest

While information may be clear, accurate, and even relevant, it may not be **interesting** to the audience. That is, the information may not be organized or delivered in an engaging manner. Therefore, as you speak, think about how you can keep your topic interesting and engaging. In most instances, you can enhance audience involvement by

- clearly organizing your ideas so it is easy for the audience to listen, being sure to craft a strong introduction, simply phrased main ideas, clear transitions, and an effective conclusion that summarizes and leaves the audience with a sense of clear closure;
- using supporting material that will gain and keep your audience's attention, including startling facts, provocative questions, engaging stories, and pithy quotes;
- displaying visual aids that help to illustrate main ideas;
- delivering your speech well using vocal variety, eye contact, and appropriate bodily movement.

Be Ethical

As you share information, be sure that you do so ethically. Consider these suggestions to ensure that you think about the ethics surrounding informative speaking:

- Avoid information overload. Inundating your audience with too much information makes it difficult for them to grasp your message. As an informative speaker, your first task is to be sure your audience understands your message. Failure to achieve this goal is, indeed, an ethical issue. Remember that a narrowed topic; a concrete, specific purpose; and a clear thesis will help you achieve this goal.
- Avoid information "underload." If you do not give your audience sufficient and appropriate information, you will not achieve the goal of informative speaking. Your audience members deserve the best and most complete information you can share with them in the time you have to speak.
- Avoid information shaping. As an informative speaker, you must carefully avoid slanting information to frame the perspective of your audience about your topic. In short, don't confuse informative and persuasive speaking. Accurate, balanced information is an important aspect of public speaking.

UNDERSTANDING THE VALUE OF INFORMATIVE SPEAKING FOR COLLEGE, CAREER, AND LIFE

Learning how to deliver effective informative speeches is valuable because you are very likely to use informative speaking in your college, career, and life experiences. For example, you may well be assigned an informative speech not only in this communication class but also in other classes. You may have written a research paper for your biology class that you will need to develop into an oral presentation to deliver to your classmates.

As you enter a career, your supervisor may ask you to share information with other employees, clients, or a board of directors. For example, you may be asked to deliver a sales or product demonstration to potential clients or customers. As a member of the community, you may be faced with coordinating a neighborhood watch program and explaining to your neighbors how such an endeavor would work. In short, informative speaking is a skill that you are likely to transfer to your everyday life now and in the future. Review the box "Communication Counts in Your Life: Connecting with Communities" for additional insight.

Interesting ■ Information that is organized or delivered in an engaging manner.

Informative speaking, like the briefing depicted here, are an important part of work life.

COMMUNICATION COUNTS IN YOUR LIFE

Connecting with Communities

As you share information both in this class and in other settings, you are engaging communities and thereby linking with a variety of people. Public speaking creates and sustains community on at least three levels.

The Immediate Community

As we speak with an audience, we develop an immediate community—that is, we seek to find and make connections with our audience. We seek to address topics of concern that we all share. Moreover, what we say and how we say it has the potential to significantly impact our audience and how they respond to us. Even though we may disagree, we still share the same space; we are a community. This is especially true in classrooms, where community can be realized, even if only for a few weeks. Working toward community proves especially helpful in a communication class and helps you prepare, practice, and present speeches. A sense of classroom community will help you build solidarity with your classmates, enhance your credibility, and encourage greater audience response, while also reducing apprehension, which, in turn, can often help you obtain a higher grade.

The Local Social Community

Public speaking, even in your classrooms, has importance for the larger social community. As you prepare to speak, think about questions, problems, issues, or possibilities that exist in your campus or geographic community. How can you address one of these matters in a way that will add to

the body of information and the communal conversation? Too often students choose trivial or relatively unimportant speech topics. We encourage you to speak to issues that truly matter to you and to your peers. Use the opportunity you have in this class to find and share knowledge that will help shape opinion, solve problems, or engage possibilities. In doing so, you will strengthen the immediate community and help forge links with the local community. In our experience, this is the path to becoming a student leader now and a leader in your future profession later.

The Larger Social Community

Public speaking also engages the larger conversation. To use an image from Kenneth Burke (1973), engaging social dialogue is like coming to a party late and entering a passionate conversation, where people are so engaged they have no time to tell you the topic of the conversation. As you listen, you contribute your own views, and then, given the pressure of time, you must leave, although the conversation continues. As you share your ideas in your class, in your community, and perhaps even in broader contexts, you contribute to the ongoing dialogue. Learning to engage this dialogue with skill, through your work in this class, provides you with important first steps in entering and maintaining the conversation. Never forget that words matter! Think about it. Our social fabric is based on the words we find in revered documents such as the Constitution of the United States and the Declaration of Independence. Words are the

(continued)

means by which we resolve conflicts, pass and adjudicate laws, and explain and understand social policy. While others' words may seem more important than our insights or contributions, to remain silent squelches the conversation. Never underestimate the value of what you have to share. We urge you to think, speak, and act, and to join the conversation. What you learn here will let you do this with excellence. Your engagement in civic and community life truly matters. Learning to speak with skill is one way to be engaged.

SUMMARY

This chapter has reviewed essential information about informative speaking. To review, we have discussed:

- the definition of informative speaking
- the types of public speaking by focus and purpose
- the importance of considering your audience in informative speaking
- the importance of applying principles of public speaking in informative speaking
- the importance of clarity in informative speaking
- the importance of accuracy in informative speaking
- the importance of relevance in informative speaking
- the importance of maintaining audience interest in informative speaking
- the value of informative speaking for campus, career, and life

QUESTIONS FOR DISCUSSION

1. Recall a memorable informative speech that you have heard recently. Why was this speech memorable? What elements of effective informative speaking can you identify in this speech?
2. What examples of jargon can you offer that you know may confuse listeners in an informative speech?
3. Consider Burke's idea that we are all participants in an ongoing conversation. What is your opinion of Burke's assertion?
4. How might you use informative speaking in your college experience outside of this class? How might you use informative speaking in your future career?

EXERCISES

1. Go to MyCommunicationLab that accompanies this book or YouTube and find an example of a student delivering an informative speech. After viewing the video, evaluate the effectiveness of this speech using the criteria of clarity, accuracy, relevance, and interest outlined in this chapter.
2. Go to http://www.myspeechclass.com/informativetopics2 .html and review the many informative speech topics listed there. Find five topics that you believe would work best for your communication class informative speech presentation. Why did you choose these topics?
3. Using one of the topics you identified in exercise two, write three different specific purpose statements using three of the five informative speech purposes outlined in this chapter.

KEY TERMS

Accuracy 221
Briefing 215
Chronological pattern 216
Clarity 220
Creativity 221
Informative speeches 212
Interesting 222

Relevancy 221
Spatial pattern 217
Speeches of definition 214
Speeches of demonstration 214
Speeches of description 214
Speeches of explanation 213

Speeches that focus on concepts 213
Speeches that focus on events 213
Speeches that focus on objects 213
Speeches that focus on people 213
Speeches that focus on processes 213
Topical pattern 217

REFERENCES

Burke, K. 1973. *The Philosophy of Literary Form*. Berkeley, CA: University of California Press.

Osborn, M., and Osborn, S. 2006. *Public speaking*. 7th ed. Boston: Houghton Mifflin.

Persuasive Speaking

LEARNING OUTCOMES After reading this chapter, you will have:

the **Knowledge** to. . .   and the **Skills** to. . .

DEFINING PERSUASION, page 228

Understand the concept of persuasion.

- Respect the power of persuasion, knowing that it can be used for positive and negative purposes.
- Know what your intentions are and be aware of your audience's level of receptivity.
- Refrain from coercing or forcing your audience to believe or act a certain way.

UNDERSTANDING THE ROLE OF ATTITUDES IN PERSUASION, page 231

Comprehend how people's attitudes impact persuasion.

- Acknowledge and respect your audience members' attitudes, values, and beliefs when creating a persuasive message.

BUILDING PERSUASIVE CREDIBILITY, page 232

Develop authority as a persuasive speaker.

- Convey your persuasive message to reinforce your credibility (character, authority, charisma, and confidence) to create a positive ethos or perceptions.
- Plan so your initial impression is positive, your persuasive message is well-received, and final impressions include understanding of the message.

CRAFTING PERSUASIVE MESSAGES, page 234

Create persuasive communication messages.

- Use emotional appeals with care to draw in your audience.
- Build in logical reasoning to support your persuasive message.
- Decide whether to state your case and support it or to let your audience deduce your purpose.
- Follow the Toulmin Model when building an argument.
- Avoid logical fallacies or arguments based on invalid reasoning.

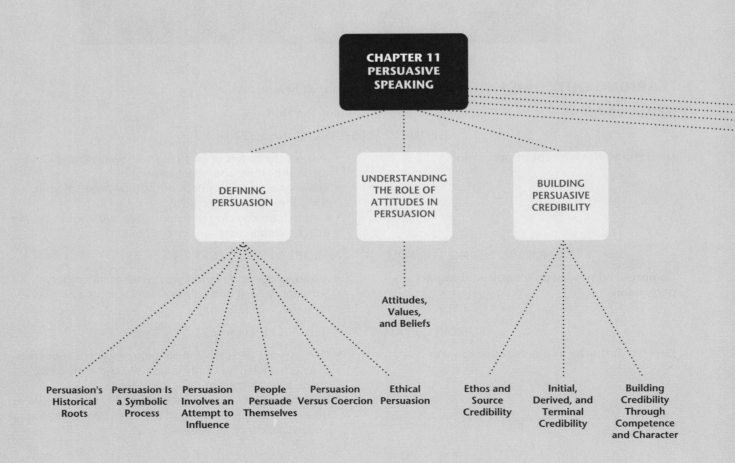

CHAPTER 11 PERSUASIVE SPEAKING

DEFINING PERSUASION

UNDERSTANDING THE ROLE OF ATTITUDES IN PERSUASION

BUILDING PERSUASIVE CREDIBILITY

Attitudes, Values, and Beliefs

Persuasion's Historical Roots

Persuasion Is a Symbolic Process

Persuasion Involves an Attempt to Influence

People Persuade Themselves

Persuasion Versus Coercion

Ethical Persuasion

Ethos and Source Credibility

Initial, Derived, and Terminal Credibility

Building Credibility Through Competence and Character

IDENTIFYING TYPES OF PERSUASIVE SPEECHES, page 238

Know the types of persuasive speeches.

- Determine the purpose or proposition of your persuasion.

ORGANIZING PERSUASIVE SPEECHES, page 240

Create well-designed persuasive speeches.

- Choose the best pattern(s) for organizing your persuasive speech.

**BECOMING A COMPETENT AND ETHICAL PERSUASIVE SPEAKER
IN COLLEGE, CAREER, AND LIFE, page 245**

Develop into a competent and principled persuasive speaker.

- Practice ethical thinking and behavior when speaking persuasively.

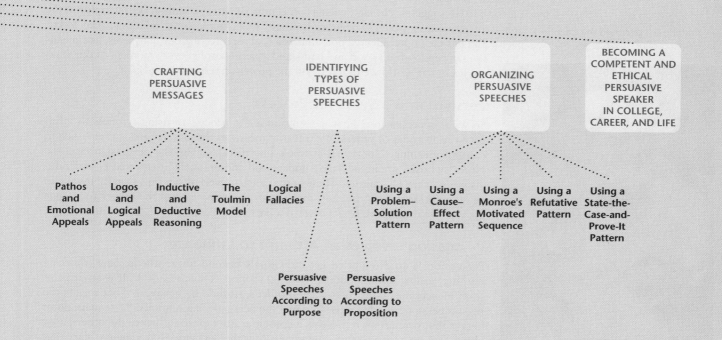

Persuasion ■ Persuasion is communication that influences how others think, feel, and act.

DEFINING PERSUASION

The term *persuasion* might make us think of a powerful, charismatic leader who convinces his followers to blindly follow him into a wilderness compound. Or it may make us think of advertising we see during a presidential campaign or a billboard on our route to school telling us to save the coral reefs. Persuasion is powerful, right? How about you? Are you apt to be swayed by the persuasive messages you see daily? Or do you have the ability to "see through" the clutter to what the persuader is trying to sell or tell you? You're not influenced, you might think. But maybe you are. Have you ever done something to help a friend when you really didn't want to? Or have you bought something you really didn't need?

Persuasion and persuasive messages surround you. Gass and Seiter (2003) define **persuasion** as the activity that "involves one or more persons who are engaged in the activity of creating, reinforcing, modifying, or extinguishing beliefs, attitudes, intentions, motivations, and/or behaviors within the constraints of a given communication situation (34). Persuasion is communication that influences how others think, feel, and act. Persuasive communication can be used for good or evil purposes and is the foundation of any change in society. Perloff (2010) suggests that the sheer number of persuasive messages that surround us grows exponentially every day; that these messages travel faster across the world than ever before; that the process of persuasion has become institutionalized; that the messages are more subtle and devious today; and that much of the persuasion we see on a daily basis is more complex and impersonal than at any other time in history. For example, when the original signers of the Declaration of Independence considered how their new nation was to be governed, white, male landowners were the people they had in mind to govern. No women, no people of color, no indentured servants had rights of any kind. How did we get from that historical moment to today? Persuasion changed attitudes. Persuasive communication has changed our attitudes toward health issues such as smoking, drinking, and safe sex. Persuasion has shaped public policy surrounding who should get health care and how much it should cost. Leaders in government use persuasion to rally the country in times of crisis. Ultimately, the study of persuasion is the study of attitude change (Perloff 2010).

Persuasion's Historical Roots

What we know about the persuasion process can be traced back to Greek and Roman cultures that precede the Bible and other religious texts. The Greek philosopher Aristotle first discussed the three most critical elements of the persuasive process: ethos, pathos, and logos (we address these later in this chapter). Persuasion is an overwhelming influence in our lives. Larson (2010) suggests, "In fact, persuasion is now the great common denominator in the arenas of economics, politics, religion, business, and interpersonal relations. And today, persuasion has the unprecedented potential as a tool for affecting our daily lives, as a means to many ends—both good and bad—and as a presence in every moment of our waking lives. The world we face rests on the power of persuasion" (2).

Aristotle first discussed the essential elements of persuasion.

Persuasion Is a Symbolic Process

So what is persuasion? First, persuasion is the process of using symbols to influence the attitudes of others. We transmit messages through language that is rich in cultural meaning. Nonverbal symbols like the U.S. flag, the peace sign, and the Nike "swoosh" are immediately understood and uniquely interpreted by individuals within the U.S. culture. These verbal and nonverbal symbols usually invoke in us an emotional response, and that emotional response has the power to change the way we think, feel, or act toward a particular person, issue, event, or message.

Persuasion Involves an Attempt to Influence

Persuasion is an attempt to get individuals beyond an apathetic view (thinking nothing, feeling nothing, doing nothing) (Benoit & Benoit 2008). It is an attempt to influence; it intends to change another's attitude or behavior. That means the person being persuaded must "know" the persuader's intentions. "The main point here is that persuasion represents a conscious attempt to influence the other party, along with an accompanying awareness that the persuadee has a mental state that is susceptible to change" (Perloff 2010, 13). So, when you get your roommate to go play basketball rather than go out with friends, you're engaging in persuasion.

People Persuade Themselves

Ultimately, the result of a persuasive act is in our own hands. No one else has control over whether you are persuaded by a message, idea, policy, or event—you persuade yourself because of that message, idea, policy, or event. The communicator provides the message, but the receiver is the one who interprets the message and acts on it. As Whalen (1996) suggests, "You can't force people to be persuaded—you can only activate their desire and show them the logic behind your ideas. You can't move a string by pushing it, you have to pull it. People are the same. Their devotion and total commitment to an idea come only when they fully understand and buy in with their total being" (5). When you decided to attend college, you likely faced some persuasive messages from a variety of sources, including teachers and parents, but, in the end, you chose to attend college and, furthermore, you chose the college you now attend.

Persuasion Versus Coercion

To understand the ways we persuade ourselves to alter our attitudes, we need to distinguish between persuasion and coercion. Persuasion requires free choice on our part. **Coercion,** in contrast, removes the free will of the person being persuaded, either directly or indirectly. Borchers (2005) suggests that "coercion is the use of force to compel an audience member to do what a persuader desires. Persuaders who use coercion deny audience members the opportunity to freely identify with them. Fundamentally, coercion denies audience members the opportunity to exercise such basic human actions as reasoning, feeling, and thinking" (65). Here is an example (an extreme one, definitely) of the distinction between a persuasive communication and a coercive one. Suppose you want to organize a picnic with your neighbors. What would happen if you went to your neighbor's house and told her that she and her family *must* join the others in the neighborhood and that she *must* pay her "fair share"; and if she doesn't submit to "voluntary compliance," then you will "enforce" her "cooperation" by hiring some goons to confiscate her property and lock her up; and if she resists then you may have to shoot her? In contrast, a persuasive attempt to organize a neighborhood picnic might involve sending a flier to everyone that announces the event, points out all of the activities that will occur, states all the fun each family would have at the event, and requests a small donation from each family to cover the food and beverages that would be served. In the first case, violence is the strategy; in the second, a nonviolent invitation is the strategy.

While persuasion and coercion are different, it is important to consider these terms on a continuum rather than as distinctly different. At either end of the continuum are pure persuasion and pure coercion, but as they come together the concepts become blurred. For example, if your boss asks you to give her a ride home in your car, is that persuasion or coercion? What is the issue that might make this lean toward the coercive end of the continuum? It is the potential *power* your boss can leverage on you in the workplace that makes this situation potentially move into the coercive realm.

Ethical Persuasion

Should persuasion be considered an ethical means of communication? Johannesen, Valde, and Whedbee (2008) suggest that persuasion contains potential ethical issues because

- persuaders attempt to influence beliefs, attitudes, values, and actions;
- persuasion requires both the persuader and the persuadee to make conscious choices among ends sought and means used to achieve the ends; and
- persuasion involves a potential judge—any of the participants or observers of the communication exchange.

Ethical persuaders are those who recognize both the importance of freedom in persuasive communication and the importance of responsibility. "Responsibility includes the elements of fulfilling duties and obligations, of being held accountable as evaluated by agreed-upon standards, and of being accountable to your own conscience. But an essential element of responsible communication, for both sender and receiver, is the exercise of thoughtful and caring judgment" (7). As Perloff (2010) suggests, "Ethical persuaders advance arguments forcefully but not aggressively. They affirm the dignity

Coercion ■ Removes the free will of the person being persuaded, either directly or indirectly.

of each person, treat audience members as free and autonomous agents, present facts and opinions fairly, and provide different perspectives on an issue to enable people to make the most thoughtful decision possible" (36). An ethical persuader presents an argument that is complete and allows the listener to ultimately make a decision with regard to his or her acceptance or attitude change. An ethical persuader makes sure that the evidence presented supports the argument that is developed. An unethical persuader intentionally complicates an argument to exploit the listener's expectations, knowledge, or emotions. An unethical persuader, essentially, manipulates truth so that the listener's ability to make a reasoned choice is undermined. Look at the following scenario (a true story, actually). Assess the degree of ethicality in the persuasive argument.

In the spring of 1982, a joint investigation by the Associated Press and the *Pontiac* (Illinois) *Daily Leader* revealed that Ann Landers had been recycling 15-year-old letters in her advice column. The investigators claimed that between April 1981 and April 1982, she ran 33 letters that had appeared in her daily column in late 1966 and early 1967. The recycled letters contained only slight changes in wording, names, and ages. She did not inform either her readers or the editors of the more than 1,000 newspapers carrying her column that she was reusing old letters. When confronted with the evidence from the investigation, she admitted recycling letters and stated she would stop immediately. The President of Field Newspaper Syndicate, which distributed the Ann Landers column, said editors were not aware of the practice of recycling, and would have advised against it if they had known. (Jaksa & Pritchard 1994)

Ask yourself the following questions:

- ■ To what extent is this an issue of the ethics of persuasion?
- ■ In what ways is an "advice column" persuasive?
- ■ What values have been violated in this situation?
- ■ If you were a newspaper editor, would you allow a columnist to "recycle" letters in your newspaper? Why or why not?
- ■ In what ways do these recycled letters take away the ability of a reader to make an informed decision?
- ■ What are the ultimate consequences of a situation like this to the credibility of Ann Landers? To her reputation? To the general trust of the public?

Persuasion, then, is judged by its consequences, a persuader's intentions, and the context in which it occurs. Take a look at the box "Communication Counts in Your Life: Persuasion in Political Ads" and discuss whether this persuasive approach fulfills the requirements for ethical persuasion.

COMMUNICATION COUNTS IN YOUR LIFE

Persuasion in Political Ads

Watch the political advertisements at the following links—one from 1969 (George Wallace) and the other from 1988 (Michael Dukakis). Consider the persuasive appeal elements used in these ads, and see if you can identify the following strategies.

    http://www.youtube.com/watch?v=4RZ4G251WR4& feature=related

    http://www.youtube.com/watch?v=EC9j6Wfdq3o& feature=related

Techniques to Get Attention

- Fear. Fear is a strong emotion that can garner immediate attention from an audience. A politician might say, "The coming recession will cause unemployment levels to rise dramatically." The fear of job loss causes many people to listen because they want to know what solution the politician is offering.
- Flattery. This is evident when politicians mention how hard people work or how upstanding and honest people are. A politician may take this a step further, aligning himself or herself with those same qualities by promising to be a hardworking, honest representative of the people.
- Bandwagon. The bandwagon technique works by playing on people's desire to be one of the crowd. No one wants to be left behind. The bandwagon technique uses topics that seem beneficial so that the person who disagrees will appear to be an outsider. "The American people want lower taxes," a candidate might say.

Techniques to Establish Trust

- **Plain Folks.** This technique gains trust and credibility by making the messenger appear to be just like the audience. Candidates may paint themselves as working moms or family men. By putting themselves on the level of the working class people, they give the impression that they understand and relate to the problems and issues important to those constituents.
- **Sentimentality.** An extension of the plain folks technique, sentimentality paints a picture of candidates in a warm, happy family relationship. Photos of candidates with their children, all smiling and happy, are an example of this technique.
- **Charisma.** Charisma is a quality that draws people to another person. It includes charm, flattery, confidence, and strength, all in one package.

Source: From "Political Persuasion Techniques: How Politicians Get the Attention of the Public and Establish Trust," by Suzanne Pitner, November 28. 2008, www.suite101.com. Reprinted by permission of the author.

UNDERSTANDING THE ROLE OF ATTITUDES IN PERSUASION

Persuasion aims at attitudes. O'Keefe (2002) explains that **attitudes** are a person's general evaluation of an object—such as persons, events, products, policies, or institutions, for example. When we evaluate an object, our evaluation can be based on semantic scales (i.e., good/bad, undesirable/desirable, positive/negative, harmful/beneficial) or on single-item measures. For example, have you ever been asked to determine on a scale from "extremely favorable" to "extremely unfavorable" where your attitude toward an object might lie? As a college student, you are likely asked to rate the instruction you receive in your classes using a numeric scale; this is an example of an evaluation of your attitudes. Attitude and behavior are linked during the persuasive process. If we feel positively toward an object, then our behavior, generally, will be consistent in support of that object.

Attitudes ■ A person's general evaluation of an object—such as persons, events, products, policies, or institutions, for example.

Values ■ General guiding principles for life.

Beliefs ■ Strongly held ideas about the nature of truth.

Attitudes, Values, and Beliefs

Because persuasion is aimed at modifying or changing attitudes, it is important to understand the relationship between attitude, value, and belief, all of which play a role in the persuasion process. Attitudes are evaluations, as we've suggested. Attitudes are learned responses that help us to determine likes and dislikes. We "learn" attitudes over the course of a lifetime, most importantly in childhood. For example, young children are not usually prone to discrimination against a particular skin color, size, shape, or ability. But over time and by imitating what they see others do, they develop prejudiced attitudes toward any number of "differences." Attitudes are also emotions: loves and hates, attractions and repulsions, joys and sorrows.

Values are general guiding principles for life. They are also potentially life goals—what we want to achieve in life. For example, we speak of "American Values" such as freedom, equality, family, wealth, and independence. These values help us evaluate a broad range of situations; they "transcend" specifics and become large and collective goals for life. If you value something, you cherish and protect it. If you do not, you are indifferent.

Beliefs, in contrast, are more specific statements we associate with values. Look at the example in Table 11.1 to see how the relationships between these concepts can be explained. Beliefs are statements of "fact" to us. We make belief statements based on

TABLE 11.1

ATTITUDES, VALUES, AND BELIEFS COMPARISON

Value	Attitude	Possible Belief
Christian truth	God is good.	There is no scientific evidence to support the theory of evolution.
Individualism	Taxes are bad.	The government should get out of the business of legislating morality.
Independence	Junk food is not harmful.	The human body can withstand a lot of punishment, so I don't have to worry about how much alcohol, sugar, fat, and caffeine I put into my body when I'm in my teens and 20s.

Ethos ■ The credibility of the speaker.

Pathos ■ The emotional appeal of the message.

Logos ■ The logic or reasoning of the message.

Credibility ■ Listener's perception of the speaker's trustworthiness, fairness, sincerity, reliability, and honesty.

Character ■ The audience's perception of the moral and ethical integrity of the speaker resulting in greater believability.

Authority ■ The audience's perception of the prevailing knowledge or experience of the speaker enhancing the resulting influence of the speaker.

Charisma ■ The audience's perception of the personal appeal and attractiveness of the speaker that typically creates an emotional response.

Competence ■ The audience's perception of the qualifications, knowledge, skills, and abilities of the speaker.

Initial credibility ■ The perceived credibility we determine before we have heard the person speak.

our values and attitudes. Beliefs are sometimes based on evidence but can, as often as not, be completely untrue. Because beliefs are based on "evidence," they are sometimes easier to change than attitudes or values. As Lucas (2007) suggests, "How successful you are in any particular persuasive speech will depend above all on how well you tailor your message to the values, attitudes, and beliefs of your audience. Persuasion is a strategic activity" (403). So, as you prepare to deliver your persuasive speech, you will need to understand your class members, who will most likely constitute your audience.

BUILDING PERSUASIVE CREDIBILITY

If you think about the persuasion process as developing a mental conversation with your audience, then it is important to understand how the speaker and his or her listeners engage in this mental conversation. What is important to a listener as the speaker attempts to guide the listener to change values, attitudes, and beliefs? As Figure 11.1 shows, listeners will focus on three elements of the persuasive speech: the credibility of the speaker (**ethos**), the emotional appeal of the message (**pathos**), and the logic or reasoning of the message (**logos**).

Ethos and Source Credibility

It is important to understand, first, that credibility is not something a speaker does or doesn't have. **Credibility** is something the listeners associate or don't associate with a speaker. As a listener, we determine or grant knowledge, expertise, or experience to a speaker. Ethos, then, is the result of the perceptions a listener has about a person and about that person's believability. Ethos is a multidimensional construct, created by our interpretations of the speaker's **character, authority, charisma,** and **competence** or experience. "Aristotle labeled the components of good character as good sense, good moral character, and goodwill. . . . The perception of good sense and good moral character depend on an audience's belief that a persuader's judgments and values are reasonable and justified" (Woodward & Denton 2009, 109–110). We are more likely to believe a speaker—to accept his or her claims and evidence—if we think the speaker sees the world as we do. We will determine the speaker to be credible if we accept that he or she has honorable intentions toward our perspective and our point of view. Ultimately, then, ethos is the listener's perception of the speaker's trustworthiness, fairness, sincerity, reliability, and honesty. If we see a speaker as credible, we acknowledge his or her expertise and reputation.

Once we have acknowledged the speaker's expertise and have determined he or she has "good character," we give the speaker's arguments legitimacy. With this legitimacy, then, we label the person as an "authority" on a specific topic or issue. Ultimately, we believe what the speaker says. Our perceptions of a person's legitimacy may come from "celebrity" or "charisma" or both. Think of celebrities who endorse products, services, and issues. Why are they chosen as spokespeople? If we associate their celebrity with legitimacy and believability, and if we determine that their values and attitudes match our own, we will be more apt to listen to and agree with them. Charisma is our perception of a person's exceptional powers and qualities. An individual with charisma inspires and motivates an audience, charging the audience members' emotions (Perloff 2010). Together, character, authority, and experience are cornerstones of effective persuasion. As Figure 11.2 exemplifies, ethos appeals to emotion.

Initial, Derived, and Terminal Credibility

When we encounter a speaker for the first time, our perceptions of his or her credibility are based on superficial factors, such as attractiveness. This we call **initial credibility**. It is the perceived credibility we determine before we have heard the person speak. We are more apt to pay attention, at least at first, to a more attractive speaker. We initially associate attractiveness with the speaker's message. "At some level, perhaps unconscious, we feel we can improve our own standing in life if we do what attractive people suggest" (Perloff 2010, 178). The elements that

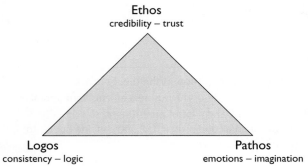

FIGURE 11.1
The Rhetorical Triangle.

Ethos
credibility – trust

Logos
consistency – logic

Pathos
emotions – imagination

impact **derived credibility** are slightly different. Derived credibility occurs throughout and as a result of the speech. Derived credibility is determined by what we learn about a speaker's education, occupation, or experience, as identified in the speech. We also create an impression of a speaker's credibility through his or her delivery and such issues as disfluencies (*um, uh, like,* or repetitive words or phrases). Another element of derived credibility comes from what sources are cited in the speech and whether the position the speaker takes on an issue or topic conforms to the listener's values and beliefs.

The final type of credibility we call **terminal credibility**. Listeners determine the speaker's terminal credibility immediately after the speech is concluded. It is, essentially, a culmination of the initial and derived credibility. Our final judgment of the speaker includes any prior relationship we might have had, our overall assessment of the power of the speech, and our assessment of the speaker's credibility, delivery, and effectiveness. Ultimately, this terminal credibility becomes that person's initial credibility the next time he or she speaks.

Building Credibility Through Competence and Character

So how can a speaker enhance his or her credibility throughout the speech? First, the speaker must engage in some degree of audience analysis to understand the values, beliefs, and attitudes of the audience. It is important to remember that in every audience there are likely those who share your values, those who are ambivalent about them, and those who disagree with you. Is your goal to change the minds of those who are opposed to you? Or is your goal to engage those who are ambivalent and try to get them to take a stronger stand? Which is more likely? As we said before, changing a deeply held value is not an easy task. Convincing someone to think more about something he or she had not previously been interested in is somewhat easier. To build credibility in either of these cases, you must enhance it. So your first job in the speech is to explain your competence and experience. What makes you credible? Explain why the audience should believe you. If you convince your audience members that you legitimately understand their point of view and that you hold values in common with your listeners, you show respect for their thoughts and feelings, and potentially enhance the likelihood they will listen to you. Remember that this is an important part of the introduction to your speech. You cannot spend an inordinate amount of time establishing your credibility, but references to your preparation and your links to the audience can help. Consider this example of a brief way to establish credibility using the topic of getting involved on campus as a first-year college student:

> Like you, I came to college with a mixture of apprehension and excitement. For the first time, I had a new sense of freedom and, yet, responsibility. I faced numerous challenges and even thought about just giving up and going home. But, I learned some important lessons early on about how to face this challenging time. One of those lessons I learned is simple but powerful: Get involved in campus life from the very beginning. That's what I did, and I encourage you to do the same.

Once you have presented your expertise and common ground, you can increase the potential success of the speech by fluent, expressive, and powerful delivery. You should take care in providing the audience with appropriate evidence and support, which we discuss in the next section, and speak with passion and conviction. Take a look at the box "Communication Counts in Your College Experience: How Do Faculty Build Credibility?" to assess how your teachers live up to the "best practices" in developing credibility.

FIGURE 11.2

An Advocacy Ad Using Ethos.

Source: Courtesy of American Academy of Physicians Assistants.

Derived credibility ■ Determined by what we learn about a speaker's education, occupation, or experience, as identified in the speech.

Terminal credibility ■ A culmination of the initial and derived credibility.

COMMUNICATION COUNTS IN YOUR COLLEGE EXPERIENCE

How Do Faculty Build Credibility?

Think of one of your current professors/instructors. Using the following list of traits, analyze how he/she has intentionally or unintentionally developed credibility with you. The first two elements refer to what you knew or did not know about this person before the class began. The final three speak to what the person has done during the class to enhance his/her credibility.

- **Competence.** Students in the class must believe that the speaker is competent to teach a particular topic before they will believe what he or she is saying. What did you know of his/her experience before the class? What did you know of his/her qualifications or expertise? Look at the syllabus for the class. In what ways are competence, qualifications, and/or expertise developed here?
- **Reputation.** Speakers have reputations. Had you heard anything about this teacher before you enrolled in his/her class? Does your school have a place, such as the student government website, where teacher ratings or evaluations can be found? Did you "ask around" about this person before taking the class? Who might you ask

who would be credible in providing you information about this person's reputation?
- **Intelligence.** Some elements that create credibility are the appearance of good thinking and relevant knowledge. How does this professor show you that he/she has sound reasoning, is well organized, and understands the importance of solid evidence in his/her presentation? Does the person refer to other "experts" in the field of study?
- **Character.** How does this person show you that he/she is trustworthy and honest? Are all expectations clear to you during the course? Are assignments returned in a timely manner? Does this person appear to you as someone with strong and appropriate values in the classroom?
- **Goodwill.** Treating the audience members in the way they would like to be treated is crucial to building credibility. Making sexist or racist jokes, rudely making fun of the audience, or appearing close-minded and mean-spirited are surefire ways to spoil credibility. Can you think of a time where your professor showed you personally that he/she had your best interests at heart?

CRAFTING PERSUASIVE MESSAGES

As Aristotle suggested, speaker credibility is critical to the success and effectiveness of a presentation. But it is not the only factor that contributes to persuasion. How the speaker develops an emotional link with the audience is also critical, as is the logic or reasoning he or she uses to develop an argument. Both pathos (emotional appeal) and logos (logical appeal) work with the speaker's credibility to create a bond between speaker and audience. First, let's look at the role of emotional appeals.

Pathos and Emotional Appeals

While establishing credibility will help convince an audience to listen to a particular speaker, the pathos or emotional appeal is the reason an audience will listen to a speaker on a specific topic. It is why the audience becomes involved with the topic or message. What are the basic emotions that a speaker might trigger in an audience? Happiness, sadness, fear, guilt? What is it about emotions that can link us to a topic? Emotions lie at the heart of our perception and interpretation of communication. Ethical use of emotional appeal can bring an audience into an issue in a personal, intimate way. But emotional appeal can also be used for purposes that are not ethical. Consider how some charismatic leaders in history, such as Hitler or Stalin used emotion to convince followers to act unethically and inhumanely. Consider also the ways that fear, in particular, is used to convince us to engage in healthy behaviors or to stop engaging in unhealthy ones.

Fear appeals are persuasive messages used to scare people into changing their attitudes by getting them to think about the negative consequences if they do not comply with the recommendations (Perloff 2010). A great deal of research has gone into the study of whether fear appeals work, and the conclusion is that they do, if they fulfill the following requirements. First, the appeal to fear must be very, very scary. We are much less likely to comply with a fear appeal if we are only slightly scared. But if we are scared out of our wits, we are much more likely to comply. Consider the issue of texting while driving. Second, the appeal to fear must suggest a solution to the problem. We need to be scared, but we also need to be able to see that we can do something about the problem, or a fear appeal does not work. Finally, the fear appeal must explain not only the costs of not taking precautionary actions, but it must also explain the benefits of changing our behavior (Perloff 2010).

So what about the guilt appeal? Think of advertisements you have seen recently that use guilt to get you to donate to a charitable organization. Do the graphic appeals of deprived children convince you to send money? Research on this type of appeal suggests that the appeal must trigger our sense of empathy and that it must also convince us that we can make a difference. If we feel empathy and guilt, but also feel that no amount of money will really change the situation, we are unlikely to donate.

The most effective ways to use fear, guilt, and other emotional appeals is through stories. The narrative, or story, creates a personal link through an extended example that "rings true" to us. The best stories allow us to become personally involved in the lives of the "characters." We can relate to them because we may have had a similar experience or know somehow who has. The story or narrative encourages us to use our imagination to envision what it might be like to share the experience. "Contemporary narratives can appear on a host of interactive technologies, such as movies shown on Web sites, video games, and virtual reality.... By transporting individuals to social realms located in the human imagination, stories can induce them to look at everyday problems through a new set of lenses" (Perloff 2010, 194). As you prepare your speech, think about stories that add human interest and that will appeal to your audience. Even a cursory Web search will yield numerous resources on which you can draw. More appropriately, however, if you have chosen a topic that holds personal concern for you, you may well have a personal story with emotional appeal that illustrates your connection to the topic. You may opt to use this story as your attention-getter, while also using it to link to your audience and enhance your credibility.

Logos and Logical Appeals

The final element of effective persuasion is the logic or reasoning we use to convince an audience to draw the same conclusions we have about a situation or issue. At the heart of the persuasive message is a claim that is made by the speaker. It is the claim that the speaker wants to draw the listeners' attention to and the claim he or she wants listeners to believe. Claims, though, do not stand on their own. The speaker must "convince" us of the validity of the claim by providing sound evidence to support it. A persuasive speaker must provide clear "message arguments" that support the claim. "Claims linked to premises and evidence are what we mean when we use the term argument" (Woodward and Denton 2009, 85). A claim is an assertion that we make, and any claim is susceptible to a challenge. When we publicly make a claim, we open ourselves to a challenge to the claim, so it is our responsibility as a speaker to support that claim with evidence and reasoning. Look at Figure 11.3, an advocacy ad, to see how an organization constructed an argument using techniques of pathos (emotions) and logos (logic), supported by evidence. How effective is this strategy?

Inductive and Deductive Reasoning

When we provide evidence and reasoning, we can reason in two ways: inductively and deductively. **Inductive reasoning** begins with specific facts, and the facts ultimately add up to the claim. If we identify enough specific evidence, then the generalized claim flows logically from it. Consider these specifics: A majority of students who graduate from college do so with more than five years' worth of expected salaries in student loan debt and with more than $10,000 in credit card debt; most college students do not know what a "credit score" is; most college students do not have a monthly budget; a significant number of college students use student

Inductive reasoning ■ Begins with specific facts, and the facts ultimately add up to the claim.

FIGURE 11.3

An Advocacy Ad Using Pathos and Logos.

Source: http://www.google.com/images?q=advocacy+ads&oe=utf-8&rls=org.mozilla:en-US:official&client=firefox-a&um=1&ie=UTF-8&source=univ&ei=VeFiTJ2VJMT48AaegKHaCQ&sa=X&oi=image_result_group&ct=title&resnum=1&ved=0CCcQsAQwAA&biw=1024&bih=605.

Deductive reasoning ■ Begins with a general claim and uses specifics to "prove" the claim.

Toulmin Model ■ A model of argument that serves as the template for developing solid, comprehensive arguments today; the components include: claim, data, warrant, backing, qualifiers, and rebuttal.

Claim ■ The statement the speaker makes that communicates what he or she wants the audience to think, feel, or act on.

Data ■ The facts that exist, from which the speaker makes the claim.

Warrant ■ The rationale for making the link between the claim and the data.

Backing ■ Additional evidence that adds power to the warrant. It consists of the facts that support the warrant.

Qualifier ■ An attempt to reduce the strength of the claim, from one that is absolute to one with exceptions.

Rebuttal ■ A more explicit reference to any exception that would invalidate the claim.

loan money for purposes other than paying for college costs; and most students pay only the minimum amount each month on credit card debt. Because of all of these reasons, college students should take a course in financial literacy.

In contrast to inductive reasoning, we can also use deductive reason. **Deductive reasoning** begins with a general claim and uses specifics to "prove" the claim. If a speaker were to claim that "the unemployment rate is increasing everywhere," then it would be up to him or her to provide examples to convince listeners—such as providing statistics about increases across geographic, socioeconomic, and career categories.

The Toulmin Model

In the 1950s, author Stephen Toulmin developed a model of argument that serves as the template for developing solid, comprehensive arguments today. The components of the **Toulmin Model** include: claim, data, warrant, backing, qualifiers, and rebuttal. Figure 11.4 shows how these components fit together to make a thorough argument.

First, as we've discussed, is the **claim**. This is the statement the speaker makes that communicates what he or she wants the audience to think, feel, or act on. An advertisement contains a claim about the product you should consider purchasing; a local politician makes a claim about a particular policy he or she wants enacted or continued. Claims can be made about facts, values, or policies, as we discuss later in this chapter. The **data** are the facts that exist, from which the speaker makes the claim. Data exist in the form of premises and evidence. Premises are the beliefs a speaker holds. We also call these premises assumptions about the world. Evidence, as we discuss earlier in the text, can be examples, statistics, testimony, or stories.

The **warrant** in Toulmin's model refers to the rationale for making the link between the claim and the data. This is where reasoning comes into the argument process. In some cases, there is a direct, explicit link between claim and data, but often there is not. When a speaker makes the claim, for example, that the United States should have government-sponsored health care, just like Canada or the UK, the speaker is using as the warrant, an argument by analogy. This type of argument "examines two similar cases to understand which qualities they share. If the two cases are alike in every way that is known, it is assumed they will be alike with regard to a characteristic known in one case, but not in the other" (Borchers 2005, 281). As we suggested, a warrant may be inductive or deductive in its link between claim and data. **Backing** is additional evidence that adds power to the warrant. It consists of the facts that support the warrant.

The additional elements in the model—qualifiers and rebuttals—both speak to how we might modify a claim to account for exceptions or oppositional claims. A **qualifier** is an attempt to reduce the strength of the claim, from one that is absolute to one with exceptions. When the speaker uses terms like "in the vast majority of cases" or suggests that something "probably" will occur, he or she is "qualifying" a claim. A **rebuttal** is a

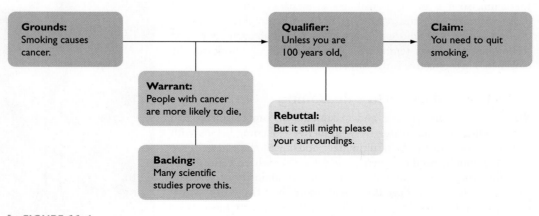

FIGURE 11.4
The Toulmin Model.

Adapted from "Uses of Reasoning," 1958, p. 105.

more explicit reference to any exception that would invalidate the claim. Consider this example of an argument:

> The government has no business regulating the Internet (claim) except in cases of child pornography (qualifier) because protecting children is more important (rebuttal). Internet providers such as Google or Craig's List police their own sites (data) and will keep us safe (warrant). The vast majority of individuals surfing the Net use self-regulated websites such as Google, and fraud and other illegal activities are rarely an issue for these users (backing).

Logical Fallacies

As the Toulmin Model suggests, a persuasive speaker who incorporates all of the critical elements of the model into his or her argument can go a long way toward increasing the likelihood that an audience will be swayed by the message. Unfortunately, some speakers may use deceptive strategies to move an audience to agree with a claim. When a speaker uses a false or incomplete idea or makes a false inference or link between claims and data or between claims and warrants, he or she has used a **logical fallacy**. Larson (2010) calls these believable arguments that are based on invalid reasoning. There are several types of logical fallacies, including the *post hoc* fallacy, *ad hominem* and *ad populum* arguments, the **fallacy of the undistributed middle**, the **"slippery slope" argument**, and the **straw man fallacy**. These are only representative fallacies; there are many more. For additional information and examples, consult http://www.don-lindsay-archive.org/skeptic/arguments.html. Table 11.2 provides a look at some of the most common logical fallacies.

Logical fallacy ■ When a speaker uses a false or incomplete idea or makes a false inference or link between claims and data or between claims and warrants.

Post hoc fallacy ■ Attempts to link two events together. If one event occurs in close proximity to another, a *post hoc* fallacy may assume the first event caused the second.

Ad hominem argument ■ Attacks a person instead of his or her position on an issue. Becomes a personal attack instead of ethical persuasion.

Ad populum argument ■ Uses popular polls to assume what is popular at any given time and to infer that if someone is in disagreement with what is popular, he or she is not to be trusted or listened to.

TABLE 11.2

COMMON LOGICAL FALLACIES

Fallacy Type	Description	Example
post hoc fallacy	Attempts to link two events together. If one event occurs in close proximity to another, a *post hoc* fallacy may assume the first event caused the second.	Football team owners who are part of the NFL draft wants us to believe that if they can just get the number one draft pick, they'll have a winning season.
ad hominem fallacy	Attacks a person instead of his or her position on an issue. Becomes a personal attack instead of ethical persuasion.	Politicians use this type of argument during election years in an effort to smear an opponent's character.
ad populum fallacy	Uses popular polls to assume what is popular at any given time and to infer that if someone is in disagreement with what is popular, he or she is not to be trusted or listened to. In essence, this is an argument to follow the crowd at a given time in history. The problem, of course, is that what is popular at one time in history (e.g., legally preventing women from voting) gives way to a completely different opinion of what is acceptable or not (e.g., women should be allowed to run for President).	Advertisers use this type of argument to convince you that "everyone" is buying this product, so you should too. You might have used this on your parents when you said you should be allowed to stay out later than your curfew because "everyone else" in your class was staying out later.
fallacy of the undistributed middle	Suggests that because a group shares one attribute, members of the group share a whole range of attributes. The problem with this type of fallacy is the faulty premise that "all" fraternity brothers have any single behavior in common other than simply membership.	All fraternity brothers are heavy drinkers; if you want to join a fraternity, you'll be expected to drink heavily too.
slippery slope fallacy	Suggests that once a set of actions has started, there is no stopping the ultimate conclusion.	If we ban automatic weapons, the NRA suggests, the second amendment supporting the "right to bear arms" will ultimately be eliminated.
straw man fallacy	Attempts to set up an easily refuted argument as a way to defeat an opposing position. When the weak argument is easily defeated, then a whole position is assumed to be invalid.	If the NRA supports "cop killer" bullets, then its whole argument in opposition to gun control of any kind is irresponsible.

Fallacy of the undistributed middle ■ Suggests that because a group shares one attribute, members of the group share a whole range of attributes.

Slippery slope fallacy ■ Suggests that once a set of actions has started, there is no stopping the ultimate conclusion.

Straw man fallacy ■ Attempts to set up an easily refuted argument as a way to defeat an opposing position. When the weak argument is easily defeated, then a whole position is assumed to be invalid.

Speech to reinforce or stimulate ■ A speech that reinforces the beliefs or behaviors to which the audience already ascribes.

If you depend on any of these fallacies in logic, you will encounter significant problems in developing a reasonable and effective argument. Ultimately, though, a model such as that developed by Toulmin can help the speaker craft a well-reasoned and logically sound position and support that position effectively.

To this point we have provided general background to understand persuasion. All of these aspects of persuasion are, however, more than theory; they influence, as we have noted, the way we present persuasive speeches. Understanding more about the intersection of persuasion theory and persuasive speaking is particularly important to you as you develop your public speaking skills.

IDENTIFYING TYPES OF PERSUASIVE SPEECHES

Just like our discussion of informative speeches, persuasive speeches come in various types. The persuader attempts to influence your knowledge, your feelings and beliefs, and/or your behavior. He or she does so by developing a position on a topic and attempting to influence your position on that topic.

Persuasive Speeches According to Purpose

As we noted earlier, unlike informative speeches, persuasive speeches fulfill one of three purposes:

■ to reinforce,
■ to change beliefs/to convince, and
■ to change behavior/to actuate.

While all three of these purposes persuade, they differ in their specifics. Let's consider each of these three purposes in more detail.

Have you heard the phrase "preaching to the choir?" When people preach to the choir, they reinforce beliefs or behaviors to which the audience already subscribes. Because this is often the purpose of sermons, this phrase uses the image of a preacher delivering a message to the choir, whose members already agree. This is a **speech to reinforce or stimulate.**

Effective persuasive speakers rely on ethos, logos, and pathos to persuade their audiences.

SAMPLE PERSUASIVE SPEECH TO REINFORCE OR STIMULATE

Topic: University parking

Specific Purpose: I want to rally my audience to fight for more student parking on campus.

Thesis: Convenient, safe, accessible parking is important to student success and can be achieved if we work together.

Main Points:

   I. Convenient, safe, accessible parking on campus is limited.
  II. Additional parking on campus is essential to student success.
 III. Students working together can convince the university to add additional parking.

Using the same example, if the speech challenges the audience to alter widely accepted beliefs, the specific purpose changes from reinforcement to motivation to accept new beliefs or alter present beliefs, even though the overall intent or general purpose remains persuasive. This is a **speech to convince.**

SAMPLE PERSUASIVE SPEECH TO CONVINCE

Topic: Scholarships for athletes

Specific Purpose: I want to persuade my audience that colleges should be required to continue scholarships for athletes who have completed their four years of eligibility as long as the players are actively pursuing their degrees.

Thesis: Athletes are legitimate students who work hard and have earned their scholarships.

Main Points:

    I. Athletes are legitimate students.

    II. Athletes work hard for their scholarship dollars.

    III. Rewarding athletes for their years of competition is the right thing to do.

In another example, if a candidate for student government asks students to cast their ballots for him, the general purpose is persuasive but the specific purpose is to motivate voters to behave in a particular manner. This is a **speech to actuate.** On the other hand, if the president of your university asks the student body to believe that a proposed tuition increase is a necessary response to economic needs, even though the general purpose is persuasive, the specific purpose changes. In this instance, the president *speaks to convince* or to alter the audience's beliefs.

SAMPLE PERSUASIVE SPEECH TO ACTUATE

Topic: Urge Congress to cut the federal budget deficit

Specific Purpose: I want to persuade my audience that they need to call on their representatives to cut the federal deficit.

Thesis: Urge your representatives to cut the federal budget deficit, which is the only fiscally responsible course given our national debit and the resulting impact on all citizens now and in the future.

Main Points:

    I. The budget deficit is skyrocketing and reducing it is the only fiscally responsible course.

    II. The federal deficit hurts each present and future citizen directly and

    III. The federal deficit must be reduced and only your representatives can effectively address this crisis; contact them today!

Although these three specific purposes for persuasive speeches differ, in each case the speaker acts as an advocate for a particular proposition or supports a specific claim. In doing so, the speaker draws on his or her credibility (ethos), employs logic and evidence (logos), and often seeks to touch the audience's emotions (pathos).

Persuasive Speeches According to Proposition

Persuasive speeches are by nature propositional; they propose and advocate a particular belief or behavior. However, the nature of the proposition for a speech may differ. Persuasive speeches may be categorized according to these various propositions: fact, value, and policy.

Propositions of fact are debatable issues that a single piece of objective evidence cannot resolve. In other words, persuasive speeches that focus on propositions of fact focus on whether a given interpretation of evidence is or is not true. Propositions of fact seek to answer the question, "Is this true or false?" For example, consider the following proposition of fact and how it can be used in a speech:

Global warming continues to increase as a result of changes in the ozone layer.

SAMPLE PERSUASIVE PROPOSITION OF FACT SPEECH

Topic: Global warming

Specific Purpose: I want to persuade my audience that global warming continues to rise as a result of damage to the ozone layer

Thesis: Damage to the ozone layer is seriously impacting global temperatures.

Main Points:

    I. The ozone layer can be explained scientifically.

    II. Damage to the ozone layer impacts global temperatures.

    III. Damage to the ozone layer is a problem created by humans.

Propositions of value focus on the worth or value of a particular person, idea, event, or object. Propositions of value seek to answer the question, "Is this good or bad, right or wrong, ethical or unethical?" Many propositions of value rest on propositions of fact—that is, you cannot argue the value of a certain proposition without

Speech to convince ■ A persuasive speech that challenges the audience to alter widely accepted beliefs.

Speech to actuate ■ A persuasive speech that motivates the audience toward a particular behavior.

Proposition of fact ■ Debatable issue that a single piece of objective evidence cannot resolve.

Proposition of value ■ Focuses on the worth or value of a particular person, idea, event, or object.

Proposition of policy ■ Focuses on a specific, preferred response to a particular problem or question.

also providing evidence regarding certain assumptions. For example, you cannot argue that the Internet is a morally compromised environment in view of the widespread presence of pornography without first establishing that pornography is, indeed, widespread on the Internet.

Consider this proposition of value and how it can be used in a speech:

> The Internet is a morally compromised environment due to the widespread presence of pornography.

SAMPLE PERSUASIVE PROPOSITION OF VALUE SPEECH

Topic: Internet pornography

Specific Purpose: I want to persuade my audience that the pervasiveness of pornography creates a morally compromised environment on the Internet.

Thesis: Internet pornography morally corrupts users of the Web.

Main Points:

  I. Internet pornography is pervasive.
 II. Internet pornography damages people.
III. Internet pornography damages the Internet.

Propositions of policy advocate a particular response or specific course of action. They are concerned with what course of action should be taken in response to a particular question. Propositions of policy espouse and argue for a specific response to a given problem. You can often identify propositions of policy by the presence of the word *should*, although some propositions of value may also employ this key word.

Consider these propositions of policy:

■ The U.S. Congress should pass legislation to ensure that executives of corporations do not propagate the kind of fraud exemplified by the executives of Lehman Brothers.

■ All parents should be required to use a child protective software program on home computers to ensure that children are not exposed to pornography.

SAMPLE PERSUASIVE PROPOSITION OF POLICY SPEECH

Topic: Child protective software

Specific Purpose: I want to persuade my audience that all new computer manufacturers should be legally required to automatically configure all new home computers with child protective software.

Thesis: Child protective software protects children and therefore should be legally mandated to on all new computers.

Main Points:

  I. Protective software is essential given numerous potential dangers for children.
 II. Protective software on computers ensures that children are not exposed to these dangers.
III. Protective software should be legally required on all new computers.

Practically, as you think about your persuasive speech topic, you will find it helpful to understand the type of speech you intend to deliver. This grounding can assist you as you work through the evidence you gather and how you use this evidence to craft and support your argument. Additionally, understanding the type of speech you intend to deliver should prove helpful in deciding on the organizational pattern you will employ. At this point, you may find it useful to review the various types of organization you can employ that we discussed in Chapter 9.

ORGANIZING PERSUASIVE SPEECHES

Persuasive speeches are usually organized in one of the five following ways. We will we show you how to apply the patterns we discussed in Chapter 9 to the development of persuasive speeches. As you can see, in each of these examples the thesis of the speech is a basic claim, and the main points of the speech provide the evidence and logical arguments to support the claim.

Using a Problem–Solution Pattern

The **problem–solution design** is the one of the simplest patterns of organization for persuasive speeches. The speaker identifies a problem and provides a way to solve the problem.

SAMPLE PERSUASIVE SPEECH USING A PROBLEM–SOLUTION PATTERN

Topic: Legalizing marijuana for medical use

Specific Purpose: I want to convince the audience that marijuana should be legal for medical use.

Thesis: Medical marijuana should be legal in all 50 states.

Main Points:

    I. There are numerous benefits of medical marijuana.

    II. There is a significant need for medical marijuana in the states where it is currently illegal.

    III. Legalizing marijuana for medical use in all 50 states would benefit patients, states, and the economy in general.

Choosing and using an appropriate organizational pattern is essential to the effective delivery of your persuasive speech.

Using a Cause–Effect Pattern

The **cause–effect pattern,** as we discussed earlier, focuses more on the significance and impact of an issue or problem than on the solution.

SAMPLE PERSUASIVE SPEECH USING A CAUSE–EFFECT PATTERN

Topic: Childhood obesity

Specific Purpose: I want to convince the audience that childhood obesity has an impact on families and communities.

Thesis: Childhood obesity is pervasive and harms children and the U.S. economy.

Main Points:

    I. Childhood obesity is pervasive in the United States

    II. There are physical and mental harms of childhood obesity

    III. There are significant economic impacts of childhood obesity

Using Monroe's Motivated Sequence

As we suggested earlier, **Monroe's Motivated Sequence** is particularly useful if you want to motivate your audience to action. This 'sequence' adds the additional step of visualization to enhance the persuasive appeal.

SAMPLE PERSUASIVE SPEECH USING MONROE'S MOTIVATED SEQUENCE

Topic: Voting is important to a democracy.

Specific Purpose: I want to convince the audience to become active participants in the democratic process by voting in all elections.

Thesis: Voting is a responsibility of all Americans and a part of a working democracy.

Main Points:

    I. Attention Step: Voting and not voting impacts you in several ways.

    II. Need Step: Voting is essential to a working democracy.

    III. Satisfaction Step: Your vote makes a difference.

    IV. Visualization Step: How voting works: It's easy and it's fun.

    V. Action Step: Register to vote today, and vote in the upcoming election.

Using a Refutative Pattern

The **refutative pattern** includes discussion of the "opposing" arguments to the claim made by the speaker and "refutes" the opposing arguments, reducing their power and enhancing the persuasiveness of the speaker's claim.

Problem–solution design ■ The speaker identifies a problem and provides a way to solve the problem.

Cause–effect pattern ■ Focusing on a problem in order to trace its roots and results.

Monroe's Motivated Sequence ■ A five step process for organizing a speech in order to inspire the audience to take action.

Refutative pattern ■ Identifying and systematically countering arguments that are opposed to a particular position or proposition.

State-the-case-and-prove-it
pattern ■ Clearly stating and claim
and then systematically providing
strong reasons and evidence to
support the claim.

SAMPLE PERSUASIVE SPEECH USING A REFUTATIVE PATTERN

Topic: Donating blood

Specific Purpose: I want to convince my audience to donate blood regularly.

Thesis: Donating blood is easy and saves lives.

Main Points:

    I. Myth: Someone else will donate. Donating blood is practiced by only about 5% of the population.

    II. Myth: It will take too much time. Donating blood takes about 45 minutes.

    III. Myth: It will hurt. Donating blood is relatively painless, no more than piercing or tattooing.

    IV. Myth: It is dangerous. Donating blood is safe, sterile, and donors are effectively screened to ensure their well-being.

    IV. Myth: They won't take my blood. Donating blood includes a screening process to ensure that you are eligible to donate.

Using a State-the-Case-and-Prove-It Pattern

The **state-the-case-and-prove-it pattern** is useful when you want to prove that something is true—or not true. The pattern puts extra focus on the evidence to "prove" your claim.

SAMPLE PERSUASIVE SPEECH USING A STATE-THE-CASE-AND-PROVE-IT PATTERN

Topic: Losing weight effectively

Specific Purpose: I want to convince the audience of the most appropriate way to lose weight.

Thesis: The most effective way to lose weight is to understand and make good eating choices—not count calories.

Main Points:

    I. Most diets don't work for several reasons

    II. The Mayo Clinic dieticians and doctors have developed a Top ten "good eating choices."

    III. There are a number of advantages of "good eating choices" approach.

    IV. Using the good eating choices approach to dieting can have significant benefits.

SAMPLE ANNOTATED FULL-SENTENCE OUTLINE OF A PERSUASIVE SPEECH

Review the annotated persuasive speech outline shown here, and look carefully at each of the specific elements of the speech. If it is helpful, develop a checklist for each of the elements identified in the outline. Creating an effective checklist can help ensure that you include all of the important parts of a good persuasive speech.

Stephanie A. Student
Communication 101, Sec. 012
November 20, 2010

> This is a speech according to purpose—the purpose is to motivate the audience to practice safe sex.

Specific Purpose: I want to persuade the audience that HIV/AIDS is still a significant problem and that using certain contraceptives or abstaining from sex will reduce the chance of contracting HIV/AIDS.

> Clear and specific thesis statement.

Thesis Statement: You can protect yourself and prevent the spread of HIV/AIDS by practicing safe sex.

> Type of organization for the speech: Point one in the speech establishes the problem; point two discusses the significance and relevance for the audience; and point three provides the solution.

Organizational Pattern: Problem–solution

Intended Audience: COMM 101 Class

INTRODUCTION

> The speaker begins with an example to gain attention and establish interest. We are told a personal story (narrative) of a friend who has been diagnosed with HIV (pathos). This kind of detail brings the topic to life and helps listeners get involved in the speech.

    I. **Attention-Getting Device:** Let me tell you about my friend Elsa. Recently she decided to get her blood tested. She decided that because she had been with many partners and took part in unprotected sex, she should be tested for HIV. When the nurse gave her the bad news, the only thought that went through her mind was, "Why me? The results must be wrong."

        Every day many adults between the ages of 18 and 25 find that they have contracted the AIDS virus. Don't be a statistic.

II. **Orientation Phase:**

    A. *Point:* Today I want to discuss how you can protect yourself from the HIV/AIDS virus.

    B. *Adaptation:* Anyone can contract this virus, and it is particularly devastating today in the population in this room: 18-to-25-year-old men and women.

    C. *Credibility:* Even if you think you know about HIV/AIDS and how to protect yourself, this speech will help you truly understand the devastation that is possible with unprotected sex. Knowing about my friend Elsa has changed my life and helped me to understand the true significance of this disease and its potential impact on our lives. Through the research I provide to you today, I hope you will be convinced of the importance of safe sex.

    D. *Enumerated preview:* I will cover three important areas today:

        1. First, the continuing problem with HIV/AIDS even today.

        2. Second, the specific risk to 18–25-year-old women and men.

        3. And third, the two easiest and most effective ways to protect yourself and why it is so important to do so.

Transition: Now, let's consider my first point.

> The speaker establishes her credibility (ethos) here—through her personal relationship and knowledge of the friend's diagnosis, and with her research support for the points she will make in the speech. This is the main claim of the speech.

> The speaker adds the final element of an effective introduction by explaining to the audience the main points she will highlight in the speech.

> The transitions between the sections of the speech and, later, between each main point, help the audience recognize the flow of the speech and make it easier to remember key points.

BODY

III. AIDS is still a growing problem today.

    A. According to the World Health Organization, since the beginning of the epidemic, more than 60 million people have been affected, and 25 million have died.

    B. In 2008 there were 2 million deaths from AIDS, and young people account for 40 percent of new HIV/AIDS cases. More than 75,000 new infections occurred in 2008 in North America alone.

        1. The Centers for Disease Control (CDC), in its July 2010 report, stated that more than 1 million people in the United States are living with AIDS, and one in five are not aware they have the disease.

        2. Individuals infected through heterosexual contact account for 31 percent of annual new HIV infections and 28 percent of people living with HIV.

        3. As a group, women account for 27 percent of annual new HIV infections and 25 percent of those living with HIV.

        4. Injection drug users represent 12 percent of annual new HIV infections and 19 percent of those living with HIV.

        5. Men who have sex with men (MSM) account for more than half (53 percent) of all new HIV infections in the United States each year, as well as nearly half (48 percent) of people living with HIV.

    C. The most common forms of transmission, according to the CDC, are unprotected sex, having multiple sexual partners, sharing needles, and being born to an infected mother.

Transition: As you can see, despite what we know of this disease and the ways to prevent it, the problem is still significant.

> This is evidence by example, from a reliable and credible source.

> This is expert testimony by a reputable person with direct experience in the disease.

> This is a dramatic statistic (fact) showing the significance of the problem.

IV. Anyone can get AIDS and 16-to-21-year-olds are at risk.

    A. The statistics for AIDS cases in this age group are significant.

        1. Young heterosexual women, especially those of minority races or ethnicities, are increasingly at risk for HIV infection through heterosexual contact. According to data from a CDC study of HIV prevalence among disadvantaged youth during the early to mid 1990s, the rate of HIV prevalence among young women aged 16–21 was 50 percent higher than the rate among young men in that age group. African American women in this study were 7 times as likely as white women and 8 times as likely as Hispanic women to be HIV-positive. Young women are at risk for sexually transmitted HIV for several reasons, including biologic vulnerability, lack of recognition of their partners' risk factors, inequality in relationships, and having sex with older men who are more likely to be infected with HIV.

        2. The presence of a sexually transmitted disease (STD) greatly increases a person's likelihood of acquiring or transmitting HIV. Some of the highest STD rates in the country are those among young people—especially young people of minority races and ethnicities.

> This is statistical data showing the relevance of the issue to the audience. Notice how the speaker identifies the sources of her "evidence" and integrates those sources deftly into the text. There are many examples of this throughout the speech. All of this is evidence or "data" for her argument.

3. Research has shown that a large proportion of young people are not concerned about becoming infected with HIV.
    a. Blacks account for about half of all people living with HIV/AIDS within each sex category, according to information from 33 states, during 2005.
    b. Among men, 41 percent living with HIV/AIDS were black
    c. Among women, 64 percent living with HIV/AIDS were black
4. So young people account for a significantly affected population.

B. Every day people our age contract this virus. The CDC reports:
    1. In 2009, 46 percent of high school students had ever had sexual intercourse, and 14 percent of high school students had had four or more sex partners during their life.
    2. In 2009, 34 percent of currently sexually active high school students did not use a condom during the last sexual intercourse.
    3. In 2002, 11 percent of males and females aged 15–19 had engaged in anal sex with someone of the opposite sex; 3 percent of males aged 15–19 had had anal sex with a male.
    4. In 2002, 55 percent of males and 54 percent of females aged 15–19 had engaged in oral sex with someone of the opposite sex.
    5. In 2006, an estimated 5,259 young people aged 13–24 in the 33 states reporting to the CDC were diagnosed with HIV/AIDS, representing about 14 percent of the persons diagnosed that year.
    6. Each year, there are approximately 19 million new STD infections, and almost half of them are among youth aged 15–24.
    7. In 2002, 12 percent of all pregnancies, or 757,000, occurred among adolescents aged 15–19.
    8. According to the *Indianapolis Star,* cases are reported to the Indiana Health Department daily.
    9. My friend Elsa is only one of four cases reported in [our city] in the last month.
    10. The CDC suggests that in this room today, possibly two of us have AIDS and don't know it; two of us have AIDS and DO know it. Of the two of us who know it, one is still having unprotected sex.

Transition: I have been sharing with you the reality and tragedy of AIDS and HIV. I ask you not to give up hope, because my final point will help convince you that there is something you can do.

V. There are easy and highly effective ways to prevent AIDS and HIV.
    A. First, the 100 percent effective prevention strategy is to abstain from sex.
        1. The passing of body fluids spreads the disease.
        2. By abstaining, you protect yourself and prevent the spread.
    B. The second way to prevent AIDS is through the use of condoms every time.
        1. If a male uses a condom, he will reduce the risk of getting or spreading HIV, according to the CDC.
        2. Wearing a condom has reduced the death rate in men and women. In fact, HIV cases in women and men 18–25 have been reduced by using a condom.
        3. Unfortunately, only 71 percent (in 2002) of sexually active men between the ages of 15 and 19 use a condom, according to Abma JC et al.
        4. Research suggests that if women request or insist on condom use with a partner, the chances of HIV infection drop.
            a. The most common reasons both women and men don't use a condom are perceptions of comfort and reluctance to ask a partner.
            b. What is more important to you? Comfort or risk of death?

Transition: Clearly, there are ways to reduce the risk of getting HIV and AIDS.

CONCLUSION

VI. *Summary:* As all of us know, AIDS and HIV continue to be a significant problem in our society, particularly in our age group. We can do something about preventing the spread of the disease. You know that anyone can get HIV. My friend Elsa, if she were here, would

---

Again the speaker draws on relevant, credible evidence to drive home the thesis of the speech.

In the case of a speech given at our university, this would be an example from a more localized source, which provides a more personal and "closer to home" look at the significance of the issue. Using the widest variety of sources upholds the principles of relatedness, relevance, and respect.

As with this statement and the one before, the speaker is attempting to establish a more personal and, thus, relevant relationship between the issue and the specific members of the audience.

This is a statistic of personal relevance to the audience. The more local and relevant the example, the more powerful the evidence is for the audience. This is also her "backing" for her argument.

Solutions are presented that are reasonable and that also "refute" the common reasons why people don't use condoms (logos). The speaker has used inductive reasoning in this speech. This is also her "qualifier"—use a condom every time you have sex.

This is the rebuttal for the arguments against using condoms.

tell you that her own behavior and lack of responsibility for using protection during sex is testament to the consequences of HIV/AIDS. She would also tell you, as she has told me, that it can happen to anyone, anywhere, anytime. But she would also say that you can do something about this epidemic; you can protect yourself. You can abstain from sex or you can use a condom.

VII. *Concluding Device:* If you choose to have unprotected sex, you may be the one in the room who hears the nurse or doctor tell you that you have HIV. You may be one of the statistics I reported earlier. Take responsibility today for your future.

> The speaker concludes the speech by restating her main points. By using an organizational system that is consistent, clear, simple, parallel, balanced, practical, and orderly, the speaker upholds elements of effective persuasion.

BIBLIOGRAPHY

Abma, JC, et al., Teenagers in the United States: Sexual activity, contraceptive use, and child-bearing, 2002, Vital and Health Statistics, 2004, Series 23, No. 24. Retrieved August 23, 2010 at http://www.guttmacher.org/pubs/fb_YMSRH.html.

Basic Information About HIV and AIDS. Centers for Disease Control. Retrieved August 12, 2010 at http://www.cdc.gov/hiv/topics/basic/index.htm#spread.

Resources About HIV and AIDs. Centers for Disease Control. Retrieved August 23, 2010 at http://www.cdc.gov/hiv/resources/qa/transmission.htm.

World Health Organization. 2009 Aids Epidemic Update. Retrieved August 12 2010 at http://data.unaids.org/pub/Report/2009/JC1700_Epi_Update_2009_en.pdf.

> Finally, the speaker concludes the speech with a powerful and personal reminder of how members of the audience can take control of and responsibility for their own lives. The speaker has continued to reinforce her credibility throughout the speech with strong evidence that is relevant and personal. Review the list of "don'ts" in the chapter in terms of the ethics of persuasion and you can see that the speaker has developed an ethical persuasive speech.

BECOMING A COMPETENT AND ETHICAL PERSUASIVE SPEAKER IN COLLEGE, CAREER, AND LIFE

How do we go about developing ethical persuasive communication? To this question, Nilsen (1966) replies, "Whatever develops, enlarges, enhances human personalities is good; whatever restricts, degrades, or injures human personalities is bad" (9). Developing and enhancing humanity means we are fostering a climate of care. This includes concern, warmth, acceptance, support, and trust. We communicate these behaviors because human beings have value. An ethical orientation also means that we seek to morally justify an action or decision by seeking good reasons to support it. We need to separate "liking" people from our belief that they have value as human beings. We can care for individuals and still disagree with them. We can care for people even if they anger and frustrate us. The persuasion process and its attempt to change attitudes create the potential for disagreement over facts, values, policies, issues, and events. Ethical persuasion, however, does not include the use of questionable techniques or fallacies. We must understand the consequences of our persuasion and that, "no matter the purpose we serve, the arguments, appeals, structure, and language we choose do shape the audience's values, thinking habits, language patterns, and level of trust" (Johannesen, Valde, & Whedbee 2008, 101).

Standards of ethics in persuasion suggest that there are criteria we can apply to the development of persuasive arguments that we develop as speakers and that we can apply to the persuasive arguments we hear in a variety of communication contexts. Johannesen, Valde, & Whedbee suggest that we look carefully at the following guidelines:

- Do not use false, fabricated, misrepresented, distorted, or irrelevant evidence to support arguments or claims;
- Do not intentionally use unsupported, misleading, or illogical reasoning;
- Do not represent yourself as informed or as an "expert" on a subject when you are not;
- Do not use irrelevant appeals to divert attention or scrutiny from the issue at hand;
- Do not ask your audience to link your idea or proposal to emotion-laden values, motives, or goals to which it actually is not related;
- Do not deceive your audience by concealing your real purpose, by concealing self-interest, by concealing the group you represent, or by concealing your position as an advocate of a viewpoint;
- Do not distort, hide, or misrepresent the number, scope, intensity, or undesirable features of consequences or effects;

- Do not use "emotional appeals" that lack a supporting basis of evidence or reasoning, or that would not be accepted if the audience members had time and opportunity to examine the subject themselves;
- Do not oversimplify complex, gradation-laden situations into simplistic two-valued, either-or, polar views or choices;
- Do not pretend certainty where tentativeness and degrees of probability would be more accurate; and
- Do not advocate something in which you do not believe yourself. (28–29)

Developing the skills to create ethical persuasive arguments and the skills to evaluate the persuasive arguments of others requires us to think critically about persuasion. "Critical thinking skills have been widely acknowledged as central to sound reasoning and decision making," write Makau and Marty (2001, 10). Critical thinking to assess the elements of a persuasive argument can help identify faulty arguments and reasoning by others and can help us respond when persuasive appeals are unethical. The ultimate response to the unethical communication behavior of others is to "blow the whistle" on the behavior—to call it out publicly. A whistleblower, according to Johannesen, Valde, and Whedbee (2008) is someone who goes outside normal communication channels to publicly expose a serious problem that is not being faced by an organization. The *Time Magazine* "Persons of the Year" for 2002 were three whistleblowers who brought attention to the unethical practices of their respective organizations: Enron, Worldcom, and the FBI. Their stories show the complexity and difficulty of the situations and also the courage it takes to expose unethical communication. See the "Communication Counts in Your Career: Will You Become a Whistleblower?" box for an example of one person's decision to become a whistleblower.

COMMUNICATION COUNTS IN YOUR CAREER

Will You Become a Whistleblower?

Earlier in the text we discussed how groupthink led to the space shuttle *Challenger* explosion. This case is also unique in that one of the engineers who worked for the Morton Thiokol company (the company responsible for the solid rocket boosters with the failed O-ring that ultimately caused the explosion) became a whistleblower during the Rogers Commission investigation into the explosion. The Rogers Commission studied testimony by NASA space flight administrators, National Space Transportation Program administrators, program managers for the various subcontractors, including Morton Thiokol managers, and engineers at Thiokol. Primarily because of the testimony of Roger Boisjoly, the Commission found that the following, in addition to the failed O-ring on the solid rocket fuel booster, were contributing factors in the explosion:

1. A "serious flaw in the decision-making process leading up to the launch of Flight 51-L" (the *Challenger* flight).
2. The waiving of launch restraints "appears to have been at the expense of flight safety."
3. A "propensity of management at Marshall (NASA's Marshall Space Flight Center) to contain potentially serious problems and to attempt to resolve them internally rather than communicate them forward" (up the chain of command).
4. Thiokol management "reversed its position and recommended the launch of 51-L, at the urging of Marshall and contrary to the views of its engineers in order to accommodate a major customer."

A great deal of the testimony during the Rogers Commission hearings focused on a teleconference between Marshall Space Flight Center and Morton Thiokol the night before the launch. Initially, Thiokol managers argued against the launch due to the potential risks of the o-ring seal at low temperatures [the expected temperature at launch on January 28, 1986 was right at freezing. Tests on the O-ring had shown the potential for "blow-by" (gas leaking from the external fuel tanks into the rocket boosters) at temperatures below 52 degrees Fahrenheit. Marshall Space Flight Center administrators demanded "proof" that the seals would fail, something Thiokol engineers could not conclusively do. Several hours into the teleconference, Marshall managers told Thiokol administrators to "take off your engineer's hat and put on your manager's hat." Thiokol managers excused the engineers from the room, and the initial "no-go" for launch decision was reversed.

This decision reversal caused considerable anxiety in the engineers at Thiokol. A report of this situation was the basis of Roger Boisjoly's whistleblowing. Without his testimony (and he was the only engineer at Thiokol willing to blow the whistle) the Commission would never have known the truth about the teleconference.

Questions for Discussion

1. Would the Thiokol engineers have been justified in blowing the whistle before the launch of *Challenger*? Should they have spoken up before the launch?

2. Should the astronauts have been informed of the risks associated with the O-rings prior to launch?
3. What persuasive techniques were operating during the teleconference the night before the launch?
4. What are the moral obligations of an organization to develop an effective communication system that can handle various points of view during critical decisions?

5. Under what circumstances do you believe you could become a whistleblower? What values matter so much to you that you would risk the consequences of whistle-blowing?

Note: Excerpts taken from *Communication Ethics: Methods of Analysis,* by James A. Jaksa and Michael S. Pritchard (1994), Belmont, CA: Wadsworth Publishing.

SUMMARY

In this chapter, we have defined persuasion and described the pervasiveness of persuasive messages. Persuasion and persuasive messages surround you. Persuasive communication can be used for good or evil purposes and is the foundation of any change in society. Persuasion is a symbolic process.

- We use verbal and nonverbal symbols to invoke an emotional response, and that emotional response has the power to change the way we think, feel, or act toward a particular person, issue, event, or message.
- The communicator provides the message, but the receiver is the one who interprets the message and acts on it.
- Persuasion requires free choice on our part. Coercion, in contrast, removes the free will of the person being persuaded—either directly or indirectly.
- Persuasion is aimed at modifying or changing attitudes. Attitudes are learned responses that help us determine likes and dislikes.
- Values are more general guiding principles for life. Beliefs are more specific statements we associate with values.
- Listeners will focus on three elements of the persuasive speech: the credibility of the speaker (ethos), the emotional appeal of the message (pathos), and the logic or reasoning of the message (logos).
- Ethos is a multidimensional construct, created by our interpretations of the speaker's character, authority, charisma, and competence or experience.
- When we encounter a speaker for the first time, our perceptions of his or her credibility are based on superficial factors. This we call initial credibility.
- Derived credibility occurs throughout and as a result of the speech. Listeners determine the speaker's terminal credibility immediately after the speech is concluded.
- While establishing credibility will help convince an audience to listen to a particular speaker, the pathos or emotional appeal is the reason an audience will listen to a speaker on a specific topic.
- The final element of effective persuasion is the logic or reasoning we use to convince an audience to draw the same conclusions we have about a situation or issue.
- Effective persuasive arguments include the elements of a claim, data, warrant, backing, qualifier, and rebuttal.
- To develop an effective and ethical persuasive argument, a speaker must avoid the use of logical fallacies such as the *ad hominem* or straw man arguments.
- Persuasive speeches may be intended to reinforce a particular attitude or belief, stimulate new ways of thinking about that attitude, or convince a listener to change an attitude or belief.
- Persuasive speeches may focus on questions of fact, value, or policy.
- Speeches may be organized as a problem–solution or a cause–effect approach. The motivated sequence design for a speech adds the element of motivating people to act on the persuasive message.
- Standards of ethics in persuasion suggest that there are criteria we can apply to the development of persuasive arguments that we develop as speakers and we can apply to the persuasive arguments we hear in a variety of communication contexts.

QUESTIONS FOR DISCUSSION

1. In what ways have you used persuasive communication to enhance your learning as a college student?
2. Provide personal examples of the persuasive messages you have encountered today. Where were they?
3. How might a different channel influence the persuasiveness of a message? Give examples of persuasive messages that might have different interpretations depending on the channel used to send and receive the message.

4. Political advertisements are perhaps the least regulated type of advertising we see today. Truth, as an essential legal requirement, does not apply to political ads. Do you think political advertising should fulfill even this basic ethical requirement? Why or why not?
5. Do you believe people really listen to a speaker only when the topic relates to their needs, values, or wishes? Why or why not?

EXERCISES

1. Think of a time when you have attempted to get a friend or a group of friends to do something you wanted them to do, but you were unsuccessful. Using at least two of the concepts from this chapter, write a brief paragraph that explains why you believe the persuasive attempt was unsuccessful.
2. Develop an argument that you would use to legitimately ask for an excused absence for a class or for time off from

work. Make sure the argument follows the Toulmin model. How does his framework enhance your ability to persuade in these contexts?
3. Do you believe that a Facebook page is a persuasive tool? Why or why not? Look at the Facebook pages of several of your "friends." Write an analysis of the ethics of the communication you see. Do you know individuals whose pages violate the recommendations for ethical persuasion?

KEY TERMS

Ad hominem argument 237
Ad populum argument 237
Attitudes 231
Authority 232
Backing 236
Beliefs 231
Cause–effect pattern 241
Character 232
Charisma 232
Claim 236
Coercion 229
Competence 232
Credibility 232
Data 236
Deductive reasoning 236

Derived credibility 233
Ethos 232
Fallacy of the undistributed middle 238
Inductive reasoning 235
Initial credibility 232
Logical fallacy 237
Logos 232
Monroe's Motivated Sequence 241
Pathos 232
Persuasion 228
Post hoc fallacy 237
Problem–solution design 241
Proposition of fact 239
Proposition of policy 240

Proposition of value 239
Qualifier 236
Rebuttal 236
Refutative pattern 241
Slippery slope fallacy 238
Speech to actuate 239
Speech to convince 239
Speech to reinforce or stimulate 238
State-the-case-and-prove-it pattern 242
Straw man fallacy 238
Terminal credibility 233
Toulmin Model 236
Values 231
Warrant 236

REFERENCES

Benoit, W. L., and Benoit, P. J. 2008. *Persuasive messages: The process of influence.* Malden, MA: Blackwell.
Borchers, T. A. 2005. *Persuasion in the media age.* 2nd ed. Boston: McGraw Hill.
Gass, R. H., and Seiter, J. S. 2003. *Persuasion, social influence, and compliance gaining.* 2nd ed. Boston: Allyn, Bacon Longman.
Jaksa, J. A., and Pritchard, M. S. 1994. *Communication ethics: Methods of analysis.* Belmont, CA: Wadsworth.
Johannesen, R. L., Valde, K. S., and Whedbee, K. E. 2008. *Ethics in human communication.* 6th ed. Long Grove, IL: Waveland.
Larson, C. U. 2010. *Persuasion: Reception and responsibility.* 12th ed. Boston: Wadsworth.
Lucas, S. E. 2007. *The art of public speaking.* 9th ed. Boston: McGraw-Hill.

Makau, J. M., and Marty, D. L. 2001. Cooperative argumentation: A model for deliberative community. Long Grove, IL: Waveland.
Nilson, T. R. 1966. *Ethics of speech communication.* Indianapolis:, IN: Bobbs-Merrill.
O'Keefe, D. J. 2002. *Persuasion: Theory and research.* 2nd ed. Thousand Oaks, CA: Sage.
Perloff, R. M. 2010. *The dynamics of persuasion: Communication and attitudes in the 21st century.* 4th ed. New York: Routledge.
Whalen, D. J. 1996. *I see what you mean: Persuasive business communication.* Thousand Oaks, CA: Sage.
Woodward, G. C., and Denton, Jr., R. E. 2009. *Persuasion and influence in American life.* 6th ed. Long Grove, IL: Waveland.

12 Groups in Discussion

LEARNING OUTCOMES After reading this chapter, you will have:

the **Knowledge** to. . .   and the **Skills** to. . .

UNDERSTANDING THE CHARACTERISTICS OF GROUPS, page 252

Become aware of characteristics of groups.

- Think about the groups you belong to and assess what kind of needs they meet.
- Consider how the characteristics of small groups apply to those you are a part of.
- Articulate what explicit or implicit "norms" or rules govern each of these groups.
- Examine how your group's identity is conveyed.

DISTINGUISHING BETWEEN INDIVIDUAL GOALS AND GROUP GOALS, page 255

Discern between personal and group goals.

- Collaborate in a group to pool resources and tackle complex projects.
- Work alone to meet personal needs or fulfill a personal agenda.

IDENTIFYING TYPES OF GROUPS, page 257

Become familiar with the types of groups and the needs they fulfill.

- Use informal groups, learning groups, and study groups to accomplish academic tasks.
- Get involved in therapy groups to learn about yourself and to solve personal issues.

- Implement problem-solving groups to tackle specific projects or tasks.
- Enjoy social groups as ways to meet your needs to belong.

DETERMINING ROLES IN GROUPS, page 258

Examine the roles individuals play in groups.

- Assume task roles to propose, clarify, and provide information.
- Take on social or maintenance roles to facilitate relationships between and among the individuals in your group.
- Avoid forcing your individual ideas on others and work for the group's benefit.

UNDERSTANDING LEADERSHIP IN GROUPS, page 259

Observe how leadership is practiced in groups.

- Identify your personal traits that are conducive to leadership.
- Consider whether your style is to control (autocratic), collaborate (democratic), or let it happen (laissez-faire).
- Determine whether you need to accomplish a task or use a process.
- Act maturely and respectfully when you assume leadership positions.
- Use your power as a leader wisely.

TRACING THE STAGES OF GROUP DEVELOPMENT, page 260

Understand the process of group development.

- Maintain focus on your group's task and social needs as you go through forming (getting to know each other), norming (working out stated and unstated rules), storming (coping with conflict), and performing (completing an assigned task or process).

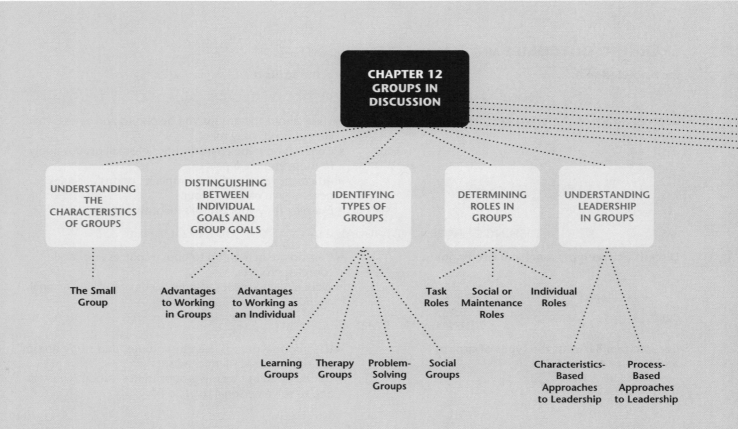

APPRECIATING CULTURE, VALUES, AND GENDER IN GROUPS, page 263

Be aware of culture, value, and gender in groups.

- Seek to understand the value system of different cultures and groups.
- Treat individuals of any gender with respect and equality.

SOLVING PROBLEMS IN GROUPS, page 264

Understand ways to resolve problems in groups.

- Foster supportive climates for problem solving by accepting other points of view, working toward common goals, and practicing empathy toward others.
- Dispel misperceptions, focus on the facts, and resolve to work together.
- Be assertive but not aggressive in resolving conflicts.

MAKING QUALITY DECISIONS IN GROUPS, page 267

Consider important points when working to make decisions as a group.

- Collaborate when making group decisions.
- Use a logical process when formulating decisions.
- Try brainstorming to think of creative solutions.
- Remain open to others points of view to avoid groupthink.

BECOMING A COMPETENT AND ETHICAL GROUP MEMBER IN COLLEGE, CAREER, AND LIFE, page 271

Become a responsible and moral group member.

- Join college, professional, and community groups to gain experience in being a good group member.

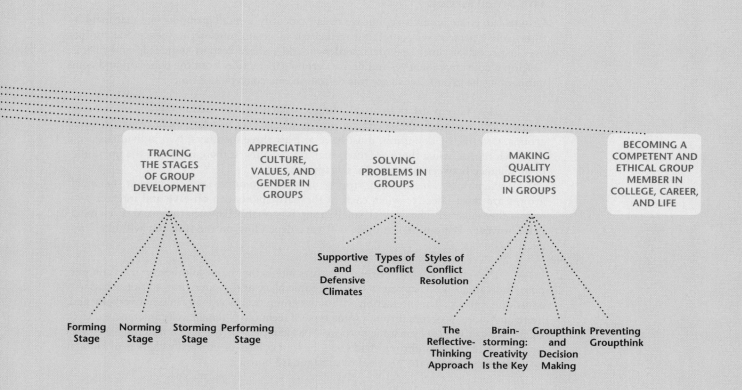

UNDERSTANDING THE CHARACTERISTICS OF GROUPS

Team ■ An organizational group working together on a class- or work-related project.

Group ■ A loose association of at least three people who come together for a wide variety of purposes.

Primary groups ■ Groups whose purpose is to meet some basic need.

Secondary groups ■ Groups that are less personal—usually shorter term (as in a work group assembled for a specific purpose).

Small group ■ Three to five persons who interact together for a purpose, influence one another over a period of time, operate interdependently, share standards and norms, develop a collective identity, and derive satisfaction from the cohesion and commitment in the group.

Many of your classes will require you to work in groups because today's workers participate in more group projects and attend more team meetings than ever before in history. Some people use the terms *group* and *team* interchangeably, but it's important to distinguish between the two. The word **team** identifies an organizational group working together on a class- or work-related project. A **group**, however, is a loose association of at least three people who come together for a wide variety of purposes. Think of a team as a type of group. Any team that is organized for a purpose can be identified as a group, but not all groups are teams. Teams—more often than groups—work together toward overall success, which some groups do not do.

Some groups are exciting and motivating; others are just plain frustrating. What makes some groups a success and others an exasperation? And what's the point of all this group work anyway? More and more organizations allow teams to make decisions that were once handled by individuals. Because organizations use groups to develop products and services and to make important organizational decisions, understanding the critical characteristics of effective group communication in decision making is essential.

You've actually spent a great deal of time in groups already. Your family is a primary group in your life, and the decision-making strategies your family uses have set the stage for how you experience other groups. Were all members of your family involved in discussion, or did your parents make the decisions and then convey them back to you? Were all opinions valued and encouraged, or were some members more credible and thus given more "speaking time" than others? Other groups in your life are also primary if the relationships are more interpersonally linked, more long term, and more influential. **Primary groups** serve to meet some basic need.

In contrast to primary groups, **secondary groups** are those that are less personal— usually shorter term (as in a work group assembled for a specific purpose). As a member of a class, you belong to a secondary group; your work group also fits into this category. In your residence hall or apartment, you belong to another secondary group. These are secondary because they may be of shorter duration. Each of these groups exists for a different purpose and each provides you with varying levels of satisfaction. Think of the most successful groups you belong to. What makes them successful? How do the groups define who you are?

The Small Group

Groups can come in any size, but we usually identify a **small group** as one that includes three to five persons who interact together for a certain purpose, influence one another over a period of time, operate interdependently, share certain standards and norms, develop a collective identity, and derive certain satisfaction from the cohesion and commitment in the group. Let's take this definition one concept at a time.

GROUP SIZE   Group size dramatically impacts the nature of the interaction among individuals. There is some disagreement among scholars as to what *small* means in small groups. Groups, by definition, must have at least three members; two individuals are a *dyad*. Moreover, when there are more than two members, there is always the possibility of an alliance between two members against the other.

So when does a small group stop being small? Some researchers suggest that small groups are most effective when each of the participants can observe and interact with every other member. The *optimal* small group is probably between three and seven members; however, the optimal number will vary depending on the task but will likely not exceed 20.

INTERACTION FOR A PURPOSE   Group members interact with one another for a certain purpose. Individuals who happen to be in the same place at the same time do not necessarily constitute a group. The interaction within the group occurs verbally and nonverbally and, more and more, it occurs through some type of technology (email, teleconferencing, etc.). Again, the group exists for some purpose. For example, did you join a fraternity or sorority because of its philanthropy? Did you join your college or university chapter of Habitat for Humanity to solve the problem of substandard housing?

MUTUAL INFLUENCE   As a member of the group, you will influence and be influenced by every other group member. The knowledge and experience each member brings to the group provides opportunities to teach one another. The attitude you bring about yourself, your priorities, and your willingness to invest time and energy in the group process can also influence the attitudes of other members. This influence is essential to understanding the next element of our definition—interdependence.

INTERDEPENDENCE   The concept of **interdependence** is at the heart of the group process and involves mutual influence. The behavior of each group member influences every other member. When you are in a group, are you the one who remains silent and listens to others? Do you take charge of the group and attempt to directly influence the decision? Do you intentionally or unintentionally speak only to certain group members and ignore others? In each of these cases, whom you communicate with and how you choose to become involved influences the way the group operates. Interdependence also means that no one person is responsible for the group product or outcome. Your level of motivation for your group's project, the manner and timing of your communication with other group members, your attitude toward your group and its members, and the investment you make (or choose not to make) in the process are impacted by every other member of the group and vice versa. While these insights are relevant to your college experience and the group work you likely encounter in a variety of situations, it will become even more important as you move into the working world.

GROUP NORMS   As members come to know one another throughout the group process, the group begins to develop a set of standards, or norms, that guide the group. **Norms** can be either **explicit** (verbally discussed and agreed on) or **implicit** (occurring through repetition of behavior that is not questioned). However they are developed, norms operate like a set of rules for what is appropriate or inappropriate behavior for members throughout the group process. Norms also encompass the shared values and beliefs of the group. Ultimately, they become the procedures by which the group operates. More often than not, the norms evolve implicitly—that is, they are not directly stated but are "accepted" by members through their silence. If Maribeth routinely arrives for group meetings 15 minutes late and none of the group members object, a norm has been created that implicitly accepts Maribeth's tardiness. If Rodney is silent throughout the majority of the group meetings and other members simply "talk around him," Rodney may rightly presume that his silence is acceptable to the group.

In other cases, group members explicitly state norms. Some of your instructors probably state in their syllabi that a certain number of absences from class during the semester may lower your grade. Your university has a set of expectations, or do's and don'ts, that were given to you in the Student Code of Conduct. These rules probably reflect expectations regarding such issues as academic dishonesty, alcohol use in the residence halls, sexual harassment, and a variety of other student behaviors and responsibilities. The key to group effectiveness with regard to norms is the degree to which they are *explicitly stated and agreed on* by members. If members know what is expected of them, they are more likely to act in accordance with the rules and to function more effectively as participants. Norms help us predict behavior and reduce our uncertainty regarding the group process. To the degree that the group depends on implicit or unstated norms only, individuals may not be operating on a common understanding, and, thus, the potential for misunderstanding and frustration increases.

It is helpful to think of norms in three categories: social, task, and procedural norms.

Social Norms.   **Social norms** guide the relationships among group members. To what degree do we self-disclose personal information during meetings? Can we express our feelings toward one another? Is disagreement acceptable to the group? How?

Task Norms.   **Task norms** focus on how decision making and problem solving occur. Will the group collaborate on a solution until all agree? Will one person's position on a subject or task simply be imposed on other group members?

Procedural Norms.   **Procedural norms** govern how members coordinate tasks. Will someone take notes at meetings? Who should group members call if they will miss a

---

Interdependence ■ Mutual influence.

Norms ■ Standards that guide a group.

Explicit norms ■ Norms that are verbally discussed and agreed on.

Implicit norms ■ Norms that occur through repetition of behavior that is not questioned.

Social norms ■ Norms that guide the relationships among group members.

Task norms ■ Norms that focus on how decision making and problem solving occur.

Procedural norms ■ Norms that govern how members coordinate tasks.

Collective identity ■ Established as a result of how the group balances social and task dimensions.

Social dimension ■ The personal relationships among group members.

Task dimension ■ The ways groups make decisions and solve problems.

Cohesion ■ The attraction that group members feel for one another and the degree to which they are willing to work together.

meeting? Who will call to remind members of a meeting? Groups frequently state procedural norms more explicitly; in contrast, social norms are more often understood implicitly. However, norms, from all three categories, that are explicitly discussed can enable the group to be more creative and, ultimately, more satisfied with the outcome.

It is difficult, however, to point out to other group members when the process is not working effectively or when frustration is building. We usually show our frustration and uncertainty nonverbally, while at the same time saying everything is all right. This inconsistency between nonverbal and verbal messages only increases frustration and uncertainty and often works to push members away from the group instead of drawing them into the process.

COLLECTIVE IDENTITY   Throughout the group process, as members interact, influence one another, and develop rules for member behavior, the group begins to establish a **collective identity**. This is established as a result of how the group balances two critical dimensions of the process—the social and task dimensions.

Groups have social purposes and task purposes. The **social dimension** involves the personal relationships among members, the socialization process within the group, and ways in which we allow others opportunities to participate in the group process, or not. The **task dimension** involves the ways groups make decisions and solve problems. How much each member becomes involved with other members, recognizes the social and task dimensions, and works toward a common purpose ultimately impacts the overall effectiveness and success of the group. The group's social and task dimensions must be recognized as having equal influence on the group.

GROUP COHESION   When members of your group are willing to work together to accomplish goals, the group becomes more cohesive. **Cohesion** refers to the attraction that group members feel for one another and the degree to which they are willing to work together. When your group simply divides up the tasks and allows individuals to work alone, you are ignoring the importance of cohesion. Of course, some tasks are best accomplished alone, but at some point the group must come together to accomplish its goals. Cohesive social relationships among group members are just as important as accomplishing the task. Understanding the diversity of members in the group can enhance the relationships among members and increase chances of success in the group. As we have discussed in earlier chapters, openness to the ways we are similar and different is critical to building and maintaining relationships in any context.

Groups have both social and task purposes.

COMMITMENT TO THE GROUP   A final concept of critical importance to effective groups is **commitment**—the willingness to focus on accomplishing a task and on developing relationships among group members. Have you ever participated in a group where members focused on everything else but the group? Perhaps their other classes, their significant others, or their jobs took precedence. We communicate commitment, or lack of commitment, both directly and indirectly. However, remember that the greater the level of commitment among members, the greater the potential for success and effectiveness of the group. When we are committed to the group, we would rather remain in the group and work toward the goal than leave the group.

Commitment ■ Group members' willingness to accomplish a task and develop relationships with each other.

Individual goals ■ The motivations of individual group members.

Group goals ■ The outcomes the whole group seeks to accomplish.

DISTINGUISHING BETWEEN INDIVIDUAL GOALS AND GROUP GOALS

Group goals provide the focus for the task that must be accomplished. As we mentioned earlier, both individual goals and group goals operate throughout the group process.

Individual goals are the motivations of individual members, whereas **group goals** involve the whole group seeking to accomplish a task. As individuals, we join groups for various reasons. They help us satisfy important psychological and social needs, such as those for affection and attention. Groups allow us to accomplish purposes that we would be unable to accomplish alone. They provide us with greater self-knowledge and awareness, as well as world knowledge through the diversity of information group members bring to the discussion. Groups also provide us with a sense of security and belonging. They provide a safe and welcoming environment and contribute to our social identity, providing us with another view of how others see us; this in turn influences our self-concept, self-esteem, and self-respect.

In essence, the group goals become the group's collective purpose. For example, many academic honor societies not only honor achievements but also assist the community through volunteer efforts. Advocacy groups like Greenpeace attempt to change or influence national policy regarding the environment. Religious and social groups seek to influence the value systems by which we operate as citizens within a community. Ultimately, the most effective groups are those in which the individuals learn to meet their individual goals while also staying focused on the group goals. Effective groups also learn to incorporate the individual goals of members within the group process. As is the case in any new relationship, one of the first steps is to engage in information sharing, which serves to reduce the uncertainty we have about what we don't know about another.

By now you should recognize the important role of groups in your personal and professional lives. Groups allow us to use a greater variety of resources in working through complex issues and problems. But when should a group make decisions? Are some decisions best made by individuals? Think back to the decision you made on where to go to college. What information did you need to make that decision, and who else was involved? Teachers? Coaches? Parents? Friends?

Advantages to Working in Groups

When a decision is complex, a group is more likely to make a better decision than an individual. Each person in the group may contribute important information and experience that any sole individual simply does not have. In the group process, we pool our resources, taking advantage of others' knowledge and experience. This pooling of resources also allows the group to identify errors and incomplete information. Working through a complex decision with others also increases our motivation to participate and, ultimately, leads to a more rewarding and satisfying experience. We develop the satisfaction of accomplishing the task and of the companionship that develops among members. When others listen to what we have to say and confirm our knowledge and experience, our self-esteem and self-confidence increase. Groups have a significant advantage as well when there is more than one

Social loafing ■ Occurs when an individual sits back and allows other group members to pick up the workload.

Hidden agenda ■ The unstated personal goals of a selfish group member.

optimal solution to a problem and when the group has significant time to engage in a discussion of alternatives.

Advantages to Working as an Individual

Although groups can be rewarding, they can also be frustrating. Probably one of the most significant potential disadvantages of working in groups is that the process simply takes more time. When groups work effectively, every individual should have the opportunity to participate and contribute to the process. Allowing everyone this opportunity is time consuming. However, the potential for effective and creative decision making is more likely when collective time and energy are invested. Individuals as decision makers work better when there is a single person who has more expertise than others in the group and thus is more qualified to analyze a situation and make a decision. When the group has collapsed into a dysfunctional mess, a single individual may be able to make a decision in the absence of group collaboration or the presence of significant personality issues. However, this should not be construed as permission for one person to take over a group if he or she thinks the group is having problems. The best strategy in this case is to attempt to work through the issues interrupting the group's process. We discuss more on this later in this chapter.

Another common disadvantage of working in groups is the potential for any individual to sit back and let others do the work. A lazy group member can increase the frustration and anger of others. **Social loafing** occurs when an individual allows others to carry the workload. When the workload of another is increased, he or she may label the loafer a "troublemaker" and ostracize him or her from the process. Social loafing can cause stress, frustration, and ostracism and can ultimately lead to poor task attainment and dysfunctional relationships among members.

As we mentioned earlier, sometimes individual and group goals are different. Group members who feel their personal goals are more important than the group's might dominate and attempt to control the group process. When personal goals become more important than group goals, the selfish member usually has a **hidden agenda** (he or she does not explicitly state that his or her goals take precedence over those of the group); this also causes increased frustration and stress. Deciding to use a group to make a decision should be based on the task itself—whether simple or complex—and on whether the group has enough time to reach a good decision. All group members should be encouraged to participate to alleviate the potential for social loafers or hidden agendas.

Social loafing occurs when one individual allows others to carry the workload.

IDENTIFYING TYPES OF GROUPS

You will be a part of a number of types of groups in your life; some, like your family, have been an intricate part of your life since you were born. Others you will join because you choose to do so. We each have our own set of reasons and needs for joining groups, and their impact on our lives is significant. Knowing why we join the groups we join and understanding the purpose of each group is essential to our ability to communicate effectively as a member.

Learning Groups

Learning groups focus on increasing members' knowledge and skills; Barbara Gross Davis (1993) from the University of California at Berkeley describes three subsets of the learning group.

THE INFORMAL LEARNING GROUP This type of learning group might be created ad hoc for a single class period.

THE FORMAL LEARNING GROUP "Formal learning groups are teams established to complete a specific task, such as perform a lab experiment, write a report, carry out a project, or prepare a position paper. These groups may complete their work in a single class session or over several weeks. Typically, students work together until the task is finished, and their project is graded" (http://teaching.berkeley.edu/bgd/collaborative.html). You can expect that throughout your college experience a large number of your classes will require a group project.

THE STUDY GROUP In this type of learning group, students either formally or informally get together to prepare for a class. Davis writes, "Study teams are of stable membership whose primary responsibility is to provide members with support, encouragement, and assistance in completing course requirements and assignments. Study teams also inform their members about lectures and assignments when someone has missed a session. The larger the class and the more complex the subject matter, the more valuable study teams can be."

Therapy Groups

Therapy or growth groups assist members in learning about themselves and solving personal problems. Individuals in these groups come together, usually with the assistance of a therapist leader or someone with substantial experience or training in the area of the group need. An exhaustive list of these groups is impossible to name here, but Alcoholics Anonymous and Mothers Against Drunk Drivers (MADD) are two well-known examples. The aim of this type of group is to enhance self-understanding of members and to provide them with a support system. This is one of the prime examples of the ways in which the group is greater than the sum of the individuals in it. Each group member can ultimately gain significantly greater understanding of himself or herself through the collective knowledge and wisdom of the group.

Problem-Solving Groups

Problem-solving groups often focus on a project external to the group, like research and development teams that design new products or services for organizations. The "problem" that exists is the impetus for the development of the group, and the group exists exclusively to solve the problem. Organizations create problem-solving groups to develop new products, analyze client services, raise funds for new projects, and a host of other issues. Problem-solving groups also can be labeled ad hoc or project committees or task forces.

Social Groups

A final type of group, **social groups**, focus primarily on the belonging needs of the participants. In your college career, you may be interested in joining a sorority or fraternity. These are primarily social groups, but they cross over into other categories depending on the extent to which they are serving needs outside the group. Many fraternities and

Learning groups ■ Groups that focus on increasing the knowledge and skills of their members.

Therapy (or growth) groups ■ Groups that assist members in learning about themselves and solving personal problems.

Problem-solving groups ■ Groups that focus on a project external to the group.

Social groups ■ Groups that focus primarily on the belonging needs of the participants.

Social groups focus on the belonging needs of members.

sororities today are engaging in a broad range of philanthropic activities as part of their mission. In fact, many of the groups discussed here cross over these categories and do not easily fit into just one.

DETERMINING ROLES IN GROUPS

Roles refer to the patterns of behavior we use in the group process. Like norms, some roles are "official" or assigned by the group. In many groups, there are offices like president, vice president, secretary, treasurer, and so forth. Other roles are understood more informally and, like norms, develop throughout the interaction process among members. Role behavior describes what individuals do, not the positions they hold. Informal roles are rarely assigned and are often not even acknowledged. Roles, like norms, belong to the group, not to individuals, though different individuals often share or trade roles at different times in the process.

Three types of roles impact group dynamics—task roles, maintenance or social roles, and individual roles.

Task Roles

Task roles assist group members in goal accomplishment. People who assume task roles *propose* new ideas, *clarify* concepts, or *provide information* to other members in the form of facts, examples, statistics, and so on. In addition, these individuals assist group discussion by offering opinions and examples based on experience. Ultimately, using task roles helps to energize the group process, motivates others to participate, and helps to organize the process of task accomplishment. For example, if LaTia makes an effort to ask other group members what they think of a specific issue or problem as a possible group presentation topic, she is exhibiting an effective task role.

Social or Maintenance Roles

Social (or maintenance) roles help members shape the relationships within the group. People who assume social or maintenance roles focus on the *relationships* among group members. These individuals offer praise or acceptance, mediate disagreements, or encourage less talkative members to participate—all behaviors that impact the group's social dimension. If Jarod makes an effort to thank group members for contributing to a lively and stimulating conversation during a meeting, he is exhibiting an effective social role.

Roles ■ The patterns of behavior we use in the group process.

Task roles ■ Roles that assist group members in goal accomplishment.

Social (or maintenance) roles ■ Roles that help members shape the relationships within the group.

Individual Roles

Individual roles offer group members opportunities to interfere with effective group process. Individuals may disrupt the group process by attempting to focus the group's attention on their own agenda rather than on the group process. Examples of individual role behavior include taking credit for someone else's contribution, attacking another member's remark, or acting in a stubborn or uncooperative manner. Behavior that shows cynicism or lack of enthusiasm for the group and behavior that attempts to gain sympathy from other members also represent individual roles.

Role behavior patterns may either assist the group process or work to inhibit effective group decisions. Every group member must be conscious of the importance of task and maintenance role behavior in the group. The group should confront individual role behavior immediately to prevent that behavior from causing communication problems for the group.

UNDERSTANDING LEADERSHIP IN GROUPS

Leadership refers to the ability to influence others. In the small group, leaders guide followers in reaching goals. Researchers have studied the phenomenon of leadership for several decades and have identified many approaches to it.

Characteristics-Based Approaches to Leadership

In early research, social scientists viewed leadership as a set of traits that an individual exhibited. The **trait approach** presumes that leaders are either born with or cultivate a set of behaviors that "guarantee" they will assume leadership positions. The needed traits included confidence, social skills, intelligence, and charisma. However, in today's society, even if you possess these traits, there is no guarantee that you will become a leader, nor is there a guarantee that these traits will help you become a leader in all situations.

In the **styles approach** to leadership, three different styles were commonly identified with leaders: (1) *autocratic leaders,* who give orders and try to control others; (2) *democratic leaders,* who engage in collective decision making by working toward consensus among group members; and (3) *laissez-faire leaders,* who rely on a "hands-off" approach to leadership and let the group process flow without assistance or input.

In the **functional approach** to leadership, two categories of functions are necessary for effective leadership: task functions and process or relational functions. The basic assumption underlying this theory is that groups vary in the type of task they want to accomplish, the time they have to accomplish it, the skills group members have to accomplish the task, and the nature of relationships among group members. Each of these factors determines the type of leadership behavior needed in the group. When the group is under pressure to solve a problem, the leader coordinates the group's activity and makes sure members have all available information. When the task involves understanding differences, perhaps related to gender or culture, the leader needs to focus on interpersonal communication issues such as honesty, respect, and support.

Process-Based Approaches to Leadership

Over time, scholars have come to understand leadership not as a set of *characteristics* associated with an individual but as a *process* that can be used by any group member or by members collectively. Researchers such as Hersey and Blanchard (1993) suggest that a more effective way of thinking about leadership is to look to **situational factors,** or group context. Leaders adopt a style or approach that meets the requirements of the situation or task as well as those of the relationships between individual group members.

Critical to this analysis is the group members' "readiness" or maturity. Readiness involves an individual's motivation, willingness to take responsibility, knowledge levels, and skills and experiences related to the task that needs to be accomplished. This theory suggests that groups change over time, and leadership should adapt appropriately to these changes. A group beginning a new task, with which it is unfamiliar, needs leadership that can clarify and simplify the task. Later in the process, once the task is clarified, leadership should focus more on the social or relational dimension of the group. Effective leadership

Individual roles ■ Roles that offer group members opportunities to interfere with effective group process.

Leadership ■ The ability to influence others.

Trait approach ■ Presumes that leaders are either born with or cultivate a set of behaviors that guarantee they will assume leadership positions.

Styles approach ■ Identifies three different leadership styles—*autocratic, democratic,* or *laissez-faire.*

Functional approach ■ Identifies two categories of functions that are necessary for effective leadership—*task functions* and *process* (or *relational*) *functions.*

Situational factors ■ Group context that influences a leader's style or approach.

Forming stage ■ The stage in which group members get to know one another and determine how the group process will occur.

Norming stage ■ The stage in which group rules and roles are developed.

in the group should vary depending upon the nature of the task, the individuals who make up the group, and the person engaging in leadership behavior. In addition, leadership skills can be learned, and any group member can adopt leadership behavior. Leadership is thus a set of skills, including the ability to understand the nature of the group and its task and the ability to adopt and modify leadership behavior depending on the group's unique requirements.

Power and leadership are linked in the group. As mentioned in an earlier chapter, every relationship has a power dimension. In the small group, power is not something a member "has" but something that is given in the context of interaction. Power is distributed throughout the group; it rarely belongs to just one person. Group members hold power in differing degrees. Finally, power that is shared by group members has the potential to increase among all participants. Effective leaders, then, must adapt their communication behavior to the power relationships among group members as well as to task or situational factors.

TRACING THE STAGES OF GROUP DEVELOPMENT

Roles often change depending on the phase of the group process. According to many researchers (Tuckman 1965; Tuckman & Jensen 1977; Wheelan & Hochberger 1996; Wheelan & Kaeser 1997), groups go through four phases:

1. forming,
2. norming,
3. storming, and
4. performing.

As Figure 12.1 shows, communication in each of the phases is distinct and serves a specific purpose (Moosbrucker 1988; Wellins, Byham, & Wilson 1991). Researchers may call these phases by different names, but essentially every group experiences, to some degree, each of these stages. The stages do not necessarily occur in order; in fact, some groups may get "stuck" in a particular stage. Other groups may revert to an "earlier" stage during the decision-making process. So while no two groups are identical in terms of the group process, each group will experience some aspects of each of the four stages, which we will now consider in greater detail.

Forming Stage

In the **forming stage**, group members try to get to know one another and to understand how the group process will occur. Like the beginning of all relationships, this is a stage of "feeling our way," of understanding and being able to predict one another's behavior. Group members begin by exchanging basic factual information such as age, hometown, major, and so on. Many groups fail at this stage of group development because group members refuse to engage in the process of relationship development and sharing of experience. This is the level at which the commitment to the group is quite low, and without strategic encouragement, some members never engage in the process. One of the ways to maximize the effectiveness of the group at this phase is to engage in an honest exchange of ideas about what the group values and expectations are. See the boxes "Communication Counts in Your College Experience: How to Engage in Classroom Group Discussion" for more specific strategies to enhance success at this phase in the group's development.

Norming Stage

In the **norming stage**, the rules and roles (often implicitly understood) are developed. Some procedures are adopted, while others are eliminated. At this stage, group members

FIGURE 12.1

Stages of Group Development.

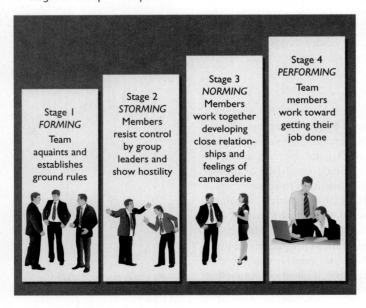

Stage 1
FORMING
Team aquaints and establishes ground rules

Stage 2
STORMING
Members resist control by group leaders and show hostility

Stage 3
NORMING
Members work together developing close relationships and feelings of camaraderie

Stage 4
PERFORMING
Team members work toward getting their job done

COMMUNICATION COUNTS IN YOUR COLLEGE EXPERIENCE

How to Engage Classroom Group Discussion

Drawing on the work of Deemer (1986), Tiberius (1990), and Gardner and Jewler (2003), here are some suggestions to enhance your participation in group discussion.

Guidelines for Interacting with Your Teacher

1. Listen for and learn the ground rules of discussion as either clearly established or implied by the teacher.
2. Avoid asking the same question repeatedly. If you don't understand a concept or explanation and you've attempted to clarify with a question or two, make an appointment with your instructor during his or her office hours for further clarification.

Guidelines for Directing Your Participation in the Group

1. Avoid characterizing your questions as "stupid" before you ever ask them, because very often someone else has the same question.
2. Work at following the conversation so you can put ideas together and make links between them. Offer your insights.
3. Provide examples drawn from your own experience or from information you gleaned in another class or through the media.
4. Ask open-ended question that further discussion, rather than squelch it with decisive statements.
5. Stick to the subject and speak briefly.
6. Avoid long stories or anecdotes.

7. Don't shift topics until there's a lull in the conversation and doing so seems appropriate. You can even ask, "Does anyone else have something to say on this subject, before we move to another topic?"
8. Don't wait to speak until every idea is complete. Speaking will often help you form your ideas in the moment.
9. Don't be afraid to disagree. If you don't share another's view, say so; explain why.
10. Offer reasons, not just reactions, although it's okay to express how you feel and how you think.
11. Criticize ideas, not people. You may disagree with someone's ideas without being unkind or uncivil to him or her as a person.
12. Encourage everyone to participate. Leave room for everyone to speak and kindly invite those who are quiet to add their comments.
13. Listen to everyone's ideas even if you don't particularly like all of the individuals or their ideas.
14. Try to paraphrase, pose a question, or encourage a classmate to say more if you don't understand what he or she has said.
15. Invite others to disagree with you and assure them that you are receptive to it.
16. Don't interrupt others while they are speaking.
17. Focus on gaining information or insight, not on winning an argument or being right.
18. Work at linking your comments to the previous speaker's insights; develop a fabric of ideas that are knit together rather than disjointed.

---

may try out different patterns of interaction to see which might fit the group. Tomoko may be silent in the meetings, and yet no group member discusses the silence directly with her; as a result, a group norm has been developed that essentially states, "Tomoko can be silent." As we discussed in Chapter 7 in the section on communication dialectics, individuals in relationships must work out the degree to which they are dependent, independent, and interdependent. The relationships among group members are no different in this regard. In developing the norms within a group, the members will enhance the potential for successful group decision making when they are interdependent. As you can see in "Communication Counts in Your Career: Dependence, Independence, and Interdependence," Stephen Covey, the author of *The 7 Habits of Highly Effective People* provides strategies for enhancing the interdependence of group members.

Storming Stage

In the **storming stage**, conflict emerges as members negatively react to norms and roles. If norms are implicitly accepted, as with Tomoko's silence, and individual members fail to speak out about this as an issue, the effectiveness of the process is compromised. Also, if members feel that a role they are uncomfortable with has been thrust upon them, they will rebel, either directly through verbal confrontation or indirectly by withdrawing from interaction with certain members. Storming is a critical stage in the group process. If the group ignores or fails to resolve conflict within this stage, decision making and satisfaction are negatively affected. Groups that are willing to risk confrontation and that work to resolve conflict during this stage are more creative and effective in the long run.

Storming stage ■ The stage in which group conflict emerges as members react to norms and rules negatively.

Dependence, Independence, and Interdependence

Groups function well when members are interdependent, which we have defined as having *mutual influence*. Here are some additional insights that may help you communicate in groups. Some of this information is drawn from Stephen Covey's book *The 7 Habits of Highly Effective People*.

Dependence

If you are *dependent,* you rely on others to get what you want; you are reliant. As a result, if you don't get what you want, you complain and blame. It's always someone else's fault. You do not see yourself as being in control of your own life; rather, your life is controlled by other people or outside forces. This is sometimes referred to as "the locus of control," or where you place control—in yourself or in others. If you locate control in yourself, you have an "internal locus of control"; if you believe others control your life, you have an "external locus of control." If you are dependent, you stress the external locus of control and your keyword of reference is *you.* As a result, like most dependent people, you will make statements such as, "It's my boss's fault that I didn't get the job done in time; he didn't give me enough time" or "My coworker makes me so mad when he isn't considerate of my feelings!" or "I didn't really want to go to the departmental picnic, but everyone else seemed to be going so what was I supposed to do?" We can symbolize dependent people by the letter *A.* The letter *A* has two stems that lean on each other and one stem that connects them. If we remove any of the three stems, the letter collapses; it cannot stand alone. If you are a dependent person, you are like the letter *A*; you cannot stand alone without the support of others.

Independence

If you are *independent,* you rely on yourself to get what you want; you are self-reliant. As Covey (1989) puts it, "You act rather than being acted upon." Or to use another of Covey's favorite words, you are "proactive." As a result, you hold yourself accountable for your behavior and the subsequent

results. You recognize that you—not others—control your life. As an independent person, you possess an internal locus of control and your keyword of reference is *I.* As a result, you make statements such as, "I didn't get the job done in time because I didn't anticipate the time demands adequately" or "I feel angry at my coworker when he is inconsiderate of how I feel" or "I decided not to go to the departmental picnic, even though I knew several others were intending to go." We can symbolize independent people by the letter *I* because this letter stands alone without requiring support.

Interdependence

If you are *interdependent,* you rely on yourself, but you recognize the value of working harmoniously with others to get what everyone wants. As a result, you don't abandon your own ideas, but you look for ways to understand and to develop mutually beneficial results for all concerned. You recognize that when people work together effectively, they can reach a new level of problem solving that joins ideas in a creative and unforeseen result. To again use Covey's (1989) language, you "think win–win," you "seek first to understand and then to be understood," and you "synergize." Although you still possess an internal locus of control, your keyword of reference is *we.* Consequently, you make statements such as, "My boss and I can work together to ensure that I finish projects in a timely fashion" or "When I feel angry at my coworker for being inconsiderate, we can work on it together so that our relationship grows" or "I can shift my view of the departmental picnic and see it as a time to work on networking and building trusting relationships, rather than satisfying an implied directive." We can symbolize interdependent people by the letter *H.* Notice that the letter *H* essentially has two *I*s and a connecting stem. The two major stems *can* stand alone, but because they are connected and can provide mutual support, they work together to create a new symbol.

The following chart summarizes this information:

	Locus of Control	Keyword	Symbol	Communication Result
Dependence	External	You	A	Complaining and blaming
Independence	Internal	I	I	Personal responsibility
Interdependence	Internal	We	H	Cooperative problem solving

Performing Stage

In the **performing stage,** groups have decided to either risk confrontation and resolve the conflict or ignore the conflict and act as if nothing is wrong. At this stage, how individuals "perform" toward each other or how the group performs toward outsiders becomes the focus of the group process. The deadline is fast approaching, the presentation is due in two days, and the group has got to get on with it. The critical challenge to the group is whether to "act" through the storming (by ignoring problems) or to address the conflict and work to resolve it.

Performing stage ■ The stage in which group members risk confrontation and resolve conflict or ignore conflict.

Through each of these stages of group development, attention to both the group's task needs and social needs is critical. Group members should not rush the task just to "get it done." They should also nurture the relationships among group members to increase motivation and satisfaction with the process and with the outcome. Attending to the group process is even more critical for groups that have long-term associations. In addition to these four phases of the group process, groups are also influenced by variables such as gender differences in communication and cultural influences within and outside the group.

APPRECIATING CULTURE, VALUES, AND GENDER IN GROUPS

The group process of developing norms, roles, and collective identity culminates in the development of a **group culture.** This encompasses the values and beliefs shared by members, the language or symbols used in interaction, the rituals that group members enact in the group process, and the behaviors that evolve from these elements. This culture, or personality, is created and maintained by the group and influenced by the larger culture in which it belongs. The larger culture significantly influences group structure and dynamics and provides a second way of examining the concept. Culture is not static but changeable, depending on the situation and needs of group members.

At the heart of group culture is the **value system** that guides the development of norms, roles, and structure. Each of us interacts in our relationships based on our individual moral principles and values. Values guide us to determine what behavior is right or wrong, and thus ethical or unethical. Values flow from the larger culture to which we belong and from the nature of the significant relationships in our lives. We come to the group and engage in interaction based on our value system, and yet we must also understand the value systems of others for the group to develop its own unique process. When individuals share their values and work collaboratively and explicitly to develop a larger set of values for the group, they maximize the potential for group effectiveness.

How can the group develop a set of values and principles that guides appropriate and ethical behavior? The principle of **equality** is at the heart of ethical groups. *Equality* refers to such things as the right to speak and be heard and to the way group norms should be applied to every group member. Philosopher Immanuel Kant suggested the rules should be created and applied to everyone with equal weight. He also admonished against using others to achieve our own selfish desires. Rather, every human being should be valued for his or her unique knowledge, experience, and potential.

Most of us also believe in the principle of honesty in communicating with others. What does it mean to you to be honest or dishonest with someone? If we are honest, we do not intentionally deceive another. When we are dishonest, we intentionally deceive directly (by direct misstatement) or indirectly (by omitting information that leads to misinterpretation). Where and how might honesty and sensitivity to others come into conflict? What other ethical principles do you think should guide interaction among group members? Review the principles of ethical communication in Chapter 1. How do these ethical principles apply in group communication?

Gender significantly influences group interaction and the development of a group culture. As we have discussed, the issue is not who are "better" communicators; the issue is trying to understand the nature of the differences in communication and working through these differences to reach a common understanding. Gender research suggests that in mixed-sex groups, men tend to determine topics of conversation and to talk more. Men also tend to focus more on the group's task dimension. In contrast, women tend to be more affirming or positive in response to others' comments and tend to focus more on the nature of the relationships among members. While there are differences in how women and men communicate, research has found little difference between the ability of women and men to solve problems or make decisions.

Group culture ■ The values and beliefs shared by group members.

Value system ■ Guides the development of norms, roles, and structure within a group.

Equality ■ Applying group norms to every member.

Culture Counts

Gender is a significant factor in group interaction.

Women, in general, tend to use a more cooperative style when interacting with group members and are more likely to share resources. For instance, when Kara gives an example from her experience, Sela shares a similar story. In this way, Sela confirms Kara's example, in effect saying, "We're the same." This sharing of similar stories, however, is often perceived by men as being weak. In contrast, men tend toward a more competitive style, often seen by women as aggressive. When Dominic tells the group of his experience, Kyle tries to "top" the story with one of his own. Kyle is saying, in effect, "My experience is even more relevant to our discussion." The point is that neither gender's approach is right or wrong in this instance. Group members must recognize that differences in style are a product of ways of thinking and behaving that have developed since early childhood. The goal for group members, then, is to understand how differences in style affect interpretation of meanings between women and men. The most effective groups are those that recognize what particular style is most appropriate to the interaction. If commitment and cohesiveness are to characterize an effective group, then a range of style options for communicating maximizes the potential for the group to succeed.

SOLVING PROBLEMS IN GROUPS

Perhaps the most important goal of every group is to develop a process by which problems may be solved, decisions may be made that prove worthwhile to the task, and satisfaction with the group process may be derived. Every group must establish a strategy that optimizes good solutions and decisions. The process developed by the group to make decisions is a reflection of the goals, norms, and roles and the group's structure and culture. Is there one perfect problem-solving strategy? No. Yet, having any strategy is better than having no strategy at all. In the next section, we explore a range of approaches that may assist groups in working toward good decisions.

Supportive and Defensive Climates

Before exploring how groups make decisions, we refer back to our discussion in Chapter 7 on the issue of **climate**. Climate is the "feel" of the group and involves the degree of cohesiveness among members, their willingness to communicate with one another, and the tone of that communication. As we discussed earlier, Gibb (1961) described two ends of a continuum in terms of climate. At one end are *supportive* climates where members feel positively toward each other and toward the group task. At the other end are *defensive* climates, characterized by individuals who monopolize the process and discount one another.

To develop a supportive climate, effective groups must have individual members who can describe one another's point of view, focus their discussion on the best solution for a problem, react honestly and spontaneously to other members' contributions, show empathy toward fellow members, minimize status differences, and remain flexible to the changing needs and information obtained by others.

In contrast, defensive groups are characterized by *evaluation,* where group members judge one another in words or tone of voice. For example, a defensive group member may show superiority and a belief in the rightness of her own opinions and not those of others. Defensiveness occurs also when group members lack sensitivity for the feelings of others or use deceit to manipulate group members. As a result, the degree to which the group develops a supportive or defensive climate significantly impacts the amount of conflict the group will encounter and will determine how that conflict is managed.

Whether the group develops a more supportive or more defensive climate will impact many other elements in the group process. For example, the group that develops a more defensive climate will likely also develop norms more implicitly than explicitly, and the potential for misunderstanding and frustration will increase. Groups that are characterized by defensiveness will find accomplishing the task much more difficult. The social dimension of defensive groups is poorly developed, and individuals will likely lack interest or motivation in the final outcome. Defensive climates encourage social loafing and free riding, as discussed earlier. Therefore, the level of satisfaction with the process is much lower in defensive groups.

In the group that has developed a supportive climate, however, the social dimension is considered as important as the task. Group members feel a strong sense of cohesion

Climate ■ The degree of cohesiveness among group members, their willingness to communicate with each other, and the tone of that communication.

and gain energy and motivation in belonging. Creativity is the most important advantage in groups with a supportive climate. Members in supportive groups are willing to engage in more creative brainstorming and are willing to take more creative risks that can lead to a more innovative and effective outcome. Supportive climates also encourage group members to engage in the process in more appropriate and ethical ways. When we communicate a sense of equality and spontaneity, and when we encourage others to do the same, we enhance the ethics of our communication and relationships. In addition, supportive group climates encourage more effective management of conflict.

Types of Conflict

The ways the group manages or mismanages conflict inevitably flow from its implicit or explicit norms. Yet conflict resolution is critical to group effectiveness and creativity. The group's ability to develop a process that will allow it to effectively proceed through the phases of the group is dependent on its ability to manage conflict. Conflict is inevitable. It is not a matter of *if* the group will experience conflict but rather *how* it will develop strategies to deal with the conflict effectively. Think back to how conflict was handled in your family. Were you taught to ignore the conflict and hope it would resolve itself? Did your family "argue it out" until consensus was reached or until participants were exhausted and gave up? Did one individual dominate the conflict process? In our culture, it is common to not manage conflict at all. Women in particular are taught that it is unacceptable to engage in conflict. Men are often taught that they must stand up for themselves and fight it out, or they're not men.

There are different types of conflict and various ways to resolve it. Miller and Steinberg (1975) have identified three types of conflict: pseudoconflict, simple or content conflict, and ego conflict.

PSEUDOCONFLICT **Pseudoconflict** is due to misperceptions; participants perceive they have a conflict, but in reality they are in agreement. Pseudoconflict often involves the mistaken notion that participants are in a win–lose situation. If I win, you lose, and if you win, I lose. To illustrate, Janine and Stephan are constantly misunderstanding each other in group discussions because their different religious backgrounds create perceptions that are barriers to agreement. These perceived differences cause them to listen poorly and misinterpret information. If they were to set aside their differences, they might realize they agree on the group's proposed solution to the task. Pseudoconflict is often called "fake" because it really doesn't exist. It is often resolved by clarifying issues and recognizing where agreement exists. One possible source of pseudoconflict may be a difference in communication style across cultures. We have mentioned several times in this text that cross-cultural communication can provide opportunities for increased knowledge, as well as problems between communicators who are unwilling to understand cultural differences. Misunderstanding as a result of cross-cultural communication is pseudoconflict because the participants in the conversation perceive disagreements and problems that are not truly intended by the other.

CONTENT CONFLICT **Content (or procedural) conflict** occurs when people disagree over facts, definitions, implications, solutions, or procedure. For example, your group's project is to investigate homelessness in your city by researching its causes and effects. As your group begins, your first question might be, "What is the definition of homelessness?" Can someone be homeless for a night? A week? Does it mean no permanent address? The group might also ask, "What subgroups make up the homeless population?" If individuals in your group disagree over the definition of homelessness or the types of people who are most likely to be homeless, the group is experiencing content conflict. Group members can resolve this type of conflict with solid research that uses credible sources in defining basic facts and implications. When individuals attempt to verify facts, test inferences, and develop concrete criteria for solutions, this conflict is managed effectively.

A related but more complicated type of conflict may occur in the group when individuals hold different values on some issue. This is more difficult to resolve because our values are personal and deeply held. For example, in your group's discussion of homelessness, members might disagree on the role of government in this issue. Some may

Pseudoconflict ■ Situation in which the parties are actually in agreement, but perceptions and misunderstanding prevent them from seeing the areas of agreement and compatibility.

Content (or procedural) conflict ■ Occurs when people disagree over facts, definitions, implications, solutions, or procedure.

Ego (or power) conflict ■ A conflict in which the issue, problem, or task becomes lost in the fight for position.

Assertive style ■ Communicating honestly and clearly explaining one's ideas and beliefs without harming another.

Aggressive style ■ Forcing one's position on others without allowing for their input.

Nonassertive style ■ Suppressing one's own feelings because of shyness, laziness, or fear that other group members will dislike you.

value government intervention in the lives of those who are less fortunate. Other members might believe that individuals must take responsibility for their own lives. Often resolutions are effective when participants "agree to disagree" about which values are *most* important and focus instead on solutions that meet the needs of as many parties as possible. Participants also must listen to one another and allow others to express their values without needing to agree.

EGO CONFLICT   Finally, groups also may encounter **ego (or power) conflict.** This type of conflict has the greatest potential for destroying the group process. In this case, participants are so intent on "winning" that they tie winning and losing to their self-concept and self-worth. The conflict becomes one of who has the most power and influence over other members. For individuals who want to win more than they want the group to win, it is unacceptable to "lose" the conflict. The issue, problem, or task becomes lost in the fight for position. Alexa wants the group to choose the portrayal of women in advertising as its topic because she has done extensive research in this area for another class. She dominates group discussions and finds problems with any other topic under discussion. It is only when participants recognize the relationship between ego and conflict strategy that resolution is possible. If this conflict is to be managed, group members must focus on the process of resolution, not on the positions of participants. Identifying the common ground among group members is essential.

Styles of Conflict Resolution

Emotions play a large role in whether conflict will be managed successfully or not. Emotions are hard to control and easy to inflame. Most of us have not been taught effective conflict management strategies, and thus we feel helpless when conflict arises. But conflict can be managed successfully in the group process. Group members may choose to manage conflict through assertiveness, aggressiveness, or nonassertiveness.

ASSERTIVENESS   The **assertive style** is often referred to as a "caring selfishness." Assertiveness's intent is to communicate honestly and explain clearly your ideas and beliefs without harming another. When you are assertive, you refuse to become a victim, yet you allow the other group members the same degree of opportunity to assert their ideas and beliefs. Assertive people recognize that rights and responsibilities apply equally to all participants. The primary focus of assertiveness is on negotiating for a solution that meets the needs of all participants.

AGGRESSIVENESS   The **aggressive style** of conflict management forces positions on others without allowing for their input. Aggressive group members are insensitive, selfish, stubborn, and pushy. The aggressive individual ignores other people's beliefs and values, refusing to recognize their validity. Often these individuals believe that to allow others their point of view automatically means they must agree with them. Usually the individual simply refuses to listen. But simply because we listen to others' points of view does not imply we must agree with them. We listen because other human beings have value. If equality is to be a principle that guides the group, every opinion, position, or point of view must be heard.

NONASSERTIVENESS   Group members who exhibit a **nonassertive style** suppress their own feelings. Individuals are afraid other group members may no longer like them if they express their feelings. Sometimes group members are simply too shy to speak up for their beliefs. Other times, group members are nonassertive because they are lazy.

Both aggressive and nonassertive styles prevent effective conflict resolution and prolong the conflict. Both of these styles stem from too much focus on self and not enough on the others involved in the conflict. However, each of us must develop a degree of assertiveness if our communication is to be effective, satisfying, and ethical. Assertiveness is an honest yet caring communication style. It is a communication strategy with many rewards, both for individuals and for the group process. If a group develops a norm of using an assertive style of conflict management, its task is accomplished more effectively with the maximum resources shared among group members. Also, the relationships among group members are more satisfying when individuals communicate with honesty and care.

Refer back to our discussion of conflict management in Chapter 7. Group members also may try to manage conflict by avoiding, competing, accommodating, or compromising. The most appropriate strategy for the greatest number of decisions, however, is collaboration. In this next section, we discuss the critical role of collaboration in the group decision-making process.

MAKING QUALITY DECISIONS IN GROUPS

Our democratic society loves to vote. Despite the fact that many Americans do not vote in elections, we still use the vote as one of the easiest ways to make a group decision. When all else fails, take a vote. After all, majority rules, right? A related strategy in choosing a solution to a problem is to flip a coin. What movie do we see tonight? Flip a coin. What restaurant shall we go to? Flip a coin. When we are trying to be more objective about a situation, we'll call in an expert. Then the decision is out of our hands. If the solution doesn't work, we can say it was the expert's fault, not ours.

In small groups, we often defer to the leader for his or her position on the issue. Again, if the solution doesn't work, we can blame it on the leader. Organizations often create a subcommittee that is charged with making decisions. Other groups simply refuse to make a decision or stall until the decision is unnecessary. In each of these cases, the strategy of choice has many problems. Ultimately, someone is dissatisfied with the outcome, either because his or her voice wasn't heard or because it was ignored. In each of these examples, the solution is dependent on one individual, and the group has failed to fulfill a critical obligation of effective group process—collaboration.

Collaboration involves assertiveness and cooperation. A collaborative group makes an effort to hear all sides of an issue, all information relevant to a decision, and all members' points of view. Collaborative groups believe that the best decisions are those that look creatively at solutions and information, and members attempt to develop solutions that meet the parameters of the problem and the needs of the participants. Collaboration involves input from all members to work toward a solution. The following model of effective decision making is an approach that has excellent potential for maximizing group collaboration.

The Reflective-Thinking Approach

A standard process in small groups occurs when the assignment has been given or the task identified; group members jump straight to the solution stage without thooughly analyzing the situation. Often these solutions are attempts to maximize efficiency (speed)—not effectiveness (suitability). The more group members are willing to work creatively and suspend judgments about a specific solution, the more the process will flow smoothly and generate the best solution in the end. The *reflective-thinking framework* was developed by John Dewey (1910) in recognition of this tendency to jump to solutions. While not a perfect strategy, it is one of the most effective and commonly used means of small-group decision making. Figure 12.2 outlines the components of the framework.

So, as we stated before, when group members are willing to work creatively and suspend judgments about a specific solution, the process will flow more smoothly and provide the best opportunity for the most effective solution. This process involves research and a clear understanding of the problem or task. Moreover, all the group's resources must be used to maximum advantage for the process to be successful. This means group members must be willing to provide input, to become part of the process, and to be committed to a collaborative group effort.

Brainstorming: Creativity Is the Key

One of the most common roadblocks to the group decision-making process is when group members fail to suggest, or refuse to think imaginatively about, possible solutions. Contemporary theorists on problem solving refer to this creativity as "thinking outside the box." Many of today's organizations now seek to recruit divergent thinkers or those who come up with new and original ideas. Divergent thinkers take risks, and brainstorming involves risks. The premise of brainstorming is that all ideas are relevant,

Collaboration ■ Incorporating assertiveness and cooperation in decision making.

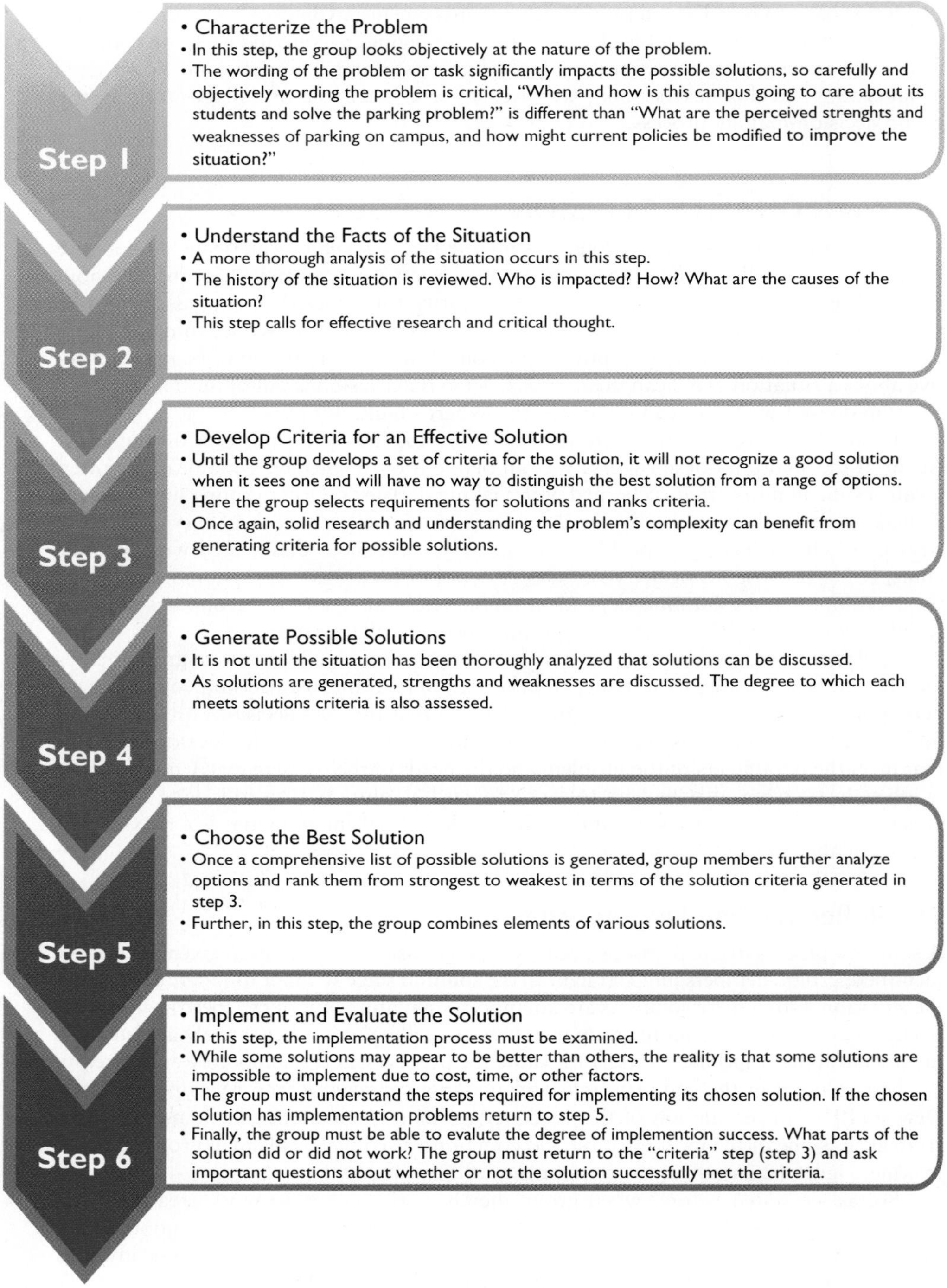

- **Characterize the Problem**
  - In this step, the group looks objectively at the nature of the problem.
  - The wording of the problem or task significantly impacts the possible solutions, so carefully and objectively wording the problem is critical, "When and how is this campus going to care about its students and solve the parking problem?" is different than "What are the perceived strenghts and weaknesses of parking on campus, and how might current policies be modified to improve the situation?"

Step 1

- **Understand the Facts of the Situation**
  - A more thorough analysis of the situation occurs in this step.
  - The history of the situation is reviewed. Who is impacted? How? What are the causes of the situation?
  - This step calls for effective research and critical thought.

Step 2

- **Develop Criteria for an Effective Solution**
  - Until the group develops a set of criteria for the solution, it will not recognize a good solution when it sees one and will have no way to distinguish the best solution from a range of options.
  - Here the group selects requirements for solutions and ranks criteria.
  - Once again, solid research and understanding the problem's complexity can benefit from generating criteria for possible solutions.

Step 3

- **Generate Possible Solutions**
  - It is not until the situation has been thoroughly analyzed that solutions can be discussed.
  - As solutions are generated, strengths and weaknesses are discussed. The degree to which each meets solutions criteria is also assessed.

Step 4

- **Choose the Best Solution**
  - Once a comprehensive list of possible solutions is generated, group members further analyze options and rank them from strongest to weakest in terms of the solution criteria generated in step 3.
  - Further, in this step, the group combines elements of various solutions.

Step 5

- **Implement and Evaluate the Solution**
  - In this step, the implementation process must be examined.
  - While some solutions may appear to be better than others, the reality is that some solutions are impossible to implement due to cost, time, or other factors.
  - The group must understand the steps required for implementing its chosen solution. If the chosen solution has implementation problems return to step 5.
  - Finally, the group must be able to evelute the degree of implemention success. What parts of the solution did or did not work? The group must return to the "criteria" step (step 3) and ask important questions about whether or not the solution successfully met the criteria.

Step 6

FIGURE 12.2
The Reflective-Thinking Approach.

at least initially. The group must create a supportive culture that encourages every member to provide his or her ideas. The first rules of brainstorming are that no idea is unacceptable and no ideas are judged. Members are encouraged to work off of one another's ideas to build, not dismantle. When judgment is suspended, members are less inhibited in making suggestions. Motivation is increased; members become more enthusiastic and, thus, take more creative risks. It is critical that group members truly suspend judgment.

Groupthink and Decision Making

Some groups, however, may get caught up in simply expediting the task or in focusing on agreement instead of on quality decision making. Psychology professor Irving R. Janis (1972) believes that ineffective decision making is often the result of a phenomenon he calls **groupthink.** Dr. Janis defines groupthink as "a mode of thinking that occurs when people are deeply involved in a cohesive group, when desire for unanimity overrides a realistic appraisal of alternatives." Thinking alike and groupthink are two different matters. Engaging in a discussion that clarifies people's positions and experiences is helpful to group decision making. Groupthink leads to bad decisions within the group.

On January 28, 1986, the space shuttle *Challenger* lifted off from the Kennedy Space Center in Florida but exploded 73 seconds later, killing all seven astronauts and a civilian on board. The civilian, Christa McAuliffe, was to become the first "teacher in space." On Saturday, February 1, 2003, the space shuttle *Columbia* broke up as it returned to Earth after a 16-day mission. The investigating bodies for both of these shuttle disasters concurred that in addition to mechanical causes for both accidents (a faulty O-ring seal for *Challenger* and foam striking a wing on *Columbia*), faulty decision making played a role. Both of these tragedies are classic cases of groupthink that resulted in catastrophe—the loss of 14 astronauts and the sullied image of the space program were just two of the many negative consequences of these bad decisions.

Janis offers eight symptoms the group must be alert to when trying to avoid groupthink:

1. **Illusion of invulnerability:** We often feel that our knowledge and experience will shelter us from bad decisions. NASA had launched 24 successful shuttle flights with faulty O-ring seals prior to the *Challenger* mission. *Columbia* was the oldest shuttle in the fleet and had landed "successfully" on each prior mission. The decision makers simply did not believe that the launches would fail.

2. **Belief in the group's inherent morality:** Group members believe they are right because they are on the "right" side or because they feel their values and beliefs are supported by some higher authority. NASA officials became so caught up in the importance of space flight and of the need to expand knowledge that they failed to recognize the safety concerns of engineers.

3. **Collective rationalization:** If we believe we are invulnerable to failure or that our decision stems from the only appropriate value system, we engage in lengthy rationalization to support our decision. Decision makers at the Marshall Space Flight Center on the night before *Challenger*'s launch went to great lengths to justify the pro-launch

Groupthink ■ A mode of thinking that occurs when people are deeply involved in a cohesive group and desire for unanimity overrides a realistic appraisal of alternatives.

decision. After the *Columbia* tragedy, NASA repeatedly suggested that foam couldn't possibly damage the shuttle wing tiles.

4. **Stereotyped views of "out-group" members:** If "outsiders" raise objections or suggest reevaluation of the decision, groups often ridicule or downplay the outsider's motivation, knowledge, or credibility. There were two engineers at Morton Thiokol (the manufacturer of the faulty O-ring seal) who argued against the launch of *Challenger* due to cold temperatures expected at the time of the launch. Tragically, upper-level decision makers at NASA succeeded in discounting the engineers' objections because the engineers could not prove absolutely that the launch would fail. After *Columbia*, memos surfaced suggesting NASA engineers also were concerned about wing tiles (Tompkins 2005).

5. **Direct pressure on dissenters:** If group "insiders" raise objections, other members may apply pressure through direct or indirect threat. In this way, dissenters are "shouted down" and may decide objections are unsafe. After the disaster, engineers reported that during the decision-making process the night before the *Challenger* launch, they saw a "look" in the eyes of their superiors at Morton Thiokol. Said engineer Roger Boisjoly, "You know that look; it's the look you get just before you get fired."

6. **Self-censorship of dissenters:** When we look at other members of the group and think they are in agreement, we simply decide not to speak, whether we have objections or not. As other engineers at Morton Thiokol observed the reaction to Boisjoly, the engineer who argued against the launch, they decided their objections would carry no weight and refused to speak up. Even Boisjoly reported that once management had overruled his objections, there was no point in pushing the subject any further, and he remained silent.

7. **Shared illusion of unanimity:** When members engage in self-censorship and fail to raise objections, their silence implies consent. We have no choice but to interpret silence as consent to our point of view without any other evidence of disagreement. Once the teleconference between Morton Thiokol and the Marshall Space Flight Center was over and the decision to launch *Challenger* had been approved, no information was passed to the next decision-making level regarding the objections of Thiokol engineers. The highest-level decision makers at NASA thus believed that the decision to launch *Challenger* had been unanimous.

8. **Emergence of mindguards:** When we believe that our position or opinion has little or no value to others, we refrain from any dissent. Over time, this feeling is modified to the point where we do not even entertain critical thoughts. Mindguards prevent us from considering another point of view; we simply "block" information from our mind or avoid sources of information that might contradict our point of view. NASA officials who were part of the *Challenger* decision refused to explore additional sources of information that might have been relevant to the issue of temperature on the launchpad at the time of the scheduled launch. Similarly, when engineers expressed concern over possible tile damage on *Columbia* missions, NASA disregarded the potential dangers of the foam.

Preventing Groupthink

Groupthink is a very dangerous phenomenon that group members must be aware of when making decisions. There are several ways the group can prevent groupthink. First, all members must understand and be alert to the symptoms of groupthink. Second, engaging in critical assessment of all decisions is crucial. At least one group member must be willing to play devil's advocate during the decision-making process to guard against faulty decisions. Using outside experts, considering alternative scenarios thoroughly, and setting aside the decision until members can consider it further are also strategies that can serve to prevent groupthink.

When group members thoroughly understand the problem or issue within the group, when the group has clearly articulated criteria for decision making, when the group has thoroughly studied a wide range of options for solving the problem, when all available information has been weighed, analyzed, and discussed clearly and openly, and when the communication within the group is open and supportive, then the potential for groupthink to occur is minimal (Wilson 2005). This true engagement in a group takes courage and commitment; but ultimately it will result in a more effective and satisfying group experience.

BECOMING A COMPETENT AND ETHICAL GROUP MEMBER IN COLLEGE, CAREER, AND LIFE

As you begin your college career, consider investigating the numerous groups on campus that can add to your college experience. Check your college website for a list of student organizations. There are a variety of student groups on campus that address a range of interests, activities, and concerns. Given that involvement with college life is fundamentally important to a student's learning, satisfaction, and development (Astin 1984), student organizations provide an immediate way for you to become linked to your campus. Investing some time in discovering and linking with student groups can help offset problems, while immeasurably enhancing your college experience.

Additionally, given that many campuses are stressing service learning and experiential learning, you are likely to be engaged in group class projects that focus on serving the needs of organizations in your community. In many courses, your instructors will expect you to engage in classroom discussion. As one international student explained, "My father told me before coming to America to the university, 'They don't care how much you know; they just want you to talk about what you do know.'" While this may be an overstatement, it is true that higher education in the United States relies heavily on oral interaction. Though you may find it difficult, we encourage you to engage in classroom discourse—offer your opinions, ask questions, draw links between classroom content and your lived experience.

When you graduate and enter the work world, group and team projects will probably be part of your job. Many corporations and businesses have moved to a "flatter" organizational structure, rather than a hierarchical one. This means that employees are often in work teams or productivity groups and have a greater share of decision making. This suggests that you should not focus on merely surviving the group experience but on making that process work for you, the group, and the organization. One of the most successful organizations in the world is the Mayo Clinic, a nonprofit service organization that has been in operation for more than 100 years. One of the founding principles of this organization is a collaborative approach to patient care that puts the needs of the patient above all other interests or issues (Berry and Seltman 2008). Each patient team is developed with an open and supportive communication climate, and information about the patient is readily accessible to every member of the team at any moment. Because every person who works at the Mayo Clinic believes in the value of patient care above all, each team enacts this value throughout the course of the patient's stay at Mayo.

When teams work well in the workplace, productivity and profit increase (Armstrong 2010) and employee turnover and absenteeism decrease. The key to success in workplace teams is communication: open, collaborative, supportive, goal-driven, and value-based.

Groups are also fundamentally important to community endeavors. Never underestimate the power of a group to influence a decision, accomplish a task, or address a community need. For example, the Boys and Girls Clubs of America—which serves 3.6 million young people in all 50 states, Puerto Rico, the Virgin Islands, and military bases at home and abroad—began in 1860 as the result of several women in Hartford, Connecticut, who decided to provide a positive alternative for boys who roamed the streets. Similar stories abound about the genesis of other organizations. Therefore, as you pursue your college education and, later, your work, remember the enduring value of community engagement as a way to contribute to and receive from others. As many testify, you are likely to find that you receive considerably more than you give.

All of us know what it feels like to work in a group that lacks cohesion and commitment. Maybe someone's individual goals became more important than the group's goals. Maybe you felt voiceless in the group process and decided to withdraw from interaction completely. The point is that, despite your past familiarity with negative group experience, you can develop more effective group communication skills.

The group communication process is inevitably complex. While you are in college, you will join some groups because of your interest in their activities and because you desire to create and maintain friendships. However, some groups will be formed for class projects and activities, and the group membership may be beyond your control. You cannot control the personalities of other group members, but you can control your communication responses to their personalities and behaviors. You can also control the ways in which you communicate—both verbally and nonverbally—about your expectations of others and of the group process, and you can control how you communicate your value judgments of

COMMUNICATION COUNTS IN YOUR LIFE

Parker Palmer's "Touchstones"

The following was *adapted from Century College Center for Teaching and Learning and the writings of Parker Palmer* http://ctlcentury.project.mnscu.edu/index.asp?Type=NONE &SEC={444F09EA-265B-41DF-AFE0-736ED1F45955}

> Formation is journeying, individually and in community, to our inner selves, our hearts and souls, to identify our true selves and our deep integrity. From this center proceeds our action. —Parker J. Palmer

Ideas that increase the likelihood of working productively in a group:

1. **Be 100 percent present, extending and presuming welcome.** Set aside the usual distractions of things undone from yesterday, things to do tomorrow. Bring all of yourself to the work.
2. **Listen deeply.** Listen intently to what is said; listen to the feelings beneath the words. Listen to yourself as well as to others. Strive to achieve a balance between listening and reflecting, speaking and acting.
3. **It is never "share or die."** You will be invited to share. The invitation is exactly that. You determine the extent to which you want to participate in discussions and activities.
4. **No fixing.** Each of us must discover our own truths, to listen to our own inner teacher, to take our own inner journey. We are not here to help right another's wrong, to "fix" what we perceive as broken in another member of the group.
5. **Suspend judgment.** Set aside your judgments. By creating a space between judgments and reactions, we can listen to the other, and to ourselves, more fully.

6. **Identify assumptions.** Our assumptions are usually invisible to us, yet they undergird our worldview. By identifying our assumptions, we can then set them aside and open our viewpoints to greater possibilities.
7. **Speak your truth.** You are invited to say what is in your heart, trusting that your voice will be heard and your contribution respected. Your truth may be different from, even the opposite of, what another person has said. Yet speaking your truth is simply that; it is not debating with, or correcting, or interpreting what another has said. Own your truth by remembering to speak only for yourself.
8. **Respect silence.** Silence is a rare gift in our busy world. After someone has spoken, take time to reflect without immediately filling the space with words. This process allows others time to fully listen before reflecting on their own reactions.
9. **Maintain confidentiality.** Create a safe space by respecting the confidential nature and content of discussions. Allow what is said in the group to remain there.
10. **When things get difficult, turn to wonder.** If you find yourself disagreeing with another, becoming judgmental, or shutting down in defense, try turning to wonder: "I wonder what brought her to this place?" "I wonder what my reaction teaches me?" "I wonder what he's feeling right now?"

Source: Used by permission of Parker J. Palmer, who has further developed this early version of the touchstones with his colleagues at the Center for Courage & Renewal. The current version can be read at http://www.couragerenewal.org/about/foundations under the "Principles of the Circle of Trust Approach."

others and of the group process. And, finally, you can control how you manage the inevitable conflict that will arise during the group process. If you focus on your success in groups during your college career, you will be able to negotiate and manage the complexity of the workplace environment more effectively during your career. Author and spiritualist Parker Palmer summarizes the essential communication skills to effective group communication in the box "Communication Counts in Your Life: Parker Palmer's 'Touchstones.'"

SUMMARY

Think about the groups you encounter in college not as something you must endure but as a way to practice the critical skills you must use in your life after college. In Chapter 1, we reported on research that suggests that communication remains among the top skills required by employers. If you use the skills and concepts described in this chapter and improve your communication in the groups you are involved with now in college, you will enhance your opportunities for employment after college, and you will position yourself to move up the career ladder faster than those who do not. But don't take our word for it—ask the successful professionals in your chosen career!

In this chapter, we have identified some essential elements of effective small-group communication:

■ Important characteristics of groups include size, interaction for a purpose, mutual influence, interdependence, norms, collective identity, cohesion, and commitment.

- Every group must balance both individual and group goals.
- Types of groups include learning, therapy, problem-solving, and social groups.
- Groups are more effective than individuals in solving complex decisions.
- Roles in groups encompass the task and social dimensions of the group.
- Dysfunctional behaviors such as hidden agendas, social loafing, and individual roles prevent effective group process.
- Leadership research has resulted in the trait approach, the styles approach, the functional approach, and the situational approach to leadership.
- Stages of group development include forming, storming, norming, and performing.
- Each group develops a unique culture and values.
- Gender plays an important role in a group's culture and decision making.
- A group's climate may develop on a continuum ranging from defensive to supportive.
- Types of conflict include pseudoconflict, content conflict, and ego conflict.
- Styles of conflict resolution include assertiveness, aggressiveness, and nonassertiveness.
- Making quality decisions in groups requires collaboration and the avoidance of groupthink.
- The reflective thinking process components include define, analyze, criteria, solutions, evaluation, and implementation.
- Brainstorming: creativity is the key.
- Groupthink prevents effective decision making.
- Making groups work in college will maximize your career success and help you contribute to your community.

QUESTIONS FOR DISCUSSION

1. What are the advantages and disadvantages of working in groups and teams?
2. How can individuals more effectively manage stress throughout the group process?
3. Describe individuals who in your experience make good leaders. What makes them stand out?

EXERCISES

1. Using the reflective thinking model, outline the process for a group research project that would reduce drinking on your campus. Or, develop a list of the most irritating habits of a small group's members. Brainstorm possible individual and group responses to these habits.
2. As a group, discuss group or organizational experiences where cultural or gender differences surfaced. Brainstorm strategies for understanding and adapting to these differences. Which "differences" are the most difficult to understand and adapt to? Discuss how stereotypes inhibited the communication between participants.

KEY TERMS

REFERENCES

Armstrong, T. nd. *Understanding team dynamics in the work-place*. Reviewed June 2, 2010 from http://www.helium.com/items/114532-understanding-team-dynamics-in-the-workplace.

Astin, A. W. 1984. Student involvement: A developmental theory for higher education. *Journal of College Student Personnel* 25:297–308.

Berry L. L., and Seltman, K. D. 2008. *Management lessons from Mayo Clinic*. New York: McGraw Hill.

Covey, S. R. 1989. *The 7 habits of highly effective people: Restoring the character ethic*. New York: Simon and Schuster.

Davis, B. G. 1993. *Tools for teaching*. Jossey-Bass: San Francisco.

Deemer, D. 1986. Structuring controversy in the classroom. In *Strategies for active teaching and learning in university class-rooms*, ed. S. F. Schomberg. Minneapolis, MN: Office of Educational Development Programs, University of Minnesota.

Dewey, J. 1910. *How we think*. Boston: D.C. Heath.

Gardner, J. N., and Jewler, A. J. 2003. *Your college experience: Strategies for success*. Belmont, CA: Wadsworth.

Gibb, J. R. 1961. Defensive communication. *Journal of Communication* 11:141–148.

Hersey, P., and Blanchard, K. H. 1993. *Management of organization*. Englewood Cliffs, NJ: Prentice Hall.

Janis, I. R. 1972. *Victims of groupthink*. Boston: Houghton Mifflin.

Miller, G. R., and Steinberg, M. 1975. *Between people: New analysis of interpersonal communication*. Chicago: Science Research Associates.

Moosbrucker, J. 1988. Developing a productivity team: Making groups at work work. In *Team building: Blue-prints for productivity and satisfaction*, eds. W. B. Reddy and K. Jamison, 88–97. San Diego: National Institute for Applied Behavioral Science and University Associates.

Tiberius, R. G. 1990. *Small group teaching: A trouble-shooting guide*. Toronto: Ontario Institute for Studies in Education Press.

Tompkins, P. K. 2005. *Apollo, Challenger, Columbia: The decline of the space program*. Los Angeles: Roxbury.

Tuckman, B. W. 1965. Developmental sequence in small groups. *Psychological Bulletin* 63:384–389.

Tuckman, B. W., and Jensen, M. A. C. 1977. Stages of small-group development revisited. *Group & Organization Studies* 2:419–427.

Wellins, R. S., Byham, W. C., and Wilson, J. M. 1991. *Empowered teams: Creating self-directed work groups that improve quality, productivity, and participation*. San Francisco: Jossey-Bass.

Wheelan, S. A., and Hochberger, J. M. 1996. Validation studies of the group development questionnaire. *Small Group Research* 27:143–170.

Wheelan, S. A., and Kaeser, R. M. 1997. The influence of task type and designated leaders on developmental patterns in groups. *Small Group Research* 24:60–83.

Wilson, G. L. 2005. *Groups in context*. 7th ed. Boston: McGraw Hill.

CHAPTER 13 Communication in Organizations

LEARNING OUTCOMES After reading this chapter, you will have:

the **Knowledge** to...   and the **Skills** to...

UNDERSTANDING THE IMPORTANCE OF COMMUNICATION IN ORGANIZATIONS, page 278

Realize the significance of communication in organizations.

- Assess your readiness to become "a new knowledge worker" against Drucker's four characteristics.

APPRECIATING ORGANIZATIONAL CULTURES, page 279

Recognize how culture is expressed and practiced in organizational cultures.

- Use language appropriate to the formality or informality of the situation.
- Listen to the organizational stories told by coworkers to learn the organization's history and culture.
- Participate in rites and rituals (company picnics, end-of-the month celebrations, etc.).
- Learn how the organization is structured from company information or through talking with others.
- Become familiar with the individuals and the roles they play in an organization.
- Attend to the organization's formal and informal rules and policies.

UNDERSTANDING ORGANIZATIONAL SYSTEMS: THE SYSTEMS MODEL, page 283

Comprehend how organizational systems operate.

- Learn how systems (individuals) are interconnected (related) in an organizational environment (structure).
- Understand the inputs (resources: personnel, services, knowledge) an organization possesses.

Understand the systems model.

- Distinguish how the wholeness or total structure of an organization contributes to its mission.
- Examine the interdependence of members of an organization and judge whether it creates positive or negative synergy.
- Assess whether an organization is open and adaptable or closed and unresponsive.
- Judge whether an organization is able to respond or adapt to feedback.
- Determine whether an organization has equifinality and can respond in various ways.

EXAMINING COMMUNICATION CONTEXTS IN ORGANIZATIONS, page 285

Consider how communication is practiced in various organizational contexts.

- Display support, respect, and empathy when engaged in superior-subordinate communication.
- Ensure communication with peers is open and ongoing.
- Use formal and informal communication networks effectively to convey and take in information.
- Use caution when representing or evaluating communication (advertising, social networking, etc.) outside of organizations.

CONFRONTING CHALLENGES IN CONTEMPORARY ORGANIZATIONS, page 289

Address communication issues in modern organizations.

- Be flexible and adaptable in responding in diverse organizations.
- Be aware of the benefits and challenges of developing personal relationships in organizations.
- Be motivated by intrinsic as well as extrinsic rewards in the relationship.

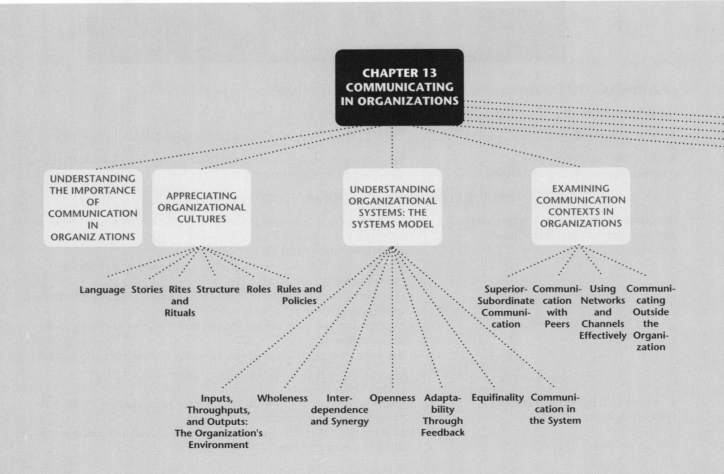

IDENTIFYING AND AVOIDING SEXUAL HARASSMENT, page 291

Recognize and avert sexual harassment.

- Treat others with respect and exhibit appropriate communication and behavior.

USING TECHNOLOGY IN ORGANIZATIONS, page 291

Employ technology in organizational communication.

- Understand and develop expertise in many types of communication technology.

PREPARING FOR THE JOB MARKET EARLY IN COLLEGE, page 292

Practice effective career searching strategies.
Understand interviewing contexts and strategies.

- Use technology, networking, and training to enhance your job search process.
- Prepare in advance by practicing for various types of interviews.
- Learn as much about an organization and its members as possible before the interview.
- Send thank you notes following your interview.

PUTTING ORGANIZATIONAL COMMUNICATION INTO PRACTICE IN COLLEGE, CAREER, AND LIFE, page 295

Employ effective organizational communication in academic settings, on the job, and in everyday life.

- Strive to be open, direct, and courteous in your communication interactions within organizations.

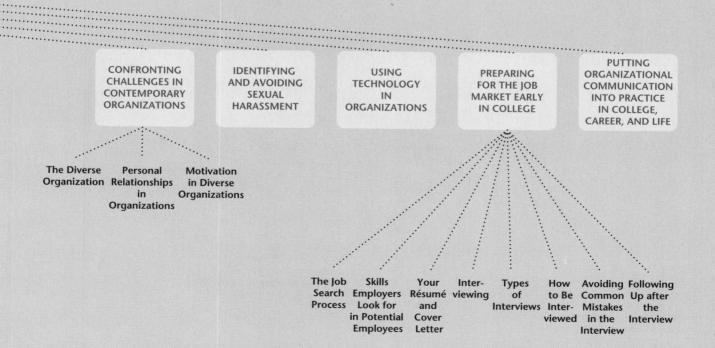

UNDERSTANDING THE IMPORTANCE OF COMMUNICATION IN ORGANIZATIONS

In the workplace today, communication effectiveness is a key variable in employee success. Much of what you have learned thus far in this text will allow you to be an effective organizational communicator. In this chapter, we explore several additional concepts that will assist you in fine-tuning your communication skills to meet the complex organizational demands. Like groups, organizations play a very important role in our lives.

Today's organizations require more teamwork than in past decades. The business world is expanding, and new markets are opening around the world; this globalization requires employees to understand and adapt to a multicultural world. Communication in this multicultural world means knowing, understanding, and adapting to different communication rules across cultures. Management theorist Peter Drucker (1992) believes that contemporary organizations are now looking for "the new knowledge worker," who possesses four key characteristics:

1. a college education,
2. the ability to apply analytical and theoretical thinking,
3. a commitment to lifelong learning, and
4. good communication skills.

Drucker suggests that the single most important characteristic of this "new knowledge worker" is his or her *ability to communicate with others who do not share the same worldview.*

The complexity of organizational life and the rapidly changing role of technology mean there are more demands on individual organizational members than ever before. Those who are successful in this changing world of work are those who develop what organizational theorist Pamela Shockley-Zalabak (2009) calls "communication competency": knowledge, skills, values, and sensitivity. As Figure 13.1 shows, employees must possess knowledge about the organization's communication environment. They need to

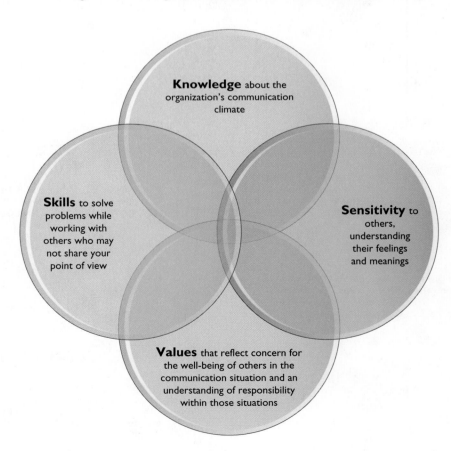

FIGURE 13.1

Communication Competency in Organizations.

possess the skills to solve problems working with others who may not share their points of view. They must be sensitive to others and understand their feelings and meanings. Their values must reflect a concern for the well-being of others in the communication situation and an understanding of responsibility within those situations.

To prepare for these complex organizations, communication competency is critical. Your present educational experiences provide an excellent opportunity to learn communication competency in organizations because the school you attend is a distinct organization that you must negotiate successfully. Many of the skills you are now developing will prepare you for the workforce. The first step in developing communication competency in organizations is understanding the cultural and systemic components of organizations.

APPRECIATING ORGANIZATIONAL CULTURES

Organizations operate as distinct cultures. An **organization's culture** represents the actions, practices, language, and artifacts of a group (Eisenberg, Goodall & Trethewey 2010). A culture is revealed *symbolically*. We understand a culture in numerous ways—by the way people explain the culture, by the tools used to create and maintain that culture, and by the values and beliefs that guide actions and practices. An organization's culture results from the accumulation of learning and behavior among a group of people and from how those individuals communicate their understanding of each other as members of the culture. As a result, communication creates and sustains culture, while simultaneously influencing how individuals communicate and interact. Many symbolic practices make up culture, including language, stories, rites and rituals, and structure.

Language

Each organization develops its own vocabulary with which it refers to its members' activity. One of the first ways organizational members learn expressed values is through the organization's mission statement. Have you read your university's mission statement? What does it tell you about the organization's value system? The vocabulary or language expresses the organization's past, present, and future values.

Language also reveals a great deal about such things as power relationships among members. For example, how a person is addressed provides information about his or her status. The level of formality or informality of language tells individuals how to act with peers, supervisors, or customers. Are supervisors in the organization referred to by their first names or addressed as Ms. Johnson, Mr. Harris, or Dr. Singh? Whether language is formal or informal may also provide insights about how organization members should dress or whether people are encouraged to discuss personal or social interests while at work. What special language or vocabulary have you come to understand as part of your university experience? The ways language is expressed are through the metaphors, stories, rituals, artifacts, and values in written documents and among organizational members (Eisenberg, Goodall & Trethewey 2010).

Stories

One way organizational members talk about their culture is through **stories and myths.** Organizational history is explained through corporate stories. These tell of past successes and failures, helping organizational members understand the type of risks that are acceptable. They provide members with an opportunity to recognize past and present "heroes" as well. Stories provide a critical socialization function for new members of the organization. They provide information about how work is done, about the appropriateness of many kinds of communication, and about the values and beliefs among organizational members. While new employees are normally provided with rule books or "standard operating procedures," stories allow new members to compare what is "written" with what is unwritten but "understood" by an organization's members. A final function of stories is that they provide opportunities for members to feel connected to one another and to the organization as a whole.

Organizational culture ■ The actions, practices, language, and artifacts of a group.

Language ■ The vocabulary that is used to refer to the activity of group members; the level of formality between members of different statuses.

Stories and myths ■ Tales of past successes and failures and of past and present heroes that help socialize new members of an organization.

Culture Counts

One of the most important rituals of college culture is the graduation ceremony.

Rites and rituals ■ Practices that symbolize the tools organizational members use to create and maintain culture.

Roles ■ Titles and/or job responsibilities.

Rules and policies ■ Standards by which organizational members make decisions.

Rites and Rituals

The organization's **rites and rituals** often symbolize the "tools" members use to create and maintain culture. Examples include the annual holiday party, the company picnic, and performance reviews. The most famous "rituals" of university life might include surviving registration, learning the maze of financial aid, and, of course, participating in graduation with all its pomp and circumstance. There are also other annual or seasonal rituals on college campuses such as homecoming parades, fund-raisers for nonprofit agencies, or tailgate parties.

Structure

An organization's structure is revealed in two ways—through the roles that individuals play and the rules and policies that govern the organization. Thus, to communicate effectively within the organization, employees must understand the roles, rules, and policies that make up the organization's underlying support and framework. Have you explored the range of services available on your campus? See "Communication Counts in Your College Experience: Using Campus Services" for assistance on finding help.

Roles

Just as power relationships are revealed by how employees address one another, organizational structure can also be identified by individuals' titles or by the **roles** they play in the group. In the university system, faculty have many titles that refer to such things as their level of education, their longevity, and their level of professional standing among their peers (see Table 13.1). A lecturer or adjunct, an instructor, an assistant professor, an associate professor, or a full professor may teach one of your classes. These titles reflect the person's teaching responsibilities, his or her rank within the organizational hierarchy, and, to some degree, his or her status among other faculty. There are, of course, other titles in the hierarchy, such as associate dean, dean, vice president, provost, president, chancellor, and trustee. These titles reflect an individual's job description and levels of responsibility within the university. Organizational charts that depict the relationships among the various offices and roles in your university will help you understand who's who and will give you a sense of how communication flows within the organization.

Rules and Policies

Another example of structure is in the **rules and policies** by which organizational members make decisions. Every organization has a set of operating policies that are mandated by various authoritative figures or bodies such as the board of trustees, the president, or department heads. When you entered your college, you probably received a student handbook or code of conduct containing your school's rules and policies. Rules are more or less formal, depending on the organization and the type of product or service they provide. Like our earlier discussion of group rules and norms, organizational rules

COMMUNICATION COUNTS IN YOUR COLLEGE EXPERIENCE

Using Campus Services

In essence, many colleges are minicommunities that offer students an array of services and opportunities. Most students spend considerable time during their first semester at college trying to negotiate the many services available on their campus. If you have not explored these, find out what your school offers by browsing through its phone directory, scrolling through an online copy of the student handbook, or looking at your college or university website. While what you find may differ from one school to the next, many college support services can be found in offices categorized under the following headings: academic outreach; technology support; health, fitness, and safety concerns; personal matters; and financial assistance. Learning to use these organizational resources can enhance and simplify your college experience.

Academic Outreach

Academic outreach services focus on helping students perform well in the classroom or providing students with opportunities to enhance what they've learned in the classroom.

- *Disability services* provide accommodations for students who are qualified under the Americans with Disabilities Act (ADA). Students who qualify for assistance may be provided with test readers, note takers, recorded textbooks, and the like.
- *International affairs* offers support and assistance to international students attending the college as well as to American students planning to study abroad. This support may be academic (such as planning on-campus workshops on understanding American culture) or social (as in putting on weekend trips to help students make friends and see local sights).
- *Job placement* may assist students in locating part- and full-time employment as well as internships or cooperative educational opportunities both during college and after graduation. Job placement may also host job fairs, résumé and interviewing workshops, and on-campus interviews.
- *Tutoring centers* provide students with one-on-one or small-group tutoring in beginning and upper-division courses. Generally, schools offer tutoring in mathematics, English, foreign languages, sciences, and other challenging courses.

Technology Support

Although many campuses have on-site computer labs and support staff, much of the learning students do now is from remote locations via the Internet using their own home computers or laptops. As a result, it is important for students to know that technical support and instruction are available and how to access them.

Health, Fitness, and Safety Concerns

Like most communities, colleges also have services to meet the health, fitness, and safety needs of their residents, whether they live on campus or commute.

- *Health center* offers students the services of physicians or nurse practitioners as well as registered or licensed nurses. Health centers may have pharmacists or lab technicians too.
- *Intramural sports* are offered at most campuses to provide students with good exercise and offer them a chance to build friendships with others. Intramural team sports are open to all students interested in some friendly

competition and normally are offered at several times throughout the day.

- *University police* protect members of the campus community and enforce the laws and regulations to provide a safe living and learning environment.

Personal Matters

Members of any community, including a campus community, have personal matters that need to be attended to. Many students today are raising children or caring for aging parents, working part or full time while going to school, or struggling with personal or family issues. Because life goes on while students are getting their education, many schools respond with services and opportunities that can positively impact students' lives both inside and outside of the classroom.

- *Campus ministries* offer students an array of denominations and services to meet their spiritual and religious needs. Some campuses have religious organizations on campus while others cooperate with local or regional churches and provide transportation to off-site services.
- *Child care centers* are found on many college campuses today. Indeed, an increasing number of students with young children are returning to college or starting school for the first time.
- *Counseling centers* offer counseling and psychological services that help facilitate students' personal development and enable them to be active members in the campus community.
- *Multicultural student centers* provide services and programs to facilitate the personal development, academic success, and retention of underrepresented minority students. In addition to its role in supporting individual students, Multicultural Student Affairs provides educational programming for the campus community to promote cultural diversity and awareness.
- *Student organizations* offer students opportunities to meet others, build skills, network with mentors, and relax with friends. Students may find opportunities with student government, academic clubs and honor societies, Greek fraternities and sororities, media organizations (radio, TV, newspaper, or website), community service clubs, and an array of special-interest groups.

Financial Assistance

Financial aid offices help qualified students identify means of financial support, such as grants and scholarships; part-time, on-campus employment; low-interest loans; or special funding sources (i.e., Veterans Administration benefits, BIA tribal grants, or ROTC scholarships for students planning to serve in the military). Normally, students' eligibility for financial assistance is determined when students file a Free Application for Federal Student Aid (FAFSA) application.

TABLE 13.1

ACADEMIC RANKS AND ROLES AT U.S. UNIVERSITIES

The following ranks (listed from highest to lowest) are common at American colleges and universities:

- **Professor Emeritus** (male) or **Professor Emerita** (female)—a title conferred at retirement on professors who have made significant contributions to their field and/or institution

- **Distinguished Professor**—usually a "named chair"; not used by all academic institutions

- **Professor**—or "Full Professor," a tenured rank; this title is used by all academic institutions

- **Associate Professor**—generally a tenured rank; some institutions award tenure only to Full Professors

- **Assistant Professor**—usually tenure-track; always the lowest rank of tenure-track faculty

- **Assistant Professor in Residence** or **Faculty in Residence**—nontenure-track; teaching-track faculty, considered a permanent position in an institution, and most likely has potential for promotion to Associate or Professor in Residence. These individuals hold a PhD or terminal degree.

- **Adjunct Professor**—an individual hired by an institution, on a temporary or limited-term basis, to teach a specific class or subject, for a specific term. Invariably, these individuals hold a PhD and are current practitioners in their fields.

- **Visiting Professor**—as the name suggests, a professor visiting from another institution to teach for a limited term

- **Lecturer**—generally have a PhD or a terminal master's degree (MBA, MFA, MPH, MPA, MSW, etc.) and are nontenured, focusing solely on teaching at the undergraduate or master's level. Some institutions may use "Lecturer" and "Instructor" interchangeably.

- **Instructor**—a nontenure-track position; instructors do not possess a PhD and are generally not assigned to any institution research. Their primary function is to teach part-time or full-time. Generally, they are limited to teaching undergraduate students.

- **Fellow, Scholar, Teaching Fellow**, or **Visiting Fellow**—generally function as an instructor while working toward a PhD or postdoctoral research experience; usually funded by an endowment or scholarship

- **Research Associate**—graduate student who is sponsored by a professor or institution and tasked with conducting specific research for said professor or institution

- **Research Assistant**—usually an undergraduate student doing an internship, or a graduate student working under an assistantship at an institution

- **Teaching Assistant**—usually a student who assists educators with administrative tasks. More commonly, this rank is given to graduate students who are teaching a course on a professor's behalf or providing supplemental instruction/tutoring for a specific class. This rank is sometimes used interchangeably with "Teaching Fellow"; some universities distinguish Teaching Assistants from Teaching Fellows, with the latter being a higher rank.

also may develop either implicitly or explicitly. As with groups, the more explicitly the rules are developed in the organization and the more rules members agree on, the more effective the organizational communication may be. Policies are formal statements about what is and is not expected of organizational members. The most common types of policies in any organization refer to such things as pay, benefits, hiring and firing, promotion, leave, and so on.

Once individuals in organizations learn how to "read" the culture, they can interpret "what it means to work here" much more effectively. Think about the last job you had. Did you learn what was expected of you by reading the corporate manual or by observing the company's day-to-day standard operating procedures? Did you get more information from watching others and hearing stories about "heroes" and "villains"? When individuals become able to interpret cultural symbols correctly, they begin to establish the knowledge and skills needed to succeed in that organization.

Understanding that an organization develops its own unique cultural characteristics can assist all members in developing a greater comprehension of the organization's "work life." Grasping the language, stories, rites, rituals, and structure can allow members to reduce uncertainty about their jobs and help them shape and adapt relationships within the organization. As a result, individuals come to know their place within the organizational system through knowledge of its culture.

UNDERSTANDING ORGANIZATIONAL SYSTEMS: THE SYSTEMS MODEL

Understanding organizations as systems means recognizing that every organization exists within a larger environment. A *system* is a set of parts (individuals) that are interconnected (in relationships) within an environment (structure). Conrad and Poole (2005) suggest that "systems thinking" enhances the effectiveness of the organization because individuals are seeking out information and adapting processes and procedures to the new information. Adaptability in organizations means in times of change the organization will be active, not reactive—thinking about the organization's "big picture," not just about one part or unit independent of others. And this is critical because an organization is not just its units or its individual workers; it is all of the units and people together that make a system.

Inputs, Throughputs, and Outputs: The Organization's Environment

The larger **environment** provides resources to the organization (input) and uses the products or services the organization creates (output). What the organization does with these products and services is called throughput. To illustrate, a university system depends on the larger environment for a variety of human, information, and fiscal resources such as students, faculty, and other employees; knowledge and information; and money from the state, benefactors, grants, and tuition fees. The university also depends on such physical resources as electricity, computers, books, equipment, and furniture. The university system generates output through its graduates, who are potential employees, and through additional knowledge and information from research, community service endeavors, and tax dollars paid by university workers. The university processes all the resources from the environment in classrooms, meetings, research projects, and other types of activities, and this becomes the essence of "throughput" at a university. An environment, then, provides an organization with a broad array of inputs or resources—goods and services, rules and regulations, people, knowledge, etc. Every system is unique, just like every college or university is unique. And every individual within the organization is connected with one another in the system.

To understand the way a system operates, we will discuss several characteristics, including wholeness, interdependence, openness, adaptability, and equifinality. Systems theorists Daniel Katz and Robert Kahn (1966) suggest that a systems approach focuses on problems of relationships, structure, and interdependence rather than on concrete objects in the organization. Let's look at the relationships between the parts (individuals) of a system and the way individuals understand and process feedback to understand the system.

Wholeness

The first characteristic of a system is **wholeness,** or the unique configuration of the system's parts. Every system is "more than the sum of its parts" (Miller 2003). Most organizations have different departments, offices, or individuals, but the way these elements coordinate activities constitutes the system. Some universities, for example, are organized by the college structure. The university has several colleges. Each college consists of several departments. In our universities, for example, the Communication Department is a part of the College of Arts and Sciences. The chair or head of our department is responsible to the college's dean. Some larger universities, on the other hand, have an entire College of Communication that consists of several different departments such as broadcasting, film studies, journalism, communication studies, and others.

In contrast, a hospital may be organized by type of medicine, such as oncology, cardiology, endocrinology, radiology, etc. In each unit there may be physicians, nurses, technicians, administrators, and other nonmedical staff who report to the head of the unit, most commonly a physician. Regardless of how the organization may be organized, each part of the system must be in communication with the other parts so that the whole runs smoothly. Though uniquely configured, it remains a whole organization; it is not a loose coalition of independent, autonomous units.

Environment ■ The larger system surrounding an organization that provides resources and uses products and services.

Wholeness ■ The unique configuration of the parts in a system.

Interdependent ■ Components of a system rely on one another to function properly.

Synergy ■ Collective energy.

Openness ■ The way a system uses feedback to adapt to changes in the larger environment.

Adaptability ■ The ability to change in response to a rapidly changing global environment.

Equifinality ■ Recognition that the end production can be produced in a number of ways.

Interdependence and Synergy

It is necessary to understand how the parts of the system function together in an **interdependent** fashion to create the whole. In a family, team, or business, the relationships among people make the group a system. As we discussed in the chapter on group communication, every part of the system can impact every other part of the system. Thus, systems theorists suggest, "the whole is greater than the sum of its parts." Collective energy, or **synergy**, increases when the parts work together. This synergy can be negative or positive. Negative synergy results from ineffective communication and misunderstanding. Positive synergy results from recognizing the interdependence between system components and competent communication within the system.

Openness

Every organization interacts differently with the environment. Environments are dynamic and changing. Today's organizations must monitor the environment and adapt to changing resources in that environment. The concept of **openness** refers to how the system uses feedback to adapt to changes in the larger environment. For example, changes can be economic (changes in the stock market, in number of customers, or in cost of supplies), political (changes in legislation that affect the organization), or human (changes in technology might require more worker training). Openness also means that organizations that exist in a larger system are constantly impacted by events in that larger system. An open system is continuously involved in scanning the environment for new information, analyzing the information for potential impact, and providing feedback to organizational stakeholders that matter to them. A closed system, in contrast, lacks the ability to assess and analyze the communication in the external environment and thus cannot respond appropriately when change occurs.

The 9/11 Commission Report analyzed a wide range of information available to military leaders and the intelligence community prior to the terrorist attacks. Despite the availability of this information, however, the Commission found that many government agencies acted like "closed systems" because they were unaccustomed to sharing information with each other; they did not scan the environment consistently and thoroughly and they did not share the information with others through feedback (Eisenberg, Goodall, & Trethewey 2010).

Adaptability Through Feedback

Changes in the larger environment, then, require organizations to adapt quickly and responsibly. To adapt to changes, the organization must become more proactive in seeking out information and must adopt a flexible approach to larger environmental change. **Adaptability** is critical to contemporary organizations, which must constantly adopt new policies, procedures, products, and services to respond to the rapidly changing global environment. After September 11, airports around the country were closed for days, and some airlines laid off thousands of employees. Other organizations set up funding mechanisms and matched employee contributions to the "September 11th Fund," which assisted victims and their families. General Electric Corporation, for example, donated $10 million to the fund. In other words, these organizations adapted to the crisis at hand with philanthropic feedback.

Organizations must also recognize that strategies that work in one situation will not necessarily work in another. Strategies are contingent on many environmental factors. For example, today's organizations must monitor the environment and create unique ways of adapting. A range of new jobs that focus on monitoring the environment—marketing, sales, public relations, and others—have opened up in organizations. Individuals in these jobs must have effective communication skills to recognize changes and to communicate those changes to others in their organization.

Equifinality

Equifinality refers to recognition that the end product (whatever output the organization produces) can be produced in several ways. Every system has the capacity to identify and develop several ways to reach its goals. For example, think of the number of options you have when choosing an Internet provider. No matter which provider you choose, you accomplish virtually the same thing—the ability to send email, surf the Internet, join a chat room, and so on. Each provider, though, has *some* unique features. Another example of equifinality can be seen in the number of colleges and universities that offer communication degrees. Although there are many different ways colleges or universities might offer this degree, each may require slightly different courses or experiences within its programs. Students achieve the same goal but travel somewhat different paths to achieve it, depending on the program's focus.

A system works best when the processes within the system (throughputs) are developed with systems principles as their foundation. Conrad and Poole (2005) summarize these principles:

1. The system is more than the sum of its parts.
2. Cause–effect relationships in systems are complex.
3. It takes time to find the right levers (the critical components of the system).
4. To understand the system, don't just focus on the system itself; look at the larger system in which it exists.
5. Systems must adapt or they perish.
6. History is important in organizational systems (we learn from history or are doomed to repeat it).
7. Systems must constantly learn and renew themselves. (29–33)

A system (organization) is more than its parts (individuals) because each person in the organization has skills, strengths, and weaknesses. As the individuals work together, they can compensate for the weaknesses of others; they "fill in the blanks." Trying to find a simple, single cause for any activity or process or outcome cannot be done. Issues of "quality" are complex, as is "customer satisfaction." Neither of these can be traced to a single source. Because of the complexity in the organization, understanding which people are the critically important ones is not easy. Yet key people become links in a complex set of relationships that "steer" the organization. And, finally, while any organization can be seen as its own "system," to understand it completely you need to look at the larger "suprasystem" that it inhabits. For example, to understand the impact of bank failures on the economic system in the year 2010, you cannot look at any single bank. Instead, focus on the role of banks in the global economic system.

Communication in the System

Through organizational communication, we gather, interpret, and use information from the environment outside the system. Communication allows the organization to coordinate the interdependent parts within the system. Openness to feedback allows an organization to adapt and adjust itself to environmental change. Communication and creativity within and throughout the system open a range of options in developing, modifying, marketing, and selling the organization's products and services. Think back to the types of advertising or marketing strategies that convinced you to attend your college or university. Did admissions counselors come to your school? Was the institution's website creative and interesting? Did you watch videos or receive a DVD? Did you receive brochures or letters? Did you go to campus and take a tour guided by a student representative? Did you speak with a faculty member? You can probably identify some key communication strategies that helped guide your decision. When you think of the "ideal company" you want to work for, do these same types of communication come to mind? Have you ever accessed the Fortune 100 Best Places to Work? What is it about these companies that makes them so positive? Think of the organization in the same way you do a product. What is the company's brand? How do its employees communicate that brand?

EXAMINING COMMUNICATION CONTEXTS IN ORGANIZATIONS

Competent organizational communication must consider its many contexts within the organization. We communicate interpersonally with peers, supervisors, and subordinates. We also communicate with customers, clients, suppliers, and others outside the organization. Additionally, gender and cultural differences add a level of complexity to

---

TABLE 13.2

FIVE PRINCIPLES TO GUIDE COMMUNICATION WITH SUPERIORS

1. *Plan a strategy.* Understand the individual and the context of your appeal.
2. *Determine why the superior should listen.* Connect your appeal to something important to your boss.
3. *Tailor the argument to the supervisor's style and characteristics.* Will he or she respond more favorably to statistics or a story? Adapt your evidence to his or her needs.
4. *Assess the supervisor's technical knowledge.* Do not assume his or her knowledge base; know it.
5. *Hone your communication skills.* Be clear and articulate in your appeals.

---

each of these contexts. Interpersonal relationships at all levels are crucial to individual and organizational success, and they are a prerequisite for effective job performance.

Superior–Subordinate Communication

Riley and Eisenberg (1991) suggest that the key to successful communication with superiors is advocacy. Employees must understand the needs of superiors and adapt communication accordingly. One of the critical principles of effective advocacy is connecting arguments to supervisors' needs and expectations. As Table 13.2 shows, Eisenberg and Goodall (1997) suggest five principles to guide communication with superiors.

Communication must always be adapted to audience knowledge, expectations, values, and beliefs. Keys to successful communication to subordinates in the organization are openness and support. Empathetic listening is critical to the success of many relationships. Subordinates commonly criticize their superiors for withholding information. They need and want to know information that impacts their work. Thus, effective supervisors pass along information to subordinates and provide them with opportunities for input into discussions that impact workplace behavior and decision making. Supportiveness in communication includes showing concern for the relationships and demonstrating respect for individuals while promoting accomplishment of tasks. Both empathetic listening and genuine support from supervisors enhance employee motivation in the workplace. These communication strategies also empower subordinates by building confidence and trust, as you can see in the box "Communication Counts in Your Career: Key Principles for Successful Organizational Relationships."

Communication with Peers

Horizontal or peer communication provides social support to individuals and builds employee morale. We have discussed effective communication in work teams and its benefits in terms of decision making and relationship maintenance. Peer communication also entails talking across departments or units and with customers or suppliers. Today, focus on customer service is essential to business success. Opportunities for feedback between units in the organization and between the organization and its customers, coupled with rapid response to that feedback, can increase organizational effectiveness and success.

Ultimately, individuals at every level of the organization must understand the complexity of its relationships and expectations. Communication that is clear, constant, and supportive within a variety of relational contexts enhances individual, team, and organizational effectiveness. The notion of feedback doesn't involve only a system's issues in the organizational communication context. As we have discussion throughout this text, feedback is a critical construct in all relationships.

Using Networks and Channels Effectively

Effective organizational communication is dependent on the appropriate use of networks and channels of communication within the organization. Who talks to whom?

COMMUNICATION COUNTS IN YOUR CAREER

Key Principles for Successful Organizational Relationships

A few years ago, a young man stormed into one of our offices without an appointment and demanded, "There are no seats left in the sections of the basic course that fit my schedule. You have to enroll me in the 12:30 P.M. Tuesday/Thursday section right now because I'm a senior, and I can't graduate unless I take this stupid course." His attitude, demeanor, and communication strategy was, to say the least, ineffective. Not surprisingly, he found that his approach failed to get him what he needed and actually hindered him.

In response, one of your authors said, in a direct but courteous manner, "Before you say more, allow me to help you. First, in the 'stupid course' in which you need to enroll, we teach principles of communication that will help you should you encounter a similar circumstance like this again in your life. However, if you think about it, you probably already know about some of these principles. So, if you'd like to go out of my office, come in again, and use what you think might be a more appropriate communication approach, I'll act as though our first encounter didn't occur. What do you say?" Sheepishly, the young man went out, knocked at the door, and this time significantly adjusted his approach; he introduced himself, softened his tone, explained what he wanted, and received the help he needed. This story illustrates an important principle: *You can more easily get what you need from others when you communicate in a kind, polite, and direct manner that affirms the other person's humanity.* This is true in both college and work contexts. Consider these key principles that can help guide your communication choices when working with others in organizations:

1. **Work on developing a trusting relationship with others.** Trusting relationships among people are the glue that holds an organization together. When you have built trust with others, you can more easily approach them and ask for assistance or offer explanations. When your immediate supervisor trusts you because you have proven that you can accomplish assignments in a timely manner with excellent results, you will get even more challenging opportunities and perhaps, eventually, a promotion.

2. **Treat everyone, regardless of rank in the organization, with respect.** Very often students (and faculty too) forget that staff and other support personnel at colleges and universities are essential to the function of the organization. They often have information power (i.e., they know what you need to know) or can help you gain access to a person,

place, or equipment you need. Practice genuine, common courtesy in your dealings with everyone because they may literally hold the key to what you need now or later.

3. **When disagreements or difficulties arise, respond—don't react.** What will you do if you disagree with the grade you received on a project? Many students tend to complain to others in the class or, in some cases, appeal the situation to someone else, without ever discussing the issue with their teacher. These are reactive responses that seek retribution, not a resolution. This can escalate the spiral of conflict with your professor who, in most instances, has more organizational power than you. However, if you respond by first approaching your professor in a kind, direct manner and asking questions to clarify the reason for your grade, you open possibilities for dialogue that will solve, rather than exacerbate, problems. Even if you are not satisfied with the result, you may uncover important insights that will help you in completing the next assignment with greater success. Response, rather than reaction, has equal application in the workplace.

4. **Don't be afraid to say you're sorry or take responsibility.** It is never easy to apologize. None of us enjoy being wrong. It is equally difficult to take responsibility to correct what we have done wrong. James Autry (2001) tells of a time in his career when he was in conflict with his immediate supervisor who micromanaged his department. Autry felt that his creativity and energy were being squelched, so he decided to accept an attractive offer from another company. Upon hearing of his resignation, the CEO of the company, who was traveling in another city, called him and asked him to delay his decision until they could talk. When the CEO returned, he apologized to Autry, explained that he had hoped the situation with Autry's supervisor would resolve itself, and promised to fix the situation if Autry would stay. Autry explains, "To make the story short, I stayed. I didn't stay for more money or power or position. I stayed because I believed the CEO. I had always believed in him as a visionary leader, but it was at that moment that I got the measure of him as an honest, authentic human being—one willing to admit mistakes who did not allow his sense of position or his ego to prevent him from apologizing to someone lower in the hierarchy" (11).

Why? How? When? Where? These were some of the questions we posed in Chapter 1 during our analysis of communication situations, including those within organizations. A network links organizational members either formally or informally and describes how information travels throughout the organization. Some formal networks are used to

A network links organizational members either formally or informally and describes how information travels throughout the organization.

disseminate critical information to all employees, while other networks are more informal and provide information on issues of socialization.

Formal networks, or channels, are used most commonly when information is communicated either up (reporting the results of a particular job) or down (giving orders or advising on policy adaptation). **Informal networks** or channels are used most commonly among peers at similar levels of the organization, although sometimes the grapevine (a common name for the most pervasive informal organizational channel) is used by many individuals at all levels. The grapevine can be a positive communication channel because it is one of the fastest ways to disseminate information. Individual members may use the grapevine to confirm information that comes from more formal channels. It assists members in interpreting and understanding information. However, the grapevine can also become a negative channel if organizational members use it as a substitute for more formal channels, such as trying to find out about critical policy or personnel changes when formal channels are lacking in information. As a result, if formal channels do not provide adequate information or allow individuals to interpret information accurately, the informal grapevine rumors replace reliable information.

Communicating Outside the Organization

Many of you will find jobs where you will be dealing with individuals outside the organization, such as customers, clients, suppliers, legislators, community leaders, and others. Managers today recognize that to ensure continued profit in the constantly changing marketplace, effective communication between the organization and its customers and other organizations is essential. Businesses must develop and nurture long-term relationships with numerous external audiences. This is not simply a matter of economics; it is also a product of expectations. Organizations are expected to accept and enact proactive social responsibility in their communities and in the broader global marketplace.

Organizational theorist Matthew Seeger (1997) suggests that organizations have four primary responsibilities to audiences both within and outside the organization:

1. philanthropic,
2. environmental,
3. product, and
4. employee

Formal networks ■ Used most commonly when information is communicated up or down.

Informal networks ■ Used most commonly when information is communicated among peers.

Philanthropic efforts include donations of time and money to local, regional, or national charities, including arts and cultural programs. Environmental responsibility concerns the organization's impact on environmental resources. Product responsibility addresses product safety and conscientious use of materials in product development and production. Finally, employee responsibility includes efforts to provide a safe and motivating workplace. In the past, a common organizational philosophy was, "Let the buyer beware!" Today, however, the reverse may be true. Let the organization beware if its products and services do not conform to customer (and other audience) expectations of social, environment, or product responsibility. Organizations, therefore, are not just about doing business but also about building relationships through service and support.

Organizations today communicate social responsibility in many ways, most commonly through their website, one of the most important channels for communicating about the ways the organization conducts itself. The advantage of the website is that the organization can control the information they present. But the downside is that the website requires the user to be the one to initiate the relationship. So many organizations today are reaching out to stakeholders through social media such as Facebook and Twitter. Check your campus website and other communication tools to see if Facebook is used to communicate to students, parents, alumni, and community members.

CONFRONTING CHALLENGES IN CONTEMPORARY ORGANIZATIONS

Historically workers could count on lifetime employment if they did a good job, but today that guarantee is gone. Communication in the workplace thus takes on greater importance as workers attempt to negotiate their jobs in an uncertain climate. Greater misunderstanding between and among supervisors and subordinates complicates that negotiation. The more misunderstanding occurs within an organization, the more workers are likely to feel fear and distrust, and the less likely they may be to communicate with others.

The Diverse Organization

The workforce today looks dramatically different from that of 20 years ago. Cultural, racial, and gender diversity have never been so pronounced. For example, the number of workers over 55 is growing. Additionally, census data tell us that the fastest-growing ethnic population in the United States is Hispanic. As a result, the white, male-dominated workforce of yesterday is being replaced by organizations filled with individuals who look, think, and act in radically different ways.

Organizations at the turn of the twentieth century and through WWI and WWII were predominantly manufacturing based. Today, the manufacturing sector is decreasing while the service industry is exploding. Another change is that workers' levels of education are much higher than ever before in history. This educated workforce demands not only pay and benefits commensurate with their levels of training and experience but also employment opportunities that are satisfying and motivating. One way to motivate workers is including them in communication and decision-making processes.

Today's educated workers also demand a more equitable balance between work and home life. Individuals want to balance their job requirements with their family's needs. In the past, all employees were expected to work the same hours, get the same benefits, and develop the same sense of loyalty to the organization. Work was work, and employers expected no intrusions from personal or family issues. Today, however, issues of child care, elder care, and other responsibilities impact employees' lives. Organizations must also consider the number of workers with substance abuse or emotional problems. Increasingly, contemporary employers must develop

Culture Counts

One way to motivate workers is including them in communication and decision-making processes.

counseling services to assist employees with substance abuse problems, family struggles, mental health issues, legal problems, child and parent care, or other personal issues.

Organizations that respond to these employees' needs with appropriate policies and benefits and who communicate with them in caring and sensitive ways will remain competitive in today's marketplace. Flexibility and adaptability, hallmarks of systems theory, must become the norm for contemporary organizations. Employees, too, must be flexible and adaptable to the diversity of individuals, values, and communication styles of their customers, superiors, coworkers, subordinates, and others.

Personal Relationships in Organizations

Because today's workforce demands more satisfying personal relationships at work, organizations must also adapt to these new expectations. Workers today spend more than 40 hours a week on the job; thus, the opportunity for enhanced social and personal relationships with coworkers is increased. Long-term relationships, both on and off the job, have the greatest potential for success when the partners are matched in such things as level of education, interests, and activities. Today we are just as likely to find these matches in our workplace as out of it.

Organizational theorists Dillard and Miller (1988) suggest that the motivation underlying romantic relationships in organizations is complex, as it involves love and ego. Employees motivated by love are looking for long-term companionship and partnership. Those motivated by ego are looking for sexual excitement and adventure. The consequences of these romantic relationships can, according to Dillard and Miller, provide improved work performance. However, negative perceptions by other employees can create problems for romantic partners. For example, if the romantic relationship ends, coworkers may continue assuming the relationship has negatively impacted the parties involved. Moving from the impersonal to the personal and to the romantic stage of a relationship with a coworker may be highly satisfying, but it could also backfire and have negative consequences both for the individuals and the organization.

Romantic relationships are not the only types of personal relationships that we might develop through our work, however. The potential for developing deep and long-lasting friendships also exists. Sharing the trials and tribulations as well as the joys and successes of our everyday work experiences with close friends adds an additional level of satisfaction to our work experience.

Motivation in Diverse Organizations

The diverse workforce consists of individuals who seek motivating and satisfying employment. But this diversity also means there is no "one-size-fits-all" motivational approach. As a result, organizations must recognize and adopt a variety of approaches to motivating workers. Although communication is the common denominator in all types of motivation, the best motivational device or strategy will fail if its message and timing are not matched to individual and organizational needs. Organizational managers must seek out information from employees about what is motivating to them. Likewise, employees must be willing to communicate their needs and expectations to their supervisors. Kreps (1991) defines **motivation** as "the degree to which an individual is personally committed to expending effort in the accomplishment of a specified activity or goal" (154). Eisenberg and Goodall (1997) suggest that communication can function in two ways to motivate: Managers can provide information and feedback about employee tasks, goals, and performance, and they can communicate encouragement, empathy, and concern.

Schutz (1958) suggests there are two levels of motivators important to individuals. The first level is primarily economic and includes such things as pay, benefits, and vacations. The second level is more subjective and includes motivators like inclusion in decision making and opportunities for input into policies, procedures, and products. These are motivating to us as workers because we feel a sense of ownership of our jobs, a sense of pride in our individual accomplishments, and a sense of being respected by others for

Motivation ■ Personal commitment to the effort of accomplishing a goal.

our knowledge and expertise. Each of us wants to engage in work that offers us personal satisfaction and professional opportunity.

The key to motivating employees, then, is to develop opportunities for collective decision making and risk taking. Effective organizational communication also requires developing multiple channels for information to flow through the organization and creating communication situations that encourage negotiation among participants.

IDENTIFYING AND AVOIDING SEXUAL HARASSMENT

As we noted earlier, an organization creates and maintains its unique culture. However, internal and external audiences demand that the culture be based on responsibility and sensitivity to issues of gender, race, ethnicity, age, and sexual orientation. Effective and ethical organizations establish cultures of equal opportunity and provide workplaces free of discriminatory actions. For example, one area of prohibited discrimination is **sexual harassment.** Sexually harassing behavior humiliates people. Although women are more commonly victims of sexual harassment, sexually hostile environmental harassment may be targeted at any individual in the organization.

According to the Equal Employment Opportunity Commission, harassment on the basis of sex violates Title VII of the Civil Rights Act of 1964. The act defines sexual harassment as "unwelcome sexual advances, requests for sexual favors, and other verbal or physical conduct of a sexual nature." Sexual harassment occurs when:

1. submission to such conduct is made, either explicitly or implicitly, a term or condition of an individual's employment;
2. submission to or rejection of such conduct is used as the basis for employment decisions affecting an individual; or
3. such conduct has the purpose or effect of unreasonably interfering with an individual's work performance or creating an intimidating, hostile, or offensive working environment.

Situations 1 and 2 are often referred to as "quid pro quo" sexual harassment and usually occur in relationships where there is an obvious power difference between the parties (such as supervisor to subordinate or faculty to student). Situation 3 is often referred to as "hostile environment" sexual harassment and more commonly occurs between coworkers or between students. Sexual harassment may be physical (such as unwanted touching, hugging, kissing, patting, pinching), verbal (such as referring to a woman as a "babe," "girl," or "honey"; discussing sexual topics or telling sexual jokes; asking personal questions of a sexual nature; or making sexual comments about a person's clothing or anatomy), or nonverbal (such as looking a person up and down, staring at someone for a prolonged time, or making sexually suggestive gestures with hands or through body movements).

It is the organization's responsibility to prevent sexual harassment by developing policies and training that educate employees about appropriate behavior and that provide them with opportunities to report harassment. Organizations should investigate these reports promptly and confidentially and should not retaliate against employees who report unacceptable behavior. Responding to this issue through education, training, and communication helps to sustain healthy interpersonal relationships among employees and can benefit the organization in numerous ways. When we work in supportive and caring organizational climates, we are motivated to be productive and creative in our professional responsibilities.

USING TECHNOLOGY IN ORGANIZATIONS

Regardless of the type of culture developed in organizations or the nature of the relationships among employees, some form of communication technology must be used. While face-to-face communication is still important in today's organizations, advanced technology has made messaging faster, made access to and processing of information much easier, and made communication with others across geographical distances much

Sexual harassment ■ Unwelcome sexual advances, requests for sexual favors, and other verbal or physical conduct of a sexual nature.

more accessible. Some technology has made the office virtually obsolete. Computer, video, and teleconferencing capabilities allow us to reach others wherever we are and whenever we want. The Internet allows us to access information from any library in the world with a few clicks of a mouse. Organizations may use computer-assisted technology to send images and voices across time and space or use computer-assisted decision-aiding technology such as databases or programs that provide information to decision makers. For example, Ganga and Lerner (2004) report that in 2001, 15 percent of employed people, almost 20 million workers, worked at least one full day a week at home. Of these, 3.4 million workers had a formal arrangement with their employers that allowed them to work at home. For the most part, these arrangements were possible because of increased technology.

The effects of this technology on contemporary organizations are significant. With the widespread use of technologies including fax, computers, overnight delivery, teleconferencing, blogs, and chat rooms, some individuals in organizations never meet their peers face-to-face. The "virtual office" is becoming more common. Eisenberg, Goodall and Trethewey (2010) define the virtual office as one that can literally be anywhere users have access to computers, modems, and phone lines, and they suggest that productivity can increase when employees have this option. Moreover, the use of virtual offices can reduce job-related stress for some employees.

To acquire and keep a good job and to remain competitive, you must understand and develop expertise in many types of communication technology. For the organization to remain competitive, training must be ongoing to meet changing technology.

Technological advancements also provide opportunities for organizations to monitor and improve employee productivity. Computerized monitoring of employees is the norm in businesses today. However, managers must recognize that abuse of individual rights and privacy (also possible because of changing technology) negatively impacts corporate culture. Employee–employer rights issues are complex and continue to cause concern for employees and employers alike. As an individual beginning your career or updating your skills for a career change, you need to know how, why, and when your behavior at work will be monitored. To counter the impact of technology that monitors your behavior, be up-to-date on the latest advances in technology and use it wisely so as not to jeopardize your job or your unit's productivity.

PREPARING FOR THE JOB MARKET EARLY IN COLLEGE

First impressions often have the most impact on whether or not a personal relationship will blossom or wither or, in the case of your professional life, whether or not you will be offered a position. All of the communication skills we have discussed so far in this text will assist you in making the best impression when you interview for the job/career you have been preparing for in college. But the interview itself is not the first step in the job-search process. Before you interview, you should first research the type of organization you want to work for and learn what the business needs and expects of its employees. Therefore, one of the first steps in your research is to develop an understanding of the qualities or skills necessary for work in a particular organization. Second, you must know how to prepare the required employment materials that will assist you in getting that job.

The Job Search Process

One of the best places to begin your research is the Internet. A host of websites provide information on every aspect of the job-search process. You can learn how to write and post a résumé, write cover letters, find job opportunities, prepare for interviews, determine commonly asked questions, and get advice on interview attire. Most companies offer a wealth of information through their websites about who they are and what they do. Many of these websites even have links aimed at potential employees. In fact, many organizations guide you through the steps for submitting an application, posting a résumé and cover letter, and requesting more information on the company.

Skills Employers Look for in Potential Employees

Despite advances and changes in technology within organizations, employers still seek candidates who can show they have effective and flexible interpersonal communication skills. As we said earlier, flexibility is critical to effective interpersonal communication in diverse and multicultural organizations. The ability to speak intelligently and assertively with colleagues, superiors, and subordinates is vital. Working effectively in groups and managing conflict in problem-solving teams are equally critical.

Key skills employers expect from workers today include self-motivation, assertiveness, ambition, as well as cultural sensitivity and understanding. Once you have developed your skills in these critical areas, you are ready to find your ideal job. After you have identified the job you want, investigated what the organization expects of you, and written and submitted your résumé and cover letter, you may be called for an interview. Remember that the résumé and cover letter may get you an interview, but the interview itself will be what lands you the job.

Your Résumé and Cover Letter

The résumé briefly describes your educational, employment, professional, and extracurricular experiences. Critical information that you must provide in the résumé includes education (college and/or graduate school); work history (both paid and volunteer); professional or academic organizational experience (fraternity, sorority, political, or professional); and awards, scholarships, military experience, and references (names, titles, work addresses, phone, and email). The résumé must be well organized, neat, and error free. A general rule is to keep the résumé to one or two pages. Use keywords and action verbs throughout the résumé to describe critical skills you have developed through your wide range of experiences. Once you have written a first draft, proof it for errors. Then have someone in your college or university career center evaluate it and offer constructive advice. You might also ask a trusted professor or mentor to assess it as well.

A cover letter should accompany your résumé unless you are hand delivering the résumé to the person conducting the interview. Simply type "cover letter guidelines" into any search engine to find many suggestions and examples.

As a general guideline, your cover letter should be no more than one page long, follow a simple business letter format, and include three paragraphs. The first paragraph should identify the job in which you are interested and how you heard about the position. The second paragraph should be what some call the "sell paragraph." Here you explain how your skills, experience, and background specifically relate to the company and its position. This paragraph should demonstrate that you have done your homework about the company and have a clear sense of how you can benefit the organization. The third paragraph should explain how you intend to follow up on the letter and should indicate that your résumé is enclosed. Like your résumé, the cover letter should be clean, correct, and concise. If you provide employers with an effective cover letter and résumé, you will be well on your way to being contacted for a job interview.

Interviewing

Before arriving for your interview, you should have conducted thorough research on the company or firm. Know some of its history, its products or services, its various offices or plants, its economic health in the past few years, and its goals and objectives. You should also know something about its employee benefits and work issues like training, promotion, and performance expectations. Again, this information can be obtained from company websites, from staff members already employed there, or from library and specialized publications that report on the status of companies worldwide. Reference books like *Dun and Bradstreet*, *Moody's*, or *Standard and Poor's* list virtually all businesses, their products, locations, and other valuable information. Doing the appropriate homework will help you understand the organization and how you can mesh with its mission and objectives. Furthermore, you will be well prepared to answer and pose questions during the interview process.

Successful applicants in today's competitive job market know themselves and express confidence during an interview.

Information-gathering interview ■ An interview in which an individual speaks to a professional working in a job he or she might like to pursue.

Employment-selection interview ■ An interview in which an individual sells himself or herself and his or her qualifications for a job.

Types of Interviews

So, you know what employers expect, you have prepared a strong résumé, and you've researched your company. Now you're ready for the interview. But what type of interview? One type of interview is the **information-gathering interview.** You may have done this type of interview when preparing a paper in one of your classes. Individuals doing survey research interview patrons in their local mall. Journalists do this type of interview when preparing for a story. In an information-gathering interview, you may have opportunities to meet a professional working in a job you might like to have someday and ask them questions. A key to effective information gathering is knowing the person you will interview and to prepare a set of specific questions in advance. Prepare open-ended questions that call for explanation rather than closed-ended questions that require simply *yes* or *no* or other one-word answers. Also, prepare follow-up questions to make sure you get all the information you need, but be prepared to deviate from your list if important information surfaces during the interview. Visit www.quintcareers.com/information_interview.html for help with drafting suitable and useful questions for the information-gathering interview.

Remember that the person or persons you interview are taking valuable time from their work to speak with you. Be courteous, attentive, and sensitive to both their verbal and nonverbal communication, and be flexible so that you can respond to their needs during the interview. Show up on time, dress appropriately, and use the interviewees' time appropriately. Take good notes, listen attentively, express your thanks, and send a follow-up thank-you letter.

If you are ready for an **employment-selection interview,** then be prepared to sell yourself and your qualifications. This means that you must be able to explain, in detail, how you can be an asset to the organization. The most common types of questions that will be asked focus on what you can bring to the job, how you have prepared for the job's responsibilities, and why the employer should hire you over other candidates. You will probably be asked to identify your strengths and weaknesses for the job as well as your goals for the next five years. Go to www.collegegrad.com/ezine/22toughi.shtml for help answering interview questions. Remember, the first five minutes of the interview are critical in establishing the impression that you are prepared and experienced and, thus, are the best candidate for the position.

How to Be Interviewed

The interviewer will also likely ask if you have any questions regarding the job and the company. Successful applicants respond to questions clearly, directly, and substantively, and they prepare questions that show they are truly interested in working for the company. Ask about the organization's working environment and culture, or inquire about a project that employees are working on. Refer to sources of information you reviewed in preparing for the interview such as the company's website or annual report. Be alert for verbal and nonverbal signals that communicate whether the interviewer is interested in continuing the interview or whether he or she is ready to end the discussion. When you think the interviewer is ready to end the interview, express appreciation for the interviewer's time and interest in your candidacy, shake his or her hand firmly, and tell the interviewer that you are truly interested in this position.

Successful applicants for a job in today's highly competitive market know themselves, express confidence, exhibit a high level of organization prior to and during an interview, and show enthusiasm and interest in the type of work they will be doing. Unsuccessful applicants fail to express themselves clearly, are unrealistic about the type of work they will be doing, are unclear about their future in the organization, or are focused on "selfish" issues like salary, benefits, or vacations.

Avoiding Common Mistakes in the Interview

Perhaps the most common mistake that interviewees make is having unrealistic expectations. These may center on the skills and knowledge the interviewee thinks he or she has or salary expectations that do not fit the job. Unrealistic expectations also can be related to communication. You may expect an employer or fellow employees to communicate more than they do, or you may believe that your communication is "enough" when an employer expects more of you. You might assume that your communication style is effective, but others might not find it to be. To avoid unrealistic expectations, engage in practice interviewing. You may be able to practice interviewing at your campus Career Center or its equivalent. Practicing for interviews can mean the difference between successfully landing a job or continuing your job search.

The impression you ultimately make at an interview may begin long before the interview is actually conducted and continue after the actual interview is completed. How much do prospective employers check on you before they call you for an interview? Do employers check your Facebook account, for example? According to an August 2009 article in *Oregon Business Report* (http://oregonbusinessreport. com/2009/08/45-employers-use-facebook-twitter-to-screen-job-candidates/), 45% of employers check Facebook and Twitter when screening employees. It is advisable to clean up your accounts if you want to make a good impression. It should be obvious as well that truthfulness in discussing your experience is essential.

Following Up After the Interview

After you complete the interview, there are a few things you can and should do to follow up. A thank-you letter can increase the odds of an interviewer remembering you and keeping you high on his or her list of candidates. This also provides you with an opportunity to add any additional information requested by the interviewer. If anyone other than the interviewer was instrumental in helping to arrange the interview, such as a secretary or administrative assistant, send him or her a thank-you letter as well. It is also wise to contact your references if the interviewer has requested letters of recommendation or communicated that he or she will be in contact with them. There is not complete agreement on whether you should call the interviewer after several days to ask about the progress of your application. However, if the interviewer has given you a deadline for a decision with regard to your hire, and the deadline has passed, it is a good idea to call and ask whether your application was successful. This phone call also communicates your continued interest in the job.

Your success in interviewing for and obtaining a position and in working within an organization is dependent on your experience, knowledge, expectations, abilities, and communication skills. We come to any organization as a person with knowledge and with a predisposition to act in certain ways; however, successful organizational communicators must learn to adapt knowledge and predispositions to the organization's goals and expectations. This means each member must balance individual skill and creativity with the organization's rules and structure. Organizations are most successful when they recognize and provide opportunities for individual creativity within their formal structure. The workforce of today and of tomorrow is increasingly diverse, and within this mix are employees with unique and valuable abilities, values, and communication styles. Valuing this diversity and providing opportunities for communicating social inclusiveness enhance the communication competency of individuals and the success of organizations.

PUTTING ORGANIZATIONAL COMMUNICATION INTO PRACTICE IN COLLEGE, CAREER, AND LIFE

Up to this point, we have largely focused on organizational communication theory and its application in the work setting. However, organizational communication also directly relates to your higher education experience because, after all, your college or university is an organization. While there are numerous issues that we might consider, let's focus on how communication flows in a college or university and what this means for you as a student.

Increasingly, higher-learning institutions are facing lean economic times. Many states face budget crises, and state legislators are calling for greater accountability from colleges. Likewise, private institutions often face equally difficult economics because the overall economy impacts donations, endowments, and other revenue streams. As a result, many colleges, both public and private, have announced tuition hikes to help defray the burgeoning costs. However, you may not be aware that such intentions even exist unless you listen to the local news or read the school newspaper. The point is this: Many decisions that impact your college experience are made by boards or administrators, and you only learn about the policies after they are instituted. Consequently, although you may have insights or information you would like to add, you do not have the opportunity to voice your concerns. This is, obviously, a communication problem. But how do you solve it? First, you need to understand the flow of communication in your college or university. This means becoming acquainted with who, how, and when decisions are made and what opportunities, if any, you have to speak to decision makers directly or indirectly through student government representation or other intermediaries. In short, if you want to add your voice, you must understand organizational structure and the flow of communication within that structure.

This may be far removed from your everyday interests, so let's consider some additional situations. Let's assume you've seen your advisor and, to your knowledge, have registered for classes for the upcoming semester. However, at the semester's start, you realize you are not registered at all! Where do you go to address this problem? How can you effectively communicate your needs when you find the appropriate contact person? These and similar organizational communication issues are an all-too-real part of college life. To respond, you have to understand organizational structure and how to get help.

To take another example, as teachers, your authors have all had students arrive unexpectedly at our office doors in tears because they thought they were all set to graduate, only to discover that they lacked one course or credit hour. How could this distressing situation occur? How could a student think he or she is ready to graduate and not be? This is a real organizational communication problem that can and does have a disturbing impact on students' lives. However, you can save yourself these heartaches by learning how your college or university's organizational communication system operates and making it work for you. In the end, it's up to you to gather and process all the information necessary to complete your college education. This means you must learn to communicate in the organization of which you are now a part.

SUMMARY

In the world of work today, structures are changing, organizational decision making is changing, and requirements for employee effectiveness are changing. As a college student, you need to understand how to negotiate the organizational environment of your institution. More importantly, once you begin your career in the working world, understanding how to develop and maintain effective organizational relationships is vital to your work success. In this chapter we have identified some essential elements of effective communication in organizational settings:

- "The new knowledge worker" today must possess four key characteristics: college education; analytical thinking; commitment to lifelong learning; and good communication skills.
- Organizations operate as distinct cultures. A culture represents the actions, practices, language, and artifacts of a group.
- A number of symbolic practices make up culture, including language, stories, rites and rituals, and structure.
- The characteristics of organizational systems include wholeness, interdependence, openness, adaptability, and equifinality.
- Effective organizational communication is dependent on the appropriate use of networks and channels of communication within the organization.

- You are entering an era when the cultural, racial, and gender diversity in organizations is more significant than ever before.
- Effective and ethical organizations establish cultures of equal opportunity, free of prohibited discriminatory actions.
- Although face-to-face communication is still important in today's organizations, technological advances have made communication faster, made access to and processing of information much easier, and made communication with others across geographical distances much more accessible.
- The job search process includes steps before, during, and after an interview.
- Organizational communication is important to successfully navigating the college environment.

QUESTIONS FOR DISCUSSION

1. What are the elements of organizational cultures?
2. What are the components of an organizational system?
3. What communication behaviors will best allow you to adapt to the diversity of the modern workplace?
4. What are the essential elements of a good résumé?
5. What must you do to effectively prepare for a job interview?
6. What questions should you be prepared for in the interview?
7. What should you do to follow up after the interview?

EXERCISES

1. Draw a floor plan for your "ideal office." Analyze the symbolic communication in that floor plan. What are you communicating to others about yourself?
2. Interview an individual working in the profession you have chosen. Ask questions about the culture in his or her organization. Ask the individual to list what he or she believes are the most effective organizational communication behaviors.
3. Develop a list of ethical principles and practices for communication in organizations. Under what circumstances would you say no to a manager or supervisor who asked you to violate your ethical values and beliefs in accomplishing some project? Under what circumstances would you "blow the whistle" on someone in your organization who violated the law?
4. Develop a list of employee and employer "rights" on the job. What limits should be placed on the rights of employers to monitor employee behavior on the job? Off the job?

KEY TERMS

Adaptability 284
Employment-selection interview 294
Environment 283
Equifinality 284
Formal networks 288
Informal networks 288
Information-gathering interview 294

Interdependent 284
Language 279
Motivation 290
Openness 284
Organizational culture 279
Rites and rituals 280
Roles 280

Rules and policies 280
Sexual harassment 291
Stories and myths 279
Synergy 284
Wholeness 283

REFERENCES

Autry, J. A. 2001. *The servant leader: How to build a creative team, develop great morale, and improve bottom-line performance.* Roseville, CA: Prima Publishing.

Conrad, C., and Poole, M. S. 2005. *Strategic organizational communication in a global economy.* 6th ed. Belmont CA: Thomson Wadsworth.

Dillard, J., and Miller, K. 1988. Intimate relationships in task environments. In *Handbook of personal relationships*, ed., S. Duck, 449–465. New York: John Wiley & Sons.

Drucker, P. 1992. *Managing for the future: The 1990s and beyond.* New York: Truman Talley Books/Dutton.

Eisenberg, E. M., and Goodall, H. L., Jr. 1997. *Organizational communication: Balancing creativity and constraint.* 2nd ed. New York: St. Martin's Press.

Eisenberg, E. M., Goodall, H. L., Jr., and Trethewey, A. 2010. *Organizational communication: Balancing creativity and constraint.* 6th ed. Boston: Bedford-St. Martin's.

Ganga, E., and Lerner, J. 2004, March 28. Working at home. *The Journal News.* Retrieved April 16, 2004, from www.thejournalnews.com/newsroom/032804/k1928wfworkingathom.html.

Katz, D., and Kahn, R. 1966. *The social psychology of organizations*. New York: John Wiley & Sons.

Kreps, G. 1991. *Organizational communication: Theory and practice*. 2nd ed. New York: Longman.

Miller, K. 2003. *Organizational communication: Approaches and processes*. 3rd ed. Belmont, CA: Thomson Wadsworth.

Oregon Business Report. *45% employers use Facebook-Twitter to screen job candidates*. Reviewed on June 4, 2010 at http://oregonbusinessreport.com/2009/08/45-employers-use-facebook-twitter-to-screen-job-candidates/.

Riley, P., and Eisenberg, E. 1991. The ACE model of management. Unpublished working papers. University of Southern California.

Schutz, W. C. 1958. *FIRO: A three-dimensional theory of interpersonal behavior*. New York: Holt, Rinehart, & Winston.

Seeger, M. W. 1997. *Ethics and organizational communication*. Cresskill, NJ: Hampton Press.

Shockley-Zalabak, P. 2009. *Fundamentals of organizational communication*. 7th ed. Boston: Pearson Allyn Bacon Longman.

14 Mass Communication and Computer Mediated Communication

LEARNING OUTCOMES After reading this chapter, you will have:

the **Knowledge** to. . .   and the **Skills** to. . .

UNDERSTANDING THE WORLD OF MEDIATED MASS COMMUNICATION, page 302

Know the definitions of "mass communication" and "mediated communication" and understand their differences.

- Identify the kinds of mass communication you use (i.e., Internet, television, newspapers).
- Examine the kinds of mediated communication involving technology that you use (i.e., texting, instant messaging, blogging, etc.).
- Consider your use of "converged" media such as e-books or on-line newspapers.
- Reflect on the types of social media you use most (i.e., Facebook, MySpace, LinkedIn, YouTube).

IDENTIFYING THE CHARACTERISTICS OF MEDIATED COMMUNICATION, page 305

Realize the different attributes of mediated communication.

- Recall instances in which Twitter or YouTube have highlighted "citizen journalists" who served a watchdog function.
- Consider ways in which your participation in Facebook is regulated or controlled.

• Examine how media ownership influences mediated mass communication.
• Identify instances where you have been the target or audience of a viral marketing campaign.

EXAMINING THE EFFECTS OF MASS COMMUNICATION, page 306

Be aware of the effects of mass communication.

• Apply the three cultural theories identified in the chapter to their roles in influencing culture.
• Identify ways that mass communication impacts your personal values, attitudes, behavior, and values.

THINKING ABOUT COMPUTER-MEDIATED COMMUNICATION AND SOCIAL MEDIA, page 310

Consider how technology mediates communication.

• Recognize ways that multitasking has positively as well as negatively impacted your academic focus, job performance, and interpersonal relationships.

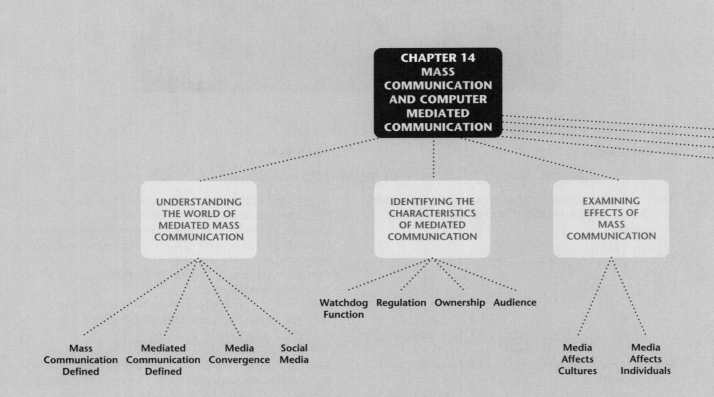

EVALUATING BLOGS AND THE CHANGING FACE OF NEWS, page 312

Assess the impact of blogs and emerging news technology.

- Consider how you and others use emerging technologies to convey information, persuade others, accomplish tasks, etc.

BEING A CRITICAL CONSUMER OF MEDIA, page 312

Analyze the components of mediated mass communication.

- Assess the message, channel, senders, receivers, context, noise, and feedback of the media messages you send and receive.

BECOMING A COMPETENT AND ETHICAL MEDIATED AND MASS COMMUNICATOR IN COLLEGE, CAREER, AND LIFE, page 315

Be a capable and more ethical mediated and mass communicator.

- Exhibit mindfulness, respect, and tolerance when engaging in mediated and mass communication.

THINKING ABOUT COMPUTER-MEDIATED COMMUNICATION AND SOCIAL MEDIA

EVALUATING BLOGS AND THE CHANGING FACE OF NEWS

BEING A CRITICAL CONSUMER OF MEDIA

BEING A COMPETENT AND ETHICAL MEDIATED AND MASS COMMUNICATOR IN COLLEGE, CAREER, AND LIFE

Critical Analysis of the Message

Critical Analysis of the Channel

Critical Analysis of Senders

Critical Analysis of Receivers and Context

Critical Analysis of Noise and Feedback

Mass medium ■ A channel that carries a message to many receivers.

Mass communication ■ Sharing information with a large audience at a given time or across an extended time frame.

Mediated communication ■ Communication that requires a technological channel to complete the communication process.

Mediated mass communication ■ Communication that relies on technology but that can also reach more than one person at the same time.

Computer mediated communication ■ Individual use of technology to communicate with one or more individuals.

UNDERSTANDING THE WORLD OF MEDIATED MASS COMMUNICATION

Think over the past week. What percentage of time were you on your Facebook page? Who were you following on Twitter? Did you a blog? Did you access a podcast? How many times did you have the radio or television on? Did you watch cable or satellite TV? How often did you access your email, enter a chat room, or use instant messaging (IM)? How often did you go online to play games, gather information, or shop? Did you use a DSL ISP (Internet service provider) or dial-up? Did you listen to a CD? How many billboards did you pass while driving? Did you read a magazine, novel, or other reading material? When did you last see a film in a theater or rent a video?

These questions make sense to you, even though they have quite a bit of jargon. The fact that you understand this specialized language indicates the pervasiveness of mass communication in our culture, to say nothing of our frequent use of it.

This pervasiveness of mediated communication in our culture and throughout the world provides us opportunities to see, hear, think, and do things that people prior to the 1950s never dreamed of. We can "travel" to faraway places through the Internet or the Discovery Channel. We can "chat" with people from every corner of the globe with a click of a mouse or the touch of a button. The media at our disposal provide opportunities to expand our knowledge and understanding of the world faster and more comprehensively than ever before. Understanding the unique characteristics of mass communication helps us reflect on its impact on our lives and learn about its influence so that we can be more astute consumers and users of these media.

Mass Communication Defined

Folkerts and Lacy (2001) distinguish between a mass medium, mass communication, and mediated communication. A **mass medium** refers to a channel that carries a message to many receivers. **Mass communication** refers to sharing information with a large audience either at a given time or across an extended time frame. An institution, such as the news media or other organization, distributes the information. Newspapers, magazines, books, films, television, radio, recordings, and the like are all channels for mass communication. The Internet, direct-mail advertising, and telemarketing are considered by some scholars to be mass communication as well, but there is some argument over this.

Mediated Communication Defined

Texting is a popular form of computer mediated communication.

Mediated communication, according to Folkerts and Lacy, requires a technological channel to complete the communication process; "Individuals may share messages using an intermediate device or mechanism, perhaps to overcome distances or obstacles or to reach a large number of other individuals" (26). Therefore, when we speak of **mediated mass communication,** we are usually focusing on communication that relies on technology but that can also reach more than one person at the same time—such as satellite or cable TV, newsmagazines or newspaper websites, radio, etc. The term used to describe individual use of technology to communicate with one or more individuals is **computer mediated communication.** Email, texting on your cell phone, IM (instant messaging), chatting on Facebook are the ways technology allows us to communicate interpersonally with others across distances (even if that distance is just across the room).

Media Convergence

According to Folkerts and Lacy (2001), in every generation, there are old media and new media. "Today, we use the term new media to refer to media forms and media content that are created and shaped by changes in technology. Therefore, the Internet became one of the new media of the twentieth century. As new media evolve, old ones change forms" (5). However, the term *new media* also is used to refer to changes in content. For example, news as presented on MTV is a new form of media content. As new technology replaces old, media forms and technologies come together; this is known as **media convergence.** Now, for example, we can access major newspapers online or read an e-book. Although you may still use media in the old form (i.e., reading the *Chicago Tribune* in its paper form), you are more likely to use media in a new form (i.e., downloading travel directions from Tampa, Florida, to St. Louis, Missouri, from MapQuest). *Convergence* simply means "coming together," and when applied to mass media, it refers to blending technology and content in new and unique ways.

New media ■ Media forms and content that are created and shaped by changes in technology.

Media convergence ■ Media forms and technologies coming together as new technology replaces old.

Social Media

For anyone under the age of 30, the world has always had the Internet, satellite television, cable access, conference calling, cell phones, and an array of technology that those who are a little older may still be trying to navigate. The bottom line is that we take our technology for granted. We want information immediately; we want entertainment at the touch of a button. For many of you in college today, social media have been with you as long as you can remember. At what age, for example, did you put up your Facebook page? One of the most important cultural changes in most of the developed world today is the fact that use of media has changed from traditional forms (i.e., TV, radio, newspapers) to what we call social media today. The most critical difference between the traditional and social media is that a primary use of social media for many of us is to establish specific relationships and to meet relational needs. Social media are used for sharing experiences and thus reducing the "space" (physical and psychological) between many individuals. Communitywealth.com lists these as the top 10 types of social media operating today: Facebook, MySpace, LinkedIn, Care2com, Twitter, YouTube, [individual] Podcast, Wiki(s), blog(s), RSS Feed (http://communitywealth.com/newsletter/august%202009/top%2010%20social%20media.htm). But this is just the tip of the iceberg as far as the options for social media are concerned. How many of the links in Table 14.1 are familiar to you?

TABLE 14.1

SOCIAL MEDIA SITES

100zakladok	Bit.ly	Bryderi.se	Designmoo
2 Tag	bizSugar	BuddyMarks	Digg
2linkme	Bleetbox	Buzzzy	Diggita
A1-Webmarks	Blinklist	Camyoo	DiggTiger
Adifni	Blip	Care2	diglog
aero	Blogger	Chiq	Digo
AIM Share	Bloggy	Cirip	Diigo
Amazon	Blogmarks	CiteULike	Dipdive
Amen Me!	Blurpalicious	ClassicalPlace	doMelhor
AOL Mail	Bobrdobr	Clickazoo	Doower
Arto	BonzoBox	Cndig	Dosti
Ask	BookmarkingNet	Colivia.de	DotNetKicks
Aviary Capture	Bookmarky.cz	Connotea	DotNetShoutout
Baang	Bordom	COSMiQ	Douban
Baidu	Box.net	Delicious	Drimio
Bebo	Brainify	DesignBump	Dropjack

Dzone	Hipstr	MySpace	Startlap
Edelight	Hitmarks	N4G	Story Follower
eKudos	Hot Bookmark	NetLog	Strands
elefanta.pl	Hotklix	Netvibes	studiVZ
eLert Gadget	Hotmail	Netvouz	Stuffpit
Email	HOTweb.lt	NewsTrust	StumbleUpon
Embarkons	HTML Validator	Newsvine	Stumpedia
euCliquei	Hyves	Nujij	Stylehive
Evernote	ideaREF!	OKNOtizie	Surfpeople
extraplay	Identi.ca	Oneview	Svejo
EzySpot	iGoogle	Orkut	Symbaloo
Fabulously40	ihavegot	Osmosus	TagMarks.de
Facebook	Instapaper	Oyyla	Tagvn
Fai Informazione	InvestorLinks	PDF Online	Tagza
Fark	iSociety	PDFmyURL	Technorati
Farkinda	iWiW	PhoneFavs	TellMyPolitician
FAVable	Jamespot	Picciz	The Web Blend
Faves	Jisko	PimpThisBlog	ThisNext
favlog	Jumptags	Ping.fm	Tip'd
Favoritus	Kaboodle	Planypus	Transferr
Flaker	Kaevur	Plaxo	Translate
Floss.pro	Kipup	Plurk	Tulinq
Fnews	kIRTSY	Polladium	Tumblr
Folkd	Kledy	PopEdition	Tusul
FollowTags	Kommenting	Posteezy	TweetMeme
fooxweb	koornk	Posterous	Twitter
forceindya	Kudos	Prati.ba	TypePad
Fresqui	Laaikit	PrintFriendly	Viadeo
FriendFeed	Ladenzeile	Propeller	Virb
Friendster	Librerio	Pusha	Visitez Mon Site
FunP	Link Ninja	Quantcast	Vyoom
fwisp	Link-a-Gogo	Read It Later	Webnews
Gabbr	LinkedIn	receeve.it	Whois Lookup
Gacetilla	LinkShares	Reddit	Windy Citizen
Gamekicker	Linkuj.cz	Rediff MyPage	WireFan
Gamesnetworks	Live	RedKum	WordPress
GiveALink	Livefavoris	Scoop.at	Worio
GlobalGrind	LiveJournal	Segnalo	Wovre
GluvSnap	LockerBlogger	Sekoman	Wykop
Gmail	Lynki	Shaveh	Xanga
Google	Mashbord	SheToldMe	Y! Mail
Google Buzz	Mawindo	Simpy	Y! Bookmarks
Google Reader	Meccho	Slashdot	Yahoo! Buzz
Gravee	meinVZ	SmakNews	Yammer
GreaterDebater	Mekusharim	SMI	Yardbarker
Grono.net	Memori.ru	SodaHead	Yazzem
Grumper	Menéame	Sonico	Yigg
Haber.gen.tr	Mindbodygreen	Speedtile	Yoolink
HackerNews	Mister Wong	Sphinn	Yorumcuyum
Hadash Hot	Mixx	Spoken To You	Youbookmarks
Hatena	Moemesto.ru	sportpost	YouMob
Hazarkor	mototagz	springpad	Zakladok.net
Hedgehogs.net	Multiply	Spruzer	Zanatic
HelloTxt	myAOL	Squidoo	ZooLoo
HEMiDEMi	Mylinkvault	Startaid	

IDENTIFYING THE CHARACTERISTICS OF MEDIATED COMMUNICATION

Media are not new, but their impact on our lives continues to be significant in our development of our sense of self, our perceptions of others, and our understanding and interpretation of the world around us. Each of us uses specific media to meet the needs we described in Chapter 6, and which we explore in more detail later in this chapter. First, though, lets look at some of the basic characteristics of media today and what function they perform in our culture.

Watchdog Function

Historically, the "watchdog" function of media has referred to the responsibility of the press to act as guardians of the public interest. The press is sometimes referred to as the fourth branch of government because it is responsible for guarding citizens' rights to have access to information and activity that impacts their lives. The press, therefore, constantly reports about government activities, the lives of "important" persons, and the activities of business: each of these provides newsworthy information to the public so that we can make informed decisions about our lives. What is interesting about today's "press" is the emergence of "citizen journalists" who diversify our source of news with blogs. Mainstream journalists also can disseminate news through blogs. Bowmann & Willis (2003) report that this participation serves to provide independent, reliable, accurate, wide-ranging and relevant information that citizens in a democracy need but in what may be to many a more credible environment. Glaser (2006) writes: "One of the main concepts behind **citizen journalism** is that mainstream media reporters and producers are not the exclusive center of knowledge on a subject—the audience knows more collectively than the reporter alone. Now, many of these Big Media outlets are trying to harness the knowledge of their audience either through comments at the end of stories they post online or by creating citizen journalist databases of contributors or sources for stories."

Regulation

Like other types of communication, mass communication involves senders, receivers, messages, channels, noise, context, and feedback. Unlike the senders in other types of communication, senders of traditional mass communication are highly regulated. This **regulation** controls content both prior to and after distribution. For example, the Federal Trade Commission (FTC) regulates commercial advertising. The FTC enforces regulation that controls what may be communicated about a commercial product or service to protect consumers from false claims that are misleading. Regulation also controls messages deemed obscene or indecent, limits access to crime scenes or courtrooms during trials involving juveniles, and protects owners of copyrighted works from use without their permission. Government regulation ends, however, where social media begin. So while the content of radio, television, and newspapers is scrutinized by the FTC, the vast majority of your social media are only regulated in so far as the creators of the site are concerned. At the time of this writing, Facebook had reached the 500 millionth user mark (Fletcher 2010). How does Facebook "police" its site with this many users? Interestingly, Facebook regulates issues of privacy and viral marketing more than any other type of content. In 2007 Facebook prevented developers from showing a different profile to friends than the one the user sees himself/herself and blocked developers from sending misleading notifications to users (Arrington 2007).

Ownership

Another distinction between the traditional mass communication process and communication in other contexts is ownership and how it impacts the content and form of mass or mediated communication. Mass communication is big business. Because of the competition for viewers, readers, and consumers, smaller companies are being swallowed up by larger media conglomerates; consequently, the ownership of many traditional media is concentrated in the hands of very few owners. Today, media conglomerates dominate. Conglomerates are collections of businesses under one ownership, such as those involving

Citizen journalism ■ The expansion of news through blogs, predominantly by non-journalists.

Regulation ■ Controls over content prior to and after its distribution.

newspapers, radio stations, television stations, cable companies, filmmaking companies, and magazine publishers. In 1993, for example, fewer than 20 corporations had majority control of the newspaper, magazine, TV, book, and movie industries (Cohen & Solomon 1993, A11). Today, the numbers are significantly smaller. Consider, for example, a conglomerate such as TimeWarner, which owns a cable TV business and an Internet service provider (AOL) while also playing a major role in the movie and print industries. Because such conglomerates are expected to produce huge profits, some critics of this concentrated ownership suggest that we now have a potential threat of a monopoly on information "by self-interested outside corporations that have no commitment to the journalistic imperative and spirit" (Day 2003, 247). This profit-motive ownership worries critics because the economic incentive to make high profits for stockholders may override an incentive to monitor government activities and provide comprehensive information to the public. Media conglomerates may be inclined to shirk their "watchdog" commitments to free press in favor of more lucrative financial ventures. This issue of ownership of traditional media may also be one of the reasons social media today are seen as more "credible" than the media conglomerate. The issues of credibility and bias are interrelated, and if consumers of media see traditional media as having bias (Is CNN too liberal? Fox News too conservative?), then citizen journalists who are not associated with the larger mainstream media may be perceived as being independent and thus more credible.

Audience

The nature of the audience constitutes yet another characteristic of mass mediated communication. The audience for a mass or mediated channel can be larger, heterogeneous, diverse, and geographically separated, or it can be highly specialized, homogeneous, and geographically close. So, for example, people from across the country can attend a professional workshop by dialing a toll-free telephone number while also logging onto a protected website. By blending these two channels, participants can share in a conference call where they can offer observations and ask questions while viewing video clips or PowerPoint slides on their computer screens. Mass and mediated communication, therefore, allow opportunities to send messages to an almost unlimited potential audience.

On the other hand, new technology allows companies and other senders the opportunity to pinpoint targeted audiences through, for example, direct mail or email advertising. Have you ever wondered how you got on a mailing list for information about a group, activity, or product you didn't want? Almost any time you make a purchase or inquire about a product or service, your name is sold to one group by another group or by one company to another company. In other words, you are a targeted consumer. At the same time, when you subscribe to a free email service or register a product you purchased online, you are probably asked to answer questions about you and your preferences. This information helps marketers send you messages that will likely interest you. Of course, you can also use search engines or other information-gathering services to find products, people, or services you are interested in. In this instance, you help marketers, companies, or others find you. You become a potential target of **viral marketing.** "Viral marketing describes any strategy that encourages individuals to pass on a marketing message to others, creating the potential for exponential growth in the message's exposure and influence. Like viruses, such strategies take advantage of rapid multiplication to explode the message to thousands, to millions" (Wilson 2005). Viral marketing uses the following strategies to help marketers find you and adapt their strategies to your needs: (1) gives away products or services; (2) exploits common motivations and behaviors; (3) uses existing communication networks; and (4) takes advantage of others' resources.

EXAMINING EFFECTS OF MASS COMMUNICATION

The pervasiveness and speed with which we have access to our world means that mass and mediated communication shape and define our culture more significantly than ever before in history. In particular, the developing world now has access to the developed world more than ever. Those of us in the developed world also have greater knowledge of the poverty, disaster, and misery of less fortunate individuals around the world. In addition to understanding the strife and suffering in our world, mass and mediated communication give us access to the richness and cultural diversity of the world. This

Viral marketing ■ Any strategy that encourages individuals to pass on a marketing message to others, creating the potential for exponential growth in the message's exposure and influence.

increased access to information causes many to ask what, ultimately, is the impact of media and mass communication on individuals and cultures? In the following sections we explore a range of effects that result from the development and use of mass and mediated communication technologies.

Media Affect Cultures

Researchers have been trying to answer the question of how media affect cultures since traditional mass communication became commonplace. Several mass media researchers believe that the pervasiveness of mass and mediated communication significantly impacts the development of cultures, which are constantly changing.

SOCIAL CONSTRUCTION/CULTIVATION THEORIES   The **social construction (or cultivation) theory** of mass communication suggests that what the media show us is one of the most important elements of our construction and interpretation of our culture. We use mass media as our primary sources of information about the world, thus giving them greater power. What we learn about the world through use of media helps us "construct" our perceptions of the world, of appropriate and inappropriate behavior, of who and what we should be. According to media researcher and developer of cultivation theory George Gerbner (1973; 1976) and his colleagues, heavy television viewing influences the values, roles, and worldview that people adopt. For example, if individuals watch a great deal of violence on TV, they believe the world is cruel and scary. Gerbner and his colleagues also suggest that television, especially television violence, impacts children more significantly than adults. Because television is primarily focused on telling stories, "television cultivates from infancy the very predispositions and preferences that used to be acquired from other primary sources" (Gerbner 1976, 17) such as children's books, nursery rhymes, and childhood songs and games.

For example, after 9/11, President Bush urged the American people not to draw inaccurate conclusions about Muslims living in the United States. The images of the Twin Towers bursting into flame, along with the indictment of al-Qaeda as the perpetrator, created the potential for U.S. citizens to draw unwarranted conclusions about all Muslims or the religion of Islam. In short, media images shape the way we think about our world. This, in turn, creates cultural stereotypes that have the power to influence our perceptions and, subsequently, the tones and tensions in our communities.

We also create more personal views of ourselves through our unique and repetitive use of media. Duck and McMahan (2010) suggest, "Beyond increased media options and a focus on specific audiences, individual members of an audience have always possessed the ability to create original and distinct media products through their individual and unique use of each media system" (353). Ask yourself what channels on your cable or satellite system you gravitate to. What music do you download on your iPod? Do you scan specific sections of a news website? What genre of novels do you read? Each time you make choices about the types of information you scan, you create an experience that is unique to you, and that helps to create a particular view of the world. In other words, you "socially construct" your view of the world through your use of specific media.

CRITICAL THEORIES: HEGEMONY AND IDEOLOGY   Critical theorists who emerged in the 1920s suggested that the economic structure of a society determines its social structure. They believed that media, primarily mainstream media, portray only those individuals, values, ideas, and interpretations that support the interests and beliefs of the power elite in this country. The elite represent a predominantly male, white perspective. The messages generated by these people are thus hegemonic, or focused on keeping the powerless silent. **Hegemony** refers to control or dominating influence by one person or group, especially by one political group over a society or one nation over others. **Ideology** is a set of beliefs, values, and opinions that shapes the way a person or a group such as a social class thinks, acts, and understands the world (Encarta 2010). For hegemony to work, though, people have to do things, willingly and happily, in their everyday lives that keep the powerful people on top. Communication professor Julia Wood (1994) suggests that one of the ways the media perpetuate hegemony is by sheer numbers. For example, in the world portrayed on television, white males make up two-thirds of the population; women over the age of 35 represent less than 10 percent of the population. However, the portrayal of stereotypical views of our culture are shifting; we now see a much greater diversity of individuals portrayed in

Culture Counts

Social construction (or cultivation) theory ■ Suggests that what the media portray is one of the most important elements of the construction and interpretation of our culture.

Hegemony ■ Control or dominating influence by one person or group, especially by one political group over a society or one nation over others.

Ideology ■ A set of beliefs, values, and opinions that shapes the way a person or a group such as a social class thinks, acts, and understands the world.

television, film, and advertising. People of color, gays and lesbians, and individuals with disabilities are seen with much greater frequency than even ten years ago. But the sheer numbers still do not portray the reality of our multicultural world. When we determine that the ways the media portray us culturally and individually is "right" we have bought into the hegemonic and ideological interpretation of the world. Some would argue that when we voluntarily support the status quo by flying the American flag, singing the National Anthem at a ball game, wearing designer labels on our clothing, shopping at chain stores, or buying greeting cards for every holiday, we voluntarily support the hegemony of society.

The media support power structures such as government, capitalism/corporations, and patriarchy in numerous ways. If a news report shows strong support for a controversial foreign policy decision, it can be said to hegemonically support the government. If a home improvement network makes it seem "normal" to own high-end granite counter tops and stainless steel appliances, it can be said to be hegemonically supporting the capitalist economic system. And if a game show includes a scantily clad woman passively standing still until the host tells her to "open the case," it can be seen as hegemonically promoting patriarchy.

CULTURAL IMPERIALISM   Scholars also note that cultural, media, and technological imperialism (Martin & Nakayama 2001) all play a definitive role in shaping and perpetuating culture. Specifically, artifacts of Western popular culture—such as music and movies—are circulated worldwide and cause the profit margins of Hollywood filmmakers to soar (Guback 1969). But how does this cultural and economic domination impact the cultures that import Western media? Although some cultures invite this influence, others, such as French Canadians, are concerned that their cultural uniqueness will be eclipsed or subordinated by Western cultural norms, beliefs, and values. As one travels the globe, the influence of Western media is obvious. For example, in Europe there are advertisements for films made in the United States and stores selling various U.S. newspapers, magazines, CDs, DVDs, and videos. Western media, due to its economic power, tend to dominate the globe; this raises important questions about cultural media imperialism.

These theoretical perspectives imply that mass and mediated communication may have a powerful influence on the development and evolution of cultures. Yet most scholars suggest that other factors are involved in the mass communication processes that mediate these powerful effects.

Media Affect Individuals

Not only does mediated mass communication affect culture; it also impacts individuals. In this section, we will consider its uses and gratifications, gatekeeping/media bias, agenda-setting, attitude-shaping, and behavioral influences.

USES AND GRATIFICATIONS   Some researchers suggest a more microscopic approach to understanding the effects of media. The **uses and gratifications theory** argues that we turn to the media to fulfill preexisting needs. We identify a specific medium—film, television show, or CD—that provides us a diversion, an emotional release, a fantasy, or a substitute companion. We turn to a specific medium for value reinforcement, sage advice, or fulfillment of unmet needs or expectations. Every choice you make in terms of the media you use, according to this theory, is a way for you to control your interactions with the media with the goal of fulfilling such gratifications as information (finding out about events, advice, basic curiosity); personal identity (reinforcing ideas and values, models for behavior); social interaction (gaining insight into social phenomena, identifying with others, finding a basis for future conversations, substituting for real-life relationships, connecting with others); and entertainment (escape, relaxation, emotional release, sexual arousal) (Katzz, Gurevitch & Haas 1973). You are an active participant in creating your media experience. At this writing, one of the most common TV genres today is the "reality show"—particularly popular are those in which the audience is a part of the process of "voting" someone on or off the show. What makes us identify with certain characters and not others, and what makes us keep coming back week after week to check on the characters? Today the range of choices for what to watch and who to follow is wide open. Cable channels, magazines, and websites are so focused, they meet the needs of even the smallest

Uses and gratifications theory
■ Argues that we turn to media to fulfill preexisting needs.

niche audience. And, this theory suggests, the reason for this range of choices is that we, the active media consumer, have determined what we need through our choices, and the media have responded.

GATEKEEPING AND MEDIA BIAS   **Gatekeeping** refers to the process of determining what is newsworthy and important enough to reach an audience. Some researchers believe this gatekeeping function of the media is their greatest power. Decisions are made every day by newspaper editors and radio or TV station managers about what stories should be covered and in what depth. Bloggers determine what is discussed on the "blogosphere" and Amazon tells us what people are buying on a daily basis. Are stories about shootings by teenagers more likely to receive news coverage if they occur in a primarily white suburb than if they occur in the inner city? Are reporters more likely to cover fighting in a country that the United States has an economic relationship with as opposed to a nation where our interests are purely humanitarian?

Further, decisions are made about where those stories should appear in the newspaper or during the newscast. Should they be on the front page or be buried in a short paragraph next to the obituaries? Should the story run in the first five minutes of the newscast with other breaking news, or should it air at the end of the newscast with the rest of the human-interest stories? The media's gatekeeping impacts the information we receive and, as a result, the interpretation or importance we ascribe to a person, place, or event.

The gatekeeping phenomenon is considered to be the place where media bias begins. Conservative media critics argue that the media have a liberal bias in their coverage of individuals, events, and issues. Liberal media critics argue that because the concentration of media ownership is primarily in the hands of conservatives, media content and coverage reflect more conservative values. Researchers on both sides of this issue have discovered biased coverage. While debate continues over whether the media are too liberal or too conservative in their coverage, during recent political election campaigns, the media coverage of both the Democrats and the Republicans was negative. Whether systematic bias exists or not, there seems to be negativity toward politicians. Media coverage, especially television, tends to focus on the sensational, the unique, and the extraordinary instead of on the trials and tribulations of everyday life.

AGENDA SETTING   Individuals who decide what should or should not be reported have enormous control, then, over what we deem to be important in the world. In this way, the media set the **agenda of news** and information. Our political agenda is set by more coverage of certain candidates or issues than others. Agendas vary among different media. Newspapers often have more time to cover an issue, an event, or a person in more depth than radio or television. Television, more than any other medium, tends to provide us information in sound bites. Even the running headlines at the bottom of the cable news screen suggest what we should be thinking and talking about.

> Newspapers provide a host of cues about the salience of the topics in the daily news—lead story on page one, other front page display, large headlines, etc. Television news also offers numerous cues about salience—the opening story on the newscast, length of time devoted to the story, etc. These cues repeated day after day effectively communicate the importance of each topic. In other words, the news media can set the agenda for the public's attention to that small group of issues around which public opinion forms. (http://sticerd.lse.ac.uk/dps/extra/McCombs.pdf)

ATTITUDE SHAPING   The media's power is even more subtle in the way our attitudes become synchronous with those represented by the media we choose to follow. The media's power to construct culture impacts individual interpretations of that culture. We learn new vocabulary and expand our language through media. We also learn what is considered "normal" in terms of height, weight, shape, hairstyles, skin color, dress, or hobbies. If you look at women's fashion magazines, for example, apparently a size zero is what all women should be aiming for. Or, perhaps, given media images, men must be tall, dark, muscular, and handsome. We who do not embody these media-manipulated images are constantly comparing ourselves to these norms and finding ourselves falling short of what is expected. The media impact our self-esteem if we can never live up to

Gatekeeping ■ The process of determining what is newsworthy and important enough to reach an audience.

Agenda of news ■ The ability of media decision makers to influence what media consumers think is important in the world.

the images portrayed as normal and desirable. Television, magazines, or movies become the yardstick by which we measure ourselves. Because we are surrounded every day by what we ought to be, to know, and to believe, our values become *framed* by these expectations. Therefore, media directly shape our attitudes and expectations about ourselves and others. More and more, scholars believe that we develop attitudes and knowledge about relationships, communities, and the world through media (Cohen & Metzger 1998).

BEHAVIORAL INFLUENCES   Once our values are shaped or framed by the expectations we see, our behavior begins to conform to the expectations as well. We begin to make *social comparisons* to the individuals portrayed by the media. We then "model" their behavior or make a commitment *not* to behave in certain ways. Perhaps, for example, some of us watch talk shows like *Dr. Phil, Montel Williams,* or *Oprah* to compare ourselves to the guests and say, "I'm *not* them!" We join a gym or try one diet after another because we look at a magazine and say, "Why can't *I* be like them?" At the extreme, some individuals, both adults and children, go so far as to copy the behavior they see in the media. This can lead to violence and tragedy. Thus, mass media consumption influences our behavior—sometimes with very negative consequences.

Passivity or *desensitization* to the violence that we see in the media also impacts our behavior. Gerbner studied this phenomenon for more than 40 years and demonstrated that desensitivity to violence is one of the most pervasive and powerful behavioral consequences of significant media exposure. The more desensitized we become to violence, the more violence we need to be entertained, as suggested by the burgeoning amount of violence on TV. For example, the Parents Television Council released a final study that looks at the trend of violence on prime time television since 1998. During the first hour of prime time (8:00–9:00 P.M.), violence increased by 41 percent. Violence was up 134 percent during the second hour of prime time (9:00–10:00 P.M.) and 63 percent during the third hour of prime time (10:00–11:00 P.M.; www.parentstv.org/).

In addition to desensitization and passivity, some critics of mediated violence suggest that viewing too much violence encourages individuals to model what they see. Television and film portray an enormous amount of violence. According to the American Psychological Association (APA), by the age of 18, children and teens will have seen 16,000 simulated murders and 200,000 acts of violence (www.healthyminds.org/mediaviolence.cfm). The APA has also reported that children and adults who watch a lot of televised violence are more likely to act violently in their everyday lives. These findings remain consistent regardless of level of education, social class, attitudes toward aggression, parental behavior, and sex-role identity.

While this discussion of the media's power is limited, it suggests that we all need to be critical consumers of media. We now turn to some principles to help you become such a consumer.

The more desensitized we become to violence, the more violence we need to be entertained.

THINKING ABOUT COMPUTER-MEDIATED COMMUNICATION AND SOCIAL MEDIA

As we indicated in Chapter 1, the channel of communication you choose to use dramatically impacts human communication. We also indicated that CMC (computer-mediated communication) has dramatically transformed the landscape of human communication. But how does CMC impact listening or the speed of relationship development? Does CMC change the nature of the relationships or the ways in which we exchange information in relationships? As we continue to increasingly rely upon CMC and other forms of technology such as cell phones and iPods, we are faced with new insights and challenges in understanding the impact of CMC.

Some contend that we are bombarded by so much information that our listening skills are rapidly declining. Multitasking has become the buzz word for many people who talk or text on their cell phones while driving a car or who respond to emails and talk on the phone simultaneously. No doubt our listening skills are compromised by our failure to give full attention to one another, but are computers and other technology the true culprits in this decline? In an article in the *New York Times* on June 7, 2010, Matt Richtel tells the story of "Mr. Campell." Campbell almost missed an email from a company offering to buy his business for $1.3 million dollars—he missed the email for 12 days amid an "electronic flood: two computer screens alive with email, instant messages, online chats, a Web browser and the computer code he was writing." His wife complains that he cannot unlink from his technology. Richtel writes, "While many people say multitasking makes them more productive, research shows otherwise. Heavy multitaskers actually have trouble focusing and shutting out irrelevant information, scientists say, and they experience more stress." Nora Volkow, director of the National Institute of Drug Abuse told Richtel, "The technology is rewiring our brains." While technology can benefit the brain by becoming more efficient at finding information, it can also mirror the addictive qualities of drugs and alcohol.

Relying upon technology creates new insights and challenges in understanding the impact of CMC.

So CMC may be seen as a call to greater listening or as part of the the demise of effective listening. There are many forms of aural information on the Web, including the various audio and video formats, streaming, Web telephone, and computer-based video conferencing. All of these channels of communication require effective listening skills, and some of us become more acute listeners. Others of us, though, consume more and more information and are constantly shifting our attention. We go to sleep with a laptop, wake up with Facebook and iPhone on the nightstand. Richtel explains, "At home, people consume 12 hours of media a day on average, when an hour spent with, say, the Internet and TV simultaneously counts as two hours. That compares with five hours a day in 1960....Computer users visit an average of 40 Web sites a day."

In contrast to the problems of multitasking as a consequence of CMC use, Walther and Burgoon (1992) suggest that CMC may speed the level of intimacy in a relationship. CMC might start out even more personal than face-to-face (FtF) interaction because people are often less concerned about the impression they are making because of the anonymity of the medium, and they are not as worried about proper turn-taking or other formalities. Therefore, in its initial stages, CMC can be more intimate that FtF communication. Computer mediated communication may even help initiate relationships that might never have begun if they had required a face-to-face meeting. For instance, are you more likely to approach a professor with a question over email or some other form of CMC than to call him or her on the phone or arrange an appointment?

Other social media such as Facebook, chat rooms, YouTube, and personal blogs are providing users with tools to develop stronger emotional attachments within non-FtF relationships. "Facebook makes us smile, shudder, squeeze into photographs so we can see ourselves online later, fret when no one responds to our witty remarks, snicker over who got fat after high school, pause during weddings to update our relationship status to Married or codify a breakup by setting our status back to single" (Fletcher 2010).

Blogs ■ Any website in which an individual or a group records information or opinions; usually diary-like and personal.

EVALUATING BLOGS AND THE CHANGING FACE OF NEWS

Blogs, as we discussed earlier, are changing the face of news today. "Blogs are popular in part because they enable easy, inexpensive self-publication of content for a potentially vast audience on the world wide web, and because they are more flexible and interactive than previous publication formats, print or digital (Herring, Scheidt, Kouper & Wright 2005, 3). "Blogs played key roles in the U.S. presidential primaries [in 2004]; bloggers were invited to cover the national conventions of both Democrats and Republicans; and blogs also played a significant role in reporting the unfolding world events from the London underground [2004 bombing] to the streets of Iraq, to the shores of Indonesia and Thailand (Bruns & Jacobs 2007, 1).

The number of blogs existing today defies quantification. Thierer reported that in 2008 there were about 112 million estimated (http://techliberation.com/2008/05/06/need-help-how-many-blogs-are-there-out-there/). Herring et al. (2005) suggest that media attention to blogs has grown in proportion to the numbers published. Their research suggests that most blogs are single-authored, personal diaries. The predominance of personal content over news content complicates the designation of these bloggers as "citizen journalists." Papacharissi (2007) confirms the diary-like structure and, through a content analysis of 260 blogs, reported that they "presented low-tech, self-referential, verbose attempts to display personal thoughts and information, with little interest for how these thoughts would be received by an audience" (37).

As individual journalists and private citizens become active publishers, commentators, and news analysts, bloggers join mainstream, traditional journalists in providing an alternative newsfeed. And all bloggers, according to Bruns and Jacobs (2007), become "produsers"—a hybrid of both potential users and potential producers of content.

> If, as blogging and other collaborative media phenomena appear to indicate, there is now an ongoing shift from production/consumption-based mass media, which *produce* a vision of society for us to consume as relatively passive audiences, to produsage-based personal media, where users are active *produsers* of a shared understanding of society which is open for others to participate in, to develop and challenge, and thus to continually co-create, then this cannot help but have a profound effect on our future. At worst, it may generate more debate and disagreement, ... at best, it may offer renewed hope for a more broad-based, democratic involvement of citizens in the issues that matter to them. (7)

A final issue regarding the use of blogs and personal messages on other social media is the potential for embarrassment by companies or organizations who find themselves highlighted or critiqued for their stupidity. In a Winter 2010 issue of *PR Strategist*, an incident involving Kevin Smith, film director and Twitter user, and Southwest Airlines is highlighted. On February 17, 2010, Smith was escorted off a Southwest Airlines flight because of his weight. As soon as he was off the plane, he sent a message to his 1.5 million-plus followers on Twitter, complete with pictures. He tweeted, "I know I'm fat, but was Captain Leysath really justified in throwing me off a flight for which I was already seated?" Southwest responded within 20 minutes with an apology, an accommodation on a later flight, and a travel voucher. A Southwest spokesperson said, "Although I'm not here to debate the decision our employees made, I can tell you that I for one have learned alot today. The communication among our employees was not as sharp as it could have been and, it's apparent that Southwest could have handled this situation differently." Corporate crisis management, customer relations, and public relations are increasingly being called to account through discussions on social media. Responding to a disgruntled customer appropriately today requires the company representative to be savvy in all media.

BEING A CRITICAL CONSUMER OF MEDIA

As we have just discussed, there are many important issues that impact what, when, and how mass communicators report (as news gatherers) or portray (as filmmakers) or analyze (as bloggers). Once you recognize these issues, you need to develop a set of critical analytical skills that will assist you in becoming more competent in your "consumption" of mass communication. Our discussion of the appropriate skills required to become a competent consumer will focus on each of the critical elements of the mass communication model: messages, channels, senders, receivers, context, feedback, and noise.

Critical Analysis of the Message

The ability to determine the degree of ambiguity in the message is important. Toward this end, we look at the use of language. The more abstract the language used, the more ambiguous the message and the more open it is to interpretation. Also, look at the message and examine the degree of reason or emotion used. Is the message informative or persuasive? Is the argument supported by appeals to our emotion or our intellect, or both? In addition, examine the message for completeness and accuracy. What information has been left out? Is the message one-sided and manipulative? Does the message convey many points of view, or just one? Today we are drowning in information; the sheer quantity is overwhelming. Our ability to interpret the array of mediated messages depends on our skill at assessing elements of the message itself.

Critical Analysis of the Channel

Media theorists McLuhan and Fiore (1967) claimed that "the medium is the message" in mass communication. They meant that the medium, or channel, influences how the message is interpreted to the degree that the meaning changes with the medium. McLuhan distinguished between hot media and cold media and explained how each impacted the ways individuals interpreted meaning. Messages relayed through print channels (cold) require us to add our own visuals, whereas more visual media like television (hot) do not require us to add to the message. We must develop and expand our own meaning more significantly with cold media. In other words, we tend to remain passive when receiving messages on television; we let the medium do the work. And the more dependent we become on visual or hot media, the less likely we are to use critical skills in assessing information.

Some media allow for elaboration and extension of information about issues, persons, or events while others do not. Newspapers and other print media, for example, have more space to devote to an article, as do blogs. Television, in contrast, tends to offer us sound bites of information, with little detail or extension. However, traditional print media, because they are delayed, are often out of date before they are published, while blogs and television can provide up-to-the-minute coverage. In the almost 40 years since McLuhan wrote about the impact of the medium, we now have electronic media that merge elements of hot and cold. The major news media outlets today (i.e., CNN, FOX, ABC, MSNBC, CBS) now have news websites and blogs where you can access news and information, complete with video and audio footage. These websites are updated constantly. We also can find much more interpretation of news in the form of news editorials and news analysis programming. As critical consumers of media, we must use a variety of mass communication channels to obtain the most comprehensive information base with regard to an issue, person, or event.

Critical Analysis of Senders

Mass media is big business. The media business exists to make a profit. Thus, part of becoming a critical consumer of media is the ability to analyze the bias or source credibility of the mediated messages you receive. To develop this critical skill, look carefully at whether the media source attributes information (facts, inferences, and conclusions) to any other source. If not, should you assume the initial source is providing fact or opinion? What is the basis of the source's expertise in providing that opinion? Another question should focus on the relationship between the source of the message and the issue, person, or event being discussed. *Conflict of interest,* according to Day (2003), "is the term used to describe a clash between professional loyalties and outside interests that undermines the credibility of a moral agent" (209). Most of us expect that the reports we read and hear are objective—that is, untainted by some relationship that would influence the information reported.

Critical Analysis of Receivers and Context

The one element of the communication model that you have the most control over is the receiver. You are it. As a member of the audience to which the mass mediated messages are sent, it is your responsibility to monitor and examine your impressions or interpretations of this communication. You can choose which messages you will attend to and how or if you will respond. One of the most powerful analytical and communication skills you can develop is recognizing when not responding is the best choice. We should not feel pressured into making decisions and acting before we have all the information we need to make good choices. We can walk away. We should also consider our emotional state when receiving these messages. Are we jumping to a conclusive interpretation because we have some emotional stake in the issue or event?

In addition, we should look at several other variables regarding the context or situation in which we receive these messages. For example, interpreting messages under conditions of danger to others or ourselves might encourage us to accept less than complete information. Do we allow the government, for instance, to have greater control of the amount and type of information we receive when our country is dealing with military or terrorist threats? Do we allow others to withhold more information or keep secrets from us when the stakes in a communication situation are high? On the flip side of this scenario, do we allow political candidates to engage in negative political advertising during a campaign because "they all do it"? How do we interpret the information individuals wish to share on their Facebook sites? What do you think about the appropriateness of "sharing" pictures of others that are unflattering or humiliating or that show the individual committing a crime? People like Mark Zuckerberg, founder of Facebook, are counting on the fact, actually investing millions in the hope, that we are willing to share everything—from what happens when we party on weekends to how we feel about our bosses, partners, and friends. Zuckerberg said, "What people want isn't complete privacy.... It's that they want control over what they share and what they don't." In 2010, Facebook had the world's largest photo collection, at more than 48 billion unique images (Fletcher 2010). We need to examine the time and place of the communication and engage in critical analysis of ourselves as receivers to become competent consumers of mass mediated messages. As we reported in Chapter 13, half of employers today are screening job applicants through Facebook.

Critical Analysis of Noise and Feedback

Noise impacts the communication situation and the meaning we develop for a mediated message. Therefore, we must be aware of the physical, physiological, and psychological noise that interferes with our examination of mass communication. For example, when you choose which television shows to watch, do you try to find those that portray characters who look, act, and believe like you? How often do you make choices about the music you listen to based on the artist and his or her looks? Can you step out of your comfort zone when making choices about what message you will expose yourself to? Exposing yourself to many points of view allows you to analyze and interpret a message more critically.

As we said earlier, in mass communication situations, opportunities for feedback may be limited. That means the critical consumers of mass mediated messages have to work harder to avail themselves of opportunities to provide feedback. Have you ever written a letter to the editor of your school or local paper? Have you ever called in to a talk show to provide your point of view? Have you ever participated in a product boycott to let a company know you objected to some action it had taken? Despite the delayed nature of this feedback, it does have power.

Keep in mind that most of us interpret silence to mean implicit consent. When you remain silent in the face of some person, issue, or event that is objectionable to you, then you communicate your acceptance of that event. This absence of feedback is also a form of communication, as we suggested at the beginning of this text. Critical and competent consumers of mass communication are willing to provide feedback despite the obstacles. They have the skills to use a variety of channels in gathering information, to analyze the credibility and bias of a source of a message, to examine themselves within the context of receiving the message, and to offer appropriate feedback to the senders of the mediated messages.

BECOMING A COMPETENT AND ETHICAL MEDIATED AND MASS COMMUNICATOR IN COLLEGE, CAREER, AND LIFE

As a student, consider how you use mass communication in your everyday life. You expose yourself to particular types of music, movies, and other forms of popular culture. You probably use the Internet in your research for class projects. Perhaps you like chat rooms and are developing relationships exclusively online. You may have instructors who use a website where they give assignments and have you turn in assignments and chat with fellow classmates or the instructor. You may have classes that invite you on "virtual tours" of the world in the course of studying and understanding other cultures. An instructor may ask you to find and develop an email relationship with a person from another culture.

Most colleges have Web-based registration and most offer courses in a variety of formats. As you can see in the box "Communication Counts in Your College Experience: Web-Based, Web-Enhanced, or Face-to-Face Courses?" you have many choices with regard to the types of classes available to you in today's college or university.

You have opportunities to get information about campus activities and even controversy through your campus newspaper, radio station, or television station. You can become even more involved in these mass communication channels by working for them. These organizations can provide you with invaluable experience.

The more you use media as your communication channel, the more you impact the nature of your relationships with others. In the place of the nonverbal elements of face-to-face communication, the "nonverbal" elements of mediated communication are significant in impacting how we interpret messages and people. Issues of tone and content of messages provide important cues to interpreting meaning, as we have suggested over the course of this text. As we discussed in earlier chapters, you communicate not only content information, you also communicate relationship information. As we discuss in the box "Communication Counts in Your Career: Ethics on the Internet," there are ethical guidelines to competent mediated communication.

Although some types of mass communication—unlike any other communication context we have discussed in this text—encourage receivers to play a passive role in receiving and interpreting its messages, they also allow you to become a more active

COMMUNICATION COUNTS IN YOUR COLLEGE EXPERIENCE:

Web-Based, Web-Enhanced, or Face-to-Face Courses?

College courses today take many forms. You might be enrolled in courses that are "Web-enhanced." Instructors might use such technology as WebCT or Blackboard to add a multimedia dimension to the learning experience. Some courses today are offered exclusively via a Web-based format. Students in a Web-based course may never meet any of the other students or the instructor face-to-face. In a Web-based or Web-enhanced class, instructors may do any of the following: offer the syllabus only online, distribute the assignments through the course website, require assignments to be turned in via email, offer opportunities for students to chat with one another through the website, require students to engage in group problem-solving exercises, and offer audio or video instruction on the website.

To enhance your success in Web-based courses, you must consider the following:

What is your level of knowledge and experience with computer technology? The more computer savvy you are, the more successful you may be.

How successful are you at managing time and meeting deadlines? Often Web-based courses are relatively unstructured, and if you are not a good time manager, you may be less successful in this course format.

Why are you taking an online course? Your attitude matters here. If you are taking the course because you are serious about it but want to maximize convenience, you may be more successful than if you simply want to get through the course without making the effort to get to a regular, on-campus class on time.

How willing are you to contact the instructor for the course? Research suggests that students who ask good questions, contact the instructor for clarification on assignments, and so on, are more likely to succeed both online and in class.

How willing are you to engage other students in "interactive" course requirements, such as email, chats, or group discussions? If you simply prefer to enroll in a class but not interact, you are less likely to succeed in the online course.

Ethics on the Internet

Netiquette refers to accepted standards for engaging in all types of interactions on the web whether in email, chat rooms, discussion boards, or blogs. While there are specific guidelines for various types of communication via the web, consider these general guidelines:

- **Maintain respect.** Remember that you are communicating with people, not machines. Show respect for the recipients in your use of language and tone. Avoid "flaming" or sending heated messages. If you are frustrated with a particular submission, write a draft that allows you to express your emotions about the topic at hand and allow at least 24 hours to lapse. Then, re-read and edit the message before sending it or simply delete it.
- **Follow standards for face to face communication.** Think about how you interact with others in conversation and the ethics you draw; use these same principles in your online interactions.
- **Pay attention to the context.** Remember that what may be acceptable in one setting on the net, may not be in another. For example, you may be able to use a kind of shorthand speech when communicating with friends that would be totally inappropriate if you are interacting on a wiki for a class discussion or a professional interchange. Also, remember that people come from different cultures and this influences how they see the world, use language, and interpret meaning. Work for clarity.

- **Write well.** Use appropriate grammar, spelling, and other mechanics. This may not be as important in some contexts, but as a general guideline write well. This is especially important when communicating with your professors. Also, avoid messages all in upper case since this appears that you are shouting. While emoticons can help indicate the tone of a message, they should be used sparingly.
- **Engage the conversation.** Share what you know or think and be a genuine part of the interaction. This does not mean that you should write lengthy papers on the subject at hand, but that you should offer your insights, questions, or observations freely.
- **Remember the time factor.** Avoid overly long messages. For example, a two page email is probably more than anyone wants or needs. Sometimes face to face conversation is better in such instances. Also, give people time to respond; not everyone is on the same time or can, necessarily, respond quickly to messages.
- **Don't invade another's territory.** Just as you would not open someone's physical mail, do not read another's email or other communication without permission; respect others' privacy.
- **Use clear identifiers.** Be sure to use correct addresses, employ subject lines, and clearly identify yourself as the sender by adding a signature line to all messages.

Mindfulness ■ The withholding of immediate judgment on a message and a search for new ways to interpret and assign meaning to a message.

participant in your community and in the world. As a consumer, you have the responsibility to play an active role in how mass communication impacts you as an individual as well as to become an active participant in our society or culture. O'Hair, Friedrich, Wiemann, and Wiemann (1997) call these responsibilities **mindfulness**. Mindfulness, they suggest, "refers to the withholding of immediate judgment on a message and a search for new categories, that is, new ways to interpret and assign meaning to a message" (494). Being mindful allows you to consider a range of possible options in interpretation, to reserve judgment, and to avoid stereotyping. You have the opportunity to engage in mindfulness during your college career and to begin a lifetime of active engagement in the activities and decisions that impact you by understanding and using the mass communication that surrounds you.

SUMMARY

- Mass or mediated communication pervades our society, impacting or constructing culture and affecting individuals in many ways.
- New and old media today converge to provide us with new ways of receiving the important news and information we need to "live" in the world.
- *Mass communication* refers to sharing information with a large audience either at a given time or across an extended time frame.
- Mass communication is often highly regulated.
- Media conglomerates dominate the mass communication context, and the economic incentive for these big businesses concerns those who evaluate the bias and credibility of sources of information.
- Cultivation theorists suggest that our use of mass mediated messages helps us construct our world and influences the values, roles, and worldview that we adopt.

- Critical theorists suggest that the economic structure of society determines its social structure. Therefore, the mainstream media in our society portray the individuals, values, ideas, and interpretations that support the powerful elite.
- Uses and gratification suggest that we use media to fulfill preexisting needs.
- Media act as gatekeepers in determining what constitutes news of importance and, therefore, sets the agenda for what we believe is important to think about.
- The goals of becoming a more critical consumer of mass communication include recognizing the impact media has on our society and on us as individuals as well as developing a set of skills that will allow us to receive and interpret mass mediated messages more critically.
- Becoming critical consumers means that we increase our awareness of what we see and how we see it, the language and structure of the messages, the impact of various channels used to disseminate messages, and the credibility and bias of the senders of those messages.

QUESTIONS FOR DISCUSSION

1. What are the pros and cons of having a small number of very large media conglomerates in control of the media?
2. *Spam* is a term used to denote the practice of bombarding people with unsolicited advertising through an Internet provider. What are your feelings on spam?
3. What do you think are the most common uses and gratifications people get from their media choices?
4. Do you think the increasing range and sophistication of technology are changing the way we engage in interpersonal relationships? Is technology allowing us to get closer to each other or pushing us further apart?
5. Discuss the impact of media gatekeeping and agenda setting. Do you think the major news media are objective in what they cover and how they cover it?
6. Have you ever worked for a company that used some technology to monitor your work? Have you ever had to take a drug test as part of your employment? In your opinion, do you think this an invasion of privacy or a normal part of everyday working life?

EXERCISES

1. Monitor your television-viewing habits for a week and summarize what you watch. Look at the gender, age, and diversity of the characters on your favorite shows. What kind of "bias" do your choices suggest?
2. Find out who owns your local cable company. Is it a part of a large media conglomerate? How extensive are the "holdings" in the conglomerate? Do you think this constitutes a monopoly of the media in your area?
3. If you haven't tried reading an e-book, find one and try it. Share your impressions with a classmate.
4. Choose a popular magazine and identify the ads that you think depict stereotypical or unreasonable expectations for women, men, people of color, or people with disabilities.
5. Identify three new ways you can become a more critical consumer of media. Use them for a month and summarize the results.
6. Search for websites that relate to ethics in mass communication. What issues, events, and people are discussed?

KEY TERMS

Agenda of news   309
Blogs   312
Citizen journalism   305
Computer mediated
   communication   302
Gatekeeping   309
Hegemony   307

Ideology   307
Mass communication   302
Mass medium   302
Media convergence   303
Mediated communication   302
Mediated mass communication   302
Mindfulness   316

New media   303
Regulation   305
Social construction (or cultivation)
   theory   307
Uses and gratifications
   theory   308
Viral marketing   306

REFERENCES

Arrington, M. 2007. *Facebook takes action against 'black hat' apps*. Retreived June 7, 2010, at http://techcrunch.com/2007/08/16/facebook-takes-action-against-black-hat-apps/.

Bruns, A., and Jacobs, J. 2007. *Uses of blogs*. New York: Peter Lang.

Cohen, J., and Metzger, M. 1998. Social affiliation and the achievement of ontological security through interpersonal and mass communication. *Critical Studies in Mass Communication, 15,* 41–60.

Cohen, J., and Solomon, N. 1993, October 23. High-tech media mergers: Good business, bad policy. *Seattle Times* A11.

Day, L. A. 2003. *Ethics in media communications: Cases and controversies.* 4th ed. Belmont, CA: Wadsworth.

Duck, S. and McMahan D. T. 2010. *Communication in everyday life.* Los Angeles: Sage.

Encarta. (2010). Retrieved July 2008 at http://encarta.msn.com/encnet/features/dictionary/dictionaryhome.aspx

Fletcher, D. 2010, May. Friends without borders. *Time* 175(21), 32–38.

Folkerts, J., and Lacy, S. 2001. *The media in your life: An introduction to mass communication.* 2nd ed. Boston: Allyn and Bacon.

Gerbner, G., and Gross, L. P. 1976, April. The scary world of TV's heavy viewer. *Psychology Today* 10:41–89.

Gerbner, G., Gross, L. P., and Melody, W. H. 1973. *Communications technology and social policy: Understanding the new "cultural revolution."* New York: Interscience Publication.

Glaser, M. 2006, September 27. *Your guide to citizen journalism.* Public Broadcasting Service. Retrieved June 7, 2010, from http://www.pbs.org/mediashift/2006/09/your-guide-to-citizen-journalism270.html.

Guback, T. 1969. *The international film industry: Western Europe and America since 1945.* Bloomington, IN: Indiana University Press.

Herring, S. C., Scheidt, L. A., Kouper, I., and Wright, E. 2005. Longitudinal content analysis of blogs: 2003–2004, 3–20.

In *Blogging, citizenship, and the future of media,* ed. M. Tremayne. New York: Routledge.

Katz, E., Gurevitch, M., & Haas, H. (1973). On the use of the mass media for important things. *American Sociological Review, 38,* 164–181.

Martin, J. K., and Nakayama, T. K. 2001. *Experiencing intercultural communication: An introduction.* Mountain View, CA: Mayfield.

McComb, M. nd. The agenda-setting role of the mass media in the shaping of public opinion. Retreived June 8, 2010, at http://sticerd.lse.ac.uk/dps/extra/McCombs.pdf.

McLuhan, M., and Fiore, Q. 1967. *The medium is the massage: An inventory of effects.* New York: Bantam Books.

Microsoft Corporation. 2007. *Educating the 21st century citizen.* Retrieved May 31, 2007, from http://findarticles.com/p/articles/mi_qa4011/is_200404/ai_n9366427.

O'Hair, D., Friedrich, G. W., Wiemann, J. M., and Wiemann, M. O. 1997. *Competent communication.* 2nd ed. New York: St. Martin's Press.

Papacharissi, Z. (2007). The Blogger Revolution? Audiences as Media Producers. Blogging, Citizenship, and the Future of Media, M. Tremayne (Ed)., Routledge.

Walther, J. B., and Burgoon, J. K. 1992, September. Relational communication in computer-mediated interaction. *Human Communication Research* 19, 50–81.

Wilson, R. F. 2005. E-mail marketing and online marketing editor. *Web Marketing Today.* Retrieved June 7, 2010, at http://www.wilsonweb.com/wmt5/viral-principles.htm.

Wood, J. T. 1994. *Gendered lives: Communication, gender, and culture.* Belmont, CA: Wadsworth.

GLOSSARY

Abstract   Complex and open to varied interpretations and understanding.

Accommodating style   Characterized by low concern for self and high concern for people.

Accuracy   Using the most current, correct, and up-to-date information in a speech.

Actual examples   Examples drawn from real-life events.

Ad hominem **argument**   Attacks a person instead of his or her position on an issue. Becomes a personal attack instead of ethical persuasion.

Ad populum **argument**   Uses popular polls to assume what is popular at any given time and to infer that if someone is in disagreement with what is popular, he or she is not to be trusted or listened to.

Adaptability   The ability to change in response to a rapidly changing global environment.

Adaptors   A wide range of movements intended to hide or "manage" emotions that we do not want to communicate directly.

Aesthetic needs   The highest level of needs; the need to see beauty for its own sake.

Affect displays   The facial movements or expressions that convey emotional meaning as well as the posture or gesture cues that convey our emotions at any given moment.

Agenda of news   The ability of media decision makers to influence what media consumers think is important in the world.

Aggressive style   Forcing one's position on others without allowing for their input.

Aggressiveness   Asserting oneself to an extreme without concern for others.

Ambushing   Occurs when a person listens carefully in order to attack what the speaker says.

Appropriateness   Possessing sensitivity suitably expressed toward a particular person, audience, or context.

Arbitrary   Created in individual persons or through cultural associations.

Articulation   Saying the sounds within words clearly.

Artifacts   A person's dress and adornments, which are a reflection of self-image and a means of communicating messages about the wearer.

Assertiveness   Ability to communicate feelings honestly and in a straightforward manner.

Assertive style   Communicating honestly and clearly explaining one's ideas and beliefs without harming another.

Associate   Signify language.

Attention   The first stage of perception; awareness of certain stimuli.

Attitude   A favorable or negative inclination toward a person, place, event, or object.

Attitudes   A person's general evaluation of an object—such as persons, events, products, policies, or institutions, for example.

Attraction   One of the factors that motivates individuals toward intimacy in an interpersonal relationship.

Attributions   Meanings assigned to actions.

Audience perspective   Considers the listeners' multiple characteristics and the resulting type of audience they comprise.

Audio and video clips   Visual aids that provide examples of ideas or claims.

Authentic dialogue   Dialogue characterized by a willingness to become fully involved with the other, a belief in the equality of each participant, and a climate of supportive communication.

Authentic listening   Seeking to truly understand the intent, feelings, and perspective of a speaker's message.

Authoritative nature of language   The rules of communication with particular others in certain communication contexts as dictated by language.

Authority   The audience's perception of the prevailing knowledge or experience of the speaker enhancing the resulting influence of the speaker.

Avoiding stage   A relationship stage in which parties go their separate ways.

Avoiding style   Characterized by low concern for self and low concern for people.

Backing   Additional evidence that adds power to the warrant. It consists of the facts that support the warrant.

Balance   Making each main point roughly the same importance and length.

Beliefs   Strongly held ideas about the nature of truth.

Blogs   Any website in which an individual or a group records information or opinions; usually diary-like and personal.

Body   Consists of main points, transitions, supporting materials.

Bonding stage   The stage of a relationship that signifies to the outside world a commitment to maintain intimacy.

Brain dominance   Refers to the side of the brain a person is more likely to use, left (logic and writing based) or right (visual and feeling based).

Brainstorming   Allowing the thought process to flow freely.

Briefing   A short presentation in an organizational setting that focuses on a process, event, or person.

Cause–effect pattern   Speech design that identifies how a certain set of conditions brings about a particular result; focusing on a problem in order to trace its roots and results.

Channel   The means by which a message is delivered from the sender to the receiver; the medium by which the message travels.

Character   The audience's perception of the moral and ethical integrity of the speaker resulting in greater believability.

Charisma   The audience's perception of the personal appeal and attractiveness of the speaker that typically creates an emotional response.

Charts and graphs   Visual aids that help an audience understand *how much* and offer comparisons of parts to a whole.

Chronemics   The study of how people use time as a nonverbal communication channel.

Chronological pattern The chronological pattern organizes ideas according to time; speech design that arranges ideas according to time.

Circumscribing stage A relationship stage in which the parties' communication with each other is significantly lessened.

Citizen journalism The expansion of news through blogs, predominantly by non-journalists.

Civility An attitude of respect for other people as unique individuals.

Claim The statement the speaker makes that communicates what he or she wants the audience to think, feel, or act on.

Clarity Clear, complete ideas that are directly related to the purpose of your presentation. The process of clearly expressing your thought; includes crafting a clear informative purpose and employing accessible language.

Climate The degree of cohesiveness among group members, their willingness to communicate with each other, and the tone of that communication.

Closure Filling in the blanks.

Co-cultures Cultures that exist within a more dominant culture.

Coercion Removes the free will of the person being persuaded, either directly or indirectly.

Cognitive orientation How a person processes information—visual, auditory, or kinesthetic; also termed *learning style*.

Cohesion The attraction that group members feel for one another and the degree to which they are willing to work together.

Collaborating style Characterized by high concern for self and high concern for people.

Collaboration Incorporating assertiveness and cooperation in decision making.

Collective identity Established as a result of how the group balances social and task dimensions.

Collectivist cultures Cultures that emphasize the group, not the individual. Cultures that emphasize the importance of the group; value less direct communication and tend to avoid conflict situations.

Commitment Group members' willingness to accomplish a task and develop relationships with each other.

Communication apprehension Fear or anxiety associated with either real or anticipated communication with another person or persons.

Competence The audience's perception of the qualifications, knowledge, skills, and abilities of the speaker.

Competent Possessing the necessary and expected combination of qualifications, knowledge, skills, and abilities.

Competing style Characterized by high concern for self and low concern for people.

Complementary relationships Relationships based on difference; each person brings characteristics that balance the characteristics of a relational partner.

Complex Incorporating intention, relation, context, and ethics.

Compromising style Characterized by moderate concern for self and moderate concern for people.

Computer mediated communication Individual use of technology to communicate with one or more individuals.

Conclusion Summarizes main ideas and cues listeners that the end of the speech is near.

Confidentiality Keeping secrets and confidences when requested.

Confirming language Language that acknowledges and directly supports the contributions of another person.

Confirming messages Messages that value the partner's presence and contributions.

Conflict The perception of incompatible goals.

Congruent messages Messages in which verbal communication and nonverbal communication match.

Connotative meaning The meaning of a word as influenced by an individual's personal history or cultural experience.

Constructive conflict Conflict in which the goal is problem solving, not hurting one another.

Content (or procedural) conflict Occurs when people disagree over facts, definitions, implications, solutions, or procedure.

Content dimension The information or request in a message.

Context A specific environment that includes a number of situational factors including physical, cultural, linguistic, social, temporal, and personal aspects.

Covert conflict Where a partner hides their anger or hostility.

Creativity Finding a novel approach to a topic that can engage your audience.

Credibility Listener's perception of the speaker's trustworthiness, fairness, sincerity, reliability, and honesty.

Critical listening A form of listening that involves analysis, synthesis, and judgment.

Cultural rules General rules that apply to all members of a culture.

Culture "The learned patterns of perception, values, and behaviors, shared by a group of people that is also dynamic and homogenous" (Martin & Nakayama 2001, 23).

Culture shock A relatively short-term feeling of disorientation or discomfort due to the unfamiliarity of surroundings and the lack of familiar cues in the environment.

Data The facts that exist, from which the speaker makes the claim.

Dating Assigning specific time periods to perceptions in order to emphasize that perceptions can shift over time.

Deductive reasoning Begins with a general claim and uses specifics to "prove" the claim.

Defensive climate A climate in which partners feel threatened and seek to protect themselves from attack.

Defensive listening The practice of attributing criticism, hostility, or attacks to the comments of others even when they are not intended.

Demonstration Visual aid that shows—sometimes with another person helping—how to do something.

Denotative meaning The objective, agreed-upon definition of a word.

Dependent relationships Relationships in which the partners rely so much on one another that their identities are enmeshed with one another.

Derived credibility Determined by what we learn about a speaker's education, occupation, or experience, as identified in the speech.

Destructive conflict   Conflict in which communication escalates, and hurting one another becomes the goal.

Developmental approach   Includes three levels of rules—cultural, sociological, and psychological—that tell us how to communicate with others.

Dialectics   Tension or opposition between interacting forces or elements.

Dialogic civility   A set of communication behaviors that include understanding the importance of public dialogue, the need for respect for one another, the extension of a sense of grace to one another, and the commitment to keep the conversation going.

Dialogue   Communicating with each other, not to each other.

Differentiating stage   A relationship stage that occurs when one or more of the parties withholds or retreats from intimacy.

Direct quotations   Word-for-word repetition of what someone has said.

Disconfirming language   Language that evaluates or judges the contributions of others.

Disconfirming messages   Messages that deny the value of a relational partner by refusing to acknowledge his or her presence and communication.

Discrimination   Unfair treatment of a given group of people based on prejudice.

Disfluencies   The fillers that some individuals add within their conversations (e.g., *um, uh, you know*).

Dominate   When one partner does not allow the other to speak.

Dominating   Occurs when others consistently refocus attention on themselves, even if they must interrupt others to do so; also termed *monopolizing* or *stage hogging*.

Doublespeak   Language deliberately constructed to disguise or distort its actual meaning.

Drawings   Visual aids that depict how things work.

Dyadic phase   The stage in which partners confront one another, talk about the relationship's strengths and problems, and try to identify solutions to the problems.

Ego (or power) conflict   A conflict in which the issue, problem, or task becomes lost in the fight for position.

Emblems   Communication behaviors that substitute for words.

Emoticons   Expressions of emotion in Internet communication.

Empathy   A purposeful attempt to understand another person's perspective.

Employment-selection interview   An interview in which an individual sells himself or herself and his or her qualifications for a job.

Enumerated preview   Arranging the main points of a speech in numerical order (e.g., first, second, third).

Environment   The larger system surrounding an organization that provides resources and uses products and services.

Equality   Applying group norms to every member.

Equifinality   Recognition that the end production can be produced in a number of ways.

Equivocal (or ambiguous)   Having multiple meanings.

Ethics   The right or best way to communicate in a given situation.

Ethnocentrism   The view that one's own culture or group is the center of the universe.

Ethos   A speaker's credibility, based on the perception of his or her goodwill, trustworthiness, competence, and appropriateness.

Euphemism   Language used to soften or be sensitive to another person.

Evaluate   Decide on the worth or value of information.

Evaluative listening   Analyzing a message in order to judge its validity, reliability, or usefulness; also termed *critical listening*.

Examples   Illustrations that help an audience visualize your point.

Experimenting stage   The stage of a relationship in which individuals begin to look for commonalities.

Expert testimony   The insights of someone who has specialized knowledge or experience and is therefore a recognized authority on a given subject.

Explicit norms   Norms that are verbally discussed and agreed on.

Extemporaneous speeches   Planned presentations that are delivered using a keyword outline that helps the speaker deliver his or her prepared comments.

Eye contact   Looking at all audience members.

Facial expressions   The ways in which an individual animates his or her face.

Fact   A piece of objective, verifiable information.

Fairness   The ethical quality of being equitable; free of favoritism or bias; acting impartially and justly, according to accepted standards.

Fallacy of the undistributed middle   Suggests that because a group shares one attribute, members of the group share a whole range of attributes.

Feedback   A verbal or nonverbal response to communication.

Fidelity   Greater clarity.

First impressions   Conclusions based on an initial meeting.

Flexibility   Ability to adapt and alter one's behaviors to accommodate changes in a relationship.

Fluency   A smooth flow of speech without frequent stumbles or fillers.

Formal networks   Used most commonly when information is communicated up or down.

Formal time   Scheduled time; used for appointments with paid professionals such as doctors, lawyers, and psychologists.

Forming stage   The stage in which group members get to know one another and determine how the group process will occur.

Functional approach   Identifies two categories of functions that are necessary for effective leadership—*task functions* and *process* (or *relational*) *functions*.

Gatekeeping   The process of determining what is newsworthy and important enough to reach an audience.

General purposes   (1) to entertain, inspire, or celebrate; (2) to inform; and (3) to persuade.

Generalized other   The common expectations within a social group that dictate acceptable beliefs and actions.

Gestures   Movements of the hands, the arms, and sometimes the shoulders, legs, or feet.

Grave-dressing phase   The stage in which each partner must come to terms with his or her perceptions of the relationship, its problems, and how to remember the relationship.

Group   A loose association of at least three people who come together for a wide variety of purposes.

Group culture   The values and beliefs shared by group members.

Group goals   The outcomes the whole group seeks to accomplish.

Groupthink   A mode of thinking that occurs when people are deeply involved in a cohesive group and desire for unanimity overrides a realistic appraisal of alternatives.

Gunnysacking   Repressing feelings to the point that an individual cannot avoid "dumping" his or her feelings onto the relational partner.

Halo effect   Drawing conclusions about an individual after observing a single factor based on the belief that certain traits, behaviors, and personality characteristics belong together.

Hate speech   Speech aimed at attacking or denigrating the status of entire groups—whites, blacks, Jews, homosexuals, and so forth.

Hearing   The physical process that allows people to perceive sounds.

Hegemony   Control or dominating influence by one person or group, especially by one political group over a society or one nation over others.

Heterosexism   A form of prejudice regarding issues of sexual orientation and the issue of whether a person's attraction to the same or opposite sex is one of choice or not.

Hidden agenda   The unstated personal goals of a selfish group member.

High-contact cultures   Cultures that engage in communication that encourages interaction, physical proximity, large gestures, and warm greetings (e.g., Arab, Latin American, and Mediterranean).

High-context culture   Culture in which more value is placed on indirectness and social harmony, and nonverbal aspects of communication play a significant role (e.g., China, Japan, Korea, Malaysia).

Honesty and truthfulness   Telling the truth and not withholding the truth.

Human communication   Negotiating symbolic meaning.

Hypothetical examples   Examples created from information the speaker has collected.

Ideology   A set of beliefs, values, and opinions that shapes the way a person or a group such as a social class thinks, acts, and understands the world.

Illustrators   Communication behaviors that accompany words to add vividness or power to them.

Immediacy   Behaviors such as direct eye contact, smiling, and facing the other person directly, and using vocal variety.

Impersonal communication   Information exchange that lacks depth, is superficial.

Implicit norms   Norms that occur through repetition of behavior that is not questioned.

Implicit personality theory   The idea that people rely on deductions based on a combination of physical characteristics, personality traits, and behaviors to draw conclusions about others.

Impression management   Strategies we use to positively influence others.

Impromptu speeches   Presentations that are given at a moment's notice, without prior planning or practice.

Incongruent messages   Messages in which verbal communication and nonverbal communication do not match.

Independent relationships   Relationships in which the partners live separate and disconnected lives.

Indexing   Qualifying generalizations when they are applied to specific circumstances.

Individual goals   The motivations of individual group members.

Individual roles   Roles that offer group members opportunities to interfere with effective group process.

Individualist cultures   Cultures that emphasize the importance of individual success.

Individualistic cultures   Cultures that place more importance on the individual within certain types of relationships; value direct, open communication.

Inductive reasoning   Begins with specific facts, and the facts ultimately add up to the claim.

Informal networks   Used most commonly when information is communicated among peers.

Informal time   Unscheduled time, often spontaneous; used for activities like dropping in on a friend or calling someone just to chat.

Informational listening   Listening to discern.

Information-gathering interview   An interview in which an individual speaks to a professional working in a job he or she might like to pursue.

Informative speeches   Speeches that instruct or assist the audience in gaining understanding; speeches in which the speaker shares information rather than attempting to sway listeners' attitudes or actions.

Initial credibility   The perceived credibility we determine before we have heard the person speak.

Initiating stage   The stage of a relationship in which the parties attempt to create an impression.

Instrumental (or functional) communication   Communication that achieves practical ends.

Integrating stage   The stage of a relationship in which two individuals become a couple.

Intensifying stage   The stage of a relationship in which individuals begin to disclose in a more personal manner.

Intentional   Purposeful.

Interaction   Turn-taking that allows each partner to engage in a conversation.

Interdependence   Mutual influence.

Interdependent   Components of a system rely on one another to function properly.

Interdependent relationships   Relationships in which the partners rely on one another but are not so dependent that they cannot make independent decisions when warranted.

Interesting Information that is organized or delivered in an engaging manner.

Interpersonal (dyadic) communication A relationship context involving two persons (a *dyad*).

Interpersonal validation When someone offers to help us, expresses interest in us, or supports us.

Interpret Assign meaning to information.

Intimacy The process of coming to know the other and yourself as a relationship develops.

Intimate space The zone of comfort only for those with whom a person is most intimate, such as a parent, lover, child, or close friend; about 0 to 18 inches.

Intrapersonal communication Internalizing messages and communicating with yourself about yourself; also termed *self-talk*.

Intrapsychic phase The stage in which an individual explores the costs and benefits of leaving a relationship.

Introduction Beginning of speech—conveys first impression to audience.

Jargon A language strategy used by a specific group to create a sense of community among group members.

Johari window A tool for analyzing a person's level of self-disclosure.

Kinesics Body behaviors including the eyes, face, gestures, and posture.

Knowledge and understanding needs Needs that make individuals curious about the world and about others.

Labels Words used to classify.

Language The vocabulary that is used to refer to the activity of group members; the level of formality between members of different statuses.

Lay testimony The views of a person who is not necessarily an expert.

Leadership The ability to influence others.

Learning groups Groups that focus on increasing the knowledge and skills of their members.

Linguistic determinism The power of language to influence interpretations of the world in a specific culture.

Listening The mental process that requires mindfulness in order to create meaning.

Logical fallacy When a speaker uses a false or incomplete idea or makes a false inference or link between claims and data or between claims and warrants.

Logos The logic or reasoning of the message.

Love and belonging needs The need for affection, support, approval, and love from friends and family.

Low-contact cultures Cultures that maintain more distance, use smaller gestures, and more formal greetings (e.g., American, German, Scandinavian).

Low-context culture Culture in which individual self-expression is valued, and messages are primarily communicated verbally (e.g., the United States).

Manuscript speeches Speeches in which the speaker reads the presentation word for word.

Maps Visual aids that help an audience understand where things occur.

Mass communication Sharing information with a large audience at a given time or across an extended time frame.

Mass medium A channel that carries a message to many receivers.

Media convergence Media forms and technologies coming together as new technology replaces old.

Mediated communication Communication that requires a technological channel to complete the communication process.

Mediated mass communication Communication that relies on technology but that can also reach more than one person at the same time.

Memorized speeches Presentations that speakers write word for word and then memorize.

Message The content one person seeks to share with another; the topic or substance of communication.

Message complexity Containing complicated ideas, numerous details, or new skills.

Message overload Receiving too many messages at the same time, making it difficult to listen.

Mindful Paying attention.

Mindfulness Willingness to create new categories of meaning and understanding in communicating in new situations; the withholding of immediate judgment on a message and a search for new ways to interpret and assign meaning to a message.

Mindlessness The use of fairly habitual or scripted ways of communicating regardless of the others in the communication experience.

Monochronic cultures Cultures that generally prefer a linear approach to activities (e.g., American, English, Swiss).

Monotone Rarely changing the pitch of one's voice.

Monroe's Motivated Sequence A five step process for organizing a speech in order to inspire the audience to take action.

Motivated sequence pattern Speech design that motivates people to act.

Motivation The reason or *why* of communication; personal commitment to the effort of accomplishing a goal.

Movement Encompasses whether the speaker stands still or moves his or her entire body.

Narratives Stories that illustrate a point or idea; usually have a clear introduction, body, and conclusion.

New media Media forms and content that are created and shaped by changes in technology.

Noise Any interference that occurs as people communicate.

Nonassertive style Suppressing one's own feelings because of shyness, laziness, or fear that other group members will dislike you.

Nonassertiveness Feeling of powerlessness and inability to express feelings honestly and comfortably.

Nonverbal communication Involves the sending and receiving of wordless messages that can be communicated by body language, postures, gestures, facial expressions, and eye contact.

Norming stage The stage in which group rules and roles are developed.

Norms Standards that guide a group.

Object adaptors Ways we manipulate objects that show emotions.

Olfactics The influence of smell in human communication.

Openness The way a system uses feedback to adapt to changes in the larger environment.

Order A clear, consistent pattern from beginning to end.

Organizational culture The actions, practices, language, and artifacts of a group.

Organizational perspective Recognizes that speakers may represent an organization and, as a result, may need to be sensitive in choosing a subject.

Overt conflict Confronting someone directly in a conflict.

Paralanguage (or vocalics) The vocal sounds we make such as pitch, volume, emphasis, or other similar sounds.

Parallelism Beginning each main idea with the same words.

Paraphrase Restating someone's ideas or feelings in your own words.

Pathos The emotional appeal of the message.

Perception The process of becoming aware of people, events, or objects and attaching meaning to that awareness.

Perception checking A process that acknowledges initial perceptions but also recognizes that there may be multiple explanations for them.

Performing stage The stage in which group members risk confrontation and resolve conflict or ignore conflict.

Personal examples Examples drawn from the speaker's own experience.

Personal perspective Takes into account an individual's knowledge, attitudes, interests, experiences, and beliefs to help generate speech topics.

Personal space The zone of comfort for family and good friends; about 18 inches to 4 feet.

Persuasion Persuasion is communication that influences how others think, feel, and act.

Persuasive speeches Speeches that stimulate an audience to reaffirm or alter beliefs or encourage the adoption of new behaviors or the continuation of past behaviors.

Phatic communication Small talk.

Photographs Visual aids that show what the speaker is discussing.

Physiological needs Biological needs necessary to sustain life, including air, water, food, sleep, and sex.

Pitch How high or low a voice is.

Plagiarism Using someone else's ideas without giving them appropriate credit.

Planning outline A rough collection of ideas and supporting material.

Pleasurable listening Listening for appreciation.

Polychronic cultures Cultures that generally prefer to do multiple things at once and view time as a flexible concept (e.g., Bolivian, African, Samoan).

Post hoc fallacy Attempts to link two events together. If one event occurs in close proximity to another, a *post hoc* fallacy may assume the first event caused the second.

Posture Overall stance.

PowerPoint Presentation software developed by Microsoft that allows speakers to prepare a slide show to accompany a speech or presentation.

Practicality Organization that helps audience understand your message.

Practical perspective Considers the availability of adequate, recent research materials and time limits for the preparation and presentation of a speech.

Prejudice A definitive negative attitude toward a group.

Preparation outline The formal, typewritten outline that clearly identifies an introduction, body, and conclusion as well as the required portions in each section.

Presentation outline The outline that contains cue words or phrases that help you recall what you have planned and practiced when you actually deliver the speech; also called the *skeletal* or *keyword outline*.

Primary groups A group whose purpose is to meet some basic need.

Problem–solution design The speaker identifies a problem and provides a way to solve the problem.

Problem–solution pattern Speech design that describes or defines a problem and then offers potential solutions.

Problem-solving groups Groups that focus on a project external to the group.

Procedural norms Norms that govern how members coordinate tasks.

Process An ongoing activity.

Pronunciation Saying words correctly.

Proposition of fact Debatable issue that a single piece of objective evidence cannot resolve.

Proposition of policy Focuses on a specific, preferred response to a particular problem or question.

Proposition of value Focuses on the worth or value of a particular person, idea, event, or object.

Proxemics The study of the use of space to communicate.

Pseudoconflict Situation in which the parties are actually in agreement, but perceptions and misunderstanding prevent them from seeing the areas of agreement and compatibility.

Pseudolistening Pretending to listen.

Psychological rules Rules that apply to the specific relationship we have with another.

Public space The widest zone of comfort, for public performances and presentations; 12 feet to the limits of our visibility or hearing.

Qualifier An attempt to reduce the strength of the claim, from one that is absolute to one with exceptions.

Racism Prejudicial feelings or beliefs we use to create labels that define and demean a group.

Rate How rapidly one speaks.

Rate (of speech) The speed with which we speak.

Rebuttal A more explicit reference to any exception that would invalidate the claim.

Receiver The target or recipient of the message.

Receiver apprehension The fear of misinterpreting, inadequately processing, and/or not being able to adjust psychologically to messages sent by others.

Reflected appraisal Accepting how others define or describe you.

Refutative pattern Speech design that presents the arguments that oppose the speaker's proposition or claim and show how they are fallacious, inadequate, inconsistent, or deficient; identifying and systematically countering arguments that are opposed to a particular position or proposition.

Regulation Controls over content prior to and after its distribution.

Regulators Cues on turn-taking in conversations.

Rejection messages Messages that acknowledge the partner's presence and communication, but do not fully accept or agree with the partner.

Relatedness Direct connectedness of your supporting materials to your topic.

Relational communication Communication that expresses emotions, strengthens bonds with others, or secures a sense of belonging.

Relational dimension Indicative of the relationship between the sender and receiver.

Relational dissolution model Identifies the intrapsychic, dyadic, social, and grave-dressing phases of relationship dissolution.

Relational listening Listening to understand, support, and empathize with others.

Relevance Applicability and understandability of supporting materials to your audience.

Relevancy Linking your topic to your audience members in such a way that they, too, are interested.

Respect Acknowledgement of what your audience members already know and showing them how to draw on and adapt their prior knowledge.

Rhetorical sensitivity Concern for self, concern for others, and a situational attitude. The ability to adapt to the widest range of communication experiences with skill, considering the most appropriate response based on a comprehensive understanding of the entire communication experience. The ability to adapt a message to the people, place, and timing of the communication.

Rigidity Inability to adapt and cope with changes that occur in a relationship.

Rites and rituals Practices that symbolize the tools organizational members use to create and maintain culture.

Roles The patterns of behavior we use in the group process; titles and/or job responsibilities.

Rules and policies Standards by which organizational members make decisions.

Safety and security needs Feeling free from violence and feeling a sense of stability in life.

Sapir-Whorf hypothesis Language is the most significant factor in determining what we see in the world and how we think about and evaluate what we see.

Scripts Mental organization patterns that help arrange information and inform behavior.

Secondary groups Groups that are less personal—usually shorter term (as in a work group assembled for a specific purpose).

Selection The second stage of perception; focusing on specific stimuli.

Selective listening Occurs when listeners focus on parts of a message that appeals to them because they like or dislike the topic at hand.

Self The sum of your personality, character, and identity.

Self-actualization needs Encompass an individual's drive to be the best that he or she can be.

Self-adaptors Ways in which we manipulate our bodies that show emotions.

Self-concept The relatively stable mental image a person holds of himself or herself.

Self-disclosure When we tell someone something about our self that they would not know unless we told them.

Self-efficacy Sense of self.

Self-esteem The value or worth a person places on himself or herself.

Self-esteem needs The needs for confidence or self-worth; they motivate individuals toward success.

Self-fulfilling prophecies Events that are more likely to transpire because someone expects them to.

Self-image Mental picture a person has of himself or herself, relatively stable over time.

Self-presentation The ways in which a person presents some of the more personal aspects of himself or herself.

Sender The originator of a message.

Sexism A form of prejudice regarding issues of gender, expectations of what is appropriate female and male behavior, and assertions on gender superiority.

Sexual harassment Unwelcome sexual advances, requests for sexual favors, and other verbal or physical conduct of a sexual nature.

Significant choice Having sufficient information about a situation to make a "good" decision.

Silence Stillness or the absence of sound.

Simplicity Stating your ideas in straightforward language.

Situational factors Group context that influences a leader's style or approach.

Situational perspective Focuses on the context of a speech in selecting a topic.

Slippery slope fallacy Suggests that once a set of actions has started, there is no stopping the ultimate conclusion.

Small group Three to five persons who interact together for a purpose, influence one another over a period of time, operate interdependently, share standards and norms, develop a collective identity, and derive satisfaction from the cohesion and commitment in the group.

Social anxiety A feeling of apprehension in any social setting in which an individual meets another for the first time.

Social comparison How a person sees himself or herself in comparison with others.

Social construction (or cultivation) theory Suggests that what the media portray is one of the most important elements of the construction and interpretation of our culture.

Social dimension The personal relationships among group members.

Social groups   Groups that focus primarily on the belonging needs of the participants.

Social loafing   Occurs when an individual sits back and allows other group members to pick up the workload.

Social (or maintenance) roles   Roles that help members shape the relationships within the group.

Social norms   Norms that guide the relationships among group members.

Social penetration model   A model depicting self-disclosure as a process that gradually reveals both breadth and depth of information.

Social phase   The stage in which partners discuss the possibility or actuality of dissolving the relationship with friends and family.

Social space   The zone of comfort for impersonal business, classroom, and general interactions; about 4 to 12 feet.

Sociological rules   Rules that apply to individuals in a particular group.

Sound bite   A brief statement taken from an audiotape or videotape and broadcast especially during a news report. (© 2011 by Merriam-Webster)

Spatial pattern   Speech design that relies on a geographical or spatial relationship. The spatial pattern organizes ideas according to how they are situated in a physical space.

Special occasion speeches   Speeches that recognize a person, place, or event.

Specific purpose   The purpose of a speech in relation to its specific topic.

Speech of explanation   A speech that explains and typically helps the audience understand an idea, concept, or process.

Speech to actuate   A persuasive speech that motivates the audience toward a particular behavior.

Speech to convince   A persuasive speech that challenges the audience to alter widely accepted beliefs.

Speech to reinforce or stimulate   A speech that reinforces the beliefs or behaviors to which the audience already ascribes.

Speeches of definition   Speeches that focus on helping your audience understand what a concept, process, or event means.

Speeches of demonstration   Speeches that concentrate on showing how a process is accomplished.

Speeches of description   Speeches that rely on mental pictures created by strategic use of pictorial language and are most likely used with speeches that focus on objects, events, and people.

Speeches of tribute   Speeches that celebrate a person, a group of people, or an event.

Speeches that focus on concepts   Speeches that help your audience understand ideas, especially philosophies, theories, ideologies, principles, or beliefs.

Speeches that focus on events   Speeches that discuss particular occurrences either historically or in present time.

Speeches that focus on objects   Speeches that teach listeners about something that is visible to the human eye.

Speeches that focus on people   Speeches that help the audience understand the life, work, personality, or uniqueness of another human being.

Speeches that focus on processes   Speeches that explain the various steps in how something is made, works, or is done.

Speeches to entertain and inspire   Special occasion speeches that are general in nature and may occur in a variety of settings.

Stagnating stage   A relationship stage in which communication disappears.

Start/stop cues   Cues that regulate interaction in a conversation.

State-the-case-and-prove-it pattern   Speech design in which the speaker sets forth a proposition or claim and then proves it systematically by offering evidence and reason to support the arguments; clearly stating and claim and then systematically providing strong reasons and evidence to support the claim.

Statistics   Numeric facts that include such information as percentages, averages, or amounts of money.

Stereotypes   Conclusions drawn from generalizations; predictive generalizations about people or situations. Over-simplified categories that people associate individuals with in order to reduce uncertainty about them.

Stories and myths   Tales of past successes and failures and of past and present heroes that help socialize new members of an organization.

Storming stage   The stage in which group conflict emerges as members react to norms and rules negatively.

Straw man fallacy   Attempts to set up an easily refuted argument as a way to defeat an opposing position. When the weak argument is easily defeated, then a whole position is assumed to be invalid.

Structured   Governed by a set of rules.

Styles approach   Identifies three different leadership styles—*autocratic, democratic,* or *laissez-faire.*

Subject   A broad area of knowledge.

Supportive climate   A climate in which partners feel comfortable and secure.

Symbolic   Representative of a particular thing, idea, concept, or event. Using words, vocal utterances, or body movement to represent a host of referents.

Symmetrical relationships   Relationships based on similarity; both individuals share traits, interests, and approaches to communication.

Synergy   Collective energy.

Tables   Visual aids that summarize information.

Task dimension   The ways groups make decisions and solve problems.

Task norms   Norms that focus on how decision making and problem solving occur.

Task roles   Roles that assist group members in goal accomplishment.

Team   An organizational group working together on a class- or work-related project.

Terminal credibility   A culmination of the initial and derived credibility.

Terminating stage   Occurs when no significant intervention is attempted at the avoiding stage.

Territoriality The characteristic of marking one's environment.

Testimony The words or ideas of another person used to support a speaker's points.

Text charts Posters, flip charts, writing on a chalkboard, and slides that preview or summarize key ideas.

Therapy (or growth) groups Groups that assist members in learning about themselves and solving personal problems.

Thesis The central idea of a speech.

Thesis statement A single, declarative sentence that summarizes the essence of a speech.

Tolerance Respect for one another.

Topic The specific focus of a speech.

Topical or categorical pattern Speech design that deals with topics or categories that relate to a main theme.

Topical pattern The topical pattern uses an interrelated set of subtopics directly related to the speech topic.

Toulmin Model A model of argument that serves as the template for developing solid, comprehensive arguments today; the components include: claim, data, warrant, backing, qualifiers, and rebuttal.

Trait approach Presumes that leaders are either born with or cultivate a set of behaviors that guarantee they will assume leadership positions.

Transactional model Depicts communication in which people act simultaneously as senders and receivers.

Transitions Provides markers between points; bridges between ideas.

Trigger words Words that stimulate a negative emotional reaction in listeners.

Turn-taking cues Cues such as eye contact, touch, and voice that communicate that the other may now take his or her turn in the conversation.

Uses and gratifications theory Argues that we turn to media to fulfill preexisting needs.

Values Deeply held convictions about the undeniable worthiness of a certain ideal; general guiding principles for life.

Value system Guides the development of norms, roles, and structure within a group.

Verbal communication Involves the sending and receiving of messages with words.

Viral marketing Any strategy that encourages individuals to pass on a marketing message to others, creating the potential for exponential growth in the message's exposure and influence.

Vocalics How the voice communicates without the use of words.

Vocal inflection Changing the pitch of one's voice.

Volume How loudly or softly one speaks.

Warrant The rationale for making the link between the claim and the data.

Wholeness The unique configuration of the parts in a system.

PHOTO CREDITS

INDEX

Bold – definition
Italics – figure
t – table

Abstract, **63–64**
Academic advisors, 133–134
Academic outreach services, 281
Academic Premier, 162
Accommodating style of conflict
    management, **139**
Accuracy, **221**
Achievers, types of, 27–28
Actual examples, **189**
Adaptability, **297**
Adaptors, **84**
Ad hominem argument, **237**, 237t
Ad populum argument, **237**, 237t
Advertisements
    advocacy, *233, 235*
    political, 230–231
Advisors, academic, 133–134
Advocacy advertisements, *233, 235*
Aesthetic needs, **107**
Affect displays, **84**
Affection, need for, 107
Age, 155
Agenda of news, **317**
Aggressiveness, **128**
Aggressive style of conflict
    management, **266**
Ambiguous, **66**
Ambiguous language, 66–67
Ambushing, **48**
American Association of Colleges and
    Universities (AAC&U), 134–135
American Psychological Association (APA),
    191, 310
Anxiety. *See* Communication apprehension
    (CA)
Apathetic audiences, 158
Apprehension. *See* Communication
    apprehension (CA)
Appropriateness
    explanation of, **43**, 44
    in interpersonal relationships, 132
    of messages, 127
Arbitrary, **62**
Aristotle, 228
Articulation, **199**
Artifacts, **89**
Ascending order, 173
Assertiveness
    explanation of, **128**
    in friendships, 130–131
    suggestions to develop, 140–141
Assertive style of conflict management, **266**
Associate, **64**
Attention, **21**, 185t
Attitudes
    academic success and, 17
    culture and, 117–118
    explanation of, **156**, 157, **231**

media impact on, 309–310
    persuasion and, 228, 231–232, 231t
    self-presentation and, 94
Attraction, 104–105
Attractiveness bias, 32t
Attributions, **32**, 32t
Audience
    adapting language to, 73–74
    attention-getting strategies to capture,
        185t, 186
    characteristics of, 153, 154t, 155–157
    choosing subject for, 158, 159t
    mediated mass communication and, 306
    for speeches, 153
    types of, 153, 154t, 157–158
Audience perspective, **153**, 158–159t
Audio clips, **194**
Auditory learners, 25t
Authentic dialogue, 118–119
Authentic listening, **48**
Authoritative nature of language, **65**
Authority, **232**
Avoiding stage of relationships, **113**
Avoiding style of conflict management,
    139–140

Baby boomers, 155t
Backing, **236**
Balance, **173**
Bandwagon technique, 230
Baxter, Leslie, 129
Beliefs
    culture and, 71–72
    explanation of, **156–157**, **231**
    persuasion and, 231–232, 231t
Bias
    attribution, 32t
    gender, 117
    media, 309
Blogs, **312**
Body movement. *See* Kinesics
Body shape/height, effects of, 85
Body (speech)
    explanation of, **182–183**
    for informative speech, 218–219
    for persuasive speech, 243–244
Boisjoly, Roger, 270
Bonding stage of relationship
    development, **112**
Boraks, David, 164
Brain dominance
    explanation of, **25**
    learning styles and, 24t, 25
Brainstorming
    in group decision making, 267–268
    for subjects and topics, 150, 153
Breathing, 198
Briefing, 215–216

Burke, Kenneth, 223
Bypassing, 63

Campus Compact, 135
Campus ministries, 281
Careers. *See also* Organizations;
    Workplace
    communication skills for, 4, 5
    informative speeches in, 222
    motivation and, 290–291
    nonsexist environments and, 70
    organizational relationships in, 287
    personal relationships and, 290
    public speaking in, 148
    self-fulfilling prophecy and, 27–28
    sexual harassment in, 291
Categorical pattern, **180**
Cause-effect pattern, 180–181, **241**
Celebratory speeches, purpose of, 160
Challenger space shuttle, 269, 270
Channels
    critical analysis of, 313
    explanation of, **8**
    listening and, 44–45, 48–49
Character
    credibility built through, 233
    explanation of, **232**
    of faculty, 234
Charisma, **232**
Charts, **192**, *192, 193*
The Chicago Manual of Style (University
    of Chicago Press), 191
Child care centers, 281
Chronemics, **90**, 93
Chronological pattern
    explanation of, **179, 216**
    informative speeches using, 216–217
Circumscribing stage of relationship
    development, **112**
Citizen journalism, 305
Civility, 53–54
Claims, **236**
Clarity
    explanation of, **220**
    in ideas, 172–173
    in informative speeches, 220–221
    verbal, 199
Class handouts, 55
Climate, in groups, 264–265
Closure, **32**
Clothing, 89, 92
Co-cultures, **46**
Coercion, **229**
Cognitive orientation, **25**
Cohesion
    explanation of, **254**
    in groups, 264–265
Cold media, **313**